T0332622

Statistical Machine Translation

The field of machine translation has recently been energized by the emergence of statistical techniques, which have brought the dream of automatic language translation closer to reality. This class-tested textbook, authored by an active researcher in the field, provides a gentle and accessible introduction to the latest methods and enables the reader to build machine translation systems for any language pair.

It provides the necessary grounding in linguistics and probabilities, and covers the major models for machine translation: word-based, phrase-based, and tree-based, as well as machine translation evaluation, language modeling, discriminative training and advanced methods to integrate linguistic annotation. The book reports on the latest research and outstanding challenges, and enables novices as well as experienced researchers to make contributions to the field. It is ideal for students at undergraduate and graduate level, or for any reader interested in the latest developments in machine translation.

PHILIPP KOEHN is a lecturer in the School of Informatics at the University of Edinburgh. He is the scientific coordinator of the European EuroMatrix project and is also involved in research funded by DARPA in the USA. He has also collaborated with leading companies in the field, such as Systran and Asia Online. He implemented the widely used decoder Pharaoh, and is leading the development of the open source machine translation toolkit Moses.

Statistical Machine Translation

Philipp Koehn
School of Informatics
University of Edinburgh

CAMBRIDGE
UNIVERSITY PRESS

University Printing House, Cambridge CB2 8BS, United Kingdom

Cambridge University Press is part of the University of Cambridge.

It furthers the University's mission by disseminating knowledge in the pursuit of
education, learning and research at the highest international levels of excellence.

www.cambridge.org
Information on this title: www.cambridge.org/9780521874151

© P. Koehn 2010

This publication is in copyright. Subject to statutory exception
and to the provisions of relevant collective licensing agreements,
no reproduction of any part may take place without the written
permission of Cambridge University Press.

First published 2010
4th printing 2013

A catalogue record for this publication is available from the British Library

ISBN 978-0-521-87415-1 Hardback

Additional resources for this publication at www.statmt.org

Cambridge University Press has no responsibility for the persistence or accuracy of
URLs for external or third-party internet websites referred to in this publication,
and does not guarantee that any content on such websites is, or will remain, accurate
or appropriate.

For Trishann and Phianna

Contents

Preface

Over the last few centuries, machines have taken on many human tasks, and lately, with the advent of digital computers, even tasks that were thought to require thinking and intelligence. Translating between languages is one of these tasks, a task for which even humans require special training.

Machine translation has a long history, but over the last decade or two, its evolution has taken on a new direction – a direction that is mirrored in other subfields of natural language processing. This new direction is grounded in the premise that language is so rich and complex that it could never be fully analyzed and distilled into a set of rules, which are then encoded into a computer program. Instead, the new direction is to develop a machine that discovers the rules of translation automatically from a large corpus of translated text, by pairing the input and output of the translation process, and learning from the statistics over the data.

Statistical machine translation has gained tremendous momentum, both in the research community and in the commercial sector. About one thousand academic papers have been published on the subject, about half of them in the past three years alone. At the same time, statistical machine translation systems have found their way to the marketplace, ranging from the first purely statistical machine translation company, Language Weaver, to the free online systems of Google and Microsoft.

This book introduces the major methods in statistical machine translation. It includes much of the recent research, but extended discussions are confined to established methodologies. Its focus is a thorough introduction to the field for students, researchers, and other interested parties, and less a reference book. Nevertheless, most of the recent research is cited in the *Further Readings* section at the end of each chapter.

I started this book about four years ago, and throughout its writing I have been supported by friends, family, and my wife Trishann, for which I am very grateful. I would not have been able to write this book without the ideas and opinions of the researchers who guide me, in this field: Kevin Knight, Franz Och, and Michael Collins. I am also indebted to colleagues for providing comments, finding mistakes, and making valuable suggestions, most notably Eleftherios Avramidis, Steven Clark, Chris Dyer, Adam Lopez, Roland Kuhn, Paola Merlo, Miles Osborne, and Ashish Venugopal. This work would also not have been accomplished without the support of the members of the statistical machine translation group at the University of Edinburgh: Miles Osborne, Phil Blunson, Trevor Cohn, Barry Haddow, Adam Lopez, Abhishek Arun, Michael Auli, Amittai Axelrod, Alexandra Birch, Chris Callison-Burch, Loïc Dugast, Hieu Hoang, David Talbot, and Josh Schroeder.

Edinburgh, October 17, 2008.

Part I
Foundations

Chapter 1
Introduction

This chapter provides a gentle introduction to the field of statistical machine translation. We review the history of the field and highlight current applications of machine translation technology. Some pointers to available resources are also given.

But first let us take a broad look at the contents of this book. We have broken up the book into three main parts: **Foundations** (Chapters 1–3), which provides essential background for novice readers, **Core Methods** (Chapters 4–8), which covers the principles of statistical machine translation in detail, and **Advanced Topics** (Chapters 9–11), which discusses more recent advances.

Chapter 1: Introduction
Chapter 2: Words, Sentences, Corpora
Chapter 3: Probability Theory
Chapter 4*: Word-Based Models
Chapter 5*: Phrase-Based Models
Chapter 6*: Decoding
Chapter 7: Language Models
Chapter 8: Evaluation
Chapter 9: Discriminative Training
Chapter 10: Integrating Linguistic Information
Chapter 11: Tree-Based Models

This book may be used in many ways for a course on machine translation or data-driven natural language processing. The three chapters flagged with a star (*) should be part of any such course. See

Figure 1.1 Dependencies between the chapters of this book.

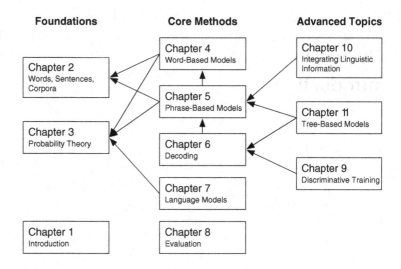

also Figure 1.1 for the dependencies between the chapters. Some suggestions for courses that last one semester or term:

- Undergraduate machine translation course: Lectures on Chapters 1–6, and optionally Chapters 7 and 8.
- Graduate machine translation course: Lectures on Chapter 1, give Chapters 2–3 as reading assignment, lectures on Chapters 4–8, and optionally Chapters 9, 10, or 11.
- Graduate data-driven NLP course: Chapters 2–7 (with stronger emphasis on Chapters 2, 3, and 7), and optionally Chapters 9 or 11.

Chapter 2 may be skipped if students have taken undergraduate classes in linguistics. Chapter 3 may be skipped if students have taken undergraduate classes in mathematics or computer science.

The web site for this book[1] provides pointers to slides that were prepared from this book, as well as a list of university classes that have used it.

1.1 Overview

In the following, we give an extended overview of the book that touches on major concepts, chapter by chapter.

1.1.1 Chapter 1: Introduction

The history of machine translation goes back over 60 years, almost immediately after the first computers had been used to break encryption

---

[1] Hosted at http://www.statmt.org/book/

codes in the war, which seemed an apt metaphor for translation: what is a foreign language but encrypted English? Methods rooted in more linguistic principles were also investigated. The field flourished, until the publication of a report by ALPAC, whose negative assessment stalled many efforts. In the 1970s the foundations for the first commercial systems were laid, and with the advent of the personal computer and the move towards translation memory tools for translators, machine translation as a practical application was meant to stay. The most recent trend is towards data-driven methods, especially statistical methods, which is the topic of this book.

Work in machine translation research is not limited to the grand goal of fully automatic, high-quality (publishable) translation. Often, rough translations are sufficient for browsing foreign material. Recent trends are also to build limited applications in combination with speech recognition, especially for hand-held devices. Machine translation may serve as a basis for post-editing, but translators are generally better served with tools such as translation memories that make use of machine translation technology, but leave them in control.

Many resources are freely available for statistical machine translation research. For many of the methods described in this book, tools are available as reference implementation. Also, many translated text collections are available either by simple web download or through the Linguistic Data Consortium. Other sources are ongoing evaluation campaigns that provide standard training and test sets, and benchmark performance.

1.1.2 Chapter 2: Word, Sentences, Corpora

Many statistical machine translation methods still take a very simple view of language: It is broken up into sentences, which are strings of words (plus punctuation which is separated out by a tokenization step). Words have a very skewed distribution in language: Some are very frequent, while many rarely occur. Words may be categorized by their part-of-speech (noun, verb, etc.) or by their meaning. Some languages exhibit rich inflectional morphology, which results in a large vocabulary. Moreover, the definition of what words are is less clear, if writing systems do not separate them by spaces (e.g. Chinese).

Moving beyond the simple notion of sentences as strings of words, one discovers a hierarchical structure of clauses, phrases and dependencies between distant words that may be best represented graphically in tree structures. One striking property of language is recursion, which enables arbitrarily deep nested constructions. Several modern linguistic theories of grammar provide formalism for representing the syntax of a sentence. Theories of discourse address the relationships between sentences.

Text collections are called corpora, and for statistical machine translation we are especially interested in parallel corpora, which are texts, paired with a translation into another language. Texts differ in style and topic, for instance transcripts of parliamentary speeches versus news wire reports. Preparing parallel texts for the purpose of statistical machine translation may require crawling the web, extracting the text from formats such as HTML, as well as document and sentence alignment.

1.1.3 Chapter 3: Probability Theory

Probabilities are used when we have to deal with events with uncertain outcomes, such as a foreign word that may translate into one of many possible English words. Mathematically, a probability distribution is a function that maps possible outcomes to values between 0 and 1. By analyzing an event, we may find that a standard distribution (such as uniform, binomial, or normal distributions) can be used to model it. Alternatively, we may collect statistics about the event and estimate the probability distributions by maximum likelihood estimation.

We typically deal with multiple uncertain events, each with a different probability distribution, for instance the translation of multiple words in a sentence. The mathematics of probability theory provides a toolset of methods that allow us to calculate more complex distributions, such as joint or conditional distributions for related events. Rules such as the chain rule or the Bayes rule allow us to reformulate distributions. Interpolation allows us to compensate for poorly estimated distributions due to sparse data.

Our methods of dealing with probabilistic events are often motivated by properties of probability distributions, such as the mean and variance in outcomes. A powerful concept is entropy, the degree of uncertainty, which guides many machine learning techniques for probabilistic models.

1.1.4 Chapter 4: Word-Based Models

The initial statistical models for machine translation are based on words as atomic units that may be translated, inserted, dropped, and reordered.

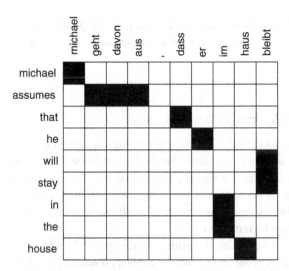

Figure 1.2 Aligning the words in a sentence pair is the first step of many statistical machine translation methods (Chapter 4).

Viewing the translation between a sentence pair as a mapping of the words on either side motivates the notion of word alignment (see Figure 1.2 for an illustration), which may be modeled with an alignment function.

Since parallel corpora provide us with sentences and their translation, but not with word alignments, we are confronted with the problem of learning from incomplete data. One way to address this is the expectation maximization algorithm, that alternately computes the probability of possible word alignments and collects counts, and builds an improved model of these alignments.

In statistical machine translation, we use both a translation model and a language model, which ensures fluent output. The combination of these models is mathematically justified by the noisy-channel model.

The original work at IBM on statistical machine translation uses word-based translation models of increasing complexity, that not only take lexical translation into account, but also model reordering as well as insertion, deletion, and duplication of words. The expectation maximization algorithm gets more computationally complex with the increasingly sophisticated models. So we have to sample the alignment space instead of being able to exhaustively consider all possible alignments.

The task of word alignment is an artifact of word-based translation models, but it is a necessary step for many other multilingual applications, and forms a research problem of its own. Automatically obtained word alignments may be evaluated by how closely they match word alignments created by humans. Recent advances in word alignment are symmetrization methods to overcome the one-to-many problem of the IBM models, integrate additional linguistic constraints, or directly align groups of words.

1.1.5 Chapter 5: Phrase-Based Models

The currently most successful approach to machine translation uses the translation of phrases as atomic units. See Figure 1.3 for an illustration. These phrases are any contiguous sequences of words, not necessarily linguistic entities. In this approach, the input sentence is broken up into a sequence of phrases; these phrases are mapped one-to-one to output phrases, which may be reordered.

Commonly, phrase models are estimated from parallel corpora that were annotated with word alignments by methods discussed in Chapter 4. All phrase pairs that are consistent with the word alignment are extracted. Probabilistic scores are assigned based on relative counts or by backing off to lexical translation probabilities.

Phrase-based models typically do not strictly follow the noisy-channel approach proposed for word-based models, but use a log-linear framework. Components such as language model, phrase translation model, lexical translation model, or reordering model are used as feature functions with appropriate weights. This framework allows the straightforward integration of additional features such as number of words created or number of phrase translations used.

Reordering in phrase models is typically modeled by a distance-based reordering cost that discourages reordering in general. Reordering is often limited to movement over a maximum number of words. The lexicalized reordering model learns different reordering behavior for each specific phrase pair (for instance in French–English, adjectives like *bleue* are more likely to be reordered).

Alternatively to learning phrase-based models from a word-aligned parallel corpus, we may also use the expectation maximization algorithm to directly find phrase alignments for sentence pairs.

Figure 1.3 Phrase-based machine translation. The input is segmented into phrases (not necessarily linguistically motivated), translated one-to-one into phrases in English and possibly reordered (Chapter 5).

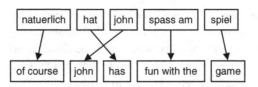

1.1.6 Chapter 6: Decoding

Probabilistic models in statistical machine translation assign a score to every possible translation of a foreign input sentence. The goal of decoding is to find the translation with the best score. In the decoding process, we construct the translation word by word, from start to finish. The word-based and phrase-based models are well suited for this, since they allow the computation of scores for partial translations.

Before translating a foreign input sentence, we first consult the translation table and look up the applicable translation options. During decoding, we store partial translations in a data structure called a hypothesis. Decoding takes the form of expanding these hypotheses by deciding on the next phrase translation, as illustrated in Figure 1.4. Due to the computational complexity of decoding (NP-complete), we need to restrict the search space. We do this by recombination, a dynamic programming technique to discard hypotheses that are not possibly part of the best translation, and by organizing the hypotheses into stacks to prune out bad ones early on. Limits on reordering also drastically reduce the search space.

When comparing hypotheses for the purpose of pruning, we also have to take the translation cost of the remaining untranslated words into account. Such future costs may be efficiently computed up front before decoding.

Variations and alternatives to the beam search stack decoding algorithm have been proposed, such as A* search, a standard search technique in artificial intelligence. Greedy hill-climbing decoding first creates a rough translation and then optimizes it by applying changes. Machine translation decoding may also be fully implemented with finite state transducer toolkits.

1.1.7 Chapter 7: Language Models

Language models measure the fluency of the output and are an essential part of statistical machine translation. They influence word choice,

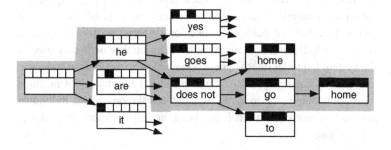

Figure 1.4 The translation process (decoding): The translation is built from left to right, and the space of possible extensions of partial translation is explored (Chapter 6).

reordering and other decisions. Mathematically, they assign each sentence a probability that indicates how likely that sentence is to occur in a text. N-gram language models use the Markov assumption to break the probability of a sentence into the product of the probability of each word, given the (limited) history of preceding words. Language models are optimized on perplexity, a measure related to how much probability is given to a set of actual English text.

The fundamental challenge in language models is handling sparse data. Just because something has not been seen in the training text does not mean that it is impossible. Methods such as add-one smoothing, deleted estimation or Good–Turing smoothing take probability mass from evident events and assign it to unseen events.

Another angle on addressing sparse data in n-gram language models is interpolation and back-off. Interpolation means that n-gram models with various orders (i.e., length of history) are combined. Back-off uses the highest order n-gram model, if the predicted word has been seen given the history, or otherwise resorts to lower-order n-gram models with shorter histories. Various methods exist to determine the back-off costs and adapt the elementary n-gram probability models. Kneser–Ney smoothing takes both the diversity of predicted words and histories into account.

Especially for English there is no lack of training data for language models. Billions, if not trillions, of words of text can be acquired. Larger language models typically lead to better results. Handling such large models, however, is a computational challenge. While the models may be trained on disk, for machine translation decoding they need to be accessed quickly, which means that they have to be stored in RAM. Efficient data structures help, and we may reduce vocabulary size and n-grams to what is needed for the translation of a specific input set. Computer clusters have also been used for very large models.

1.1.8 Chapter 8: Evaluation

A hotly debated topic in machine translation is evaluation, since there are many valid translations for each input sentence (see Figure 1.5 for an illustration). At some point, we need some quantitative way to assess the quality of machine translation systems, or at least a way to be able to tell if one system is better than another or if a change in the system led to an improvement. One way is to ask human judges to assess the adequacy (preservation of meaning) and fluency of machine translation output, or to rank different translations of an individual sentence. Other criteria, such as speed, are also relevant in practical deployments.

这个 机场 的 安全 工作 由 以色列 方面 负责 .
Israeli officials are responsible for airport security.
Israel is in charge of the security at this airport.
The security work for this airport is the responsibility of the Israel government.
Israeli side was in charge of the security of this airport.
Israel is responsible for the airport's security.
Israel is responsible for safety work at this airport.
Israel presides over the security of the airport.
Israel took charge of the airport security.
The safety of this airport is taken charge of by Israel.
This airport's security is the responsibility of the Israeli security officials.

Figure 1.5 Ten different translations of the same Chinese sentence (Chapter 8).

Due to the high cost of human evaluation, automatic evaluation metrics have been proposed for machine translation. Typically, they compare the output of machine translation systems against human translations. Common metrics measure the overlap in words and word sequences, as well as word order. Advanced metrics also take synonyms, morphological variation, or preservation of syntactic relations into account. Evaluation metrics are evaluated by their correlation to human judgment.

One question in evaluation is: Are measured differences statistically significant or are they just due to random effects in a limited test set? Statistics offer methods to measure confidence intervals and assess pairwise comparison, but they may not be applicable to more complex evaluation metrics. For these cases, we may employ bootstrap resampling.

The ultimate test for machine translation is its usefulness in performing tasks that involve translated material. We may compare post-editing time vs. full human translation time. Tests for the understanding of translated content may also be used.

1.1.9 Chapter 9: Discriminative Training

The statistical learning paradigm behind word-based models and largely behind phrase-based models is generative modeling, which estimates probability distributions based on counts given in the data. In contrast to this, discriminative training directly optimizes translation performance by reducing some measure of translation error.

An essential first step for discriminative training methods is to find a sample of candidate translations for an input sentence. By converting the search graph of the beam search decoding process into a word lattice, we are able to extract n-best lists of the most likely translations.

Re-ranking methods allow the consideration of additional properties to pick the best translation out of a list of candidate translations. Re-ranking is a supervised learning problem, since we are able to build a training corpus of input sentence, candidate translations, and label one of the candidate translations as correct using a reference translation. Properties of each translation are represented as features. One popular method for this task is maximum entropy modeling.

Modern statistical machine translation models are optimized in a parameter tuning stage. Typically, the model is broken up into several components, and the component weights have to be optimized. By examining the effect of different parameter settings on n-best lists of candidate translations, we search for the optimal setting. Using a variant of Powell search, we find the optimal setting for one parameter at a time. Using the simplex algorithm, we explore the space of parameter settings along the bisector of a triangle of three parameter settings.

An ambitious goal is to train all parameters of a statistical machine translation model with discriminative training, replacing all generative models, for instance phrase translation probabilities. Since we are optimizing some measure of translation, we must choose this measure carefully. We may use gradient descent methods such as the perceptron algorithm.

Related to discriminative training are posterior methods that also operate on sets of candidate translations. In minimum Bayes risk decoding, we choose the translation that is most similar to the most probable translations (instead of the most probable translation). Confidence estimation methods may assign more confidence to parts of the output translation on which more candidate translations agree. Combination of output from different translation systems may be done along the same lines: we include in the consensus translation the parts on which most systems agree.

1.1.10 Chapter 10: Integrating Linguistic Information

Some aspects of translation pose specific problems that may be addressed with methods that are sensitive to the underlying linguistic phenomena. The translation of numbers or names is different from the translation of regular words: There are very many of them, but their translation is relatively straightforward. However, name translation is difficult if the input and output languages use different writing systems, and hence names may need to be transliterated. Transliteration models are often implemented using finite state transducers. There is a difference between transliteration of foreign names and the back-transliteration of English names from a foreign writing system.

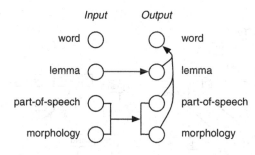

Figure 1.6 Factored translation models allow the separate translation of lemma and morphological features (Chapter 10).

Morphology poses a special problem to machine translation, especially when dealing with highly inflected languages with large vocabularies of surface forms. If the input language is morphologically rich, it may help to simplify it. If both input and output language models are inflected, we may want to build models that translate lemma and morphemes separately (see Figure 1.6). Related to the problems caused by morphology is the problem of splitting compound words.

If the input and output languages have different syntactic structures, sequence models (word-based or phrase-based) have difficulties with the increased amount of reordering during translation, especially long-range reordering. We may want to define reordering rules, based on syntactic annotation (part-of-speech tags or syntactic trees), which restructure the input sentence into the order of the output sentence. These rules may be devised manually or learned automatically from word-aligned sentence pairs annotated with syntactic markup.

Linguistic annotation may also be exploited in a re-scoring approach. By generating n-best lists of candidate translations, we annotate these with additional linguistic markup, which allows us to give preference to translations that show more grammatical coherence with the input and more grammatical agreement within itself. We also consider overall syntactic parse probability.

Factored translation models are an extension of phrase-based models that integrate linguistic annotation (or any other so-called factors). Each word is represented as a vector of factors, instead of a simple token. A phrase mapping is decomposed into several steps that either translate input factors to output factors or generate target factors to other target factors.

1.1.11 Chapter 11: Tree-Based Models

Since modern linguistic theories of language use tree structures to represent sentences, it is only natural to think about translation models that also use trees. Formal theories of syntax use grammars to create trees,

Figure 1.7 Statistical machine translation systems may also exploit syntactic structure, such as phrase structure or dependency structure (Chapter 11).

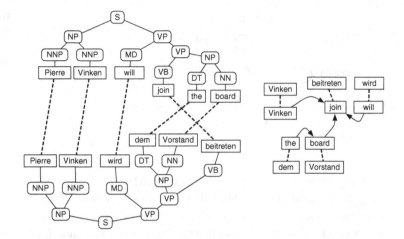

which we extend to synchronous grammars that create pairs of trees, one for the input sentence and the other for the output sentence. See Figure 1.7 for an illustration.

One way to learn synchronous grammars is based on the method for building phrase models. First, we extract all rules that are consistent with the word alignment which is created by some other method. Then, by allowing phrases to include other phrases, we create hierarchical phrase pairs. With syntactic markup, we create grammar rules with non-terminal nodes covering underlying phrase mappings. Probability distributions for grammar rules may be estimated based on relative counts.

The beam search decoding algorithm for phrase models does not work for tree-based models, since we are not able to build the translation from left to right in a straightforward way. Instead, we adopt the chart parsing algorithm to do decoding by parsing. An efficient implementation incorporates methods for recombination and pruning. Due to the increased complexity of tree-based decoding, we may want to binarize the grammar. Also, efficient methods to access grammar rules are required.

1.2 History of Machine Translation

The history of machine translation is one of great hopes and disappointments. We seem currently to be riding another wave of excitement, so it is worth keeping in mind the lessons of the past.

1.2.1 The Beginning

Efforts to build machine translation systems started almost as soon as electronic computers came into existence. Computers were used in

Britain to crack the German Enigma code in World War II and decoding language codes seemed like an apt metaphor for machine translation. Warren Weaver, one of the pioneering minds in machine translation, wrote in 1947:

> *When I look at an article in Russian, I say: 'This is really written in English, but it has been coded in some strange symbols. I will now proceed to decode'.* [Weaver, 1947, 1949]

The emergence of electronic brains created all kinds of expectations and some researchers hoped to solve the problem of machine translation early on. Major funding went into the field.

Some of the principles of machine translation that were established in the early days remain valid today. Not only are we still talking about *decoding* a foreign language and using such modeling techniques as the noisy-channel model, it also appears that the funding for the field of machine translation is still driven by the same motivation as code breaking. Governments, especially that of the United States, seem to be most willing to tackle the languages of countries that are taken to be a threat to national security, be it militarily or economically.

In the early days, many approaches were explored, ranging from simple **direct translation** methods that map input to output with basic rules, through more sophisticated **transfer** methods that employ morphological and syntactic analysis, and up to **interlingua** methods that use an abstract meaning representation.

interlingua

1.2.2 The ALPAC Report and Its Consequences

The early days were characterized by great optimism. Promises of imminent breakthroughs were in the air, and the impression was created that mechanical translation (as it was then called) would soon be solved. In the **Georgetown experiment**, the translation of Russian to English was demonstrated, suggesting that the problem was almost solved. On the other hand, sceptics made the claim that some problems, especially those related to semantic disambiguation, are impossible to solve by automatic means.

Georgetown experiment

The flurry of activity surrounding machine translation came to a grinding halt with the issue of the **ALPAC report** in 1966. US funding agencies commissioned the Automatic Language Processing Advisory Committee to carry out a study of the realities of machine translation.

ALPAC report

The study showed, among other things, that post-editing machine translation output was not cheaper or faster than full human translation. It established that only about $20 million was spent on translation in the US annually. There was very little Russian scientific literature worth translating and there was no shortage of human translators. The committee suggested that there was no advantage in using machine translation systems. Funding should rather go into basic linguistic research and the development of methods to improve human translation.

Funding for machine translation in the United States stopped almost entirely as a consequence. While the ALPAC report may have unfairly considered only the goal of high-quality translation, the experience shows the dangers of over-promising the abilities of machine translation systems.

1.2.3 First Commercial Systems

Despite sharply reduced research efforts, the foundations of commercial translations were nevertheless laid in the decade after the ALPAC report. One early fully functioning system is the **Météo** system for translating weather forecasts, which was developed at the University of Montreal. It has been operating since 1976.

Météo

Systran **Systran** was founded in 1968. Its Russian–English system has been used by the US Air Force since 1970. A French–English version was bought by the European Commission in 1976, and thereafter systems for more European language pairs were developed. Other commercial systems that came to the market in the 1980s were the **Logos** and **METAL** systems.

Logos
METAL

The Pan American Health Organization in Washington has successfully developed and widely used a system for translating Spanish to English and back since the 1970s. In the late 1980s, Japanese computer companies built translation systems for Japanese and English. During the 1990s, the more widespread use of desktop computer systems led to the development of **computer aided translation** systems for human translators by companies such as **Trados**.

computer aided translation
Trados

1.2.4 Research in Interlingua-Based Systems

A research trend in the 1980s and 1990s was the focus on the development of systems that use **interlingua** to represent meaning independent of a specific language. Syntactic formalism grew more sophisticated, including reversible grammars that may be used for both analysis and generation. The notion of representing meaning in a formal way tied together several strands of research both from artificial intelligence and computational linguistics.

interlingua

One example in the development of interlingua-based systems is the CATALYST project at Carnegie Mellon University (CMU), which was developed for the translation of technical manuals of Caterpillar Tractor. Another example is the Pangloss system that was developed at New Mexico State University, the University of Southern California, and CMU. The development of interlingua systems was also an important element in the large German Verbmobil project (1993–2000).

The attraction of developing such systems is easy to see. Translating involves expressing meaning in different languages, so a proper theory of meaning seems to address this problem at a more fundamental level than the low-level mapping of lexical or syntactic units. The problem of representing meaning in a formal way is one of the grand challenges of artificial intelligence with interesting philosophical implications.

1.2.5 Data-Driven Methods

Since language translation is burdened with so many decisions that are hard to formalize, it may be better to learn how to translate from past translation examples. This idea is also motivation for **translation memory** systems for human translators that store and retrieve matching translation examples for a given new input text.

translation memory

Early efforts based on this idea are **example-based translation** systems that have been built especially in Japan since the 1980s. These systems try to find a sentence similar to the input sentence in a parallel corpus, and make the appropriate changes to its stored translation.

example-based translation

In the late 1980s, the idea of statistical machine translation was born in the labs of IBM Research in the wake of successes of statistical methods in speech recognition. By modeling the translation task as a statistical optimization problem, the Candide project put machine translation on a solid mathematical foundation.

The emergence of statistical machine translation was ground-breaking. In retrospect it seems that the world was not quite ready for it. Throughout the 1990s, most researchers still focused on syntax-based and interlingua systems, which was tied in with work in semantic representations. Most of the original researchers at IBM left the field and found fortunes on Wall Street instead.

While research on statistical methods for machine translation continued throughout the 1990s to some degree (their success in the German Verbmobil project is one highlight), the approach gathered full steam only around the year 2000. A number of factors contributed to this.

In 1998, participants at a Johns Hopkins University workshop re-implemented most of the IBM methods and made the resulting tools

DARPA   widely available. **DARPA**, the leading funding agency in the United States, showed great interest in statistical machine translation and funded the large TIDES and GALE programs. The US response to the events of September 11, 2001 also played a role in the renewed interest in the automatic translation of foreign languages, especially Arabic.

Another factor in the rise of statistical methods is the increase in computing power and data storage, along with the increasing availability of digital text resources as a consequence of the growth of the Internet. Nowadays, anyone can download parallel corpora along with standard tools from the web and build a machine translation system on a typical home computer.

1.2.6 Current Developers

Statistical machine translation systems are currently being developed in a large number of academic and commercial research labs. Some of these efforts have led to the founding of new companies. Language Weaver was the first company, founded in 2002, that fully embraced the new paradigm and promised *translation by numbers*. Commercial statistical machine translation systems are also being developed by large software companies such as IBM, Microsoft, and Google.

At the same time, traditional machine translation companies, such as the market leader Systran, are integrating statistical methods into their systems. Its system also demonstrates the usefulness of machine translation today. Internet users translate 50 million web pages a day, using systems, hosted by Google, Yahoo, Microsoft, and others.

There is a great deal of excitement in the air, when leading research groups gather at venues such as the yearly NIST evaluation workshop in Washington, D.C. Ideas about the latest methods are exchanged in the light of continuing improvements of machine translation performance that raise the hope that one day machine translation will not only be very useful, but that it will also be *good*.

1.2.7 State of the Art

How good is statistical machine translation today? This question opens a can of worms. In fact, we devote an entire chapter to attempts to address it (Chapter 8). Let us answer it here with a few translation examples.

Figure 1.8 shows the output for a relatively easy language pair, French–English. The excerpt is taken from the University of Edinburgh systems submission to the 2005 WMT shared task. This system is

---

French input

Nous savons trés bien que les Traités actuels ne suffisent pas et qu'il sera nécessaire à l'avenir de développer une structure plus efficace et différente pour l'Union, une structure plus constitutionnelle qui indique clairement quelles sont les compétences des États membres et quelles sont les compétences de l'Union.

Statistical machine translation

We know very well that the current treaties are not enough and that in the future it will be necessary to develop a different and more effective structure for the union, a constitutional structure which clearly indicates what are the responsibilities of the member states and what are the competences of the union.

Human translation

We know all too well that the present Treaties are inadequate and that the Union will need a better and different structure in future, a more constitutional structure which clearly distinguishes the powers of the Member States and those of the Union.

Figure 1.8 Example of French–English statistical machine translation output (University of Edinburgh system on WMT 2005 shared task evaluation set).

Arabic input

اعتبر تيرى رود لارسن الموفد السابق للامم المتحدة الى الشرق الاوسط ان الوضع فى هذه المنطقة لم يكن يوما على درجة الخطورة التى هو عليها اليوم مشبها المنطقة ب " برميل بارود بفتيل مشتعل " .

Statistical machine translation

Former envoy Terje Roed Larsen, the United Nations to the Middle East that the situation in this region was not as serious as it is today, comparing the region "powder keg burning".

Human translation

Terje Roed-Larsen, the former United Nations Middle East envoy, considered the situation in the region as having never been as dangerous as it is today and compared the region to a "powder keg with a lit fuse".

Figure 1.9 Example of Arabic–English statistical machine translation output (University of Edinburgh system on NIST 2006 evaluation set).

---

trained on nearly 40 million words of parallel text that was collected mostly from the European Parliament proceedings and from a much smaller collection of news commentaries. The example displayed is the first sentence of the test set.

Figure 1.9 shows the output for a more difficult language pair, Arabic–English. Again, the excerpt is taken from a recent version of the statistical machine translation system developed at the University of Edinburgh. This system is trained on about 200 million words of parallel text that has been made available through the LDC and the GALE program. The example displayed is the first line from the 2006 NIST evaluation set.

Figure 1.10 shows the output for a very difficult language pair, Chinese–English. Again, training data is provided by the LDC, a

Figure 1.10 Example of Chinese–English statistical machine translation output (University of Edinburgh system on NIST 2006 evaluation set).

Chinese input

伦敦每日快报指出,两台记载黛安娜王妃一九九七年巴黎死亡车祸调查资料的手提电脑,被从前大都会警察总长的办公室里偷走.

Statistical machine translation

The London Daily Express pointed out that the death of Princess Diana in 1997 Paris car accident investigation information portable computers, the former city police chief in the offices of stolen.

Human translation

London's Daily Express noted that two laptops with inquiry data on the 1997 Paris car accident that caused the death of Princess Diana were stolen from the office of a former metropolitan police commissioner.

---

parallel text with about 200 million English words, and the excerpt is the first sentence taken from the 2006 NIST evaluation set.

1.3 Applications

The usefulness of machine translation technology rises with its quality. Machine translation does not have to be perfect to be useful, **crummy** machine translation also has its applications.

crummy

The use of machine translation may be broken up broadly into three categories: (a) **assimilation**, the translation of foreign material for the purpose of understanding the content; (b) **dissemination**, translating text for publication in other languages; and (c) **communication**, such as the translation of emails, chat room discussions, and so on. Each of these uses requires a different speed and quality.

assimilation
dissemination
communication

1.3.1 Fully-Automatic High-Quality Machine Translation

The holy grail of machine translation is expressed in the cumbersome acronym FAHQMT, which stands for fully-automatic high-quality machine translation. Given the complexity of language and the many unsolved problems in machine translation, this goal has been reached only for **limited domain** applications.

limited domain

Take the example of weather forecasts, or summaries of sports events. The set of possible sentences in these domains is sufficiently constrained that it is possible to write translation rules that capture all possibilities. Machine translation systems for automatic use have also been built for interactive applications such as rail or flight information or appointment scheduling.

Another way to achieve high-quality machine translation is by **controlled language**. Multinational companies have to produce documentation for their products in many languages. One way to achieve that is to author the documentation in a constrained version of English that machine translation systems are able to translate.

controlled language

Statistical machine translation systems also reach very high performance when they translate documentation for new products using very similar documentation of old products as training material.

1.3.2 Gisting

The most widespread use of machine translation is **gisting**, for instance the translation of web pages with online translation services by users themselves who want to understand what is written in a foreign language. Translation does not have to be perfect to bring across the meaning. For instance, if a user is able to translate a technical support page from English into his native Spanish and understand enough to solve his technical problem, then machine translation has proven its usefulness.

gisting

The translation services of Systran which currently support the translation functions of web sites such as Yahoo and Google translate 500 million words a day.[2] This vast number is testament to the usefulness of machine translation which is not perfect, but good enough.

The possibility of gisting foreign texts also drives the use of machine translation technology by intelligence agencies. Currently major funding for machine translation research comes from the US defense department, which is interested in tracking news reports and other communications from countries of concern.

Machine translation is the first step toward information extraction and ultimately analysis of large amounts of foreign material. If analysts find truly interesting pieces of information, it will be passed on to a human translator. But human translators are not needed (and not even available) to translate all foreign texts that are potentially of interest.

1.3.3 Integration with Speech Technologies

An exciting direction for machine translation is its combination with speech technologies. It opens up a wide range of uses such as translating telephone conversations or audio broadcasts.

---

[2] According to Jean Senellart, Systran, 2007.

speech recognition The field of machine translation is following trends in **speech recognition** with some lag time. Statistical methods in speech recognition revolutionized the field in the 1980s and many commercial companies using statistical speech recognition methods were founded in the 1990s and now dominate the field.

Many ideas from speech recognition find their way into statistical machine translation. The close collaboration of speech researchers with machine translation researchers in recent research programs such as the GALE program (funded by DARPA) and the TC-STAR program (funded by the European Commission) nurtures this knowledge transfer between disciplines.

The methods used in modern speech recognition and statistical machine translation are similar, so the integration of the two technologies is fairly straightforward. In its easiest form the best output of the speech recognizer is passed on to the machine translation system. But since both technologies operate on probabilistic models it is also possible to pass on word lattices with confidence scores.

Current testbed applications are the translation of broadcast news, parliament speeches, and travel domain conversations. There are systems in use today that monitor news broadcasts in foreign languages and perform speech translation in real time. Speech-to-speech translation of live presentations in public forums has also been demonstrated.

1.3.4 Translation on Hand-Held Devices

hand-held devices The increasing computing power in **hand-held devices** makes it possible to run machine translation systems on them, even if the systems have to be scaled down to match their memory limitations. Experimental systems have been developed to assist foreign health workers in developing countries and to support soldiers in the field.

An obvious commercial use is hand-held devices for tourists. Hand-held dictionaries are already commercially successful and extending them to include the capability to translate full sentences and to recognize spoken language is on the horizon of what is currently technically possible. You can buy hand-held devices that translate Japanese to English for tourists.

An interesting extension to hand-held translators is the capability to translate text in images. By applying optical character recognition (OCR) to the camera capabilities that are now standard with hand-held devices of any kind, it is possible to translate signs, directions at train stations, or restaurant menus. Since these are all very limited domain sublanguages applications (or **sublanguages**), there is no need for a fully-fledged general machine translation system.

1.3.5 Post-Editing

If the goal of translation is to produce publishable high-quality text, machine translation may act as a first step to producing a rough translation. In the second step, a human post-editor may then correct the output to the desired level of quality.

Post-editing machine translation output (also called human aided machine translation) is cost-efficient if the effort of post-editing is less than the effort of translation from scratch. The efficiency rises with the quality of machine translation. If the machine translation system reliably brings the meaning across, the post-editor does not need to know the foreign input language. Since bilingual speakers are much harder to come by than monolingual speakers, this reduces the cost of correcting the output.

One may also imagine a scenario in which a monolingual post-editor fixes the mistakes in fluency of the English output and a second bilingual post-editor fixes the mistakes in meaning. Note that if the monolingual post-editor knows something about the subject matter of the text, he will catch many mistakes in meaning already.

Post-editing

1.3.6 Tools for Translators

Human translators are generally more comfortable with tools that support them in the task of translation rather than being reduced to post-editing machine translation output. Machine translation technology can be exploited to create an interactive environment for translators that increases their productivity.

Translation memory systems that look for text matches in large collections of previously translated material are commonly used by professional translators today.

More interactive tools for translators are being developed. Statistical machine translation technology is used not only to find the most likely translation of an input sentence, but also to assess the system's confidence that the proposed translation is accurate. If the confidence does not meet a certain threshold, it is better not to distract the human translator with error-prone output.

Translation memory

1.4 Available Resources

To build a statistical machine translation system for a particular language pair, all one needs is a parallel corpus for that language and a generic statistical machine translation toolkit.

Fortunately, the research community in the field provides tools for many of the methods described in this book. In fact, all necessary tools to build a baseline machine translation system are freely available, along with parallel corpora for many language pairs. With these tools it is possible to have a system up and running within a few days.

This book is not an application manual for existing tools, but rather describes the underlying methods. The set of available tools and their use is changing too fast to be able to provide a comprehensive overview that will not be outdated soon after publication of this book. Instead, we will maintain a list of tools and resources at the book's web site.[3]

Still, we would like to give an overview of what is currently available to provide a starting point for the reader. Two great resources for publications on statistical machine translations are the **ACL Anthology**[4] and the **Machine Translation Archive**.[5]

ACL Anthology

Machine Translation Archive

1.4.1 Tools

Some researchers in statistical machine translation have made their tools available. These are all targeted at fellow researchers, and typically designed for UNIX systems. That implies that they are generally not very polished and sometimes lack sufficient documentation. On the other hand, their source code is typically available, so they can be inspected and modified.

GIZA++

GIZA++[6] is an implementation of the IBM word-based models (Chapter 4), and it is commonly used nowadays for word alignment. The code was developed at a Johns Hopkins University summer workshop and later refined by Franz Och.

SRILM

SRILM[7] is a tool for language modeling (Chapter 7). It has a long history of contributions from Johns Hopkins University summer workshop participants, and is maintained by Andreas Stolcke at SRI. Also in use is the language modeling software developed by **IRST**,[8] which provides efficient methods for handling very large models.

IRST

Moses

Moses[9] is an implementation of a phrase-based decoder (Chapter 6), including training (Chapter 5). It was developed at the University

---

[3] The book's web site is at http://www.statmt.org/book/

[4] ACL Anthology is available at http://acl.ldc.upenn.edu/

[5] Machine Translation Archive is available at http://www.mt-archive.info/

[6] GIZA++ is available at http://www.fjoch.com/GIZA++.html

[7] SRILM is available at http://www.speech.sri.com/projects/srilm/

[8] IRSTLM is available at http://sourceforge.net/projects/irstlm/

[9] Moses is available at http://www.statmt.org/moses/

of Edinburgh and enhanced during a Johns Hopkins University summer
workshop. It is the successor to **Pharaoh**,[10] which was developed at
the University of Southern California. **Thot**[11] is an alternative training
package for phrase-based models.

    SAMT[12] is a system for tree-based models (Chapter 11), which was
developed at Carnegie Mellon University. It is maintained by Andreas
Zollmann and Ashish Venugopal.

    The **BLEU**[13] scoring tool is most commonly used to evalu-
ate machine translation performance (Chapter 8). Recently, the
METEOR[14] metric has gained popularity as well.

    Also note that many researchers make their tools available on
request, even if they do not have an official release mechanism in place.

1.4.2 Corpora

The **LDC**[15] (Linguistic Data Consortium) releases a large number of
parallel corpora, most notably a large set of resources for Arabic–
English, Chinese–English, and French–English (Canadian Hansard).
Also large monolingual corpora are made available, for instance the
English **Gigaword** corpus that contains several billion words of news
reports.

    The **Europarl**[16] corpus is a collection of proceedings of the Euro-
pean Parliament, which is translated across eleven languages. It consists
of about 40 million words per language.

    The **OPUS**[17] initiative collects various parallel corpora, includ-
ing the localization and documentation of open source software. The
Acquis Communautaire[18] corpus is a collection of legal documents
signed by European Union member countries, available in over 20
languages.

1.4.3 Evaluation Campaigns

Improving machine translation performance is partly driven by competitive evaluation campaigns that compare machine translation systems

---

[10] Pharaoh is available at http://www.isi.edu/licensed-sw/pharaoh/
[11] Thot is available at http://thot.sourceforge.net/
[12] SAMS is available at http://www.cs.cmu.edu/~zollmann/samt/
[13] BLEU is available at http://www.nist.gov/speech/tests/mt/scoring/
[14] METEOR is available at http://www.cs.cmu.edu/~alavie/METEOR/
[15] LDC is hosted at http://www.ldc.upenn.edu/
[16] Europarl is available at http://www.statmt.org/europarl/
[17] OPUS is available at http://logos.uio.no/opus/
[18] Acquis Communautaire is available at http://langtech.jrc.it/JRC-Acquis.html

of leading research groups on a yearly basis. These campaigns also generate standard test sets, manual evaluation data, and reference performance numbers.

NIST   The **NIST**[19] (National Institute of Standards and Technology) evaluation is the oldest and most prestigious evaluation campaign, focusing on Arabic–English and Chinese–English. It releases manual evaluation data through the LDC.

IWSLT   The **IWSLT**[20] (International Workshop on Spoken Language Translation) evaluation campaign has a stronger focus on speech translation in a limited travel domain. It is centered on translation between English and Asian languages such as Chinese, Japanese, and Korean, but more recently also Italian.

WMT   The **WMT**[21] (Workshop on Statistical Machine Translation) evaluation campaign targets translation between European languages. It has

EuroMatrix   recently been supported by the **EuroMatrix**[22] project. A similar evalu-
TC-STAR   ation campaign was organized by the European **TC-STAR**[23] project.

1.5 Summary

1.5.1 Core Concepts

The field of machine translation has had its ups and downs, triggered by over-selling of the technological abilities, such as in the **Georgetown experiment**, and overly sceptical assessments such as the **ALPAC report**. Much of the history of machine translation systems is also the history of the involvement of funding agencies such as **DARPA**.

Early approaches to machine translation are **direct translation**, **transfer**, and **interlingua** methods. Some of the early commercial systems developed in the 1970s and 1980s, such as **Météo**, **Systran**, **Logos**, **METAL**, are still around today. Another commercial use of translation technology is **computer aided translation**, such as the **translation memory** system developed by **Trados**. An early data-driven method is **example-based translation**.

The main uses of translation are **assimilation**, **dissemination**, and **communication**, which creates many different avenues for translation technology to replace or augment human translation efforts. The requirements for quality differ; **crummy** translation may be often good enough, for instance for translation of web pages.

The problem of machine translation may be reduced by restriction to a **limited domain**, or the use of a **controlled language** when

---

[19] NIST evaluation is hosted at http://www.nist.gov/speech/tests/mt/
[20] IWSLT 2007 is hosted at http://iwslt07.itc.it/
[21] WMT 2007 is hosted at http://www.statmt.org/wmt07/
[22] Euromatrix is hosted at http://www.euromatrix.net/
[23] TC-STAR is hosted at http://www.tc-star.org/

authoring text with its translation in mind. Such limited use of language is also called a **sublanguage**.

1.5.2 Further Reading

General introduction – For non-statistical methods of machine translation, refer to the books by Arnold *et al.* [1994] and by Hutchins and Somers [1992]. For the history of machine translation, Hutchins [2007] gives a concise overview. Gaspari and Hutchins [2007] report on the recent rise of online machine translation services and usage patterns. See also the famous ALPAC report [Pierce and Carroll, 1966]. A recent survey of work in statistical machine translation is presented by Lopez [2008a].

Statistical machine translation and other methods – Statistical machine translation is related to other data-driven methods in machine translation, such as the earlier work on example-based machine translation [Somers, 1999]. Contrast this to systems that are based on hand-crafted rules. The distinctions between these categories are getting blurred. Borrowing from different approaches is called the hybrid approach to machine translation. Statistical methods, especially the use of the language model, may be integrated in rule-based systems [Knight *et al.*, 1994; Habash and Dorr, 2002]. Parsing and translation decisions may be learned from data [Hermjakob and Mooney, 1997]. Multiple scoring functions may decide between the alternatives generated by the transfer-based system [Carl, 2007]. Statistical methods may be used to learn rules for traditional rule-based systems [Font Llitjós and Vogel, 2007]. Conversely, translations from rule-based systems may be used as additional phrase translations in statistical systems [Chen *et al.*, 2007c]. Rule-based systems may be used to generate training data for statistical methods [Hu *et al.*, 2007], essentially having the statistical method relearn the rule-based system [Dugast *et al.*, 2008]. Often statistical machine translation is used as a fall-back for methods that frequently fail to produce output, but are more accurate when they do [Chai *et al.*, 2006]. Statistical machine translation models may also be used to automatically post-edit the output of interlingual [Seneff *et al.*, 2006] or rule-based systems [Simard *et al.*, 2007]. Additional markup from the rule-based system may be exploited for tighter integration [Ueffing *et al.*, 2008]. Such post-editing may alleviate the need to customize rule-based systems to a specific domain [Isabelle *et al.*, 2007]. Related to this, refer to the further reading on system combination in Chapter 9. Labaka *et al.* [2007] compare different machine translation approaches for the Basque–Spanish language pair.

Available software – Popular implementations of statistical machine translations are Pharaoh [Koehn, 2004a], which was succeeded by the open source Moses [Koehn *et al.*, 2007]. Phramer [Olteanu *et al.*, 2006a] is a Java implementation of a phrase-based statistical system. Thot [Ortiz-Martínez *et al.*, 2005] is a toolkit to train phrase-based models for these decoders. Available implementations of tree-based decoders are Hiero [Chiang *et al.*, 2005] and SAMT [Zollmann *et al.*, 2007]. GIZA++ [Och and Ney, 2003] and MTTK [Deng and Byrne, 2006] are tools for word alignment; Hunalign[24] [Varga *et al.*, 2005] is a popular tool for sentence alignment. Cattoni *et al.* [2006] present a web demo for their phrase-based system. An online tool for machine translation evaluation is presented by Eck *et al.* [2006b]. Yawat is a web-based tool to view and create word alignments [Germann, 2007, 2008].

Competitions – The development of statistical machine translation systems is driven by translation competitions, most notably annual competitions organized by DARPA on Arabic–English and Chinese–English in an open news domain (since 2001). The International Workshop on Spoken Language Translation (IWSLT) [Akiba *et al.*, 2004a; Eck and Hori, 2005; Paul, 2006; Fordyce, 2007] is an annual competition on translating Asian languages and Arabic into English in a more limited speech travel domain. The WMT campaign is a competition on European languages mostly using the European Parliament proceedings [Koehn and Monz, 2005, 2006; Callison-Burch *et al.*, 2007, 2008].

Research groups – Statistical machine translation models have been developed by a number of research groups, such as:

- ATR, Japan [Zhang *et al.*, 2006b; Finch *et al.*, 2007]
- Cambridge University [Blackwood *et al.*, 2008a]
- Carnegie Mellon University [Vogel *et al.*, 2003; Zollmann *et al.*, 2007; Lane *et al.*, 2007; Bach *et al.*, 2008; Hanneman *et al.*, 2008]
- Charles University, Prague [Bojar and Hajič, 2008; Zabokrtsky *et al.*, 2008]
- Dublin City University [Stroppa and Way, 2006; Hassan *et al.*, 2007a; Tinsley *et al.*, 2008]
- Google [Och, 2005]
- IBM [Lee, 2005, 2006]
- Inesc-ID, Lisbon, Portugal [Graça *et al.*, 2007]
- Institute for Infocomm Research, Singapore [Chen *et al.*, 2007b]
- Institute of Computing Technology, Beijing, China [He *et al.*, 2007]
- Fundazione Bruno Kessler, formerly ITC-irst [Cettolo *et al.*, 2005; Chen *et al.*, 2006a; Bertoldi *et al.*, 2007]
- Hong Kong University of Science and Technology [Shen *et al.*, 2007b]
- Johns Hopkins University [Kumar *et al.*, 2004]
- LIMSI, France [Schwenk *et al.*, 2006a; Déchelotte *et al.*, 2008]
- Microsoft

[24] http://mokk.bme.hu/resources/hunalign

- MIT Lincoln Labs [Shen *et al.*, 2005, 2006a, 2007a]
- National Laboratory for Pattern Recognition in China [Pang *et al.*, 2005; Zhou *et al.*, 2007].
- National Research Council in Canada [Sadat *et al.*, 2005; Johnson *et al.*, 2006; Ueffing *et al.*, 2007b]
- National Research Institute of Electronics and Cryptology, Turkey [Mermer *et al.*, 2007]
- National University of Defense Technology, China [Chao and Li, 2007b]
- NTT, Japan [Tsukada *et al.*, 2005; Watanabe *et al.*, 2006c,a, 2007a]
- Polytechnic University of Catalunya, Barcelona [Crego *et al.*, 2005; Giménez and Màrquez, 2006; Costa-jussà *et al.*, 2006b,a; Crego *et al.*, 2006b; Civera and Juan, 2007; Lambert *et al.*, 2007b; Khalilov *et al.*, 2008]
- Polytechnic University of Valencia [Alabau *et al.*, 2007b]
- RWTH Aachen [Ney *et al.*, 2001; Bender *et al.*, 2004; Mauser *et al.*, 2006, 2007]
- Saarland University [Chen *et al.*, 2007c; Eisele *et al.*, 2008]
- Systran [Dugast *et al.*, 2007, 2008]
- Technical University of Valencia [Casacuberta and Vidal, 2004; Costa-jussà and Fonollosa, 2007]
- Tottori University, Japan [Murakami *et al.*, 2007]
- University College London [Wang and Shawe-Taylor, 2008]
- University J. Fournier, Grenoble [Besacier *et al.*, 2007]
- University of Caen Basse-Normandie [Lepage and Denoual, 2005; Lepage and Lardilleux, 2007]
- University of California, Berkeley [Nakov and Hearst, 2007; Nakov, 2008]
- University of Edinburgh [Koehn *et al.*, 2005; Koehn and Schroeder, 2007; Schroeder and Koehn, 2007; Koehn *et al.*, 2008]
- University of Karlsruhe [Eck *et al.*, 2006a; Paulik *et al.*, 2007; Lane *et al.*, 2007]
- University of Linköping [Holmqvist *et al.*, 2007; Stymne *et al.*, 2008]
- University of Le Mans [Schwenk *et al.*, 2008]
- University of Maryland [Chiang *et al.*, 2005; Dyer, 2007a,b]
- University of Montreal [Langlais *et al.*, 2005; Patry *et al.*, 2006, 2007]
- University of Paris, LIMSI [Schwenk, 2007]
- University of Southern California/ISI [DeNeefe and Knight, 2005]
- University of Texas at Dallas [Olteanu *et al.*, 2006a]
- University of Washington [Kirchhoff *et al.*, 2006; Kirchhoff and Yang, 2007; Axelrod *et al.*, 2008]
- Xerox Research Centre Europe [Nikoulina and Dymetman, 2008b]
- Xiamen University, China [Chen *et al.*, 2006c, 2007d]

Speech translation – There has been increasing interest in integrating speech recognition and machine translation [Zhang *et al.*, 2004b]. In speech-to-speech translation systems, a speech generator needs to be added as final step [Sumita *et al.*, 2007]. Vilar *et al.* [2005] gives an overview of the work of integrating speech recognition and machine translation in the TC-Star project. Often n-best lists are passed from the speech recognizer to the translation system [Lee *et al.*, 2007]. Interfacing the output of a speech recognizer and a machine translation system raises problems such as sentence segmentation and punctuation prediction [Matusov *et al.*, 2006a]; this may require extension of the lattice that is passed to the machine translation component [Bertoldi *et al.*, 2007]. For limited domains, real-time speech-to-speech systems have been implemented and deployed in the field, such as for *force protection* [Bach *et al.*, 2007]. It is not too much of a step to simultaneously translate speech into multiple languages [Pérez *et al.*, 2007a,b].

Computer aided translation – By giving human translators access to the inner workings of a machine translation system, they may fix errors at various stages, such as changing the source sentences or its linguistic analysis [Varga and Yokoyama, 2007]. The TransType project [Langlais *et al.*, 2000; Foster *et al.*, 2002; Bender *et al.*, 2005] developed an interactive translation tool which predicts the most appropriate extension of a partial translation by quick re-translation based on user input [Tomás and Casacuberta, 2006]. Word graphs allow for quicker re-translations [Och *et al.*, 2003; Civera *et al.*, 2004, 2006] and confidence metrics indicate how much should be presented to the user as reliable prediction [Ueffing and Ney, 2005, 2007]. Macklovitch [2004] describes how users interacted with the TransType tool. Conversely, the input to a translation system may be automatically examined for phrases that are difficult to translate [Mohit and Hwa, 2007]. A user of a translation tool would like to have types of information, such as suggested translations for idioms, unknown words, and names [Abekawa and Kageura, 2007]. Macklovitch *et al.* [2005] present a tool that visualizes the user interactions. Human post-editing data may be mined to improve the performance of machine translation, as shown for transfer-based systems [Llitjos *et al.*, 2007]. Machine translation may also be used for interactive tutoring tools for foreign language learners [Wang and Seneff, 2007]. Macklovitch [1994] shows how alignment methods may be used to spot errors in human translations.

1.5.3 Exercises

1. (⋆) What are the hardest problems in translations for
   (a) human translators?
   (b) machine translation systems?

2. (⋆) Given that the main uses of translation technology are assimilation, dissemination, and communication, describe how these uses differ in terms of
   (a) demands for quality;
   (b) requirements for speed;
   (c) willingness to spend money;
   (d) size of the market.
3. (⋆) The dominant method for building a machine translation system has evolved from being based on transfer rules over interlingua to statistics. Which of these methods is best suited to deal with the following translation problems?:
   (a) a word has multiple translations;
   (b) when translating from French to English, often adjectives and nouns are swapped;
   (c) a metaphorical expression that cannot be translated literally;
   (d) a particular concept in one language has no clear equivalent in the other;
   (e) translation from or to languages with a rich morphology.

Chapter 2
Words, Sentences, Corpora

This chapter is intended for readers who have little or no background in natural language processing. We introduce basic linguistics concepts and explain their relevance to statistical machine translation. Starting with words and their linguistic properties, we move up to sentences, issues of syntax and semantics. We also discuss the role text corpora play in the building of a statistical machine translation system and the basic methods used to obtain and prepare these data sources.

2.1 Words

Intuitively, the basic atomic unit of meaning is a **word**. For instance, the word *house* evokes the mental image of a rectangular building with a roof and smoking chimney, which may be surrounded by grass and trees and inhabited by a happy family. When *house* is used in a text, the reader adapts this meaning based on the context (*her grandmother's house* is different from the *White House*), but we are able to claim that almost all uses of *house* are connected to that basic unit of meaning.

word

There are smaller units, such as syllables or sounds, but a *hou* or *s* do not evoke the mental image or meaning of *house*. The notion of a word seems straightforward for English readers. The text you are reading right now has its words clearly separated by spaces, so they stand out as units.

Interestingly, this representation and the way we understand words is not always that obvious. In spoken language, we do not pause between words, a fact that is somewhat surprising: We seem to *hear* separate words, we can clearly make them out. However, when listening to an unknown foreign language, our ability to discern different words is lost, and we recognize speech as being a stream of sounds without many pauses.

Some writing systems also do not clearly mark words as unique units. For instance Chinese is typically written without spaces between words, so the inventory of words is not clear. To illustrate this problem with an English example: We consider *homework* a single word, but it is really composed of two words. It refers to *work* we do at *home*. Besides such compounding, there are also morphological phenomena that slightly muddle the clear notion of words: Is *Joe's* one or two words, as *doesn't* is really the orthographic merger of two words?

Another direction that challenges our notion of words as atomic units of meaning is idiomatic expressions. Consider the sentence *She's gone off the deep end.* The words in the phrase *off the deep end* all have distinct meanings that are not related to the meaning of the phrase *crazy.* Note that this problem of non-compositional phrases is a problem for translation. While we assume that we can often translate word-by-word, this is clearly not possible for such cases.

2.1.1 Tokenization

tokenization One of the basic text processing steps is **tokenization**, the breaking up of raw text into words. For languages that use the Latin alphabet, this is mainly an issue of splitting off punctuation.

For writing systems that do not already provide spaces between words, it is a more challenging task. Much work has gone into the breaking up of Chinese text, a process referred to as **Chinese word**
Chinese word segmentation **segmentation**. For this task, we need a lexicon of possible words and a method to resolve ambiguities between different possible segmentations (for instance: prefer more frequent words).

But even for English there are some tokenization issues that do not have straightforward answers:

- What should we do with the possessive marker in *Joe's*, or merged words such as *doesn't*? Typically these are broken up. For instance, the possessive marker *'s* is considered a word in its own right.
- How about hyphenated words such as *co-operate*, *so-called*, or *high-risk*? There seems to be little benefit of breaking up *co-operate*, but *high-risk* is really made up of two words.

When tokenizing text for machine translation, the main guiding principle is that we want to reduce text to a sequence of tokens from a small inventory. We do not want to learn different translations for *house*, depending on whether it is followed by a comma (*house,*), surrounded by quotes (*"house"*), and so on.

Some languages, such as German, are famous for creating new words by **compounding** existing words. Some of these words – *kinder-garten, zeitgeist, weltschmerz*, and so on – have even found their way into the English language. Compounding is very productive in creating new words, for instance *Neuwortgenerierung* (new word generation) is a perfectly fine German word, although it cannot be found in any document on the web.[1] Breaking up compound words may be part of the tokenization stage for some languages.

compounding

Related to tokenization is the issue of words that occur in lower-cased or uppercased form in text. The items *house, House*, and *HOUSE* may all occur in a large text collection, in the middle of a sentence, at the beginning of a sentence, or in a headline, respectively. It is the same word, so we would like to normalize case, typically by **lowercas-ing** or **truecasing**. The latter preserves uppercase in names, allowing the distinction between *Mr Fisher* and *a fisher*.

lowercasing

truecasing

Figure 2.1 gives an example of tokenization and lowercasing. Here we decided to break up hyphenated words and introduced the special token @-@ for the hyphen to distinguish it from a dash.

At the other end of the translation processing pipeline, we would like to present users with text in its natural form, so we have to **detok-enize** it to reattach punctuation, and undo all other tokenization steps. We also have to **recase**, so that sentences start with an uppercase character, and names (*Mr Fisher*) are distinguished from regular nouns.

detokenization

recasing

All these pre-processing and post-processing steps are typically done with dedicated tools, so that the machine translation system only has to deal with the problem of translating tokenized lowercased text in one language into tokenized lowercased text in another.

2.1.2 Distribution of Words

What are the words of the English language? This seems to be an open-ended question, since new words are constantly coined and others

Raw text	My son's friend, however, plays a high-risk game.
Tokenized	My son 's friend , however , plays a high @-@ risk game .
Lowercased	my son 's friend , however , plays a high @-@ risk game .

Figure 2.1 Tokenization and lowercasing: Basic data processing steps for machine translation. Besides splitting off punctuation, hyphenated and merged words may be broken up.

[1] According to a Google search in early 2007.

Figure 2.2 The most
frequent words in the English
Europarl corpus. The left-hand
table displays the 10 most
frequent tokens (including
punctuation), the right-hand
table displays the 10 most
frequent content words.

Frequency in text	Token	Frequency in text	Content word
1,929,379	the	129,851	european
1,297,736	,	110,072	mr
956,902	.	98,073	commission
901,174	of	71,111	president
841,661	to	67,518	parliament
684,869	and	64,620	union
582,592	in	58,506	report
452,491	that	57,490	council
424,895	is	54,079	states
424,552	a	49,965	member

fall out of use. The vocabulary of English words is a very fluid concept.

A more practical question is: How many English words are used in a corpus? To answer this question, let us take a closer look at the **Europarl** corpus, a collection of debate transcripts from the proceedings of the European Parliament. The corpus contains about 29 million English words (about one million sentences). Following our definition of word in the previous section (after tokenization and lowercasing), we can find 86,699 different words in this corpus.

Some words are more frequent than others. See Figure 2.2 for the most frequent words in this corpus. The top 10 words are all **function words**; the most common is *the*, which occurs 1,929,379 times. Given that there are 86,699 different words, it is astonishing that this one word makes up almost 7% of the corpus. The top 10 words (this includes the comma and end-of-sentence period token) together account for 30% of the corpus.

On the tail end of the distribution we have a large number of rare words. In this corpus 33,447 words (out of 86,699 unique words) occur once, for instance *cornflakes, mathematicians,* or *tazhikhistan*. This makes for a very skewed distribution of words; see Figure 2.3 for graphs that show the word counts. Ranking words by their frequency and plotting their rank against their frequency shows the extreme contrast between a few very frequent words against the great mass of rare words. In fact, to make the information visible in the graph we had to use log scales on the coordinate axes.

Note that the skewedness of the distribution is not due just to the contrast between frequent function words and infrequent **content words**. The second table in Figure 2.2 displays the top 10 content words: *european* occurs 129,851 times, followed by a list of a few more very frequent content words.

This examination of the Europarl corpus has highlighted the distribution of words in English use. But it does not clearly answer the

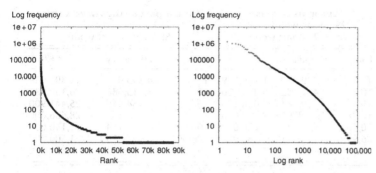

Figure 2.3 Distribution of words in text: The graphs display the words sorted by their rank in the Europarl corpus. At the top of the list, some words are very frequent (*the* occurs 1,929,379 times), but there is a large tail of words that occur only once (33,447 words occur once, for instance *cornflakes*, *mathematicians*, or *tazhikhistan*). Note the use of the log scale in the graphs.

question about the size of the English vocabulary. This is complicated by the way we define **words** as space-separated sequences of characters, which includes names and numbers. With even larger corpora of billions or even trillions of words, the number of unique tokens increases dramatically from 86,699 to millions. The supply of unique numbers is infinite, and new names constantly crop up. The vocabulary of very large text collections increases for other reasons too. In practice, misspellings show up, and even foreign text material may be included.

A famous formula for the distribution of words in a corpus is **Zipf's law**. According to this, the product of the rank r of each word (sorted by frequency) and its frequency f is roughly a constant. If we reformulate $r \times f = c$ into $\log f = \log c - \log r$, then we get a linear relationship between the logs of frequency and rank. Consider the right-hand graph in Figure 2.3, where we used log scales when plotting frequency against rank. The points in the graph lie roughly on a line.

Another attempt at verifying Zipf's law is Figure 2.4. When examining the frequency of the 1st, 10th, 100th, etc. most frequent word, the product $r \times f$ is roughly the same order of magnitude. The value of the product, however, does drop off for the rarer words.

When you take another look at the right-hand graph in Figure 2.3, you see the same drop-off. While the points first seem to follow a line, the curve declines more steeply around rank 1000. This means that rare words are not as frequent as Zipf's law predicts.

One useful question in determining how big a corpus we need is: How much text do we need to collect to see a sufficient number of occurrences of rare words such as *cornflakes*, *mathematicians*, or *tazhikhistan*? Let us say we want enough occurrences for the 10,000

Zipf's law

Figure 2.4 Verifying Zipf's law for two corpora: Product of rank (*r*) and frequency (*f*) is roughly constant for most words, but drops off for the lowest ranked words.

Europarl corpus			Xinhua part of Gigaword corpus		
29 million words total			252 million words total		
86,699 distinct words			887,629 distinct words		
Rank	Frequency	$r*f$	Rank	Frequency	$r*f$
1	1,929,379	1,929,379	1	14,395,939	14,395,939
10	424,552	4,245,520	10	3,015,088	30,150,880
100	30,384	3,038,400	100	254,419	25,441,900
1000	2793	2,793,000	1000	28,666	28,666,000
10,000	70	700,000	10,000	1114	11,140,000
86,999	1	86,999	100,000	15	1,500,000
			887,629	1	887,629

most frequent words. More specifically, we want a corpus in which the 10,000th most frequent word occurs at least 10,000 times.

Using Zipf's law, we make the following simple calculation. We assume that the most frequent word *the* makes up 6% of all words and that $r \times f$ is constant. Hence $r \times f = 0.06s$ where s is the corpus size. If we solve the equation for s, we get $s = \frac{1}{0.06} r \times f$. With $r = 10,000$ and $f = 10,000$, we get $s = 1.67$ billion words.

2.1.3 Parts of Speech

noun   Words differ in the role they play. Some, called **nouns**, refer to objects in the real world (*house*), or at least abstract objects (*freedom*). Others

preposition   play a functional role in a sentence, for instance **prepositions** such as *in*.

Roughly, we can divide words into two broad categories. On the one

content word   hand there are **content words** that refer to objects, actions, or proper-

function word   ties. On the other hand there are **function words** that tell us how these content words relate to each other.

open-class word   Linguists also refer to these two categories as **open-class words** and

closed-class word   **closed-class words**. Content words are open-class words, because there is not a finite set of them, but rather new words are formed and adapted all the time, when new objects (e.g., *Google*), or types of objects (e.g., *web site*) enter our mental world. Function words, however, come from a fixed class of words that does not change – at least not more often than every few decades or centuries (the word *whom* is currently falling out of use).

From a machine translation point of view, both content words and function words pose challenges, albeit different ones. The problem with content words is simply that there are too many of them and new ones are always being introduced. Hence we need large text collections that span many topics and domains to have a reasonable chance of getting almost all of them.

Function words pose different challenges. There are fairly few of them, and we will encounter them very frequently in large text collections. However, languages differ greatly in their function words. Consider the most frequent word in English, *the*. When translating into German, we have to choose *der, die, das, dem, den* or *des* as a possible translation, a problem of morphology, which we will address in the next section. Even worse, determiners like *the* do not have an equivalent in Chinese. When translating from Chinese, we have to figure out when to insert *the, a*, or nothing.

What makes function words tricky for machine translation is that they fulfill a specific role of how words relate together in one language. This type of role may not exist in another language. For instance, Japanese marks the subject of the sentence with a special post-position (*wa*). When translating into Japanese, we must have some means of establishing which noun phrase is the subject and where we need to insert *wa*.

Let us not dwell on all these troubles and save them for later chapters of this book. Instead, now is a good time to get more familiar with the syntactically different categories of words that are commonly called **parts of speech**. See Figure 2.5 for a detailed break-down.   part of speech

Open-class words fall into three broad categories: words that describe objects (**nouns**), actions (**verbs**), and properties. The latter are distinguished into properties that qualify nouns (**adjectives**), and those that qualify verbs and adjectives (**adverbs**).

Closed-class words are a mixed bag. They include fairly obvious parts of speech such as **determiners**, **pronouns** that refer to nouns, **prepositions** that qualify the role of noun phrases, and **coordinating conjunctions** such as *and*. But there are also more exotic parts of speech such as the **existential** *there*, as in *there is a problem*, which appears first like a pronoun, but it does not refer to anything. Real text is interspersed with **numbers**, the **possessive marker** *'s*, **list item markers** (*I., II., III.*), various **symbols** (*$, £*, maybe even smiley faces :}), **foreign words**, and **interjections** (*oh*).

Detecting the parts of speech of words in a text is a well-established task in natural language processing. The canonical solution is to label a large amount of text with part-of-speech tags, and then train a **tagger**   tagger
using common machine learning methods.

The problem is not trivial, since some words are ambiguous in their part-of-speech. For instance, *like* may be a verb, adverb, preposition, and interjection, depending on the context. Moreover, we need to classify previously unseen words. They will most likely be content words, and hopefully context and word ending provide sufficient clues. For

Figure 2.5 Part-of-speech
tags of the Penn tree bank.

- **Nouns** refer to abstract or real objects in the word. Nouns (singular: *house*/NN, plural: *houses*/NNS) are distinguished from proper nouns (singular: *Britain*/NP, plural: *Americas*/NPS)
- **Verbs** refer to actions. Base form: *go*/VB, past tense: *went*/VBD, past participle: *gone*/VBN, gerund: *going*/VBG, 3rd person singular present: *goes*/VBZ, other singular present: *am*/VBP. Special cases: modals *can*/MD, particles *switch on*/RP.
- **Adjectives** refer to properties of nouns. Regular: *green*/JJ, comparative: *greener*/JJR, superlative: *greenest*/JJS
- **Adverbs** refer to properties of verbs or adjectives. Regular: *happily*/RB, comparative: *ran faster*/RBR, superlative: *ran fastest*/RBS, wh-adverbs: *how*/WRB *fast*
- **Determiners** (also called **articles**) qualify or replace nouns. Regular: *the*/DT *house*, pre-determiner: *all*/PDT *the houses*, wh-determiner: *which*/WDT.
- **Pronouns** refer to previously mentioned nouns. Personal pronoun: *she*/PP, possessive pronoun: *her*/PP$, wh-pronoun: *who*/WP, possessive wh-pronoun: *whose*/WP$.
- **Prepositions** precede noun phrases or clauses and indicate their role in the sentence: *from*/IN *here*. Special case *to*/TO.
- **Coordinating conjunctions**: *and*/CC.
- **Numbers**: *17*/CD
- **Possessive marker**: *Joe 's*/POS
- **List item markers**: *A.*/LS
- **Symbols**: *$*/SYM
- **Foreign words**: *de*/FW *facto*/FW
- **Interjections**: *oh*/UH

English, many part-of-speech taggers that are freely available achieve an accuracy above 98%.

2.1.4 Morphology

morphology   Typically the meaning of a word is refined by placing other words around it. For instance *small house* gives additional information about the type of *house*, or *the house* indicates that the *house* was mentioned before.

But another way to further qualify the meaning of a word is to change its spelling slightly. For instance, by adding an *s* to the end of *house*, thus becoming *houses*, we indicate that there is more than one *house*.

English has very limited morphological variation of words. Nouns may be changed due to their **count** (singular vs. plural). Verbs are changed due to their **tense** (as in *walk, walked, walking*) and to a very limited degree to their **person** and count (*walks*).

count
tense
person

Tense and auxiliary verbs

Note that even this limited morphology is not truly necessary in a language. We could always indicate count by adding additional qualifiers such as *one* and *many*. The same is true for tense, which in fact is often indicated by additional auxiliary verbs, as the following list of English tenses indicates:

- simple present: *walk*
- present continuous: *is walking*
- past: *walked*
- present perfect: *have walked*
- past perfect: *had walked*
- future: *will walk*
- future perfect: *will have walked*

Case and prepositions

Many other languages use morphology to express additional information. One of them is **case**. A sentence often contains several noun phrases, but which are the object and the subject? For instance, given the bag of words *eat, lion, zebra*, we need to indicate who is eating whom. In English this is done by sentence order: the subject comes before the verb, hence we write *the lion eats the zebra*.

case

Other languages, such as German, allow more flexibility in sentence order. To still be able to communicate the role of the noun phrases, they are morphologically changed. Consider the following four sentences:

1. *Der Löwe frißt das Zebra.*
2. *Den Löwen frißt das Zebra.*
3. *Das Zebra frißt der Löwe.*
4. *Das Zebra frißt den Löwen.*

In sentences 1 and 3 the lion is doing the eating, while in sentences 2 and 4 the zebra is returning the favor. This is indicated by the change of the noun phrase referring to the lion from subject case *der Löwe* to object case *den Löwen*.

German has four cases, so there are two more: genitive indicating ownership relationships similar to the possessive marker in English (*the lion's food*) and another object case which is handy when there are more than two objects, as in *The man gives the woman the book*. Note that cases do show up in English in pronouns: *he, him, himself*, indicating that English went through a process of losing morphological case over time.

Latin has two further cases, vocative (for the entity that is addressed as in *John, I'm eating dinner!*) and ablative (used for instance to indicate location). Finnish has 15 cases. Why so many? We argued that English does not need case morphology, since it uses sentence position to indicate the role of noun phrases in a sentence. This is not the whole story, since English also has another tool to indicate the role of noun phrases: preposition **prepositions**.

Consider the following examples that indicate the power of prepositions in English. One little word changes the meaning of the sentence dramatically.

- I go *to* the house.
- I go *from* the house.
- I go *in* the house.
- I go *on* the house.
- I go *by* the house.
- I go *through* the house.

However, the meaning of prepositions is not easy to define. Sometimes the meaning is clear, especially when they indicate movement or relative location. But they are used for many different purposes, some of them fairly abstract. It is hard to pin down when to use which preposition. Consider the following three examples:

- Let's meet *at* 9am.
- Let's meet *on* Sunday.
- Let's meet *in* December.

Prepositions rarely match well between languages, which makes their translation difficult. In this way their role is similar to case: some languages have many, some have few, and their use and meaning is often hard to define.

Gender

gender Let us conclude with one more grammatical element that affects the morphology of some languages: **gender**. In English, it shows up only in pronouns (*she, he, her, his*). English also has simple rules for noun gender: animate objects take their sexual gender, and inanimate objects are neutral. There are a few exceptions (e.g., countries and named ships are female).

Not so in many other languages. German and French have genders other than neutral for all kinds of inanimate objects. And they do not

Case	Singular			Plural		
	male	fem.	n.	male	fem.	n.
nominative (subject)	der	die	das	die	die	die
genitive (possessive)	des	der	des	der	der	der
dative (indirect object)	dem	der	dem	den	den	den
accusative (direct object)	den	die	das	die	die	die

Figure 2.6 Morphology of the definite determiner in German (in English always *the*). It varies depending on count, case, and gender. Each word form is highly ambiguous: *der* is male singular nominative, but also female singular genitive/dative, as well as plural genitive for any gender.

follow any obvious pattern and do not agree well even between these two related languages. For instance, in German the moon is male and the sun is female, in French it is the opposite. Gender affects the morphology of nouns, adjectives, and even determiners. See Figure 2.6 for an illustration of the full morphological table for the German analogue to *the*.

Morphology and machine translation

Morphology creates various challenges for machine translation. While some languages express the relationships between words mostly with location or function words, others use morphological variation of words. The appropriate transfer of relevant information is not straightforward.

The more morphological variation a language exhibits, the larger its vocabulary of surface forms. One solution would be simply to acquire large amounts of training data, so that all surface forms occur frequently enough. However, the reality of limited training data puts morphologically richer languages at a disadvantage. Moreover, translating into morphologically rich languages often requires additional information for choosing the correct word form that may not be readily available in the input language.

2.1.5 Lexical Semantics

lexical semantics

The task of translation is to take words and sentences in one language and produce words and sentences with the same **meaning** in another language. Unfortunately, meaning is a very difficult concept to deal with. What is the meaning of a word like *house*? What properties does an object in the world need to be called a *house*? How about the *House of Windsor*, which is not a physical house at all?

meaning

Instead of answering all these questions, let us focus on the problems of word meaning that are relevant for machine translation.

The first major problem stems from the fact that a word may have different meanings. Linguists draw a distinction between **polysemy** and **homonymy**. Homonyms are words that are completely unrelated, but are spelled the same way, for instance *can* is both a modal (*you can do it!*) and a container (*a can of beans*). Polysemy refers to words with different meanings (also called **word senses**), such as *interest*, which has meanings indicating curiosity (*interest in football*), a stake (*a 5% interest in Google*), or the fee paid for a loan (*interest rate of 4.9%*).

polysemy
homonymy

word sense

The definition of word senses, like everything else in semantics, is a difficult business. How many senses does the word *interest* have? We just listed three, but maybe we could consider the meaning of *interest* in the phrase *the national interest* as a different sense, since it is not curiosity per se, but rather a common goal. **WordNet**,[2] a widely used database for lexical semantics, lists seven different senses for the word *interest*.

WorldNet

Fortunately, translation provides a clear basis for defining relevant word senses. A word has multiple senses if it has multiple translations into another language. For instance, the three meanings of *interest* we listed above result in different translations into German: *Interesse* (curiosity sense), *Anteil* (stake sense) and *Zins* (money sense).

The task of determining the right word sense for a word in a given context is called **word sense disambiguation**. Research in this area has shown that the word context, such as closely neighboring words and content words in a larger window, is a good indicator for word sense. Statistical machine translation systems consider local context in the form of language models (Chapter 7) and within phrase translation models (Chapter 5), so they typically do not require a special word sense disambiguation component.

disambiguation

Words, or to be more precise, word senses, may be organized according to their relationship to each other. For instance: A *dog* is a *mammal*, which is an *animal*. Such **is-a**, or **hypernym**, **relationships** form the organizing principle of an **ontology**, as illustrated in Figure 2.7. The illustration is an excerpt of WordNet.

hypernym relationship
ontology

Besides hypernym relationships, ontologies may also contain other relationships between words, such as **part-of**, for instance a *wheel* is part of a *car*, or **member-of**, for instance a *wolf* is part of a *pack*.

---

[2] You can browse WordNet at http://wordnet.princeton.edu/

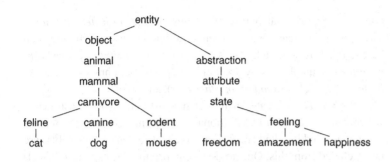

Figure 2.7 Hypernym, or *is-a*, relationships between words: a simplified example from the WordNet ontology.

Efforts to build large-scale ontologies have been as ambitious as the Cyc project, which attempted to encode all facts in the world as relationships between senses.

2.2 Sentences

If words are the atomic units of meaning, then **sentences** are the next step: the basic means to combine concepts into something new, a new idea, a description of a recent event, and so on.

sentence

2.2.1 Sentence Structure

Let us look first at the simple sentence

Jane bought the house.

The central element of the sentence is the **verb** *bought*. It requires a buyer and an object to be bought: the **subject** *Jane* and the **object** *the house*. Other verbs require a different number of objects. Some do not require any at all (so-called **intransitive verbs**), for instance *Jane swims*. Some require two, for instance *Jane gave Joe the book*. How many and what objects a verb requires is called the **valency** of the verb.

verb
subject
object

intransitive verb

valency

Objects that are required by the verb are also called **arguments** (think of a programming function that takes a number of arguments). Additional information may be added to the sentence, which takes the form of **adjuncts**. The sentence *Jane bought the house* may be augmented with a prepositional phrase such as *from Jim* and *without hesitation*, or adverbs such as *yesterday* and *cheaply*. The distinction between arguments and adjuncts is not always straight-forward. Moreover, different meanings of a verb may have different valency.

argument

adjuncts

Adjuncts and arguments do not have to be simple. Noun phrases such as *the house* may be extended by adjectives, e.g., *the beautiful house* or prepositional phrases *the house in the posh neighborhood.* These extensions can be again seen as adjuncts. Furthermore, they can be extended as well, adjectives by adverbs (*beautiful* becomes *very beautiful*), noun phrases by additional prepositional phrases (*the house in the posh neighborhood across the river*), and so on.

recursion

This ability to create such nested constructions of constituents, which can be extended by additional constituents, is a striking feature of language and is called **recursion**. Note that sentences themselves are not excluded from this. Our original sentence may be expanded by relative clauses to *Jane who recently won the lottery bought the house that was just put on the market.*

clause

Let us refine our notion of sentence: A sentence may consist of one or more **clauses**, each of which consists of a verb with arguments and adjuncts. Clauses may be adjuncts and arguments themselves, as in *I proposed to go swimming.*

structural ambiguity

The recursive expansion of sentences into nested construction causes a lot of problems for the analysis of language. One especially egregious problem for automatic sentence processing is the introduction of **structural ambiguity**. Consider the three sentences:

- *Joe eats steak with a knife.*
- *Jim eats steak with ketchup.*
- *Jane watches the man with the telescope.*

All three sentences end in an adjunct prepositional phrase. In the first sentence the adjunct belongs to the verb (the *eating* happens with a *knife*). In the second sentence the adjunct informs the object (the *steak* has *ketchup* on it). But how about the third sentence? Does Jane use a *telescope* to watch the man, or does the man have it?

prepositional phrase attachment

scope

Structural ambiguity is introduced not only by adjuncts (such as the classic **prepositional phrase attachment** problem illustrated above). Connectives also introduce ambiguity because their **scope** is not always clear. Consider the sentence: *Jim washes the dishes and watches television with Jane.* Is *Jane* helping with the dishes or is she just joining for television?

The reason why structural ambiguity is such a hard problem for automatic natural language processing systems is that the ambiguity is often resolved semantically. Humans are not confused, because only one reading makes sense. Furthermore, speakers and writers avoid ambiguity when it is not obvious what the right reading is. However, what is obvious for a human is not obvious for a machine. How should your desktop computer know that *steak* and *knife* do not make a tasty meal?

2.2.2 Theories of Grammar

There are several competing grammar formalisms, for which computational methods have been developed. Great influence has been exerted by efforts to build the **Penn tree bank** in the early 1990s. Currently, about one million words have been annotated with syntactic information, so-called parse trees. Figure 2.8 shows one sentence from that collection.

    Parse trees illustrate ideas about grammatical structure that we discuss above. The recursive nature of language is reflected by the structure of the tree. Just like trees in nature, the initial stem branches out recursively until we reach the leaves (words). Unlike natural trees, syntactic trees grow from top to bottom.

    On the top of the tree – the root if you will – is the sentence node S, which branches out into the subject noun phrase NP-SBJ and the verb phrase VP (see Figure 2.8). After picking up the modal, the verb phrase branches out into the main verb and its object and adjunct. Subject and object are grouped together as noun phrases (NP). The subject noun phrase *Pierre Vinken* is further informed by the adjective phrase *61 years old*.

Phrase structure grammar

The introduction of the notion of **phrases** – be it noun phrases, prepositional phrases, verb phrases, adjective phrases, etc. – provides the basis for talking about levels in the parse tree between the sentence node on top and the parts of speech and words at the bottom.

    The role of these phrasal types is clearly visible in the example in Figure 2.8. Phrases are groups of words and introduce an additional level of abstraction. This allows us to explore the relationship between

Penn tree bank

Parse tree

phrase

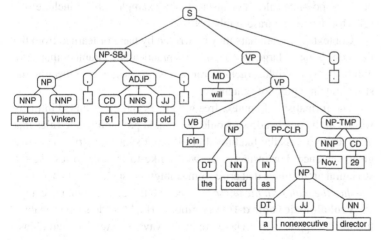

Figure 2.8 Parse tree from the Penn tree bank for the sentence *Pierre Vinken, 61 years old, will join the board as a nonexecutive director Nov. 29.*

different types of phrases, i.e., to define the relationship between word groups. Note that for instance the concept of subject and object, that we have already used, refers to a phrasal unit and not a single word.

The idea of phrase structure grammar is further developed in formalisms such as **generalized phrase structure grammar** (GPSG) or **head-driven phrase structure grammar** (HPSG). These formalisms are the basis for scientific theories of language.

phrase structure grammar

Context-free grammars

In this book, we are mostly concerned with computational methods to deal with language, and less with explaining how the human mind uses language. In respect to grammar, we are interested in formalisms that allow us to define all possible English sentences, and rule out impossible word combinations.

context-free grammar

nonterminal symbol

terminal symbol

A widely used formalism is called **context-free grammar** (CFG). This formalism consists of a set of **nonterminal** (part-of-speech tags and phrase categories) and **terminal symbols** (words), as well as rules that have a single nonterminal symbol on the left-hand side and at least one symbol (terminal or nonterminal) on the right-hand side.

English grammar may be expressed by context-free rules such as:

- S → NP VP
- NP → NNP ADJP
- NP → NNP NNP
- VP → VB NP PP NP
- VB → *join*

Note how these rules mirror the branching of the tree structure in Figure 2.8. Also, note that for a single nonterminal symbol, there may be many possible rules. For instance, the examples above include two rules for the noun phrase symbol NP.

Context-free grammars may be written by hand or learned from the Penn tree bank. A large number of rules practically guarantees that there will be many possible structures for each single sentence, reflecting the structural ambiguity of sentences.

The formalism of context-free grammars can be extended in many ways. On the one hand, we would like to add probabilities to rules that allow us to assess the likelihood of different syntactic structures for a given sentence. For instance, we would like to be able to resolve the structural ambiguities that arise from ambiguous sentences such as *Jane watches the man with the telescope* (recall our discussion on page 46).

Probabilistic context-free grammars (PCFG) add such probabilities to rule applications. There are many ways to extend a noun phrase

NP, but some are more likely than others. By assigning a probability distribution to the possible right-hand sides of an expansion of a non-terminal on the left-hand side, we have a probabilistic framework to assign different probabilities to different syntactic structures for a sentence.

Note that assigning probability distributions to a context-free grammar implies the independence of all rule applications in a parse tree. This is a very strong assumption, which severely limits the power of this formalism.

In fact, our discussion of the prepositional phrase attachment problem suggested that the most important information that leads us to the correct attachment decisions is semantic in nature (e.g., *steak with knife* is not a good food combination, *ketchup* is not a good instrument for eating). But other types of information may be relevant. For instance in German, the syntactic case of a noun phrase is essential to decide if it is the subject or object of the sentence, or if it relates to other noun phrases.

Consequently, instead of representing the constituents in the parse trees with simple labels, maybe it is better to use **feature structures** to include all relevant information. When we encounter attachment decisions, the features will inform us whether certain rule applications are possible or not.

feature structure

The method to check if feature structures that refer to the right-hand side of a CFG rule are compatible and how to generate the resulting structure on the left-hand side of the rule is called **unification**.

unification

Dependency structure
An alternative way to represent syntactic structure is demonstrated in Figure 2.9. In this **dependency structure**, we only display the relationship of words to each other, without any reference to phrases or phrase structure. For instance, an adjective such as *nonexecutive* relates to a noun such as *director*.

dependency structure

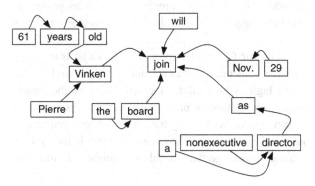

Figure 2.9 Dependency structure for the sentence from Figure 2.8. The central word is the verb; others depend on it, with more words recursively attached. Dependencies may be labeled by types such as subject, object, adjunct, etc.

Comparing this representation with the parse tree in Figure 2.8, it contains both more and less information, but also shares a lot of similarities. If you take a word such as *director* and include both its dependents *a* and *nonexecutive*, then you have a set of words that forms a constituent in the parse tree. This is true for all other words as well. For each such word set or constituent, the dependency structure explicitly indicates one word as the **head word**, on which the others depend. In our example the noun *director* is the head word of the phrase *a nonexecutive director* and the verb *join* is the head word of the entire sentence. The syntax tree lacks this information.

head word

But the parse tree has other information that is missing in the dependency structure. Each constituent has a label, for instance, *the nonexecutive director* is an NP. The tree also preserves the order of the words. The parse tree also has more inherent structure and constituents than the dependency structure. For instance, the verb *join* has five dependants in the dependency structure. In the parse tree, these dependants are associated with the verb in three stages: first the subject, then the modal, and finally the remaining object and adjuncts.

Note that both parse trees and dependency structure may be extended to incorporate additional information. The concept of a head word is a very useful one, it is often integrated into phrase structure grammar. Conversely, dependency relationships are often labeled with types such as subject, object, adjunct, etc.

Lexical functional grammar

deep structure
Lexical functional grammar

From early on, linguists have drawn a distinction between the surface structure of language and underlying **deep structure**, which is more closely related to the expressed meaning. **Lexical functional grammar** (LFG) makes this distinction by having two representations of a sentence. Besides the constituent structure, called the **c-structure**, there is also the functional structure, called the **f-structure**.

c-structure
f-structure

See Figure 2.10 for an example: the f-structure for our example sentence. Word order is ignored, but representation includes grammatical information about subject, object and adjunct as well as tense and definiteness.

LFG uses the syntactic f-structure representation as a basis to derive the semantics of the sentence. Semantics may be expressed in the form of **predicate logic**, which allows the processing of the meaning of a sentence with a theorem prover. We will not discuss such semantic formalisms in this book. They have not yet been used in statistical machine translation because their main problem is the lack of formalized semantic knowledge that would be required for empirical approaches.

predicate logic

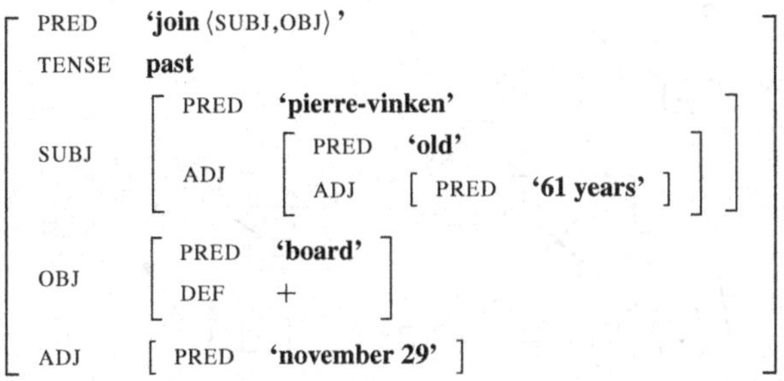

$$
\begin{bmatrix}
\text{PRED} & \text{`join} \langle \text{SUBJ,OBJ} \rangle \text{'} \\
\text{TENSE} & \textbf{past} \\
\text{SUBJ} & \begin{bmatrix} \text{PRED} & \text{`pierre-vinken'} \\ \text{ADJ} & \begin{bmatrix} \text{PRED} & \text{`old'} \\ \text{ADJ} & \begin{bmatrix} \text{PRED} & \text{`61 years'} \end{bmatrix} \end{bmatrix} \end{bmatrix} \\
\text{OBJ} & \begin{bmatrix} \text{PRED} & \text{`board'} \\ \text{DEF} & + \end{bmatrix} \\
\text{ADJ} & \begin{bmatrix} \text{PRED} & \text{`november 29'} \end{bmatrix}
\end{bmatrix}
$$

Figure 2.10 F-structure of the sentence from Figure 2.8. In the lexical functional grammar (LFG) formalism, the constituent structure (c-structure) is mirrored by a representation of the sentence that captures its syntax.

Combinatory categorical grammar

Let us conclude our short survey of grammar formalisms with **combinatory categorical grammar** (CCG). It relies more heavily on the lexicon to guide the syntactic processing of a sentence. For instance, verbs are annotated with the type of objects they take:

combinatory categorical grammar

- *swim:* S\NP
- *eat:* (S\NP)/NP
- *give:* ((S\NP)/NP)/NP

The intransitive verb *swim* requires an NP on the left to form a sentence S. The transitive verbs *eat* and *give* require additional NPs on the right. Having such additional information about the grammatical behavior of words encoded in the form of functional types in the lexicon helps to reduce the number of structural ambiguities.

2.2.3 Translation of Sentence Structure

The fact that languages differ in their syntactic structure causes some of the hardest problems for machine translation. Different syntactic structure requires the reordering of words and the insertion and deletion of function words during translation.

Sometimes, the restructuring required to translate from one language to another is not very difficult to describe. Look at the example in Figure 2.11. When using a modal and main verb (as in our continuing example: *will join*), English places these together after the subject. In German, they are split. While the modal is typically also after the subject, the main verb is placed at the end of the clause. This means, for our example sentence, that when translating from English to German the main verb needs to be moved to the end of the sentence.

The required change is straightforward to describe in syntactic terms. This is also reflected by the fact that the phrase structure parse trees of our German and English example sentences are very similar. Their discourse structure is even identical. In terms of context-free

Figure 2.11 German and English differ in their syntactic structure, resulting in changes of word order. The movement of the main verb from after the modal (in English) to the end of the sentence (in German) is reflected by one different rule application (VP→VP NP in English vs. VP→NP VP in German). The dependency structure is the same for both languages.

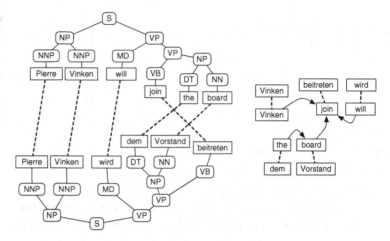

grammar rule applications, the only difference is the use of the rule VP→VP NP in English as opposed to VP→NP VP in German when the VP is expanded after taking up the modal.

Syntactic structure appears to be a good aid to handling restructuring when translating from one language to another. However, syntactic annotation such as phrase structure parse trees or dependency structures do not occur in raw text and need to be obtained by automatic tools. Moreover, syntactic annotation adds a layer of complexity, making the models more cumbersome to deal with. Nevertheless, building statistical machine translation systems that are based on syntactic representations offers exciting opportunities. We discuss this further in Chapters 10 and 11.

2.2.4 Discourse

Much current research in statistical machine translation is focused on the translation of single sentences. While translation from one language to another is almost always possible by translating texts sentence-by-sentence (with the occasional splitting and merging of neighboring sentences), some translation problems cannot be resolved on the sentence level alone.

co-reference
anaphor

One problem is the translation of **co-references** or **anaphora**. While the first mention of an entity is typically fleshed out (e.g., *the President George Bush*, it may be later referred to only by a pronoun (*he*) or an abbreviated description (*the president*). This may result in ambiguity in later sentences. What if *the president* is translated differently for a male or female office holder? What if there is a different translation depending if we are talking about the president of a

country or a company or a student club? A later mention may not have
sufficient information, so we need to backtrack to previous mentions, a
problem called **anaphor resolution**.

anaphor resolution

Another document-level property is **topic**, the general subject matter of the text. In a sports article the English word *bat* is translated
differently from in an article on cave animals. It may be helpful to
detect the topic of a document and use this information when translating
sentences.

topic

2.3 Corpora

Statistical machine translation systems are trained on translated texts.
In this section we will define this type of data more closely and discuss
the collection and preparation of texts for the methods discussed in this
book.

2.3.1 Types of Text

One thing you will hear immediately from sellers and users of machine
translation systems is that there is no general-purpose translation system. Instead, machine translation is used for particular text types.
A system that works excellently when translating scientific neuro-
science articles may be very bad at translating chat room conversations
between teenagers. Words and phrases have different meanings in different **domains**, and the rendering of their translation also has to fit the
expected style in the domain.

domains

Machine translation is applied to both written and spoken language.
To work with textual machine translation systems, spoken language has
to be converted into written form. This implies either manual transcrip-
tion, possibly including polishing by removing restarts and filler words
(*I really believe, um, believe that we should do this.*), or the use of
automatic speech recognition systems. The **modality** of communication matters. Spoken language is different from written text. It is often
ungrammatical, full of unfinished sentences and (especially in the case
of dialogue) reliant on gestures and mutually understood knowledge.
Much of this is also true for informal uses of written text, such as
Internet chat, email, and text messages.

modality

Another dimension of text types is **topic**. Much of the currently
available translated text comes from international organizations, such as
the United Nations or the European Union. For instance the European
Parliament proceedings cover many political, economic, and cultural
matters, but may be a bad source to learn how to translate texts in a
specialized scientific domain.

topic

Historically, many machine translation systems were developed for
limited domain a **limited domain**, such as weather reports, travel information systems
or manuals for technical equipment. Restricting the domain simplifies
the machine translation problem dramatically. For instance, vocabulary
is limited or can be controlled. While limited domain machine translation remains a valuable application and research area, most current
statistical machine translation research focuses on open domain systems, or at least very large domains, such as the translation of news
stories.

At the time of this writing, the three major evaluation campaigns
focus their attention on different domains (and different language
pairs):

NIST
- The **NIST** Arabic–English and Chinese–English task is mainly concerned
with the translation of news stories, although this is being expanded to cover
Internet newsgroup postings, and other such materials. Training material is
translated news sources and a large United Nations corpus.

IWSLT
- The **IWSLT** task, mostly on Asian languages into English, uses a limited
travel conversation domain, and also puts much focus on the translation of
speech recognition output or transcripts.

WMT
- The **TC-STAR** and **ACL WMT** tasks use the European Parliament proceedings as training and testing material. **TC-STAR** also includes speech input,
and the **ACL WMT** task is widening the domain into news commentary.

A lot of interesting training material (translated books, product
manuals, etc.) is not in the public domain, so it is rarely available to
researchers in the field. Commercial companies, however, are able to
build dedicated statistical machine translation systems for clients that
already have large amounts of translated texts in their domain of interest
(for instance, product manuals from previous years).

2.3.2 Acquiring Parallel Corpora

parallel corpus A **parallel corpus** is a collection of text, paired with translations into
another language. Several parallel corpora have recently become avail-
able. These are often in the order of tens to hundreds of millions of
words. Some are available on the web,[3] many more are distributed by
the Linguistic Data Consortium[4] of the University of Pennsylvania.

Alternatively, you may want to crawl the web for parallel data.
Many web sites are translated into multiple languages, and some news

---

[3] For instance the Europarl corpus at http://www.statmt.org/europarl/ and
the Acquis Communautaire corpus at http://wt.jrc.it/lt/Acquis/
[4] http://ldc.upenn.edu/

organizations such as the BBC publish their stories for a multilingual audience. Acquiring parallel corpora from the web is sometimes straightforward, but is often complicated for a number of reasons.

First, there are the technical issues of crawling a web site and extracting text from the downloaded HTML pages. Then, we need to identify which pages in one language correspond to which documents in the other language, a problem known as **document alignment**. In the simplest case, the URL of the page or the structure of the web site gives sufficient clues. However, often the ideal of directly translated web pages does not exist. For instance, almost all news sites that serve a multilingual readership do not directly translate their news reports. Instead, they adapt reports for the different audiences, excluding or adding material to suit their varied backgrounds.

document alignment

If documents are not directly translated, for instance an English news report by the BBC that is rewritten for a French audience, there may still be chunks that are indeed direct translations. Finding matching paragraphs and sentences in this environment is an interesting challenge that has received some attention from the research community.

There have been some efforts to learn translation models from **comparable corpora**. These are corpora in two different languages, in the same domain, but not direct translations. For instance, comparable corpora are the *New York Times* news archives and the French newspaper *Le Monde*'s archives. They will often talk about the same events, but they are not translations of each other. Learning from comparable corpora has been shown to be effective to some degree, for instance by taking advantage of the fact that a word that occurs in a particular context has a translation that occurs in a similar (translated) context. However, parallel text is much more powerful evidence for translational equivalence.

comparable corpus

2.3.3 Sentence Alignment

Given a parallel corpus, which consists of directly translated text, there is still one processing step that is performed to make this corpus useful for the type of statistical machine translation models that we discuss in this book, namely the task of **sentence alignment**.

sentence alignment

Text is rarely translated word by word, and it is not always translated sentence by sentence. Long sentences may be broken up, or short sentences may be merged. There are even some languages where the clear indication of a sentence end is not part of the writing system (for instance, Thai).

Since sentence alignment is such an essential step in corpus preparation for statistical machine translation, the topic has received much

Figure 2.12 Sentence alignment: given a document and its translation, we need to find sentences that are translations of each other.

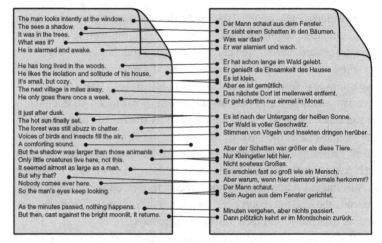

attention from very early on. See Figure 2.12 for an illustration of the problem.

Let us define the task of sentence alignment formally. Given the sentences $f_1,...,f_{n_f}$ in the foreign language to the sentences $e_1,...,e_{n_e}$ in English, a sentence alignment S consists of a list of **sentence pairs** $s_1,...,s_n$.

sentence pairs

Each sentence pair s_i is a pair of sets

$$s_i = (\{f_{\text{start-f}(i)}, ..., f_{\text{end-f}(i)}\}, \{e_{\text{start-e}(i)}, ..., e_{\text{end-e}(i)}\}) \qquad (2.1)$$

Typically, we assume that sentences are translated in sequence. This assumption implies that

$$\begin{aligned} \text{start-f}(i) &= \text{end-f}(i-1) + 1 \\ \text{start-e}(i) &= \text{end-e}(i-1) + 1 \end{aligned} \qquad (2.2)$$

Other straightforward restrictions are

$$\begin{aligned} \text{start-f}(1) &= 1 \\ \text{start-e}(1) &= 1 \\ \text{end-f}(n) &= n_f \\ \text{end-e}(n) &= n_e \\ \text{start-f}(i) &\leq \text{end-f}(i) \\ \text{start-e}(i) &\leq \text{end-e}(i) \end{aligned} \qquad (2.3)$$

alignment type

The **alignment type** of a sentence pair is the number of sentences in each set, i.e.,

$$\begin{aligned} \text{type} &= |\{f_{\text{start-f}(i)}, ..., f_{\text{end-f}(i)}\}| - |\{e_{\text{start-e}(i)}, ..., e_{\text{end-e}(i)}| \\ &= \text{end-f}(i) - \text{start-f}(i) + 1 - \text{end-e}(i) - \text{start-e}(i) + 1 \end{aligned} \qquad (2.4)$$

For instance, a 1–1 alignment is an alignment where one foreign sentence is aligned to one English sentence. In a 1–2 alignment, a foreign sentence is aligned to two English sentences. A 0–1 alignment indicates an English sentence that is not aligned to anything, and so on.

All sentences need to be accounted for, and each sentence may only occur in one sentence pair. Hence, we are looking for a **sentence alignment** $S = \{s_1, ..., s_n\}$ that fulfills this requirement and is optimal in terms of some measure of matching quality of all its sentence pairs.

sentence alignment

$$\text{score}(S) = \prod_i^n \text{match}(s_i) \tag{2.5}$$

One early approach by Gale and Church [1993] uses two components to define the **match function**: a probability distribution for the alignment type and a distance measure that considers the number of words or letters in each of the sentences.

match function

For instance, the Gale–Church algorithm includes the probability for alignment types

$$\text{type-match}(s_i) = \begin{cases} 0.89 & \text{if type}(s_i) = 1\text{–}1 \\ 0.0099 & \text{if type}(s_i) = 1\text{–}0 \text{ or } 0\text{–}1 \\ 0.089 & \text{if type}(s_i) = 2\text{–}1 \text{ or } 1\text{–}2 \\ 0.011 & \text{if type}(s_i) = 2\text{–}2 \end{cases} \tag{2.6}$$

Later approaches include lexical clues in their approaches, i.e., they use bilingual dictionaries and boost sentence pairs that have many word translations.

Given these mathematical models for sentence alignments, it is possible to efficiently search the space of possible sentence alignments and find the highest scoring one. The algorithms for sentence alignment make use of dynamic programming and pruning. We discuss these techniques in Chapter 6 on decoding and in Section 8.2.2, where we discuss the Levenshtein distance in the context of word error rate.

2.4 Summary

2.4.1 Core Concepts

This chapter presented some basic linguistic concepts that are used throughout the book. Text is made up of a sequence of **words**, which are separated by a **tokenization** process. Some languages allow the joining of words into **compounds**. Depending on its position in the sentence, the same word may be rendered with a leading uppercase or lowercase letter. Hence, for machine translation, we may want to **lowercase** or **truecase** text before decoding, but we will have to **recase** it afterwards. We also have to undo tokenization by a **detokenization** step.

According to **Zipf's law** words are distributed very unevenly in text. Some very frequent words make up most of the text, and a long tail of words only occurs rarely. Words may be classified by their **part-of-speech**, or more broadly into **content words** (**open-class words**) or **function words** (**closed-class words**). Parts of speech are **noun**, **verb**, **adjective**, **adverb**, **determiner**, **pronoun**, **preposition**, **conjunction**, **possessive marker**, **list marker**, **symbols**, **foreign words**, **interjection**, **punctuation**, or more fine-grained distinctions (e.g., plural nouns vs. singular nouns). A part-of-speech **tagger** is used to assign automatically parts of speech to each word in a text.

Surface forms of words may differ due to **morphology**. For instance in English nouns differ due to **count** (**singular** or **plural**), and verbs differ due to **person** (*you swim* vs. *he swims*) and **tense**. Other languages also inflect words due to **case**, **gender**, etc.

Lexical **semantics**, the study of **meaning** of words, plays a role in machine translation, especially in the case of **polysemy** or **homonymy**, when a word has several **word senses**, and hence distinct translations.

Words are grouped together into **sentences**, and each may consist of several **clauses**. Each clause consists of a verb and its **arguments**, which are its **subject** and **objects**, and additional **adjuncts** such as prepositional phrases or adverbs. **Recursion** is a striking property of language which implies that clauses may contain subclauses, noun phrases may contain relative clauses, which in turn may contain subclauses, and so on.

Syntactically, due to **structural ambiguity**, a sentence may have several interpretations, especially due to **prepositional phrase attachment** and coordination. The syntactic analysis of sentences is a great concern for linguistics. Many grammar formalisms have been proposed such as **generalized phrase structure grammar** (GPSG) or **head-driven phrase structure grammar** (HPSG). A mathematical formalism to define grammars are **context-free grammars** (CFG), which operate on a set of symbols (either **terminals**, or **nonterminals**) and **rules**. This formalism has been extended to **probabilistic context-free grammar** (PCFG), which includes probability distributions over the rule set.

Other grammar formalisms use **feature structures** for nonterminals, which are combined by a process of **unification**. Often the surface structure (as it appears in text) is distinguished from the **deep structure** (which relates to the meaning of the sentence). For instance, **lexical functional grammar** (LFG) uses a separate **c-structure** and

f-structure representation and uses **predicate logic** to formalize semantics. **Dependency structure** formalisms focus on the relationship between words and introduce the notion of a **head word**. **Combinatory categorical grammars** (CCG) encode syntactic relations between words at the word level.

The study of **discourse** examines the relationship between sentences in a text. One issue is the use of **co-reference** (or **anaphor**), i.e., repeatedly referring to the same object, often in different ways. The task of resolving co-references is called **anaphor resolution**. Language resources may be categorized by their **topic** or **modality of communication**. Many early machine translation systems were built only for a **limited domain**.

For statistical machine translation, we need a collection of texts, or **corpus**, to train our systems. Especially, we need a **parallel corpus**, a text paired with its translation. To create such a parallel corpus from, for instance, web sources, we may have to use **document alignment** methods to find translated texts. We further need **sentence alignment** to match up **sentence pairs**. **Comparable corpora**, corpora in different languages with the same subject matter, have also been exploited for machine translation.

2.4.2 Further Reading

General background – There are several textbooks on natural language processing that may serve as background to the material presented here. Good general introductions are given by Manning and Schütze [1999] as well as Jurafsky and Martin [2008].

Collecting parallel corpora – The web is one of the main sources for parallel corpora today. Resnik [1999] describes a method to automatically find such data. Fukushima *et al.* [2006] use a dictionary to detect parallel documents, while Li and Liu [2008] use a number of criteria such as similarity of the URL and page content. Acquiring parallel corpora, however, typically requires some manual involvement [Martin *et al.*, 2003; Koehn, 2005], including the matching of documents [Utiyama and Isahara, 2003]. Uchiyama and Isahara [2007] report on the efforts to build a Japanese–English patent corpus and Macken *et al.* [2007] on efforts on a broad-based Dutch–English corpus. A discussion of the pitfalls during the construction of parallel corpora is given by Kaalep and Veskis [2007]. Parallel corpora may also be built by translating text for this purpose [Germann, 2001]. It may be useful to focus on the most relevant new sentences, using methods such as active learning [Majithia *et al.*, 2005]. Translation memories may also be a useful training resource [Langlais and Simard, 2002]. Other methods focus on fishing the web for the translation of particular terms [Nagata *et al.*, 2001] or noun phrases [Cao and Li, 2002]. It is not clear whether it matters in which translation direction the parallel corpus was constructed, of if both sides were translated from a third language. van Halteren [2008] shows that it is possible to reliably detect the source language in English texts from the European Parliament proceedings, so the original source language does have some effect.

Pivot languages – Machine translation systems for a language pair may also be generated when resources in connection to a pivot (or bridge) language exist, for instance parallel corpora from each language into the pivot language [Callison-Burch and Osborne, 2003]. Pivoting works better if the bridge language is closely related to the other two languages [Babych *et al.*, 2007a]. It may be better to combine translation tables than simply tying machine translation systems together [Utiyama and Isahara, 2007]. By using pivot languages in triangulation, existing phrase translation tables may be enriched, leading to better translation quality [Wu and Wang, 2007b], especially when using multiple pivot languages [Cohn and Lapata, 2007]. When constructing translation dictionaries via a bridge language [Tsunakawa *et al.*, 2008], additional resources such as ontologies may help [Varga and Yokoyama, 2007].

Sentence alignment – Sentence alignment was a very active field of research in the early days of statistical machine translation. We present in this book a method based on sentence length, measured in words [Brown *et al.*, 1991b; Gale and Church, 1991, 1993] or characters [Church, 1993]. Other methods may use alignment chains [Melamed, 1996c, 1999], model omissions [Melamed, 1996b], distinguish between large-scale segmentation of text and detailed sentence alignment [Simard and Plamondon, 1996], and apply line detection methods from image processing to detect large-scale alignment patterns [Chang and Chen, 1997; Melamed, 1997b]. Kay and Röscheisen [1993] propose an iterative algorithm that uses spelling similarity and word co-occurrences to drive sentence alignment. Several researchers proposed including lexical information [Chen, 1993; Dagan *et al.*, 1993; Utsuro *et al.*, 1994; Wu, 1994; Haruno and Yamazaki, 1996; Chuang and Chang, 2002; Kueng and Su, 2002; Moore, 2002; Nightingale and Tanaka, 2003; Aswani and Gaizauskas, 2005], content words [Papageorgiou *et al.*, 1994], numbers and n-grams [Davis *et al.*, 1995]. Sentence alignment may also be improved by a third language in multilingual corpora [Simard, 1999]. More effort is needed to align very noisy corpora [Zhao *et al.*, 2003]. Different sentence alignment methods are compared by Singh and Husain [2005]. Xu *et al.* [2006a] propose a method that iteratively performs binary splits of a document to obtain a sentence alignment. Enright and Kondrak [2007] use a simple and fast method for document alignment that relies on overlap of rare but identically spelled words, which are mostly cognates, names, and numbers.

Comparable corpora – Parallel sentences may also be mined from comparable corpora [Munteanu and Marcu, 2005], such as news stories written on the same topic in different languages. Methods have been proposed to extract matching phrases [Tanaka, 2002] or web pages [Smith, 2002] from such large collections. Munteanu and Marcu [2002] use suffix trees, and in later work log-likelihood ratios [Munteanu et al., 2004] to detect parallel sentences. Instead of full sentences, parallel sentence fragments may be extracted from comparable corpora [Munteanu and Marcu, 2006]. Quirk et al. [2007] propose a generative model for the same task. Extraction of paraphrased sentences from monolingual data may be done using similar methods, such as word overlap and tf/idf [Nelken and Shieber, 2006].

Dictionary – For language pairs for which no parallel corpora are available but translation dictionaries exist, basic gloss translation may be improved by glossing source corpora and using frequency statistics to restructure the gloss, thus creating a parallel corpus from which a translation model may be learned [Pytlik and Yarowsky, 2006].

Corpus cleaning – Statistical machine translation models are generally assumed to be fairly robust to noisy data, such as data that includes misalignments. However, data cleaning has been shown to help [Vogel, 2003]. Often, for instance in the case of news reports that are rewritten for a different audience during translation, documents are not very parallel, so the task of sentence alignment becomes more a task of sentence extraction [Fung and Cheung, 2004b,a]. For good performance it has proven crucial, especially when only small amounts of training data are available, to exploit all of the data, whether by augmenting phrase translation tables to include all words or breaking up sentences that are too long [Mermer et al., 2007].

Domain adaptation – Machine translation systems are often built for very specific domains, such as movie and television subtitles [Volk and Harder, 2007]. A translation model may be trained only from sentences in a parallel corpus that are similar to the input sentence [Hildebrand et al., 2005], which may be determined by language model perplexity [Yasuda et al., 2008]. Also, a domain-specific language model may be obtained by including only sentences that are similar to the ones in the target domain [Sethy et al., 2006]. We may detect such sentences using the tf/idf method common in information retrieval and then boost the count of these sentences [Lü et al., 2007]. In a more graded approach, sentences may be weighted by how well they match the target domain [Bach et al., 2008]. Instead of discarding some of the training data, the mixture-model approach weights submodels trained on data from different domains and combines them [Foster and Kuhn, 2007]. Mixture models may also be used to automatically cluster domains [Civera and Juan, 2007]. Such submodels may be combined as components in the standard log-linear model [Koehn and Schroeder, 2007]. When dealing with multiple domain-specific translation models, input sentences need to be classified to the correct domain, which may be done using a language model or information retrieval approach [Xu *et al.*, 2007]. If the classifier returns proportions on how well the input falls into some of the classes, this may be used to dynamically weight the domain models [Finch and Sumita, 2008]. Wu *et al.* [2008] present methods that exploit domain-specific monolingual corpora and dictionaries. Related to domain adaptation is the problem of adapting machine translation systems to different regional language uses [Cheng *et al.*, 2004].

Truecasing – Truecasing with an HMM is discussed by Lita *et al.* [2003], who mainly rely on a language model. A machine learning approach allows the integration of additional features, such as properties of the source language [Wang *et al.*, 2006b].

2.4.3 Exercises

1. (⋆) Obtain the description of the part-of-speech tags used in the Penn treebank[5] and annotate the following sentences:
   (a) *Time flies like an arrow.*
   (b) *Joe reads the book by the famous author to his sister.*
   (c) *It is getting wet because it is raining.*
   (d) *Jane likes to go to Hoboken.*
2. (⋆) Build a parse tree for each of the sentences in Question 1.
3. (⋆⋆) Download the TreeTagger[6] and tag the sentences in Question 1 with part-of-speech tags.
4. (⋆⋆) Download the Berkeley parser[7] and parse the sentences in Question 1.
5. (⋆⋆) Implement the Gale–Church algorithm for sentence aligning and test it on the Europarl[8] corpus. Check how well the aligner holds up, when randomly dropping or merging sentences on one side.

---

[5] Available at ftp://ftp.cis.upenn.edu/pub/treebank/doc/tagguide.ps.gz
[6] Available at http://www.ims.uni-stuttgart.de/projekte/corplex/TreeTagger/
[7] Available at http://nlp.cs.berkeley.edu/pages/Parsing.html
[8] Available at http://www.statmt.org/europarl/

Chapter 3
Probability Theory

This chapter will introduce concepts in statistics, probability theory, and information theory. It is not a comprehensive treatment, but will give the reader a general understanding of the principles on which the methods in this book are based.

3.1 Estimating Probability Distributions

The use of **probability** in daily life is often difficult. It seems that the human mind is best suited to dealing with certainties and clear outcomes for planned actions. Probability theory is used when outcomes are less certain, and many possibilities exist.

probability

Consider the statement in a weather report: *On Monday, there is a 20% chance of rain.* What does that reference to *20% chance* mean? Ultimately, we only have to wait for Monday, and see if it rains or not. So, this seems to be less a statement about facts than about our knowledge of the facts. In other words, it reflects our uncertainty about the facts (in this case, the future weather).

For the human mind dealing with probabilistic events creates complexities. To address a 20% chance of rain, we cannot decide to carry 20% of an umbrella. We either risk carrying unnecessary weight with us or risk getting wet. So, a typical response to this piece of information is to decide that it will not rain and ignore the less likely possibility. We do this all the time. On any given day, there may be an earthquake, riots in the streets, a flu epidemic, attack by foreign armies, and so on – all events that are not likely, but possible.

But to actually consider all these possible events would overload our brains.

3.1.1 Estimation by Analysis

Let us consider a simpler example, the cast of a dice. There is a reason why probability theory has it roots in the study of casino games. The cast of a dice (or the draw of a card, or the resting place of the ball on the roulette wheel) represents an uncertain outcome, whose understanding may provide enormous profit, and where (unless there is cheating involved) all knowable facts are given. Given that a dice has six sides, the chance that it lands on any of them is therefore $\frac{1}{6}$. Or in other words: *If I cast a dice, there is a 16.7% chance that it lands on 6.*

We reach the estimate of $16\frac{2}{3}\%$ by analyzing the event. We consider all possible outcomes, draw the conclusion that all of them are equally likely and compute the only estimate that matches these facts.

3.1.2 Common Probability Distributions

probability distribution

Probability theory provides a toolbox of common **probability distributions** for us to use, once we have analyzed a problem. The probability distribution we used for the cast of a dice is called the uniform distribution **uniform distribution**, since all possible outcomes have the same uniform probability.

The uniform distribution also applies to an even simpler probabilistic event: the flip of a coin. It comes up either *heads* or *tails*, with equal probability 0.5. But what if we flip a coin multiple times, and count how many times *heads* comes up? If we flip a coin twice, it is more likely that we end up with an overall count of one *head* than with either none or two. We know this by taking a closer look at all the possible outcomes (*heads–heads*, *heads–tails*, *tails–heads*, *tails–tails*), which are all equally likely. Two of them contain one *head*, while only one contains two heads and only one contains zero heads.

Figure 3.1 displays the probability charts for the coin-flipping event with one, two, and seven flips of a coin. Seven flips means that there are $2^7 = 128$ different events to be examined. Fortunately, there is a handy formula to compute the probability for this type of scenario. It is called binomial distribution the **binomial distribution** and the probability that k out of n times the event with probability p occurs is:

$$
\begin{aligned}
b(n, k; p) &= \binom{n}{k} p^k (1-p)^{n-k} \\
&= \frac{n!}{(n-k)!\, k!} p^k (1-p)^{n-k}
\end{aligned}
\tag{3.1}
$$

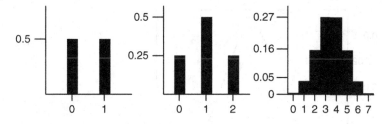

Figure 3.1 Binomial distribution: How likely is it that k times out of n *heads* comes up when flipping a coin? The three graphs display the probabilities for all possible *heads* counts for a series of one, two, and seven coin flips.

Consider another example of the use of the binomial distribution. A politician who considers running for office may want to know if it is worth the effort. He wants to commission an opinion poll where n people are asked if they would vote for him. If the true probability of a random person voting for him is p, then the binomial distribution lets us compute how many (k) people out of the n we expect to give a positive answer. This type of reasoning allows polling institutes to compute the margin of error of their polls, and adjust their sample size accordingly (we will come back to this in Chapter 8 when discussing machine translation evaluation).

In the limit, the binomial distribution approximates the **normal distribution**, which is also known as the **bell curve** or **Gaussian distribution**. Many natural phenomena are assumed to follow the normal distribution, such as the heights of individuals in a population.

normal distribution

bell curve

Gaussian distribution

The formula for the normal distribution is

$$p(x) = \frac{1}{\sigma\sqrt{2\pi}} \exp\left(-\frac{(x-\mu)^2}{2\sigma^2}\right) \qquad (3.2)$$

where μ is the mean and σ^2 is the variance (σ is the standard deviation). We discuss the computation of mean and variance in Section 3.3.1. Note that this is a probability density function for real-valued values of x. To compute a probability for an interval of values, we need to integrate the area under the curve.

The normal distribution is probably best known for its use in the computation of the intelligence quotient (IQ). See Figure 3.2 for an illustration. The IQ is computed as follows. First, we devise a test with questions that test reasoning skills (and not knowledge). Given the test scores of a population of individuals who represent society as a whole, we first compute the average test score and assign individuals with this score the IQ of 100.

Then, we compute the variance (the average of the squares of the distances from the mean test score). The standard deviation is the square root of the variance. Individuals with a test score of one standard deviation higher than the average are declared to have an IQ of 115. People

Figure 3.2 Normal distribution for the distribution of the Intelligence Quotient (mean 100, standard deviation 15).

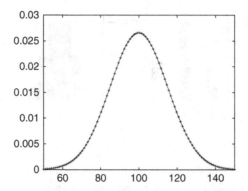

with scores that are two standard deviations higher are assigned the IQ of 130, and so on. Similar assignments are made for below-average test scores.

The normal distribution allows the computation of probability estimates for the IQ scores. For instance, individuals with an IQ of 115 score higher on IQ tests than 84% of the general population (an IQ of 130 corresponds to the 96% percentile, and an IQ of 145 to the 99.9% percentile).

3.1.3 Estimation from Statistics

Often, it is not possible to derive estimates about probability distributions by inspection alone. For instance, we will not be able to predict Monday's weather by armchair reasoning. What we can do instead is gather facts and statistics. Already in the use of the normal distribution, we collected statistics about the average and standard deviation of

data sample   a **data sample**.

In the case of the dice, we may suspect that a particular dice that is handed to us is crooked. In other words, we do not trust that all possible outcomes are equally likely. To estimate the probability distribution for this particular dice, we may collect a data sample by sitting down, casting a dice many times and recording the outcomes. Then, we estimate the probabilities based on these counts. If out of a million casts of the dice, the number 6 came up 200,000 times, we compute the probability of that event as $\frac{200,000}{1000,000} = 0.2$.

Intuitively, we need a large sample of events to estimate probability distributions reliably. If we cast a dice only 10 times, and end up twice with the number 6, we would hesitate to conclude that the dice is crooked and biased towards this number.

law of large numbers   According to the **law of large numbers**, our probability estimate based on counts gets increasingly accurate, the more counts we collect. See Figure 3.3 for an illustration. The more often we cast a perfect

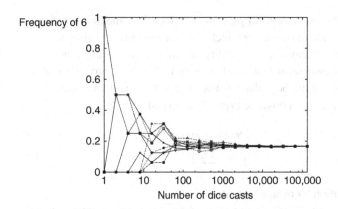

Frequency of 6

Number of dice casts

Figure 3.3 Illustration of the law of large numbers: In 10 experimental runs, we record how often a perfect dice ends up with 6 on top. While initially the ratio is not representative of the true probability $\frac{1}{6}$, it converges with the increasing number of recorded events.

dice, the closer the relative frequency of a 6 approximates its theoretical probability.

Let us return to our original challenge to predict Monday's weather. Here, we could also collect a sample, for instance, by counting on how many days in the last 10 years it rained. If it rained on 730 days out of 3650, then the chance that it will rain on Monday is like that of any other day: $\frac{730}{3650} = 20\%$. Admittedly, this is not a very informative weather forecast. It would be a good idea to incorporate a bit more information into our model besides the fact that Monday is *a day*. Maybe today's weather, or the season, or an upcoming storm front matter. To be able to do this, we need to get a better understanding of mathematical probability theory.

3.2 Calculating Probability Distributions

The preceding section discusses methods for creating probability distributions for random events either by using standard distributions (e.g., uniform, binomial, normal) or by estimating distributions based on counts from a data sample. Mathematical probability theory allows us to take this further by building more complex probability distributions and analyzing their properties.

3.2.1 Formal Definitions

The notion of a **random variable** X allows us to capture the inherent nature of uncertainty. We are familiar with variables in math that have fixed values, for instance $a = 4$. A random variable may have several different values, and we can find out how likely each value is with a **probability function** p.

random variable

probability function

For instance, if the random variable X contains the outcome of the cast of a perfect dice, we know that $p(X = 6) = \frac{1}{6}$. This is typically denoted by the shorthand $p(6) = \frac{1}{6}$, which is sometimes confusing, since we have to remember which p we are currently referring to.

Mathematically, a probability function is a typical function as known elsewhere in mathematics, with two distinct properties. Probabilities have to be values between 0 and 1, and the sum of the probabilities of all possible events have to add up to 1:

$$\forall x : 0 \leq p(x) \leq 1 \tag{3.3}$$

$$\sum_x p(x) = 1 \tag{3.4}$$

(The notation $\forall x$ means "for all x.")

Probability distributions may be defined over any number of events, even infinitely many.

3.2.2 Joint Probability Distributions

Sometimes, and very often in this book, we want to deal with many random variables at the same time. Suppose we want to consider both the cast of a dice and the flip of a coin. So, we introduce two random variables, D (dice) and C (coin), respectively. For these, we define a joint probability distribution $p(D = d, C = c)$, or for short $p(d, c)$.

joint probability distribution

How likely is it that we cast a 6 and get *heads*? Given that there are six different but equally likely outcomes for the dice cast and two different but equally likely outcomes for the coin flip, there are a total of 12 different combinations of both outcomes, which are equally likely, hence $p(6, heads) = \frac{1}{12}$. Could we also have computed this probability from the elementary probability distributions $p(d)$ and $p(c)$?

Before we answer this question, let us introduce the concept of *independence* of random variables. Two variables are independent if the value of one variable has no impact on the second, and vice versa. Formally, independence is defined as follows:

independence

$$X \text{ and } Y \text{ are independent} \Leftrightarrow \forall x, y : p(x, y) = p(x)\, p(y) \tag{3.5}$$

The cast of a dice and the flip of a coin are independent so we are able to compute:

$$p(6, \text{heads}) = p(6)\, p(\text{heads}) = \frac{1}{6} \times \frac{1}{2} = \frac{1}{12} \tag{3.6}$$

Let us look at another example, where the random variable T refers to today's weather ($t \in \{\text{rain, no-rain}\}$) and M refers to tomorrow's weather. We estimate the probability distribution $p(T, M)$ for these two random variables by observing the weather over, say, the past 10 years, collecting counts and computing probabilities in the following table:

$p(T, M)$	rain tomorrow	no rain tomorrow
rain today	0.12	0.08
no rain today	0.08	0.72

The probability that it rains on any given day is 0.20 (this number can be deduced from the table by adding up the values in the appropriate row or column). Intuitively, today's weather is not independent of tomorrow's weather, and it is easy to show that the independence condition is violated:

$$p(\text{rain}, \text{rain}) = 0.12$$
$$p(\text{rain})\, p(\text{rain}) = 0.2 \times 0.2 = 0.04$$

(3.7)

3.2.3 Conditional Probability Distributions

Joint probability distributions give us information about how two random variables relate to each other. However, if we are in the business of prediction, we would like to answer the following question: *If it rains today, how likely is it that it will rain tomorrow?*

This is where **conditional probability distributions** come into play. The probability of y given x is denoted as $p(y|x)$ and defined as

conditional probability distribution

$$p(y|x) = \frac{p(x, y)}{p(x)}$$

(3.8)

We can now answer the question about tomorrow's chance of rain, given the joint probability distribution from the previous section:

$$p(\text{rain}|\text{rain}) = \frac{p(\text{rain}, \text{rain})}{p(\text{rain})} = \frac{0.12}{0.2} = 0.6$$

(3.9)

$$p(\text{rain}|\text{no-rain}) = \frac{p(\text{rain}, \text{no-rain})}{p(\text{no-rain})} = \frac{0.08}{0.8} = 0.1$$

Equation (3.8), the definition of a conditional probability distribution, is often used in a reformulated way called the **chain rule**:

chain rule

$$p(x, y) = p(x)p(y|x)$$

(3.10)

Conditional probability distributions are also called **marginal distributions**, and the process of computing them from joint probability distributions is called **marginalizing out** the random variable X.

marginal distribution

marginalizing out

Note that for two independent random variables X and Y, the conditional probability distribution $p(y|x)$ is the same as simply $p(y)$.

3.2.4 Bayes Rule

Let us introduce another rule, the **Bayes rule**, that follows straightforwardly from the definition of conditional probabilities:

Bayes rule

$$p(x|y) = \frac{p(y|x)\, p(x)}{p(y)}$$

(3.11)

posterior distribution
prior distribution

This rule a conditional probability distribution $p(x|y)$ expresses in terms of its inverse $p(y|x)$ (called the **posterior**) and the two elementary probability distributions $p(x)$ (called the **prior**) and $p(y)$ (which typically plays less of a role).

One use of this rule is in Bayesian model estimation. Here, we have two random variables: a data sample D and a model M. We are interested in the most probable model that fits the data:

$$\text{argmax}_M\, p(M|D) = \text{argmax}_M\, \frac{p(D|M)\, p(M)}{p(D)}$$
$$= \text{argmax}_M\, p(D|M)\, p(M) \tag{3.12}$$

The best model M is selected by considering how well it explains the data sample, $p(D|M)$, and how likely it is to be a good model in general, $p(M)$. The prior $p(M)$ may be used to prefer simpler models over more complex ones, or to introduce a bias towards an expected type of model.

3.2.5 Interpolation

In practice, and at several points in this book, we have several ways to estimate the probability distribution for a random variable. The most common reason for this is that we have large samples with general information and small samples that are more specific, but less reliable. So we typically have two ways to estimate the probability distribution resulting in two functions p_1 and p_2.

interpolation   By **interpolation** we can combine two probability distributions p_1 and p_2 for the same random variable X by giving each a fixed weight and adding them. If we give the first the weight $0 \leq \lambda \leq 1$, then we have $1 - \lambda$ left for the second:

$$p(x) = \lambda\, p_1(x) + (1 - \lambda)\, p_2(x) \tag{3.13}$$

A common application of interpolation arises from data samples that take different conditions into account. For instance, we may want to predict tomorrow's weather M based on today's weather T, and also based on the current calendar day D (in order to consider typical seasonal weather patterns).

We now want to estimate the conditional probability distribution $p(m|t, d)$ from weather statistics. Conditioning on specific days leads to small data samples in estimation (for instance, there may be hardly any rainy days on August 1st in Los Angeles). Hence, it may be more practical to interpolate this distribution with the more robust $p(m|t)$:

$$p_{\text{interpolated}}(m|t, d) = \lambda\, p(m|t, d) + (1 - \lambda)\, p(m|t) \tag{3.14}$$

Besides considering different condition, we may have different methodologies for estimating probability distributions. The strategy in the machine learning community for combining several the results of methods is called **classifier combination** or **ensemble learning** and may be done by simple interpolation.

classifier combination
ensemble learning

3.3 Properties of Probability Distributions

When talking about the properties of probability distributions, some important concepts are frequently used. Here, we will briefly introduce the mean, variance, expectation, entropy, and mutual information.

3.3.1 Mean and Variance

Often, we choose to represent the possible outcomes of uncertain events with numerical values. For instance, the result of casting a dice and the temperature have obvious numerical representations (1–6 and degrees centigrade, respectively). Binary outcomes such as *rain* vs. *no-rain* can be represented by the numbers 0 and 1.

Numerical values for an uncertain event allow the computation of the **mean** $\bar{x}$ for a data sample $\{x_1, \ldots, x_n\}$ with the formula

mean

$$\bar{x} = \frac{1}{n} \sum_i x_i \tag{3.15}$$

For instance, if we recorded the outcomes from 10 casts of a dice as $\{5, 6, 4, 2, 1, 3, 4, 3, 2, 4\}$, then the mean is

$$\bar{x} = \frac{1}{10}(5 + 6 + 4 + 2 + 1 + 3 + 4 + 3 + 2 + 4) = \frac{34}{10} = 3.4 \tag{3.16}$$

Another interesting property of a data sample is how much individual events diverge from the mean. This is called the **variance** and it is computed as the geometric mean of the difference between each individual event's value and the mean:

variance

$$\sigma^2 = \frac{1}{n} \sum_i (x_i - \bar{x})^2 \tag{3.17}$$

In our example above, the variance σ^2 is

$$\sigma^2 = \frac{1}{10}((5 - 3.4)^2 + (6 - 3.4)^2 + (4 - 3.4)^2 + (2 - 3.4)^2$$
$$+ (1 - 3.4)^2 + (3 - 3.4)^2 + (4 - 3.4)^2 + (3 - 3.4)^2$$
$$+ (2 - 3.4)^2 + (4 - 3.4)^2) = \frac{20.4}{10} = 2.4 \tag{3.18}$$

3.3.2 Expectation and Variance

We have defined mean and variance as properties of data samples. But these notions can also be applied to probability distributions. The mean *expectation* of a probability distribution is called the **expectation** and it is defined as

$$E[X] = \sum_{x \in X} x\, p(x) \tag{3.19}$$

The possible values x_i for the random variable X are weighted by their corresponding probability. For instance, if buying a lottery ticket brings a one-in-a-million change of winning \$100,000, then we say that the expected win is 10 cents, as the following computation shows:

$$E[X] = 100,000 \times \frac{1}{1,000,000} + 0 \times \frac{999,999}{1,000,000} = 0.10 \tag{3.20}$$

variance   The definition of **variance** for probability distributions follows straightforwardly from the definition of variance for data samples:

$$\text{Var}[X] = \sum_{x \in X} (x - E[X])^2\, p(x) \tag{3.21}$$

In a way, the variance is the expected squared difference between each value of the random variable and its expected value, so an equivalent definition of variance is

$$\text{Var}[X] = E[(X - E[X])^2] \tag{3.22}$$

If we estimate a probability distribution from a data sample, we may require that the mean of the data sample matches the expectation of the probability distribution, and also that the variance of the data sample and the variance of the estimated distribution are the same.

Note how this plays out if we assume that the data are distributed according to the normal distribution. Given a data sample, we compute its mean and variance. These are the only two parameters we need to determine a normal distribution.

3.3.3 Entropy

entropy   A concept widely used across many scientific disciplines is **entropy**, which roughly is a measure of disorder. You may remember it from the laws of thermodynamics, which state that unless energy is added to a system its entropy never decreases. Nature tends towards disorder. In probability theory entropy is roughly a measure of uncertainty of outcomes. When making predictions, we want to expend energy to increase the certainty of our predictions (i.e. decrease the entropy).

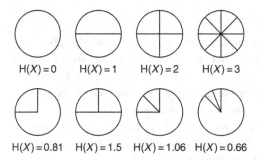

$H(X) = 0$ $H(X) = 1$ $H(X) = 2$ $H(X) = 3$

$H(X) = 0.81$ $H(X) = 1.5$ $H(X) = 1.06$ $H(X) = 0.66$

Figure 3.4 Illustration of the entropy of a random variable X: If possible events are equally likely, then entropy $E(X)$ increases by 1 with each doubling of the number of events (top row of examples). Entropy is lower if the probabilities are less evenly distributed (lower row of examples).

The definition of entropy of a random variable is

$$H(X) = -\sum_{x \in X} p(x) \log_2 p(x) \tag{3.23}$$

Figure 3.4 shows how entropy reflects uncertainty. If a random variable X has one certain outcome, its entropy is 0. If there are two equally likely outcomes, its entropy is 1. If there are four equally likely outcomes, its entropy is 2, and so on. With each doubling of equally likely values for X, entropy increases by 1.

Entropy is lower if the probability is distributed unevenly. If one of two possible outcomes has $\frac{1}{4}$ probability (and the other has $\frac{3}{4}$ probability), the entropy is 0.81, which is less than 1. It is possible that even if there are three possible outcomes the entropy is below 1, which is the entropy for two equally likely events. One example is a random variable with values that have probabilities $\frac{1}{16}$, $\frac{1}{16}$, and $\frac{7}{8}$. Its entropy is 0.66.

We can formulate our goal of learning good predictive models in terms of entropy. We would like to reduce the entropy (increase the certainty of outcomes) by adding additional information about possible outcomes in a given situation.

Entropy, as we have defined it, has a very natural explanation in **information theory**. If we are trying to communicate a set of events, and have to encode each event with a binary code, then entropy is a lower bound on the number of bits needed per event to encode a message. One example: if there are four equally likely events, then we encode them with 00, 01, 10, 11, i.e., we always need 2 bits. Another example: if we have one event with probability 50%, and two events with probability 25%, then we encode them with 0, 10, 11, respectively, and need on average $(0.5 \times 1 + 0.25 \times 2 + 0.25 \times 2)$ 1.5 bits per event to communicate a message. Note how this correlates nicely with news worthiness. *Dog bites man*, a common event, receives scarcely a mention, while *man bites dog*, an uncommon event, is a news story.

information theory

3.3.4 Mutual Information

We are often interested in the extent to which knowledge about one random variable X impacts our certainty over the outcome of another random variable Y. Recall our motivating example of tomorrow's weather. If we know something about today's weather, it should help us to make better predictions about tomorrow's weather.

We just introduced a measure of certainty that we called entropy. We will now use this concept to qualify the relation between two random variables. First, let us define **joint entropy** $H(X, Y)$:

joint entropy

$$H(X, Y) = - \sum_{x \in X, y \in Y} p(x, y) \log_2 p(x, y) \tag{3.24}$$

Nothing too surprising here: joint entropy is simply the entropy when we consider two random variables at the same time. With joint entropy in hand, we can define **conditional entropy**:

conditional entropy

$$H(Y|X) = H(X, Y) - H(X) \tag{3.25}$$

Intuitively, conditional entropy measures how much uncertainty is removed when one of the random variables is known. Coming back to our example: one day's weather X may be fairly uncertain, and the prediction of the weather of any two consecutive days X, Y is even more so (measured as $H(X, Y)$). Removing the uncertainty about the weather of the first day (measured as $H(X)$) leaves much less uncertainty about the following day's weather (measured as $H(Y|X)$). How much depends on how related the two events are.

Note that it is not necessarily the case that $H(X|Y) = H(Y|X)$. In other words, one random variable may say a lot about the other, but not the other way around (a simple example: X is the number on the dice, Y indicates whether it is an odd number). Therefore, we intro-

mutual information

duce another, symmetric measure called **mutual information**. The mutual information $I(X; Y)$ between two random variables X and Y is defined as

$$I(X; Y) = \sum_{x \in X, y \in Y} p(x, y) \log \frac{p(x, y)}{p(x)\, p(y)} \tag{3.26}$$

To understand this better, let us first look at the extreme cases. If the two random variables X and Y are independent of each other, then $p(x, y) = p(x)\, p(y)$ and hence $I(X; Y) = 0$. In other words they share no mutual information. If knowledge about X perfectly predicts Y, then $p(x, y) = p(x)$, and $I(X; Y) = H(Y)$. In this case, the shared mutual information encompasses all the uncertainty about Y.

Probability table

X \ Y	rain tomorrow	no rain tomorrow
rain today	0.12	0.08
no rain today	0.08	0.72

Measure	Computation	Value
$H(X) = H(Y)$	$-\sum_{x \in X} p(x) \log_2 p(x)$ $= -(0.2 \times \log_2 0.2 + 0.8 \times \log_2 0.8)$	0.722
$H(X, Y)$	$-\sum_{x \in X, y \in Y} p(x, y) \log_2 p(x, y)$ $= -(0.12 \times \log_2 0.12 + 0.08 \times \log_2 0.08$ $+0.08 \times \log_2 0.08 + 0.72 \times \log_2 0.72)$	1.291
$H(Y \mid X)$	$H(X, Y) - H(X)$ $= 1.291 - 0.722$	0.569
$I(X; Y)$	$H(X) + H(Y) - H(X, Y)$ $= 0.722 + 0.722 - 1.291$	0.153

Figure 3.5 Example of entropy $H(X)$, joint entropy $H(X, Y)$, conditional entropy $H(Y \mid X)$ and mutual information $I(X; Y)$. The probabilities of rain today X and rain tomorrow Y are related, indicated by the mutual information $I(X; Y) = 0.153$.

Mutual information relates to the entropy measures for X and Y as follows (see also Figure 3.5):

$$I(X; Y) = H(X) - H(X \mid Y)$$
$$= H(Y) - H(Y \mid X)$$
$$= H(X) + H(Y) - H(X, Y) \tag{3.27}$$

Figure 3.5 applies the measures to our weather example. Each day's weather has an entropy of 0.722. If the weather of two subsequent days were independent of each other, the joint entropy would be $2 \times 0.722 = 1.444$, but it is 1.291, indicating mutual information of 0.153. Or, to look at it another way, knowledge about today's weather reduces the entropy of tomorrow's weather from 0.722 to the conditional entropy of 0.569.

3.4 Summary

3.4.1 Core Concepts

This chapter introduced the concept of **probability distributions** which are used to model events with uncertain outcomes. We may analyze a specific event and model it by standard distributions such as the **uniform distributions**, the **binomial distribution**, or the **normal distribution** (also called a **bell curve** or **Gaussian distribution**). We may also collect a data **sample** and use it as a basis for estimating a probability distribution. The **law of large numbers** says that the larger the data sample, the closer the data will be to the true probability distribution.

Mathematical probability theory provides us with a rich tool box for calculating probability distributions. An uncertain event is expressed by a **random variable** and its **probability function**. We define **joint probability** distributions for multiple random variables, and can compute these straightforwardly if the variables are **independent** of each other. We use the **chain rule** to compute **conditional probability** distributions (also called **marginal distributions**) of one event taking place given the outcome of another event. The **Bayes rule** allows us to reformulate a conditional probability distribution into a **prior** and a **posterior**. Multiple probability distributions can be combined by **interpolation**, which may be used in **classifier combination** or **ensemble learning** methods.

We are often interested in certain properties of data samples, such as the **mean** (average of all values in the data) and **variance** (divergence from the mean). The corresponding properties of probability distributions are called **expectation** and variance. **Entropy** measures the degree of uncertainty of a probabilistic event. The concept is also used in **information theory**, which provides an intuitive interpretation of entropy. Measures such as **joint entropy**, **conditional entropy** and **mutual information** allow us to analyze the relationship between different probability distributions.

3.4.2 Further Reading

A good introduction to probability theory and information is given by Cover and Thomas [1991]. For an application of probabilistic methods to the related field of speech recognition, see the book by Jelinek [1998].

3.4.3 Exercises

1. (⋆) If we flip a coin 10 times, we might get the outcome *HTTHTHTHTT* (*H* for *heads*, *T* for *tails*).
   (a) Estimate a distribution by maximum likelihood estimation.
   (b) We want to test the quality of the estimation. We flip the coin five times and get *HHTTH*. What is the probability of this outcome according to (a) the estimated distribution, and (b) the uniform distribution?
2. (⋆) If we roll a dice 10 times, we might get the outcome 4,2,6,6,2,1,4,3,6,5.
   (a) Estimate the mean and variance of this sample.
   (b) Assuming a uniform distribution, what is the expectation and variance for a dice roll?

3. (⋆) Computations with probability distributions:
   (a) Prove that $p(y|x) = p(y)$ if X and Y are independent.
   (b) Derive the Bayes rule.
4. (⋆) In our example of weather predictions, we find for the joint probability for the weather of two days in sequence that $p(\text{rain}, \text{no-rain}) = p(\text{no-rain}, \text{rain})$. Give an intuitive argument why this is the case and prove the equation mathematically.
5. (⋆⋆) Obtain a text corpus that is tokenized and split into sentences, such as the Europarl corpus.[1] Collect statistics on the length of sentences (in words) and the length of words (in characters).
   (a) Compute the mean and variance for these samples.
   (b) If you plot the samples, are they normally distributed?
6. (⋆⋆) Obtain a text corpus that is tokenized, such as the Europarl corpus, and take a subset of it. Collect statistics over the frequency of words and the length of words (in characters).
   (a) Use the statistics to estimate probability distributions for both events, and for each event by itself.
   (b) Compute the entropy for each of the distributions.
   (c) Compute the conditional entropy and mutual information between the two events.

---

[1] Available at http://www.statmt.org/europarl/

Part II
Core Methods

Chapter 4
Word-Based Models

In this chapter, we discuss word-based models. The models stem from the original work on statistical machine translation by the IBM Candide project in the late 1980s and early 1990s. While this approach does not constitute the state of the art anymore, many of the principles and methods are still current today.

Reviewing this seminal work will introduce many concepts that underpin other statistical machine translation models, such as generative modeling, the expectation maximization algorithm, and the noisy-channel model. At the end of the chapter, we will also look at word alignment as a problem in itself.

4.1 Machine Translation by Translating Words

We start this chapter with a simple model for machine translation that is based solely on **lexical translation**, the translation of words in isolation. This requires a dictionary that maps words from one language to another.

lexical translation

4.1.1 Lexical Translation

If we open a common bilingual dictionary, say, German–English, we may find an entry[1] like

> **Haus** — *house, building, home, household, shell.*

---

[1] This example is a simplified version of the entry in HarperCollins [1998].

Most words have multiple translations. Some are more likely than others. In this example, the translation *house* will often be correct when translating *Haus* into English. Others are common as well – *building, home* – while some are used only in certain circumstances. For instance, the *Haus* of a snail is its *shell*.

4.1.2 Collecting a Statistic

statistics

The notion of statistical machine translation implies the use of **statistics**. What kind of statistics would be useful for deciding how to translate *Haus*? If we had a large collection of German texts, paired with translations into English, we could count how often *Haus* is translated into each of the given choices.

Figure 4.1 displays the possible outcome of such an exercise in data collection. The word *Haus* occurs 10,000 times in our hypothetical text collection. It is translated 8000 times into *house*, 1600 times into *building*, and so on.

Note that this exercise simplifies the data dramatically. We completely ignore the context of the occurrences of these instances; we strip the problem of translating the word *Haus* down to a very simple question. Given no outside knowledge, what are the possible translations, and how often do they occur?

4.1.3 Estimating a Probability Distribution

lexical translation probability distribution

We now want to estimate a **lexical translation probability distribution** from these counts. This function will help us to answer a question that will arise when we have to translate new German text: What is the most likely English translation for a foreign word like *Haus*?

To put it formally, we want to find a function

$$p_f : e \to p_f(e) \qquad (4.1)$$

that, given a foreign word f (here *Haus*), returns a probability, for each choice of English translation e, that indicates how likely that translation is.

Figure 4.1 Hypothetical counts for different translations of the German word *Haus* into English. This statistic is the basis for the estimation of a lexical translation probability distribution.

Translation of *Haus*	Count
house	8000
building	1600
home	200
household	150
shell	50

The function should return a high value if an English candidate word e is a common translation. It returns a low value if an English candidate word e is a rare translation. It returns 0 if the English translation e is impossible.

The definition of probability distribution requires the function p_f to have two properties:

$$\sum_e p_f(e) = 1 \qquad (4.2)$$

$$\forall e : 0 \leq p_f(e) \leq 1 \qquad (4.3)$$

How do we derive a probability distribution given the counts in Figure 4.1? One straightforward way is to use the ratio of the counts. We have 10,000 occurrences of the word *Haus* in our text collection. In 8000 instances, it is translated as *house*. Dividing these two numbers gives a ratio of 0.8, so we set $p_{\text{Haus}}(\text{house}) = 0.8$.

If we do this for all five choices, we end up with the function

$$p_f(e) = \begin{cases} 0.8 & \text{if } e = house \\ 0.16 & \text{if } e = building \\ 0.02 & \text{if } e = home \\ 0.015 & \text{if } e = household \\ 0.005 & \text{if } e = shell \end{cases} \qquad (4.4)$$

This method of obtaining a probability distribution from data is not only very intuitive, it also has a strong theoretical motivation. There are many ways we could build a model for the given data (for instance, reserving some probability mass for unseen events). This type of estimation is also called **maximum likelihood estimation**, since it maximizes the likelihood of the data.

maximum likelihood estimation

4.1.4 Alignment

Armed with probability distributions for lexical translation, we can make a leap to our first model of statistical machine translation, which uses only lexical translation probabilities.

Let us look at an example. Figure 4.2 shows probability distributions for the translation of four German words into English. We now denote the probability of translating a foreign word f into an English word e with the conditional probability function $t(e|f)$, to more clearly denote this probability distribution as a *translation probability*. The corresponding translation tables are often called **T-tables**.

T-tables

Figure 4.2 Lexical translation probability tables for four German words: *das, Haus, ist, klein*.

das		**Haus**		**ist**		**klein**	
e	*t(e|f)*	*e*	*t(e|f)*	*e*	*t(e|f)*	*e*	*t(e|f)*
the	0.7	house	0.8	is	0.8	small	0.4
that	0.15	building	0.16	's	0.16	little	0.4
which	0.075	home	0.02	exists	0.02	short	0.1
who	0.05	household	0.015	has	0.015	minor	0.06
this	0.025	shell	0.005	are	0.005	petty	0.04

Let us start by translating the German sentence

das Haus ist klein

We decide to translate the sentence word by word into English. One possible translation is

the house is small

alignment · Implicit in this translation is an **alignment**, meaning a mapping from German words to English words. We translated the German word *das* to the English word *the*. This alignment between input words and output words can be illustrated by a diagram:

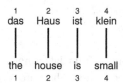

alignment function · An alignment can be formalized with an **alignment function** *a*. This function maps, in our example, each English output word at position *j* to a German output at position *i*:

$$a : j \rightarrow i \qquad (4.5)$$

Note that although we translate from German to English, the alignment function maps English word positions to German word positions. In our example, this function would provide the mappings:

$$a : \{1 \rightarrow 1, 2 \rightarrow 2, 3 \rightarrow 3, 4 \rightarrow 4\} \qquad (4.6)$$

This is a very simple alignment, since the German words and their English counterparts are in exactly the same order. While many languages do indeed have similar word order, a foreign language may have sentences in a different word order than is possible in English. This means that words have to be reordered during translation, as the following example illustrates:

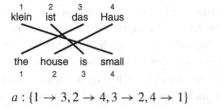

$$a : \{1 \rightarrow 3, 2 \rightarrow 4, 3 \rightarrow 2, 4 \rightarrow 1\}$$

Besides having different word order, languages may also differ in how many words are necessary to express the same concept. In the following example one German word requires two English words to capture the same meaning:

```
1      2      3    4
das   Haus   ist  klitzeklein

 |     |      |   / \

the   house   is  very  small
1      2      3    4     5
```

$$a : \{1 \rightarrow 1, 2 \rightarrow 2, 3 \rightarrow 3, 4 \rightarrow 4, 5 \rightarrow 4\}$$

Languages may have words that have no clear equivalent in English and that should simply be dropped during translation. One example of this is the German flavoring particle *ja*, as in the sentence pair below:

```
1     2     3    4    5
das  Haus  ist  ja  klein

 \    \     \   /

the  house  is  small
1     2     3   4
```

$$a : \{1 \rightarrow 1, 2 \rightarrow 2, 3 \rightarrow 3, 4 \rightarrow 5\}$$

Conversely, some words in the English output may have no relation to any of the German input words. To model this, we introduce a special **NULL token** that is treated just like another input word. Why do we need this NULL token? We still want to align each English word to a German input word, so that the alignment function is fully defined.

In the example below the English function word *do* does not have a clear equivalent in German:

```
0     1    2     3   4     5     6
NULL  ich  gehe  ja  nicht  zum  haus

 X     X    /    /

i  do  not  go  to  the  house
1  2   3    4   5    6    7
```

$$a : \{1 \rightarrow 1, 2 \rightarrow 0, 3 \rightarrow 4, 4 \rightarrow 2, 5 \rightarrow 5, 6 \rightarrow 5, 7 \rightarrow 6\}$$

We have just laid the foundations for an **alignment model** based on words that allows for dropping, adding, and duplication of words during

NULL token

alignment model

translation. We have also introduced a convention that we will follow throughout the book. We will refer to the input as the foreign language, and the output language as English. Of course all of our methods also work for translation from English or between two foreign languages.

Note that, in our alignment model, each output word is linked to exactly one input word (including the imaginary NULL token), as defined by the alignment function. The same is not true in the other direction: an input may be linked to multiple output words, or none at all. This is a glaring problem that will eventually haunt us. But we will ignore it for now and leave the resolution of this asymmetry to the end of this chapter.

4.1.5 IBM Model 1

Lexical translation probabilities and the notion of alignment allow us to define a model that generates a number of different translations for a sentence, each with a different probability. This model is called **IBM Model 1**.

IBM Model 1

Let us step back and state our motivation for this. We do not directly try to model a translation probability distribution for full sentences, since it is hard to estimate such a distribution – most sentences occur only once, even in large text collections. Therefore, we break up the process into smaller steps, in our case into the translation of individual words. It is much more promising to collect sufficient statistics for the estimation of probability distributions for the translation of individual words.

This method of modeling – breaking up the process of generating the data into smaller steps, modeling the smaller steps with probability distributions, and combining the steps into a coherent story – is called **generative modeling**.

generative modeling

Let us now turn to IBM Model 1, which is a generative model for sentence translation, based solely on lexical translation probability distributions. For each output word e that is produced by our model from an input word f, we want to factor in the translation probability $p(e|f)$, and nothing else.

We define the translation probability for a foreign sentence $\mathbf{f} = (f_1, ..., f_{l_f})$ of length l_f to an English sentence $\mathbf{e} = (e_1, ..., e_{l_e})$ of length l_e with an alignment of each English word e_j to a foreign word f_i according to the alignment function $a : j \rightarrow i$ as follows:

$$p(\mathbf{e}, a|\mathbf{f}) = \frac{\epsilon}{(l_f + 1)^{l_e}} \prod_{j=1}^{l_e} t(e_j|f_{a(j)}) \qquad (4.7)$$

Let us take a closer look at this formula. The core is a product over the lexical translation probabilities for all l_e generated output words e_j. The fraction before the product is necessary for normalization. Since we include the special NULL token, there are actually $l_f + 1$ input words. Hence, there are $(l_f + 1)^{l_e}$ different alignments that map $l_f + 1$ input words into l_e output words. The parameter ϵ is a normalization constant, so that $p(\mathbf{e}, a|\mathbf{f})$ is a proper probability distribution, meaning that the probabilities of all possible English translations $\mathbf{e}$ and alignments a sum up to one:[2] $\sum_{\mathbf{e},a} p(\mathbf{e}, a|\mathbf{f}) = 1$.

To conclude, we apply this model to our original example, repeated below:

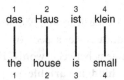

Four words are translated, and hence four lexical translation probabilities must be factored in:

$$p(e, a|f) = \frac{\epsilon}{5^4} \times t(\text{the}|\text{das}) \times t(\text{house}|\text{Haus}) \times t(\text{is}|\text{ist}) \times t(\text{small}|\text{klein})$$

$$= \frac{\epsilon}{5^4} \times 0.7 \times 0.8 \times 0.8 \times 0.4$$

$$= 0.0029\epsilon \tag{4.8}$$

The probability of translating the German sentence as *the house is small* is hence 0.0029ϵ. We have translated our first sentence using a statistical machine translation model.

4.2 Learning Lexical Translation Models

We have introduced a model for translating sentences based on lexical translation probability distributions. So far, we have assumed that we already have these translation probability distributions. We will now describe a method that allows us to **learn** these translation probability distributions from sentence-aligned parallel text (text paired with a translation, sentence-by-sentence). This method is the expectation maximization algorithm.

learning translation probability distributions

---

[2] We cite the formula for IBM Model 1 as presented by Brown *et al.* [1993]. They define $\epsilon = p(l_e|l_f)$ as a uniform length probability. However, given that any output length is possible and $\sum p(\mathbf{e}, a|f, l_f) = 1$, ϵ would have to be infinitesimally small. If IBM Model 1 is used only for model estimation and not for translation (as we do here), this does not matter.

4.2.1 The Problem of Incomplete Data

We described earlier (Section 4.1.2) a method for estimating lexical translation probability distributions: For any input word f, we go through a large collection of text, take note of how each instance is translated, collect counts and then estimate a probability distribution of these counts using maximum likelihood estimation.

There is one slight flaw with this strategy. While it is reasonable to assume that we can collect large amounts of *sentence-aligned* parallel texts from existing sources, these data are not *word-aligned*. For each foreign input word f, we do not know which of the words in the English sentence is its translation. In other words, we lack the alignment function a for this data.

incomplete data

hidden variable

We are facing a typical problem for machine learning. We want to estimate our model from **incomplete data**. One aspect of our model is hidden from plain view: the alignment between words. For this reason, the alignment is considered a **hidden variable** in our model.

We have a chicken and egg problem. If we had the word alignments marked up in our data, it would be trivial to estimate the lexical translation model. We simply collect counts and perform maximum likelihood estimation. On the other hand, if we had the model given to us, it would be possible to estimate the most likely alignment between words for each sentence pair.

In other words: Given the model, we could fill in the gap in our data. Given the complete data, we could estimate the model. Unfortunately, we have neither.

4.2.2 The Expectation Maximization Algorithm

EM algorithm

The **expectation maximization algorithm**, or **EM algorithm**, addresses the situation of incomplete data. It is an iterative learning method that fills in the gaps in the data and trains a model in alternating steps.

The EM algorithm works as follows:

1. Initialize the model, typically with uniform distributions.
2. Apply the model to the data (expectation step).
3. Learn the model from the data (maximization step).
4. Iterate steps 2 and 3 until convergence.

First, we initialize the model. Without prior knowledge, uniform probability distributions are a good starting point. For our case of lexical translation this means that each input word f may be translated with equal probability into any output word *e*. Another option would be to start with randomized translation probabilities.

In the expectation step, we apply the model to the data. We fill in the gaps in our data with the most likely values. In our case, what is missing is the alignment between words. Therefore, we need to find the most likely alignments. Initially, all alignments are equally likely, but further along, we will prefer alignments where, e.g., the German word *Haus* is aligned to its most likely translation *house*.

In the maximization step, we learn the model from the data. The data are now augmented with guesses for the gaps. We may simply consider the best guess according to our model, but it is better to consider all possible guesses and weight them with their corresponding probabilities. Sometimes it is not possible to efficiently compute all possible guesses, so we have to resort to sampling. We learn the model with maximum likelihood estimation, using partial counts collected from the weighted alternatives.

We iterate through the two steps until convergence. There are some mathematical guarantees for the EM algorithm. For one, the perplexity of the model is guaranteed not to increase at every iteration. In some circumstances, as for instance in our case of IBM Model 1, the EM algorithm is guaranteed to reach a global minimum.

4.2.3 EM for IBM Model 1

Let us now have a more detailed look at applying the EM algorithm to IBM Model 1. This process pretty much follows the outline in the previous section. We first initialize the model with uniform translation probability distributions, apply this model to the data, collect counts to estimate the improved model, and iterate.

When applying the model to the data, we need to compute the probabilities of different alignments given a sentence pair in the data. To put it more formally, we need to compute $p(a|\mathbf{e}, \mathbf{f})$, the probability of an alignment given the English and foreign sentences.

Applying the chain rule (recall Section 3.2.3 on page 69) gives us:

$$p(a|\mathbf{e}, \mathbf{f}) = \frac{p(\mathbf{e}, a|\mathbf{f})}{p(\mathbf{e}|\mathbf{f})} \tag{4.9}$$

We still need to derive $p(\mathbf{e}|\mathbf{f})$, the probability of translating the sentence **f** into **e** with any alignment:

$$p(\mathbf{e}|\mathbf{f}) = \sum_{a} p(\mathbf{e}, a|\mathbf{f})$$

$$= \sum_{a(1)=0}^{l_f} \ldots \sum_{a(l_e)=0}^{l_f} p(\mathbf{e}, a|\mathbf{f})$$

$$= \sum_{a(1)=0}^{l_f} \cdots \sum_{a(l_e)=0}^{l_f} \frac{\epsilon}{(l_f+1)^{l_e}} \prod_{j=1}^{l_e} t(e_j|f_{a(j)})$$

$$= \frac{\epsilon}{(l_f+1)^{l_e}} \sum_{a(1)=0}^{l_f} \cdots \sum_{a(l_e)=0}^{l_f} \prod_{j=1}^{l_e} t(e_j|f_{a(j)})$$

$$= \frac{\epsilon}{(l_f+1)^{l_e}} \prod_{j=1}^{l_e} \sum_{i=0}^{l_f} t(e_j|f_i) \tag{4.10}$$

Note the significance of the last step. Instead of performing a sum over an exponential number $l_f{}^{l_e}$ of products, we reduced the computational complexity to linear in l_f and l_e (since $l_f \sim l_e$, computing $p(\mathbf{e}|\mathbf{f})$ is roughly quadratic with respect to sentence length).

alignment probability   Let us now put Equations (4.9) and (4.10) together:

$$p(a|\mathbf{e},\mathbf{f}) = \frac{p(\mathbf{e},a|\mathbf{f})}{p(\mathbf{e}|\mathbf{f})}$$

$$= \frac{\frac{\epsilon}{(l_f+1)^{l_e}} \prod_{j=1}^{l_e} t(e_j|f_{a(j)})}{\frac{\epsilon}{(l_f+1)^{l_e}} \prod_{j=1}^{l_e} \sum_{i=0}^{l_f} t(e_j|f_i)}$$

$$= \prod_{j=1}^{l_e} \frac{t(e_j|f_{a(j)})}{\sum_{i=0}^{l_f} t(e_j|f_i)} \tag{4.11}$$

We have now laid the mathematical foundation for the E-step in the EM algorithm. Formula (4.11) defines how to apply the model to the data, to place probabilities on different ways to fill the gaps in the incomplete data.

In the M-step, we need to collect counts for word translations over all possible alignments, weighted by their probability. For this purpose, count function   let us define a **count function** c that collects evidence from a sentence pair $(\mathbf{e},\mathbf{f})$ that a particular input word f translates into the output word e:

$$c(e|f; \mathbf{e},\mathbf{f}) = \sum_a p(a|\mathbf{e},\mathbf{f}) \sum_{j=1}^{l_e} \delta(e,e_j)\delta(f,f_{a(j)}) \tag{4.12}$$

The Kronecker delta function $\delta(x,y)$ is 1 if $x = y$ and 0 otherwise. When we plug in the formula for $p(a|\mathbf{e},\mathbf{f})$ from Equation (4.11) and perform the same simplifications as in Equation (4.10), we arrive at

$$c(e|f; \mathbf{e},\mathbf{f}) = \frac{t(e|f)}{\sum_{i=0}^{l_f} t(e|f_i)} \sum_{j=1}^{l_e} \delta(e,e_j) \sum_{i=0}^{l_f} \delta(f,f_i) \tag{4.13}$$

```
Input: set of sentence pairs (e, f)    14:      // collect counts
Output: translation prob. t(e|f)       15:      for all words e in e do
 1: initialize t(e|f) uniformly        16:        for all words f in f do
 2: while not converged do             17:          count(e|f) += ──t(e|f)──
                                                                   s-total(e)
 3:   // initialize                    18:          total(f) += ──t(e|f)──
                                                                 s-total(e)
 4:   count(e|f) = 0 for all e,f       19:        end for
 5:   total(f) = 0 for all f           20:      end for
 6:   for all sentence pairs (e,f) do  21:   end for
 7:     // compute normalization       22:   // estimate probabilities
 8:     for all words e in e do        23:   for all foreign words f do
 9:       s-total(e) = 0               24:     for all English words e do
10:       for all words f in f do      25:       t(e|f) = ──count(e|f)──
                                                          total(f)
11:         s-total(e) += t(e|f)       26:     end for
12:     end for                        27:   end for
13:   end for                          28: end while
```

Figure 4.3 EM training algorithm for IBM Model 1.

Given these counts, we can estimate the new translation probability distribution by

$$t(e|f) = \frac{\sum_{(\mathbf{e},\mathbf{f})} c(e|f; \mathbf{e}, \mathbf{f})}{\sum_e \sum_{(\mathbf{e},\mathbf{f})} c(e|f; \mathbf{e}, \mathbf{f})} \tag{4.14}$$

Figure 4.3 shows a pseudo-code implementation of the EM algorithm applied to IBM Model 1. We first initialize the probability distribution $t(e|f)$ uniformly. Then we collect counts for evidence that a particular English output word e is aligned to a particular foreign input word f. For every co-occurrence in a sentence pair, we add the probability $t(e|f)$ to the count. Finally, by normalizing these counts, we can estimate a new probability distribution $t(e|f)$.

The time complexity of the algorithm is linear with the number of sentences and quadratic in sentence length. Note that, although we have an exponential number of possible alignments, we were able to reduce EM training to a quadratic problem.

Example

Let us take a look at how the algorithm works on a simple example. Figure 4.4 presents a few iterations on a tiny three-sentence corpus with four input words *(das,ein,buch,haus)* and four output words *(the,a,book,house)*. For this example, there is no NULL token.

Initially, the translation probability distribution t is set to be uniform. All translation probabilities $t(e|f)$ from the German words to the English words are $\frac{1}{4} = 0.25$.

Given this initial model, we collect counts in the first iteration of the EM algorithm. All alignments are equally likely. The pairs (*the, das*) and (*book, buch*) occur twice, while the other lexical translation pairs occur only once, except for pairs like (*book, haus*), which never co-occur. Normalizing these counts yields a new lexical translation probability distribution.

At each iteration, the probability estimates are refined. Ultimately, the model converges to the desired results, for instance $t(\text{book}|\text{buch}) = 1$.

4.2.4 Perplexity

convergence of EM

We have been somewhat vague about the formal properties and the **convergence behavior** of the EM algorithm. Let us step back and consider what we are trying to accomplish.

We are given some data with missing information (the alignments). Conversely, we also have a model with unknown parameters (the lexical translation probabilities). The goal of the EM algorithm is to find a model that best fits the data.

How can we measure whether we have accomplished this goal? Our model is a model for translation, and its quality will ultimately be measured by how well it translates new, previously unseen sentences. At this point, however, we have the training data and we can measure how well our model translates this data.

We have a model for $p(\mathbf{e}|\mathbf{f})$. Given the input side of the training data, how likely is the output side of the training data according to our model? Let us look at the starting point of our example in Figure 4.4. The second input sentence is *das buch*. How likely is the translation *the*

e	f	Initial	1st it.	2nd it.	3rd it.	...	Final
the	*das*	0.25	0.5	0.6364	0.7479	...	1
book	*das*	0.25	0.25	0.1818	0.1208	...	0
house	*das*	0.25	0.25	0.1818	0.1313	...	0
the	*buch*	0.25	0.25	0.1818	0.1208	...	0
book	*buch*	0.25	0.5	0.6364	0.7479	...	1
a	*buch*	0.25	0.25	0.1818	0.1313	...	0
book	*ein*	0.25	0.5	0.4286	0.3466	...	0
a	*ein*	0.25	0.5	0.5714	0.6534	...	1
the	*haus*	0.25	0.5	0.4286	0.3466	...	0
house	*haus*	0.25	0.5	0.5714	0.6534	...	1

Figure 4.4 Application of IBM Model 1 EM training: Given the three sentence pairs { (*das haus, the house*), (*das buch, the book*), (*ein buch, a book*) } the algorithm quickly converges to values for $t(e|f)$.

book? We can plug the numbers from the initial uniform distribution into Equation (4.10):[3]

$$p(\mathbf{e}|\mathbf{f}) = \frac{\epsilon}{l_f^{l_e}} \sum_{j=1}^{l_e} \sum_{i=1}^{l_f} t(e_j|f_i) \tag{4.15}$$

In the uniform probability distribution all $t(e|f) = 0.25$, so we have

$$p(\text{the book}|\text{das buch}) = \frac{\epsilon}{2^2}(0.25 + 0.25)\,(0.25 + 0.25) = 0.0625\epsilon \tag{4.16}$$

After the first iteration, the probabilities $t(e|f)$ are updated to

$$t(e|f) = \begin{cases} 0.5 & \text{if } e = \text{the and } f = \text{das} \\ 0.25 & \text{if } e = \text{the and } f = \text{buch} \\ 0.25 & \text{if } e = \text{book and } f = \text{das} \\ 0.5 & \text{if } e = \text{book and } f = \text{buch} \end{cases} \tag{4.17}$$

and hence

$$p(\text{the book}|\text{das buch}) = \frac{\epsilon}{2^2}(0.5 + 0.25)\,(0.25 + 0.5) = 0.140625\epsilon \tag{4.18}$$

This ultimately converges to

$$t(e|f) = \begin{cases} 1 & \text{if } e = \text{the and } f = \text{das} \\ 0 & \text{if } e = \text{the and } f = \text{buch} \\ 0 & \text{if } e = \text{book and } f = \text{das} \\ 1 & \text{if } e = \text{book and } f = \text{buch} \end{cases} \tag{4.19}$$

and hence

$$p(\text{the book}|\text{das buch}) = \frac{\epsilon}{2^2}(1 + 0)\,(0 + 1) = 0.25 \tag{4.20}$$

The translation probabilities for the other sentences can be computed the same way. Figure 4.5 gives the translation probabilities for the sentences in the training data. We see a steady improvement of the likelihood of the output side of our parallel corpus, given the input side and our model.

We can measure this progress by the **perplexity** of the model. In statistical machine translation, perplexity PP is defined as

$$\log_2 PP = -\sum_s \log_2 p(\mathbf{e}_s|\mathbf{f}_s) \tag{4.21}$$

Theoretically, the perplexity is guaranteed to decrease or stay the same at each iteration. This also guarantees that EM training converges to

perplexity

---

[3] The formula is slightly adapted, since we ignored the NULL token in our example.

	Initial	1st it.	2nd it.	3rd it.	...	Final
p (the haus|das haus)	0.0625	0.1875	0.1905	0.1913	...	0.1875
p (the book|das buch)	0.0625	0.1406	0.1790	0.2075	...	0.25
p (a book|ein buch)	0.0625	0.1875	0.1907	0.1913	...	0.1875
perplexity (ϵ=1)	4095	202.3	153.6	131.6	...	113.8

Figure 4.5 Progress of $p(e_s|f_s)$ and perplexity during EM training using IBM Model 1 on the example corpus in Figure 4.4 (assuming $\epsilon = 1$).

a local minimum. In the case of IBM Model 1, the EM training will eventually reach a global minimum.

Figure 4.5 gives numbers for sentence translation probability and perplexity during EM training on the example corpus. The perplexity steadily decreases from 4096 initially to 113.8 in the limit.

4.3 Ensuring Fluent Output

We have introduced a word-based translation model, IBM Model 1.

context   When translating a word, this model ignores the **context** surrounding the word. In fact, practically all the word-based models we present in this chapter do this. But often context matters.

Recall our lexical translation tables from Figure 4.2 on page 84. The T-table for *klein* gave equal probability mass to *small* and *little*. Both are valid translations. However, depending on the context, one translation

fluent output   is more appropriate, more **fluent**, than the other.

4.3.1 Empirical Evidence for Fluent Output

In the context of, say, step, *small step* is a better translation than *little step*. How do we know this? Or, more importantly, how could a computer system know this? We could let it look up the frequency of the

Google count   two phrases using Google:[4]

- *small step*: 2,070,000 occurrences in the Google index;
- *little step*: 257,000 occurrences in the Google index.

What we have here is a measure of what makes good English. A mathematical model of this measure is called a language model, or formally $p(\mathbf{e})$, the probability of an English string $\mathbf{e}$.

---

[4] You can get the frequency of a phrase from the web site http://www.google.com/ by typing in the phrase in quotes, e.g. `"little step"`. The cited numbers were retrieved in 2005.

4.3.2 Language Model

Relying on Google counts is a neat trick, but even the vastness of the world wide web has it limits. If we enter longer and longer sentences, it is increasingly likely that their Google count will be 0.

Hence, we need to engage again in generative modeling, i.e., breaking up the computation of the probability of long sentences into smaller steps, for which we can collect sufficient statistics. The most common method for language modeling is the use of **n-gram language models**.

Let us step through the mathematics of **trigram language models** (i.e., using n-gram language models with n = 3):

$$p(\mathbf{e}) = p(e_1, e_2, ..., e_n)$$
$$= p(e_1)p(e_2|e_1) \cdots p(e_n|e_1, e_2, ..., e_{n-1})$$
$$\simeq p(e_1)p(e_2|e_1) \cdots p(e_n|e_{n-2}, e_{n-1}) \qquad (4.22)$$

We decompose the whole-sentence probability into single-word probabilities, using the chain rule. Then, we make the independence assumption that only the previous two words matter for predicting a word.

To estimate the probabilities for a trigram language model, we need to collect statistics for three-word sequences from large amounts of text. In statistical machine translation, we use the English side of the parallel corpus, but may also include additional text resources.

Chapter 7 has more detail on how language models are built.

4.3.3 Noisy-Channel Model

How can we combine a language model and our translation model? Recall that we want to find the best translation **e** for an input sentence **f**. We now apply the Bayes rule to include $p(e)$:

$$\text{argmax}_{\mathbf{e}} p(\mathbf{e}|\mathbf{f}) = \text{argmax}_{\mathbf{e}} \frac{p(\mathbf{f}|\mathbf{e})p(\mathbf{e})}{p(\mathbf{f})}$$
$$= \text{argmax}_{\mathbf{e}} p(\mathbf{f}|\mathbf{e})p(\mathbf{e}) \qquad (4.23)$$

Note that, mathematically, the translation direction has changed from $p(e|f)$ to $p(f|e)$. This can create a lot of confusion, since the concept of what constitutes the source language differs between the mathematics of the model and the actual application. We try to avoid confusion as much as possible by sticking to the notation $p(e|f)$ when formulating a translation model.

Combining a language model and translation model in this way is called the **noisy-channel model**. This method is widely used in speech recognition, but can be traced back to early **information theory**.

n-gram language models

noisy-channel model

information theory

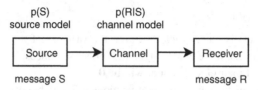

Figure 4.6 Noisy-channel model: A message is passed through a noisy channel to the receiver. The message may be corrupted by noise in the process. The message is reconstructed using a source model for source messages $p(S)$ and a channel model for corruption in the channel $p(R|S)$.

Shannon [1948] developed the noisy-channel model for his work on error correcting codes. In this scenario, a message is passed through a noisy channel, such as a low-quality telephone line, from a source S to a receiver R. See Figure 4.6 for an illustration.

The receiver only gets a corrupted message R. The challenge is now to reconstruct the original message using knowledge about possible source messages and knowledge about the distortions caused by the noise of the channel.

Also consider the example of fixing errors in optical character recognition (OCR). Scanning text from printed books and converting the scanned image into computer readable text is an error-prone process. But we know a lot about what the original input (source) text may have looked like, and we also know a lot about possible distortions in this channel: confusions between l, I, and 1 are more likely than confusions between A and b.

We can also apply the noisy-channel model to the translation problem. Somewhat presumptuously, we assume that the foreign speaker actually wanted to utter an English sentence, but everything got distorted in a noisy channel and out came a foreign sentence.

4.4 Higher IBM Models

We have presented, with IBM Model 1, a model for machine translation. However, on closer inspection, the model has many flaws. The model is very weak in terms of reordering, as well as adding and dropping words. In fact, according to IBM Model 1, the best translation for any input is the empty string (see Exercise 3 at the end of this chapter).

Five models of increasing complexity were proposed in the original work on statistical machine translation at IBM. The advances of the five

IBM models   **IBM models** are:

- IBM Model 1: lexical translation;
- IBM Model 2: adds absolute alignment model;
- IBM Model 3: adds fertility model;

- IBM Model 4: adds relative alignment model;
- IBM Model 5: fixes deficiency.

Alignment models introduce an explicit model for reordering words in a sentence. More often than not, words that follow each other in one language have translations that follow each other in the output language. However, IBM Model 1 treats all possible reorderings as equally likely.

Fertility is the notion that input words produce a specific number of output words in the output language. Most often, of course, one word in the input language translates into one single word in the output language. But some words produce multiple words or get dropped (producing zero words). A model for the fertility of words addresses this aspect of translation.

Adding additional components increases the complexity of training the models, but the general principles that we introduced for IBM Model 1 stay the same. We define the models mathematically and then devise an EM algorithm for training.

This incremental march towards more complex models does not serve didactic purposes only. All the IBM models are relevant, because EM training starts with the simplest Model 1 for a few iterations, and then proceeds through iterations of the more complex models all the way to IBM Model 5.

4.4.1 IBM Model 2

In **IBM Model 2**, we add an explicit model for alignment. In IBM Model 1, we do not have a probabilistic model for this aspect of translation. As a consequence, according to IBM Model 1 the translation probabilities for the following two alternative translations are the same:

IBM Model 2

IBM Model 2 addresses the issue of alignment with an explicit model for alignment based on the positions of the input and output words. The translation of a foreign input word in position i to an English word in position j is modeled by an **alignment probability distribution**

alignment probability distribution

$$a(i \mid j, l_e, l_f) \tag{4.24}$$

Recall that the length of the input sentence $\mathbf{f}$ is denoted as l_f, and the length of the output sentence $\mathbf{e}$ is l_e. We can view translation under IBM Model 2 as a two-step process with a lexical translation step and an alignment step:

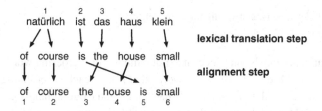

The first step is lexical translation as in IBM Model 1, again modeled by the translation probability $t(e|f)$. The second step is the alignment step. For instance, translating *ist* into *is* has a lexical translation probability of $t(is|ist)$ and an alignment probability of $a(2|5,6,5)$ – the 5th English word is aligned to the 2nd foreign word.

Note that the alignment function a maps each English output word j to a foreign input position $a(j)$ and the alignment probability distribution is also set up in this reverse direction.

The two steps are combined mathematically to form IBM Model 2:

$$p(\mathbf{e},a|\mathbf{f}) = \epsilon \prod_{j=1}^{l_e} t(e_j|f_{a(j)}) \, a(a(j)|j,l_e,l_f) \tag{4.25}$$

Fortunately, adding the alignment probability distribution does not make EM training much more complex. Recall that the number of possible word alignments for a sentence pair is exponential with the number of words. However, for IBM Model 1, we were able to reduce the complexity of computing $p(\mathbf{e}|\mathbf{f})$ to a polynomial problem. We can apply the same trick to IBM Model 2. Here is the derivation of $p(\mathbf{e}|\mathbf{f})$ for Model 2 (similar to Equation 4.10):

$$p(\mathbf{e}|\mathbf{f}) = \sum_a p(\mathbf{e},a|\mathbf{f})$$

$$= \epsilon \sum_{a(1)=0}^{l_f} \cdots \sum_{a(l_e)=0}^{l_f} \prod_{j=1}^{l_e} t(e_j|f_{a(j)}) \, a(a(j)|j,l_e,l_f)$$

$$= \epsilon \prod_{j=1}^{l_e} \sum_{i=0}^{l_f} t(e_j|f_i) \, a(i|j,l_e,l_f) \tag{4.26}$$

Using this equation, we can compute efficiently $p(a|\mathbf{e},\mathbf{f})$ which gives rise to the computation of fractional counts for lexical translation with the formula

$$c(e|f;\mathbf{e},\mathbf{f}) = \sum_{j=1}^{l_e} \sum_{i=0}^{l_f} \frac{t(e|f) \, a(i|j,l_e,l_f) \, \delta(e,e_j) \, \delta(f,f_i)}{\sum_{i'=0}^{l_f} t(e|f_{i'}) \, a(i'|j,l_e,l_f)} \tag{4.27}$$

Figure 4.7 EM training
algorithm for IBM Model 2.

```
Input: set of sentence pairs (e,f)
Output: probability distributions t (lexical translation)
        and a (alignment)
 1: carry over t(e|f) from Model 1
 2: initialize a(i|j,l_e,l_f) = 1/(l_f+1) for all i,j,l_e,l_f
 3: while not converged do
 4:     // initialize
 5:     count(e|f) = 0 for all e,f
 6:     total(f) = 0 for all f
 7:     count_a(i|j,l_e,l_f) = 0 for all i,j,l_e,l_f
 8:     total_a(j,l_e,l_f) = 0 for all j,l_e,l_f
 9:     for all sentence pairs (e,f) do
10:         l_e = length(e), l_f = length(f)
11:         // compute normalization
12:         for j = 1 .. l_e do // all word positions in e
13:             s-total(e_j) = 0
14:             for i = 0 .. l_f do // all word positions in f
15:                 s-total(e_j) += t(e_j|f_i) * a(i|j,l_e,l_f)
16:             end for
17:         end for
18:         // collect counts
19:         for j = 1 .. l_e do // all word positions in e
20:             for i = 0 .. l_f do // all word positions in f
21:                 c = t(e_j|f_i) * a(i|j,l_e,l_f) / s-total(e_j)
22:                 count(e_j|f_i) += c
23:                 total(f_i) += c
24:                 count_a(i|j,l_e,l_f) += c
25:                 total_a(j,l_e,l_f) += c
26:             end for
27:         end for
28:     end for
29:     // estimate probabilities
30:     t(e|f) = 0 for all e,f
31:     a(i|j,l_e,l_f) = 0 for all i,j,l_e,l_f
32:     for all e,f do
33:         t(e|f) = count(e|f) / total(f)
34:     end for
35:     for all i,j,l_e,l_f do
36:         a(i|j,l_e,l_f) = count_a(i|j,l_e,l_f) / total_a(j,l_e,l_f)
37:     end for
38: end while
```

and the computation of counts for alignment with the formula

$$c(i|j,l_e,l_f;\mathbf{e},\mathbf{f}) = \frac{t(e_j|f_i)\,a(i|j,l_e,l_f)}{\sum_{i'=0}^{l_f} t(e_j|f_{i'})\,a(i'|j,l_e,l_f)} \qquad (4.28)$$

The algorithm for training Model 2 is very similar to that for IBM Model 1. For a pseudo-code specification see Figure 4.7.

Instead of initializing the probability distributions $t(e|f)$ and $a(i|j,l_e,l_f)$ uniformly, we initialize them with the estimations we get from a few iterations of Model 1 training.

The lexical translation probability distribution estimates can be taken verbatim from the Model 1 training. Since Model 1 is a special case of Model 2 with $a(i|j, l_e, l_f)$ fixed to $\frac{1}{l_f+1}$, we initialize the distribution as such. Collecting counts and estimations for the distribution a is done in the same way as for the lexical translation probability t.

4.4.2 IBM Model 3

So far, we have not explicitly modeled how many words are generated from each input word. In most cases, a German word translates to one single English word. However, some German words like *zum* typically translate to two English words, i.e., *to the*. Others, such as the flavoring particle *ja*, get dropped.

fertility We now want to model the **fertility** of input words directly with a probability distribution

$$n(\phi|f) \tag{4.29}$$

For each foreign word f, this probability distribution indicates how many $\phi = 0, 1, 2, ...$ output words it usually translates to. Returning to the examples above, we expect for instance, that

$$n(1|\text{haus}) \simeq 1$$
$$n(2|\text{zum}) \simeq 1$$
$$n(0|\text{ja}) \simeq 1 \tag{4.30}$$

Fertility deals explicitly with dropping input words by allowing $\phi = 0$. But there is also the issue of adding words. Recall that we introduced the NULL token to account for words in the output that have no correspondent in the input. For instance, the English word *do* is often inserted when translating verbal negations into English. In the IBM models these added words are generated by the special NULL token.

We could model the fertility of the NULL token in the same way as for all the other words by the conditional distribution $n(\phi|\text{NULL})$. However, the number of inserted words clearly depends on the sen-
NULL insertion tence length, so we choose to model **NULL insertion** as a special step. After the fertility step, we introduce one NULL token with probability p_1 after each generated word, or no NULL token with probability $p_0 = 1 - p_1$.

The addition of fertility and NULL token insertion increases the
IBM Model 3 translation process in **IBM Model 3** to four steps:

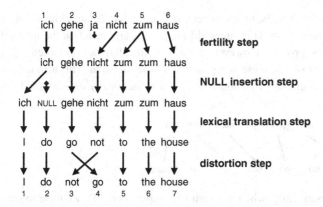

To review, each of these four steps is modeled probabilistically:

- Fertility is modeled by the distribution $n(\phi|f)$. For instance, duplication of the German word *zum* has the probability $n(2|zum)$.
- NULL insertion is modeled by the probabilities p_1 and $p_0 = 1 - p_1$. For instance, the probability p_1 is factored in for the insertion of NULL after *ich*, and the probability p_0 is factored in for no such insertion after *nicht*.
- Lexical translation is handled by the probability distribution $t(e|f)$ as in IBM Model 1. For instance, translating *nicht* into *not* is done with probability $p(\text{not}|\text{nicht})$.
- Distortion is modeled almost the same way as in IBM Model 2 with a probability distribution $d(j|i, l_e, l_f)$, which predicts the English output word position j based on the foreign input word position i and the respective sentence lengths. For instance, the placement of *go* as the 4th word of the seven-word English sentence as a translation of *gehe*, which was the 2nd word in the six-word German sentence, has probability $d(4|2, 7, 6)$.

Note that we called the last step **distortion** instead of alignment. We make this distinction since we can produce the same translation with the same alignment in a different way:

distortion

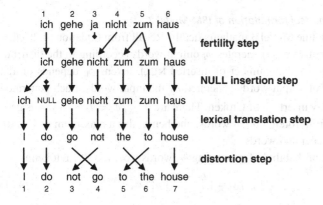

In contrast to the previous version, here *to* and *the* are switched after lexical translation. This subtle difference has an impact on the internal translation process. However, if we draw the alignment between input and output words, these two productions are identical. This also means that the alignment function $a : j \rightarrow i$ is identically defined for both versions.

Consequently, when we want to compute $p(\mathbf{e}, a|\mathbf{f})$, we have to sum up the probabilities of each possible production (also called **tableau**). Since this only occurs when a foreign word produces multiple output words, it is not very complicated: all the productions have the same probability. This is spelled out in more detail below in the mathematical formulation of IBM Model 3.

Let us take some time to emphasize the differences between the alignment function $a : j \rightarrow i$, the IBM Model 2 alignment probability distribution a, and the IBM Model 3 distortion probability distribution d:

alignment function
- The **alignment function** a defines, for a specific alignment, at which position i the foreign word is located that generated the English word at position j. The probability distributions indicate how likely such an alignment is, based on word positions and sentence lengths.

alignment probability distribution
- The IBM Model 2 **alignment probability distribution** $a(i|j, l_e, l_f)$ is formulated in the same direction as the alignment function: it predicts foreign input word positions conditioned on English output word positions.

distortion probability distribution
- The IBM Model 3 **distortion probability distribution** $d(j|i, l_e, l_f)$ is set up in the translation direction, predicting output word positions based on input word positions.

Mathematical formulation of IBM Model 3

Let us define Model 3 mathematically. Recall from Equation (4.29) that each input word f_i generates ϕ_i output words according to the distribution $n(\phi_i|f_i)$. The number of inserted NULL tokens ϕ_0 depends on the number of output words generated by the input words. Each generated word may insert a NULL token. There are $\sum_{i=1}^{l_f} \phi_i = l_e - \phi_0$ words generated from foreign input words, and hence also a maximum of $l_e - \phi_0$ NULL generated words.

The probability of generating ϕ_0 words from the NULL token is

$$p(\phi_0) = \binom{l_e - \phi_0}{\phi_0} p_1^{\phi_0} p_0^{l_e - 2\phi_0} \tag{4.31}$$

Again, p_0 is the probability that no NULL token is inserted after a conventionally generated word, p_1 is the probability that one NULL is generated. The combinatorial term $\binom{l_e - \phi_0}{\phi_0}$ arises from the situation that a fixed number of NULL tokens may be inserted after different sets of conventionally generated words: there are ϕ_0 out of $l_e - \phi_0$ positions to choose from.

We can combine fertility and NULL token insertion by

$$\binom{l_e - \phi_0}{\phi_0} p_1^{\phi_0} p_0^{l_e - 2\phi_0} \prod_{i=1}^{l_f} \phi_i! \; n(\phi_i | f_i) \tag{4.32}$$

For each foreign input word we factor in the fertility probability $n(\phi_i | f_i)$. The factorial $\phi_i!$ stems from the multiple tableaux for one alignment, if $\phi_i > 1$ (recall our discussion of the difference between distortion and alignment).

To finish up, let us combine the three elements of Model 3 – fertility, lexical translation, and distortion – in one formula:

$$p(\mathbf{e}|\mathbf{f}) = \sum_a p(\mathbf{e}, a | \mathbf{f})$$

$$= \sum_{a(1)=0}^{l_f} \cdots \sum_{a(l_e)=0}^{l_f} \binom{l_e - \phi_0}{\phi_0} p_1^{\phi_0} p_0^{l_e - 2\phi_0} \prod_{i=1}^{l_f} \phi_i! \; n(\phi_i | f_i)$$

$$\times \prod_{j=1}^{l_e} t(e_j | f_{a(j)}) \, d(j | a(j), l_e, l_f) \tag{4.33}$$

As in Models 1 and 2, we have an exponential number of possible alignments. For those models, we were able to simplify the formula and reduce the complexity to polynomial, allowing for efficient exhaustive count collection over all possible alignments. Unfortunately, this is no longer the case for Model 3.

4.4.3 Training for Model 3: Sampling the Alignment Space

The exponential cost of exhaustive count collection is just too high for even relatively short sentences. To still be able to train Model 3, we have to resort to sampling from the space of possible alignments, instead of exhaustively considering all alignments. If we consider a subset of all alignments that make up most of the probability mass, we should still be able to collect representative counts and estimate valid probability distributions.

To ensure that our sample of alignments contains most of the probability mass, we first find the most probable alignment, and also add small variations of it to the sample set.

This creates two tasks for the training procedure: (1) finding the most probable alignment and (2) collecting additional variations that we consider for sampling.

Finding the most probable alignment for Model 2 can be done efficiently in polynomial time. However, finding the most probable alignment for Model 3 is computationally much harder. So, we resort to a heuristic: **hill climbing**.

hill climbing

Imagine the space of possible alignments between two sentences as a landscape, where the height of every location (i.e., alignment) is given by its probability. We would like to climb to the highest point in this landscape. Unfortunately, we do not have a bird's eye view of the landscape that would allow us instantly to spot the highest point. In fact, deep fog prevents us from seeing very far at all. However, if we are at a certain spot, we can look at the immediate vicinity and gauge the steepest route up. We climb until we reach a peak.

A peak may be only a local maximum, so there are no guarantees that we find the highest point. The more rugged the terrain, the more likely we are to get stuck on a small knoll. Intuitively, it helps to drop in at various locations and start climbing.

Since we can compute the best alignment according to Model 2 efficiently, this is as good a starting point as any for the Model 3 hill climbing. From this alignment, we consider neighboring alignments and move to the one with the highest probability.

neighboring alignments

We define **neighboring alignments** formally as alignments that differ by a move or a swap:

move
- Two alignments a_1 and a_2 differ by a **move** if the alignments differ only in the alignment for one word j:

$$\exists j : a_1(j) \neq a_2(j), \forall j' \neq j : a_1(j') = a_2(j') \tag{4.34}$$

(The notation $\exists j$ means "there exists a j".)

swap
- Two alignments a_1 and a_2 differ by a **swap** if they agree in the alignments for all words, except for two, for which the alignment points are switched:

$$\exists j_1, j_2 : j_1 \neq j_2,$$
$$a_1(j_1) = a_2(j_2), a_1(j_2) = a_2(j_1), a_2(j_2) \neq a_2(j_1), \tag{4.35}$$
$$\forall j' \neq j_1, j_2 : a_1(j') = a_2(j')$$

We build a set of good alignments for count collection by including not only the best alignment we find with the hill-climbing method, but also all of its neighbors. This gives a set of alignments that we hope will include the most probable alignments, and hence most of the probability mass. Sampling implies that we now pretend that this is an adequate representation of the space of possible alignments and normalize each alignment probability, so that they all add up to one.

Recall our concern that the hill-climbing method would get stuck at a local maximum. We suggested that it would be good to start the search at various points. This is the idea behind **pegging**. For all i, j, we peg the   pegging
alignment $a(j) = i$ (i.e., we keep that alignment point fixed) and find the best alignment by hill climbing (without changing the alignment for j). This gives us an additional alignment for sampling, so we add it and its neighbors to the sample set.

Implementation of training

Figure 4.8 contains a pseudo-code implementation of Model 3 training. The main training loop consists of three steps: sampling of the alignment space, collecting the counts, and estimating the probability distributions.

For the sampling of the alignment space, we do pegging and hill climbing. Recall that pegging means that one word alignment is fixed. The starting point is the best alignment according to Model 2. Hill climbing to the best alignment is done in the function hillclimb(a, j). The function neighboring(a) generates a set of neighboring alignments.

Note that we did not specify the implementation of the computation of the probability of an alignment, denoted by the function probability(a). It follows straightforwardly from Equation (4.33). We do not need to explicitly normalize $p(\mathbf{e}, a|\mathbf{f})$ to $p(a|\mathbf{e}, \mathbf{f})$, since we normalize over the samples using the variable c_{total}.

In the initial iteration, we do not have estimates for all the probability distributions and we use alignment probabilities according to Model 2 instead.

It is possible to have a more efficient implementation of Model 3 training. For instance, the computation of probabilities for neighboring alignments is very similar, and updates can be calculated faster by computing the impact of change, instead of recomputing everything.

For instance, if we move the alignment of an output word e_j from the input word f_i to the input word $f_{i'}$, we can compactly compute the change in the alignment probability by

$$p(a'|\mathbf{e}, \mathbf{f}) = p(a|\mathbf{e}, \mathbf{f}) \frac{\phi_{i'} + 1}{\phi_i} \frac{n(\phi_{i'} + 1|f_{i'})}{n(\phi_{i'}|f_{i'})} \frac{n(\phi_i - 1|f_i)}{n(\phi_i|f_i)} \frac{t(e_j|f_{i'})}{t(e_j|f_i)} \frac{d(j|i', l_e, l_f)}{d(j|i, l_e, l_f)}$$

$$(4.36)$$

Similar update formulae can be derived for swaps or for changes with NULL generated words.

4.4.4 IBM Model 4

Model 3 is already a powerful model for statistical machine translation that accounts for the major transformations in a word-based

```
Input: set of sentence pairs (e,f)
Output: t (lexical) and d (distortion), n (fertility), and p₀ (null insertion).
 1: carry over t(e|f) from Model 2
 2: carry over d(i|j,lₑ,lf) from Model 2
 3: while not converged do
 4:   set all count* and total* to 0
 5:   for all sentence pairs (e,f) do
 6:     A = sample( e, f )
 7:     // collect counts
 8:     c_total = 0
 9:     for all a ∈ A do c_total += probability( a, e, f );
10:     for all a ∈ A do
11:       c = probability( a, e, f ) / c_total
12:       for j = 0 .. length(f) do
13:         count_t(e_j|f_a(j)) += c; total_t(f_a(j)) += c // lexical translation
14:         count_d(j|a(j),lₑ,lf) += c; total_d(a(j),lₑ,lf) += c // distortion
15:         if a(j) == 0 then null++; // null insertion
16:       end for
17:       count_p1 += null * c; count_p0 += (length(e) - 2 * null) * c
18:       for i = 1 .. length(e) do // fertility
19:         fertility = 0
20:         for j = 0 .. length(f) do
21:           if i == a(j) do fertility++
22:         end for
23:         count_f(fertility|f_i) += c; total_f(f_i) += c
24:       end for
25:     end for
26:   end for
27:   // estimate probability distribution
28:   t(e|f) = 0 for all e,f
29:   d(j|i,lₑ,lf) = 0 for all i,j,lₑ,lf
30:   φ(n|f) = 0 for all f,n
31:   for all (e,f) in domain( count_t ) do t(e|f) = count_t(e|f) / total_t(f)
32:   for all (i,j,lₑ,lf) in domain( count_d ) do d(j|i,lₑ,lf) =
       count_d(j|i,lₑ,lf) / total_d(i,lₑ,lf)
33:   for all (φ,f) in domain( count_f ) do n(φ|f) = count_f(φ|f) / total_f(f)
34:   p₁ = count_p1 / (count_p1 + count_p0); p₀ = 1 - p₁
35: end while
function sample(e, f)
 1: for j = 0 .. length(f) do
 2:   for i = 1 .. length(e) do
 3:     a(j) = i // pegging one alignment point
 4:     for all j', j' ≠ j do // find best alignment according to Model 2
 5:       a(j') = argmax_i' t(e_j'|f_i') d(i'|j', length(e), length(f))
 6:     end for
 7:     a = hillclimb(a,j)
 8:     add neighboring(a,j) to set A
 9:   end for
10: end for
11: return A
```

Figure 4.8 EM training algorithm for IBM Model 3 *(continued on the next page).*

```
(continued from previous page)

function hillclimb(a,jpegged)
 1: repeat
 2:    aold = a
 3:    for all aneighbor in neighboring(a,jpegged) do
 4:       if probability(aneighbor) > probability(a) then a = aneighbor
 5:    end for
 6: until a == aold
 7: return a
function neighboring(a,jpegged)
 1: N = {} // set of neighboring alignments
 2: for j' = 0 .. length(f), j' ≠ jpegged do // moves
 3:    for i' = 1 .. length(e) do
 4:       a' = a; a'(j') = i'
 5:       add a' to set N
 6:    end for
 7: end for
 8: for j1 = 0 .. length(f), j1 != jpegged do // swaps
 9:    for for j2 = 0 .. length(f), j2 != jpegged, j2 != j1 do
10:       a' = a; swap a'(j1), a'(j2)
11:       add a' to set N
12:    end for
13: end for
14: return N
```

Figure 4.8 *(continued)*

translation process: translation of words (T-table), reordering (distortion), insertion of words (NULL insertion), dropping of words (words with fertility 0), and one-to-many translation (fertility).

IBM Model 4 further improves on Model 3. One problem with Model 3 is the formulation of the distortion probability distribution $d(j|i, l_e, l_f)$. For large input and output sentences (large values for l_e and l_f), we will have sparse and not very realistic estimates for movements. In the translation process, large phrases tend to move together. Words that are adjacent in the input tend to be next to each other in the output. For instance, whether the 22nd input word is translated into the 22nd output word depends to a large degree on what happened to the previous 21 words. It especially depends on the placement of the translation of the preceding input word.   *IBM Model 4*

For Model 4, we introduce a **relative distortion** model. In this model, the placement of the translation of an input word is typically based on the placement of the translation of the proceeding input word. The issue of relative distortion gets a bit convoluted, since we are   *relative distortion*

Figure 4.9 Distortion in IBM Model 4: Foreign words with nonzero fertility form cepts (here five cepts), which contain English words e_j. The center $\odot_i$ of a cept π_i is *ceiling(avg(j))*. Distortion of each English word is modeled by a probability distribution: (a) for NULL generated words such as *do*: uniform; (b) for first words in a cept such as *not*: based on the distance between the word and the center of the preceding word $(j - \odot_{i-1})$; (c) for subsequent words in a cept such as *the*: distance to the previous word in the cept. The probability distributions d_1 and $d_{>1}$ are learnt from the data. They are conditioned using lexical information; see text for details.

Alignment

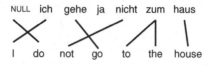

Foreign words and cepts

cept π_i	π_1	π_2	π_3	π_4	π_5
foreign position [i]	1	2	4	5	6
foreign word $f_{[i]}$	ich	gehe	nicht	zum	haus
English words {e_j}	I	go	not	to,the	house
English positions {j}	1	4	3	5,6	7
center of cept $\odot_i$	1	4	3	6	7

English words e_j and distortion

j	1	2	3	4	5	6	7
e_j	I	do	not	go	to	the	house
in cept $\pi_{i,k}$	$\pi_{1,0}$	$\pi_{0,0}$	$\pi_{3,0}$	$\pi_{2,0}$	$\pi_{4,0}$	$\pi_{4,1}$	$\pi_{5,0}$
$\odot_{i-1}$	0	–	4	1	3	–	6
$j - \odot_{i-1}$	+1	–	−1	+3	+2	–	+1
distortion	$d_1(+1)$	1	$d_1(-1)$	$d_1(+3)$	$d_1(+2)$	$d_{>1}(+1)$	$d_1(+1)$

dealing with placement in the input and the output, aggravated by the fact that words may be added or dropped, or translated one-to-many.

cept

For clarification, let us first introduce some terminology. See Figure 4.9 for an example to illustrate this. Each input word f_i that is aligned to at least one output word forms a **cept**. Figure 4.9 tabulates the five cepts π_i for the six German input words – the flavoring particle *ja* is untranslated and thus does not form a cept.

We define the operator [i] to map the cept with index i back to its corresponding foreign input word position. For instance, in our example, the last cept π_5 maps to input word position 6, i.e., [5] = 6. Most cepts contain one English word, except for cept π_4 that belongs to the fertility-2 word *zum*, which generates the two English words *to* and *the*.

center of a cept

The **center of a cept** is defined as the ceiling of the average of the output word positions for that cept. For instance, the fourth cept π_4 (belonging to *zum*) is aligned to output words in positions 5 and 6. The average of 5 and 6 is 5.5, and the ceiling of 5.5 is 6. We use the symbol $\odot_i$ to denote the center of cept i, e.g., $\odot_4 = 6$.

How does this scheme using cepts determine distortion for English words? For each output word, we now define its **relative distortion**. We distinguish between three cases: (a) words that are generated by the NULL token, (b) the first word in a cept, and (c) subsequent words in a cept:

relative distortion

(a) Words generated by the NULL token are uniformly distributed.
(b) For the likelihood of placements of the first word of a cept, we use the probability distribution

$$d_1(j - \odot_{i-1}) \tag{4.37}$$

Placement is defined as English word position j relative to the center of the preceding cept $\odot_{i-1}$. Refer again to Figure 4.9 for an example. The word *not*, English word position 3, is generated by cept π_3. The center of the preceding cept π_2 is $\odot_2 = 4$. Thus we have a relative distortion of -1, reflecting the backward movement of this word. In the case of translation in sequence, distortion is always $+1$: *house* and *I* are examples of this.
(c) For the placement of subsequent words in a cept, we consider the placement of the previous word in the cept, using the probability distribution

$$d_{>1}(j - \pi_{i,k-1}) \tag{4.38}$$

$\pi_{i,k}$ refers to the word position of the kth word in the ith cept. We have one example of this in Figure 4.9. The English word *the* is the second word in the 4th cept (German word *zum*); the preceding English word in the cept is *to*. The position of *to* is $\pi_{4,0} = 5$, and the position of *the* is $j = 6$, thus we factor in $d_{>1}(+1)$

Word classes

We may want to introduce richer conditioning on distortion. For instance, some words tend to get reordered during translation, while others remain in order. A typical example of this is adjective–noun inversion when translating French to English. Adjectives get moved back, when preceded by a noun. For instance, *affaires extérieur* becomes *external affairs*.

We may be tempted to condition the distortion probability distribution in Equations (4.37)–(4.38) on the words e_j and $f_{[i-1]}$:

$$\begin{aligned} \text{for initial word in cept:} \quad & d_1(j - \odot_{i-1}|f_{[i-1]}, e_j) \\ \text{for additional words:} \quad & d_{>1}(j - \pi_{i,k-1}|e_j) \end{aligned} \tag{4.39}$$

However, we will find ourselves in a situation where for most e_j and $f_{[i-1]}$, we will not be able to collect sufficient statistics to estimate realistic probability distributions.

word classes
To enjoy some of the benefits of both a lexicalized model and sufficient statistics, Model 4 introduces **word classes**. When we group the vocabulary of a language into, say, 50 classes, we can condition the probability distributions on these classes. The result is an almost lexicalized model, but with sufficient statistics.

To put this more formally, we introduce two functions $\mathcal{A}(f)$ and $\mathcal{B}(e)$ that map words to their word classes. This allows us to reformulate Equation (4.39) as

$$
\begin{aligned}
&\text{for initial word in cept:}\quad d_1(j - \odot_{i-1} | \mathcal{A}(f_{[i-1]}), \mathcal{B}(e_j)) \\
&\text{for additional words:}\quad d_{>1}(j - \pi_{i,k-1} | \mathcal{B}(e_j))
\end{aligned}
\tag{4.40}
$$

There are many ways to define the word class functions $\mathcal{A}$ and $\mathcal{B}$. One option is to use part-of-speech tags. Typically, this means that we have to annotate the parallel corpus with automatic tools. An alternative way, the one followed by the original Model 4, is to automatically cluster words into a fixed number of word classes.

Training for Model 4

The problems that we discussed for Model 3 training also apply to Model 4 training. Again, an exhaustive evaluation of all possible alignments is computationally prohibitive for all but the shortest sentence pairs. So, we have to resort to the same hill-climbing strategy we used for Model 3.

Even some of the efficient update formulae used to compute probabilities for neighboring alignments for Model 3 are not applicable to Model 4. When the alignment of an output word is moved, this may affect the value for up to two centers of cepts and the distortion of several words.

For this reason, in the original Model 4 specification, a hill-climbing method based on Model 3 probability scores is used. We will not lay out Model 4 training in detail here; it pretty much follows Model 3 training, as specified in Figure 4.8.

4.4.5 IBM Model 5

IBM Model 5
deficiency
To motivate **IBM Model 5**, we have to discuss an issue that we have ignored so far: **deficiency**. There is a problem with Model 3 and Model 4. According to these models, it is possible that multiple output words may be placed in the same position. Of course, this is not possible in practice.

In other words, some impossible alignments have positive probability according to the models. The goal of generative modeling and the EM algorithm is to find a model that best fits the data. If the model allows for impossible outcomes, probability mass is wasted.

Model 5 fixes this problem and eliminates deficiency. It also resolves the problem of multiple tableaux for the same alignment (recall our discussion on page 102).

When translating words with Model 3 and Model 4, nothing prohibits the placement of an output word into a position that has already been filled. However, we would like to place words only into **vacant word positions**. Model 5 keeps track of the number of vacant positions and allows placement only into these positions.

vacant word positions

The distortion model is similar to IBM Model 4, except it is based on vacancies. If we denote with v_j the number of vacancies in the English output interval $[1;j]$, we can formulate the IBM Model 5 distortion probabilities as follows:

$$\text{for initial word in cept: } d_1(v_j|\mathcal{B}(e_j), v_{\odot_{i-1}}, v_{\max})$$
$$\text{for additional words: } d_{>1}(v_j - v_{\pi_{i,k-1}}|\mathcal{B}(e_j), v_{\max'}) \tag{4.41}$$

To motivate these probability distributions from the viewpoint of Model 4, we still have a relative reordering model, since we condition on the number of vacancies at the center of the previous cept $v_{\odot_{i-1}}$. But we are creating a closed world of possible outcomes by $v_{\max}$ – the maximum number of available vacancies.

When placing additional words ($d_{>1}$), the maximum number of available vacancies $v_{\max'}$ takes into account the constraint that additional words can only be placed after already placed words. We define $v_{\pi_{i,k-1}}$ as the number of vacancies at the position of the previously placed English word, and hence $v_j - v_{\pi_{i,k-1}}$ is the number of skipped vacant spots plus 1.

We view alignment according to Model 5 as a process that steps through one foreign input word at a time, places words into English output positions and keeps track of vacant English positions. At the start, the fertility of foreign input words has already been selected, which means that the number of English output positions is fixed.

Figure 4.10 illustrates the alignment process for the same example as used previously for Model 4. How do we keep track of vacancies in the English output positions? At any given time in the process, we compute for each position how many vacancies exist up to (and including) that position (see the middle part of the table).

The number of positions is set by the already decided fertilities of foreign words. In the example of Figure 4.10, the English output sentence has length 7. The NULL token and foreign words $f_{[1]}$ to $f_{[5]}$ generate English words and place them in vacant positions:

- First, the NULL token places the English word *do* in position 2. Distortion of NULL generated words is handled by a uniform distribution, as in Models 3 and 4.

Alignment

NULL ich gehe ja nicht zum haus

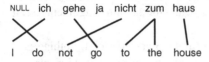

I do not go to the house

Vacancies v_j and placement of English words e_j

cept		vacancies							parameters for d_1			
$f_{[i]}$	$\pi_{i,k}$	v_1	v_2	v_3	v_4	v_5	v_6	v_7	j	v_j	v_{max}	$v_{\odot_{i-1}}$
		I	do	not	go	to	the	house				
NULL	$\pi_{0,1}$	1	**2**	3	4	5	6	7	2	–	–	–
ich	$\pi_{1,1}$	**1**	–	2	3	4	5	6	1	1	6	0
gehe	$\pi_{2,1}$	–	–	1	**2**	3	4	5	4	2	5	0
nicht	$\pi_{3,1}$	–	–	**1**	–	2	3	4	3	1	4	1
zum	$\pi_{4,1}$	–	–	–	–	**1**	2	–	5	1	2	0
	$\pi_{4,2}$	–	–	–	–	–	**1**	2	6	–	–	–
haus	$\pi_{5,1}$	–	–	–	–	–	–	**1**	7	1	1	0

Figure 4.10 Alignment in IBM Model 5: While using relative alignment similar to Model 4, Model 5 considers the number of vacancies to eliminate deficiency. The table illustrates the process of aligning English words to the foreign cepts: one row per English word e_j, ordered by the foreign cepts π_j. NULL generated words are aligned first, with uniform probability (here the English *do* is NULL generated). At each step, the number of vacancies up to a position is tracked. For instance, after taking out position 2 for the null generated *do*, the number of vacancies is decreased by 1 for positions 3–7 and position 2 is eliminated as a potential alignment output. On the right-hand side, the parameters for the distortion probability distribution $d_1(v_j|v_{\odot_{i-1}}, v_{max})$ are tracked: the number of vacancies up to the alignment position v_j, the number of vacancies at the previous cept's center $v_{\odot_{i-1}}$, and the available number of vacancies v_{max}. Note how this scheme addresses the issue of deficiency: since words may be placed only in available slots, no probability mass is wasted on impossible outcomes.

- Then, $f_{[1]}$, the German *ich*, places the English word *I* in position 1. There is one vacancy up to position 1 at this point. The number of vacant positions is 6.
- $f_{[2]}$ places the English word *go* in position 4, the second of five vacancies.
- Continuing, $f_{[3]}$ places the English word *not* in position 3, the first of four vacancies. Since the previous cept was translated out of order, the number of vacancies $v_{\odot_{i-1}}$ at the center of that previous cept is 1 (the center $\odot_{i-1}$ is position 4).
- $f_{[4]}$ generates two English words: *to* (e_5) and *the* (e_6). The English words have to be placed according to their English order, so e_5 has to be placed before e_6.

This also implies that the first word of this cept cannot be placed at position 7, the last vacant position. For both choices two positions are available.

- Finally, $f_{[5]}$ fills the last available position with the English word *house*.

How does this model eliminate deficiency? First of all, no words can be placed into positions that are already taken. Secondly, at any point in the process, the probabilities of all remaining options add up to 1. This is very intuitive, since the distortion probabilities are conditioned on the maximum number of vacancies v_{max}, and the number of vacancies v_j at possible positions is always between 1 and that maximum number, i.e. $1 \leq v_j \leq v_{max}$.

The same is true for the probability distribution $d_{>1}$ that is used for the placement of subsequent words in a cept: $1 \leq v_j - v_{\pi_{i,k-1}} \leq v_{max'}$.

Note that we no longer condition on the word class of foreign words, only on the English $\mathcal{B}(e_j)$. Conditioning on both the maximum number of vacancies v_{max} (to eliminate deficiency) and the number of vacancies at the previous cept's center (to create a relative reordering model) raises concerns about data sparsity that we do not want to aggravate with additional conditioning.

This concludes our discussion of the IBM models. We moved from simplistic but efficient IBM Model 1 to a very complex IBM Model 5, which addresses many issues in translation but is very hard to train. While the IBM models are no longer the state of the art in translation modeling, they are still the state of the art in word alignment, with a little trick which we will discuss in the next section.

4.5 Word Alignment

One important notion that the IBM models introduced is that of a **word alignment** between a sentence and its translation. In this section, we will develop this concept further, point out problems with word alignment, discuss how word alignment quality is measured and present a method for word alignment that is based on the IBM models, but fixes their most glaring problem: their limitation to one-to-many alignments.

4.5.1 The Task of Word Alignment

One way to visualize the task of word alignment is by a matrix as in Figure 4.11. Here, alignments between words (for instance between the German *haus* and the English *house*) are represented by points in the **alignment matrix**.

Word alignments do not have to be one-to-one. Words may have multiple or no alignment points. For instance, the English word *assumes*

Figure 4.11 Word alignment: Words in the English sentence (rows) are aligned to words in the German sentence (columns) as indicated by the filled points in the matrix.

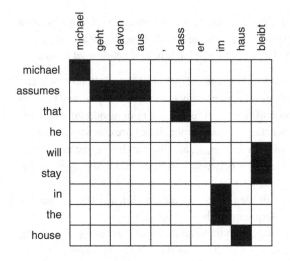

Figure 4.12 Problematic word alignment: (a) Is the English word *does* aligned with the German *wohnt* or *nicht* or neither? (b) How do the idioms *kicked the bucket* and *biss ins gras* match up? Outside this exceptional context, *bucket* is never a good translation for *gras*.

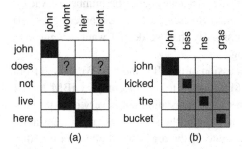

is aligned to the three German words *geht davon aus*; the German comma is not aligned to any English word.

However, it is not always easy to establish what the correct word alignment should be. One obvious problem is that some function words have no clear equivalent in the other language. See, for instance, the example in Figure 4.12a. How do you align the English word *does* in the sentence pair *john does not live here*, *john wohnt hier nicht*? Reasonable arguments can be made for three choices:

- Since it does not have a clear equivalent in German, we may decide that it should be unaligned.
- However, the word *does* is somewhat connected with *live*, since it contains the number and tense information for that verb. So it should be aligned to *wohnt*, the German translation of *live*.
- A third point of view is that *does* only appeared in the sentence because the sentence was negated. Without the negation, the English sentence would be *john lives here*. So *does* somehow goes together with *not* and hence should be aligned to *nicht*, the German translation of *not*.

Let us take a look at another problematic case: **idioms**. For instance, consider the sentence pair *jim kicked the bucket, jim biss ins gras* (see Figure 4.12b). The expression *kicked the bucket* is an idiomatic expression synonymous with *died*. In this example, its translation *biss ins gras* is also an idiomatic expression with the same meaning, which literally translates as *bit into the grass*.

idioms

One might argue that a proper word alignment for this sentence pair aligns the verbs *kicked* and *biss*, the nouns *bucket* and *gras*, and the function words *the* and *ins*. But outside this very unusual context *bucket* is never a good translation for *gras*, so this is a bit of a stretch.

What we have here is really a **phrasal alignment** that cannot be decomposed further, the same way the idiom *kicked the bucket* is a phrase whose meaning cannot be derived by decomposing it into its words.

phrasal alignment

4.5.2 Measuring Word Alignment Quality

In recent years, a number of competitions for word alignment methods have been organized. The quality of the methods is measured by the performance on a test set for which a gold standard has been established by human annotators. To create a good gold standard, annotators have to follow strict guidelines which solve the issues we have just raised in one way or another.

For instance, one approach to these problematic cases is to distinguish **sure alignment points** and **possible alignment points**. This may mean, for instance, in the alignment between the two idiomatic expressions that all alignment points between each of the words are labeled as possible alignment points.

sure alignment point
possible alignment point

A common metric for evaluation of word alignments is the **alignment error rate** (AER), which is defined as

alignment error rate

$$\text{AER}(S, P; A) = -\frac{|A \cap S| + |A \cap P|}{|A| + |S|} \qquad (4.42)$$

The quality of an alignment A is measured against a gold standard alignment that contains sure (S) and possible (P) alignment points. A perfect error of 0% can be achieved by an alignment that has all of the sure alignment points and some of the possible alignment points.

One way to deal with the questionable alignment points in the examples of Figure 4.12 is to label them as possible alignment points. This is not a completely satisfactory assessment of, for instance, phrasal alignment. Nevertheless, having gold standard word alignments and an error metric laid the foundation for improvements in alignment methods by

Figure 4.13 Symmetrization of IBM model alignments: Since these models are not capable of aligning multiple input words to an output word, both a German–English and an English–German alignment will be faulty. However, these alignments can be merged by taking the intersection (black) or union (gray) of the sets of alignment points.

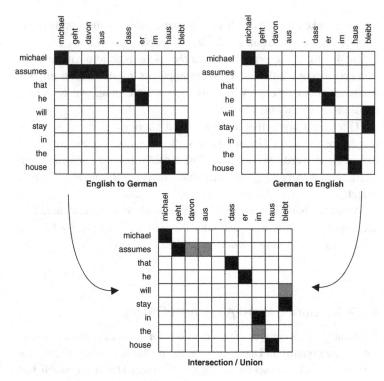

competitive evaluations of alignment quality. In the next section, we will discuss one such method.

4.5.3 Word Alignment Based on IBM Models

A by-product of the IBM models for word-based statistical machine translation is that they establish a word alignment for each sentence pair. While it is true that during the EM training fractional counts are collected over a probability distribution of possible alignments, one word alignment sticks out: the most probable alignment, also called the **Viterbi alignment**. To use the IBM models for word alignment, we let the model training run its course and output the Viterbi alignment of the last iteration.

However, there is one fundamental problem with the IBM models. Recall that an IBM model generates English words e_j from an aligned foreign word $f_{a(j)}$ with the probability $t(e_j|f_{a(j)})$. Each English word can be traced back to exactly one particular foreign word (or the NULL token). This means that each English word is aligned to (at most) one foreign word. It is not possible to end up with an alignment of one English word to multiple foreign words.

Viterbi alignment

However, this kind of alignment is common, as seen in one of our previous examples, repeated in Figure 4.13. The figure displays an optimistic outcome of IBM model training for the sentence pairs. When training to obtain a translation model from English to foreign, it is possible to generate the foreign word sequence *geht davon aus* from the English *assumes*, but when translating *will* and *stay*, only one of them can generate the German word *bleibt* and thus be aligned to it.

Conversely, in the translation direction from foreign to English, we can generate *will stay* from *bleibt*, but can no longer generate *assume* from all three words in the phrase *geht davon aus*.

The trick is now to run IBM model training in both directions. The two resulting word alignments can then be merged by, for instance, taking the intersection or the union of alignment points of each alignment. This process is called **symmetrization of word alignments**.

symmetrization of word alignments

In our example, the union of the alignments (taking all alignment points that occur in either of the two directional alignments) matches the desired outcome. In practice, this is less often the case, since when dealing with real data, faulty alignment points are established and the union will contain all faulty alignment points.

Generally, the intersection will contain reliably good alignment points (a high **precision** of the alignment points, to use a concept from information retrieval), but not all of them. The union will contain most of the desired alignment points (a high **recall** of the alignment points), but also additional faulty points.

precision

recall

So rather than taking the union or the intersection, we may want to explore the space between these two extremes. We may want to take all the alignment points in the intersection (which are reliable), and add some of the points from the union (which are the most reliable candidates for additional points). A couple of heuristics have been proposed for this. These heuristics typically exploit the observation that good alignment points neighbor other alignment points. Starting with the alignment points in the intersection, neighboring candidate alignment points from the union are progressively added.

Figure 4.14 presents pseudo-code for one such method. **Neighboring** is here defined to include the diagonal neighborhood of existing points. The algorithm starts with the intersection of the alignments. In the growing step, neighboring alignment points that are in the union but not in the intersection are added. In the final step, alignment points for words that are still unaligned are added.

neighboring alignment points

Such growing heuristics that symmetrize word alignments derived from IBM model training are currently the best known methods for word alignment. By tightly integrating symmetrization and IBM model

Figure 4.14 Pseudo-code for a symmetrization heuristic that settles on a set of alignment points between the intersection and the union of two IBM model alignments.

```
GROW-DIAG-FINAL(e2f,f2e):
  neighboring = ((-1,0),(0,-1),(1,0),(0,1),
                 (-1,-1),(-1,1),(1,-1),(1,1))
  alignment = intersect(e2f,f2e);
  GROW-DIAG(); FINAL(e2f); FINAL(f2e);

GROW-DIAG():
  iterate until no new points added
    for english word e = 0 ... en
      for foreign word f = 0 ... fn
        if ( e aligned with f )
          for each neighboring point ( e-new, f-new ):
            if ( ( e-new not aligned or f-new not aligned ) and
                 ( e-new, f-new ) in union( e2f, f2e ) )
              add alignment point ( e-new, f-new )
FINAL(a):
  for english word e-new = 0 ... en
    for foreign word f-new = 0 ... fn
      if ( ( e-new not aligned or f-new not aligned ) and
           ( e-new, f-new ) in union( e2f, f2e) )
        add alignment point ( e-new, f-new )
```

training (symmetrizing word alignments after every iteration of IBM model training), even better performance can be achieved.

4.6 Summary

4.6.1 Core Concepts

This chapter introduced many important concepts of statistical machine translation. We described in detail the first statistical machine translation models, the **IBM models**, which follow an approach to machine translation that is based on statistics collected over a parallel corpus of translated text. The models break up the translation process into a number of small steps, for which sufficient statistics can be collected, a method called **generative modeling**.

The IBM models are based on word translation, which is modeled by a **lexical translation** probability distribution. This distribution (among others) is trained from data by collecting counts for word translations using **maximum likelihood estimation**. One important element is missing in the data: information about **alignment** between input and output words, a **hidden variable** in the model. We are faced with a problem of **incomplete data**, which is addressed by the **EM algorithm** (expectation maximization). How well the model fits the data can be measured by its **perplexity**.

The IBM models use a modeling technique called the **noisy-channel model**, which allows them to break up the translation task into a translation model and a language model, which ensures fluent output.

IBM Model 1 uses only lexical translation probabilities, Model 2 adds an **absolute alignment model**, Model 3 adds a **fertility** model, Model 4 replaces the absolute alignment model with a **relative alignment model**, and Model 5 fixes a problem with **deficiency** in the model (assigning probability mass to impossible alignments).

One important concept introduced by the IBM models is the **word alignment** between a sentence and its translation. The task of word alignment is interesting in itself for a variety of uses. The quality of word alignment can be measured with the **alignment error rate** (AER). One method to improve word alignment is the **symmetrization** of IBM model alignments.

4.6.2 Further Reading

Word alignment based on co-occurence – Early work in word alignment focused on co-occurence statistics to find evidence for word associations [Kaji and Aizono, 1996]. These methods do not model a word alignment, and hence may find evidence for the alignment of a word to multiple translations, a problem called indirect association, which may be overcome by enforcing one-to-one alignments [Melamed, 1996a]. Kumano and Hirakawa [1994] augment this method with an existing bilingual dictionary. Sato and Nakanishi [1998] use a maximum entropy model for word associations. Ker and Chang [1996] group words together into sense classes from a thesaurus to improve word alignment accuracy. Co-occurence counts may also be used for phrase alignment, although this typically requires more efficient data for storing all phrases [Cromieres, 2006]. Chatterjee and Agrawal [2006] extend a recency vector approach [Fung and McKeown, 1994] with additional constraints. Lardilleux and Lepage [2008] iteratively match the longest common subsequences from sentence pairs and align the remainder.

IBM models – Our presentation of the IBM models follows the description by Brown *et al.* [1993], who originally presented the statistical machine translation approach in earlier papers [Brown *et al.*, 1988, 1990]. Wu and Xia [1994] apply IBM Model 1 to a Chinese–English corpus. For an introduction see also the introductions by Knight [1997, 1999b]. Note that our presentation downplays the noisy-channel model to give a simpler presentation. During a 1999 Johns Hopkins University workshop, the IBM models were implemented in a toolkit called GIZA [Al-Onaizan *et al.*, 1999], later refined into GIZA++ by Och and

Ney [2000]. GIZA++ is open source and widely used. Instead of hill climbing to the Viterbi alignment, algorithms such as estimation of distributions may be employed [Rodríguez *et al.*, 2006]. The stochastic modeling approach for translation is described by Ney [2001]. Several reports show how statistical machine translation allows rapid development with limited resources [Foster *et al.*, 2003; Oard and Och, 2003].

Symmetrization – Symmetrizing IBM model alignments was first proposed by Och and Ney [2003b] and may be improved by already symmetrizing during the IBM model training [Matusov *et al.*, 2004], or by explicitly modeling the agreement between the two alignments and optimizing it during EM training [Liang *et al.*, 2006b]. Different word alignments obtained with various IBM models and symmetrization methods may also be combined using a maximum entropy approach [Ayan and Dorr, 2006b; Ganchev *et al.*, 2008]. Crego and Habash [2008] use constraints over syntactic chunks to guide symmetrization.

Extensions to IBM models – A variation on the IBM models is the HMM model which uses relative distortion but not fertility [Vogel *et al.*, 1996]. This model was extended by treating jumps to other source words differently from repeated translations of the same source word [Toutanova *et al.*, 2002], and conditioning jumps on the source word [He, 2007]. IBM models have been extended using maximum entropy models [Foster, 2000b] to include position [Foster, 2000a], part-of-speech tag information [Kim *et al.*, 2000], even in the EM training algorithm [García-Varea *et al.*, 2002b,a]. Improvements have also been obtained by adding bilingual dictionaries [Wu and Wang, 2004b] and context vectors estimated from monolingual corpora [Wang and Zhou, 2004], lemmatizing words [Dejean *et al.*, 2003; Popovic and Ney, 2004; Pianta and Bentivogli, 2004], interpolating lemma and word aligment models [Zhang and Sumita, 2007], as well as smoothing [Moore, 2004]. Mixture models for word translation probabilities have been explored to automatically learn topic-dependent translation models [Zhao and Xing, 2006; Civera and Juan, 2006]. Packing words that typically occur in many-to-one alignments into a single token may improve alignment quality [Ma *et al.*, 2007].

Other iterative methods for word alignment, use of linguistic annotation – Word alignment methods have evolved into iterative algorithms, for instance the competitive linking algorithm by Melamed [1995, 1996c, 1997c, 2000] or bilingual bracketing [Wu, 1997]. Tufis [2002] extends a simple co-occurrence method to align words. These methods have been extended to exploit part-of-speech information [Chang and Chen, 1994; Tiedemann, 2003] in constraint methods [Tiedemann, 2004], translation divergences [Dorr *et al.*, 2002], compositionality constraints [Simard and Langlais, 2003], and syntactic constraints [Cherry and Lin, 2003; Lin and Cherry, 2003; Zhao and Vogel, 2003]. Fraser and Marcu [2005] improve word alignments by stemming words in the input and output languages, thus generalizing over morphological variants. Syntactic constraints may derive from formal criteria of obtaining parallel tree structures, such as the ITG constraint, or from syntactic relationships between words on either side [Cherry and Lin, 2006a]. Such constraints may be modeled as priors in the generative model [Deng and Gao, 2007].

Targeting word alignments to syntax-based models – Syntax-based machine translation models may have different requirements for word alignment. DeNero and Klein [2007] consider the effect of word alignment on rule extraction in a HMM alignment model. Rules from a syntax-based machine translation model may also be used to improve word alignments using an EM realignment method [May and Knight, 2007].

Discriminative approaches to word alignment – The machine learning community has discovered word alignment as an interesting structured prediction problem. Training translation models from sentences annotated with correct word alignments, results are typically much better than from the unsupervised approach [Callison-Burch *et al.*, 2004], but such data do not exist in large quantities. Discriminative word alignment methods typically generate statistics over a large unlabeled corpus which may have been aligned with some baseline method such as the IBM models, which form the basis for features that are optimized during machine learning over a much smaller labeled corpus. Discriminative approaches may use the perceptron algorithm [Moore, 2005; Moore *et al.*, 2006], maximum entropy models [Ittycheriah and Roukos, 2005], neural networks [Ayan *et al.*, 2005], max-margin methods [Taskar *et al.*, 2005], boosting [Wu and Wang, 2005; Wu *et al.*, 2006], support vector machines [Cherry and Lin, 2006b], conditional random fields [Blunsom and Cohn, 2006; Niehues and Vogel, 2008] or MIRA [Venkatapathy and Joshi, 2007]. Such methods allow the integration of features such as a more flexible fertility model and interactions between consecutive words [Lacoste-Julien *et al.*, 2006]. Smaller parallel corpora especially benefit from more attention to less frequent words [Zhang *et al.*, 2005a]. Discriminative models open a path to adding additional features such as ITG constraint [Chao and Li, 2007a]. Related to the discriminative approach, posterior methods use agreement in the n-best alignments to adjust alignment points [Kumar and Byrne, 2002].

Discriminative symmetrization – Starting from a word alignment resulting from the IBM models, additional features may be defined to assess each alignment point. Fraser and Marcu [2006] use additional features during symmetrization, either to be used in re-ranking or integrated into the search. Such features may form the basis for a classifier that adds one alignment point at a time [Ren *et al.*, 2007], possibly based on a skeleton of highly likely alignment points [Ma *et al.*, 2008], or deletes alignment points one at a time from the symmetrized union alignment [Fossum *et al.*, 2008]. Fraser and Marcu [2007a] present a generative model that allows many-to-many alignments which is trained from unlabeled data, but may be improved with small amounts of labeled data.

Combining word aligners – Tufis *et al.* [2006] combine different word aligners with heuristics. Schrader [2006] combines statistical methods with manual rules. Elming and Habash [2007] combine word aligners that operate under different morphological analysis of one of the languages – Arabic. Huang *et al.* [2005] discuss the issue of interpolating word alignment models trained on data from multiple domains. Word alignment in a specific domain may also be improved with a dictionary obtained from a general domain [Wu and Wang, 2004a]. Combining different word aligners may also improve performance [Ayan *et al.*, 2004]. The log-linear modeling approach may be used for the combination of word alignment models with simpler models, for instance based on part-of-speech tags [Liu *et al.*, 2005].

Evaluation of word alignment – To better understand the word alignment problem, parallel corpora have been annotated with word alignments for language pairs such as German–English, French–English, and Romanian–English. These have been the basis for competitions on word alignment [Mihalcea and Pedersen, 2003; Martin *et al.*, 2005]. The relationship between alignment quality and machine translation performance is under some discussion [Langlais *et al.*, 1998; Fraser and Marcu, 2007b]. Vilar *et al.* [2006] point to mismatches between alignment error rate and machine translation performance. New measures have been proposed to overcome the weakness of alignment error rate [Carl and Fissaha, 2003]. Giving less weight to alignment points that connect multiple aligned words improves correlation [Davis *et al.*, 2007]. Lopez and Resnik [2006] show the impact of word alignment quality on phrase-based models. Ayan and Dorr [2006a] compare alignment quality and machine translation performance and also stress the interaction with the phrase extraction method. Albeit computationally very expensive, word alignment quality may also be directly optimized on machine translation performance [Lambert *et al.*, 2007a].

Pivot languages – Pivot or bridge languages have been used to improve word alignments, such as in the case of Chinese–Japanese, where only large parallel corpora of these languages paired with English exist [Wang *et al.*, 2006a]. Bridge languages were also explored by Kumar *et al.* [2007].

Aligning longer units – Instead of tackling the full word alignment problem, more targeted work focuses on terminology extraction, for instance the extraction of domain-specific lexicons [Resnik and Melamed, 1997], noun phrases [Kupiec, 1993; van der Eijk, 1993; Fung, 1995b], collocations [Smadja *et al.*, 1996; Echizen-ya *et al.*, 2003; Orliac and Dillinger, 2003], non-compositional compounds [Melamed, 1997a], named entities [Moore, 2003], technical terms [Macken *et al.*, 2008], or other word sequences [Kitamura and Matsumoto, 1996; Ahrenberg *et al.*, 1998; Martinez *et al.*, 1999; Sun *et al.*, 2000; Moore, 2001; Yamamoto *et al.*, 2001; Baobao *et al.*, 2002; Wang and Zhou, 2002]. Translation for noun phrases may be learned by checking automatically translated candidate translations against frequency counts on the web [Robitaille *et al.*, 2006; Tonoike *et al.*, 2006].

Learning bilingual dictionaries from comparable corpora – It is also possible to extract terminologies from non-parallel comparable corpora. If only monolingual corpora are available, the first task is to find words that are translations of each other. Often, a seed lexicon is needed, which may be identically spelled words or cognates [Koehn and Knight, 2002b], although attempts have been made without such a seed but relying purely on co-occurrence statistics [Rapp, 1995] or generative models based on canonical correlation analysis [Haghighi *et al.*, 2008]. Several criteria may be used to find matching words, such as co-occurrence vectors based on mutual information [Fung, 1997; Kaji, 2004] or id/idf [Fung and Yee, 1998; Chiao and Zweigenbaum, 2002], co-occurrence vectors with considerations of ambiguous words [Tanaka and Iwasaki, 1996] or reduced using latent semantic analysis [Kim *et al.*, 2002] or Fisher kernels [Gaussier *et al.*, 2004], heterogeneity of the word context [Fung, 1995a], distributional similarity [Rapp, 1999], semantic relationship vectors [Diab and Finch, 2000], spelling similarity [Schulz *et al.*, 2004], automatically constructed thesauri [Babych *et al.*, 2007b], syntactic templates for the word context [Otero, 2007]. Other resources such as Wikipedia or WordNet may help with the construction of dictionaries [Ramírez *et al.*, 2008]. These methods may also be applied for collocations, not just single words [Lü and Zhou, 2004; Daille and Morin, 2008]. If monolingual corpora and bilingual dictionaries are available, the task is to find word senses or sets of mutually translated words across multiple languages. Kikui [1998] uses context vectors to disambiguate words, then adds an initial clustering step [Kikui, 1999]. Koehn and Knight [2000] use a language model to learn translation probabilities for ambiguous words using the EM algorithm. Sammer and Soderland [2007] use pointwise mutual information to match contexts in which words occur to separate out different senses of a word. Li and Li [2004] apply the Yarowski algorithm [Yarowsky, 1994] to bootstrap bilingual word translation models for ambiguous words. The use of bridge languages has been shown to be useful [Mann and Yarowsky, 2001; Schafer and Yarowsky, 2002]. Otero [2005] extends the use of the DICE coefficient with local context to better deal with polysemous words. Comparable corpora also allow the construction of translation models between a formal language and a dialect [Hwa *et al.*, 2006].

Lexical choice – Related to the problem of translating words is the problem of word sense disambiguation. When a word has several senses, these senses may have different translations. Early work [Brown *et al.*, 1991a] tried to integrate word sense disambiguation methods in statistical machine translation. These methods include local [García-Varea *et al.*, 2001] or broader context [Vickrey *et al.*, 2005] or dictionary information [Lee and Kim, 2002] in the lexical translation decision, although straightforward application of word sense disambiguation methods does not always lead to improvements [Carpuat and Wu, 2005].

Machine translation without word alignments – While word alignment is generally assumed to be an essential element of statistical translation models, methods have been proposed that first generate a bag of words from the source bag of words and then apply an ordering model [Venkatapathy and Bangalore, 2007; Bangalore *et al.*, 2007].

4.6.3 Exercises

1. (⋆) Given the translation tables in Section 4.1.5 on page 86, compute the translation probabilities for the following translations of the German sentence *das Haus ist klein*:
   - the house is small
   - the house is little
   - small house the is
   - the

   Assume the most likely alignment.

   (a) Is the IBM Model 1 translation model by itself a good model for finding the best translation?

   (b) Explain how the noisy-channel model elevates some of the problems of IBM Model 1 as a translation model.

2. (★★) Derive Equation (4.13) with a proof by induction. Why does this trick not work for IBM Models 3–5?

3. (★★) Implement IBM Model 1 and duplicate the experiment described in Figure 4.4. How does the training behave when you add the sentence pair *(ein haus, a house)*?

4. (★★) Implement IBM Model 2 and run it on a toy corpus. Download the Europarl corpus and train a model on a language pair of your choice.

5. (★★) Obtain the software package GIZA++[5] that implements the IBM models.

   (a) Run IBM model training on a parallel corpus such as Europarl.[6]

   (b) Implement a growing heuristic to merge word alignments that were generated by bidirectional IBM model training.

---

[5] Available at http://www.fjoch.com/GIZA++.html
[6] Available at http://www.statmt.org/europarl/

Chapter 5
Phrase-Based Models

The currently best performing statistical machine translation systems are based on phrase-based models: models that translate small word sequences at a time. This chapter explains the basic principles of phrase-based models and how they are trained, and takes a more detailed look at extensions to the main components: the translation model and the reordering model. The next chapter will explain the algorithms that are used to translate sentences using these models.

5.1 Standard Model

First, we lay out the standard model for phrase-based statistical machine translation. While there are many variations, these can all be seen as extensions to this model.

5.1.1 Motivation for Phrase-Based Models

The previous chapter introduced models for machine translation that were based on the translation of words. But words may not be the best candidates for the smallest units for translation. Sometimes one word in a foreign language translates into two English words, or vice versa. Word-based models often break down in these cases.

Consider Figure 5.1, which illustrations how phrase-based models work. The German input sentence is first segmented into so-called **phrases** (any multiword units). Then, each phrase is translated into an English phrase. Finally, phrases may be reordered. In Figure 5.1, the six German words and eight English words are mapped as five phrase pairs.

phrase

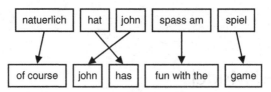

Figure 5.1 Phrase-based machine translation: The input is segmented into phrases (not necessarily linguistically motivated), translated one-to-one into phrases in English and possibly reordered.

The English phrases have to be reordered, so that the verb follows the subject.

The German word *natuerlich* best translates into *of course*. To capture this, we would like to have a translation table that maps not words but phrases. A **phrase translation table** of English translations for the German *natuerlich* may look like the following:

phrase translation table

Translation	Probability $p(e|f)$
of course	0.5
naturally	0.3
of course ,	0.15
, of course ,	0.05

It is important to point out that current phrase-based models are not rooted in any deep linguistic notion of the concept phrase. One of the phrases in Figure 5.1 is *fun with the*. This is an unusual grouping. Most syntactic theories would segment the sentence into the noun phrase *fun* and the prepositional phrase *with the game*.

However, learning the translation of *spass am* as *fun with the* is very useful. German and English prepositions do not match very well. But the context provides useful clues about how they have to be translated. The German *am* has many possible translations in English. Translating it as *with the* is rather unusual (more common is *on the* or *at the*), but in the context of following *spass* it is the dominant translation.

Let's recap. We have illustrated two benefits of translation based on phrases instead of words. For one, words may not be the best atomic units for translation, due to frequent one-to-many mappings (and vice versa). Secondly, translating word groups instead of single words helps to resolve translation ambiguities. There is a third benefit: if we have large training corpora, we can learn longer and longer useful phrases, sometimes even memorize the translation of entire sentences. Finally, the model is conceptually much simpler. We do away with the complex notions of fertility, insertion and deletion of the word-based model.

Intuitively, a model that does not allow the arbitrary adding and dropping of words makes more sense.

5.1.2 Mathematical Definition

Let us now define the phrase-based statistical machine translation model mathematically. First, we apply the Bayes rule to invert the translation direction and integrate a language model p_{LM}. Hence, the best English translation e_{best} for a foreign input sentence f is defined as

$$e_{best} = \text{argmax}_e\, p(e|f)$$
$$= \text{argmax}_e\, p(f|e)\, p_{LM}(e) \qquad (5.1)$$

This is exactly the same reformulation that we have already seen for word-based models (see Equation 4.23). For the phrase-based model, we decompose $p(f|e)$ further into

$$p(\bar{f}_1^I|\bar{e}_1^I) = \prod_{i=1}^{I} \phi(\bar{f}_i|\bar{e}_i)\, d(\text{start}_i - \text{end}_{i-1} - 1) \qquad (5.2)$$

The foreign sentence f is broken up into I phrases $\bar{f}_i$. Note that this process of segmentation is not modeled explicitly. This means that any segmentation is equally likely.

Each foreign phrase $\bar{f}_i$ is translated into an English phrase $\bar{e}_i$. Since we mathematically inverted the translation direction in the noisy channel, the phrase translation probability $\phi(\bar{f}_i|\bar{e}_i)$ is modelled as a translation from English to foreign.

Reordering is handled by a **distance-based reordering model**. We consider reordering relative to the previous phrase. We define start$_i$ as the position of the first word of the foreign input phrase that translates to the ith English phrase, and end$_i$ as the position of the last word of that foreign phrase. Reordering distance is computed as start$_i$ − end$_{i-1}$ − 1.

distance-based reordering model

The reordering distance is the number of words skipped (either forward or backward) when taking foreign words out of sequence. If two phrases are translated in sequence, then start$_i$ = end$_{i-1}$ + 1; i.e., the position of the first word of phrase i is the same as the the position of the last word of the previous phrase plus one. In this case, a reordering cost of $d(0)$ is applied. See Figure 5.2 for an example.

What is the probability of d? Instead of estimating reordering probabilities from data, we apply an exponentially decaying cost function $d(x) = \alpha^{|x|}$ with an appropriate value for the parameter $\alpha \in [0, 1]$ so that d is a proper probability distribution.[1] This formula simply means

---

[1] Actually, we do not worry too much about turning d into a proper probability distribution, because we weight model components according to their importance in a log-linear model. We will describe this in Section 5.3.1 on page 136.

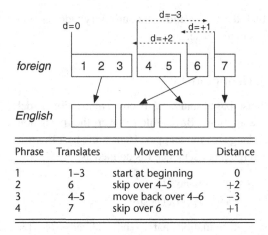

Figure 5.2 Distance-based reordering: Reordering distance is measured on the foreign input side. In the illustration each foreign phrase is annotated with a dashed arrow indicating the extent of reordering. For instance the 2nd English phrase translates the foreign word 6, skipping over the words 4–5, a distance of +2.

Phrase	Translates	Movement	Distance
1	1–3	start at beginning	0
2	6	skip over 4–5	+2
3	4–5	move back over 4–6	−3
4	7	skip over 6	+1

that movements of phrases over large distances are more expensive than shorter movements or no movement at all.

Note that this reordering model is very similar to the one in word-based models. We could even learn reordering probabilities from the data, but this is not typically done in phrase-based models.

What we have just described is a simple phrase-based statistical machine translation model. Only the phrase translation table is learnt from data, reordering is handled by a predefined model. We will describe one method to learn a phrase translation table in the next section and then discuss some extensions to the standard model, both to the translation model and to the reordering model.

5.2 Learning a Phrase Translation Table

Clearly, the power of phrase-based translation rests on a good phrase translation table. There are many ways to acquire such a table. We will present here one method in detail. First, we create a word alignment between each sentence pair of the parallel corpus, and then **extract phrase pairs** that are consistent with this word alignment.

phrase extraction

5.2.1 Extracting Phrases from a Word Alignment

Consider the word alignment in Figure 5.3, which should be familiar from the previous chapter. Given this word alignment we would like to extract phrase pairs that are consistent with it, for example matching the English phrase *assumes that* with the German phrase *geht davon aus, dass*.

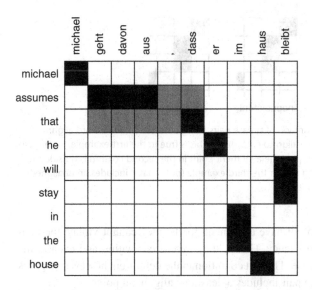

Figure 5.3 Extracting a phrase from a word alignment: The English phrase *assumes that* and the German phrase *geht davon aus, dass* are aligned, because their words are aligned to each other.

If we have to translate a German sentence that contains the phrase *geht davon aus, dass* then we can use the evidence of this phrasal alignment to translate the phrase as *assumes that*. Useful phrases for translation may be shorter or longer than this example. Shorter phrases occur more frequently, so they will more often be applicable to previously unseen sentences. Longer phrases capture more local context and help us to translate larger chunks of text at one time, maybe even occasionally an entire sentence.

Hence, when extracting phrase pairs, we want to collect both short and long phrases, since all of them are useful.

5.2.2 Definition of Consistency

Coming back to the example in Figure 5.3, we collected each phrase pair from the sentence pair using the word alignment because its words match up consistently. Let us put the definition of **consistent with a word alignment** on a more formal footing.

We call a phrase pair $(\bar{f}, \bar{e})$ consistent with an alignment A, if all words $f_1, ..., f_n$ in $\bar{f}$ that have alignment points in A have these with words $e_1, ..., e_n$ in $\bar{e}$ and vice versa:

$$(\bar{e}, \bar{f}) \text{ consistent with } A \Leftrightarrow$$
$$\forall e_i \in \bar{e} : (e_i, f_j) \in A \Rightarrow f_j \in \bar{f}$$
$$\text{AND } \forall f_j \in \bar{f} : (e_i, f_j) \in A \Rightarrow e_i \in \bar{e} \tag{5.3}$$
$$\text{AND } \exists e_i \in \bar{e}, f_j \in \bar{f} : (e_i, f_j) \in A$$

Figure 5.4 illustrates what kind of phrase pairs this definition includes and excludes. Note especially the case of unaligned words.

consistent with a word alignment

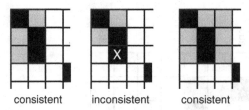

consistent   inconsistent   consistent

Figure 5.4 Definition of phrase pairs being consistent with a word alignment: All words have to align to each other. This is true in the first example, violated in the second example (one alignment point in the second column is outside the phrase pair), and true in the third example (note that it includes an unaligned word on the right).

Since they do not have alignment points, they cannot violate the condition for consistency. Hence, they may occur within and even at the edges of a phrase. The last condition in the definition, however, requires that the phrase pair includes at least one alignment point.

5.2.3 Phrase Extraction Algorithm

Given the definition of consistency, we now want to devise an algorithm that extracts all consistent phrase pairs from a word-aligned sentence pair.

Such an algorithm is sketched out in Figure 5.5. The idea is to loop over all possible English phrases and find the minimal foreign phrase that matches each of them. Matching is done by identifying all alignment points for the English phrase and finding the shortest foreign phrase that includes all the foreign counterparts for the English words.

The following has to be taken into account:

- If the English phrase contains only unaligned words, we do not want to match it against the foreign sentence.
- If the matched minimal foreign phrase has additional alignment points outside the English phrase, we cannot extract this phrase pair. In fact, no phrase pair can be extracted for this English phrase.
- Other foreign phrases than the minimally matched foreign phrase may be consistent with the English phrase. If the foreign phrase borders unaligned words, then it is extended to these words, and the extended phrase is also added as a translation of the English phrase.

One way to look at the role of alignment points in extracting phrases is that they act as constraints for which phrase pairs can be extracted. The fewer alignment points there are, the more phrase pairs can be extracted (this observation is not valid in the extreme: with no alignment points at all, no phrase pairs can be extracted).

```
Input: word alignment A for sentence pair (e, f)
Output: set of phrase pairs BP
 1: for e_start = 1 ... length(e) do
 2:   for e_end = e_start ... length(e) do
 3:     // find the minimally matching foreign phrase
 4:     (f_start, f_end) = ( length(f), 0 )
 5:     for all (e, f) ∈ A do
 6:       if e_start ≤ e ≤ e_end then
 7:         f_start = min( f, f_start )
 8:         f_end = max( f, f_end )
 9:       end if
10:     end for
11:     add extract(f_start, f_end, e_start, e_end) to set BP
12:   end for
13: end for
function extract(f_start, f_end, e_start, e_end)
 1: return {} if f_end == 0 // check if at least one alignment point
 2: // check if alignment points violate consistency
 3: for all (e, f) ∈ A do
 4:   return {} if f_start ≤ f ≤ f_end and (e < e_start or e > e_end)
 5: end for
 6: // add phrase pairs (incl. additional unaligned f)
 7: E = {}
 8: f_s = f_start
 9: repeat
10:   f_e = f_end
11:   repeat
12:     add phrase pair (e_start .. e_end, f_s .. f_e) to set E
13:     f_e++
14:   until f_e aligned
15:   f_s--
16: until f_s aligned
17: return E
```

Figure 5.5 Phrase extraction algorithm: For each English phrase e_{start} .. e_{end}, the minimal phrase of aligned foreign words is identified f_{start} .. f_{end}. Words in the foreign phrase are not allowed to be aligned with English words outside the English phrase. This pair of phrases is added, along with additional phrase pairs that include additional unaligned foreign words at the edge of the foreign phrase.

5.2.4 Example

Let us turn back to our example sentence pair (from Figure 5.3). What phrase pairs are consistent with the word alignment, and hence will be extracted by our algorithm? Figure 5.6 displays the complete list.

It is possible that for some English phrases, we are not able to extract matching German phrases. This happens, for instance, when multiple English words are aligned to one German word: *in the* are both aligned to the German *im*, so that no individual match for either *in* or *the* can be extracted.

Figure 5.6 Extracted phrase pairs from the word alignment in Figure 5.3: For some English phrases, multiple mappings are extracted (e.g., *that* translates to *dass* with and without preceding comma); for some English phrases, no mappings can be found (e.g., *the* or *he will*).

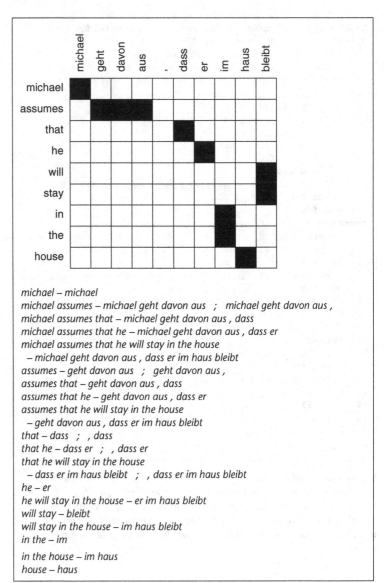

michael – michael
michael assumes – michael geht davon aus   ;   michael geht davon aus ,
michael assumes that – michael geht davon aus , dass
michael assumes that he – michael geht davon aus , dass er
michael assumes that he will stay in the house
 – michael geht davon aus , dass er im haus bleibt
assumes – geht davon aus   ;   geht davon aus ,
assumes that – geht davon aus , dass
assumes that he – geht davon aus , dass er
assumes that he will stay in the house
 – geht davon aus , dass er im haus bleibt
that – dass   ;   , dass
that he – dass er   ;   , dass er
that he will stay in the house
 – dass er im haus bleibt   ;   , dass er im haus bleibt
he – er
he will stay in the house – er im haus bleibt
will stay – bleibt
will stay in the house – im haus bleibt
in the – im
in the house – im haus
house – haus

This also happens when the English words align with German words that enclose other German words that align back to English words that are not in the original phrase. See the example of *he will stay*, which aligns to *er ... bleibt*, words that enclose *im haus*, which aligns back to *in the house*. Here, it is not possible to match *he will stay* to any German phrase, since the only matching German phrase has a gap.

Unaligned words may lead to multiple matches for an English phrase: for instance, *that* matches to *dass* with and without the preceding unaligned comma on the German side.

Note some numbers for this example: there are 9 English words and 10 German words, matched by 11 alignment points. There are 36 distinct contiguous English phrases and 45 distinct contiguous German phrases. 24 phrase pairs are extracted.

Obviously, allowing phrase pairs of any length leads to a huge number of extracted phrase pairs. In well-behaved alignments without reordering, the number of extracted phrases is roughly quadratic in the number of words. However, most long phrases observed in the training data will never occur in the test data. Hence, to reduce the number of extracted phrases and keep the phrase translation table manageable, we may want to enforce a maximum phrase length.

Another reason there are a huge number of extracted phrases is unaligned words. Observe the effect of the unaligned comma on the German side. If it were aligned to *that*, five fewer phrase pairs would be extractable. However, while handling a large number of extracted phrases may cause computational problems, it is less clear whether this hinders our ultimate purpose: improving the quality of the output of our machine translation system.

5.2.5 Estimating Phrase Translation Probabilities

So far, we have only discussed how to collect a set of phrase pairs. More is needed to turn this set into a probabilistic phrase translation table.

It is worth noting that what unfolds here is different from the generative modeling of the IBM models, presented in the previous chapter. Previously, we had a mathematical model that explained, in a generative story, how words in the input sentence are translated into words in the output sentence. This story gave different probabilities for different alignments between input and output sentences, and counts for word translation (and other model components) were based on the relative weight of these alignments.

In contrast to this, here we do not choose among different phrase alignments. Quite purposely, we do not make a choice between, for instance, a more fine-grained alignment with many small phrases or a coarser alignment with a few large phrases. Phrases of any length may come in handy, and we do not want to eliminate any of them.

These practical considerations lead us to a different estimation technique for the conditional probability distributions of the phrase translation table. For each sentence pair, we extract a number of phrase pairs. Then, we count in how many sentence pairs a particular phrase pair is extracted and store this number in count($\bar{e},\bar{f}$). Finally, the translation probability $\phi(\bar{f}|\bar{e})$ is estimated by the relative frequency:

$$\phi(\bar{f}|\bar{e}) = \frac{\text{count}(\bar{e},\bar{f})}{\sum_{\bar{f}_i} \text{count}(\bar{e},\bar{f}_i)} \qquad (5.4)$$

We may want to take into consideration the case when one phrase is matched to multiple phrases in a particular sentence pair, which frequently occurs when there are unaligned words. To reflect the degree of uncertainty, we could assign, for each of the matches, fractional counts that add up to one.

Size of the phrase table

For large parallel corpora of millions of sentences, the extracted phrase translation tables easily require several gigabytes of memory. This may be too much to fit into the working memory of a machine. This causes problems for estimating phrase translation probabilities and later the use of these tables to translate new sentences.

For the estimation of the phrase translation probabilities, not all phrase pairs have to be loaded into memory. It is possible to efficiently estimate the probability distribution by storing and sorting the extracted phrases on disk. Similarly, when using the translation table for the translation of a single sentence, only a small fraction of it is needed and may be loaded on demand.

5.3 Extensions to the Translation Model

So far in this chapter, we have described the standard model for phrase-based statistical machine translation. Even this relatively simple version achieves generally better translation quality than the word-based statistical IBM models. In the rest of this chapter, we will extend the model, achieving further improvement of translation performance.

5.3.1 Log-Linear Models

The standard model described so far consists of three factors:

- the phrase translation table $\phi(\bar{f}|\bar{e})$;
- the reordering model d;
- the language model $p_{\text{LM}}(e)$.

These three model components are multiplied together to form our phrase-based model   **phrase-based statistical machine translation model**:

$$e_{\text{best}} = \text{argmax}_e \prod_{i=1}^{I} \phi(\bar{f}_i|\bar{e}_i)\, d(\text{start}_i - \text{end}_{i-1} - 1) \prod_{i=1}^{|e|} p_{\text{LM}}(e_i|e_1...e_{i-1})$$

$$(5.5)$$

Another way to describe this setup is that there are three components that contribute to producing the best possible translation, by ensuring that

- the foreign phrases match the English words (ϕ);
- phrases are reordered appropriately (d);
- the output is fluent English (p_{LM}).

When we use our system, we may observe that the words between input and output match up pretty well, but that the output is not very good English. Hence, we are inclined to give the language model more weight. Formally, we can do this by introducing **weights** $\lambda_\phi, \lambda_d, \lambda_{LM}$ weighting of components that let us scale the contributions of each of the three components:

$$e_{best} = \text{argmax}_e \prod_{i=1}^{I} \phi(\bar{f}_i|\bar{e}_i)^{\lambda_\phi} \; d(\text{start}_i - \text{end}_{i-1} - 1)^{\lambda_d} \prod_{i=1}^{|e|} p_{LM}(e_i|e_1...e_{i-1})^{\lambda_{LM}}$$

(5.6)

What have we done here? Our original justification for decomposing the model into a translation model and a language model was the noisy-channel model. We applied the Bayes rule, which is a mathematically correct transformation. However, we followed that up with a number of independence assumptions that are not strictly correct, but are necessary to decompose the model further into probability distributions for which we have sufficient statistics.

The assumption behind the translation model that the translation of a phrase does not depend on surrounding phrases is such a necessary but inaccurate assumption. Similarly, the trigram language model assumption states that the probability of an English word depends only on a window of two previous words. It is not hard to come up with counterexamples for either of these assumption.

By adding weights, we are guided more by practical concerns than by mathematical rigor. However, we do come up with a model structure that is well known in the machine learning community: a **log-linear**   log-linear model **model**. Log-linear models have the following form:

$$p(x) = \exp \sum_{i=1}^{n} \lambda_i h_i(x)$$

(5.7)

Equation (5.6) fits this form with

- number of feature function $n = 3$;
- random variable $x = (e, f, \text{start}, \text{end})$;
- feature function $h_1 = \log \phi$;
- feature function $h_2 = \log d$;
- feature function $h_3 = \log p_{LM}$.

To make this more apparent, here is a reformulation of Equation (5.6):

$$p(e, a|f) = \exp\left[\lambda_\phi \sum_{i=1}^{I} \log \phi(\bar{f}_i|\bar{e}_i)\right.$$

$$+ \lambda_d \sum_{i=1}^{I} \log d(a_i - b_{i-1} - 1)$$

$$\left.+ \lambda_{LM} \sum_{i=1}^{|e|} \log p_{LM}(e_i|e_1...e_{i-1})\right] \qquad (5.8)$$

Log-linear models are widely used in the machine learning community. For instance, naive Bayes, maximum entropy, and perceptron learning methods are all based on log-linear models.

In this framework, we view each data point (here: a sentence translation) as a vector of features, and the model as a set of corresponding feature functions. The feature functions are trained separately, and combined assuming that they are independent of each other.

We already gave one reason for moving our model structure towards log-linear models: the weighting of the different model components may lead to improvement in translation quality. Another motivation is that this structure allows us naturally to include additional model components in the form of feature functions. We will do exactly this in the remainder of this chapter.

5.3.2 Bidirectional Translation Probabilities

The Bayes rule led us to invert the conditioning of translation probabilities: $p(e|f) = p(e) \, p(f|e) \, p(f)^{-1}$. However, we may have some second thoughts about this in light of the phrase-based model we are now considering.

It may be that in the training data a rare long English phrase $\bar{e}$ exists that mistakenly gets mapped to a common foreign phrase $\bar{f}$. In this case $\varphi(\bar{f}|\bar{e})$ is very high, maybe even 1. If we encounter the phrase $\bar{f}$ again in the test data, this erroneous phrase translation may be used to produce the highest probability translation: The translation model likes it – high $\varphi(\bar{f}|\bar{e})$ – and the language model may like it as well, if $\bar{e}$ is made up of common English n-grams.

In this case it would be better to use the conditioning of phrase translation probabilities in the actual translation direction, i.e., $\phi(\bar{e}|\bar{f})$. Having moved beyond the noisy-channel model, we may very well use the direct translation probabilities. It is even possible to use both
bidirectional translation · **translation directions**, $\phi(\bar{e}|\bar{f})$ and $\phi(\bar{f}|\bar{e})$, as feature functions.

In practice, a model using both translation directions, with the proper weight setting, often outperforms a model that uses only the Bayes-motivated inverse translation direction, or only the direct translation direction.

5.3.3 Lexical Weighting

Some infrequent phrase pairs may cause problems, especially if they are collected from noisy data. If both of the phrases $\bar{e}, \bar{f}$ only occur once then $\phi(\bar{e}|\bar{f}) = \phi(\bar{f}|\bar{e}) = 1$. This often overestimates how reliable rare phrase pairs are.

How can we judge if a rare phrase pair is reliable? If we decompose it into its word translations, we can check how well they match up. This is called **lexical weighting**; it is basically a smoothing method. We back off to probability distributions (lexical translation), for which we have richer statistics and hence more reliable probability estimates.

lexical weighting

Many different lexical weighting methods have been proposed in the literature. Most of them are inspired by the word-based IBM models. Even using the relatively simple IBM Model 1 has been shown to be effective.

Let us describe one such weighting method. Recall that we extracted phrase pairs from a word alignment. Consequently, for each phrase pair, we also have the alignment between the words in the phrases available to us. Based on this alignment, we can compute the lexical translation probability of a phrase $\bar{e}$ given the phrase $\bar{f}$ by, for instance:

$$\text{lex}(\bar{e}|\bar{f}, a) = \prod_{i=1}^{\text{length}(\bar{e})} \frac{1}{|\{j|(i,j) \in a\}|} \sum_{\forall(i,j) \in a} w(e_i|f_j) \qquad (5.9)$$

In this lexical weighting scheme, each of the English words e_i is generated by aligned foreign words f_j with the word translation probability $w(e_i|f_j)$. If an English word is aligned to multiple foreign words, the average of the corresponding word translation probabilities is taken. If an English word is not aligned to any foreign word, we say it is aligned to the NULL word, which is also factored in as a word translation probability.

In Figure 5.7 the English phrase *does not assume* is paired with the German *geht nicht davon aus*. The lexical weight for this phrase pair is the product of three factors, one for each English word. The English word *not* is aligned to *nicht*, so the factor is $w(\text{not}|\text{nicht})$. The English word *does* is not aligned to any foreign word, so the factor is $w(\text{does}|\text{NULL})$. The English word *assume* is aligned to three German words *geht davon aus*, so the factor is the average of the three corresponding word translation probabilities.

Figure 5.7 Lexical weight of a phrase pair $(\bar{e}, \bar{f})$ given an alignment a and a lexical translation probability distribution w: Each English word has to be explained by foreign words using the distribution w. If aligned to multiple foreign words, the average is taken. If unaligned, $w(e_i|\text{NULL})$ is factored in.

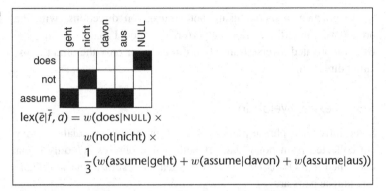

$$\text{lex}(\bar{e}|\bar{f}, a) = w(\text{does}|\text{NULL}) \times$$
$$w(\text{not}|\text{nicht}) \times$$
$$\frac{1}{3}(w(\text{assume}|\text{geht}) + w(\text{assume}|\text{davon}) + w(\text{assume}|\text{aus}))$$

The lexical translation probabilities $w(e_i|f_j)$ are estimated from the word-aligned corpus. Counts are taken, and relative frequency estimation yields the probability distribution. Again, unaligned words are taken to be aligned to NULL.

Finally, as we pointed out in the previous section, it may be useful to use both translation directions in the model: $\text{lex}(\bar{e}|\bar{f}, a)$ and $\text{lex}(\bar{f}|\bar{e}, a)$.

5.3.4 Word Penalty

So far, we have not explicitly modeled the output length in terms of number of words. Yet one component of the system prefers shorter translations: the language model, simply because fewer trigrams have to be scored.

word penalty   To guard against output that is too short (or too long), we introduce a **word penalty** that adds a factor ω for each produced word. If $\omega < 1$ we increase the scores of shorter translations. If $\omega > 1$ we prefer longer translations.

This parameter is very effective in tuning output length and often improves translation quality significantly.

5.3.5 Phrase Penalty

Before any phrase translations can be applied to a new input sentence, the sentence has to be segmented into foreign phrases. This segmentation is not explicit in the model that we have presented so far. In effect, all segmentations are equally likely, and only the chosen phrase translations with their translation, reordering, and language model scores determine indirectly the input sentence segmentation.

What is better: longer phrases or shorter phrases? A simple way to bias towards fewer and hence longer phrases or towards more and hence shorter phrases is to introduce a factor ρ for each phrase translation, a
phrase penalty   **phrase penalty**. Analogous to the word penalty ω discussed above, if

$\rho < 1$ we prefer fewer (longer) phrases, and if $\rho > 1$ we prefer more (shorter) phrases.

In practice, if the model has the choice of using a longer phrase translation, it tends to use it. This is preferable because longer phrases include more context. Of course, longer phrases are less frequent and hence less statistically reliable, but we have addressed this problem with lexical weighting, which discounts bad phrase pairs.

Several researchers have explored other avenues for modeling phrase segmentation. One tempting approach is to prefer segmentation along linguistically motivated constituent boundaries. However, this has not been shown to be useful. There are many examples of good phrase translations that cross such boundaries. Recall our initial example, where we produced the English *fun with the*. Such a segmentation within a prepositional phrase is unintuitive from a linguistic point of view. However, it has been shown to be beneficial in phrase-based models. In this case, the translation of the preposition depends more strongly on the preceding noun *fun* than on the following words. Learning such a non-constituent phrase pair captures the dependency.

5.3.6 Phrase Translation as a Classification Problem

One inherent concern with the decomposition of the translation of a sentence into the independent translation of phrases is the loss of context when making translation predictions. The translation of an ambiguous word may depend on other words in the sentence. For instance, the translation of *bat* will be different, if the word *pitcher* or *cave* occurs in the same sentence. Findings in research on word sense disambiguation have shown that a context window of, say, 50–100 words surrounding the ambiguous word may be helpful in determining its meaning.

How can we include such **contextual information** in the phrase translation table? Borrowing ideas from the field of machine learning, we can view phrase translation as a **classification** task. An input phrase translates into one of a fixed set of possible output phrases. So, we have to classify a phrase into its correct translation category.

contextual information

classification

One method for building such phrase translation classifiers is maximum entropy modeling, which we describe in detail in Section 9.2.4 of this book. This method allows the conditioning of phrase translation not only on the input phrase but on any feature that may be found in the training data. Typically, for computational reasons, we restrict such models to properties of the input sentence.

5.4 Extensions to the Reordering Model

So far, we have introduced only a relatively simple reordering model for phrase-based statistical machine translation. Like the reordering model for the IBM Models 3–5, it is based on movement distance. However, it is not conditioned on words or word classes and not even trained on the data.

In this section, we will take a closer look at the issue of reordering, discuss restrictions on reordering, and describe a lexicalized reordering model.

5.4.1 Reordering Limits

Reordering is one of the hardest problems in machine translation. However, it manifests itself differently for different language pairs. Much recent statistical machine translation research has been driven by language pairs such as Chinese–English, Arabic–English and French–English. While these pairs represent a diverse set of input languages, they have one thing in common: restricting reordering to short local movements is sufficient for the translation of most sentences.

Contrast this to the situation when translating from Japanese or German. These languages have a different syntactic structure from English. Most importantly, for the task of reordering, they are (in the case of German mostly) verb-final, meaning the verb occurs at the end of the sentence. The movement of the verb from the end of the sentence to the position just after the subject at the beginning of the sentence is often a move over a large number of words, which would be penalized heavily by the relative distance reordering model.

Our reordering model generally punishes movement. It is up to the language model to justify the placement of words in a different order in the output. For the local changes required when translating from, say, French, this works reasonably well. A typical move in French is the switching of adjectives and nouns, such as when *affaires extérieur* becomes *external affairs*. The improvement in language model score for *external affairs* over *affairs external* is much higher than the reordering cost involved in the movement.

Given that reordering is mostly driven by the language model, and grudgingly allowed by the reordering model, one has to consider the limitations of the language model used in phrase-based statistical machine translation. It is typically based on trigrams, so only a window of three words is considered in making decisions on what is good English. This window is too small for making adequate judgments about overall grammaticalness of the sentence.

Given the weaknesses of the reordering model, it may not come as a surprise that limiting reordering to **monotone translation** is not very harmful. Allowing no reordering at all has other benefits: the search problem for finding the optimal translation according to the model is reduced in complexity from exponential to polynomial, making search algorithms much faster.

monotone translation

Allowing **limited reordering**, however, yields better translation results than allowing no reordering at all. If we permit moves within a window of a few words, we allow the local reordering required when translating Arabic–English (subject–verb, adjective–noun) or French–English (adjective–noun). Since this is also something that the language model can handle, it often represents the best we can do with reordering. Larger reordering windows or completely unrestricted reordering often leads to worse translations.

limited reordering

5.4.2 Lexicalized Reordering

The reordering model that we proposed for phrase-based statistical machine translation is only conditioned on movement distance and nothing else. However, as we have observed, some phrases are reordered more frequently than others. For instance, a French adjective like *extérieur* typically gets switched with the preceding noun, when translated into English.

Hence, we want to consider a **lexicalized reordering model** that conditions reordering on the actual phrases. One concern, of course, is the problem of sparse data. A particular phrase pair may occur only a few times in the training data, making it hard to estimate reliable probability distributions from these statistics.

lexicalized reordering model

Therefore, in the lexicalized reordering model we present here, we consider only three reordering types: (m) monotone order; (s) swap with previous phrase; and (d) discontinuous. Figure 5.8 illustrates these three different types of **orientation** of a phrase.

orientation

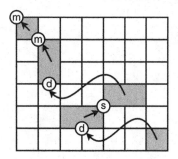

Figure 5.8 Three different orientations of phrases in the lexicalized reordering model: (m) monotone; (s) swap; (d) discontinuous.

To put it more formally, we want to introduce a reordering model p_o that predicts an orientation type m,s,d given the phrase pair currently used in translation:

$$\text{orientation} \in \{m, s, d\}$$
$$p_o(\text{orientation}|\bar{f}, \bar{e}) \tag{5.10}$$

How can we learn such a probability distribution from the data? Again, we go back to the word alignment that was the basis for our phrase table. When we extract each phrase pair, we also extract its orientation type in that specific occurrence.

See Figure 5.9 for an illustration. Looking at the word alignment matrix, we note for each extracted phrase pair its corresponding orientation type (rows relate to English output words, columns to foreign input words). The orientation type can be detected if we check for word alignment points to the top left or to the top right of the extracted phrase pair. An alignment point to the top left signifies that the preceding English word is aligned to the preceding foreign word. An alignment point to the top right indicates that the preceding English word is aligned to the following foreign word.

The orientation type is detected as follows:

- **monotone**: if a word alignment point to the top left exists, we have evidence for monotone orientation;
- **swap**: if a word alignment point to the top right exists, we have evidence for a swap with the previous phrase;
- **discontinuous**: if no word alignment point exists to top left or to the top right, we have neither monotone order nor a swap, and hence evidence for discontinuous orientation.

We count how often each extracted phrase pair is found with each of the three orientation types. The probability distribution p_o is then estimated based on these counts using the maximum likelihood principle:

$$p_o(\text{orientation}|\bar{f}, \bar{e}) = \frac{\text{count}(\text{orientation}, \bar{e}, \bar{f})}{\sum_o \text{count}(o, \bar{e}, \bar{f})} \tag{5.11}$$

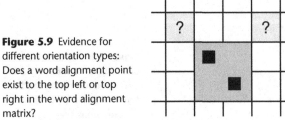

Figure 5.9 Evidence for different orientation types: Does a word alignment point exist to the top left or top right in the word alignment matrix?

Given the sparse statistics of the orientation types, we may want to smooth the counts with the unconditioned maximum-likelihood probability distribution with some factor σ:

$$p_o(\text{orientation}) = \frac{\sum_{\bar{f}} \sum_{\bar{e}} \text{count}(\text{orientation}, \bar{e}, \bar{f})}{\sum_o \sum_{\bar{f}} \sum_{\bar{e}} \text{count}(o, \bar{e}, \bar{f})} \tag{5.12}$$

$$p_o(\text{orientation}|\bar{f}, \bar{e}) = \frac{\sigma\, p(\text{orientation}) + \text{count}(\text{orientation}, \bar{e}, \bar{f})}{\sigma + \sum_o \text{count}(o, \bar{e}, \bar{f})} \tag{5.13}$$

There are a number of variations on this lexicalized reordering model based on orientation types:

- Certain phrases may not only flag, if they themselves are moved out of order, but also if subsequent phrases are reordered. A lexicalized reordering model for this decision could be learnt in addition, using the same method.
- Due to sparse data concerns, we may want to condition the probability distribution only on the foreign phrase (or the English phrase).
- To further reduce the complexity of the model, we might merge the orientation types swap and discontinuous, leaving a binary decision about **monotonicity** of the phrase order.

monotonicity

These variations have been shown to be occasionally beneficial for certain training corpus sizes and language pairs.

5.5 EM Training of Phrase-Based Models

We described in Section 5.2 a method for creating a phrase translation table from a word-aligned parallel corpus. The phrase alignment is done in two steps. First a word alignment is established using expectation maximization (EM) training. Then, we extract phrases that are consistent with the word alignment.

But why the detour over word alignments? Is it not possible to directly align phrases in a sentence pair? In this section, we will discuss a method that does just that.

Recall the intuition behind EM training for word-based models. We laid out a generative model that explains the data but has hidden parameters (the word alignment) that are not directly observable. Here, we want to build a phrase model. As before, the words in the parallel text are observable, but not the phrasal alignment between them.

5.5.1 A Joint Model for Phrasal Alignment

We define a generative model in which a pair of foreign and English phrases is generated by a **concept**. Formally, first a number of concepts $c = c_1...c_n$ are generated. Then each concept c_i generates a

concept

joint model

phrase pair $(\bar{e}_i, \bar{f}_i)$ with probability $p(\bar{e}_i, \bar{f}_i | c_i)$. Since both foreign and English phrases are generated by the model, this model is called a **joint model**. Each phrase is placed at a specific position *pos* in the sentence. The phrase pairs form the sentence pair $\mathbf{f} = \bar{f}_1 \ldots \bar{f}_n$, $\mathbf{e} = \bar{e}_1 \ldots \bar{e}_n$, with an English output order defined by *pos*. Hence, the combined probability of the sentence pair $\mathbf{e}, \mathbf{f}$ generated by this generative process is

$$p(\mathbf{e}, \mathbf{f}) = \prod_{i=1}^{n} p(\bar{e}_i, \bar{f}_i | c_i) \, d(\text{pos}(e_i) | \text{pos}(e_{i-1})) \tag{5.14}$$

There are many ways to define the distortion (reordering) probability d. We may choose a fixed distance-based reordering model as in the standard model. Note that we can also learn the probability distribution properly from the parallel corpus, since we have a generative model that explains the data.

Figure 5.10 gives an example sentence pair. Five concepts $c_1, \ldots, c_5$ generate the sentence pair (*of course john has fun with the game, natuerlich hat john spass am spiel*). The first concept generates (*of course, natuerlich*), the second concept generates (*has, hat*), and so on. Note that the concepts c_2 and c_3 create phrases that are in different orders in German and English.

Although the notion of *concept* suggests that meaning is attached to these originators of phrase pairs, we actually only use one universal concept that generates all phrase pairs. Hence, the generating probability is simply $t(\bar{e}, \bar{f}) = p(\bar{e}, \bar{f} | c)$.

5.5.2 Complexity of the Alignment Space

Before we turn to training the model, first some comments on the complexity of the space of possible alignments. If we limit ourselves to contiguous phrases, a phrase may start at any position and end at any position thereafter. This means that from a sentence with length n, we can identify $O(n^2)$ phrases.

The complexity of possible phrases in the English sentence is $O(n^2)$, and the complexity of possible phrases in the foreign sentence is $O(n^2)$ as well. Without any prior knowledge, any phrase in the English

Figure 5.10 Example of a joint model that directly aligns foreign and English phrases: Five concepts generate the sentence pair.

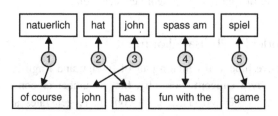

sentence may be mapped to any phrase in the foreign sentence. So, a concept may generate any of $O(n^4)$ phrase pairs.

How many different ways are there to generate a sentence pair of length n each? First of all, m concepts have to be chosen with $1 \leq m \leq n$. If we generate phrases in the sequence of, say, English words, we still have $O(n^3)$ choices when aligning a phrase pair. Since we have to make m such choices, we end up with a complexity of $O(m^{n^3})$ for the space of possible phrasal alignments for a sentence pair, clearly a space that is too large to search exhaustively in a straightforward way.

Another problem we need to consider is the enormous inventory of possible phrases for each side of the parallel corpus, and the resulting size of the bilingual phrase translation table. During training, we have to consider not only the $O(n)$ different phrases of the highest-probability Viterbi alignment, but all $O(n^4)$ possible phrase pairs. Given modern training corpus sizes of maybe a million sentences, this number easily becomes too large to be stored in memory, or even on disk.

Contrast this with the phrase alignment method based on word alignments that we discussed before. The word alignment points effectively restrict the space of possible phrase alignments to a small fraction of the space considered for the joint model. In fact, this allows us to exhaustively collect all remaining possible phrase alignments as entries in the phrase translation table.

5.5.3 Training the Model

Setting aside the complexities of the alignment space for a moment, the basic method for expectation maximization (EM) training of the joint phrase model is very simple:

- Initialize: We begin with a uniform joint model, meaning all $p(\bar{e}, \bar{f})$ phrase pair probabilities are the same.
- Expectation step: We use the joint model to estimate the likelihood of all possible phrase alignments for all sentence pairs. This allows us to collect counts for phrase pairs $(\bar{e}, \bar{f})$, weighted with the probability of the alignment in which they occur.
- Maximization step: Given the counts, we can update the estimate of the probability of the joint model $p(\bar{e}, \bar{f})$ by maximum likelihood estimation.

Given the complexity of the alignment space, we need to take a few short-cuts to be able to train the model. First, we want to reduce the number of phrase pairs that we consider for inclusion in the phrase translation table. Secondly, we need to limit the space of possible alignments for count collection (expectation step).

To limit the phrase inventory, we consider only phrases (on each side) that occur at least a few times (say, five times). An exception is made for phrases consisting of only one word. We may also want to enforce a minimum number of co-occurrences of a phrase pair.

Let us now consider a method to make count collection for phrasal alignments for a particular sentence pair feasible (expectation step). You may recall the analogous discussion for the word-based IBM Models 3–5 (see Section 4.4.2 from page 100 onward). There, as here, we have to deal with an exponential space of possible alignments, which we cannot efficiently evaluate exhaustively for long sentences.

greedy search heuristic   Instead, we employ a **greedy search heuristic** that is efficient enough to find a high-probability phrase alignment in reasonable time, but is not guaranteed to find the optimal alignment. Count collection then proceeds to sample the space around the best alignment found by the search heuristic.

The greedy search for the best alignment works as follows. First, we greedily create an initial alignment, by using the highest probability $t(\bar{e}, \bar{f})$ entries in the phrase translation table. Then, we hill-climb towards the highest probability alignment by (a) breaking and merging concepts, (b) moving words across concepts, and (c) swapping words between concepts.

High-probability alignments for collecting counts may be sampled in the neighborhood of the highest probability alignment. Alternatively, all phrase alignments seen during the greedy hill-climbing process may be taken as the sample for collecting counts.

This training procedure makes the direct EM training of the joint phrase model feasible, but it is still a computationally expensive process, in terms of both time and space. The application of this training routine is currently limited to small corpora, and even for those, cluster computers are commonly used to perform the training. In terms of performance, results are generally no better than learning a phrase table using word alignments, the method we described earlier.

5.6 Summary

5.6.1 Core Concepts

This chapter introduced **phrase-based** statistical machine translation models, which are based on the translation of **phrases** instead of words as atomic units. We define a phrase as a contiguous multiword sequence, without any linguistic motivation. Phrases are mapped one-to-one based on a **phrase translation table**, and may be reordered.

The phrase translation table may be learnt based on a word alignment. All phrase pairs that are **consistent with the word alignment** are added to the phrase table. At the end of the chapter we presented an alternative method, which learns phrasal alignments directly from a parallel corpus. According to a **joint model**, each phrase pair is generated from a **concept**. This model is trained using the expectation maximization (EM) algorithm, in a way similar to the word-based IBM model presented in the previous chapter.

We initially presented a simple **distance-based reordering** model, and then suggested a **lexicalized reordering** model. The lexicalized reordering model predicts the **orientation** of a phrase: either **monotone**, **discontinuous**, or **swap**. One variant of the orientation model checks only for **monotonicity** of the phrases.

Different model components in the phrase model are combined in a **log-linear model**, in which each component is a factor which may be weighted. We extended the original translation model by introducing additional model components: **bidirectional translation** probabilities, **lexical weighting**, **word penalty** and **phrase penalty**.

5.6.2 Further Reading

Introduction – Modern statistical phrase-based models are rooted in work by Och and Weber [1998]; Och *et al.* [1999]; Och [2002]; and Och and Ney [2004] on alignment template models. These models defined phrases over word classes that were then instantiated with words. Translating with the use of phrases in a statistical framework was also proposed by Melamed [1997b]; Wang and Waibel [1998]; Venugopal *et al.* [2003]; and Watanabe *et al.* [2003]. Marcu [2001] proposes the use of phrases within word-based model decoding. The use of log-linear models was proposed by Och and Ney [2002]. Our description follows Koehn *et al.* [2003], which is similar to the model by Zens *et al.* [2002] and Zens and Ney [2004]. Tribble *et al.* [2003] suggest the use of overlapping phrases. Lopez and Resnik [2006] show the contribution of the different components of a phrase-based model.

Learning translation models – Several methods to extract phrases from a parallel corpus have been proposed. Most make use of word alignments [Tillmann, 2003; Zhang *et al.*, 2003; Zhao and Vogel, 2005; Zhang and Vogel, 2005a; Setiawan *et al.*, 2005]. One may restrict extraction of phrase pairs to the smallest phrases that cover the sentence [Mariño *et al.*, 2005]. Lambert and Banchs [2005] compare this restrictive method with the method described in this book and propose some refinements. Phrase alignment may be done directly from sentence-aligned corpora using a probabilistic model [Shin *et al.*, 1996], pattern mining methods [Yamamoto *et al.*, 2003], or matrix factorization [Goutte *et al.*, 2004]. IBM Model 1 probabilities may be used to separate words aligned to each phrase from words outside it [Vogel, 2005], a method also used for splitting long sentences [Xu *et al.*, 2005]. Zhao *et al.* [2004b] use a measure based on the td-idf score from information retrieval to score phrase translations. Additional feature scores may also be used during the parameter tuning of the decoder to determine which phrase pairs should be discarded [Deng *et al.*, 2008]. Kim and Vogel [2007] use an iterative method that adds extracted phrases to the parallel corpus to bootstrap better alignments and extract better phrases. Turchi *et al.* [2008] give an overall analysis of the learning problem for phrase-based machine translation.

EM training of phrase models – The joint phrase model we described is taken from Marcu and Wong [2002], who also propose an improved model initialization over that presented here. The joint model may also be improved by constraining it with alignment points from the intersection of IBM model alignments [Birch *et al.*, 2006a,b] or by not strictly requiring a unique phrase alignment [Moore and Quirk, 2007b]. DeNero *et al.* [2006] point to some problems when using EM training with conditional probabilities. Cherry and Lin [2007] show that the ITG constraint helps the joint phrase model approach, partly by enabling a faster algorithm with fewer search errors. The phrase alignment problem is NP-complete [DeNero and Klein, 2008].

Refinements of phrase models – Usually, the segmentation of the source is not modeled, or only a phrase count feature is used, but adding a source phrase segmentation model may be beneficial [Blackwood *et al.*, 2008b]. Models may allow word insertion to account for spurious function words [Xu, 2005], or allow for words to be dropped by translating them into the empty phrase [Li *et al.*, 2008].

Context features in translation – Phrase translation may be informed by additional context features, for instance by applying methods used in word sense disambiguation [Carpuat *et al.*, 2006]. Such features may be integrated using a maximum entropy model [Bangalore *et al.*, 2006], using support vector machines [Giménez and Màrquez, 2007a], or by directly integrating more complex word sense disambiguation components, such as an ensemble of different machine learning methods [Carpuat and Wu, 2007a,b]. Ittycheriah and Roukos [2007] propose a maximum entropy model for phrase translation. Syntactic context dependencies may be added to phrase translations in the phrase-based approach, for instance verb–argument relationships

[Hwang and Sasaki, 2005], or the syntactic structure underlying each phrase translation [Sun et al., 2007]. Gimpel and Smith [2008] add features around the context of a source phrase into a probabilistic back-off model.

Smoothing – Smoothing the phrase translation probability using discounting methods that are common in language modeling has been shown to improve performance [Foster et al., 2006]. Continuous space models implemented as neural networks allow smoothing of phrase translation table probabilities [Schwenk et al., 2007].

Paraphrasing – More robust translation models may be generated by paraphrasing phrase translation entries [Callison-Burch et al., 2006a] or the parallel corpus [Nakov and Hearst, 2007]. Paraphrases may be extracted from a parallel corpus [Bannard and Callison-Burch, 2005]; for more accuracy the dependency structure may be exploited [Hwang et al., 2008].

Use of dictionaries – Existing bilingual dictionaries may simply be added as additional parallel data to the training data. This can, however, miss the right context in which these words occur. Okuma et al. [2007] propose inserting phrases into the phrase tables that adapt existing entries with a very similar word to the dictionary word by replacing it with the dictionary word.

Pruning large translation models – Quirk and Menezes [2006] argue that extracting only minimal phrases, i.e. the smallest phrase pairs that map each entire sentence pair, does not hurt performance. This is also the basis of the n-gram translation model [Mariño et al., 2006; Costa-jussà et al., 2007], a variant of the phrase-based model. Discarding unlikely phrase pairs based on significance tests on their more-than-random occurrence reduces the phrase table drastically and may even yield increases in performance [Johnson et al., 2007]. Wu and Wang [2007a] propose a method for filtering the noise in the phrase translation table based on a log likelihood ratio. Kutsumi et al. [2005] use a support vector machine for cleaning phrase tables. Such considerations may also be taken into account in a second-pass phrase extraction stage that does not extract bad phrase pairs [Zettlemoyer and Moore, 2007]. When faced with porting phrase-based models to small devices such as PDAs [Zhang and Vogel, 2007], the translation table has to be reduced to fit a fixed amount of memory. Eck et al. [2007a,b] prune the translation table based on how often a phrase pair was considered during decoding and how often it was used in the best translation.

Suffix arrays for storing translation models – With the increasing size of available parallel corpora and translation models, efficient use of working memory becomes an issue, motivating the development of parallel infrastructures for training such as Google's MapReduce [Dyer *et al.*, 2008a]. Alternatively, the translation table may be represented in a suffix array as proposed for a searchable translation memory [Callison-Burch *et al.*, 2005a] and integrated into the decoder [Zhang and Vogel, 2005b]. Callison-Burch *et al.* [2005b] propose a suffix-tree structure to keep corpora in memory and extract phrase translations on the fly. The hierarchical phrase-based model (see Chapter 11) may also be stored in such a way [Lopez, 2007] and allows for much bigger models [Lopez, 2008b]. Suffix arrays may also be used to quickly learn phrase alignments from a parallel corpus without the use of a word alignment [McNamee and Mayfield, 2006]. Related to this is the idea of prefix data structures for the translation which allow quicker access and storage of the model on disk for on-demand retrieval of applicable translation options [Zens and Ney, 2007].

Lexicalized reordering – The lexicalized reordering model was first proposed by Tillmann [2004]; our description follows Koehn *et al.* [2005]. A similar model was proposed by Ohashi *et al.* [2005]. These models have been integrated in finite-state implementations [Kumar and Byrne, 2005]. Nagata *et al.* [2006] extend lexicalized reordering models with better generalization by conditioning on words instead of phrases and clustering words into classes. Similarly, Xiong *et al.* [2006] and Zens and Ney [2006a] use a maximum entropy classifier to learn better reordering probabilities. Features over the source syntax tree may be included in such reordering models [Xiong *et al.*, 2008b] as well as in the translation model [Xiong *et al.*, 2008a]. They may also predict reordering distance [Al-Onaizan and Papineni, 2006].

Phrase-based models and example-based translation – Phrase-based SMT is related to example-based machine translation (EBMT) [Somers, 1999]. Some recent systems blur the distinction between the two fields [Groves and Way, 2005; Paul *et al.*, 2005; Tinsley *et al.*, 2008]. Various combinations of methods from SMT and EBMT are explored by Groves and Way [2006]. Similar convergence takes place when combining statistical machine translation with translation memory, for instance by looking for similar sentences in the training data and replacing the mismatch with a translation chosen with statistical translation methods [Hewavitharana *et al.*, 2005]. Along these lines, phrase-based models may be improved by dynamically constructing translations for unknown phrases by using similar phrases that differ in a word or two and inserting lexical translations for the mismatched words [He *et al.*, 2008b]. Statistical machine translation models may be used to select the best translation from several example-based systems [Paul and Sumita, 2006].

5.6.3 Exercises

1. (⋆) Consider the following three-word alignment examples.

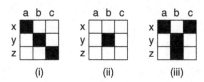

   For each, which and how many phrase pairs can be extracted? What
   do these examples suggest about the relationship between number of
   alignment points and number of extracted phrase pairs?
2. (⋆) Explain how the estimation of phrase translation probabilities can
   be efficiently handled without keeping all phrase pairs in memory,
   but keeping them in a big file on disk.
3. (⋆) The proposed lexicalized reordering model learns an orientation probability distribution for every phrase pair. What simplified
   alternatives would you suggest?
4. (⋆) If the phrase model were extended to allow phrases that have
   gaps on the input side only, what does this mean for the complexity
   of the phrase table?
5. (⋆⋆) Sketch out a pseudo-code implementation for EM training of
   the joint model.
6. (⋆⋆) Implement the phrase extraction algorithm and test it on a word-
   aligned parallel corpus.

Chapter 6
Decoding

In the two previous chapters we presented two models for machine translation, one based on the translation of words, and another based on the translation of phrases as atomic units. Both models were defined as mathematical formulae that, given a possible translation, assign a probabilistic score to it.

The task of **decoding** in machine translation is to find the best scor-   decoding
ing translation according to these formulae. This is a hard problem, since there is an exponential number of choices, given a specific input sentence. In fact, it has been shown that the decoding problem for the presented machine translation models is NP-complete [Knight, 1999a]. In other words, exhaustively examining all possible translations, scoring them, and picking the best is computationally too expensive for an input sentence of even modest length.

In this chapter, we will present a number of techniques that make it possible to efficiently carry out the search for the best translation. These methods are called **heuristic search** methods. This means that there is   heuristic search
no guarantee that they will find the best translation, but we do hope to find it often enough, or at least a translation that is very close to it.

Will decoding find a good translation for a given input? Note that there are two types of error that may prevent this. A **search error**   search error
is the failure to find the best translation according to the model, in other words, the highest-probability translation. It is a consequence of the heuristic nature of the decoding method, which is unable to explore the entire **search space** (the set of possible translations). It is   search space
the goal of this chapter to present methods that lead to a low search error.

155

model error

The other type of error is the **model error**. The highest-probability translation according to the model may not be a good translation at all. In this chapter, we are not concerned with this type of error. Of course, at the end of the day, what we want from our machine translation system is to come up with good translations that capture the meaning of the original and express it in fluent English. However, we have to address model errors by coming up with better models, such as adding components to a log-linear model as described in Section 5.3.1 on page 136. We cannot

fortuitous search error

rely on **fortuitous search errors** that come up with a better translation even though it has lower probability than the highest-probability translation according to the model.

6.1 Translation Process

translation process

To gain some insight into the **translation process**, let us walk through one example of how a human translator might approach the translation of one sentence. We will do this with the phrase-based translation model in mind. It may be a bit too audacious to claim that the phrase-based model is a good model for human translation, but it serves our purpose here.

6.1.1 Translating a Sentence

In our example here, we are confronted with the following German sentence that we would like to translate into English:

er   geht   ja   nicht   nach   hause

With the phrase-based model in mind, we will try to translate this sentence by picking out short text chunks that we know how to translate. By doing this repeatedly we will able to stitch together an English translation. There are many ways to approach this: we will try to build the English sentence piece by piece, starting at the beginning.

Without further ado, we pick a phrase in the input and come up with a translation for it. Let us start modestly by taking the German word *er* and translating it as *he*:

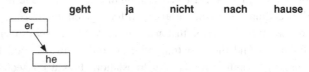

In the illustration above we indicate the phrases we used by boxes, as we did in the chapter on phrase-based models. The boxes also help us to indicate which parts of the foreign input sentence we have already covered.

Note that we started with the first German word, but we are not required to do so. While we are building the English sentence in sequence, we may pick German words out of sequence. In fact, we will do so in the next step, where we translate *ja nicht* as *does not*:

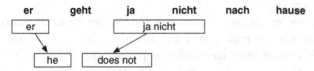

We have discussed the notion of **reordering**: input words and their translations do not have to occur in the same order. In this example, when translating from German to English, the negation particle (*nicht* or *not*) occurs in different positions: before the verb in English, after the verb in German.

reordering

In the translation process, this difference is accommodated by the possibility of picking words out of sequence in the input language when we are building the output sentence in sequence.

To finish up, we need to translate the remaining German words. We do so in two steps, first by translating *geht* as *go*, and then translating the phrase *nach hause* as *home*:

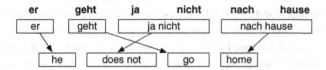

After these steps, we have exhausted all German words in the input sentence. Since we are not allowed to translate a word twice, we know that we are done.

Note that this example followed the phrase-based model, but it should be clear that the translation process for word-based models is similar. We also construct the output sentence from left to right in sequence and mark off input words.

6.1.2 Computing the Sentence Translation Probability

In the previous two chapters on word-based and phrase-based models for statistical machine translation, we introduced formulae to compute the probability of a translation given an input sentence.

Recall the basic formula for the phrase-based model (Equations 5.1 and 5.2):

$$\mathbf{e}_{\text{best}} = \text{argmax}_{\mathbf{e}} \prod_{i=1}^{I} \phi(\bar{f}_i|\bar{e}_i) \, d(\text{start}_i - \text{end}_{i-1} - 1) \, p_{\text{LM}}(\mathbf{e}) \qquad (6.1)$$

Several components contribute to the overall score: the phrase translation probability ϕ, the reordering model d and the language model p_{LM}. Given all $i = 1, ..., I$ input phrases $\bar{f}_i$ and output phrases $\bar{e}_i$ and their positions start$_i$ and end$_i$, it is straightforward to compute the probability of the translation.

partial scoring

Moreover, during the translation process, we are able to compute **partial scores** for the partial translations we have constructed. So, instead of computing the translation probability for the whole translation only when it is completed, we can incrementally add to the score as we are constructing it.

Each time we add one phrase translation, we have to factor in the scores from the three model components in the formula:

- **Translation model**: When we pick an input phrase $\bar{f}_i$ to be translated as an output phrase $\bar{e}_i$, we consult the phrase translation table ϕ to look up the translation probability for this phrase pair.
- **Reordering model**: For reordering, we have to keep track of the end position in the input of the previous phrase we have translated, end$_{i-1}$. We also know where we are picking our current phrase and hence we have its start position in the input, start$_i$. Armed with these two numbers, we can consult the distortion probability distribution d to get the reordering cost.
- **Language model**: We will discuss language modeling in detail in Chapter 7. There we will describe how the probability of a sentence is computed using n-grams, for instance bigrams (2-grams): The probability that a sentence starts with *he* is $p_{\mathrm{LM}}(\text{he}| <s>)$. The probability that *he* is followed by *does* is $p_{\mathrm{LM}}(\text{does}|\text{he})$, and so on. This means, for our application of language models to translation, that once we add new words to the end of the sequence, we can compute their language model impact by consulting the language model p_{LM}. For this we need to keep track of the last $n - 1$ words we have added, since they form the history of the language model (the part of the probability we are conditioning on).

Reviewing the three model components – phrase translation, reordering, and language model – indicates that whenever we add a new translated phrase to our partially constructed translation, we can already compute its model cost. All we need to know is the identity of the phrase pair, its location in the input, and some information about the sequence we have constructed so far.

6.2 Beam Search

Having established two principles of the translation process – constructing the output sentence in sequence from left to right and incremental computation of sentence translation probability – we are now well prepared to face the reality of decoding.

6.2.1 Translation Options

First of all, in our illustration of the translation process in the previous section, we picked the phrase translations that made sense to us. The computer has less intuition. It is confronted with many options when deciding how to translate the sentence. Consulting the phrase translation table shows that many sequences in the input sentence could be translated in many different ways.

For a given input sentence, such as *er geht ja nicht nach hause*, we can consult our phrase table and look up all **translation options**, i.e., the phrase translations that apply to this input sentence. What does that look like? In Figure 6.1 we display the top four choices for all phrases in the input, using an actual phrase table (learnt from the Europarl corpus).

translation option

We can find the phrases for the right translation in this collection of translation options, but there are also many other choices. In fact, the actual Europarl phrase translation table provides a staggering 2,727 translation options for this sentence. The decoding problem is to find adequate phrase translations and place them together in a fluent English sentence. This is the search problem we are trying to solve.

As a side-note, the figure also illustrates nicely that word-by-word translation using the top-1 translation of each word is not a good approach to machine translation. For this sentence, it would result in the puzzling sequence of words *he is yes not after house*, which is not only bad English, but also a poor reflection of the meaning of the input sentence.

6.2.2 Decoding by Hypothesis Expansion

Armed with the notion of a translation process that builds the output sentence sequentially and a set of translation options to choose from, we can now appreciate the computer's decoding challenge.

In our search heuristic, we also want to build the output sentence from left to right in sequence by adding one phrase translation at a time.

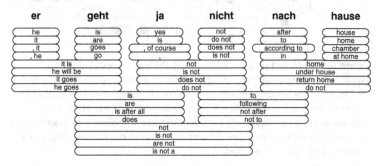

Figure 6.1 Translation options: Top four translations for phrases in the German input sentence *er geht ja nicht nach hause*. The phrases are taken from a phrase table learnt from the Europarl corpus. This is just the tip of the iceberg: the phrase table provides 2,727 translation options for this sentence.

During the search, we are constructing partial translations that we call **hypotheses**.

From a programming point of view, you can think of a hypothesis as a data structure that contains certain information about the partial translation, e.g., what English output words have been produced so far, which foreign input words have been covered, the partial score, etc.

The starting point is the **empty hypothesis**. The empty hypothesis has no words translated and hence empty output. Since no probabilities have been factored in at this point, its partial probability score is 1.

We are **expanding** a hypothesis when we pick one of the translation options and construct a new hypothesis.

For instance, initially, we may decide to translate the German one-word phrase *er* as its first option *he*. This means placing the English phrase *he* at the beginning of the sentence, checking off the German word *er*, and computing all the probability costs, as described in the previous section. This results in a new hypothesis that is linked to the initial empty hypothesis.

But, we may instead decide to expand the initial hypothesis by translating the German word *geht* as *are* (the second translation option for this one-word phrase – see Figure 6.1). Again, we have to mark off the German, attach the English, and add the translation costs. This results in a different hypothesis.

The decoding process of hypothesis expansion is carried out recursively, as illustrated in Figure 6.2. Hypotheses are expanded into new

hypothesis — (margin)

empty hypothesis — (margin)

hypothesis expansion — (margin)

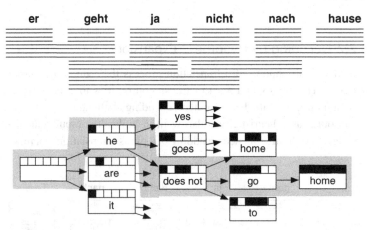

Figure 6.2 Decoding process: Starting with the initial empty hypothesis, hypotheses are expanded by picking translation options (indicated by the lines; see Figure 6.1 for details) and applying the current hypothesis. This results in a new hypothesis in the search graph. Each hypothesis in this illustration is pictured as a box containing the most recently added English, a coverage vector of translated German words (the squares on top, filled black if covered), and a pointer from its parent hypothesis.

hypotheses by applying phrase translations to input phrases that have not been covered yet. This process continues until all hypotheses have been expanded.

A hypothesis that covers all input words cannot be expanded any further and forms an end point in the **search graph**. Given all such completed hypotheses, we have to find the one with the best probability score: this is the end point of the best path through the search graph. In other words, when we track back (using the pointers) through the search graph, we find the best-scoring translation.

search graph

6.2.3 Computational Complexity

Time for reflection: We have proposed a search heuristic that lets us find all possible translations for the input sentence, given a set of translation options. This heuristic is fairly efficient: if two translations differ only in the way the last word is translated, they share the same hypothesis path up to the last hypothesis, and this common path has to be computed only once.

However, the size of the search space grows roughly exponentially in the length of the input sentence. This makes our search heuristic computationally prohibitive for any large sentence. Recall that machine translation decoding has been shown to be NP-complete.

If we want to be able to translate long sentences, we need to address this complexity problem. We will do so in two steps. In the next section we show that we can reduce the number of hypotheses by hypothesis recombination. However, this is not sufficient, and we have to resort to pruning methods that make estimates of which hypotheses to drop early, at the risk of failing to find the best path.

6.2.4 Hypothesis Recombination

Hypothesis recombination takes advantage of the fact that matching hypotheses can be reached by different paths. See Figure 6.3 for an illustration. Given the translation options, we may translate the first two German words separately into *it* and *is*. But it is also possible to get

Hypothesis recombination

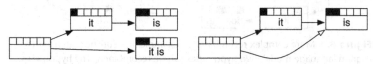

Figure 6.3 Recombination example: Two hypothesis paths lead to two matching hypotheses: they have the same number of foreign words translated, and the same English words in the output, but different scores. In the heuristic search they can be recombined, and the worse hypothesis is dropped.

this translation with a single translation option that translates the two German words as a phrase into *it is*.

Note that the two resulting hypotheses are not identical: although they have identical coverage of already translated German words and identical output of English words, they do differ in their probability scores. Using two phrase translations results in a different score than using one phrase translation.

One of the hypotheses will have a lower score than the other. The argument that we can drop the worse-scoring hypothesis is as follows: The worse hypothesis can never be part of the best overall path. In any path that includes the worse hypothesis, we can replace it with the better hypothesis, and get a better score. Thus, we can drop the worse hypothesis.

Identical English output is not required for hypothesis recombination, as the example in Figure 6.4 shows. Here we consider two paths that start with different translations for the first German word *er*, namely *it* and *he*. But then each path continues with the same translation option, skipping one German word, and translating *ja nicht* as *does not*.

We have two hypotheses that look similar: they are identical in their German coverage, but differ slightly in the English output. However, recall the argument that allows us to recombine hypotheses. If any path starting from the worse hypothesis can also be used to extend the better hypothesis with the *same* costs, then we can safely drop the worse hypothesis, since it can never be part of the best path.

It does not matter in our two examples that the two hypothesis paths differ in their first English word. All subsequent phrase translation costs are independent of already generated English words. The language model is sensitive to only a few of the latest words in the output. A typical trigram language model uses as its history the two latest English words. However, in our example, these two words are identical: both hypothesis paths have output that ends in *does not*. In conclusion, from a subsequent search point of view the two hypotheses are identical and can be recombined.

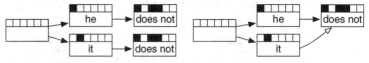

Figure 6.4 More complex recombination example: In heuristic search with a trigram language model, two hypotheses can be recombined. The hypotheses are the same with respect to subsequent costs. The language model considers the last two words produced (*does not*), but not the third-to-last word. All other later costs are independent of the words produced so far.

You may have noted that in the illustrations, we did not simply erase the worse hypothesis, but kept an arc that connects its parent hypothesis with the better hypothesis. For finding the best translation, this arc is not required, but we will later discuss methods to also find the second best path, the third best path, and so on. For this purpose, we would like to preserve the full search graph. Keeping the arcs enables this.

Note that different model components place different constraints on the possibility of hypothesis recombination:

- **Translation model:** The translation models we discussed here treat each phrase translation independent of each other, so they place no constraints on hypothesis recombination.
- **Language model:** An n-gram language model uses the last $n - 1$ words as history to compute the probability of the next word. Hence, two hypotheses that differ in their last $n - 1$ words cannot be recombined.
- **Reordering model:** We introduced two reordering models in the previous chapter on phrase-based models. For both models, the sentence position of the last foreign input phrase that was translated matters in addition to the sentence position of the current foreign input phrase. So, if two hypotheses differ with respect to this sentence position, they cannot be recombined.

Recombining hypotheses is very helpful in reducing spurious ambiguity in the search. The method reduces the problem of having to consider two hypothesis paths that differ only in internal representation such as different phrase segmentation. This leads to a tighter and more efficient search. However, it does not solve the problem that machine translation decoding has exponential complexity. To address this problem, we have to employ riskier methods for search space reduction, which we will discuss next.

6.2.5 Stack Decoding

Given that the decoding problem is too complex to allow an efficient algorithm that is guaranteed to find the best translation according to the model, we have to resort to a heuristic search that reduces the search space. If it appears early on that a hypothesis is bad, we may want to drop it and ignore all future expansions. However, we can never be certain that this hypothesis will not redeem itself later and lead to the best overall translation.

Dropping hypotheses early leads to the problem of search error. In heuristic search, search error is a fact of life that we try to reduce as much as possible, but will never eliminate. To know with certainty that a hypothesis is bad, we need to find its best path to completion. However, this is too expensive.

How can we make good guesses at which hypotheses are likely to be too bad to lead to the best translation? The exponential explosion of the search space creates too many hypotheses, and at some point fairly early on we need to take a set of hypotheses, compare them, and drop the bad ones. It does not reduce the search space enough only to choose among hypotheses that are *identical* from a search point of view (this is what we already do with hypothesis recombination); however, we want to consider hypotheses that are at least comparable.

hypothesis stack

pruning

To this end, we would like to organize hypotheses into **hypothesis stacks**. If the stacks get too large, we **prune** out the worst hypotheses in the stack. One way to organize hypothesis stacks is based on the **number of foreign words translated**. One stack contains all hypotheses that have translated one foreign word, another stack contains all hypotheses that have translated two foreign words in their path, and so on.

Note the following concern. Are hypotheses that have the same number of words translated truly comparable? Some parts of the sentence may be easier to translate than others, and this should be taken into consideration. We will save this thought for later, and come back to it in Section 6.3 on future cost estimation.

Figure 6.5 illustrates the organization of hypotheses based on number of foreign words covered. Stack 0 contains only one hypothesis: the empty hypothesis. Through hypothesis expansion (applying a translation option to a hypothesis) additional words are translated, and the resulting new hypothesis is placed in a stack further down.

The notion of organizing hypotheses in stacks and expanding hypotheses from stacks leads to a very compact search heuristic. Figure 6.6 gives a pseudo-code specification. We iterate through all stacks, all hypotheses in each stack, and all translation options to create new hypotheses.

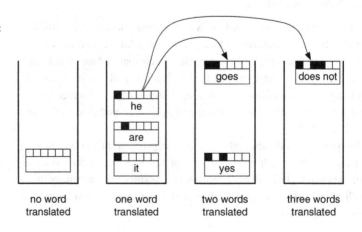

Figure 6.5 Hypothesis stacks: All hypotheses with the same number of words translated are placed in the same stack (coverage is indicated by black squares at the top of each hypothesis box). This figure also illustrates hypothesis expansion in a stack decoder: a translation option is applied to a hypothesis, creating a new hypothesis that is dropped into a stack further down.

no word translated   one word translated   two words translated   three words translated

```
 1: place empty hypothesis into stack 0
 2: for all stacks 0...n-1 do
 3:   for all hypotheses in stack do
 4:     for all translation options do
 5:       if applicable then
 6:         create new hypothesis
 7:         place in stack
 8:         recombine with existing hypothesis if possible
 9:         prune stack if too big
10:       end if
11:     end for
12:   end for
13: end for
```

Figure 6.6 Pseudo-code for the stack decoding heuristic described in Section 6.2.5.

6.2.6 Histogram Pruning and Threshold Pruning

Of course, the exponential nature of machine translation decoding leads to very large numbers of hypotheses in the stacks. Since each stack contains comparable hypotheses (they cover the same number of foreign input words), we use pruning to drop bad hypotheses based on their partial score.

There are two approaches to pruning. In **histogram pruning**, we keep a maximum number n of hypotheses in the stack. The stack size n has a direct relation to decoding speed. Under the assumption that all stacks are filled and all translation options are applicable all the time, the number of hypothesis expansions is equal to the maximum stack size times the number of translation options times the length of the input sentence.

histogram pruning

Let us put the computational time complexity of decoding into a formula:

$$O \text{ (max stack size} \times \text{translation options} \times \text{sentence length)} \qquad (6.2)$$

Note that the number of translation options is linear with sentence length. Hence, the complexity formula can be simplified to

$$O \text{ (max stack size} \times \text{sentence length}^2) \qquad (6.3)$$

If hypothesis expansion is the only computational cost, the cost of stack decoding is quadratic with sentence length, quite an improvement from the original exponential cost. This improvement comes, however, at the risk of not finding the best translation according to the model.

The second approach to pruning, **threshold pruning**, exploits the following observation: sometimes there is a large difference in score between the best hypothesis in the stack and the worst, sometimes they are very close. Histogram pruning is very inconsistent with regard to

threshold pruning

pruning out bad hypotheses: sometimes relatively bad hypotheses are allowed to survive, sometimes hypotheses that are only slightly worse than the best hypothesis are pruned out.

Threshold pruning proposes a fixed threshold α, by which a hypothesis is allowed to be worse than the best one in the stack. If the score of a hypothesis is α times worse than the best hypothesis, it is pruned out.

This threshold can be visualized as a beam of light that shines through the search space. The beam follows the (presumably) best hypothesis path, but with a certain width it also illuminates neighboring hypotheses that differ not too much in score from the best one. Hence **beam search** the name **beam search**, which is the title of this section.

The impact on the computational cost of decoding, given different thresholds α, is less predictable, but roughly the same quadratic complexity holds here too. In practice, today's machine translation decoders use both histogram pruning and threshold pruning. Threshold pruning has some nicer theoretical properties, while histogram pruning is more reliable in terms of computational cost. By the choice of the two limits, stack size n and beam threshold α, it is easy to emphasize one pruning method over the other.

6.2.7 Reordering Limits

If you are familiar with the statistical approach to speech recognition or tagging methods for problems such as part-of-speech tagging and syntactic chunking, the decoding approach we have presented so far will sound vaguely familiar (in all these problems, input is mapped to output in a sequential word-by-word process). However, one distinct property makes machine translation decoding much harder: the input may be processed not linearly, but in any order.

Reordering is one of the hard problems in machine translation, both from a computational and from a modeling point of view. For some language pairs, such as French–English, limited local reordering almost suffices (nouns and adjectives flip positions). Translating other languages into English requires major surgery. In German, the main verb is often at the end of the sentence. The same is true for Japanese, where almost everything is arranged in the opposite order to English: the verb is at the end, prepositions become post-positioned markers, and so on.

The phrase-based machine translation model we presented in the previous chapter, and for which we are now devising decoding methods, is fairly weak in regard to large-scale restructuring of sentences. We proposed some advanced models only for local reordering. Large-scale restructuring is driven by syntactic differences in language, and we will need to come back to that problem in the later chapters on syntax-based approaches to machine translation.

Nevertheless, popular language pairs among statistical machine translation researchers, such as French–English, Chinese–English, and Arabic–English, appear to be a good fit for phrase-based models despite their limited capabilities in global reordering. Some early work in statistical machine translation even ignored completely the reordering problem and limited itself to so-called **monotone decoding**, where the input sentence has to be processed in order. monotone decoding

A compromise between allowing any reordering and allowing only monotone decoding is achieved by the introduction of **reordering limits**. When taking phrases out of sequence, a maximum of d words may be skipped. reordering limit

In practice, statistical machine translation researchers found that beyond a certain reordering limit d (typically 5–8 words), machine translation performance does not improve and may even deteriorate. This deterioration reflects either more search errors or a weak reordering model that does not properly discount bad large-scale reordering.

Note the effect of the introduction of reordering limits on computational complexity: with limited reordering, only a limited number of translation options is available at any step. In other words, the number of translation options available no longer grows with sentence length. This removes one of the linear dependencies on sentence length and reduces Equation (6.3) to

$$O \text{ (max stack size} \times \text{sentence length)} \tag{6.4}$$

With decoding speed linear in sentence length, we are now very comfortable translating even the longest sentences. Pruning limits (in the form of maximum stack size and beam threshold) allow us to trade off between translation speed and search error.

6.3 Future Cost Estimation

We have argued for a beam-search stack decoding algorithm, where we organize comparable hypotheses (partial translations) into stacks and prune out bad hypotheses when the stacks get too big. Pruning out hypotheses is risky, and a key to minimizing search errors is to base the pruning decision on the right measure.

6.3.1 Varying Translation Difficulty

We proposed comparing all hypotheses that have the same number of foreign words translated and pruning out the ones that have the worst probability score. However, there is a problem with this approach. Some

the tourism initiative addresses this for the first time

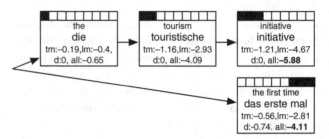

Figure 6.7 Translating the easy part first: The hypothesis that translates (out of order) *the first time* has a better score (−4.11) than the correct hypothesis that starts with the hard words *the tourism initiative* at the beginning of the sentence. Both translated three words, and the worse-scoring (−5.88) but correct hypothesis may be pruned out. Scores are scaled log-probabilities from an English–German model trained on Europarl data (tm: translation model, lm: language model, d: reordering model).

parts of the sentence may be easier to translate than others, and hypotheses that translate the easy parts first are unfairly preferred to ones that do not.

For example, the translation of unusual nouns and names is usually more expensive than the translation of common function words. While translation model costs are similar, the language model prefers common words over unusual ones. See Figure 6.7 for an example of this problem. When translating the English sentence *the tourism initiative addresses this for the first time*, the hard words are at the beginning, and the easy words towards the end. A hypothesis that skips ahead and translates the easy part first has a better probability score than one that takes on the hard part directly, even taking reordering costs into account. In the example, translating first *the first time* yields a better score (−4.11) than translating first *the tourism initiative* (−5.88). Pruning based on these scores puts the latter hypothesis at an unfair disadvantage. After all, the first hypothesis still has to tackle the hard part of the sentence.

future cost

We would like to base pruning decisions not only on the probability score of the hypothesis, but also on some measure of **future cost**, i.e., the expected cost of translating the rest of the sentence. Keep in mind that it is computationally too expensive to compute the expected cost exactly, because this would involve finding the best completion of the hypothesis, which is precisely the search problem we are trying to solve.

outside cost
rest cost

Hence, we need to estimate the future cost. This is also called **outside cost** or **rest cost** estimation. Adding a future cost estimate to the partial probability score leads to a much better basis for pruning decisions.

6.3.2 Estimating Future Cost for Translation Options

Computing a future cost estimate means estimating how hard it is to translate the untranslated part of the input sentence. How can we efficiently estimate the expected translation cost for part of a sentence? Let us start simply and consider the estimation of the cost of applying a specific translation option. Recall that there are three major model components, and each affects the model score:

- **Translation model:** For a given translation option, we can quickly look up its translation cost from the phrase translation table.
- **Language model:** We cannot compute the actual language model cost of applying a translation option when we do not know the preceding words. A good estimate in most cases, however, is the language model cost without context: the unigram probability of the first word of the output phrase, the bigram probability of the second word, and so on.
- **Reordering model:** We know very little about the reordering of the translation option, so we ignore this for the future cost estimation.

Once we have future cost estimates for all translation options, we can estimate the cheapest cost for translating any span of input words covered by the phrase translation table.

Why the cheapest? When translating the rest of the sentence, we want to find the best path to completion. Of course, we would like to use the cheapest translation option, unless a combination of other translation options gives an even better score. So, we do not expect to have a completion more expensive than the one given by the cheapest options (of course, there is no guarantee, because the language model cost is only an estimate and the real cost may turn out differently).

Figure 6.8 illustrates the future costs computed for all spans covered by the translation table in our example sentence. For some parts of the sentence, we can find only one-word matches in the translation table. For instance, the English *tourism initiative* does not occur in the training

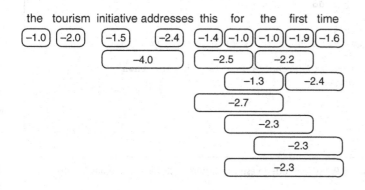

Figure 6.8 Future cost estimates of input phrases covered by the translation table: For each covered span, the cost of the cheapest translation option is displayed. Future cost estimates take translation model and language model probabilities into account.

data, so we do not have a phrase translation for it. Not surprisingly, we have a translation for the English *for the first time* in the translation table, since it is a commonly occurring phrase.

The values of the future cost estimates for the translation options confirm our intuition that the translation of common function words is cheaper than the translation of unusual nouns – translating *tourism* is twice as expensive (-2.0) as translating either *for* or *the* (-1.0). Using a phrase translation, e.g., for *for the first time* (-2.3), is generally cheaper than using one-word phrases (-1.0, -1.0, -1.9, and -1.6 add up to -5.5). The costs reported here are weighted log-probabilities from an English–German translation model trained on the Europarl corpus.

6.3.3 Estimating Future Cost for Any Input Span

We need future cost estimates not only for spans of input words that are covered by phrase translations in the translation table, but also for longer spans. We will compute these using the future cost estimates for the covered spans. There are complex interactions between translation options in actual search (e.g., language model effects and reordering), but we will ignore them for the purpose of future cost estimation.

We can very efficiently compute the future cost using a dynamic programming algorithm that is sketched out in Figure 6.9. The cheapest cost estimate for a span is either the cheapest cost for a translation option or the cheapest sum of costs for a pair of spans that cover it completely.

Figure 6.10 gives cost estimates for all spans in our example sentence. The first four words in the sentence are much harder to translate (*the tourism initiative addresses*, estimate: -6.9) than the last four words (*for the first time*, estimate: -2.3).

```
 1: for length = 1 .. n do
 2:   for start = 1...n+1-length do
 3:     end = start+length
 4:     cost(start,end) = infinity
 5:     cost(start,end) = translation option cost estimate if exists
 6:     for i=start..end-1 do
 7:       if cost(start,i) + cost(i+1,end) < cost(start,end) then
 8:         update cost(start,end)
 9:       end if
10:     end for
11:   end for
12: end for
```

Figure 6.9 Pseudo-code to estimate future costs for spans of any length.

first	future cost estimate for n words (from first)								
word	1	2	3	4	5	6	7	8	9
the	−1.0	−3.0	−4.5	−6.9	−8.3	−9.3	−9.6	−10.6	−10.6
tourism	−2.0	−3.5	−5.9	−7.3	−8.3	−8.6	−9.6	−9.6	
initiative	−1.5	−3.9	−5.3	−6.3	−6.6	−7.6	−7.6		
addresses	−2.4	−3.8	−4.8	−5.1	−6.1	−6.1			
this	−1.4	−2.4	−2.7	−3.7	−3.7				
for	−1.0	−1.3	−2.3	−2.3					
the	−1.0	−2.2	−2.3						
first	−1.9	−2.4							
time	−1.6								

Figure 6.10 Future cost estimates indicate the difficulty of translating parts of the input sentence *the tourism initiative addresses this for the first time*. Numbers are scaled log-scores from an English–German translation model trained on the Europarl corpus. Some words are easier to translate than others, especially common functions words such as *for* (−1.0) and *the* (−1.0), as opposed to infrequent verbs or nouns such as *addresses* (−2.4) or *tourism* (−2.0). The four-word phrase *for the first time* (−2.3) is much easier to translate than the three-word phrase *tourism initiative addresses* (−5.9).

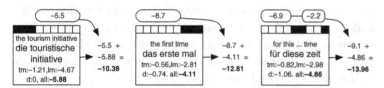

Figure 6.11 Combining probability score and future cost: While the probability score alone may be misleading, adding an estimate of the expected future cost gives a more realistic basis for pruning out bad hypotheses. Here, the hypothesis that tackles the hard part of the sentence *the tourism initiative* has the worse score (−5.88 against −4.11, −4.86), which is offset by a cheaper future cost estimate (−5.5 against −8.7, −9.1), resulting in an overall better score than the two competing hypotheses that cover simpler parts of the sentence (−10.38 against −12.81, −13.96).

6.3.4 Using Future Cost in the Search

We now have in our hands the tool we need to discount hypotheses that translate the easy part of the sentence first. By adding up the partial score and the future cost estimate, we have a much better measure of the quality of a hypothesis. Basing pruning decisions on this measure will lead to lower search error than using just the probability score.

Recall our example, shown again in Figure 6.11, where the hypothesis that skipped the start of the sentence and translated the easy *the first time* had a better score (−4.11) than the hypothesis that tackled head-on *the tourism initiative* (−5.88). Adding in the future cost estimates levels the playing field and puts the better hypothesis ahead (−10.38 vs. −12.81).

It may happen that skipping words leads to several contiguous spans in the input sentence that have not been covered yet. In this case, we simply add up the cost estimates for each span. Since we are ignoring interaction between translation options in the future cost estimation, we can also ignore interaction between uncovered spans that are separated by translated words.

Note that we have ignored reordering costs in the future cost estimates so far. However, we may want to take these into account. If a hypothesis creates coverage gaps, this means that some reordering cost will have to be added further down in the path. Computing the minimum distance of the required jumps gives a good measure of the cheapest expected reordering cost. Adding this to the future cost estimate may reduce search errors.

6.4 Other Decoding Algorithms

We presented in detail a beam-search stack decoder for phrase-based models, which is the most commonly used decoding algorithm. The same type of decoder may be used for word-based models. We now review several other decoding algorithms that have been proposed in the literature, to conclude this chapter.

6.4.1 Beam Search Based on Coverage Stacks

Organizing hypotheses in stacks based on the number of translated foreign input words introduced the additional complexity of future cost estimation. However, if we were to have a stack for each span of foreign input words covered, we could do away with that.

If we only compare hypotheses that translate the same span of foreign words, their future cost estimates, as we defined them, are the same, so we can ignore them. Note that it is still possible to make search errors: while one hypothesis may look better than the alternatives at a given point in the search, it may end with an English word that leads to worse language model scores in the next step, and will not be part of the best path.

coverage stacks   The problem with such **coverage stacks** is that there is an exponential number of them, which makes this approach computationally infeasible. However, recall our argument in Section 6.2.7 for the use of reordering limits. A reordering limit will reduce the number of possible foreign word coverage vectors to a number that is linear with sentence length (albeit still exponential with the reordering limit). So, coverage stack decoding with reordering limits is practical.

6.4.2 A* Search

The beam search we have presented here is very similar to **A* search**, which is described in many artificial intelligence textbooks. A* search allows pruning of the search space that is risk free, in other words, prevents search error.

A* search

A* search puts constraints on the heuristic that is used to estimate future cost. A* search uses an **admissible heuristic**, which requires that the estimated cost is never an overestimate. Note how this can be used to safely prune out hypotheses: if the partial score plus estimated future cost for a hypothesis is worse than the score for the cheapest completed hypothesis path, we can safely remove it from the search.

admissible heuristic

Admissible heuristic for machine translation decoding
The future cost heuristic that we described in detail in Section 6.3 is not an admissible heuristic: it may over- or underestimate actual translation costs. How can we adapt this heuristic? We ignore reordering costs and use the actual phrase translation cost from the translation table, so we do not run the risk of overestimating these components of cost.

However, the language model cost is a rough estimate, ignoring the preceding context, so it may over- or underestimate the actual translation cost. We can get optimistic language model estimates instead by considering the most advantageous history. For instance, for the probability of the first word in a phrase, we need to find the highest probability given any history.

Search algorithm
For A* search to be efficient, we need to quickly establish an early candidate for the cheapest actual completed cost. Hence, we follow a depth-first approach, illustrated in Figure 6.12.

We first expand a hypothesis path all the way to completion. To accomplish this, we perform all possible hypothesis expansions of a hypothesis and then proceed with the one that has the cheapest cost estimate, e.g., partial score and the heuristic future cost estimate. Then, we can explore alternative hypothesis expansions and discard hypotheses whose cost estimate is worse than the score for the cheapest completed hypothesis.

Depth-first search implies that we prefer the expansion of hypotheses that are closest to completion. Only when we have expanded all hypotheses that can be completed in one step, do we back off to hypotheses that can be completed in two steps, and so on. Contrast this with the **breadth-first search** in the stack decoding algorithm that we described earlier: here, we reach completed hypotheses only after

Depth-first search

breadth-first search

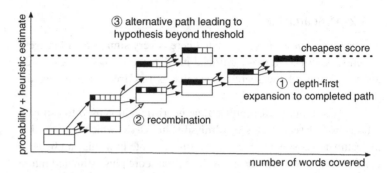

Figure 6.12 A* search: (1) First, one hypothesis path is expanded to completion, establishing the cheapest actual score. (2) Hypotheses may also be recombined as in stack decoding. (3) If an alternative expansion leads to a cost estimate better than the cheapest score threshold, it is pruned. Not pictured: New cheaper hypothesis tightens the cheapest score threshold. Note that hypothesis expansion never worsens the overall cost estimate, since actual costs are never better than estimated costs.

covering the whole breadth of the extensions that cover one foreign word, then two foreign words, and so on.

agenda-driven search   A third search strategy, called **agenda-driven search**, is to always expand the cheapest hypothesis. We organize hypotheses that have not been expanded yet on a prioritized list, i.e., the agenda. By following this agenda, we expect to find more quickly better completed hypotheses that can improve the cheapest actual cost. Once no hypothesis with a better cost estimate than the cheapest score exists, we are done.

While A* search is very efficient in cutting down the search space, there is no guarantee that it finishes in polynomial time (recall that machine translation decoding is NP-complete). Another problem with A* search is that it requires an admissible heuristic, meaning a future cost estimate that is never an underestimate. This may lead to less realistic cost estimates.

6.4.3 Greedy Hill-Climbing Decoding

greedy hill climbing   A completely different approach to decoding is **greedy hill climbing**. First, we generate a rough initial translation, and then we apply a number of changes to improve it. We do this iteratively, until no improving step can be found.

The initial translation may be as simple as the lexical translation of every word, without reordering, with the best translation for each word. We may consider language model probabilities when picking the word translations, or perform monotone decoding using the full translation table.

The steps to improve a translation may include the following:

- change the translation of a word or phrase;
- combine the translation of two words into a phrase;
- split up the translation of a phrase into two smaller phrase translations;
- move parts of the English output into a different position;
- swap parts of the English output with the English output at a different part of the sentence.

All possible steps are considered, and only those that lead to an improvement are applied. There are a number of variants. We may always apply a step, if it leads to an improvement, or search for the best improvement at any point. We may also want to look two steps ahead to be able to apply two steps that first decrease translation probability, but then more than make up for it.

The advantage of this decoding approach is that we always have a full translation of the sentence in front of us. This enables the addition of model components that score **global properties**. For instance, does the English output contain a verb? Also, it is an **anytime method**: at any time, we can stop the translation process if we are satisfied with the output or are bound by time constraints (e.g., a maximum of 5 seconds of decoding time per sentence).

global properties

anytime method

The main disadvantage of this decoding method is its limitation to a much smaller search space than the beam-search approach. We may get stuck in local optima, where a sequence of two or more steps is needed to reach a better translation. In contrast, the dynamic programming element of recombining hypotheses allows the beam search to efficiently consider many more possible translations than the hill-climbing search.

6.4.4 Finite State Transducer Decoding

Finally, a popular choice in building machine translation decoders is the use of finite state machine toolkits. The search graph of the machine translation decoding process is in essence a huge probabilistic **finite state transducer**. Transitions between states are hypothesis expansions. Transition probability is the added model costs incurred by that expansion.

finite state transducer

Using finite state machine toolkits has great appeal. We do not need to implement a decoding algorithm. We only need to construct the finite state transducer for the translation of one sentence. This implies defining the state space and the transitions between states using the phrase translation table.

On the other hand, we are not able to integrate heuristics for future cost estimation, but have to rely on the general-purpose search of the finite state toolkit. As a consequence, researchers typically restrict reordering fairly severely, because otherwise the number of states in the search graphs becomes unmanageably big.

A purpose-built decoder for machine translation is usually more efficient. However, if the goal is to quickly try many different models, finite state transducers provide faster turnaround.

6.5 Summary

6.5.1 Core Concepts

This chapter described **decoding** algorithms that use statistical machine translation models and find the best possible translation for a given input sentence. Due to the exponential complexity of the search space, we employ **heuristic search** methods.

Heuristic search is not guaranteed to find the best translation and hence may lead to **search errors**. Contrast this type of error to **model errors** which are the result of the model giving a bad translation the highest probability. While it is possible to have **fortuitous search errors**, which occur when the search finds a translation that is lower scoring (according to the model) but better (according to human assessment), we cannot rely on these.

We described the **translation process** of building a translation from an input and used it as motivation for the search algorithm. Of course, in statistical machine translation we have to deal with many **translation options** given an input sentence. Search is formulated as a succession of **hypotheses** (in essence partial translations), starting with an **empty hypothesis** (nothing is translated), and using **hypothesis expansion** to build new ones.

The search space can be reduced by **hypothesis recombination**, but this is not sufficient. We hence proposed a **stack decoding** heuristic, in which hypotheses are organized in **hypothesis stacks**, based on the number of foreign words translated. The size of the stacks is reduced by **pruning**. We distinguished between **histogram pruning**, which limits the number of hypotheses per stack, and **threshold pruning**, which discards hypotheses that are worse than the best hypothesis in a stack by at least a certain factor. The search space is typically also reduced by imposing **reordering limits**.

For a fair comparison of hypotheses that have covered different parts of the input sentence, we have to take into account an estimate of the **future cost** of translating the rest of the input sentence. This estimate is also called **rest cost** or **outside cost**.

We reviewed a number of alternative search heuristics. Beam search based on **coverage stacks** is a viable alternative when strict reordering limits are employed, and it does away with future cost estimation. **A* search** is guaranteed to find the best translation when the future cost estimate is an **admissible heuristic**.

A* search is usually performed as **depth-first search** (complete a translation as soon as possible), while the stack decoding is an example of **breadth-first search** (expand all hypotheses at the same pace). Another search strategy uses an **agenda** to expand the hypotheses that are most promising at any given time.

Greedy hill climbing starts with an initial translation, and recursively improves it by changing it in steps. This search method exhibits **anytime** behavior, meaning it can be interrupted at any time (e.g., by a time constraint) and have ready a complete translation (maybe not the best possible).

Finally, **finite state transducers** have been used for machine translation decoding, which takes advantage of existing finite state toolkits.

6.5.2 Further Reading

Stack decoding – The stack decoding algorithm presented here has its roots in work by Tillmann *et al.* [1997], who describe a dynamic programming algorithm, similar to techniques for hidden Markov models, for monotone decoding of word-based models. Allowing for reordering makes decoding more complex. Efficient A* search makes the translation of short sentences possible [Och *et al.*, 2001]. However, longer sentences require pruning [Wang and Waibel, 1997; Nießen *et al.*, 1998] or restrictions on reordering [Tillmann and Ney, 2000] or both [Tillmann and Ney, 2003]. Ortiz-Martínez *et al.* [2006] compare different types of stack decoding with varying numbers of stacks. Delaney *et al.* [2006] speed up stack decoding with A* pruning. Moore and Quirk [2007a] stress the importance of threshold pruning and the avoidance of expanding doomed hypotheses. Some efficiency may be gained by collapsing contexts that are invariant to the language model [Li and Khudanpur, 2008].

Reordering constraints – Matusov *et al.* [2005] constrain reordering when the input word sequence was consistently translated monotonically in the training data. Zens and Ney [2003], Zens *et al.* [2004] and Kanthak *et al.* [2005] compare different reordering constraints and their effect on translation performance, including the formal grammar ITG constraint, which may be further restricted by insisting on a match to source-side syntax [Yamamoto *et al.*, 2008]. Similarly, reordering may be restricted to maintain syntactic cohesion [Cherry, 2008]. Ge *et al.* [2008] integrate other linguistically inspired reordering models into a phrase-based decoder. Dreyer *et al.* [2007] compare reordering constraints in terms of oracle BLEU, i.e., the maximum possible BLEU score.

Decoding for word-based models – Several decoding methods for word-based models are compared by Germann *et al.* [2001], who introduce a greedy search [Germann, 2003] and integer programming search method. Search errors of the greedy decoder may be reduced by a better initialization, for instance using an example-based machine translation system for seeding the search [Paul *et al.*, 2004]. A decoding algorithm based on alternately optimizing alignment (given translation) and translation (given alignment) is proposed by Udupa *et al.* [2004].

Decoding with finite state toolkits – Instead of devising a dedicated decoding algorithm for statistical machine translation, finite state tools may be used, both for word-based [Bangalore and Riccardi, 2000, 2001; Tsukada and Nagata, 2004; Casacuberta and Vidal, 2004], alignment template [Kumar and Byrne, 2003], and phrase-based models. The use of finite state toolkits also allows for the training of word-based and phrase-based models. The implementation by Deng and Byrne [2005] is available as the MTTK toolkit [Deng and Byrne, 2006]. Similarly, the IBM models may be implemented using graphical model toolkits [Filali and Bilmes, 2007]. Pérez *et al.* [2007] compare finite state implementations of word-based and phrase-based models.

Decoding complexity – Knight [1999a] showed that the decoding problem is NP-complete. Udupa and Maji [2006] provide further complexity analysis for training and decoding with IBM models.

6.5.3 Exercises

1. (⋆) Given the following input and phrase translation options:

das	ist	das	Haus	von	Nikolaus
the	is	the	house	of	Nicholas
that		that		from	
that's		house		Nicholas'	

decode the input by hand with the stack decoding that we described in Figure 6.6 on page 165. For simplification, assume no reordering. Draw the search graph constructed during decoding assuming recombination when using

(a) a trigram language model;
(b) a bigram language model;
(c) a unigram language model.

2. (⋆) Given the input and phrase translation options:

das	ist	das	Haus
the	is	the	house
that	's	that	home
this	are	this	building

how many possible translations for the input sentence exist
   (a) without reordering;
   (b) with reordering?
3. (⋆⋆) Implement a stack decoder, as sketched out in pseudo-code in
   Figure 6.6 on page 165. For simplification, you may ignore language
   model scoring. Test the decoder on the example phrase tables from
   Questions 1 and 2, after adding arbitrary translation probabilities,
   (a) without recombination;
   (b) with recombination under a trigram language model.
4. (⋆⋆) Install Moses[1] and follow the step-by-step guide to train a
   model using the Europarl corpus.[2]
5. (⋆⋆⋆) Recent research supports the use of maximum entropy classifiers to include more context in translation decisions. Using the
   open-source Moses system as a starting point, implement maximum
   entropy classifiers that predict
   (a) an output phrase given an input phrase and other words in the
       sentence as features;
   (b) reordering distance based on word movement, and syntactic
       properties over the input part-of-speech tags and input syntactic
       tree.
6. (⋆⋆⋆) Implement A* search in Moses.

---

[1] Available at http://www.statmt.org/moses/
[2] Available at http://www.statmt.org/europarl/

Chapter 7

Language Models

One essential component of any statistical machine translation system is the **language model**, which measures how likely it is that a sequence language model of words would be uttered by an English speaker. It is easy to see the benefits of such a model. Obviously, we want a machine translation system not only to produce output words that are true to the original in meaning, but also to string them together in fluent English sentences.

In fact, the language model typically does much more than just enable fluent output. It supports difficult decisions about word order and word translation. For instance, a probabilistic language model p_{LM} should prefer correct word order to incorrect word order:

$$p_{LM}(\text{the house is small}) > p_{LM}(\text{small the is house}) \qquad (7.1)$$

Formally, a language model is a function that takes an English sentence and returns the probability that it was produced by an English speaker. According to the example above, it is more likely that an English speaker would utter the sentence *the house is small* than the sentence *small the is house*. Hence, a good language model p_{LM} assigns a higher probability to the first sentence.

This preference of the language model helps a statistical machine translation system to find the right word order. Another area where the language model aids translation is word choice. If a foreign word (such as the German *Haus*) has multiple translations (*house, home, ...*), lexical translation probabilities already give preference to the more common translation (*house*). But in specific contexts, other translations

181

may be preferred. Again, the language model steps in. It gives higher probability to the more natural word choice in context, for instance:

$$p_{\text{LM}}(\text{I am going home}) > p_{\text{LM}}(\text{I am going house}) \qquad (7.2)$$

This chapter presents the dominant language modeling methodology, n-gram language models, along with smoothing and back-off methods that address issues of data sparseness, the problems that arise from having to build models with limited training data.

7.1 N-Gram Language Models

n-gram   The leading method for language models is **n-gram** language modeling. N-gram language models are based on statistics of how likely words are to follow each other. Recall the last example. If we analyze a large amount of text, we will observe that the word *home* follows the word *going* more often than the word *house* does. We will be exploiting such statistics.

Formally, in language modeling, we want to compute the probability of a string $W = w_1, w_2, ..., w_n$. Intuitively, $p(W)$ is the probability that if we pick a sequence of English words at random (by opening a random book or magazine at a random place, or by listening to a conversation) it turns out to be W.

How can we compute $p(W)$? The typical approach to statistical estimation calls for first collecting a large amount of text and counting how often W occurs in it. However, most long sequences of words will not occur in the text at all. So we have to break down the computation of $p(W)$ into smaller steps, for which we can collect sufficient statistics and estimate probability distributions.

sparse data   Dealing with **sparse data** that limits us to collecting sufficient statistics to estimate reliable probability distributions is the fundamental problem in language modeling. In this chapter, we will examine methods that address this issue.

7.1.1 Markov Chain

In n-gram language modeling, we break up the process of predicting one word   ing a word sequence W into **predicting one word** at a time. We first decompose the probability using the chain rule:

$$p(w_1, w_2, ..., w_n) = p(w_1)\, p(w_2|w_1)\, ...\, p(w_n|w_1, w_2, ..., w_{n-1}) \qquad (7.3)$$

The language model probability $p(w_1, w_2, ..., w_n)$ is a product of word history   probabilities given a **history** of preceding words. To be able to estimate these word probability distributions, we limit the history to m words:

$$p(w_n|w_1, w_2, ..., w_{n-1}) \simeq p(w_n|w_{n-m}, ..., w_{n-2}, w_{n-1}) \qquad (7.4)$$

This type of model, where we step through a sequence (here: a sequence of words), and consider for the transitions only a limited history, is called a **Markov chain**. The number of previous states (here: words) is the **order** of the model.

Markov chain
order

The **Markov assumption** states that only a limited number of previous words affect the probability of the next word. It is technically wrong, and it is not too hard to come up with counterexamples that demonstrate that a longer history is needed. However, limited data restrict the collection of reliable statistics to short histories.

Markov assumption

Typically, we choose the actual number of words in the history based on how much training data we have. More training data allows for longer histories. Most commonly, **trigram** language models are used. They consider a two-word history to predict the third word. This requires the collection of statistics over sequences of three words, so-called 3-grams (trigrams). Language models may also be estimated over 2-grams (**bigrams**), single words (**unigrams**), or any other order of n-grams.

trigram

bigram
unigram

7.1.2 Estimation

In its simplest form, the estimation of trigram word prediction probabilities $p(w_3|w_1, w_2)$ is straightforward. We count how often in our training corpus the sequence w_1, w_2 is followed by the word w_3, as opposed to other words. According to maximum likelihood estimation, we compute:

$$p(w_3|w_1, w_2) = \frac{\text{count}(w_1, w_2, w_3)}{\sum_w \text{count}(w_1, w_2, w)} \qquad (7.5)$$

Figure 7.1 gives some examples of how this estimation works on real data, in this case the European parliament corpus. We consider three different histories: *the green, the red*, and *the blue*. The words that most frequently follow are quite different for the different histories. For instance *the red cross* is a frequent trigram in the Europarl corpus, which also mentions *the green party* a lot, a political organization.

the green (total: 1748)			the red (total: 225)			the blue (total: 54)		
Word	Count	Prob.	Word	Count	Prob.	Word	Count	Prob.
paper	801	0.458	cross	123	0.547	box	16	0.296
group	640	0.367	tape	31	0.138	.	6	0.111
light	110	0.063	army	9	0.040	flag	6	0.111
party	27	0.015	card	7	0.031	,	3	0.056
ecu	21	0.012	,	5	0.022	angel	3	0.056

Figure 7.1 Counts for trigrams and estimated word probabilities based on a two-word history: 123 out of 225 trigrams in the Europarl corpus that start with *the red* end with *cross*, so the maximum likelihood probability is 0.547.

Let us look at one example of the maximum likelihood estimation of word probabilities given a two-word history. There are 225 occurrences of trigrams that start with *the red* in the Europarl corpus. In 123 of them, the third word is *cross*, hence the maximum likelihood estimation for $p_{LM}(\text{cross}|\text{the red})$ is $\frac{123}{225} \simeq 0.547$.

7.1.3 Perplexity

Language models differ in many ways. How much text are they trained on? Are they using bigrams, trigrams, or even 4-grams? What kind of smoothing techniques are used (more on that below starting with Section 7.2)?

To guide decisions when building a language model, we need a measure of a model's quality. Our premise for language modeling is that a model should give good English text a high probability and bad text a low probability.

If we have some held-out sample text, we can compute the probability that our language model assigns to it. A better language model should assign a higher probability to this text.

This is the idea behind the common evaluation metric for language models, **perplexity**. It is based on the **cross-entropy**, which is defined as

perplexity
cross-entropy

$$H(p_{LM}) = -\frac{1}{n} \log p_{LM}(w_1, w_2, ..., w_n)$$

$$= -\frac{1}{n} \sum_{i=1}^{n} \log p_{LM}(w_i|w_1, ..., w_{i-1}) \qquad (7.6)$$

Perplexity is a simple transformation of cross-entropy:

$$PP = 2^{H(p_{LM})} \qquad (7.7)$$

More on the mathematical derivation of cross-entropy and perplexity later. Let us first develop some intuition about what these metrics mean. Given a language model trained on the Europarl corpus, we want to assess its perplexity on a sentence from a section of the corpus that is not included in training. Our example sentence is:

I would like to commend the rapporteur on his work.

Using a trigram language model,[1] the probability of the trigrams for this sentence are given in Figure 7.2. We frame the sentence with markers for sentence start <s> and sentence end </s>. This allows us to properly model the probability of *i* being the first word of the sentence, by

---

[1] We report numbers using language models trained on the Europarl corpus using Kneser–Ney smoothing, computed with the SRILM toolkit.

Prediction	p_{LM}	$-\log_2 p_{\text{LM}}$
$p_{\text{LM}}(i\|</s><s>)$	0.109	3.197
$p_{\text{LM}}(\text{would}\|<s>i)$	0.144	2.791
$p_{\text{LM}}(\text{like}\|i \text{ would})$	0.489	1.031
$p_{\text{LM}}(\text{to}\|\text{would like})$	0.905	0.144
$p_{\text{LM}}(\text{commend}\|\text{like to})$	0.002	8.794
$p_{\text{LM}}(\text{the}\|\text{to commend})$	0.472	1.084
$p_{\text{LM}}(\text{rapporteur}\|\text{commend the})$	0.147	2.763
$p_{\text{LM}}(\text{on}\|\text{the rapporteur})$	0.056	4.150
$p_{\text{LM}}(\text{his}\|\text{rapporteur on})$	0.194	2.367
$p_{\text{LM}}(\text{work}\|\text{on his})$	0.089	3.498
$p_{\text{LM}}(.\|\text{his work})$	0.290	1.785
$p_{\text{LM}}(</s>\|\text{work .})$	0.99999	0.000014
	Average	2.634

Figure 7.2 Computation of perplexity for the sentence *I would like to commend the rapporteur on his work:* For each word, the language model provides a probability. The average of the negative log of these word prediction probabilities is the cross-entropy H, here 2.634. Perplexity is 2^H.

looking at $p_{\text{LM}}(i|</s><s>)$. We also include the probability for the end of the sentence: $p_{\text{LM}}(</s>|\text{work.})$

The language model provides for each word a probability, which indicates how likely it is that the word would occur next in the sentence, given the previous two-word history. According to the language model, the probability that a sentence starts with the personal pronoun *i* is 0.109043, a fairly probable sentence start for the Europarl corpus from which the language model is built.

The next words are also fairly common: *would* with probability 0.144, *like* with probability 0.489, and the almost certain *to* after that (probability 0.904). Now many words may follow, most likely verbs, but *commend* is a rather unusual verb, even for this corpus. Its language model probability in this context is only 0.002.

The cross-entropy is the average of the negative logarithm of the word probabilities. In Figure 7.2, next to each probability you can find its negative $\log_2$. Highly expected words, such as the end of sentence marker </s> following the period (0.000014), are balanced against less expected words, such as *commend* (8.794). In this example, the cross-entropy is 2.634, and hence the perplexity is $2^{2.634} = 6.206$.

Note that we do not simply count how many words the language model would have guessed right (e.g., the most likely word following *the green* is *paper*, etc.). The measure of perplexity is based on how much probability mass is given to the actually occurring words. A good model of English would not waste any probability mass on impossible sequences of English words, so more of it is available for possible sequences, and most of it concentrated on the most likely sequences.

Figure 7.3 compares language models of different order, from unigram to 4-gram. It gives negative log-probabilities and the resulting perplexity for our example sentence. Not surprisingly, the higher order n-gram models are better at predicting words, resulting in a lower perplexity.

Figure 7.3 Negative $\log_2$ probabilities for word prediction for unigram to 4-gram language models: A longer history allows more accurate prediction of words, resulting in lower perplexity.

Word	Unigram	Bigram	Trigram	4-gram
i	6.684	3.197	3.197	3.197
would	8.342	2.884	2.791	2.791
like	9.129	2.026	1.031	1.290
to	5.081	0.402	0.144	0.113
commend	15.487	12.335	8.794	8.633
the	3.885	1.402	1.084	0.880
rapporteur	10.840	7.319	2.763	2.350
on	6.765	4.140	4.150	1.862
his	10.678	7.316	2.367	1.978
work	9.993	4.816	3.498	2.394
.	4.896	3.020	1.785	1.510
</s>	4.828	0.005	0.000	0.000
Average	8.051	4.072	2.634	2.251
Perplexity	265.136	16.817	6.206	4.758

Mathematical derivation of perplexity

entropy   Perplexity is based on the the concept of **entropy**, which measures uncertainty in a probability distribution. Mathematically, it is defined as

$$H(p) = - \sum_x p(x) \log_2 p(x) \tag{7.8}$$

If a distribution has very certain outcomes, then entropy is low. In the extreme case, if the distribution has only one event x with probability $p(x) = 1$, the entropy is 0. The more events that are possible with significant probability, the higher the entropy. If there are two equally likely events with $p(x) = 0.5$ each, then $H(p) = 1$; if there are four equally likely events, then $H(p) = 2$; and so on.

Entropy is a common notion in the sciences and also in computer science, since it is related to how many bits are necessary to encode messages from a source. More frequent messages (think: more probable events) are encoded with shorter bit sequences, to save overall on the length over several messages.

If we consider the event of observing a sequence of words $W_1^n = w_1, ..., w_n$ from a language L, we can compute the entropy for this probability distribution in the same way:

$$H(p(W_1^n)) = - \sum_{W_1^n \in L} p(W_1^n) \log p(W_1^n) \tag{7.9}$$

This computation of entropy will strongly depend on the length n of the sequences. Longer sequences are generally less likely than shorter sequences. To have a more meaningful measure, we want to compute entropy rate   entropy per word, also called the **entropy rate**:

$$\frac{1}{n} H(p(W_1^n)) = -\frac{1}{n} \sum_{W_1^n \in L} p(W_1^n) \log p(W_1^n) \tag{7.10}$$

We can bring this argument to its logical conclusion by attempting to measure the **true entropy of a language** L given its true probability distribution p. Instead of limiting the calculation to a fixed sequence of length n, we need to consider the observation of infinitely long sequences:

true entropy of a language

$$
\begin{aligned}
H(L) &= \lim_{n \to \inf} -\frac{1}{n} H(p(W_1^n)) \\
&= \lim_{n \to \inf} -\frac{1}{n} \sum_{W_1^n \in L} p(W_1^n) \log p(W_1^n)
\end{aligned}
\tag{7.11}
$$

Instead of computing the probability of all sequences of infinite length, we can simplify this equation to:

$$
H(L) = \lim_{n \to \inf} -\frac{1}{n} \log p(W_1^n)
\tag{7.12}
$$

For a mathematical justification of this last step, refer to the Shannon–McMillan–Breiman theorem. This is explained, for instance, by Cover and Thomas [1991, Chapter 15].

There have been attempts to measure the true entropy of a language such as English. See the box on page 188 for a historical account. In language modeling we are trying to produce a model that predicts the next word, given a history of preceding words. An instructive game is to measure human performance at this task.

In practice, we do not have access to the true probability distribution p, only a model p_{LM} for it. When we replace p with p_{LM} in Equation (7.12), we obtain the formula for the **cross-entropy**:

cross-entropy

$$
H(L, p_{\text{LM}}) = \lim_{n \to \inf} -\frac{1}{n} \log p_{\text{LM}}(W_1^n)
\tag{7.13}
$$

The true entropy of a language $H(L)$ is a lower bound for the cross-entropy of a model p_{LM}:

$$
H(L) \le H(L, p_{\text{LM}})
\tag{7.14}
$$

A good language model achieves a cross-entropy close to the true entropy of the language, so this becomes a convenient measure for the quality of language models.

In practice, we do not have infinite sequences of words, but only a limited test set. However, we can still use this formula to approximate the cross-entropy of a model p_{LM}. If you look back at Figure 7.3, this is exactly what we did for our example, with the additional step of converting cross-entropy into perplexity. For more realistic estimates of perplexity, we need of course a larger sample of thousands of words or even more.

Estimating the entropy of English

Take a newspaper article and try to predict the next word given what has already been said in the article. You will often find it very easy to guess. Obviously language is very redundant, and we can make do with many fewer letters and words to communicate the same meaning.

compression

Compression – Anybody who has ever used a file compression program such as bzip2 will know that we can compress text considerably. Usual ASCII encoding uses 8 bits per letter. When we compress the English Europarl corpus, we can reduce its size from 15 MB to 3 MB. So, its 27 million characters require on average only 1.7 bits each.

Shannon's guessing game

Shannon's guessing game – What is the minimum number of bits required to store text? Shannon [1951] introduced the guessing game to estimate the entropy of English. He worked on the character level, ignoring case and punctuation, leaving 26 characters and the space symbol. A human subject is asked to predict the next letter in the sequence given the preceding text, and we record how many guesses were necessary for each letter.

We can convert the sequence of letters into a sequence of numbers of guesses. This sequence can also be interpreted as follows: A perfect model of English will have a ranking of the predictions for the next letter, based on their probabilities. By telling this model that the next letter is, say, the 5th guess, it is able to reconstruct the text. Given this sequence, we can estimate the probability p_1 that a letter is the first choice, p_2 that it is the second choice, and so. With this distribution p, we are able to compute the entropy using Equation (7.8):

$$H(p) = -\sum_{i=1}^{27} p_i(x) \log p_i(x)$$

gambling estimate

Gambling estimate – Cover and King [1978] propose a gambling estimate of the entropy of English. To be able to have probabilities directly associated with letter predictions, participants in this game are asked to bet a certain amount for each next letter. The size of the bets directly correlate to probabilities.

Both methods estimate entropy at about 1.3 bits per character.

7.2 Count Smoothing

We have so far ignored the following problem: What if an n-gram has not been seen in training, but then shows up in the test sentence we want to score? Using the formula for maximum likelihood

estimation in Equation (7.5), we would assign **unseen n-grams** a   unseen n-gram
probability of 0.

Such a low probability seems a bit harsh, and it is also not very useful in practice. If we want to compare different possible translations for a sentence, and all of them contain unseen n-grams, then each of these sentences receives a language model estimate of 0, and we have nothing interesting to say about their relative quality. Since we do not want to give any string of English words zero probability, we need to assign some probability to unseen n-grams.

Also consider n-grams that *do* occur in the training corpus. If an n-gram occurs once in the training data, how often do we expect it to occur again in a corpus of equal size? Exactly once, or more, or less?

When we move to higher order n-gram models, the problem of unseen n-grams becomes more severe. While these models enable us to capture more context, it is less likely that a higher order n-gram has been observed before in a training corpus.

This section will discuss various methods for adjusting the **empirical counts** that we observe in the training corpus to the **expected**   empirical count
counts of n-grams in previously unseen text.   expected count

7.2.1 Add-One Smoothing

The simplest form of adapting empirical counts is to add a fixed number (say, 1) to every count. This will eliminate counts of zero. Since probabilities still have to add up to one, we need to consider these additional imaginary occurrences of n-grams when estimating probabilities.

Instead of simply using the count c and the total number of n-grams n for the maximum likelihood estimation of the probability p by

$$p = \frac{c}{n} \qquad (7.15)$$

we now adjust this to

$$p = \frac{c+1}{n+v} \qquad (7.16)$$

where v is the total number of possible n-grams.

If we have a vocabulary size of, say, 86,700 distinct tokens, the number of possible bigrams is $86,700^2 = 7,516,890,000$, just over 7.5 billion. Contrast this number with the size of the Europarl corpus, which has 30 million words, and hence a total number of 30 million bigrams. We quickly notice that **add-one smoothing** gives undue credence to   add-one smoothing
counts that we do not observe.

We can remedy this by **add-α smoothing**, adding a smaller number   add-α smoothing
$\alpha < 1$ instead of one:

$$p = \frac{c+\alpha}{n+\alpha v} \qquad (7.17)$$

Figure 7.4 Add-one smoothing: Counts are adjusted by adding 1 (or a lower value $\alpha = 0.005$), given a corpus size of $n = 29{,}564{,}160$ tokens and a vocabulary size of $v = 86{,}700$ tokens. The table displays raw count, adjusted count after adding a value $(1, \alpha = 0.00017)$ and renormalization, and actual test count.

Count c	$(c+1)\dfrac{n}{n+v^2}$	$(c+\alpha)\dfrac{n}{n+\alpha v^2}$	Test count t_c
	Adjusted count		
0	0.00378	0.00016	0.00016
1	0.00755	0.95725	0.46235
2	0.01133	1.91433	1.39946
3	0.01511	2.87141	2.34307
4	0.01888	3.82850	3.35202
5	0.02266	4.78558	4.35234
6	0.02644	5.74266	5.33762
8	0.03399	7.65683	7.15074
10	0.04155	9.57100	9.11927
20	0.07931	19.14183	18.95948

But what is a good value for α? We may determine this value by experimentation, e.g., by trying out different values and settling on the value that optimizes perplexity on a held-out test set.

Figure 7.4 shows how this works out in practice, given the Europarl corpus. Counts are adjusted either by adding one or by adding $\alpha = 0.00017$. The latter number is optimized for a match between the adjusted counts and test counts of unseen bigrams.

Add-one smoothing clearly gives too much weight to unseen n-grams. Their adjusted count is 0.00378 vs. the test count of only 0.00016. As a consequence, not much probability mass is left for observed n-grams. All n-grams in the table, even the ones occurring 20 times in training, are adjusted to a count below 1.

Add-α smoothing assigns the correct adjusted count to unseen n-grams since this is how we set α. But the other adjusted counts are still off. Singletons are adjusted to a count of 0.95725, while the test count is less than half of that (0.46235).

7.2.2 Deleted Estimation

Adjusting counts has to address the question: If we observe an n-gram c times in the training corpus, what does that really mean? How often do we expect it to see in the future?

To be able to answer this question, we need a second corpus. Pooling together all n-grams that appear some fixed number of times in the training corpus, how often do they occur in the second corpus? How many new, previously unseen n-grams do we encounter in the second corpus? How many that have we already seen once, twice, etc.?

This is clearly a function of the size of the original training corpus and the expansiveness of the text domain. Figure 7.5 gives some

Count r	Count of counts N_r	Count in held-out T_r	Exp. count $E[r] = T_r/N_r$
0	7,515,623,434	938,504	0.00012
1	753,777	353,383	0.46900
2	170,913	239,736	1.40322
3	78,614	189,686	2.41381
4	46,769	157,485	3.36860
5	31,413	134,653	4.28820
6	22,520	122,079	5.42301
8	13,586	99,668	7.33892
10	9,106	85,666	9.41129
20	2,797	53,262	19.04992

Figure 7.5 Deleted estimation: In half of the Europarl corpus 753,777 distinct bigrams occur exactly once. These n-grams occur 353,383 times in the held-out set. For each of these n-grams, the expected count is $\frac{353,383}{753,777} = 0.46900$.

numbers for such a study on the example of the Europarl corpus. We split it into one half for training (i.e., collecting counts for n-grams) and the other half for validating these counts.

The distribution of n-gram counts has a **long tail**, meaning a long list of rare n-grams – of the 1,266,566 bigrams in this corpus, more than half, 753,777, occur only once. Such a skewed distribution is typical for natural language. It is often called a **Zipfian distribution**. On the other hand, we have a few events that are very frequent. The most frequent word bigram *of the* occurs 283,846 times.

long tail

Zipfian distribution

Let us come back to our discussion of empirical and expected counts. According to the table, 753,777 bigrams occur exactly once in the training corpus (half of the entire Europarl corpus). These bigrams occur 353,383 times in the held-out corpus (the other half of the Europarl corpus). Thus, on average, each of these singleton bigrams occurred $\frac{353,383}{753,777} = 0.469$ times. This answers our original question: If an n-gram occurs once in the training corpus, how often do we expect it to occur in a corpus of equal size? It turns out that the answer is 0.469 times in this case.

Bigrams not previously observed in the training corpus occur 938,504 times in the held-out corpus. Since there are 7,515,623,434 distinct unseen n-grams, each of them occurs on average $\frac{938,504}{7515,623,434} = 0.00012$ times.

Adjusting real counts to these expected counts will give us better estimates both for seen and unseen events, and also eliminate the problem of zeros in computing language model probabilities.

By using half of the corpus for validation, we lose it as training data for count collection. But this is easy to remedy. By alternating between training and held-out corpus – meaning we first use one half as training corpus and the other as held-out corpus, and then switch around – we can make use of all the data. We then average the count-of-counts and counts in held-out data that we collect in one direction (N_r^a and T_r^a) with the ones we collect in the other direction (N_r^b and T_r^b):

$$r_{\text{del}} = \frac{T_r^a + T_r^b}{N_r^a + N_r^b} \quad \text{where } r = \text{count}(w_1, ..., w_n)$$

The expected counts are not entirely accurate. They are estimated with only half of the training data. With more training data, for instance, we would expect to encounter fewer unseen n-grams in new data. We can alleviate this by taking 90% of the corpus for training and 10% for validation, or even 99% for training and 1% for validation.

deleted estimation   The name **deleted estimation** for the technique we just described derives from the fact that we leave one part of the training corpus out for validation. How well does deleted estimation work? If you compare the expected counts as computed in Figure 7.5 with the test counts in Figure 7.4, you see that our estimates come very close.

7.2.3 Good–Turing Smoothing

The idea behind all the smoothing methods we have discussed so far is to get a better assessment of what it means that an n-gram occurs c times in a corpus. Based on this evidence, we would like to know how often we expect to find it in the future.

In other words, we need to adjust the actual count to the expected count. This relates to the probability p, the probability we are ultimately trying to estimate from the counts.

Some mathematical analysis (see the detailed derivation below) leads us to a straightforward formula to calculate the expected count r^* from the actual count r and using count-of-counts statistics:

$$r^* = (r + 1)\frac{N_{r+1}}{N_r} \tag{7.18}$$

To apply this formula, we need to collect statistics on how many n-grams occur once in the training corpus (N_1), how many occur twice (N_2), etc., as well as how many n-grams do not occur in the corpus at all (N_0).

See Figure 7.6 for these numbers in the same Europarl corpus we have used so far. Out of a possible $86{,}700^2 = 7{,}516{,}890{,}000$ n-grams, most never occur in the corpus ($N_0 = 7{,}514{,}941{,}065$, to be exact). $N_1 = 1{,}132{,}844$ n-grams occur once in the corpus.

According to Equation (7.18), this leads to an adjusted count for unseen n-grams of $(0 + 1)\frac{N_1}{N_0} = \frac{1{,}132{,}844}{7{,}514{,}941{,}065} = 0.00015$. This is very close to the actual expected count as validated on the test set, which is 0.00016. The other adjusted counts are very adequate as well.

Count r	Count of counts N_r	Adjusted count r^*	Test count t
0	7,514,941,065	0.00015	0.00016
1	1,132,844	0.46539	0.46235
2	263,611	1.40679	1.39946
3	123,615	2.38767	2.34307
4	73,788	3.33753	3.35202
5	49,254	4.36967	4.35234
6	35,869	5.32928	5.33762
8	21,693	7.43798	7.15074
10	14,880	9.31304	9.11927
20	4,546	19.54487	18.95948

Figure 7.6 Good–Turing smoothing: Based on the count-of-counts N_r, the empirical counts are adjusted to $r^* = (r + 1)\dfrac{N_{r+1}}{N_r}$, a fairly accurate count when compared against the test count.

Good–Turing smoothing provides a principled way to adjust counts. It is also fairly simple computationally – all you need to do is collect counts-of-counts on the training corpus.   Good–Turing smoothing

One caveat: The method fails for large r for which frequently $N_r = 0$, or counts-of-counts are simply unreliable. This can be addressed either by curve-fitting the formula or by simply not adjusting the counts for frequent n-grams.

Derivation of Good–Turing smoothing

Since the derivation of Good–Turing smoothing is a bit tricky, we will first introduce a few concepts that will come in handy later.

Each n-gram α occurs with a probability p at any point in the text. In other words, if we pick an n-gram at random out of any text, it is the n-gram α with the probability p. Unfortunately, we do not have access to the true probabilities of n-grams, otherwise things would be much easier (and we would not have to deal with estimating these probabilities).

If we assume that all occurrences of an n-gram α are independent of each other – if it occurs once, it does not affect the fixed probability p of it occurring again – then the number of times it will occur in a corpus of size N follows the binomial distribution

$$p(c(\alpha) = r) = b(r; N, p_i) = \binom{N}{r} p^r (1 - p)^{N-r} \qquad (7.19)$$

The goal of Good–Turing smoothing is to compute the *expected count* c^* for n-grams, versus the *empirical count* c that we observe in a fixed training corpus. The expected count of an n-gram α follows from (7.19) pretty straightforwardly:

$$E(c^*(\alpha)) = \sum_{r=0}^{N} r\, p(c(\alpha) = r)$$

$$= \sum_{r=0}^{N} r \binom{N}{r} p^r (1 - p)^{N-r} \qquad (7.20)$$

As noted before, we do not have access to the true probability p of the n-gram α, so we cannot use this simple formula. So, we have to find another way.

Before we get to this, let us introduce another useful concept, the expected number of n-grams that occur with a certain frequency r, which we denote by $E_N(N_r)$. If we have a finite number s of n-grams that we denote by $\alpha_1, ..., \alpha_s$ that occur with respective probabilities $p_1, ..., p_s$, then each of them may occur with frequency r, so the overall expected number of such n-grams is

$$E_N(N_r) = \sum_{i=1}^{s} p(c(\alpha_i) = r)$$

$$= \sum_{i=1}^{s} \binom{N}{r} p_i^r (1 - p_i)^{N-r} \tag{7.21}$$

Again, we cannot compute this number because we do not have access to the n-gram probabilities p_i, but we actually have a pretty good idea of how many n-grams occur r times in a corpus of N n-grams. This is exactly what we counted previously (see for instance Figure 7.5 on page 191). While of course these counts collected over a large corpus N_r are not the same as true expected counts $E_N(N_r)$, we can still claim that $E_N(N_r) \simeq N_r$, at least for small r.

Let us now move to the derivation of Good–Turing smoothing. Recall that our goal is to compute expected counts c^* for n-grams, based on the actual counts c. Or, to put this into mathematical terms:

$$E(c^*(\alpha)|c(\alpha) = r) \tag{7.22}$$

Let us say for the sake of this mathematical argument that we do not know much about the n-gram α, except that it occurred r times in the training corpus of N n-grams. It may be any of the s n-grams $\alpha_1, ..., \alpha_s$; we do not even know which one.

So we adapt the formula in Equation (7.20) to:

$$E(c^*(\alpha)|c(\alpha) = r) = \sum_{i=1}^{s} N \, p_i \, p(\alpha = \alpha_i | c(\alpha) = r) \tag{7.23}$$

Each n-gram α_i occurs with probability p_i, but we are only interested in it to the degree with which we believe it is our n-gram α, of which we only know that it occurs r times in the training corpus.

Any of the n-grams α_i may occur r times in a corpus with N n-grams, but some more likely than others, depending on its occurrence probability p_i. Devoid of any additional knowledge, we can say that

$$p(\alpha = \alpha_i | c(\alpha) = r) = \frac{p(c(\alpha_i) = r)}{\sum_{j=1}^{s} p(c(\alpha_j) = r)} \tag{7.24}$$

Let us put Equations (7.23) and (7.24) together, and check what we have so far:

$$
\begin{aligned}
E(c^*(\alpha)|c(\alpha) = r) &= \sum_{i=1}^{s} N\, p_i \, \frac{p(c(\alpha_i) = r)}{\sum_{j=1}^{s} p(c(\alpha_j) = r)} \\
&= \frac{\sum_{i=1}^{s} N\, p_i \, p(c(\alpha_i) = r)}{\sum_{j=1}^{s} p(c(\alpha_j) = r)}
\end{aligned}
\tag{7.25}
$$

Eyeballing this formula, we quickly recognize that the denominator is the formula for $E_N(N_r)$ (see Equation 7.21), for which we claim to have reliable estimates. The numerator is not too different from that either, so we can massage it a bit:

$$
\begin{aligned}
\sum_{i=1}^{s} N\, p_i \, p(c(\alpha_i) = r) &= \sum_{i=1}^{s} N\, p_i \binom{N}{r} p_i^{r} (1 - p_i)^{N-r} \\
&= \sum_{i=1}^{s} N \, \frac{N!}{N-r!\, r!} p_i^{r+1}(1 - p_i)^{N-r} \\
&= \sum_{i=1}^{s} N \, \frac{(r+1)}{N+1} \frac{N+1!}{N-r!\, r+1!} p_i^{r+1}(1 - p_i)^{N-r} \\
&= (r+1) \frac{N}{N+1} E_{N+1}(N_{r+1}) \\
&\simeq (r+1)\, E_{N+1}(N_{r+1})
\end{aligned}
\tag{7.26}
$$

Putting this back into Equation (7.25) gives us the formula for Good–Turing smoothing (recall Equation 7.18 on page 192)

$$
\begin{aligned}
r^* &= E(c^*(\alpha)|c(\alpha) = r) \\
&= \frac{(r+1)\, E_{N+1}(N_{r+1})}{E_N(N_r)} \\
&\simeq (r+1)\frac{N_{r+1}}{N_r}
\end{aligned}
\tag{7.27}
$$

7.2.4 Evaluation

To conclude this section on count smoothing, we use all of the methods we have just described to build bigram language models and check how well they work. We adjust the counts according to the different methods, and then use these counts to estimate bigram probabilities

$$
p(w_2|w_1) = \frac{\text{count}(w_1, w_2)}{\sum_i \text{count}(w_1, w_i)}
\tag{7.28}
$$

Since we smoothed out all zero-counts, all bigram probabilities $p(w_2|w_1)$ are positive. Given these probabilities, we can measure the quality of the resulting language models by computing their perplexity on the held-out test set. This is the same test set we used to compute test counts.

Figure 7.7 Evaluation of count smoothing methods: Perplexity for language models trained on the Europarl corpus. Add-α smoothing is optimized on the test set.

Smoothing method	Perplexity
Add-one	383.2
Add-α ($\alpha = 0.00017$)	113.2*
Deleted estimation	113.4
Good–Turing	112.9

Results are given in Figure 7.7. Besides add-one smoothing, which gives too much probability mass to unseen events, all smoothing methods have similar performance, with Good–Turing smoothing coming out slightly ahead. The results for add-α smoothing are unrealistically good, since we optimized the value $\alpha = 0.00017$ on the set we are are testing on.

The small difference between deleted estimation and Good–Turing is partly due to the way we applied deleted estimation. Estimating and validating counts on half the corpus is less reliable than taking the whole corpus into account.

7.3 Interpolation and Back-off

We have already argued that higher order n-grams allow the consideration of a larger context and lead to better language models (see Figure 7.3 on page 186). However, given limited training data, many fluent n-grams of higher order will not be observed.

For instance, we may never observe the two alternative n-grams

- *Scottish beer drinkers*
- *Scottish beer eaters*

if our training corpus hardly mentions *Scottish beer*.

Note that these alternatives may arise if we translate from a foreign language which has a word that equally likely translates to *drinkers* and *eaters*. Our hope is that the language model will aid us in the decision that *drinkers* is the preferred translation in this context.

In the previous section we discuss methods that assign positive probabilities to n-grams with zero count. However, these methods treat all n-grams with the same count the same, and hence make no distinction between the two alternative n-grams above.

In our example, the additional context of *Scottish* adds little valuable information; it just causes a sparse data problem. Hence in this case, we would prefer to only use a bigram language model that draws the distinction between the alternatives

- *beer drinkers*
- *beer eaters*

for which we more likely have evidence in the corpus.

7.3.1 Interpolation

Higher order n-grams may provide valuable additional context, but lower order n-grams are more robust. The idea of **interpolation** is to combine lower order and higher order n-gram language models.

interpolation

We first build n-gram language models p_n for several orders (say $n = 1, 2, 3$), as described in the previous section. This may include Good–Turing smoothing or other count adjusting smoothing techniques, but we may also simply rely on the interpolation with lower order n-grams to remedy zero counts.

Then, we build an interpolated language model p_I by linear combination of the language models p_n:

$$p_I(w_3|w_1, w_2) = \lambda_1\, p_1(w_3)$$
$$\times \lambda_2\, p_2(w_3|w_2)$$
$$\times \lambda_3\, p_3(w_3|w_1, w_2) \qquad (7.29)$$

Each n-gram language model p_n contributes its assessment, which is weighted by a factor λ_n. With a lot of training data, we can trust the higher order language models more and assign them higher weights.

To ensure that the interpolated language model p_I is a proper probability distribution, we require that

$$\forall \lambda_n : 0 \le \lambda_n \le 1$$
$$\sum_n \lambda_n = 1 \qquad (7.30)$$

We are left with the task of deciding how much weight is given to the unigram language model (λ_1), and how much is given to the bigram (λ_2) and trigram (λ_3). This may be done by optimizing these parameters on a held-out set.

7.3.2 Recursive Interpolation

Recall that the idea behind interpolating different order n-gram language models is that we would like to use higher order n-gram language models if we have sufficient evidence, but otherwise we rely on the lower order n-gram models.

It is useful to change Equation (7.29) into a definition of **recursive interpolation**:

recursive interpolation

$$p_n^I(w_i|w_{i-n+1}, ..., w_{i-1}) = \lambda_{w_{i-n+1},...,w_{i-1}} p_n(w_i|w_{i-n+1}, ..., w_{i-1})$$
$$+ (1 - \lambda_{w_{i-n+1},...,w_{i-1}}) p_{n-1}^I(w_i|w_{i-n+2}, ..., w_{i-1}) \qquad (7.31)$$

The λ parameters set the degree of how much we trust the n-gram language model p_n, or if we would rather back off to a lower order model. We may want to make this depend on a particular history $w_{i-n+1}, ..., w_{i-1}$. For instance, if we have seen this history many times before, we are more inclined to trust its prediction.

It is possible to optimize the λ parameters on a held-out training set using EM training. In practice, we do not want to learn for each history a different λ parameter, since this would require large amounts of held-out data. Hence, we may group histories into buckets, for instance based on their frequency in the corpus.

7.3.3 Back-off

We initially motivated smoothing by the need to address the problem of unseen n-grams. If we have seen an n-gram, we can estimate probabilities for word predictions. Otherwise, it seems to be a good idea to back off to lower order n-grams with richer statistics.

back-off   This idea leads us to a recursive definition of **back-off**:

$$p_n^{BO}(w_i|w_{i-n+1}, ..., w_{i-1})$$

$$= \begin{cases} d_n(w_{i-n+1}, ..., w_{i-1})\, p_n(w_i|w_{i-n+1}, ..., w_{i-1}) \\ \qquad \text{if count}_n(w_{i-n+1}, ..., w_i) > 0 \\ \alpha_n(w_{i-n+1}, ..., w_{i-1})\, p_{n-1}^{BO}(w_i|w_{i-n+2}, ..., w_{i-1}) \\ \qquad \text{else} \end{cases} \qquad (7.32)$$

We build a back-off language model p_n^{BO} from the raw language models p_n. If we have seen an n-gram (count(...) > 0), we use the raw language model probability, otherwise we back off to the lower order back-off p_{n-1}^{BO}.

Since we have to ensure that overall probabilities add up to 1 for a history $w_{i-n+1}, ..., w_{i-1}$, we introduce a discounting function d. Probabilities from the raw language model p_n are discounted by a factor $0 \le d \le 1$, and the remaining probability mass is given to the back-off model.

The discounting function d is conditioned on the history of the n-gram. One idea is to group histories based on their frequency in the corpus. If we have seen the history very frequently, we would trust predictions based on this history more, and therefore set a fairly high value for $d_n(w_1, ..., w_{n-1})$. On the other hand, for rare histories, we assume that we have seen only a small fraction of possible predicted words w_n, and therefore give more weight to the back-off, resulting in a lower value for d.

Another way to compute the discounting parameters d is to employ Good–Turing smoothing. This reduces the counts and the remaining probability mass is given to the α parameters.

7.3.4 Diversity of Predicted Words

Witten and Bell [1991] turn our attention to the diversity of words that follow a history. Consider the bigram histories *spite* and *constant*. Both words occur 993 times in the Europarl corpus. Any smoothing method that is based on this count alone would treat these histories the same.

The word *spite* occurs 993 times in the corpus, but we observe only nine different words that follow it. In fact, it is almost always followed by *of* (979 times), due to the common expression *in spite of*. Words such as *yours* (three times) or *towards* (two times) also follow *spite*, but this is rather exceptional.

Contrast this with the word *constant*, which also occurs 993 times in the corpus. However, we find 415 different words that follow it. Some stand out – *and* (42 times), *concern* (27 times), *pressure* (26 times) – but there is a huge tail of words that are seen only once after *constant*, to be precise 268 different words.

How likely is it to encounter a previously unseen bigram that starts with *spite* versus one that starts with *constant*? In the case of *spite* this would be highly unusual. In the case of *constant*, we would not be very surprised. **Witten–Bell smoothing** takes the diversity of possible extensions of a history into account.

Witten–Bell smoothing

When defining Witten–Bell smoothing we follow the template of recursive interpolation (recall Equation 7.31). First, let us define the number of possible extensions of a history $w_1, ..., w_{i-1}$ seen in the training data as

$$N_{1+}(w_1, ..., w_{n-1}, \bullet) = |\{w_n : c(w_1, ..., w_{n-1}, w_n) > 0\}| \quad (7.33)$$

Based on this, we define the lambda parameters in Equation (7.31) as

$$1 - \lambda_{w_1,...,w_{n-1}} = \frac{N_{1+}(w_1, ..., w_{n-1}, \bullet)}{N_{1+}(w_1, ..., w_{n-1}, \bullet) + \sum_{w_n} c(w_1, ..., w_{n-1}, w_n)} \quad (7.34)$$

Let us apply this to our two examples:

$$1 - \lambda_{\text{spite}} = \frac{N_{1+}(\text{spite}, \bullet)}{N_{1+}(\text{spite}, \bullet) + \sum_{w_n} c(\text{spite}, w_n)}$$

$$= \frac{9}{9 + 993} = 0.00898$$

$$\quad (7.35)$$

$$1 - \lambda_{\text{constant}} = \frac{N_{1+}(\text{constant}, \bullet)}{N_{1+}(\text{constant}, \bullet) + \sum_{w_n} c(\text{constant}, w_n)}$$

$$= \frac{415}{415 + 993} = 0.29474$$

The lambda values follow our intuition about how much weight should be given to the back-off model. For *spite*, we give it little weight

(0.00898), indicating that we have a good idea of what follows this word. For *constant*, we reserve much more probability mass for unseen events (0.29474).

Another informative example is a history that occurs only once. Here we set the lambda parameter to $\frac{1}{1+1} = 0.5$, also allowing for the high likelihood of unseen events.

7.3.5 Diversity of Histories

To conclude our review of smoothing methods, we add one more consideration, which will lead us to the most commonly used smoothing method today, **Kneser–Ney smoothing** [Kneser and Ney, 1995].

Consider the role of the lower order n-gram models in the back-off models we have discussed so far. We rely on them if the history of higher order language models is rare or otherwise inconclusive. So, we may want to build the lower order n-gram models that fit this specific role.

The word *york* is a fairly frequent word in the Europarl corpus, it occurs there 477 times (as frequent as *foods*, *indicates* and *providers*). So, in a unigram language model, it would be given a respectable probability. However, when it occurs, it almost always directly follows *new* (473 times), forming the name of the American city New York. So, we expect *york* to be very likely after we have seen *new*, but otherwise it is a very rare word – it occurs otherwise only in rare mentions of the English city York: *in york* (once), *to york* (once) and *of york* (twice).

Recall that the unigram model is only used if the bigram model is inconclusive. We do not expect *york* much as the second word in unseen bigrams. So, in a back-off unigram model, we would want to give the word *york* much less probability than its raw count suggests.

In other words, we want to take the **diversity of histories** into account. To this end, we define the count of histories for a word as

$$N_{1+}(\bullet w) = |\{w_i : c(w_i, w) > 0\}| \qquad (7.36)$$

Recall that the usual maximum likelihood estimation of a unigram language model is

$$p_{\text{ML}}(w) = \frac{c(w)}{\sum_i c(w_i)} \qquad (7.37)$$

In Kneser–Ney smoothing, we replace the raw counts with the count of histories for a word:

$$p_{\text{KN}}(w) = \frac{N_{1+}(\bullet w)}{\sum_{w_i} N_{1+}(\bullet w_i)} \qquad (7.38)$$

To come back to our example, instead of using the raw count of 477 for the word *york*, we now use the much lower count of four different

Kneser–Ney smoothing

diversity of histories

one-word histories. Contrast this with the equally frequent *indicates*, which occurs with 172 different one-word histories. Basing probabilities on the counts of histories results in a much higher unigram back-off probability for *indicates* than for *york*.

7.3.6 Modified Kneser–Ney Smoothing

We have argued for the interpolation of higher order n-gram models with lower order n-gram models. We have discussed methods that assign proper probability mass to each, and how the component n-gram models should be built. Now we have to put everything together.

First of all, let us combine the ideas behind interpolation and back-off and redefine our interpolation function as:

$$p_I(w_n|w_1, ..., w_{n-1})$$

$$= \begin{cases} \alpha(w_n|w_1, ..., w_{n-1}) & \text{if } c(w_1, ..., w_n) > 0 \\ \gamma(w_1, ..., w_{n-1}) \, p_I(w_n|w_2, ..., w_{n-1}) & \text{otherwise} \end{cases}$$

$$(7.39)$$

Two functions are involved. For each n-gram in the corpus, we have a function α that relates to its probability. For each history, we have a function γ that relates to the probability mass reserved for unseen words following this history.

This formulation of interpolated back-off will guide us now in our definition of modified Kneser–Ney smoothing below.

Formula for α for highest order n-gram model
Chen and Goodman [1998] suggest a modified version of Kneser–Ney smoothing, which uses a method called **absolute discounting** to reduce the probability mass for seen events. For $c(w_1, ..., w_n) > 0$, absolute discounting implies we subtract a fixed value D with $0 \le D \le 1$ from the raw counts for the highest order n-gram model:

absolute discounting

$$\alpha(w_n|w_1, ..., w_{n-1}) = \frac{c(w_1, ..., w_n) - D}{\sum_w c(w_1, ..., w_{n-1}, w)} \qquad (7.40)$$

Chen and Goodman [1998] argue that better results can be achieved by subtracting not a fixed value D from each n-gram count, but the discounting value should depend on the n-gram count itself. They suggest using three different discount values:

$$D(c) = \begin{cases} D_1 & \text{if } c = 1 \\ D_2 & \text{if } c = 2 \\ D_{3+} & \text{if } c \ge 3 \end{cases} \qquad (7.41)$$

It turns out that optimal discounting parameters D_1, D_2, D_{3+} can be computed quite easily:

$$Y = \frac{N_1}{N_1 + 2N_2}$$

$$D_1 = 1 - 2Y\frac{N_2}{N_1}$$

$$D_2 = 2 - 3Y\frac{N_3}{N_2} \tag{7.42}$$

$$D_{3+} = 3 - 4Y\frac{N_4}{N_3}$$

The values N_c are the counts of n-grams with exactly count c. Compare the discounting formulae for D_i to Good–Turing smoothing, which we discussed in Section 7.2.3 on page 192. Alternatively, the D_i parameter can be optimized using held-out data.

Formula for γ for highest order n-gram model

The probability mass we set aside through discounting is available for unseen events, which leads to a very straightforward definition of the γ function:

$$\gamma(w_1, ..., w_{n-1}) = \frac{\sum_{i \in \{1,2,3+\}} D_i N_i(w_1, ..., w_{n-1}\bullet)}{\sum_{w_n} c(w_1, ..., w_n)} \tag{7.43}$$

where the N_i for $i \in \{1, 2, 3+\}$ are computed based on the count of extensions of a history $w_1, ..., w_{n-1}$ with count 1, 2, and 3 or more, respectively.

We subtracted D_1 from each n-gram with count 1, so we have D_1 times the number of n-grams with count 1 available for γ, and so on. Note that the formula for γ resembles the formula we derived for Witten–Bell smoothing (Section 7.3.4 on page 199) where we argued for taking the diversity of predicted words into account, and not just basing the discounted probability mass on the frequency of a history.

Formula for α for lower order n-gram models

We argued that for lower order n-grams it is better to base the estimation of the probability distribution on the count of histories $N_{1+}(\bullet w)$ in which a word may appear, instead of the raw counts.

This leads us to change the formula for computing α for lower order n-gram models slightly from Equation (7.38) to

$$\alpha(w_n|w_1, ..., w_{n-1}) = \frac{N_{1+}(\bullet w_1, ..., w_n) - D}{\sum_w N_{1+}(\bullet w_1, ..., w_{n-1}, w)} \tag{7.44}$$

Again, we use three different values for D (D_1, D_2, D_{3+}), estimated as specified in Equation (7.42), based on the count of the history $w_1, ..., w_{n-1}$.

Formula for γ for lower order n-gram models

As for the highest order n-gram model, the probability mass that was set aside by discounting the observed counts is available for the γ function:

$$\gamma(w_1, ..., w_{n-1}) = \frac{\sum_{i \in \{1,2,3+\}} D_i N_i(w_1, ..., w_{n-1} \bullet)}{\sum_{w_n} c(w_1, ..., w_n)} \qquad (7.45)$$

Interpolated back-off

The back-off models we defined rely on the highest order n-gram that matches the history and predicted words. If these are sparse, they may be not very reliable. If two different n-grams with the same history occur once in the training data, we assign their predicted words the same probability. However, one may be an outlier, and the other an under-representative sample of a relatively common occurrence. Keep in mind that if a history is not very frequent, then the observed n-grams with that history are sparse counts.

To remedy this, we may always consider the lower order back-off models, even if we have seen the n-gram. We can do this simply by adapting the α function into an interpolated α_I function by adding the back-off probability:

$$\alpha_I(w_n|w_1, ..., w_{n-1}) = \alpha(w_n|w_1, ..., w_{n-1})$$
$$+ \gamma(w_1, ..., w_{n-1}) \, p_I(w_n|w_2, ..., w_{n-1}) \qquad (7.46)$$

Note that the values for the γ function need to be reduced accordingly.

7.3.7 Evaluation

Figure 7.8 compares the smoothing methods we described in this section. The figure shows perplexity results for different order n-gram language models, trained on the Europarl corpus. The increasingly sophisticated smoothing methods result in better (lower) perplexity.

Good–Turing smoothing is used here as a back-off method. Probability mass for unseen events is reserved for the lower order language model, which is estimated the same way.

Modified Kneser–Ney smoothing and especially the interpolated variant leads to lower perplexity, by about 5–10%. There is also a great

Smoothing method	Bigram	Trigram	4-gram
Good–Turing	96.2	62.9	59.9
Witten–Bell	97.1	63.8	60.4
Modified Kneser–Ney	95.4	61.6	58.6
Interpolated modified Kneser–Ney	94.5	59.3	54.0

Figure 7.8 Evaluation of smoothing methods: Perplexity for language models trained on the Europarl corpus.

benefit from using larger n-grams. Overall, the 4-gram interpolated modified Kneser–Ney language model has nearly half the perplexity of the bigram Good–Turing language model.

7.4 Managing the Size of the Model

Fortunately, we have access to vast quantities of monolingual text for many languages, especially English, and their use has been shown to be beneficial in statistical machine translation systems, especially if they cover a domain similar to the test data.

Parallel texts often contain tens to hundreds of millions of words of English. A Gigaword corpus of several billion words is available through the Linguistic Data Consortium (LDC). It is also not too hard to write a web crawler that downloads even more text, up to trillions of English words.

On the other hand, using language models trained on such large corpora in a machine translation decoder becomes a challenge. Once the language model no longer fits into the working memory of the machine, we have to resort to clever methods to manage the size of the models. This final section of the chapter will discuss such methods.

7.4.1 Number of Unique N-Grams

First, let us get a sense of the size of language models. How many distinct n-grams can we find in a large corpus? Figure 7.9 has some numbers for the Europarl corpus. This corpus of 29,501,088 words has 86,700 unique English words (including punctuation as well as beginning-of-sentence and end-of-sentence markers). This number is vocabulary size   also referred to as the **vocabulary size**.

Given this vocabulary size, $86{,}700^2 = 7{,}516{,}890{,}000$, about 7.5 billion, bigrams are possible. However, we find only about 2 million distinct bigrams in the corpus. Not every sequence of two words that is possible actually occurs in English text, which is more or less the point of n-gram language models.

Figure 7.9 Number of unique n-grams in the English part of the Europarl corpus, which comprises 29,501,088 tokens (words and punctuation).

Order	Unique n-grams	Singletons
unigram	86,700	33,447 (38.6%)
bigram	1,948,935	1,132,844 (58.1%)
trigram	8,092,798	6,022,286 (74.4%)
4-gram	15,303,847	13,081,621 (85.5%)
5-gram	19,882,175	18,324,577 (92.2%)

For larger n-grams, the count seems to be more constrained by the actual corpus size. We find that about every second 4-gram is unique in the corpus. While the number of possible n-grams is polynomial with vocabulary size, the number is also bound to be linear with the corpus size. Check Figure 7.9 again. The number of unique n-grams grows rapidly from 86,700 unigrams to 1,948,935 bigrams. But for the highest order the growth stalls; there are not many more unique 5-grams than unique 4-grams: 19,882,175 vs. 15,303,847. But then, the corpus size is 29,501,088, which is an upper limit on the number of unique n-grams.

Most of the unique higher order n-grams are **singletons**, i.e., they occur only once. For 5-grams, the ratio of singletons is 92.2%. Since there is diminishing value in such rarely occurring events, higher order singletons are often excluded from language model estimation, typically starting with trigrams.

singletons

7.4.2 Estimation on Disk

The first challenge is to *build* a language model that is too large to fit into the working memory of the computer. However, none of the estimation and smoothing methods require that everything is stored in memory.

Consider the maximum likelihood estimation of a conditional probability distribution. Given a history, we need to sum over all possible word predictions. So, we need to loop twice over the n-grams with a shared history: once to get their counts, and then – given the total count – to estimate their probability. To avoid reading n-gram counts from disk twice, we may want to store all n-grams with a shared history in memory. After writing out the estimated probabilities, we can delete the respective n-grams and their counts from the working memory. The number of n-grams we have to keep in memory at any time is bounded by the vocabulary size.

To enable such **estimation on disk** we need a file of all n-grams with counts, sorted by their histories. This can be done – again, on disk – by first going through the corpus and writing all occurring n-grams into a file, and then sorting it by history and collecting counts. Standard UNIX tools (`sort`, `uniq`) are available to do this very efficiently.

estimation on disk

Smoothing methods require additional statistics. For Good–Turing discounting, we need the counts of counts, i.e. how many n-grams occur once, how many occur twice, etc. These statistics are obtained straightforwardly from the n-gram count file.

Kneser–Ney smoothing requires additional statistics on the number of distinct predicted words for a given history, and the number of distinct histories for a given word. The latter requires an n-gram count file, sorted by predicted word, but again these statistics can be obtained by linearly processing sorted n-gram count files.

7.4.3 Efficient Data Structures

We need to store large language models both memory-efficiently and in a way that allows us to retrieve probabilities in a time-efficient manner.

trie   Typically, this is done using a data structure known as a **trie**.

Consider the following: We want to store the 4-gram probabilities for *the very large majority* and for *the very large number*. They share the history *the very large*, so we would like to store the probabilities for the two 4-grams without storing the histories twice. Even *the very big event* shares the first two words in the history, so we would like to avoid storing the common part of its history separately as well.

Figure 7.10 shows a fragment of a trie that contains language model probabilities. Each word in the history is a node that points to a list of possible extensions, i.e., subsequent words in existing histories. The final node is a table of language model probabilities for all possible predictions given the history of the preceding path.

When we want to look up the probability for an n-gram, we walk through the trie by following the words of the history until we reach the word prediction table, where we look up the language model probability.

In this case, the language model probability is simply the 4-gram probability stored in the language model:

$$p_{\text{LM}}(majority|the\ very\ large) = p_4(majority|the\ very\ large)$$
$$= \exp(-1.147) \tag{7.47}$$

What happens when the 4-gram does not exist in the language model, i.e., when we want to look up the language model probability for *the very large amount*?

Let us state again the back-off formula for interpolated language models (compare with Equation 7.39 on page 201):

$$p_{\text{LM}}(w_n|w_1, ..., w_{n-1})$$
$$= \begin{cases} p_n(w_n|w_1, ..., w_{n-1}) & \text{if } c(w_1, ..., w_n) > 0 \\ \text{backoff}(w_1, ..., w_{n-1})\, p_{\text{LM}}(w_n|w_2, ..., w_{n-1}) & \text{otherwise} \end{cases}$$
$$\tag{7.48}$$

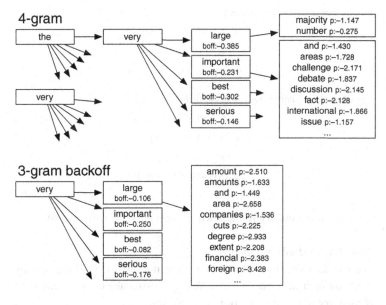

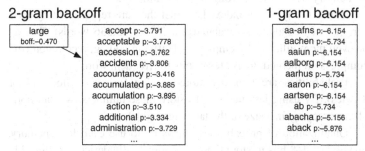

Figure 7.10 Language model probabilities stored in a trie: Starting with the first word of the history, we traverse the trie to the predicted word. If not found, we add a back-off cost and back off to a lower order language model. For instance *the very large amount* does not occur in the 4-gram LM, so we compute its LM probability by adding the back-off cost for *the very large* exp(-0.385) to the trigram language model cost for *very large amount* exp(-2.510).

If we do not find the n-gram in the language model, i.e., $c(w_1, ..., w_n) = 0$, we back off to lower order n-gram statistics. This implies a back-off cost which depends on the history. In the trie data structure, the back-off costs are stored at the penultimate nodes (the end point of the history).

In the case of *the very large amount*, we find probabilities at the trigram order. The language model probability is therefore (see also Figure 7.10):

$$p_{LM}(amount|the\ very\ large) = \text{backoff}(the\ very\ large)$$
$$\times\ p_3(amount|very\ large)$$
$$= \exp(-0.385 + -2.510) \qquad (7.49)$$

If we do not find the n-gram at reduced order, we back off further, incurring back-off costs, until we reach a prediction. See the following two examples which are ultimately resolved as bigram and unigram:

$$p_{LM}(action|the\ very\ large) = backoff(the\ very\ large)$$
$$+ backoff(very\ large)$$
$$+ p_2(action|large)$$
$$= \exp(-0.385 + -0.106 + -3.510)$$

$$p_{LM}(aaron|the\ very\ large) = backoff(the\ very\ large)$$
$$\times backoff(very\ large)$$
$$\times backoff(large)$$
$$\times p_1(aaron)$$
$$= \exp(-0.385 + -0.106 + -0.470 + -6.154)$$
$$(7.50)$$

Note that if the history is unknown, we can back off with no cost.

Fewer bits to store probabilities

The trie data structure allows us to store n-grams more compactly by grouping their histories together. We may also make more efficient use of memory when storing words and probabilities.

Words are typically indexed, so that they are represented by integers (two bytes allow a vocabulary of $2^{16} = 65,536$ words). We can be even more efficient by employing Huffman coding, a common data compression method, to use fewer bits for frequent words.

Probabilities are typically stored in log format as floats (4 or 8 bytes). By using less memory to store these numbers, we can trade off accuracy against size of the language model.

Quantization of probabilities allows us to use even less memory, maybe just 4–8 bits to store these probabilities [Federico and Bertoldi, 2006]. The occurring probability values are grouped into bins, forming a code table. The bin number is stored in the trie data structure, or more specifically, in the word prediction table for a given history.

7.4.4 Reducing Vocabulary Size

We will now look at various ways to cut down on the number of n-grams that need to be stored in memory. First, let us focus on the vocabulary. It is true that there is a somewhat limited number of words that constitute the English language, maybe around 100,000. But if we process large collections of text, we will quickly find that the count of unique tokens easily rises to a multiple of that number.

Names, numbers, misspellings, and random material in the corpus will continually create new tokens. Numbers are an especially fertile source for new tokens in text, since there are infinitely many of them. Since different numbers in text do not behave that differently from each other, we could simply group them all together into a special NUMBER **token**.

However, not all numbers occur in text in the same way. For instance, we may still want to be able to make a distinction in the case:

$$p_{\text{LM}}(\text{I pay 950.00 in May 2007}) > p_{\text{LM}}(\text{I pay 2007 in May 950.00}) \quad (7.51)$$

This would not be possible if we reduced this distinction to

$$p_{\text{LM}}(\text{I pay NUM in May NUM}) = p_{\text{LM}}(\text{I pay NUM in May NUM}) \quad (7.52)$$

A trick that is often applied here is to replace all digits with a unique symbol, such as @, or 5. So we are still able to distinguish between four-digit integers like *2007* (replaced by *5555*), which often follow words like *May*, and fractional numbers like *950.00* (replaced by *555.55*):

$$p_{\text{LM}}(\text{I pay 555.55 in May 5555}) > p_{\text{LM}}(\text{I pay 5555 in May 555.55}) \quad (7.53)$$

In our effort to reduce the vocabulary size for the language model, let us consider how the language model will be used. It is part of an application where one module produces words. A speech recognizer only produces words that are in the vocabulary of recognizable words. Similarly, a machine translation system only produces words that are in the translation table.

When using a language model for these applications, we can safely discard specifics about words that cannot be produced by the system. We may simply replace all **un-producible tokens** with a special token UNKNOWN.

One has to keep in mind the impact of this on various smoothing methods. For instance, Kneser–Ney smoothing is sensitive to the number of *different* words that may occur in a specific position. If we collapse many different words into the same token, we may not be able to count this number correctly anymore.

7.4.5 Extracting Relevant n-Grams

Our concerns about the size of the language model arise from the limitations of modern computers that (currently) have main memories of a few gigabytes. However, modern disk array storage is measured in terabytes, which would fit even the largest collection of English text, so one idea is to keep language models on disk.

While it is possible to build huge language models from corpora such as the Gigaword corpus or data collected from the web, only a fraction of it will be required when translating a particular segment of text. The translation model will produce only a small number of English words, given the foreign input words and the translation tables. At most, we need the probabilities for n-grams that contain only these English words.

Hence, we may want to filter the language model down to the n-grams that are needed for decoding a specific segment of a foreign sentence. The language model on disk may be huge, but the language model needed for decoding and kept in the working memory of the machine is much smaller.

bag-of-words   Figure 7.11 gives some idea of the size of the language model needed for decoding one sentence using the **bag-of-words** approach to language model filtering. When translating one sentence, we consult the phrase translation table and obtain the English words that may be produced by the model. We then restrict the language model to this bag of English words, i.e., we filter out all n-grams that contain at least one word that is not in this bag. Such n-grams could never be requested during decoding, so we can exclude them.

To illustrate this on one example, we examine how many 5-grams are left after bag-of-words filtering. We use the Europarl corpus (about 30 million words). The language model includes all 5-grams that occur at least twice. The test set is taken from the WMT 2006 shared task [Koehn and Monz, 2006], which comes from a held-out portion of the Europarl corpus plus additional News Commentary texts.

For most sentences, filtering limits the ratio of required 5-grams to about 3–5% of the total; some really long sentences of over 80 words in length require more than 10% of all 5-grams. This is still a remarkably

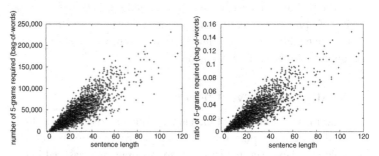

Figure 7.11 Number of 5-grams required to translate one sentence (bag of words approach): This graph plots the sentence length against the number of 5-grams that contain only English words that occur in the translation options, for one sentence each. The right-hand graph displays the ratio of 5-grams required to all 5-grams in the language model (German–English phrase model trained on Europarl, tested on WMT 2006 test set).

high ratio: It means that some 100,000 5-grams include only the few hundred words that are considered during the decoding of one sentence.

7.4.6 Loading N-Grams on Demand

The bag-of-words approach to language model filtering may overestimate the subset of the language model that is needed for decoding. So, it may be preferable to load n-gram statistics only **on demand**. A much   on demand larger set of n-grams could be stored on disk or on a cluster of networked machines.

This raises the question: how many n-gram requests are really made to the language model during decoding? Figure 7.12 answers this question for the example setting we just described.

The number of n-grams grows linearly with the input sentence length, here about 5,000 distinct 5-gram requests are made for each input word that is decoded (the total number of 5-gram requests is about five times this rate). This number depends on the number of translation options (here a maximum of 20 per input phrase), reordering limit (here 6), and stack size of the decoder (here 100).

When we request an n-gram probability, this n-gram may not exist, and the language model backs off to lower order n-grams. Figure 7.13 shows at what order 5-gram requests to the language model are resolved in this experiment. Only 0.75% of 5-gram requests match an existing 5-gram in the model. This is largely due to the nature of the decoding algorithm that produces a lot of nonsensical English word combinations. Most 5-gram requests are resolved as trigrams (24.4%), bigrams (53.0%), or unigrams (16.5%).

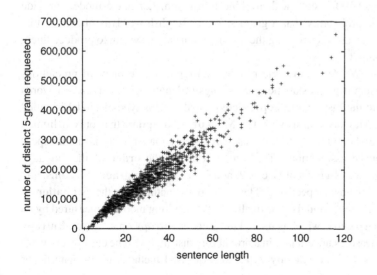

Figure 7.12 Number of distinct 5-gram language model requests: The graph plots the sentence length against the number of distinct 5-gram requests when translating one sentence each.

	5-gram	4-gram	Trigram	Bigram	Unigram
Resolved at order	0.75%	5.3%	24.4%	53.0%	16.5%
Unique resolutions	0.75%	2.1%	4.1%	3.1%	0.1%

Figure 7.13 Resolution of 5-gram decoder requests to the language model. Only a small fraction (0.75%) match a 5-gram in the language model; most often the language model backs off to bigrams (53.0%) or trigrams (24.4%). Hits to lower order n-grams are resolved with a few distinct n-grams; most clearly unigram resolutions end up at only a handful of words. On average, of 1,000 unique 5-gram requests, 165 are resolved as unigrams (16.5%) and hit the same word (0.1%).

Many distinct 5-gram requests that are resolved as, say, bigrams may resolve as the same bigram. For instance, looking up the probabilities for *doll chinese fireworks he says* and *commission fish institution he says* may both be resolved as $p_2(\text{says}|\text{he})$, since the full histories are unknown. This means that even fewer existing n-gram statistics are used than the number of 5,000 distinct n-gram requests per input word suggests. According to the findings, only about 500 distinct n-grams per input word need to be stored (we are ignoring here the storage of back-off histories).

7.5 Summary

7.5.1 Core Concepts

This chapter described the estimation and efficient use of **language models** for statistical machine translation. Language models provide the probability that a given string of English words is uttered in that language, thus helping the machine translation system to produce fluent output.

We decompose the problem into a sequence of word predictions using **n-gram** statistics, i.e., strings of length n. The first $n - 1$ words are the **history** of the **predicted word** n. This type of model is called a **Markov chain**, with the **Markov assumption** that only a limited number of $n - 1$ previous word states matter (this is an independence assumption). The size n is called the **order** of the language model. N-grams of size 1, 2, and 3 are called **unigrams**, **bigrams**, and **trigrams**, respectively. There are many methods for the **estimation of language models**. The quality of the resulting model is measured by its **perplexity**, which is related to its **cross-entropy** on a test set. **Entropy** measures uncertainty in a probability distribution. The entropy per word is called the **entropy rate**. We discussed methods to estimate upper bounds for the **true entropy of a language** L, starting with Shannon's guessing game.

Since we will not observe all possible n-grams in a finite training corpus, we have to deal with the problem of **sparse data**. By **smoothing** the **empirical counts** we mean discounting the actual counts and saving some probability mass for unseen events. Ideally, the discounted counts match **expected counts** of a word given a history. The simplest form of smoothing is **add-one smoothing**, where we add one to any event. Due to the very skewed **Zipfian distribution** of words and n-grams in a natural language, this tends to overestimate unseen events. This can be somewhat alleviated by adding not 1, but a small value α. A more principled way to find estimates for the expected counts is **deleted estimation**, where we use part of the data as training data to count n-grams, and the remaining part to validate the counts by checking how often n-grams of a certain count actually occur. Another way of discounting is **Good–Turing smoothing**, which does not require held-out validation data.

Besides discounting counts in an n-gram model of fixed size n, we may also use **interpolation** to combine higher order n-gram models with lower order n-gram models. In **recursive interpolation**, we assign some weight λ to the higher order n-gram model, and the remaining weight to the interpolated lower order n-gram model. In **back-off** models, we use higher order n-gram models if the history exists with a minimum count, otherwise we back off to the lower order n-gram back-off model. There are several methods for defining the weights given to the higher order and to the lower order back-off model. **Witten–Bell smoothing** takes the diversity of predicted words for a given history into account. **Kneser–Ney smoothing** also considers the diversity of histories of a given predicted word for the estimation of lower order back-off models. Modified Kneser–Ney smoothing uses **absolute discounting**, which subtracts a fixed number D from each observed count (with special handling of counts 1 and 2).

Large monolingual corpora allow the estimation of large language models that do not fit into the working memory of modern computers, but we can resort to **estimation on disk**. Also, using such large language models in a statistical machine translation decoder is a problem. Language model size is often reduced by eliminating **singletons**, i.e., n-grams that occur only once. We can also reduce **vocabulary size** by simplifying numbers and removing words that cannot be generated by the translation model. Language models are stored in an efficient data structure called a **trie**. Efficiency can be further improved by using fewer bits to store word indexes and language model probabilities. When translating a single sentence, the required size of the language model to be stored in memory can be further reduced by **bag-of-words filtering**, or by requesting n-grams **on demand** from disk or a cluster of machines.

7.5.2 Further Reading

Introduction – The discount methods we present in this chapter were proposed by Good [1953] – see also the description by Gale and Sampson [1995] – Witten and Bell [1991], as well as Kneser and Ney [1995]. A good introduction to the topic of language modelling is given by Chen and Goodman [1998]. Instead of training language models, large corpora can also be exploited by checking whether potential translations occur in them as sentences [Soricut *et al.*, 2002].

Targeted language models – Zhao *et al.* [2004a] describe a method for extracting training data for targeted language models based on similarity to the n-best output of a first decoding stage. Hasan and Ney [2005] cluster sentences according to syntactic types (i.e., questions vs. statements), train a separate language model for each cluster and interpolate it with the full language model for coverage.

Use of morphology in language models – Factored language models are also used in statistical machine translation systems [Kirchhoff and Yang, 2005]. For morphologically rich languages, better language models may predict individual morphemes. Sarikaya and Deng [2007] propose a joint morphological-lexical language model that uses maximum entropy classifiers to predict each morpheme.

Using very large language models – Very large language models that require more space than the available working memory may be distributed over a cluster of machines, but may not need sophisticated smoothing methods [Brants *et al.*, 2007]. Alternatively, storing the language model on disk using memory mapping is an option [Federico and Cettolo, 2007]. Methods for quantizing language model probabilities are presented by Federico and Bertoldi [2006], who also examine this for translation model probabilities. Alternatively, lossy data structures such as bloom filters may be used to store very large language models efficiently [Talbot and Osborne, 2007a,b]. Schwenk *et al.* [2006b] introduce continuous space language models that are trained using neural networks. The use of very large language models is often reduced to a re-ranking stage [Olteanu *et al.*, 2006b].

7.5.3 Exercises

1. (⋆) Given the following statistics:

Count of counts statistics:

Count	Count of counts
1	5000
2	1600
3	800
4	500
5	300

The word *beer* occurs as history in three bigrams in the data:

Count	Bigram
4	*beer drinker*
4	*beer lover*
2	*beer glass*

   (a) What are the discounted counts under Good–Turing discounting for the three given bigrams?
   (b) The amounts from discounting counts are given to a back-off unigram model. Using such a back-off model, what are the probabilities for the following bigrams?
       (i) $p(\text{drinker}|\text{beer})$
       (ii) $p(\text{glass}|\text{beer})$
       (iii) $p(\text{mug}|\text{beer})$
   Note: $p(\text{mug}) = 0.01$. State any assumptions that you make.
2. (⋆⋆) Download the SRILM language modeling toolkit[2] and train a language model using the English text from the Europarl corpus[3].
3. (⋆⋆) Some decoding algorithms require the computation of the cheapest context a word or phrase may occur in. Given the ARPA file format used in the SRILM language modeling toolkit, implement a function that computes
   (a) the cost of the cheapest word following a given context;
   (b) the cost of the cheapest context a given word may occur in.
4. (⋆⋆) Implement a program to estimate a language model in a number of steps. You may want to compare the output of your program against the SRILM language modeling toolkit.
   (a) Collect distinct bigrams from a corpus and compute their counts.
   (b) Compute the count of counts.
   (c) Implement Good–Turing discounting for the bigram counts with the unigram model as back-off.

---

[2] Available at http://www.speech.sri.com/projects/srilm/
[3] Available at http://www.statmt.org/europarl/

(d) Make this program flexible, so it works with arbitrary n-gram sizes (e.g., trigram with bigram and unigram as back-off).

(e) Implement Kneser–Ney discounting.

(f) Implement interpolated Kneser–Ney discounting.

(g) Use the language model to generate random English sentences.

5. (★★★) Adapt your language model estimation program so that it works efficiently with on-disk data files and minimal use of RAM.

Chapter 8
Evaluation

How good are statistical machine translation systems today? This simple question is very hard to answer. In contrast to other natural language tasks, such as speech recognition, there is no single right answer that we can expect a machine translation system to match. If you ask several different translators to translate one sentence, you will receive several different answers.

Figure 8.1 illustrates this quite clearly for a short Chinese sentence. All ten translators came up with different translations for the sentence. This example from a 2001 NIST evaluation set is typical: translators almost never agree on a translation, even for a short sentence.

So how should we evaluate machine translation quality? We may ask human annotators to judge the quality of translations. Or, we may compare the similarity of the output of a machine translation system with translations generated by human translators. But ultimately, machine translation is not an end in itself. So, we may want to consider how much machine-translated output helps people to accomplish a task, e.g., get the salient information from a foreign-language text, or post-edit machine translation output for publication.

This chapter presents a variety of evaluation methods that have been used in the machine translation community. **Machine translation evaluation** is currently a very active field of research, and a hotly debated issue.

machine translation evaluation

Figure 8.1 Ten different translations of the same Chinese sentence (a typical example from the 2001 NIST evaluation set).

这个 机场 的 安全 工作 由 以色列 方面 负责 .
Israeli officials are responsible for airport security.
Israel is in charge of the security at this airport.
The security work for this airport is the responsibility of the Israel government.
Israeli side was in charge of the security of this airport.
Israel is responsible for the airport's security.
Israel is responsible for safety work at this airport.
Israel presides over the security of the airport.
Israel took charge of the airport security.
The safety of this airport is taken charge of by Israel.
This airport's security is the responsibility of the Israeli security officials.

8.1 Manual Evaluation

An obvious method for evaluating machine translation output is to look at the output and judge by hand whether it is correct or not. Bilingual evaluators who understand both the input and output language are best qualified to make this judgment. Such bilingual evaluators are not always available, so we often have to resort to monolingual evaluators who understand only the target language but are able to judge system
reference translation   output when given a **reference translation**.

Typically, such evaluation is done sentence by sentence, but a longer document context may be essential to carry out the judgments. For instance, the resolution of pronouns may only be faithfully evaluated in context.

8.1.1 Fluency and Adequacy

Manual evaluations using a harsh correctness standard – is the translation perfect or not? – have been done, although usually only on short sentences, where there is a reasonable chance that no mistakes are made by the machine translation system. A more common approach is to use a graded scale when eliciting judgments from the human evaluators.

Moreover, correctness may be too broad a measure. It is therefore more common to use the two criteria fluency and adequacy:

fluency   **Fluency:** Is the output good fluent English? This involves both grammatical correctness and idiomatic word choices.

adequacy   **Adequacy:** Does the output convey the same meaning as the input sentence? Is part of the message lost, added, or distorted?

See Figure 8.2 for an example from an evaluation tool that elicits fluency and adequacy judgments from a human annotator. The annotator is given the following definitions of adequacy and fluency:

Adequacy	
5	all meaning
4	most meaning
3	much meaning
2	little meaning
1	none

Fluency	
5	flawless English
4	good English
3	non-native English
2	disfluent English
1	incomprehensible

These definitions are very vague, and it is difficult for evaluators to be consistent in their application. Also, some evaluators may generally be more lenient when assigning scores (say, giving an average of 4) than others (say, giving an average of 2).

For example, in the evaluation presented by Koehn and Monz [2005] the average fluency judgement per judge ranged from 2.33 to 3.67, the average adequacy judgement per judge ranged from 2.56 to 4.13. See also Figure 8.3 for the judgments given out by the five most prolific judges (over 1000 judgments each).

We would therefore like to **normalize** the judgments. Ideally, all evaluators use scores around the same average. The average $\bar{x}$ of a set of judgments $\{x_1, ..., x_n\}$ is defined as

normalizing evaluations

$$\bar{x} = \frac{1}{n} \sum_{i=1}^{n} x_i \tag{8.1}$$

If we want all judges to have the same average, say 3, then we need to adjust the individual scores x_i by adding in an adjustment value $3 - \bar{x}$. We may also adjust the variance of scores in the same way.

Judge Sentence

You have already judged 14 of 3064 sentences, taking 86.4 seconds per sentence.

Source: les deux pays constituent plutôt un laboratoire nécessaire au fonctionnement interne de l'ue .

Reference: rather , the two countries form a laboratory needed for the internal working of the eu .

Translation	Adequacy	Fluency
both countries are rather a necessary laboratory the internal operation of the eu .	1 2 3 4 5	1 2 3 4 5
both countries are a necessary laboratory at internal functioning of the eu .	1 2 3 4 5	1 2 3 4 5
the two countries are rather a laboratory necessary for the internal workings of the eu .	1 2 3 4 5	1 2 3 4 5
the two countries are rather a laboratory for the internal workings of the eu .	1 2 3 4 5	1 2 3 4 5
the two countries are rather a necessary laboratory internal workings of the eu .	1 2 3 4 5	1 2 3 4 5
Annotator: Philipp Koehn **Task:** WMT06 French-English		Annotate
Instructions	5= All Meaning 4= Most Meaning 3= Much Meaning 2= Little Meaning 1= None	5= Flawless English 4= Good English 3= Non-native English 2= Disfluent English 1= Incomprehensible

Figure 8.2 Evaluation tool to elicit judgments of translation quality: Five different system outputs are presented, to be scored on a scale of 1–5 for fluency (good English) and adequacy (correct meaning).

Figure 8.3 Histograms of adequacy judgments by different human evaluators in the WMT 2006 evaluation: Different evaluators use the scale 1–5 in remarkably different ways. The same is true for fluency judgments.

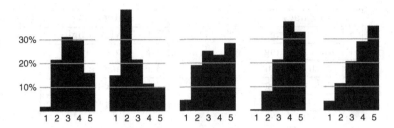

Judging adequacy is tricky. The human mind is quite adept at filling in missing information. Consider the following: If you first read the system output, you may be very puzzled by its meaning, which only becomes clear after reading the reference translation (or input sentence). But if you first read the reference or input sentence and then read the system output, you may not notice that the system output is very garbled and may come to the conclusion that the gist of the meaning can be found in there. The latter may also be the case if you have sufficient domain knowledge that helps you understand the meaning the sentence.

Recent evaluation campaigns have shown that judgments of fluency and adequacy are closely related. This may be not completely surprising, since a sentence in garbled English typically also carries less meaning. But this may also point to the difficulty that humans have in distinguishing the two criteria.

ranking translations   Instead of judging fluency and adequacy on an absolute scale, it is typically easier to **rank** two or more systems against each other on a sentence-by-sentence basis. In the case of two systems, the question *Is system output A better than system output B, or worse, or indistinguishable?* is typically answered by human evaluators in a more consistent manner than questions about adequacy or fluency.

8.1.2 Goals for Evaluation

Before we move on to other evaluation metrics, let us review what we expect from such a metric.

low-cost metric   From a practical point of view, a metric should have **low cost**; i.e., it should be possible to quickly and cheaply carry out evaluations of a new system, of a new domain, etc. Cost is the major disadvantage of evaluation metrics that include human evaluators, especially bilingual evaluators. Cost may be measured in time or money spent on the evaluation. Fully automatic metrics may be **tunable**, i.e., directly used in the automatic system optimization.

meaningful metric   For an evaluation metric to rank systems against each other is useful, but ideally we would like to have a **meaningful** metric. Recall that the leading question of this chapter was *How good is statistical machine translation today?* Does an adequacy score of 3.5 really answer that, or does it say more about the leniency of the evaluator?

Moreover, we want an evaluation metric to be **consistent**. Consistency should be maintained across many dimensions. Different evaluators using the same metric should come to the same conclusions. This is called **inter-annotator agreement**. But we would also like the evaluation on one part of the test corpus to be consistent with the evaluation on another part. If there is high fluctuation, i.e., the metric is not **stable**, this means that we need large test corpora to ensure that the results are reliable.

consistent metric

inter-annotator agreement

stable metric

Finally, we want an evaluation metric to come up with the **correct** result. Here, unfortunately we are missing one essential element. We can compare outcomes from one evaluation metric against another, but there is no real ground truth. Since fluency and adequacy judgments are currently seen as the metrics that are closest to ground truth, new metrics are generally assessed by how much they correlate with these judgments.

correct judgment

8.1.3 Other Evaluation Criteria

In this chapter, we are primarily concerned with evaluation metrics that reflect how good the machine translation output quality is. For the practical deployment of machine translation systems in an operational environment, several other issues are important.

One issue is **speed**. We as researchers are somewhat concerned with this issue, since we would like our experiments to finish quickly, so we can examine their results. Typical statistical machine translation research systems have speeds of about 10–100 words per second, but this may not be fast enough for practical deployment. Of course, there is a trade-off between speed and quality: Higher translation speeds may be obtained with some loss of quality, for instance by more pruning in decoding that leads to more search errors.

system speed

The **size** of the system plays an important role, even for research systems, which have to run on the available machines. Use of machine translation systems in the field, e.g., on hand-held devices, carries with it tighter constraints on system size.

system size

Other issues come from the **integration** of a machine translation system into the workflow of an application environment. Does the system interface well with other applications? Is it easy to use? Is it reliable (does it crash)? In this book, we are less concerned with these questions, but they do play an important role in the usefulness of machine

integration into workflow

translation systems. Often, machine translation is not used, simply because it is too complicated.

When deploying machine translation systems in a specific environment to translate documents from a specific domain, the system's support for **domain adaptation** and **customization** plays a major role. Users prefer a system to act predictably and may want to correct common errors.

domain adaptation
customization

8.2 Automatic Evaluation

When it comes to evaluating machine translation systems, we tend to put most trust into the judgment of human evaluators who look at the output of several systems, examine it sentence by sentence, assess each sentence, and conclude with an overall score for each system.

This method, however, has one major disadvantage. It takes a lot of time, and if the evaluators expect to be paid, also a lot of money. The typical statistical machine translation researcher, on the other hand, has no money and would like to carry out evaluations very frequently, often many per day to examine different system configurations.

Therefore, we prefer to have an automatic method for assessing the quality of machine translation output. Ideally, we would like a computer program to tell us quickly whether our system got better after a change, or not. This is the objective of **automatic machine translation evaluation**.

automatic evaluation

Much progress has recently been made in this field, to the point that machine translation researchers trust automatic evaluation metrics and design their systems based on the rise and fall of automatic evaluation scores. However, automatic evaluation metrics are under constant debate and their true value in distinguishing better and worse systems is often called into question. We will come back to this discussion in Section 8.2.5; let us first get a better understanding of automatic evaluation methods.

8.2.1 Precision and Recall

How could we possibly expect a computer to assess the quality of a translation? All automatic evaluation metrics use the same trick. Each system translation is compared against one or more human translations of the same sentence. The human translations are called **reference translations**. We have argued at the beginning of this chapter that it is too much to ask of a machine translation system, or a human translator for that matter, to match a reference translation exactly. But a translation that is very similar to a reference translation is more likely to be

reference translation

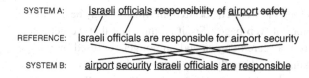

SYSTEM A: Israeli officials ~~responsibility~~ of airport ~~safety~~

REFERENCE: Israeli officials are responsible for airport security

SYSTEM B: airport security Israeli officials are responsible

Figure 8.4 Matching words in the system output to the reference translation: System A has three correct words, while all six of System B's words are correct.

correct than one that differs substantially. The challenge for automatic evaluation metrics is to come up with a good similarity measure.

Let us start with an evaluation metric based on word matches. Check the first example in Figure 8.4. System A's output is *Israeli officials responsibility of airport safety*, which shares three words (*Israeli*, *officials* and *airport*) with the reference translation *Israeli officials are responsible for airport security*.

System A's output has six words in total, so three correct words out of six is a ratio of 50%. This type of metric is called **precision**. System B's output is *airport security Israeli officials are responsible*. The output has six words, and all them are also in the reference translation. Six correct out of six gives a nice 100% precision.

There are clearly problems with System B's output, despite the perfect precision. First, the words are out of order, the phrase *airport security* should be moved to the end of the sentence. Focusing on word matches alone and ignoring their order has obvious short-comings. But also in terms of word matches, the translation is not perfect. The reference translation has one more word, *for*, so should we not consider this as well?

So, instead of computing how many of the words that a system generates are correct, we may compute how many of the words that a system *should* generate are correct. This metric is called **recall**. In contrast to precision, we divide the number of correct words by the length of the reference translation, instead of the length of the system output:

$$\text{precision} = \frac{\text{correct}}{\text{output-length}} \tag{8.2}$$

$$\text{recall} = \frac{\text{correct}}{\text{reference-length}} \tag{8.3}$$

Both of these metrics can be deliberately tricked. We may produce translations only for words that we are sure of. The output will be very short, but we will have a very high precision (but low recall). Correspondingly, we may output all kinds of words, so the chance is high that we match all the words in the reference translation. The output will be very long, but we will have very high recall (but low precision).

Precision and recall are common metrics in natural language processing, and in some applications one is more important than the other.

precision

recall

Consider searching the web. The desired information may be contained in a large number of web pages. So, it is important that we get a few good results from a search engine and do not get confused by a large number of mismatches. Usually, there is no need to retrieve all pages. In this application, precision is more important than recall.

In machine translation, we are typically equally interested in precision and recall. We do not want to output wrong words, but we do not want to miss out on anything either. A common way to combine precision and recall is the **f-measure**, which is defined as the harmonic mean of the two metrics:

f-measure

$$\text{f-measure} = \frac{\text{precision} \times \text{recall}}{(\text{precision} + \text{recall})/2} \tag{8.4}$$

In our case, this can be reformulated as

$$\text{f-measure} = \frac{\text{correct}}{(\text{output-length} + \text{reference-length})/2} \tag{8.5}$$

Let us consider one more variation on this. **Position-independent error rate** (PER) is occasionally used in machine translation evaluation. It is similar to recall in that it uses the reference length as a divisor. It is an error rate, so we measure mismatches, not matches. To overcome the problem of too long translations, the metric also considers superfluous words that need to be deleted as wrong:

position-independent error rate

$$\text{PER} = 1 - \frac{\text{correct} - \max(0, \text{output-length} - \text{reference-length})}{\text{reference-length}} \tag{8.6}$$

In summary, the scores for the two systems using word-order insensitive precision, recall, and f-measure are:

Metric	System A	System B
precision	50%	100%
recall	43%	86%
f-measure	46%	92%
PER	57%	14%

8.2.2 Word Error Rate

word error rate

Levenshtein distance

Word error rate (WER), one of the first automatic evaluation metrics applied to statistical machine translation, is borrowed from speech recognition and takes word order into account. It employs the **Levenshtein distance**, which is defined as the minimum number of editing steps – insertions, deletions, and substitutions – needed to match two sequences.

		Israeli	officials	responsibility	of	airport	safety
	0	1	2	3	4	5	6
Israeli	1	0	1	2	3	4	5
officials	2	1	0	1	2	3	4
are	3	2	1	1	2	3	4
responsible	4	3	2	2	2	3	4
for	5	4	3	3	3	3	4
airport	6	5	4	4	4	3	4
security	7	6	5	5	5	4	4

		airport	security	Israeli	officials	are	responsible
	0	1	2	3	4	5	6
Israeli	1	1	2	2	3	4	5
officials	2	2	2	3	2	3	4
are	3	3	3	3	3	2	3
responsible	4	4	4	4	4	3	2
for	5	5	5	5	5	4	3
airport	6	5	6	6	6	5	4
security	7	6	5	6	7	6	5

Figure 8.5 Two examples for the computation of the Levenshtein distance between output (on top) and reference translation (on the left): The distance is defined as the lowest-cost path (in grey) from the beginning of both sentences (top-left corner) to the end of both sentences (bottom-right corner), using word matches (cost 0, dark colors), or the editing steps of substitutions, insertions, and deletions (cost 1, light colors).

See Figure 8.5 for an illustration. The task of finding the minimum number of editing steps can be seen as finding the optimal path through the word alignment matrix of output sentence (across) and reference translation (down). Using a dynamic programming approach, we start at the top left corner (beginning of both sentences), and fill each point in the matrix with the cheapest cost of either:

match: if the point is a word match, take the cost from the point which is diagonally to the left-top;

substitution: if the point is not a word match, take the cost from the point which is diagonally to the left-top, add one;

insertion: take the cost from the point to the left, add one;

deletion: take the cost from the point above, add one.

Given the Levenshtein distance, we can compute the word error rate. Word error rate normalizes the number of editing steps by the length of the reference translation:

$$\text{WER} = \frac{\text{substitutions} + \text{insertions} + \text{deletions}}{\text{reference-length}} \qquad (8.7)$$

The requirement of matching words in order may seem too harsh. Note that one of the human translations in Figure 8.1 was *This airport's security is the responsibility of the Israeli security officials*, which is a perfectly fine translation, but in the opposite order to the reference translation, so it will be marked with a very high word error rate.

In summary, the scores for the two systems using word error rate are:

Metric	System A	System B
word error rate (WER)	57%	71%

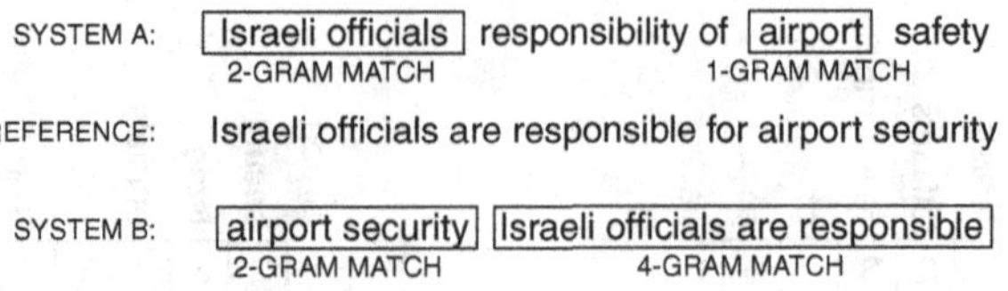

Figure 8.6 The BLEU score is based on n-gram matches with the reference translation.

SYSTEM A: ⸤Israeli officials⸥ responsibility of ⸤airport⸥ safety
             2-GRAM MATCH   1-GRAM MATCH

REFERENCE: Israeli officials are responsible for airport security

SYSTEM B: ⸤airport security⸥ ⸤Israeli officials are responsible⸥
             2-GRAM MATCH   4-GRAM MATCH

8.2.3 BLEU: A Bilingual Evaluation Understudy

BLEU metric

The currently most popular automatic evaluation metric, the **BLEU metric**, has an elegant solution to the role of word order. It works similarly to position-independent word error rate, but considers matches of larger n-grams with the reference translation.

See Figure 8.6 for an illustration of n-gram matches in our previous example. System A's output matches are a 2-gram match for *Israeli officials* and a 1-gram match for *airport*. All output words of System B match: *airport security* is a 2-gram match and *Israeli officials are responsible* is a 4-gram match.

Given the n-gram matches, we can compute n-gram precision, i.e., the ratio of correct n-grams of a certain order n in relation to the total number of generated n-grams of that order:

- System A: 1-gram precision 3/6, 2-gram precision 1/5, 3-gram precision 0/4, 4-gram precision 0/3.
- System B: 1-gram precision 6/6, 2-gram precision 4/5, 3-gram precision 2/4, 4-gram precision 1/3.

The BLEU metric is defined as

$$\text{BLEU-n} = \text{brevity-penalty} \exp \sum_{i=1}^{n} \lambda_i \log \text{precision}_i$$

$$\text{brevity-penalty} = \min\left(1, \frac{\text{output-length}}{\text{reference-length}}\right)$$

(8.8)

brevity penalty

The problem with precision-based metrics – no penalty for dropping words – is addressed by BLEU with a **brevity penalty**. The penalty reduces the score if the output is too short. The maximum order n for n-grams to be matched is typically set to 4. This metric is then called BLEU-4. Moreover, the weights λ_i for the different precisions are typically set to 1, which simplifies the BLEU-4 formula to

$$\text{BLEU-4} = \min\left(1, \frac{\text{output-length}}{\text{reference-length}}\right) \prod_{i=1}^{4} \text{precision}_i$$

(8.9)

Note that the BLEU score is 0 if any of the n-gram precisions is 0, meaning no n-grams of a particular length are matched anywhere in the output. Since n-gram precisions of 0 especially for 4-grams often occur on the sentence level, BLEU scores are commonly computed over the entire test set.

Another innovation of the BLEU score is the use of **multiple reference translations**. Given the variability in translation, it is harsh to require matches of the system output against a single human reference translation. If multiple human reference translations are used, it is more likely that all acceptable translations of ambiguous parts of the sentences show up.

multiple reference translations

See Figure 8.7 for an example. Originally, System A did not get any credit for the output of *responsibility of*, which is not a wrong translation. Indeed, the words do show up in one of the reference translations.

The use of multiple reference translations works as follows. If an n-gram in the output has a match in any of the reference translations, it is counted as correct. If an n-gram occurs multiple times in the output (for instance the English word *the* often shows up repeatedly), it has to occur in a single reference translation the same number of times for all occurrences to be marked as correct. If reference translations have fewer occurrences of the n-gram, it is marked as correct only that many times.

Multiple reference translations complicate the issue of reference length. In multiple-reference BLEU for each output sentence the closest length of any of the reference translations is determined and taken as the reference length. If two reference lengths are equally close, but one is shorter and one longer, the shorter one is taken. For instance, given an output length of 10 and lengths of reference sentences 8, 9, 11, and 15, the reference length for that sentence is 9 (both 9 and 11 are equally close, but 9 is smaller).

In summary, the various precisions, brevity penalty, and BLEU scores for two example sentences from Figure 8.6 on the facing page are (see Figure 8.7 for the multiple references):

Metric	Single reference		Multiple reference	
	System A	System B	System A	System B
precision (1-gram)	3/6	6/6	5/6	6/6
precision (2-gram)	1/5	4/5	2/5	4/5
precision (3-gram)	0/4	2/4	0/4	2/4
precision (4-gram)	0/3	1/3	0/3	1/3
brevity penalty	6/7	6/7	6/7	6/7
BLEU-1	42%	86%	71%	86%
BLEU-2	9%	69%	29%	69%
BLEU-3	0%	34%	0%	34%
BLEU-4	0%	11%	0%	11%

Figure 8.7 Additional n-gram matches by using multiple reference translations, accounting for variability in acceptable translations.

SYSTEM:

| Israeli officials | responsibility of | airport | safety |
| 2-GRAM MATCH | 2-GRAM MATCH | 1-GRAM | |

REFERENCES:

Israeli officials are responsible for airport security
Israel is in charge of the security at this airport
The security work for this airport is the responsibility of the Israel government
Israeli side was in charge of the security of this airport

8.2.4 METEOR

Recently, many variations and extensions to the BLEU metric have been proposed. One point of discussion, for instance, is the role of precision and recall in machine translation evaluation. The case is made that recall is more important to ensure that the complete meaning is captured by the output.

METEOR metric   One more recent metric, **METEOR**, incorporates a stronger emphasis on recall, and also introduces a couple of novel ideas. One perceived flaw of BLEU is that it gives no credit to near matches. Recall that one of our example system outputs used the noun *responsibility*, but the reference used the adjective *responsible*. Both carry the same meaning, but since the words are not the same, BLEU counts this as an error. By stemming the two words, i.e., reducing them to their stems, we are able to match them.

Another way to detect near misses is using synonyms, or semantically closely related words. The human translations in the lead example of this chapter (Figure 8.1) give some examples for this. Translators varied in their use of *security* and *safety*, as well as *responsibility* and *charge*. Often, these word choices are irrelevant in bringing across the meaning of the sentences and should not be penalized.

METEOR incorporates the use of stemming and synonyms by first matching the surface forms of the words, and then backing off to stems and finally semantic classes. The latter are determined using Wordnet, a popular ontology of English words that also exists for other languages.

The main drawback of METEOR is that its method and formula for computing a score is much more complicated that BLEU's. The matching process involves computationally expensive word alignment. There are many more parameters – such as the relative weight of recall to precision, the weight for stemming or synonym matches – that have to be tuned.

8.2.5 The Evaluation Debate

The use of automatic evaluation metrics in machine translation is under constant debate in the research community. It seems to be hard to believe that simplistic metrics such as the BLEU score do properly reflect differences in meaning between system output and reference translations (or input, for that matter). Another reason for this debate is that these automatic metrics are almost exclusively used by *statistical* machine translation researchers, and their claims are often questioned by practitioners of machine translation by different means.

The main points of **critique** are:

critique of BLEU

- BLEU ignores the relative relevance of different words. Some words matter more than others. One of the most glaring examples is the word *not*, which, if omitted, will cause very misleading translations. Names and core concepts are also important words, much more so than, e.g., determiners and punctuation, which are often irrelevant. However, all words are treated the same way by the metrics we presented here.
- BLEU operates only on a very local level and does not address overall grammatical coherence. System output may look good on an n-gram basis, but very muddled beyond that. There is a suspicion that this biases the metric in favor of phrase-based statistical systems, which are good at producing good n-grams, but less able to produce grammatically coherent sentences.
- The actual BLEU scores are meaningless. Nobody knows what a BLEU score of 30% means, since the actual number depends on many factors, such as the number of reference translations, the language pair, the domain, and even the tokenization scheme used to break up the output and reference into words.
- Recent experiments computed so-called human BLEU scores, where a human reference translation was scored against other human reference translations. Such human BLEU scores are barely higher (if at all) than BLEU scores computed for machine translation output, even though the human translations are of much higher quality.

Many of these arguments were also brought up initially by current users of BLEU, and all of them also apply broadly to any other automatic evaluation metric. There are counter-arguments; the most convincing is shown in Figure 8.8. The graph in the figure plots system performance as measured by automatic scores against human judgement scores for submissions to the 2002 machine translation evaluation on Arabic–English, organized by NIST.

In this analysis, systems with low automatic scores also received low human judgement scores, and systems with high automatic scores also received high human judgement scores. What this shows is a high **correlation** between human and automatic scores. This is what we expect from a good automatic evaluation metric, and this is what evaluation metrics should be assessed on.

human–automatic correlation

8.2.6 Evaluation of Evaluation Metrics

The most widely used method for computing the correlation between two metrics is the **Pearson correlation coefficient**. Formally, we are

Pearson correlation coefficient

Figure 8.8 Correlation between an automatic metric (here: NIST score) and human judgment (fluency, adequacy). Illustration by George Doddington.

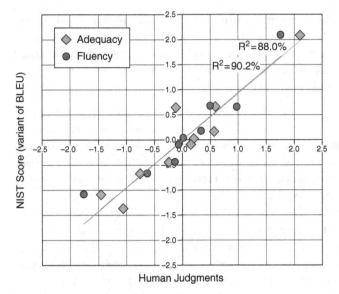

Figure 8.9 Typical interpretation of the correlation coefficient r_{xy}.

Correlation	Negative	Positive
small	−0.29 to −0.10	0.10 to 0.29
medium	−0.49 to −0.30	0.30 to 0.49
large	−1.00 to −0.50	0.50 to 1.00

faced with a set of data points $\{(x_i, y_i)\}$ that contain values for two variables x, y. The Pearson correlation coefficient r_{xy} between the two variables is defined as

$$r_{xy} = \frac{\sum_i (x_i - \bar{x})(y_i - \bar{y})}{(n - 1)\, s_x\, s_y} \tag{8.10}$$

To compute the coefficient r_{xy} we first need to compute the sample means $\bar{x}, \bar{y}$ and the sample variances s_x, s_y of the two variables x and y:

$$\bar{x} = \frac{1}{n} \sum_{i=1}^{n} x_i$$

$$s_x^2 = \frac{1}{n-1} \sum_{i=1}^{n} (x_i - \bar{x})^2 \tag{8.11}$$

What counts as a good correlation between perfect correlation ($r_{xy} = 1$) and total independence between the variables ($r_{xy} = 0$) is anybody's guess. Figure 8.9 gives a typical interpretation of the correlation coefficient. If our goal is to compare different automatic evaluation metrics with respect to their correlation with a manual metric, the answer is straightforward: a higher correlation is better.

8.2.7 Evidence of Shortcomings of Automatic Metrics

Recent evaluation campaigns have revealed exceptions to the correla-   shortcomings of BLEU
tion of manual and automatic scores for some special cases.

In the 2005 NIST evaluations on Arabic–English, one of the submissions was a system that was improved by human post-editing. The
post-editing was done by monolingual speakers of the target language
with no knowledge of the source language. The post-editing effort led
to only small increases in the automatic BLEU score, but to large
improvements in both fluency and adequacy judgments in the manual
evaluation. See Figure 8.10a,b.

Secondly, in an experiment comparing a commercial rule-based
machine translation system with two instances of a statistical system
(one trained on the full data set, the other on 1/64th of it), the automatic BLEU score failed to reflect the human judgment. The worse
statistical system, although given much lower judgments by humans,
still achieved a higher BLEU score than the rule-based system. Human
evaluators scored the rule-based system and the better statistical system
similarly; the BLEU scores, however, were 18% and 30%, respectively.
See Figure 8.10c.

The WMT 2006 evaluation campaign confirmed the latter result –
again a rule-based system participated along with a range of statistical
systems. Interestingly, the correlation of scores was much higher when
the systems were tested on out-of-domain test data. While the rule-
based system was not developed for a specific domain, the statistical

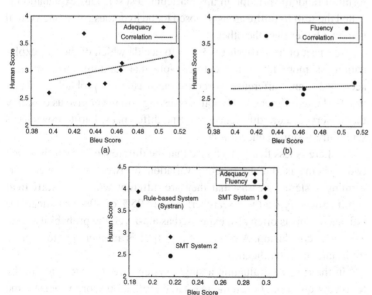

Figure 8.10 Examples of lack of correlation between BLEU and manual judgment. Manually post-edited machine translation is scored low by BLEU, but high by humans, both in terms of adequacy (a) and fluency (b). A rule-based system receives a much lower BLEU score than a comparable statistical system that is trained and evaluated on the Europarl corpus (c).

systems were trained on Europarl data, but the out-of-domain test data set was political and economic commentary. This finding seems to suggest that part of the explanation for the lack of correlation is that automatic scores are overly literal and reward the right choice of jargon much more strongly than human evaluators.

The state of the current debate on automatic evaluation metrics evolves around a general consensus that automatic metrics are an essential tool for system development of statistical machine translation systems, but not fully suited to computing scores that allow us to rank systems of different types against each other. Developing evaluation metrics for this purpose is still an open challenge to the research community.

8.3 Hypothesis Testing

Machine translation evaluation is typically carried out in the following manner. Two (or more) machine translation systems produce translations for a set of test sentences. For each system's output an evaluation score is obtained, either by eliciting human judgments, or by computing automatic scores using reference translations.

If this leads to different scores for different systems, we would like to conclude that one system is better than the other. But there may also be another explanation for the different scores. Both systems are actually performing equally well, and the two different scores are just a result of random variation in this particular test set. This explanation is called the **null hypothesis**, as opposed to the hypothesis that one system is in fact better than the other.

null hypothesis

The task of **hypothesis testing** is to decide which of the two explanations is more likely to be true. Note that random variation may account for any difference in scores, but it is a less probable explanation for large differences. Hypothesis testing will never give us certainty that observed score differences are true differences, but it allows us to set arbitrary significance levels.

hypothesis testing

If there is less than 1% chance that the difference in score between two systems is due to random variation of two equally well performing systems, we say that they are different with 99% **statistical significance**. Typically, researchers require 95% or 99% statistical significance. This is often also expressed as a **p-level**, the probability of an erroneous conclusion. A p-level of $p < 0.01$ is another way to express 99% statistical significance.

statistical significance

p-level

In the case of evaluating a single system, we are interested in the following question: Given the measured evaluation score x, what is the true evaluation score? Or, to phrase it as a question that we are actually able to answer: With a statistical significance of, say, 95%, what is the range of scores that includes the true score? This range is called the **confidence interval**. It is typically computed with a distance d around the measured score x, i.e., the interval $[x - d, x + d]$.

confidence interval

8.3.1 Computing Confidence Intervals

Let us consider the simplest form of evaluation that we have presented so far. Given the system output, a human evaluator judges each sentence translation to be either correct or false. If, say, 100 sentence translations are evaluated, and 30 are found correct, what can we say about the true translation score of the system? Our best guess is 30%, but that may be a few percent off. How much off, is the question to be answered by statistical significance tests.

Given a set of n sentences, we can compute the sample mean $\bar{x}$ and variance s^2 of the individual sentence scores x_i:

$$\bar{x} = \frac{1}{n} \sum_{i=1}^{n} x_i$$

$$s^2 = \frac{1}{n-1} \sum_{i=1}^{n} (x_i - \bar{x})^2 \tag{8.12}$$

What we are really interested in is, however, the true mean μ (the true translation score). Let us assume that the sentence scores are distributed according to the normal distribution. See Figure 8.11 for an illustration. Given the sample mean $\bar{x}$ and sample variance s^2, we estimate the probability distribution for true translation quality. We are now interested in a confidence interval $[\bar{x} - d, \bar{x} + d]$ around the mean sentence score. The true translation quality (or the true mean μ) lies within the confidence interval with a certain probability (the statistical significance level).

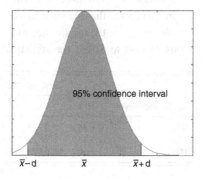

95% confidence interval

$\bar{x}-d$ $\bar{x}$ $\bar{x}+d$

Figure 8.11 With probability $q = 0.95$, the true score lies in an interval $[\bar{x} - d, \bar{x} + d]$ around the sample score $\bar{x}$.

Note the relationship between the degree of statistical significance and the confidence interval. The degree of statistical significance is indicated by the fraction of the area under the curve that is shaded. The confidence interval is indicated by the boundaries on the x-axis. A larger statistical significance, a large shaded area, pushes the boundaries of the confidence interval outward.

Since we do not know the true mean μ and variance σ^2, we cannot model the distribution of sentence scores with the normal distribution. However, we can use Student's t-distribution, which approximates the normal distribution for large n.

The function that maps between a confidence interval $[\bar{x} - d, \bar{x} + d]$ and the statistical significance level can be obtained by integrating over the distribution. However, in case of Student's t-distribution, the integral cannot be evaluated in closed form, but we can use numerical methods.

The size of the confidence interval can be computed by

$$d = t \cdot \frac{s}{\sqrt{n}} \tag{8.13}$$

The factor t depends on the desired p-level of statistical significance and the sample size. See Figure 8.12 for typical values.

Let us review the assumptions underlying this method of defining the confidence intervals. We randomly draw test sentences and score them with the system. The confidence interval gives an indication of what the likely true average error is, if it were computed on an infinite number of test sentences.

8.3.2 Pairwise Comparison

We are usually not interested in the absolute value of evaluation scores. As we have argued, these scores are often hard to interpret. More typically, we are interested in the comparison of two (or more) systems. We want to render a judgment, to decide whether one system is indeed better than the other. This may involve comparing different systems in a competition or, as is more often the case, comparing a baseline system against a change that we want to assess.

We may use the confidence intervals that we computed in the previous section to assess the statistical significance of the difference in

Figure 8.12 Values for t for different sizes and significance levels (to be used in Formula 8.13).

	Test sample size			
Significance level	100	300	600	∞
99%	2.6259	2.5923	2.5841	2.5759
95%	1.9849	1.9679	1.9639	1.9600
90%	1.6602	1.6499	1.6474	1.6449

scores. If the confidence intervals do not overlap, we are able to state that the two systems do in fact have different performance at the given statistical significance level.

Alternatively, instead of using confidence intervals, we may want to compute the statistical significance of score differences directly for that **pairwise comparison**. For instance, given a test set of 100 sentences, if we find one system doing better on 40 sentences, and worse on 60 sentences, is that difference statistically significant?

pairwise comparison

The **sign test** allows us to compute how likely it is that two equal systems would come up with such a sample of performance differences. The binomial distribution is used to model such a scenario. If system A is better at translating a sentence with probability p_A, and system B is better with probability p_B ($=1 - p_A$), then the probability of system A being better on $k = 40$ sentences out of a sample of $n = 100$ sentences is

sign test

$$\binom{n}{k} p_A^k \, p_B^{n-k} = \frac{n!}{k! \, (n-k)!} \, p_A^k \, p_B^{n-k} \tag{8.14}$$

According to the null hypothesis $p_A = p_B = 0.5$, so the formula simplifies to

$$\binom{n}{k} p^k \, (1-p)^{n-k} = \binom{n}{k} 0.5^n = \frac{n!}{k! \, (n-k)!} \, 0.5^n \tag{8.15}$$

The particular outcome of system A being better on exactly 40 sentences is unlikely, so we want to compute the whole range of $k \in [0, 40]$, when considering the null hypothesis:

$$p(0..k; n) = \sum_{i=0}^{k} \binom{n}{i} 0.5^n \tag{8.16}$$

This formula computes the probability that, given two equally well performing systems, one system is better on up to k out of n sentences. If such an outcome is unlikely (say, with a p-level of $p \leq 0.05$), we reject the null hypothesis, and conclude that the difference reflects a difference in quality between the systems. Note that when using this formula, we ignore sentences where the two systems are scored the same.

For our example, we plug the numbers $n = 100$ and $k = 40$ into the formula for the sign test and we get $p = 0.0569$. So, we cannot say with statistical significance at a p-level of $p \leq 0.05$ that the systems differ. See Figure 8.13 for more illustrations of this formula. It gives the minimum number of k out of n to achieve statistical significance at different p-levels. In our example of 100 sentences, one system has to be better in at least 61 cases (and the other better in at most 39 cases) to achieve statistical significance at p-level $p \leq 0.05$.

Figure 8.13 Examples for the sign test: Given a number of sentences *n*, one system has to be better in at least *k* sentences to achieve statistical significance at the specified p-level.

n	$p \leq 0.01$		$p \leq 0.05$		$p \leq 0.10$	
5	–	–	–	–	$k = 5$	$\frac{k}{n} = 1.00$
10	$k = 10$	$\frac{k}{n} = 1.00$	$k \geq 9$	$\frac{k}{n} \geq 0.90$	$k \geq 9$	$\frac{k}{n} \geq 0.90$
20	$k \geq 17$	$\frac{k}{n} \geq 0.85$	$k \geq 15$	$\frac{k}{n} \geq 0.75$	$k \geq 15$	$\frac{k}{n} \geq 0.75$
50	$k \geq 35$	$\frac{k}{n} \geq 0.70$	$k \geq 33$	$\frac{k}{n} \geq 0.66$	$k \geq 32$	$\frac{k}{n} \geq 0.64$
100	$k \geq 64$	$\frac{k}{n} \geq 0.64$	$k \geq 61$	$\frac{k}{n} \geq 0.61$	$k \geq 59$	$\frac{k}{n} \geq 0.59$

8.3.3 Bootstrap Resampling

We have described methods for computing confidence intervals and statistical significance of test score differences. However, the methods operate under the assumption that we can compute scores for single sentences. This assumption does not hold for the canonical metric in machine translation, the BLEU score, since it is not computed on the sentence level.

One solution to this problem is to break up the test set into blocks of, say, 10–20 sentences, and compute BLEU scores for each. Then we are able to resort to the presented methods, and for instance apply the sign test on these blocks. If one system outperforms the other in translating significantly more blocks better, the difference is statistically significant.

bootstrap resampling   An alternative method is called **bootstrap resampling**. Let us first consider the case of estimating confidence intervals. The pairwise comparison task is very similar.

Consider the following: Let us say that we are using a test set of 2,000 sentences that we sampled from a large collection of available test sentences. We then proceed to compute the BLEU score for this set. But how likely is that score to be representative of the true BLEU score computed on a test of near-infinite size?

If we were to repeatedly sample test sets of 2,000 sentences, and compute the BLEU score on each of them, we would get a distribution of scores that looks like the bell curve in Figure 8.11. With enough test set samples, say 1,000, we can then empirically determine the 95% confidence interval. By ignoring the 25 highest and 25 lowest BLEU scores, we are left with an interval that contains 95% of the scores.

To restate the argument: if we pick one of the test set samples at random, then with 95% probability it will be in the interval between the extreme tails of the distribution. Hence, a truly representative test set sample will also lie with 95% probability in this interval.

Of course, taking 1,000 test sets of 2,000 sentences means translating 2 million sentences, and if we were able to do that, we could most likely come up with a tighter confidence interval using the sign test on blocks, as mentioned above.

Therefore, we apply the following trick. We sample the 1,000 test sets from the *same* 2,000 sentences of the initial test set, with replacement. Since we are allowed to take the same sentences more than once, we will likely come up with 1,000 different test sets, and therefore 1,000 different test scores. We then move on and compute the confidence interval, as if these sets were truly independent samples.

We will not go into the theoretical arguments about bootstrap resampling here; the reader is referred to Efron and Tibshirani [1993]. Intuitively, bootstrap resampling uses the variability in the test sets, as does the sign test, to draw conclusions about statistical significance. If the system translated most parts of the test set with very similar performance, then we are more likely to trust the resulting score, as opposed to a test set translation with parts of widely different performance.

The application of bootstrap resampling to the pairwise comparison of different systems is straightforward. We compute both systems' scores on the resampled test set, and check which system is better. If one system is better on at least 950 samples, then it is deemed to be statistically significantly better at the $p \leq 0.05$ p-level.

8.4 Task-Oriented Evaluation

So far we have discussed various manual and automatic evaluation metrics that aim to judge the quality – or relative quality in the form of a ranking – of machine translation output. These metrics take into account that most sentences will have some errors in them, and they give some measurement of the error rate. The reduction of this error rate is the goal of research activity in the field of machine translation.

But maybe the question *How good is machine translation?* is the wrong question to ask, maybe a better question is *Is machine translation good enough?* Machine translation is not an end itself; it is used to support some kind of task, perhaps supporting the efforts of a human translator to more efficiently translate documents for publication, or perhaps helping someone to understand the contents of a document in an unknown foreign language.

If these are the uses of machine translation, then machine translation will ultimately be evaluated in the marketplace on how well it supports these tasks.

8.4.1 Cost of Post-Editing

Consider this scenario of the use of machine translation systems: first a foreign document is translated with a machine translation system, then a human translator corrects the errors, and submits a final high-quality translation for publication.

For this scenario to work, the human translator will only make a few corrections. An evaluation metric that reflects this may count the minimum number of required corrections.

We have already presented one metric that compares the system output with a reference translation in terms of editing steps. **Levenshtein distance** (Section 8.2.2 on page 224) counted the number of insertions, deletions, and substitutions needed to transform the system output to match the reference translation.

Levenshtein distance

One disadvantage of the Levenshtein distance is that mismatches in word order require the deletion and re-insertion of the misplaced words. We may remedy this by adding an editing step that allows the movement of word sequences from one part of the output to another. This is something a human post-editor would do with the cut-and-paste function of a word processor.

translation error rate
cover disjoint error rate

Some evaluation metrics based on such editing steps have been proposed, including **translation error rate** (TER) and **cover disjoint error rate** (CDER). The metrics are based on the Levenshtein distance, but add block movement (also called a jump) as an editing step. The computation of TER scores is actually not trivial: finding the shortest sequence of editing steps is a computationally hard problem. It is, in fact, NP-complete. CDER is computationally less complex, due to a relaxation of the alignment requirements.

The metrics TER and CDER still suffer from one short-coming. The system output may be an acceptable translation, but different from the reference translation. Hence, the error measured by these metrics does not do justice to the system.

human translation error rate

Alternatively, we may ask a human evaluator to post-edit the system output and count how many editing steps were undertaken. One example of a metric that is designed in such a manner is the **human translation error rate** (HTER), used in recent DARPA evaluations. Here, a human annotator has to find the minimum number of insertions, deletions, substitutions, and shifts to convert the system output into an acceptable translation. HTER is defined as the number of editing steps divided by the number of words in the acceptable translation.

Finding the minimum number of editing steps is often a time-consuming task. It does not reflect what a human post-editor would do. A post-editor would try to spend as little time as possible to correct the sentence. This may involve more editing steps than indicated by HTER scores. If the output is very muddled, human translators are justified in simply deleting the machine translation and writing a new translation from scratch, instead of fiddling with the broken output.

post-editing time

When considering **post-editing time**, one also has to take into consideration the time spent on reading the system output. If the human translator reads buggy machine translation output, discards it, and then writes his own translation, he will have spent more time than if he were not using machine translation technology at all.

Error-prone machine output may not only result in more time spent on translation, it may also disrupt the work flow of translators. This added frustration may be one reason today's human translators rarely use full-fledged machine translation systems to support their work.

Note that a good translation tool for human translators is sometimes better off not providing any translation at all. See also our discussion of applications of machine translation technology to aid translators in Section 1.3.

8.4.2 Content Understanding Tests

Let us now consider metrics that try to assess whether machine translation output is good enough that a human reader is able to **understand the content** of the translated document.

Note that the bar for machine translation is lower here. A translation that has muddled grammar and misplaced or missing function words may still be fully informative. We are constantly confronted with incorrect English – most spontaneous speech is ungrammatical – but that does not prevent us from understanding it.

Extracting meaning from text requires increasing levels of understanding:

1. Basic facts: Who is talked about? Where and when do the events take place? Detect names, numbers, and dates. What is the main gist of the story?
2. Detailed relationships between the elements of the text: How do the entities relate to each other? What is the order of events? What causality exists between them?
3. Nuance and author intent: How are the facts characterized and emphasized? Why did the author express them in the given manner? What is the subtext?

If we hand a translated text to human evaluators and ask them questions that range in difficulty, we can measure how well they are able to understand the text. We then take the ratio of correctly answered questions as a judgment of how well the machine translation system retained the meaning of the text. The question may be broken down by the levels mentioned above or other categories. We may also measure the time spent on answering the questions – good machine translation output should be faster to read and comprehend.

Of course, this test measures not only the capability of the machine translation system to provide understandable text, but also the capability

understanding tests

of the human evaluator. This cuts both ways. The evaluator's reading proficiency and ability to answer test questions in his native language limits his ability to answer such questions on machine translated output. On the other hand, a clever test subject with broad knowledge about the subject matter at hand may be able to fill in missing or mistranslated content.

8.5 Summary

8.5.1 Core Concepts

This chapter addressed the issue of **evaluating** machine translation performance. This is a hard problem, since a foreign sentence may have many different correct translations. We may be able to provide some **reference translations**, but we cannot expect machine translation systems (or even human translators) to match these exactly.

Manual evaluation metrics ask a human evaluator to render an assessment of the translation performance, say, on a sentence-by-sentence basis. **Adequacy** measures how much meaning is retained in the translation, while **fluency** measures whether the output is good English. Different human evaluators tend to differ in their leniency or harshness when assigning scores, so we have to **normalize** these to make them comparable. Human evaluators are more consistent in **ranking** different translated sentences against each other than in assigning absolute scores.

We would like to use evaluation metrics that are **low cost** in terms of time and money spent, result in **meaningful** numbers, and are **consistent**. By consistent we mean **inter-annotator agreement** – different evaluators should come to the same assessment – and **stable** with respect to different parts of the text. Most importantly, we expect a metric to be **correct**, i.e., indicating actual performance and ranking better systems higher than worse ones. Besides quality metrics, we may also consider, in the evaluation of machine translation systems, matters such as **speed** and **size** of the system, ease of **integration** into an application environment, and support for **domain adaptation** and **customization**.

Since manual evaluation is very labor intensive, it would be preferable to have reliable automatic evaluation metrics for daily use. When comparing system output with reference translations, we may consider the **precision** and **recall** of words. **Word error rate** (WER) uses the **Levenshtein distance** to compute the minimum number of edits needed to get from the system output to the reference translation.

While WER leads to very low scores when the word order is wrong, **position-independent word error rate** (PER) ignores word order when matching output and reference. The currently most popular metric is **BLEU**, which uses n-gram matches with the reference and also makes use of **multiple reference translations** to account for variability. The **METEOR** metric also considers matches on the lemma-level and synonym matches. Evaluation of evaluation metrics is done by measuring correlation with human judgments, which may be computed using the **Pearson correlation coefficient**.

With **hypothesis testing**, we are able to assess the **statistical significance** of score differences. We distinguish genuine performance differences from the **null hypothesis**, i.e., random variation in evaluation scores of systems performing equally well. We assess significance with a minimum specified **p-level** of certainty. We may compute a **confidence interval** around the measured score, but more often we are interested in the **pairwise comparison** of systems. The **sign test** is one method that is used for such sentence-level scores. It does not easily apply to the BLEU score, for which we may resort to **bootstrap resampling**.

Task-oriented evaluation metrics attempt to directly measure the utility of machine translation for performing a specific task. If the task is to produce high-quality translations, we may measure the **post-editing time** required to correct machine translation output. In a similar vein, the **translation error rate** measures the number of editing steps required to reach a reference translation, and the **human translation error rate** measures how many editing steps a human post-editor has to perform to reach an acceptable translation. Extracting information from translated text material is the motivation for **understanding tests**, which measure how well a human evaluator is able to answer questions about a foreign text given machine translation output.

8.5.2 Further Reading

Evaluation campaigns – The first machine translation evaluation campaign, in which both statistical and traditional rule-based machine translation systems participated, was organized by ARPA in the early 1990s. White *et al.* [1994] present results and discuss in detail the experience with different evaluation strategies. The straightforward application of metrics for human translators proved difficult, and was abandoned along with measurements of productivity of human-assisted translation, which hinges to a large degree on the quality of the support tools and the level of expertise of the translator. Ultimately, only reading comprehension tests with multiple choice questions and adequacy and fluency judgments were used in the final evaluation. Hamon *et al.* [2007b] discuss the evaluation of a speech-to-speech translation system.

Manual metrics – King *et al.* [2003] present a large range of evaluation metrics for machine translation systems that go well beyond the translation quality measures to which we devoted the bulk of this chapter. Miller and Vanni [2005] propose *clarity* and *coherence* as manual metrics. Reeder [2004] shows the correlation between fluency and the number of words it takes to distinguish between human and machine translations. Grading standards for essays from foreign language learners may be used for machine translation evaluation. Using these standards reveals that machine translation has trouble with basic levels, but scores relatively high in advanced categories [Reeder, 2006a]. A manual metric that can be automated is one that asks for specific translation errors – the questions may be based on past errors [Uchimoto *et al.*, 2007]. Vilar *et al.* [2007a] argue for pairwise system comparisons as a metric, which leads to higher inter- and intra-annotator agreement [Callison-Burch *et al.*, 2007].

Task-based metrics – Task-based evaluation of machine translation tests the usefulness of machine translation directly, for instance the ability of human consumers of machine translation output to answer who, when, and where questions [Voss and Tate, 2006]. Jones *et al.* [2006] use a foreign language learner test for measuring speech-to-speech machine translation performance. The adaptation of such a test (the Defense Language Proficiency Test, DLPT) for machine translation revealed that Arabic–English machine translation performance achieves a passing grade up to level 2+, but performs relatively weakly on basic levels.

Word error rate – Word error rate was first used for the evaluation of statistical machine translation by Tillmann *et al.* [1997], who also introduce the position-independent error rate. Allowing block movement [Leusch *et al.*, 2003] leads to the definition of the CDER metric [Leusch *et al.*, 2006]. TER allows for arbitrary block movements [Snover *et al.*, 2006]. MAXSIM uses an efficient polynomial matching algorithm that also uses lemma and part-of-speech tag matches [Chan and Ng, 2008]. The way automatic evaluation metrics work also depends on the tokenization of system output and reference translations [Leusch *et al.*, 2005].

N-gram matching metrics – The BLEU evaluation metric is based on n-grams not words [Papineni *et al.*, 2001]. Several variants of n-gram matching have been proposed: weighting n-grams based on their frequency [Babych and Hartley, 2004], or other complexity metrics

[Babych *et al.*, 2004]. GTM is based on precision and recall [Melamed *et al.*, 2003; Turian *et al.*, 2003]. Echizen-ya and Araki [2007] propose IMPACT, which is more sensitive to the longest matching n-grams. A metric may benefit from using an explicit alignment of system output and reference while maintaining the advantages of n-gram based methods such as BLEU [Liu and Gildea, 2006] and by training such a metric to correlate to human judgment [Liu and Gildea, 2007]. Lavie *et al.* [2004] emphasize the importance of recall and stemmed matches in evaluation, which led to the development of the METEOR metric [Banerjee and Lavie, 2005; Lavie and Agarwal, 2007]. Partial credit for stemmed matches may also be applied to BLEU and TER [Agarwal and Lavie, 2008].

Syntax-based metrics – Metrics may be sensitive to syntactic information [Liu and Gildea, 2005]. A more syntactic approach to machine translation may consider the matching of dependency structures of reference and system output [Owczarzak *et al.*, 2007a], possibly including dependency labels [Owczarzak *et al.*, 2007b]. A wide range of linguistic features for evaluation is explored by Giménez and Màrquez [2007b]. A method based on latent semantic analysis has been proposed for machine translation evaluation [Reeder, 2006b].

Analytical metrics – Automatic metrics may also help in pinpointing the type of errors that machine translation systems make. For instance the relationship of WER and PER indicates the severity of reordering problems, and the relationship of BLEU on stemmed words and surface forms indicates the need for better morphological generation [Popovic *et al.*, 2006]. We may also gain insight into the types of errors by examining word error rates for different parts of speech [Popovic and Ney, 2007].

Evaluation without reference – Some researchers investigate methods that allow automatic evaluation without the use of a reference translation. Gamon *et al.* [2005] train a model that combines the language model probability of the output with syntactic and semantic features. Albrecht and Hwa [2007b, 2008] propose to learn a metric from human judgments and pseudo-reference translations, which are generated by using other machine translation systems that are not necessarily better.

Correlation of automatic and manual metrics – The credibility of automatic evaluation metrics rests on their correlation with reliable human judgments. Coughlin [2003] finds evidence in support of BLEU in a total of 124 evaluations for many European language pairs. Other evaluation campaigns continuously assess correlation of human and automatic metrics, such as in the CESTA campaign [Surcin *et al.*, 2005; Hamon *et al.*, 2007a]. Yasuda *et al.* [2003] and Finch *et al.* [2004]

investigate the required number of reference translations. The number of reference translations may be increased by paraphrasing [Finch *et al.*, 2004; Owczarzak *et al.*, 2006a]. The same idea is behind changing the reference translation by paraphrasing to make it more similar to the reference [Kauchak and Barzilay, 2006], or to attempt to paraphrase unmatched words in the system output [Zhou *et al.*, 2006]. Hamon and Mostefa [2008] find that the quality of the reference translation is not very important. Akiba *et al.* [2003] show strong correlation for BLEU only if the systems are of similar type. BLEU tends to correlate less when comparing human translators with machine translation systems [Culy and Riehemann, 2003; Popescu-Belis, 2003], or when comparing statistical and rule-based systems [Callison-Burch *et al.*, 2006b]. Amigó *et al.* [2006] find that the relationship between manual metrics that measure human acceptability and the automatic metrics that check the similarity of system output with human translations is a bit more complex.

Trained metrics – Albrecht and Hwa [2007a] argue for the general advantages of learning evaluation metrics from a large number of features, although Sun *et al.* [2008] point out that carefully designed features may be more important. Jones and Rusk [2000] propose a method that learns automatically to distinguish human translations from machine translations. Since in practice the purpose of evaluation is to distinguish good translations from bad translations, it may be beneficial to view evaluation as a ranking task [Ye *et al.*, 2007b; Duh, 2008]. Lin and Och [2004] propose a metric for the evaluation of evaluation metrics, which does not require human judgment data for correlation. The metric is based on the rank given to a reference translation among machine translations. Multiple metrics may be combined uniformly [Giménez and Màrquez, 2008b], or by adding metrics greedily until no improvement is seen [Giménez and Màrquez, 2008a].

Difficulty to translate – The difficulty of translating a text may depend on many factors, such as source, genre, or dialect, some of which may be determined automatically [Kirchhoff *et al.*, 2007]. Uchimoto *et al.* [2005] suggests using back-translation to assess which input words will cause problems, and then prompting the user of an interactive machine translation system to rephrase the input.

Statistical significance – Our description of the bootstrap resampling method [Efron and Tibshirani, 1993] for estimating statistical significance follows the description by Koehn [2004b]. For further comments on this technique, see the work by Riezler and Maxwell [2005]. Estrella *et al.* [2007] examine how big the test set needs to be for a reliable comparison of different machine translation systems.

8.5.3 Exercises

1. (⋆) Consider the following system output and reference translation:
   Reference: *The large dog chased the man across the street.*
   System: *The big dog chases a man across the street.*
   (a) Draw a matrix with system words on one axis and reference words on the other (as in Figure 8.5). Compute the word error rate.
   (b) Determine the precision for unigrams to 4-grams, and compute the BLEU score (ignoring the brevity penalty).
   (c) One suggested change to n-gram metrics is the use of partial credit for synonym matches or for the right lemma but wrong morphological form. Compute an adapted BLEU score where synonym and lemma matches count as 50% correct. State your assumptions about what constitutes a synonym.

2. (⋆) We want to test how many sentences a machine translation system translates correctly. We use test sets of various sizes and count how many sentences are correct. Compute the 90%, 95% and 99% confidence intervals for the following cases:

Size of test set	Correct
100 sentences	77 sentences
300 sentences	231 sentences
1000 sentences	765 sentences

3. (⋆⋆) Implement a bootstrap resampling method to measure the confidence intervals for the test sets in Question 2. How would you empirically test if bootstrap resampling is reliable for such a scenario?

4. (⋆⋆) Judge some sentences at http://www.statmt.org/ wmt08/judge/. Afterwards, describe what are the most severe problems in bad translations:
   (a) missing words;
   (b) mistranslated words;
   (c) added words;
   (d) reordering errors;
   (e) ungrammatical output.

5. (⋆⋆⋆) Download human judgment data from a recent evaluation campaign, such as the ACL WMT 2008 shared task,[1] and carry out various statistical analyses of the data, such as:

---

[1] Available at http://www.statmt.org/wmt08/results.html

(a) Plot human judgment against BLEU score for all systems for a language pair and check for patterns (e.g., rule-based vs. statistical systems).

(b) Does intra-annotator agreement improve over time?

(c) Does intra-annotator agreement correlate with time spent on evaluations?

Part III
Advanced Topics

Chapter 9
Discriminative Training

This book presents a variety of statistical machine translation models, such as word-based models (Chapter 4), phrase-based models (Chapter 5), and tree-based models (Chapter 11). When we describe these models, we mostly follow a generative modeling approach. We break up the translation problem (sentence translation) into smaller steps (say, into the translation of phrases) and build component models for these steps using maximum likelihood estimation.

By decomposing the bigger problem into smaller steps we stay within a mathematically coherent formulation of the problem – the decomposition is done using rules such as the chain rule or the Bayes rule. We throw in a few independence assumptions which are less mathematically justified (say, the translation of one phrase is independent of the others), but otherwise the mathematically sound decomposition gives us a straightforward way to combine the different component models.

In this chapter, we depart from generative modeling and embrace a different mindset. We want to directly optimize translation performance. We use machine learning methods to **discriminate** between good translations and bad translations and then to adjust our models to give preference to good translations.

discriminative training

To give a quick overview of the approach: Possible translations of a sentence, so-called **candidate translations**, are represented using a set of **features**. Each feature derives from one property of the translation, and its **feature weight** indicates its relative importance. The task of the machine learning method is to find good feature weights. When applying the model to the translation of a foreign input sentence, the

candidate translation
feature
feature weight

feature value

feature values of each candidate translation are weighted according to the model and combined to give an overall score. The highest scoring candidate is the best translation according to the model.

two-pass approach

re-ranking approach

One realization of discriminative training is a so-called **two-pass approach** or **re-ranking approach** to machine translation. In the first pass, we generate a set of candidate translations for a given input sentence. In the second pass, we add additional features and re-score the candidate translations according to a discriminative model. The main motivation for this approach is that it allows for complex features that would be too expensive to use during the original search.

Another realization of discriminative training is to optimize the features that are used during the decoding process. We distinguish in our presentation here between (a) parameter tuning where only a handful of features are optimized, typically the weights of the traditional components such as the language model, and (b) large-scale discriminative training using millions of features, such as features that indicate the use of a specific phrase translation.

In this chapter, we first look at how to generate good candidate translations and then examine models and methods for combining features and learning feature weights (Section 9.1), discuss the issues and methods in discriminative training (Section 9.2–9.4), and conclude with a section on the related topic of posterior methods (Section 9.5).

9.1 Finding Candidate Translations

The number of possible translations for a sentence grows exponentially with the sentence length, given our machine translation models. Hence, it is computationally infeasible to list all of them, even for short sentences. In practice, we are not interested in *all* translations that our models are able to generate. Most possible translations are very unlikely, and we are really only interested in the good ones.

Recall how we address this problem in Chapter 6 on decoding. Since it is not possible to find the best translation for a given input sentence by listing all of them, we use a beam-search decoding algorithm that reduces the search space by using hypothesis recombination and pruning techniques.

In decoding, we are interested in only the *one* best translation for an input sentence. Now, we are interested in a larger set of promising translations: the candidate translations.

9.1.1 Search Graph

The decoding search algorithm explores the space of possible translations by expanding the most promising partial translations. We can

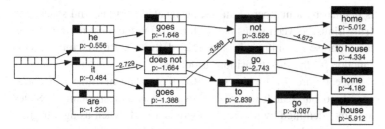

Figure 9.1 Search graph from beam-search decoding (see Chapter 6, particularly Figure 6.2): Hypotheses are represented by rectangles, containing the last added English phrase and the partial translation probability (in log-probability form). The translation process proceeds by hypothesis expansion, where new partial translations form by attaching a new phrase translation to an existing hypothesis. Paths may be merged by hypothesis recombination (white arrowheads).

represent the search process by a **search graph**, as illustrated in Figure 9.1.

search graph

In beam-search decoding, the search for the best translation proceeds through hypothesis expansions. A hypothesis is a partial translation, represented in the figure as a box (containing a sequence of squares representing the foreign word coverage, the last added English phrase, the score of the hypothesis, and an arrow pointing to it from its parent).

Each intermediate hypothesis may expand into many new hypotheses through the application of new phrase translations. Different paths may be merged when they reach hypotheses that are indistinguishable from the point of view of future expansions. This merging of paths is called hypothesis recombination (Section 6.2.4), a standard dynamic programming technique.

Note that hypothesis recombination enriches the search graph. Without it, the number of full paths in the search graph is limited to the number of completed hypotheses that cover the whole sentence. But by allowing alternative paths *to* each hypothesis, we effectively add many more paths. In our example, four completed hypotheses are displayed. The three instances of hypothesis recombination (indicated by white arrowheads) lead to 10 different full paths. This example is, of course, a vast simplification. Typically, many more hypotheses are created during decoding, thus many more full paths exist in the search graph.

9.1.2 Word Lattice

We would like to use the search graph to extract the best translations of the input sentence. For this purpose, we convert the search graph into another data structure. The data structure we use is one that is very common in computer science: a **finite state machine**. Such a machine

finite state machine

states	is defined by a number of **states**, designated start and end states, and
transitions	**transitions** between states. At each transition the most recently trans-
weighted finite state machine	lated phrase is emitted. In a **weighted finite state machine**, a cost

function for the state transitions is defined.

See Figure 9.2 for the weighted finite state machine that corresponds to our search graph. The structure is almost identical. States are now identified by the last two words added (when using a trigram language model, transitions from a state depend on the last two words in the history). The states themselves no longer hold any probability scores; these can now be found at the transitions. Each transition cost is the difference between the costs of the hypotheses that the transition connects. Note that we no longer make a distinction between transitions from regular and recombined hypothesis expansions.

Finite state machine

Formally, a finite state machine is a quintuple $(\Sigma, S, s_0, \delta, F)$, where

- Σ is the alphabet of output symbols (in our case, the emitted phrases);
- S is a finite set of states;
- s_0 is an initial state ($s_0 \in S$) (in our case, the initial hypothesis);
- δ is the state transition function $\delta : S \times \Sigma \rightarrow S$;
- F is the set of final states (in our case, representing hypotheses that have covered all input words).

In a weighted finite state machine, an additional function π is added for the probability distributions for the emissions from each state:

$$\pi : S \times \Sigma \times S \rightarrow \mathbf{R} \qquad (9.1)$$

word lattice   In the **word lattice** of Figure 9.2, the states are given by the last two[1] English output words and the foreign word coverage vector.

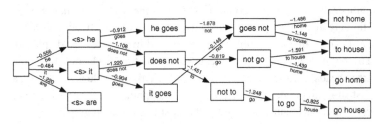

Figure 9.2 Word lattice: We converted the search graph from Figure 9.1 into a weighted finite state machine. This graph is a compact representation of the most promising translations that may be mined for n-best lists.

---

[1] Recall that the number of two relevant English output words in this example comes from the length of the history in a trigram language model.

The transitions are given by the hypothesis extensions, which output a phrase from the alphabet of emitted phrases.

The transition costs (the cost of each hypothesis expansion) are not normalized (all choices do not add up to 1), so the cost function π is not a probability distribution. We could remedy this by adding *dead-end* states that take up the remaining probability mass, so that we can formally treat the word graph as a **probabilistic finite state machine**.

probabilistic finite state machine

9.1.3 N-Best List

A word lattice is an efficient way to store many different translations. Its compact format is due to the common subpaths that many different translations share. However, dealing with so many different translations, even if they are stored efficiently, is computationally too complex for the methods presented here.

If we are interested only in the top n translations, it is better to use a simple list of the translations along with their scores (called the **n-best list**). See Figure 9.3 for the n-best list extracted from the word lattice in Figure 9.2. Note how the list also contains translations that are not represented as final states in the search graph (Figure 9.1), but derive from recombination.

n-best list

Extracting the top n paths from a finite state machine is a well-known problem with efficient solutions. Applying these solutions to the finite state machine created from the search graph is straightforward. Let us quickly describe one such method.

The key insight is that for each state in the graph, there is one **best path** to the beginning. In fact, we already discovered the best path from start to end during the heuristic beam search of the decoding process. Alternative paths take a **detour** from the best path on at least one state of the graph. By detour we mean a suboptimal transition to the previous

best path

detour

Rank	Score	Sentence
1	−4.182	he does not go home
2	−4.334	he does not go to house
3	−4.672	he goes not to house
4	−4.715	it goes not to house
5	−5.012	he goes not home
6	−5.055	it goes not home
7	−5.247	it does not go home
8	−5.399	it does not go to house
9	−5.912	he does not to go house
10	−6.977	it does not to go house

Figure 9.3 N-best list: The top 10 translations for the input sentence *Er geht ja nicht nach Hause* according to the word lattice from Figure 9.2.

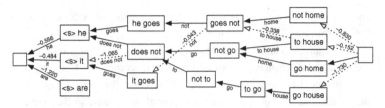

Figure 9.4 Representation of the graph for n-best list generation: Transitions point back to the best previous state to reach the current state (solid lines, filled arrowheads), or to detours that carry additional costs (dotted lines, white arrowheads). The graph also contains a unique end state. To generate an n-best list, detours are selected, starting with the shortest.

state. The detours are also already discovered during the search: they are the recombinations of expanded hypotheses (see Section 6.2.4 on page 161). When recombining hypotheses, the better transition is preserved as the best path; the other may be recorded as a detour.

First, we need a representation of the search graph that makes a distinction between optimal state transitions and detours. See Figure 9.4 for an illustration of this for our example sentence. The new graph also contains a unique end state, which points to the best path and contains detour links to the other complete paths.

Each detour carries an additional cost. In short, the algorithm to generate an n-best list selects detours from existing base paths to find the next best path for the n-best list. This requires that we maintain a sorted list of detours and the cost of the resulting path.

The algorithm proceeds as follows:

1. The first base path is the best path. It is added to the n-best list as the first best translation. All detour transitions from it are recorded in a list that contains triples ⟨base path, detour transition, added cost⟩. The added cost in this case is simply the cost of the detour. The list is sorted by added cost.
2. The cheapest detour is selected from the list (and removed from the list). The base path is a list of states $b = (s_0, ..., s_i, ..., s_{final})$. The detour is a transition s_d, s_i from a state $s_d \notin b$ to a state in the base path $s_i \in b$. Taking this detour leads to a new path. It starts with the best path to s_d and then continues with the states $s_i, ..., s_{final}$. The new path is added to the n-best list.
3. Any detour transitions that occur in the new path *before* s_d are added to the list of detours. The base path is the new path, and the added cost is the cost of the detour transitions plus the cost of the new path.
4. We iterate from step 2 until the required size of the n-best list is filled.

See Figure 9.5 for an illustration of the state of the algorithm after step 1, given our example. The best path is highlighted as the base path, and four detours are considered.

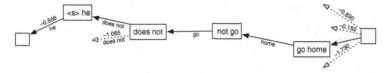

Figure 9.5 Illustration of first step of n-best list extraction: The best path and its detours. The cheapest detour has an additional cost of −0.152, and is selected as the second best path.

9.2 Principles of Discriminative Methods

The word-based models presented in Chapter 4 are an example of generative models. Generative models break down the translation process into smaller steps that we are able to model with probability distributions estimated by maximum likelihood estimation. But now, armed with n-best lists, we can take a completely different look at learning machine translation models.

Each of the candidate translations in the n-best list is represented by a set of features. Anything relevant may be encoded as a **feature**: number of words in the translation, language model score, use of a particular phrase translation, and so on. The features help us to decide how likely it is that each candidate translation is correct. A **feature weight** indicates the importance of each feature.

feature

feature weight

How do we apply models that make use of a feature representation of candidate translations? See Figure 9.6 for an illustration of one approach, **re-ranking**. The base model generates an n-best list of candidate translations. For each candidate, a number of additional features are computed. Then, the re-ranker chooses the best translation among them.

re-ranking

The re-ranker is trained on translation examples generated from the training data. Each example is an input sentence and its n-best candidate translations, which are labeled for correctness using the reference translations. Each candidate translation is represented by a set of features. Training the re-ranker consists essentially of setting a weight for each feature, so that the correct translation for an input sentence is also the best one according to the model.

In contrast to a re-ranking approach, we may want to learn weights for features that are used directly by the decoder. All these approaches have in common that they formulate machine translation as a supervised learning problem, need to define a measure of correctness (the learning goal), and represent translations with a set of features.

9.2.1 Representing Translations with Features

We typically think of a translation as a string of words. From a machine learning point of view, a translation is a training example that is represented by a set of features. What are good features?

Figure 9.6 Machine translation as a re-ranking problem: The initial generative model is used to create an n-best list of candidates. This n-best list may be enriched with additional features. In the training phase, the reference translations are used to learn the best feature weights. When applying this approach to new test data, the weights are applied in the re-ranking phase (second pass) of the decoding process.

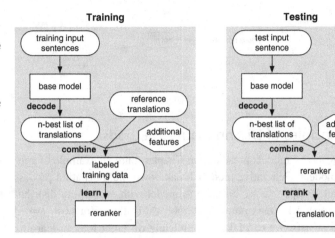

In Chapters 4 and 5 we introduced word-based and phrase-based statistical machine translation models that break down translation probability into smaller components, such as the translation model (that measures how well words or phrases match between input and output), the language model (that measures how well formed the output is), and the reordering model (that measures the likelihood of the movements of words and phrases). These components are typically broken up even further: the translation model may include phrase and lexical translation probabilities as well as phrase and word counts.

In our new approach to machine translation, we can view each model component as a feature. Note that these kinds of features are few in number and the result of rather complex computations (for instance, some require the alignment of input and output words, a nontrivial task). The models are generative and are estimated with maximum likelihood estimation (recall that when the German *haus* is aligned in 80% of all occurrences to *house*, we estimate its translation probability as $p = 0.80$).

model components as features

We now use these **model components as features**. To give two examples: The feature function for the language model component is the language model probability of the English translation **e** of the input sentence **f**. The feature function for the backward phrase translation probabilities is the product of the probabilities for all the phrase translations $\phi(\bar{f}_i|\bar{e}_i)$. We define these two features h_1 and h_2 formally as

$$h_1(x) = h_1(\mathbf{e}, \mathbf{f}, \mathbf{a}) = p_{\text{LM}}(\mathbf{e})$$
$$h_2(x) = h_2(\mathbf{e}, \mathbf{f}, \mathbf{a}) = \prod_i \phi(\bar{f}_i|\bar{e}_i) \qquad (9.2)$$

If we view the components of a phrase-based model as features, then each translation is represented by a vector of about 10–15

real-numbered **feature values**. The goal of the machine learning   feature value
method is to find out how much weight should be given to each of the
features. This particular setup for discriminative training, where only a
handful of features are used, is often referred to as **parameter tuning**.   parameter tuning

Taking the discriminative training approach further, we may decide
to use many features: millions or more. For instance, instead of learning phrase translation probabilities by maximum likelihood estimation,
we may want to define a feature for each phrase translation, such as a
feature indicating whether one candidate translation has the translation,
say, *the house* for the German input *das haus*:

$$h_3(x) = h_3(\mathbf{e}, \mathbf{f}, \mathbf{a}) = \sum_i \delta(\bar{e}_i, \text{the house})\, \delta(\bar{f}_i, \text{das haus}) \qquad (9.3)$$

If this is generally the property of a good translation, it should be a
beneficial feature. Each translation is represented by a subset of active
features. If we want to stick to the view of a vector representation of
training examples, a feature value is a binary flag that indicates whether
the feature is present or not.

Finally, the re-ranking approach allows us to introduce new features
that are not part of the base model used in decoding. For instance, good
output sentences should contain a verb. So, we could introduce a feature
that indicates whether the candidate translation has a verb. Note that we
have access to the full input sentence and candidate translation, so any
global property of the sentence translation may be used as a feature:

$$h_4(x) = h_4(\mathbf{e}, \mathbf{f}, \mathbf{a}) = \begin{cases} 1 & \text{if } \exists e_i \in \mathbf{e},\, e_i \text{ is verb} \\ 0 & \text{otherwise} \end{cases} \qquad (9.4)$$

Currently, re-ranking and parameter tuning are common methods used in competitive statistical machine translation systems, while
discriminative training with millions of features is at the edge of
the research frontier. So we will first describe popular methods for
re-ranking and parameter tuning before reviewing research on large-
scale discriminative training.

9.2.2 Labeling Correctness of Translations

In the overview description of the re-ranking approach to machine translation, we quickly glossed over one difficult question. Given an n-best
list of candidate translations, how do we **label one as correct**? Even if   labeling correctness
we have access to a reference translation, this is a hard problem for two
reasons.

First, the n-best list generated by the base model may include a
translation that is as good as the reference translation. How do we

determine that it is also correct, if it does not match the reference translation?

Second, the base model may not come up with an acceptable translation at all. For instance, it may simply not be able to correctly translate one of the input words, or the translation may require complex restructuring that the model does not allow. If none of the candidate translations is correct, how do we learn something from this sentence?

The problem of labeling a translation as correct is related to the more general problem of **machine translation evaluation**. We discussed the issue of evaluation at length in Chapter 8. There, we propose a solution that evolves around similarity measures between system translations and reference translations. According to this view, the most correct translation in the n-best list is the one that is most similar to the reference translation.

machine translation evaluation

The similarity measure may take properties such as number of word matches, word order, and number of substring matches into account, or even more sophisticated properties of system output and reference translations (stemming, synonym matches). For instance, word error rate is based on the number of word matches in sequence (words out of sequence are thrown out). The widely use BLEU score rewards matches of longer sequences, typically up to 4-grams.

We may use a similarity measure to label the most correct translation. Some of the learning methods we explore in this chapter also work with gradual judgment. Say, improving from a 40% correct translation to a 60% correct translation is better than improving from a 55% correct translation to a 56% correct translation. See Figure 9.7 for an illustration. For the input sentence *er geht ja nicht nach hause*, 10 candidate translations are generated by the base model. Each candidate translation is paired with feature values and an error score, in this case word error rate.

9.2.3 Supervised Learning

Now that we have candidate translations represented with features and labeled for correctness, let us set up machine translation as a **supervised classification** problem. Given a set of candidate translations X, we would like to learn how to classify translations as correct or wrong. In other words, we would like to learn a function

supervised classification

$$f : x \in X \to \begin{cases} \text{correct} & \text{if } x \text{ is a correct translation example} \\ \text{wrong} & \text{otherwise} \end{cases} \tag{9.5}$$

Translation	Feature values						Error
it is not under house	−32.22	−9.93	−19.00	−5.08	−8.22	−5	0.8
he is not under house	−34.50	−7.40	−16.33	−5.01	−8.15	−5	0.6
it is not a home	−28.49	−12.74	−19.29	−3.74	−8.42	−5	0.6
it is not to go home	−32.53	−10.34	−20.87	−4.38	−13.11	−6	0.8
it is not for house	−31.75	−17.25	−20.43	−4.90	−6.90	−5	0.8
he is not to go home	−35.79	−10.95	−18.20	−4.85	−13.04	−6	0.6
he does not home	−32.64	−11.84	−16.98	−3.67	−8.76	−4	**0.2**
it is not packing	−32.26	−10.63	−17.65	−5.08	−9.89	−4	0.8
he is not packing	−34.55	−8.10	−14.98	−5.01	−9.82	−4	0.6
he is not for home	−36.70	−13.52	−17.09	−6.22	−7.82	−5	0.4

Figure 9.7 Translations for the German input sentence *er geht ja nicht nach hause*: Each candidate translation is paired with feature values for six component models (log-probabilities for language model, phrase and word translation models, and a word count feature), as well as an error score (word error rate with respect to the English reference translation *he does not go home*). The goal of discriminative training is to rank the best translation according to the error metric (the candidate translation *he does not home*) on top by giving the features appropriate weights.

An example x in machine translation consists of an input sentence $\mathbf{f}$ and its translation $\mathbf{e}$ with an alignment $\mathbf{a}$ (formally $x = \langle \mathbf{e}, \mathbf{f}, \mathbf{a} \rangle$). Each example $x \in X$ in our training set is represented by a set of features. Formally, each feature is defined as a **feature function** h that maps an example to the feature value $h(x)$.   feature function

The learning task is to discover the **classification function**   classification function

$$f(x) = f(h_1(x), ..., h_n(x)) \rightarrow y \qquad (9.6)$$

Instead of learning a classifier that gives a class $y \in \{\text{correct, wrong}\}$, we may want to learn a probabilistic model that tells us how likely it is that an example belongs to the class of correct translations. We use this probabilistic model to re-rank the n-best list of candidate translations and pick as best translation the one that is deemed correct with the highest likelihood. The model does not need to be a proper probabilistic model, as long as it provides a scoring function that allows us to pick the best translation out of a list of choices.

Typically, the function used to compute the translation probability of an input sentence $\mathbf{f}$ into an output sentence $\mathbf{e}$ with an alignment $\mathbf{a}$ is modeled as a log-linear combination of the feature functions h_i and their weights λ_i:

$$p(\mathbf{e}, \mathbf{a} | \mathbf{f}) = f(x) = \exp \sum_{i=1}^{n} \lambda_i h_i(x) \qquad (9.7)$$

Given this probabilistic model, we can pick the best translation according to the model with the decision rule:

$$\mathbf{e}_{\text{best}} = \text{argmax}_{\mathbf{e}} \, p(\mathbf{e}, \mathbf{a} | \mathbf{f}) \qquad (9.8)$$

How do we know that we have successfully learned a good classification function? We can check how well it classifies the training examples, in other words the **training error**. But ultimately, we want to use the classifier to identify correct translations in unseen test examples; in other words we are interested in the **test error**. It may happen that overly eager reduction of training errors leads to more test errors, a problem called **over-fitting**.

training error

test error

over-fitting

Let us contrast this approach, in which we learn machine translation models, to the methods described in Chapters 4 and 5 on word-based and phrase-based models. In these generative models, we break the translation process into smaller steps (assuming independence) and estimate the component models for the smaller steps with maximum likelihood estimation. Now, we are trying to identify and properly weight the features that discriminate between good and bad examples, in our case between correct and wrong translations. Hence the name **discriminative training**.

discriminative training

The key to successful application of machine learning is the definition of the learning objective, the selection of good features, known as **feature engineering**, and the application of an appropriate learning method. We will examine good ways to address these issues in the context of machine translation in the following sections.

feature engineering

9.2.4 Maximum Entropy

Let us now finally look at one specific method for training discriminative models. A popular optimization method for log-linear models is the **maximum entropy** approach. This has been successfully applied to the re-ranking problem in statistical machine translation [Och and Ney, 2002].

maximum entropy

Maximum entropy is based on the simple principle that after accounting for all the evidence the simplest model should be chosen. By simplest we mean the most uniform, which is the model with the highest entropy.

Consider what the maximum entropy principle means in practice for, say, learning word translation probabilities. Suppose that a dictionary gives the French words *dans, à, de,* and *pour* as possible French translations for the English *in*. We do not know the probabilities of each of the word translation choices, but we do know that they add up to 1:

$$p(\text{dans}|\text{in}) + p(\text{á}|\text{in}) + p(\text{de}|\text{in}) + p(\text{pour}|\text{in}) = 1 \qquad (9.9)$$

If this is all we know, then the most uniform model assigns all four words equal translation probability

$$
\begin{aligned}
p(\text{dans}|\text{in}) &= 0.25 \\
p(\text{á}|\text{in}) &= 0.25 \\
p(\text{de}|\text{in}) &= 0.25 \\
p(\text{pour}|\text{in}) &= 0.25
\end{aligned}
\qquad (9.10)
$$

This model has an entropy of 2, the highest possible entropy for a model with four outcomes. If we consult a parallel corpus, we may find that the English *in* is translated with 30% frequency as *dans*. To adapt our model to conform to this observation, we have to adjust the probabilities to

$$
\begin{aligned}
p(\text{dans}|\text{in}) &= 0.30 \\
p(\text{á}|\text{in}) &= 0.233 \\
p(\text{de}|\text{in}) &= 0.233 \\
p(\text{pour}|\text{in}) &= 0.233
\end{aligned}
\qquad (9.11)
$$

The two observations we accounted for in our model (there are only four possible translations, and one translation has a certain frequency) are very basic, but the maximum entropy framework allows the inclusion of many possible features. For instance, we may observe that the English *in* is almost always translated as *à* if the following English word is *Canada*.

With many more such observations as constraints on our model, the estimation of the maximum entropy model becomes more complicated. Let us put the framework on a more formal footing, and then examine training methods.

Formal definition

Within the maximum entropy framework, we encode statistical observations as features. For instance, the two observations above are encoded as

$$
h_1(x, y) = \begin{cases} 1 & \text{if } x = in \text{ and } y \in \{dans, \grave{a}, de, pour\} \\ 0 & \text{otherwise} \end{cases}
$$

$$
\qquad (9.12)
$$

$$
h_2(x, y) = \begin{cases} 1 & \text{if } x = in \text{ and } y = dans \\ 0 & \text{otherwise} \end{cases}
$$

Features are not required to be binary they may have integer or real values. Recall that we may want to use the language model probability of the translation as a feature in a sentence-level machine translation model. The learning algorithm described below only requires that the feature values are nonnegative.

constraints

The statistics for these features in the training data are enforced as **constraints** on the model. We require that the expected value of a feature h matches its empirical distribution.

The empirical distribution of the feature $\tilde{p}(h)$ follows from the empirical distribution of examples $\tilde{p}(x, y)$:

$$\tilde{p}(h) = \sum_{x,y} \tilde{p}(x, y) \, h(x, y) \qquad (9.13)$$

The expected value of h according to the conditional probability model $p(y|x)$ is

$$p(h) = \sum_{x,y} \tilde{p}(x) \, p(y|x) \, h(x, y) \qquad (9.14)$$

We enforce the constraint that the expected value and the empirical distribution of each feature match $(p(h) = \tilde{p}(h))$; otherwise we want to have the most uniform model. Formally, the most uniform model is the model with maximum entropy, where the entropy measure is derived from conditional entropy:

$$H(p) = -\sum_{x,y} \tilde{p}(x) \, p(y|x) \, \log p(y|x) \qquad (9.15)$$

Learning: improved iterative scaling

The model $p(y|x)$ we are learning takes the form of a log-linear model

$$p(y|x) = \frac{1}{Z(x)} \exp \sum_{i} \lambda_i \, h_i(x, y) \qquad (9.16)$$

where $Z(x)$ is the normalization constant determined by the requirement that $\sum_y p(y|x) = 1$ for all x.

The learning task is to find the parameter weights λ_i. We start with $\lambda_i = 0$ for all weights. Then, we compute changes $\Delta\lambda_i$ and apply them. We iterate this process until the λ_i converge.

improved iterative scaling

In the **improved iterative scaling** algorithm, the changes are computed as the solution to the equation

$$\sum_{x,y} \tilde{p}(x) \, p(y|x) \, h_i(x, y) \, \exp(\, \Delta\lambda_i \, h^{\#}(x, y) \,) = \tilde{p}(h_i) \qquad (9.17)$$

where $h^{\#}(x, y) = \sum_{i=1}^{n} h_i(x, y)$, i.e., the sum of all feature values for an example. If we enforce that $h^{\#}$ is constant, i.e., $h^{\#}(x, y) = M$ for all x, y, which can be done with a filler feature $h_{n+1}(x, y) = M - \sum_{i=1}^{n} h_i(x, y)$, then the update formula is given by

$$\Delta\lambda_i = \frac{1}{M} \log \frac{\tilde{p}(h_i)}{p(h_i)} \qquad (9.18)$$

Fairly straightforward alternative numerical methods for computing $\Delta\lambda_i$ exist for the case when there is not a fixed feature value sum M.

Feature selection

The maximum entropy framework allows the inclusion of a large number of features of many different types. For instance, for our word translation model, we may want to consider features that take surrounding context words into account:

$$h(x, y) = \begin{cases} 1 & \text{if } x = in \text{ and next-word}(x) = Canada \text{ and } y = \grave{a} \\ 0 & \text{otherwise} \end{cases} \qquad (9.19)$$

It is often tempting to define a large number of features, but this then causes computational and over-fitting problems. Therefore, a **feature selection** method is often applied that decides which features are included in the model, and which are left out.

A basic feature selection method adds one feature at a time. Having measuring the impact of all possible features, the feature that improves the model the most is added. The quality of a model is often measured by the probability of the training data given the model. By also considering the likelihood of unseen test data, we can safeguard against over-fitting.

One can measure a model's likelihood gain resulting from one added feature by adding the feature to the model, learning the feature weights, and computing the training data likelihood. But this is computationally too expensive. More practical is to keep the feature weights for the other features constant and try to find only the optimal weight for the added feature. Adding more than one feature at a time also speeds up the feature selection process.

9.3 Parameter Tuning

Recall the **log-linear model** that is commonly used in statistical machine translation. The overall translation probability $p(x)$ is a combination of several components $h_i(x)$, weighted by parameters λ_i:

$$p(x) = \exp \sum_{i=1}^{n} \lambda_i h_i(x) \qquad (9.20)$$

We have not said much about how to set the parameters λ_i. But now, with our notion of machine translation as a machine learning problem

feature selection

log-linear model

parameter tuning in mind, we know how to view this task. **Parameter tuning** consists of learning the feature weights λ_i for the features h_i.

9.3.1 Experimental Setup

Maximum entropy is one machine learning method that can be used to learn the feature weights. We discuss two more methods, Powell search and the simplex algorithm, below. But we first take a closer look at the experimental setup.

Machine translation models are typically estimated from parallel corpora with tens to hundreds of millions of words. Language models may use even more data: billions and even a trillion words have been used in recent research systems. In parameter tuning, we only have to set a handful of feature weights (say, 10–15), so such excessively large training corpora are not necessary. In practice, hundreds or thousands of sentences suffice.

tuning set
development set

The training set used for parameter tuning is called the **tuning set** (or **development set**), and it is kept separate from the original training data for the estimation of translation and language models. It is, in a way, a true representation of actual test sets, which also consist of previous unseen data. Small tuning sets also support the adaptation of the model to specific domains and text types.

Parameter tuning is done with a specific error metric in mind. We want to tweak the parameters λ_i so that we achieve, say, the optimal BLEU score (see Section 8.2.3 on page 226) on the tuning set.

minimum error rate training

Hence parameter tuning is often called **minimum error rate training** (MERT). Optimizing on metrics such as BLEU introduces a new problem, since this metric does not operate on a per-sentence level, but only on the entire set.

Recall that the starting point for parameter tuning is a tuning set of maybe a thousand sentences, which we have translated (using a baseline setting of parameter values) into a collection of n-best lists. For all possible settings of parameters, we now study the effect on the n-best lists. Different translations come out on top, and for these translations we can measure the overall translation error, using metrics such as BLEU.

But here is the problem. Even with only 10–15 features, the space of possible feature values is too large to be exhaustively searched in any reasonable time. It is, after all, a 10–15 dimensional space over the real numbers. So, we need good heuristic methods for searching this space. We discuss two methods below: Powell search (Section 9.3.2) and the simplex algorithm (Section 9.3.3).

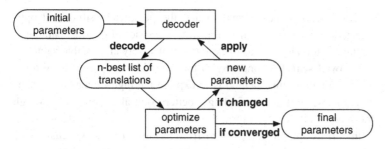

Figure 9.8 Iterative parameter tuning: The decoder generates an n-best list of candidate translations that is used to optimize the parameters (feature weights). This process loops by running the decoder with the new setting. The generated n-best lists for each iteration may be merged.

Another problem is that the original set of n-best lists may be a bad sample of the set of possible translations. They lead us to settle on an optimal parameter setting for this set of n-best lists, but when we use them in the decoder they may produce completely different translations.

One example: If the translations in the n-best lists are on average too long, the optimal parameter setting learnt from them may prefer the shortest possible translation. Plugging these parameter values into the decoder leads then to excessively short translations.

To address the problem, we **iterate** over the training process multiple times. We first translate the tuning set using a baseline setting, generate n-best lists, and find the optimal parameters. Then, we run the decoder again with the new parameter setting, generate new n-best lists, merge the lists, and again find optimal parameters. We iterate until the process converges, or for a fixed number of iterations (say, 5–10). See Figure 9.8 for an illustration of this process.

iterative parameter tuning

9.3.2 Powell Search

The problem of parameter tuning, as we define it, is to find values for a set of parameters (the feature weights $\lambda_1, ..., \lambda_n$ for the features $h_1, ..., h_n$), so that the resulting machine translation error is minimized. The function that maps parameter values to error scores is fully defined and known. Either, we consult a set of n-best lists to find out which translations rise to the top with the specified parameters, or we run the decoder with the parameter values. The resulting translations can be scored with the automatic error function, thus giving us the error score for the parameter values.

What makes this a hard problem is that the function that maps parameters to machine translation error scores is expensive to compute and overly complex. We are not able to use analytical methods (compute derivatives, and find optima) to find the parameter setting that optimizes the error score. At the same time, the space of possible parameter settings is too large for us to explore exhaustively all possible values.

Powell search   **Powell search** is one way to look for the best parameter setting. The idea behind this method is to explore the high-dimensional space of parameter settings by finding a better point along one line through the space. In its simplest form this means that we vary one parameter at a time. If its optimal value differs from its current value, we change the current value, and then optimize the next parameter. If multiple parameters may be changed at a given time, we find the single parameter change with the highest impact on the score and make that change. If there are no more single parameter changes that improve the error score, we are finished.

Visualize this search as trying to find the highest point in the streets of San Francisco, where a grid of streets is placed on uneven terrain. We are able to find the highest point along one street and go to it, and then to try the same along the cross street. But we are not able to move diagonally. There is no guarantee that we will find the highest point in the city. Also, the end point of the search depends on where we start. As elsewhere in this book, we are addressing a computationally hard problem with a heuristic that is not guaranteed to deliver the best result, but will, we hope, produce a good one.

Searching for the best value a single parameter at a time still seems a daunting task. Some parameters have real-numbered values, so there is an infinite number of possible values to consider. But only at a small number of threshold points does the top translation for any input sentence change. We take advantage of this insight in our efficient methods for finding the optimal value for a parameter by first computing the threshold points for each sentence.

Finding threshold points for one sentence

Let us begin with the elementary problem of finding the top translation for a single sentence given a value for the parameter λ_c that we are considering changing. Recall that the overall probability of a translation is

$$p(x) = \exp \sum_{i=1}^{n} \lambda_i h_i(x) \tag{9.21}$$

The sentence that comes out on top is

$$x_{\text{best}}(\lambda_1, ..., \lambda_n) = \text{argmax}_x \exp \sum_{i=1}^{n} \lambda_i h_i(x) \tag{9.22}$$

Note that we leave all $\lambda_i, i \neq c$ unchanged, so we can define

$$u(x) = \sum_{i \neq c} \lambda_i h_i(x) \tag{9.23}$$

as a value for each candidate translation x that is independent of the changing parameter λ_c. Equation (9.22) can then be written

$$x_{\text{best}}(\lambda_c) = \text{argmax}_x \exp(\lambda_c h_c(x) + u(x)) \qquad (9.24)$$

Because the exponential function is monotone, it has no effect on argmax, so we can drop it:

$$x_{\text{best}}(\lambda_c) = \text{argmax}_x \lambda_c h_c(x) + u(x) \qquad (9.25)$$

What we have with the last equation is a representation of the probability score for one translation as a linear function. See Figure 9.9 for an illustration of the lines that represent five different translations. Lines differ in their incline $h_c(x)$ and offset $u(x)$. Our goal is to find which of the lines includes the highest point at each value for λ_c.

Note that when varying the parameter λ_c the best translation x_{best} can only change at intersections of lines. The intersection between two lines, i.e., the point where two translations x_1 and x_2 have the same score with the same λ_c, is given by the equation

$$\lambda_c h_c(x_1) + u(x_1) = \lambda_c h_c(x_2) + u(x_2) \qquad (9.26)$$

Recall that the feature function h_c and the unchanged term u are given, so this equation can be solved straightforwardly to find the value λ_c where the two lines intersect.

The insight that the ranking of translations changes only at intersection points limits the number of values for λ_c that we have to examine to a finite set, instead of exploring all possible values. We call the values for λ_c where the top-rated translation $x_{\text{best}}(\lambda_c)$ changes **threshold points**.   threshold points

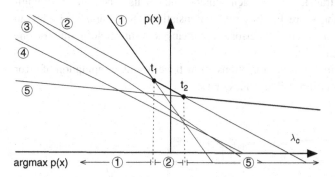

Figure 9.9 When varying one parameter λ_c, the probability score of each translation x for a sentence is given by a linear formula (each translation is represented by a line, labeled with a numbered). Which translation has the best score changes at threshold points (intersections between lines). In this example, the best translation is (1) for $\lambda_c \in [-\inf, t_1]$, (2) for $\lambda_c \in [t_1, t_2]$, and (5) for $\lambda_c \in [t_2, \inf]$.

Note a number of additional observations that lead to an efficient algorithm for finding the highest scoring translation $x_{\text{best}}(\lambda_c)$ for each value of λ_c:

- The best translation for $\lambda_c \rightarrow -\inf$ is the one with the steepest declining line, i.e., the one with the lowest feature value $h_c(x)$. In case of a tie, a higher value for the offset $u(x)$ decides.
- Let us say that x_i is the best translation for an interval that starts at $-\inf$ or some other point. To find the point where the translation x_i is no longer $x_{\text{best}}(\lambda_c)$, one has to compute all its intersections with other lines. The closest intersection after the beginning of the interval is the threshold point to the next best translation x_{i+1}. Note that we only have to consider intersections with lines with a higher incline, i.e., $h_c(x_{i+1}) > h_c(x_i)$.

With this in mind, our algorithm for finding all threshold points is reduced in complexity from $O(n^2)$ (the number of all intersection points) to $O(kn)$, where k is the average number of different translations that are ranked on top per sentence (typically only 3–4): in other words, linear with the size of the n-best list.

Combining threshold points

The method above for finding threshold points operates on one sentence and its n-best list of candidate translations. We now want to compute the overall error for a set of sentences given λ_c. So, we need to find the threshold points for all sentences, and collect them. Then, we compute the error (e.g., the BLEU score) for each relevant interval of values of λ_c by re-ranking the n-best lists, picking the top translation for each sentence out of its n-best list, and computing the score for this set of translations. See Figure 9.10 for an illustration of how the error score changes at threshold points for one parameter.

Again, a few optimizations allow the efficient computation of error scores for all possible values of λ_c:

Figure 9.10 The effect of changing one parameter on the BLEU score: a very rugged error surface. The right-hand graph is a detailed view of the peak (this graph was generated by varying the distortion weight in an Arabic–English model).

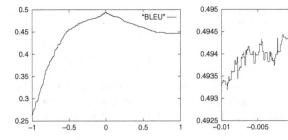

```
Input: sentences with n-best list of translations, initial parameter values
 1:  repeat
 2:    for all parameter do
 3:      set of threshold points T = {}
 4:      for all sentence do
 5:        for all translation do
 6:          compute line l: parameter value → score
 7:        end for
 8:        find line l with steepest descent
 9:        while find line l2 that intersects with l first do
10:          add parameter value at intersection to set of threshold points T
11:          l = l2
12:        end while
13:      end for
14:      sort set of threshold points T by parameter value
15:      compute score for value before first threshold point
16:      for all threshold point t ∈ T do
17:        compute score for value after threshold point t
18:        if highest do record max score and threshold point t
19:      end for
20:      if max score is higher than current do update parameter value
21:    end for
22:  until no changes to parameter values applied
```

Figure 9.11 Pseudo-code for the parameter tuning algorithm using Powell search.

- When constructing the n-best lists of candidate translations, we also compute each translation's impact on the error score. In the case of the BLEU score, we record its length and count the n-gram matches with the reference translations.
- When finding the threshold points, we record not only the value for λ_c, but also the effect on the error score when changing from one translation to another. If there is no effect, we do not even need to store the threshold point at all.

After computing threshold points for each sentence, we collect them all. We efficiently compute the error score for all possible values of λ_c by starting with the minimal value for λ, and then step through all threshold points in sequence, apply the changes to the error score, and detect the interval for λ_c that yields the best error score. The complete algorithm is shown in Figure 9.11.

Regenerating the n-best lists

The parameter tuning process may yield parameter values that are optimal for the n-best list of translations, but not good as parameters for the decoder. In other words, the sample of translations in the n-best lists may lead us to an area of the search space where the best translations according to the model are not well represented in the initial n-best lists.

Hence, it is often important to iterate the process of parameter tuning. First, we generate n-best lists with a basic parameter setting. Then, we find the optimal parameter setting according to this n-best list. Then we iterate: we again generate n-best lists with this new setting. We either add new translations in this list to the ones in the original list, or replace them. Consequently, we try to find the optimal parameter setting again. This iteration is repeated either a fixed number of times (typically 5–10 times), or until no new parameter setting is found. In practice, Powell search easily gets stuck at local minima. Hence, we carry out the search repeatedly from multiple random starting points.

9.3.3 Simplex Algorithm

simplex algorithm

We now look at another popular method for parameter tuning, the **simplex algorithm**. Again, we are looking for a set of parameter values $\{\lambda_j\}$ for a set of feature functions $\{h_j\}$ that optimize translation performance on a set of foreign sentences $\{\mathbf{f}_i\}$, as measured by a scoring function against a set of reference translations $\{\mathbf{e}_i^{\text{ref}}\}$

$$\text{score}\left(\{\mathbf{e}_i^* = \text{argmax}_{\mathbf{e}_i} \exp \sum_j h_j(\mathbf{e}_i, \mathbf{f}_i)\,\lambda_j\}, \{\mathbf{e}_i^{\text{ref}}\}\right) \qquad (9.27)$$

The optimization requires that we compute the error score, and hence obtain the best translations (according to the model) for many different parameter settings. Obtaining the best translation requires running the machine translation decoding process, which is computationally expensive. To keep the computational cost down, we may use an n-best list of the most likely translations instead of running the decoder. In addition (or instead) we may also want to reduce the number of times we have to compute the error score. Compared with Powell search, the simplex algorithm requires fewer such computations.

The intuition behind the algorithm is similar to gradient descent methods. If we find the direction in which the error decreases, then we can update our parameter setting by moving into that direction. Typically, in gradient descent methods, the direction is computed by taking the derivative of the error function. Given the non-smooth error function that we are trying to optimize and the computational complexity of computing that error function, the derivative cannot be computed for theoretical and practical reasons.

The simplex algorithm approximates the computation of the direction of lowest error. In the case of two parameter values, the algorithm starts with three points, i.e., randomly chosen parameter settings, which form a triangle (for n parameter values $n + 1$ points are needed). For each of these points, we evaluate the corresponding error score. Given

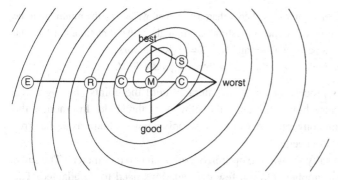

Figure 9.12 Simplex algorithm: Given the three points (possible parameter settings), the line between the worst point and the midpoint (M) between the best and good points is searched for a new edge to the triangle. Considered are the reflection point (R), the extension of the reflection point (E), and contractions (C) between M and worst as well as M and R. A fallback is the triangle of best, M, and S (the midpoint between best and worst).

the error scores, we name the three points *best*, *worst*, and the one in-between *good*.

Considering the triangle that is formed by these three points, we expect the error to decrease when we move along the line from the *worst* point (the top of the triangle) through the center of the base of the triangle which connects the two other points. See Figure 9.12 for an illustration.

The simplex algorithm considers the following points as a replacement for the *worst* point:

- Let M be the midpoint between *best* and *good* (the center of the base of the triangle): $M = \frac{1}{2}(best + good)$. Let R be the reflection of the *worst* point across the baseline of the triangle: $R = M + (M - worst)$. Let E be the extension of that point further down: $E = M + 2(M - worst)$. If R is better than *worst*, we are moving in the right direction. We do not know whether we are moving far enough, so we also consider E:
  case 1: if error(E) < error(R) < error(*worst*), replace *worst* with E
  case 2: else if error(R) < error(*worst*), replace *worst* with R.
- If R is worse than *worst*, then we conclude that both R and E are too far down the line from *worst* through M. We therefore consider points that are closer to the base. Let C_1 be the midpoint between *worst* and M: $C_1 = M + \frac{1}{2}(M - worst)$. Let C_2 be the midpoint between M and R: $C_2 = M + \frac{3}{2}(M - worst)$.
  case 3: if error(C_1) < error(*worst*) and error(C_1) < error(C_2), replace *worst* with C_1;
  case 4: if error(C_2) < error(*worst*) and error(C_2) < error(C_1), replace *worst* with C_2.

- If neither C_1 nor C_2 is better than *worst*, then we expect the minimum to be close to *best*. We therefore shrink the triangle in that direction. Let S be the midpoint between *worst* and *best*: $S = \frac{1}{2}(best + worst)$.

  case 5: replace *worst* with S and replace *good* with M.

This process of updates is iterated until the points converge, i.e., the distance between them falls below a set threshold. In practice, the algorithm converges very quickly, so only a few evaluations of the error function are needed.

Typically we want to optimize more than two parameters. The same algorithm applies. Only a few computations need to be adapted. The number of points increases to $n + 1$ for n parameters. The midpoint M is the center of all points except *worst*. In case 5 all *good* points need to be moved towards midpoints closer to *best*.

9.4 Large-Scale Discriminative Training

In the section above on parameter tuning, we discussed methods for setting the parameter weights for, say, 10–15 components of a statistical machine translation model (language model, phrase translation model, lexical translation model, etc.). We now want to embark on a more ambitious project: the discriminative learning of the **millions of parameters** that make up the component models.

millions of parameters

For instance, instead of learning the translation probability of the phrase translation ϕ(the house|das haus) based on the relative frequency of the words (maximum likelihood estimation), we now want to learn how useful this phrase translation is and set an appropriate feature weight. Given the millions of entries in a phrase translation table, it is easy to see how we end up with millions of features this way.

The large number of features means that we can no longer restrict ourselves to a small tuning set (where *das haus* may not occur at all), but have to train over the entire parallel corpus of maybe millions of sentence pairs.

In an iterative training process, we use an initial model to translate the sentences in the training corpus one by one. Depending on the learning method, we apply some comparison between the best translation according to the model and the reference translation. If they differ, we discount the features that occur in the current model's best translation and promote the features in the reference translation.

The development of methods for training millions of features on millions of sentence pairs is an ongoing area of research. Nevertheless, we are able to distill some lessons and guidance for future work in this area. We take a closer look at the major training issues and describe methods inspired by gradient descent.

9.4.1 Training Issues

Applying large-scale discriminative training methods to machine translation requires us to address issues such as scaling, matching the reference translation, and over-fitting.

Scaling to large training corpora increases computational costs. Note the size of the training data in this case: if we are generating 1,000-best lists for millions of sentence pairs, we are dealing with billions of training examples. The number of features may be larger still. We can take some comfort in the fact that most of the training methods lend themselves to fairly simple parallelization, so that computer clusters can be used.

Due to the large size of the training corpus, it is often beneficial to apply frequent updates instead of just one update after going through all training examples. This is called **online learning**. Not all learning methods support this, however.

We discussed above (in Section 9.2.2 on page 257) the problems of **finding a correct translation** using the model. We may not be able to match the reference translation, and maybe not even an otherwise acceptable translation. We may resort to finding a **substitute** for the reference translation, a translation that can be produced by the model and is similar to the reference translation. Another solution is to discard that sentence pair from the training data. A third solution is called **early updating**. We carry out a normal search for the best translation according to the model. We keep track of when the reference translation can no longer be found, i.e., when it falls out of the beam of the search. With early updating, the learning method only updates the features involved up to this point, i.e., the features that cause the reference translation to fall out of the beam.

A common problem in machine learning is **over-fitting**. Since we optimize translation performance directly on the training data it is possible to learn a model that does well on this data set, but badly on previously unseen sentences.

Consider the over-fitting problem in phrase-based models. The model may learn to translate each sentence with one large phrase pair, leading to perfect performance on the training data, but it is not a useful model for translating unseen test data. This is an extreme example, but any training of phrase models has to deal with the problem that long phrase pairs do well on training data, but are generally less useful.

Scaling to large training corpora

online learning

finding a correct translation

substitute translation

early updating

over-fitting

Over-fitting is mostly a problem of over-estimating the value of infrequent features, and hence a lack of generalization. One way to address this is by eliminating features that occur less than a minimum number of times; another is to smooth the learnt feature weight by a prior. Moreover, at the end of this section we discuss a technique called regularization.

Over-fitting may also be addressed by the jack-knife: learning phrase translation pairs from one part of the corpus and optimizing their weights on another part.

9.4.2 Objective Function

Several machine learning methods may be used for large-scale discriminative training. We have already introduced maximum entropy models in the context of re-ranking, and these have been applied to this more complex problem as well.

Maximum entropy learning is guided by matching the expectations of the empirical and expected feature values in the training data. In contrast to this, we may directly optimize a measure of machine translation error (as we have proposed in the section on parameter tuning). There are many ways to define an error metric. The error metric we adopted for parameter tuning, the BLEU score, has the disadvantage that it is not a sentence-level error metric, but operates on the document level. The methods we discuss in this section need to compute the error on the sentence level, so that BLEU cannot be applied. However, we may use sentence-level error metrics that approximate document-level BLEU.

objective function
loss function
Let us take a look at a few other ways to define the **objective function** (also called the **loss function**) of the learning problem. To define such a learning goal formally, let us first introduce a few concepts. Given a set of input sentences $\mathbf{f}_i$, we are considering candidate translations $\mathbf{e}_{i,j}$. Given a parameter setting $\bar{\lambda}$, we assign to each candidate translation a score $S(\mathbf{e}_{i,j}, \bar{\lambda})$. Let us assume that the candidate translations $\mathbf{e}_{i,j}$ for an input sentence $\mathbf{f}_i$ are sorted according to their scores, i.e., $\mathbf{e}_{i,1}$ is the highest scoring translation. $\mathbf{e}_{i,\text{ref}}$ is the reference translation.

The first obvious candidate for measuring error is to compute how many sentences were wrongly translated. We can define this **sentence error** as follows (the definition uses the truth function TRUE(s), which is 1 if the statement s is true, and 0 otherwise):

$$\text{SENTENCEERROR}(\bar{\lambda}) = \sum_i \text{TRUE}(\mathbf{e}_{i,1} \neq \mathbf{e}_{i,\text{ref}}) \qquad (9.28)$$

This can be a bad choice for measuring error in machine translation performance. For longer sentences, it is unlikely that we are able to match the reference translation exactly, and the metric makes no distinction between near misses and translations that are completely off the mark.

Another error metric, **ranking error**, looks at where the reference translation ranks according to the scoring method with respect to the other candidate translations. Naturally, we would like the reference translation to come out on top, but given the choice between rank 2 and rank 100, we would prefer it to be ranked at the higher spot. This leads us to define the ranking error as

ranking error

$$\text{RANKINGERROR}(\bar{\lambda}) = \sum_i \sum_j \text{TRUE}(S(e_{i,j}, \bar{\lambda}) > S(e_{i,\text{ref}}, \bar{\lambda})) \qquad (9.29)$$

An alternative way to derive a gradual error metric is to directly consider the scores assigned by the scoring function. If the scoring function is a probability function (and if it is not, it is easy to normalize it to be one), we want to have most probability mass assigned to the correct translation. The likelihood of the training data is the product of all reference sentence probabilities

$$\text{LIKELIHOOD}(\bar{\lambda}) = \prod_i \frac{S(e_{i,\text{ref}}, \bar{\lambda})}{\sum_j S(e_{i,j}, \bar{\lambda})} \qquad (9.30)$$

It is customary to use the logarithm of this value, which is called the **log-likelihood**. If we want to use it as an error metric that we aim to minimize (instead of a term to maximum), we adapt it further by taking the inverse. This new metric is then called the **log-loss**, and its definition follows straightforwardly from the definition of likelihood:

log-likelihood

log-loss

$$\text{LOGLOSS}(\bar{\lambda}) = \sum_i -\log \frac{S(e_{i,\text{ref}}, \bar{\lambda})}{\sum_j S(e_{i,j}, \bar{\lambda})} \qquad (9.31)$$

9.4.3 Gradient Descent

With an objective function on hand, the training of the parameter set $\bar{\lambda}$ becomes a well-defined problem. Typically we follow an iterative strategy. Starting with a set of values for the parameters, we would like to change them so that the error is reduced.

Many methods are inspired by the idea of **gradient descent**. We can compute the error for each point in the high dimensional space of possible parameter settings. We would like to move from the current point in the direction where lower errors may be found. Basic analysis tells us that we can take the derivative of the error function with respect to the λ settings to find that direction:

gradient descent

$$\text{UPDATE}(\bar{\lambda}) = \frac{\delta \text{ERROR}(\bar{\lambda})}{\delta \bar{\lambda}} \qquad (9.32)$$

Figure 9.13 Gradient descent methods: Taking the derivative of the error function with respect to the parameter λ, we compute the direction of the reduced error. We move in that direction, until we reach an optimum.

The update can be computed for each single parameter value separately. It is also common to define a learning rate μ by which the derivative is scaled. This gives us the update formula for each parameter λ_i as

$$\text{UPDATE}(\lambda_i) = \mu \frac{\delta \text{ERROR}(\lambda_i)}{\delta \lambda_i} \qquad (9.33)$$

The learning rate may be adjusted during the learning process – first allowing large changes and later reducing the learning rate to enable fine-tuning of a setting. This may be accomplished by constructing a **momentum term** that is the sum of the recent changes, with discounting of older updates.

momentum term

See Figure 9.13 for an example of how gradient descent learning plays out. Given a starting point, we compute the derivative and move in that direction. We may escape local optima by moving over them. We may also overshoot, forcing us to move back.

We are only guaranteed to reach the global optimum if the error function is convex. This is typically not the case for error metrics in machine translation (recall the plot of the BLEU score for a single parameter in Figure 9.10 on page 268). Moreover, it is typically not possible to take the derivative of the error function and hence compute the gradient. Nevertheless, the concept of gradient descent serves as underlying motivation for many other machine learning methods. They incrementally adjust parameter values along the direction of falling error scores.

9.4.4 Perceptron

perceptron

Let us take a look at the **perceptron** algorithm, an error correcting machine learning method that is similar to gradient descent. It is attractive because it is a very simple algorithm, for which convergence proofs exist under certain circumstances [Collins, 2002].

Figure 9.14 displays pseudo-code for the algorithm. We iterate over the training data, sentence by sentence. If the model predicts a best translation of the sentence different from the reference translation, then

```
Input: set of sentence pairs (e, f), set of features
Output: set of weights λ for each feature
 1:  λ_i = 0  for all i
 2:  while not converged do
 3:    for all foreign sentences  f do
 4:      e_best = best translation according to model
 5:      e_ref = reference translation
 6:      if e_best ≠ e_ref then
 7:        for all features feature_i do
 8:          λ_i += feature_i(f, e_ref) − feature_i(f, e_best)
 9:        end for
10:      end if
11:    end for
12:  end while
```

Figure 9.14 Perceptron algorithm: The algorithm updates the feature weights λ_i if it makes a prediction error on a single sentence.

we update the feature weights for each feature involved. The update is the difference between the feature values. In essence, we promote features that are expressed more strongly in the reference translation than in the model translation, and discount features for which the opposite is the case.

The perceptron algorithm is an online learning method. By this we mean that the algorithm makes predictions while it is still learning. Contrast this with **batch learning** such as maximum likelihood esti- batch learning mation, where we first collect and analyze all the training data and then apply it to make predictions. When learning a model with the perceptron algorithm, we update the model with each training example.

Under certain circumstances, it can be shown that the perceptron algorithm is guaranteed to converge. The most important requirement is that the data are linearly separable, i.e., that a solution exists that separates the correct translations from the wrong ones.

9.4.5 Regularization

Of course, convergence on the training data is not necessarily the best possible outcome of the learning process. Recall our discussion of over-fitting. We may get the best possible performance on the training data but end up with a model that is not general enough to perform well on unseen test data.

To prevent over-fitting, we may want to recall one principle of machine learning that we have already encountered in maximum entropy estimation. All things being equal, we prefer a simpler model. We may want to include this principle in the objective function. This is called **regularization**. To put this formally, the learning goal is both regularization low error and low model complexity:

$$\text{LEARNINGGOAL}(\bar{\lambda}) = \text{ERROR}(\bar{\lambda}) + \text{MODELCOMPLEXITY}(\bar{\lambda}) \quad (9.34)$$

For the log-linear models we are considering here a simpler model has fewer features, and the features do not have extreme weights. For instance, if a feature occurs very rarely, and our learning method decides that it has a large impact, then we run the risk of being misled by noise. Think of a feature that corresponds to the use of the translation of a long phrase that only applies in one sentence. It may be better to suppress such a feature.

To give an example for regularization for the sentence error, see the equation below, where we include the squared value of the feature weights in the objective function:

$$\text{LEARNINGGOAL}(\bar{\lambda}) = \sum_i \text{TRUE}(\mathbf{e}_{i,1} \neq \mathbf{e}_{i,\text{ref}}) + \sum_j \lambda_j^2 \qquad (9.35)$$

This formula implies that we prefer low feature values while having a low error. A good feature reduces the error more than its feature weight burdens the model with additional complexity.

9.5 Posterior Methods and System Combination

We conclude this chapter with a class of methods that operate on n-best lists and that have been shown to be useful for many purposes. These methods are based on posterior probabilities, which are computed using some measure of similarity between the most likely translations.

9.5.1 Minimum Bayes Risk

The decoding heuristic we presented in Chapter 6 tries to find the most likely translation given the input. In other words, the decision rule

maximum a posteriori   for selecting the output translation $\mathbf{e}_{\text{best}}$ is the **maximum a posteriori** (MAP) translation

$$\mathbf{e}_{\text{best}}^{\text{MAP}} = \text{argmax}_{\mathbf{e}} \ p(\mathbf{e}, \mathbf{a}|\mathbf{f}) \qquad (9.36)$$

Note that even if the foreign input sentence $\mathbf{f}$ can be translated with different alignments $\mathbf{a}$ into the same output sentence $\mathbf{e}$, we rely only on the alignment that gives us the highest probability. But what if there are other alignments that lead us to the same translation $\mathbf{e}$? Do they not give us more confidence that $\mathbf{e}$ is a good translation? So, instead of relying on only one alignment $\mathbf{a}$ to indicate that $\mathbf{e}$ is a good translation, we may want to sum the probabilities over all alignments. This gives us the decision rule

$$\mathbf{e}_{\text{best}}^{\text{SUM}} = \text{argmax}_{\mathbf{e}} \sum_{\mathbf{a}} p(\mathbf{e}, \mathbf{a}|\mathbf{f}) \qquad (9.37)$$

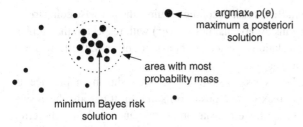

Figure 9.15 Minimum Bayes risk (MBR) decoding: This graph displays potential translations as circles, whose sizes indicate their translation probability. The traditional *maximum a priori* (MAP) decision rule picks the most probable translation. MBR decoding also considers neighboring translations, and favors translations in areas with many highly probable translations.

The intuition behind **minimum Bayes risk decoding** takes this argument a bit further. Consider the situation in Figure 9.15. The maximum a posteriori translation may be an outlier. Most of the probability mass may be concentrated in a different area of the search space. Given the uncertainties in our probability estimates, why risk betting on that outlier if we are more confident that the best translation is somewhere in the dense area?

minimum Bayes risk decoding

Formally, the decision rule for minimum Bayes risk decoding is

$$e_{\text{best}}^{\text{MBR}} = \text{argmax}_{\mathbf{e}} \sum_{\mathbf{e'},\mathbf{a'}} L((\mathbf{e}, \mathbf{a}), (\mathbf{e'}, \mathbf{a'}))\, p(\mathbf{e'}, \mathbf{a'}|\mathbf{f}) \tag{9.38}$$

The translation $e_{\text{best}}^{\text{MBR}}$ that is selected by this decision rule can be viewed as a **consensus translation**, since it is not only very probable but also similar to the other very probable translations.

consensus translation

We need to define a loss function L to measure the similarity of translations. It is advantageous to select a loss function that is related to the error function with which we score translations against reference translations. We introduced a number of error functions in Chapter 8 on evaluation. If we measure translation quality by, say, the BLEU score, then we do best to also use BLEU as a loss function in minimum Bayes risk decoding:

$$L((\mathbf{e}, \mathbf{a}), (\mathbf{e'}, \mathbf{a'})) = \text{BLEU}(\mathbf{e}, \mathbf{e'}) \tag{9.39}$$

Note that the traditional maximum a posteriori decoder is a special case of minimum Bayes risk decoding with the loss function

$$L((\mathbf{e}, \mathbf{a}), (\mathbf{e'}, \mathbf{a'})) = \begin{cases} 1 & \text{if } \mathbf{e} = \mathbf{e'} \text{ and } \mathbf{a} = \mathbf{a'} \\ 0 & \text{otherwise} \end{cases} \tag{9.40}$$

How does this work out in practice? Of course, it is not possible to explore the space of all possible translations, so we have to limit ourselves to a manageable set of the most likely translations. The decision rule of minimum Bayes risk decoding requires the pairwise comparison of all possible translations, making it $O(n^2)$ with respect to the number n of possible translations. Hence, we consider only, say, the 1,000 most probable translations.

Minimum Bayes risk decoding has been shown in practice to improve over the maximum a posteriori solution. It has also been successfully used to optimize translation performance with specific error functions.

9.5.2 Confidence Estimation

As discussed above, the goal of minimum Bayes risk decoding is to find the translation that we believe to be more likely to be correct than the maximum a posteriori translation. We do this by finding a high-probability translation that is similar to other high-probability translations.

confidence estimation Related to this problem of trusting a high-scoring translation is the problem of **confidence estimation**. If a machine translation decoder outputs a translation, it is often useful to know how confident the decoder is that the translation is correct.

There are several applications for this, for instance interactive translation aids. If a human translator is aided by a translation tool, this tool should not provide the translator with its translation when it is uncertain that the translation is correct. Consumers of machine translation also benefit from indications of text portions that are more likely to be wrong. Another application is system combination, which we discuss in the next section.

One method for confidence estimation follows from the same principle as minimum Bayes risk decoding. If most of the high-probability translations agree on how a particular word is translated, we trust its translation more than if there is great variety.

Let us define this formally. We want to know the confidence for a specific word e at position i. First, we generate an n-best list of sentence translations $\{e_j\}$ for the input sentence $\mathbf{f}$. We normalize the probabilities, so that the probabilities for all the translations we sampled add up to one:

$$\sum_j p(\mathbf{e}_j|\mathbf{f}) = 1 \qquad (9.41)$$

word posterior probability The **word posterior probability** of an English output word e occurring in a particular output position i is the sum of the probabilities of translations $\mathbf{e}_j$ where the ith word $e_{j,i}$ is the word e:

$$p_i(e|\mathbf{f}) = \sum_j \delta(e, e_{j,i})\, p(\mathbf{e}_j|\mathbf{f}) \qquad (9.42)$$

The word posterior probability $p_i(e|\mathbf{f})$ is a measure of how sure the model is about the translation of the word e at position i, meaning how confident the model is about this particular word translation.

Tying the confidence measure for word e to a specific word position i is questionable for long sentences, where several translations may contain the word e, but at different positions due to changes elsewhere in the sentences. Hence, more refined confidence estimation methods for translations for words in the output rely on alignments to the source (is e a translation of a particular input word f?), or use methods like Levenshtein distance to align the sentence translations.

9.5.3 System Combination

Different machine translation systems have different strengths and weaknesses. If we have access to several systems, it may be a good idea to **combine** them to get overall better translations. There are many ways to approach this, for instance by swapping components and sharing resources.

system combination

Here, we describe a method that takes the output of different systems without any additional annotation and combines them into a **consensus translation**. We do not attempt to pursue any deeper integration of the systems, so we have to make no assumptions about how these systems work.

consensus translation

Consider the three translations in Figure 9.16, produced by three different systems for the same input sentence. We could simply choose the translation of the system that we trust the most. But instead, we may be able to construct an even better translation out of the parts of the different system outputs.

To be able to pick and choose from different translations, we first introduce a new data structure, called a **confusion network**. It is related

confusion network

System translations

it_1 $does_2$ not_3 go_4 $home_7$
he_1 $goes_4$ not_3 to_5 the_6 $home_7$
he_1 $does_2$ not_3 go_4 $house_7$

Confusion network

| $it_{0.33}$ | $does_{0.67}$ | $not_{1.00}$ | $go_{0.67}$ | $\epsilon_{0.67}$ | $\epsilon_{0.67}$ | $home_{0.67}$ |
| $he_{0.67}$ | $\epsilon_{0.33}$ | | $goes_{0.33}$ | $to_{0.33}$ | $the_{0.33}$ | $house_{0.33}$ |

Figure 9.16 Confusion network: Translations from three different systems are converted into a linear sequence of alternative word choices (including the empty word ϵ), allowing the construction of a consensus translation. Note that this representation requires the alignment of the sentences at the word level and special treatment of reordering.

to the word lattice we introduced in Section 9.1.2, but has a simpler form. In a linear sequence, we may pick a word out of each column. If we draw this as a word lattice with state transitions, each translation has to move through the same states. The graph of this lattice reminds sausage some people of a **sausage**, which is a colloquial name for this type of graph.

Each word in the confusion network is annotated with a probability. In the example, we computed for each word the maximum likelihood probability that it occurs in one of the system translations. We may take a more refined approach for estimating the word probabilities. Some systems may be more reliable than others, so we may want to give their output more weight. Also, when picking out a consensus translation, we may not just simply select the most likely words, but also take language model probabilities into account, thus having some assurance of fluent output.

Note that it is not trivial to construct a confusion network out of a set of system translations. For instance, we placed the words *go* and *goes* in the same column, but why? We need to have some evidence that these two words are interchangeable. This evidence may either come from word alignments to the source, or by aligning the output sentences using word alignment methods discussed in Section 4.5. Also, methods that originate in evaluation metrics research have been used to match sentences, since it is a similar problem to align system outputs to a reference translation.

There is one more issue with the construction of the consensus network: word order. Note that not all the sentences are in the same order. In the first translation, the word *go* follows the word *not*, while in the second translation, the word *goes* occurs before *not*.

Since the confusion network allows us to arrive at a consensus translation that contains word choices different from any single system output, we may be tempted to pursue the same flexibility for word order – in other words to allow the consensus translation to have a word order that does not match any single system output. However, we typically prefer methods that are simpler and avoid too much complexity.

The following methods have been proposed:

skeleton
- Use the order of the output of the best system as a **skeleton**. Align all other system outputs to this sentence.
- Same as above, but do not always pick the output of the best overall system; rather decide on a sentence-by-sentence basis, which takes overall quality of the system and minimum Bayes risk calculations with regard to other system outputs into account (i.e., bias towards the system output that agrees most with all other system outputs).

- Same as above, but establish not only one linear skeleton, but a lattice from all system outputs, and weight each path with overall system quality and minimum Bayes risk scores.
- Same as above, but align sentences to the growing confusion network iteratively, i.e., using the words in the skeleton and prior system outputs to match words.

One final note on system combination: Since it has evolved as a successful strategy, it is also applied as a lazy way to resolve design decisions. Systems may be built with different morphological preprocessing or word alignment methods. Instead of carefully composing the best possible method, we may simply build different systems for any of the possible choices, translate an input sentence with each of these systems, and combine their outputs.

9.6 Summary

9.6.1 Core Concepts

This chapter presented methods for **discriminative training**, in which the translation task is modeled so that each possible **candidate translation** is represented by **feature values** for a set of **features**. In the learning stage, each feature is assigned a **feature weight** which reflects its relevance to good translations. The discriminative training approach enables a **two-pass** or **re-ranking** approach to machine translation, where in the first stage a baseline model generates candidate translations and in the second stage additional features support the selection of the best translation. Discriminative training also enables direct optimization of translation performance.

Candidate translations may be extracted by converting the **search graph** of a statistical machine translation decoder into a **word lattice**, which is typically represented by a **weighted finite state machine**, which is a probabilistic version of a **finite state machine** where state transitions are modeled by probability distributions. The word lattice may also be mined to generate an **n-best list**.

Discriminative training for statistical machine translation is an instance of **supervised learning**. We prepare a training set of input sentences paired with candidate translations, of which at least one is labeled as correct (based on similarity or identity to the reference translation). One popular method for this type of supervised learning is the **maximum entropy** approach, in which feature weights are set by the **improved iterative scaling** algorithm. Typically **feature selection** plays an important role in choosing a set of high-quality features.

Any modern statistical machine translation system includes a **parameter tuning** stage in training to set optimal values for important system parameters, typically weights in a log-linear system model the contributions of a handful of components such as the language model. **Powell search** optimizes one parameter at a time, while the **simplex algorithm** searches for the direction of greatest improvement in the parameter space.

A current research challenge in statistical machine translation is **large-scale discriminative training**, in which probability estimates are completely replaced by features and feature values, resulting in millions of features. Training directly attempts to optimize an **objective function** (or **loss function**), which is related to some measure of translation quality. In **gradient descent** methods, the steepest direction of improvement in the feature space is followed. In the **perceptron** algorithm, the feature sets of the current system output and reference translation are compared and their weights adjusted. By **regularization** we take the model complexity into account and prefer simpler models.

Related to discriminative training are **posterior methods**, where the probability distribution over a sample of the best candidate translations is exploited. In **minimum Bayes risk decoding**, we prefer a translation that is similar to other high-probability translations. **Confidence estimation** for words in the output may use posterior methods by checking if a particular output word is in most high-probability translations. **System combination**, the combination of the output of several machine translation systems, uses the same principle and prefers words in the output that many systems agree on.

9.6.2 Further Reading

Word graphs – The generation of word graphs from the search graph of the decoding process was first described by Ueffing et al. [2002]. Zens and Ney [2005] describe additional pruning methods to achieve a more compact graph. Word graphs may be converted into confusion networks or mined for n-best lists. Alternatively, the n-best list may be extended with additional candidate translations generated with a language model that is trained on the n-best list [Chen et al., 2007a] or from overlapping n-grams in the original n-best list [Chen et al., 2008b].

Parameter tuning – Our description of minimum error rate training follows the original proposal by Och [2003]. Properties of this method are discussed by Moore and Quirk [2008]. Cer et al. [2008] discuss regularizing methods that average BLEU scores over a small window to smooth over the curves. Many researchers also report on using the simplex algorithm [Nelder and Mead, 1965]. The implementation of these methods is described by Press *et al.* [1997]. Tuning may use multiple reference translations, or even additional reference translations generated by paraphrasing the existing reference [Madnani *et al.*, 2007].

Re-ranking – Minimum error rate training is used for re-ranking [Och *et al.*, 2004]; other proposed methods are based on ordinal regression to separate good translations from bad ones [Shen *et al.*, 2004] and SPSA [Lambert and Banchs, 2006]. Duh and Kirchhoff [2008] use boosting to improve over the log-linear model without any additional features. Hasan *et al.* [2007] examine how big n-best lists can be and still provide gains, considering both Oracle-BLEU and actual re-ranking performance, and see gains with n-best lists of up to 10,000. The use of a log-linear model imposes certain restrictions on features that may be relaxed using other machine learning approaches such as kernel methods or Gaussian mixture models [Nguyen *et al.*, 2007]. See work by Chen *et al.* [2007b] and Patry *et al.* [2007] for some recent examples of the type of features used in re-ranking.

Large-scale discriminative training – Large-scale discriminative training methods that optimize millions of features over the entire training corpus have emerged more recently. Tillmann and Zhang [2005] add a binary feature for each phrase translation table entry and train feature weights using a stochastic gradient descent method. Kernel regression methods may be applied to the same task [Wang *et al.*, 2007c; Wang and Shawe-Taylor, 2008]. Wellington *et al.* [2006a] applies discriminative training to a tree translation model. Large-scale discriminative training may also use the perceptron algorithm [Liang *et al.*, 2006a] or variations thereof [Tillmann and Zhang, 2006] to directly optimize on error metrics such as BLEU. Arun and Koehn [2007] compare MIRA and the perceptron algorithm and point out some of the problems on the road to large-scale discriminative training. This approach has also been applied to a variant of the hierarchical phrase model [Watanabe *et al.*, 2007b,a]. Blunsom *et al.* [2008] argue the importance of performing feature updates on all derivations of translation, not just the most likely one, to address spurious ambiguity. Machine translation may be framed as a structured prediction problem, which is a current strain of machine learning research. Zhang *et al.* [2008b] frame ITG decoding in such a way and propose a discriminative training method following the SEARN algorithm [Daumé III *et al.*, 2006].

Minimum Bayes risk – Minimum Bayes risk decoding was introduced initially for n-best-list re-ranking [Kumar and Byrne, 2004], and has been shown to be beneficial for many translation tasks [Ehling *et al.*, 2007]. Optimizing for the expected error, not the actual error, may also be done in parameter tuning [Smith and Eisner, 2006a]. Related to minimum Bayes risk is the use of n-gram posterior probabilities in re-ranking [Zens and Ney, 2006b; Alabau *et al.*, 2007a,b].

Confidence measures – Our description of confidence measures is largely based on the work by Ueffing *et al.* [2003] and Ueffing and Ney [2007]. Other researchers extend this work using machine learning methods [Blatz *et al.*, 2004] or to multiple, especially non-statistical, systems [Akiba *et al.*, 2004b]. Sanchis *et al.* [2007] combine a number of features in a smoothed naive Bayes model. Confidence measures have been used for computer-aided translation tools [Ueffing and Ney, 2005]. Confidence measures have also been used in a self-training method. By translating additional input language text, we bootstrap a parallel corpus to train an additional translation table, but it helps if we filter the bootstrapped corpus using confidence metrics [Ueffing, 2006]. This may also be done iteratively, by retraining the model and adding more sentences each time [Ueffing *et al.*, 2007a]. Alternatively, the original training data may be discarded and the phrase table (and other components) only trained from the n-best lists [Chen *et al.*, 2008a].

System combination – System combination is also called Multi-Engine Machine Translation [Nomoto, 2003], and may take the form of a classifier that decides which system's output to trust [Zwarts and Dras, 2008]. The prevailing idea is to combine the output of different systems without deeper integration of their architectures, which has been very successful in speech recognition [Fiscus, 1997] and follows a machine learning paradigm called ensemble learning. Bangalore *et al.* [2002] use a confusion network representation for the computation of consensus translations of different off-the-shelf systems, while van Zaanen and Somers [2005] use a word graph and Jayaraman and Lavie [2005] use a decoder to search through possible combinations, possibly augmented with a phrase translation table [Eisele *et al.*, 2008]. Eisele [2005] compares a statistical and a heuristic method. Our description follows work by Rosti *et al.* [2007a,b] who propose the construction of confusion networks by aligning the different system outputs, which may be improved by a incremental alignment process [Rosti *et al.*, 2008]. Matusov *et al.* [2006b] use IBM models to align the words in the different system translations, while Karakos *et al.* [2008] suggest limiting alignments with the ITG constraint. Word alignment may be aided by using information about synonyms, which may be provided by Wordnet synsets [Ayan *et al.*, 2008]. Huang and Papineni [2007] use some of the internals of the translation systems, such as phrase segmentation, to guide combination. Macherey and Och [2007] look at various properties of system combination methods, such as the relative quality of the systems and how well they correlate, and their effect on success.

System combination may also be used to combine systems that use the same methodology, but are trained on corpora with different morphological preprocessing [Lee, 2006], or different word alignment methods [Kumar *et al.*, 2007].

9.6.3 Exercises

1. (⋆) Given the following search graph:

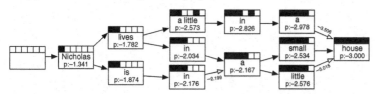

(a) Convert the search graph into a phrase lattice with back-pointers as in Figure 9.4.

(b) Extract the 10 most probable paths through the graph.

2. (⋆) Given the following n-best translations and feature scores:

	h_1	h_2	h_3
small is the house	0.4	0.4	0.4
a small house is	0.6	0.7	0.2
the house is small	0.2	0.6	0.3

find weights for the features in a log-linear model to rank the third translation on top of the n-best list (highest probability).

3. (⋆) Construct a confusion network for the following sentences:

> *the old man bought the small house yesterday*
> *a gentlemen bought the cottage the day before*
> *the grandfather bought a small hut earlier*
> *the man purchased the tiny house yesterday*
> *the old gentlemen obtained the house yesterday*

4. (⋆⋆) Implement an algorithm that extracts an n-best list from a search graph. To test your program, obtain a search graph from a machine translation system using the Moses system.[2]

5. (⋆⋆) Implement a basic re-ranking framework, using the Moses system and maximum entropy toolkit such as Yasmet.[3]

6. (⋆⋆) Implement minimum Bayes risk decoding with BLEU as loss function and test it on an n-best list.

---

[2] Available at http://www.statmt.org/moses/
[3] Available at http://www.fjoch.com/YASMET.html

Chapter 10
Integrating Linguistic Information

The models we have discussed so far make no use of syntactic annotation. Both word-based models (Chapter 4) and phrase-based models (Chapter 5) operate on the surface form of words. In this and the next chapter we discuss methods that attempt to improve the quality of statistical machine translation by exploiting syntactic annotation in various ways. This chapter focuses on methods that extend the phrase-based approach, and the next chapter introduces a new framework that is based on the type of tree structures and grammars that are most commonly used in syntactic theory.

Output from phrase-based systems may look like this (translation from French using Europarl data):

> *We know very well that the current treaties are not enough and that it will be necessary in future to develop a structure more effective and different for the union, a more constitutional structure which makes it clear what are the competence of member states and what are the powers of the union.*

While all the content words are translated correctly and the sentences seems coherent at a local level, there are problems with overall grammaticality. There are problems with the placement of verbs and adjectives, which make the output hard to read.

The argument for including **syntactic annotation** in statistical machine translation models rests on various points, such as:

syntactic annotation

- **Reordering for syntactic reasons:** Often the reordering of words necessary during translation can be easily described using syntactic terms. When translating French–English, adjectives have to be moved from behind the noun to

reordering

in front of the verb (note the erroneous *a structure more effective and different* in the example above). In German–English, the verb often has to be moved from the end of the sentence to the position after the subject. German sentences also allow the object to come before the subject, so these have to be switched. Having concepts such as *verb* or *subject* available to the model will make the formulation of such reordering much more straightforward.

function words
- **Better explanation for function words:** Function words are typically not translated one-to-one from one language to another. Some types of function words may not even exist in some languages. For instance, Chinese lacks determiners. Function words such as prepositions may be used very differently in different languages. They define how the content words in a sentence relate to each other, and this relation may be expressed in various different forms (for instance by word order). The deletion, addition, and translation of function words is often better explained by the underlying syntactic relation. For instance the French preposition *de* in *entreprises de transports* causes a word order change in English to *haulage companies*.

conditioning on related words
- **Conditioning on syntactically related words:** The tough problem of word choice when multiple translations of a word are possible is tackled in phrase-based systems by allowing words to be translated with their context (by translating phrases) and by the use of a language model. Both these means only use the context of directly neighboring words. But for instance for the translation of a verb, its subject and object may be very important. For instance *make sense* translates to German as *ergibt Sinn* while *make a plan* translates as *erstellt einen Plan*. Note that any number of words may appear between verb and object (*make really not all that much sense*). This suggests that we should condition word translation on syntactically related words.

syntactic language models
- **Use of syntactic language models:** Traditional n-gram language models build on the local coherence of words. If neighboring words match up nicely, the language model probability is better. However, its local scope limits the language model from detecting long-distance grammatical problems such as the example in Figure 10.1. The sentence *The house is the man is small* consists only of good trigrams, but it is syntactically flawed. It contains two

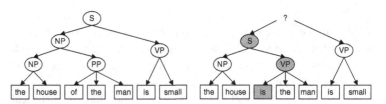

Figure 10.1 Syntactic language models: While both sentences contain good trigrams, the left-hand sentence has a straightforward syntactic parse, while parsing the right-hand sentence causes problems due to its two verbs. By utilizing this type of syntactic information, we may be able to produce more grammatical output.

verbs. By including the need for a viable syntactic parse tree in the language model, we may be able to produce more grammatical output.

The argument against syntactic annotation is that this type of markup does not occur in sentences originally, and has to be added using automatic tools. These tools can have a significant error rate (for instance, parsing performance is often no better than 90%), so while syntax may be useful in theory, it may not be available in practice. Also, adding syntactic annotation makes models more complex and harder to deal with (for instance, increasing search errors).

As always, the argument has to be fought out in practice, by showing empirically that models that incorporate syntactic annotation outperform traditional models.

10.1 Transliteration

The methods presented throughout this book are based on the assumption that translation takes place between sequences of word tokens from a finite set. There are a few exceptions where this assumption breaks down, most notably numbers and names. There are infinitely many possible numbers and names, quite literally.

10.1.1 Numbers and Names

Translation of **numbers** and **names** is trivial between, say, German and English, since both use the same writing system (the Latin alphabet), so names and numbers are written almost identically. The odd exception is the use of punctuation in large and fractional numbers such as 12,345.67 (English), which is written 12.345,67 in German.

Large numbers in European languages are simplified using a system based on the factor 1000: thousands, millions, billions, trillions, etc. In Chinese, the corresponding system is based on the factor 10,000. The Chinese 5.23萬 translates as 52,300 in English.

A statistical machine translation system cannot be expected to efficiently and robustly learn translation entries for all possible numbers. Since it is relatively straightforward to capture number translation with a small rule-based component, we may want to separate this out into a processing step that detects numbers in the input and instructs the machine translation system to use specified translations for them.

Der Dow stieg um <NUM english="*0.65*"> *0,65* </NUM> *Prozent.*

The **XML markup** instructs the machine translation decoder on the specified translation for the number in the sentence. The same strategy

numbers
names

XML markup

can be useful for the translation of names, especially if we have not seen them before in our training data.

10.1.2 Name Translation

Name translation is a serious challenge if the input and output languages use different writing systems, for instance in the case of Japanese–English translation. Most writing systems are phonetic, i.e., they transcribe the sounds of the languages, be it syllables (Chinese, Japanese kanji) or individual consonants and vowels (Latin, Arabic, Japanese katakana). In Chinese, the relationship between characters and meaning is stronger than the relationship between characters and sounds, but the rendering of foreign names is based on the phonetics of characters.

transliteration   Since translating names is essentially a process of mapping letters (or characters), it is called **transliteration**. Figure 10.2 illustrates of how a name may be transliterated from Japanese to English. In both the English alphabet and the Japanese katakana, letters can be mapped to sounds. Since the sounds should be very similar, we should be able to match them up.

Note that the process of mapping Japanese katakana to Japanese sounds to English sounds to English letters is ambiguous at every step. While the mapping of Japanese katakana to Japanese sounds is exceptionally exact, Japanese sounds do not map exactly to English sounds. For instance the distinction between *r* and *l* in English is not made in Japanese. The mapping of English sounds to English letters is famously ambiguous. For instance the pronunciation of the English *kn* is the same as *n*.

10.1.3 A Finite State Approach to Transliteration

Given the ambiguity of mapping letters to sounds and back, as well as the lack of clear rules to govern mapping, the transliteration problem is well suited to the statistical approach.

Transliteration resembles the general machine translation problem. It mostly breaks down to the mapping of ambiguous smaller units. In fact, it is a simpler problem, since we do not expect any reordering

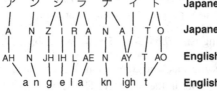

Figure 10.2 Transliteration from Japanese to English of the name *Angela Knight* (adapted from Knight and Graehl [1997a]).

to take place. This allows us to use simpler modeling techniques. Here, we describe how **finite state transducers** may be used to model transliteration.

finite state transducer

First, we break up the translation into a number of steps:

$$p(e_{\text{LETTER}}, f_{\text{LETTER}}) = \sum_{e_{\text{SOUND}}, f_{\text{SOUND}}} p(e_{\text{LETTER}})$$

$$\times\, p(e_{\text{SOUND}}|e_{\text{LETTER}})$$
$$\times\, p(f_{\text{SOUND}}|e_{\text{SOUND}})$$
$$\times\, p(f_{\text{LETTER}}|f_{\text{SOUND}}) \qquad (10.1)$$

Note that we are interested in the best English word $e_{\text{LETTER}}^{\text{best}}$ that maximizes the conditional probability $p(e_{\text{LETTER}}|f_{\text{LETTER}})$. However, this is equivalent to maximizing the joint probability distribution:

$$e_{\text{LETTER}}^{\text{best}} = \text{argmax}_{e_{\text{LETTER}}} p(e_{\text{LETTER}}|f_{\text{LETTER}})$$
$$= \text{argmax}_{e_{\text{LETTER}}} p(e_{\text{LETTER}}, f_{\text{LETTER}}) \qquad (10.2)$$

We now want to model each step by a finite state transducer. Finite state toolkits allow the combination of these transducers, so all we need to do is to define each of them. Refer to Figure 10.3 for some background on combining finite state transducers.

Let us now take a look at each step that we need to model.

English word model $p(e_{\text{LETTER}})$

English word model

This model is similar in spirit to the language models discussed in Chapter 7. So, we can use an n-gram sequence model over letters, just as we used n-gram models over words in regular language modeling. Given the limited inventory of letters, it should be possible to use a high order of n.

We need to keep in mind, however, that this does not prevent us from generating English letter sequences that have never been observed in English, as names or otherwise. However, it may be preferable to restrict our models to generating letter sequences that are proper English names. Figure 10.3 indicates how an inventory of words or names may be encoded in a finite state transducer.

English pronunciation model $p(e_{\text{SOUND}}|e_{\text{LETTER}})$

English pronunciation model

Phonetic dictionaries such as the CMU Pronunciation Dictionary[1] provide a large inventory of English words and their phonetic realization. This lexicon contains phonetic entries such as AYS for *ice*, IH N AH F for *enough*, or N EY SH AH N for *nation*.

---

[1] Available online at http://www.speech.cs.cmu.edu/cgi-bin/cmudict

A **finite state transducer** consists of a number of states. When transitioning between states an input symbol is consumed and an output symbol is emitted. Here is a simple example for a finite state transducer that takes English letters and outputs English words:

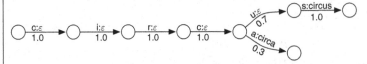

The transitions are annotated with probabilities. The finite state transducer above implements a simple language model $p(e)$ on words, emitting either *circus* or *circa*.

The following finite state transducer implements a letter translation model $p(f|e)$ from German letters (indicated with uppercase) to English letters (indicated with lowercase). The transducer only has one state, meaning that the translation of a letter does not depend on previously translated letters:

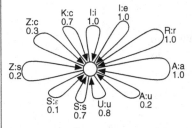

There is considerable ambiguity in the translation of a letter. For instance, the English letter c may be mapped to K ($p = 0.7$) or Z ($p = 0.3$). The two transducers may be combined into a single finite state transducer. This is usually done with finite state machine toolkits and may result in very large finite state machines. In our simple case we are still able draw the graph of the combined transducer:

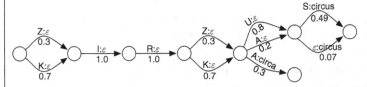

This combined transducer implements the probability distribution $p(e)\ p(f|e) = p(f, e)$. What happens if we input the German word *ZIRKA* into the transducer? The transducer allows us to take two different paths, outputting either *circa* (with combined probability 0.063) or *circus* (probability 0.00294).

Figure 10.3 Combining finite state transducers.

To obtain mappings on the level of letters, we need to align the letter representation of each word with its phonetic representation. This problem is similar to the word alignment problem, but again, it is simpler since no reordering takes place. We may learn alignment models using the expectation maximization algorithm and simple mapping models, similar to IBM Model 1.

Note that phonetic dictionaries do not have to include any names since we are trying to learn something more fundamental: the translation of letters into phonemes. However, if the dictionary includes all the names we possibly want to generate, we may want to directly encode it. The dictionary may even completely replace the English word model.

English to foreign sound conversion model $p(f_{\text{SOUND}}|e_{\text{SOUND}})$

Languages differ in the sounds they use. To just give two examples: the German *ch* has no equivalent in English, and Japanese uses the same sound for the English *l* and *r*, which lies somewhere between the two.

To be able to train a model that maps English sounds to foreign sounds, we need a parallel corpus of words with their pronunciation in both languages. If we only have access to parallel data without pronunciation annotation, we can use the other transducers we are building to identify the most likely phoneme sequence for each word in both languages.

Training a model from this data is similar to the training of the English pronunciation model: we need to establish the alignment between phonemes, which then allows us to estimate letter translation probabilities.

Foreign spelling model $p(f_{\text{LETTER}}|f_{\text{SOUND}})$

The foreign spelling model is the converse of the English pronunciation model, and similar methods may be used. For languages such as Japanese, with its very close match of spelling and pronunciation, we can also simply build spelling models by hand.

10.1.4 Resources

The approach we have outlined relies on the existence of phonetic dictionaries for both input and output languages. Such resources are not always available. However, recent research has shown that the detour over phonemes may not be necessary; we may also directly map source letters to output letters without loss of performance. In this case, there is no need for phonetic dictionaries, just a parallel corpus of names.

Research has also demonstrated the usefulness of plentiful output language resources. Possible names may be validated by checking them against the web.

10.1.5 Back-Transliteration and Translation

back-transliteration

Our example in Figure 10.2 on page 292 illustrates one category of name translation, which is called **back-transliteration**. In the example, an English name, spelled in Japanese katakana, is translated back into English characters.

Contrast this with the transliteration task of translating Japanese names into English. In the case of English names, there is one correct answer, the spelling of the person's name as it was originally spelled in his or her country. Things are not so straightforward if the name originates in the foreign language. For instance, the Arabic name *Yasser Arafat* is also often spelled *Yasir Arafat*, and the name *Osama bin Laden* also occurs as *Usama bin Laden* (for instance on the FBI Most Wanted list).

For the problem of back-transliteration, a large inventory of English names will be very helpful in determining what letter sequences represent valid names. Such resources are less reliable for the straight transliteration task. The name may never have been transliterated into English at all, and an inventory will not resolve the issue of multiple valid spellings.

For downstream applications of machine translation, having multiple spellings of foreign names constitutes a problem. How do we know that *Yasir* and *Yasser* refer to the same person? For the training of machine translation systems, multiple spellings are a source of noise that may lead to sparse data problems. It is hence useful to standardize on a consistent rendering of foreign names into English.

There is another question we need to consider. When do we transliterate and when do we translate? For instance, when referring to the *FBI* in a non-English language, we may want to translate *Federal Bureau of Investigation* (say, into the German *Bundeskriminalamt*), or transliterate either the acronym or full name. Some names are always transliterated, some are always translated, and for some both choices are valid. This means that a name translation system needs to be aware of when to transliterate and when to translate. Let us also acknowledge that the task of identifying names in a text is a far from trivial problem.

10.2 Morphology

content word

One way to divide up words in a language is to take the view that they fall into two categories: **content words** that carry meaning by referring to real and abstract objects, actions, and properties (called nouns,

verbs, and adjectives/adverbs) on the one hand, and **function words**   function word
that inform us about the relationships between the content words on the
other. The relationship between content words is also encoded in word
order and **morphology**.   morphology

Languages differ in the way they encode relationships between
words. For instance English makes heavy use of word order and function words, but less of morphology. By contrast, Latin makes heavy use
of morphology and less of function words, and has a relatively free word
order.

Some basic principles of morphology are discussed in Section 2.1.4.
Please refer to that section to become familiar with syntactic concepts such as case, count and gender. Here, we take a closer look at
how to address the problem of translating information expressed by
morphology.

10.2.1 Morphemes

Languages differ in morphological complexity. English morphology
is limited mainly to verb form changes due to tense, and noun form
changes due to count. Other languages such as German or Finnish
have a much richer morphology. Rich morphology implies that for each
lemma (for instance, *house*), many word forms exist (*house, houses*).
This leads to **sparse data** problems for statistical machine transla-   sparse data
tion. We may have seen one morphological variant (word form) of
a word, but not the others. Since our typical models are based on
the surface form of words, we will not be able to translate unseen
forms.

See Figure 10.4 for an illustration of the effect of rich morphology
on **vocabulary sizes** and out-of-vocabulary rates. In this analysis of the   vocabulary size
Europarl corpus, Finnish has five times the vocabulary size of English,
resulting in an almost ten-fold greater out-of-vocabulary rate. German
lies somewhere between the two languages.

To give one example for rich morphology: while in English adjectives have only one form (for instance, *big*), this is not the case in

	English	German	Finnish
Vocabulary size	65,888	195,290	358,344
Unknown word rate	0.22%	0.78%	1.82%

Figure 10.4 Vocabulary size and effect on the unknown word rate: Numbers
reported for 15 million words of the Europarl corpus for vocabulary collection
and unknown word rate on additional 2000 sentences (data from the 2005 ACL
workshop shared task).

German, where there are six word forms for each adjective (*groß*, *große*,
großem, *großen*, *großer*, *großes*).

stem   A first step is to split each word form into its **stem** and **morphemes**.
morpheme We can break up the German adjective form *großes* into *groß* +*es*. Note
that it is not always straightforward to detect the meaning of a morpheme from its surface realization. Consider the following examples of
English past tense word forms:

- *talked* → *talk* (STEM) + +*ed* (MORPHEME)
- *produced* → *produce* (STEM) + +*d* (MORPHEME)
- *made* → *make* (STEM) + -*ke*+*de* (MORPHEME)

The three morphemes +*ed*, +*d*, and -*ke*+*de* play the same role; they all
indicate past tense. Hence, it may be better to represent them not by
the change pattern to the stem, but by their syntactic role, in this case
+PAST.

However, morphology is often very ambiguous. The German adjective change pattern +*e* indicates either (a) singular, indefinite, nominative, (b) singular, definite, female, nominative or dative, (c) accusative,
plural, or (d) indefinite, nominative, plural. Morphological analyzers
may not always be able to provide the correct syntactic role for each
word in a sentence.

Note that we take here a rather restrictive view on morphology.
Consider the English words: *nation, national, nationally, nationalize,
nationalism, nationalistic*. They all derive from the same root form.
The morphological changes allow the root form to be converted into all
types of content words: noun, verb, adjective, and adverb. When considering morphology, we may want to take these changes into account.
On the other hand, some of these changes affect the meaning of the
word, resulting in very different translations into another language. For
instance, *nation* has a quite different meaning from *nationalism*, and
these translate differently into German (*Volk* vs. *Nationalismus*).

10.2.2 Simplifying Rich Morphology

Much recent statistical machine translation has focused on translation
rich input morphology   into English. Often, the input language has a much **richer morphology**,
as is the case with German, Turkish, and Arabic. The additional word
forms on the input side create sparse data problems that make the
translation of rare or unseen word forms difficult. How can we use
morphological analysis to reduce this problem?

German   **German**

Here is a simple German example sentence, with decomposition of
words into lemmas and morphemes, as well as an English translation:

Er	wohnt	in	einem	großen	Haus
Er	wohnen -en+t	in	ein +em	groß +en	Haus +ε
He	lives	in	a	big	house

The sentence contains four German words that have a morphological analysis. Their English translations are either words that do not have morphological variants (*a, big*), or that may also be inflected (*lives, houses*).

The two English words *a* and *big* are not changed due to their syntactic role. In these cases the morphemes on the German side do not provide any apparently useful information for lexical translation. So, we may be able to translate German sentences better if we remove these superfluous morphemes.

In contrast, the English word *house* does have morphological variants, one for singular and one for plural. However, the German word *Haus* is additionally inflected for case, resulting in five distinct word forms: *Haus, Hause, Hauses, Häuser, Häusern*. So, German has additional morphological information associated with this noun that is redundant from a lexical translation point of view. We may reduce the morpheme to a simple flag indicating either singular or plural.

Taking these considerations into account, we should be able to translate the German sentence into English better if we process it into the following format:

$$Er \mid wohnen+\text{3P-SGL} \mid in \mid ein \mid groß \mid Haus+\text{SGL}$$

Turkish

Turkish

Let us look at a language with an even richer morphology. Here is a short Turkish sentence (from Oflazer and Durgar El-Kahlout [2007]):

$$Sonuçlarına_1 \; dayanılarak_2 \; bir_3 \; ortakliği_4 \; oluşturulacaktır_5.$$

and its English translation

a$_3$ **partnership**$_4$ *will be* **drawn-up**$_5$ *on the* **basis**$_2$ *of* **conclusions**$_1$.

Word alignments are indicated by subscripted numbers. Many of the English function words have no equivalent in Turkish – not only tense markers such as *will be*, but also prepositions such as *on* and *of*. In Turkish, their role is realized as morphological suffixes.

A morphological analyzer for Turkish may give us the following analysis of our example sentence (note that the lexical morphemes given here do not directly match the surface forms of the joined words due to word-internal phenomena such as vowel harmony and morphotactics, i.e., rules about the ordering of morphemes):

$$Sonuç +lar +sh +na \; daya +hnhl +yarak$$
$$bir \; ortaklık +sh \; oluş +dhr +hl +yacak +dhr$$

At this level of analysis, we are able to establish alignments to English function words and morphemes:

sonuç	+lar	+sh	+na			daya+hnhl	+yarak
conclusion	+s		of	the		basis	on

bir		ortaklık	+sh		oluş	+dhr	+hl	+yacak	+dhr
a		partnership			draw up	+ed		will	be

This example suggests that languages such as Turkish have morphemes that we may want to treat like independent words (the equivalent of, say, auxiliary verbs or prepositions) when translating into English.

Arabic

Arabic

Another morphologically rich language, Arabic, has recently received much attention in statistical machine translation circles. Base forms of Arabic words may be extended in several ways:

$$[\text{CONJ}+ [\text{PART}+ [al+ \text{BASE} +\text{PRON}]]]$$

clitics

Morphemes (called **clitics** in Arabic) may be prefixes or suffixes. For instance, the definite determiner *al* (English *the*) is a prefix, while pronominal morphemes +PRON such as +*hm* for *their/them* are suffixes.

Different type of prefixes are attached in a fixed order. The prefix *al* comes first. Then one of a set of particle pro-clitics PART+ may be attached, for instance *l*+ (English *to/for*), *b*+ (English *by/with*), *k*+ (English *as/such*), or the verbal *s*+ (English future tense *will*). Outermost conjunctive pro-clitics CONJ+ may be attached, for instance *w*+ for the English *and* or *f*+ for the English *then*.

We may address Arabic morphology in the context of machine translation the same way we suggested for German and Turkish. Some morphemes are more akin to English words, and should be separated out as tokens. Others mark properties such as tense that are also expressed morphologically in English, and we may prefer to keep them attached to the word. A third class of morphemes has no equivalent in English and it may be best to drop them.

Note that morphological treatment of text is not restricted to foreign languages. It is standard practice to break up English possessive forms into the tokens. To give an example: *John's* is broken up into the tokens *John* and *'s*.

10.2.3 Translating Rich Morphology

morphologically rich

We discussed above how to simplify rich morphology in the case when a morphologically rich input language is translated into a morphologically poor output language. Simplification is a less viable strategy when the output language is **morphologically rich**.

Recall our original premise for statistical machine translation. Since the problem of mapping an input sentence to an output sentence with one probabilistic translation table would suffer from sparse data problems, we decided to break it up into smaller steps: the translation of words (or phrases).

Now, when faced with sparse data problems due to rich morphology, we may want to apply the same strategy. We would like to build a generative model for the translation of morphologically rich words by breaking up word translation into separate steps for the translation of word stem and morphological properties.

Such a generative model might look like this:

$$p\,(s_e, m_e | s_f, m_f) = p\,(s_e | s_f, m_f)\,p\,(m_e | s_e, s_f, m_f)$$
$$\simeq p\,(s_e | s_f)\,p\,(m_e | m_f) \tag{10.3}$$

First, we apply the chain rule to break up the problem of translating a foreign word (with stem s_f and morphology m_f) into an English word (with stem s_e and morphology m_e). This gives us separate probability distributions for first predicting the stem s_e and then the morphology m_e. To overcome data sparseness, we simplify these two distributions so that the translation of the English stem s_e is only conditioned on the foreign stem s_f, and the translation of the English morphology m_e is only conditioned on the foreign morphology m_f.

Note that this model assumes that there is a deterministic mapping between the morphological analysis of a word (s_e, m_e) and its surface form e. If this is not the case, our generative model will be a bit more complex:

$$p(e|f) = \sum_{(s_e, m_e)} p(e|s_e, m_e) \sum_{(s_f, m_f)} p(s_e, m_e | s_f, m_f)\,p(s_f, m_f | f) \tag{10.4}$$

In this model, we have to sum over all possible morphological decompositions (s_e, m_e) of the English word e and all possible morphological decompositions (s_f, m_f) of the foreign word f.

Generative morphological models are currently not generally used in statistical machine translation systems, but they have been proposed for word alignment and are one motivation for the factored models that we discuss later in Section 10.5.

10.2.4 Word Splitting

Related to the problem of inflectional morphology is the **compounding of words** into new bigger words, a feature of several European languages such as German, Dutch, and Finnish, but also present in English. To give two examples: *homework* is typical written as one word

compounding of words

Figure 10.5 Possible
decomposition of the German
compound noun *Aktionsplan*
into smaller German nouns.

(20 times more common than its split version *home work*, according
to a web search), and *website* is common (albeit only half as frequent as
web site).

The generative nature of merging existing words into new words
that express distinct concepts leads to even more severe sparse data
problems than inflectional morphology. Since the new words created
this way may never have been used before, simply relying on larger
training corpora will not solve this problem.

Figure 10.5 gives an example of a German noun compound, *Aktionsplan*, and its possible decomposition into the existing German nouns
Aktion, *Plan*, *Akt* and *Ion*. In German the process of compounding nouns
follows relatively simple rules that may introduce filler letters such as
the *s* between *Aktion* and *Plan*.

If the goal is to split German compounds into words that correspond to English words, then the correct decomposition of *Aktionsplan*
is *Aktion* and *Plan*. Splitting a compound into the sequence of the most
frequent words (using the geometric average of word frequencies) has
been demonstrated to be a effective strategy.

Within the context of phrase-based translation models, the over-
eager strategy of splitting a word into as many valid words as possible
does not lead to worse results. This is due to the ability of phrase-based
models to learn many-to-many mappings, which allow phrase pairs such
as *(akt ion, action)*.

word segmentation

Note that the problem of word splitting is related to the problem
of **word segmentation** in languages such as Chinese, where typically
no spaces at all are used to separate words. A method similar to the
one proposed here for word splitting applies to the problem of Chinese
word segmentation. Given a lexicon of valid Chinese words, we explore
possible segmentations and settle on the one that includes only valid
words, and is optimal under some scoring method (such as using the
fewest words possible or preferring frequent words).

10.3 Syntactic Restructuring

Traditional phrase-based statistical machine translation models deal
well with language pairs that require no or only local reordering.
The first statistical machine translation systems were developed for
French–English. Both are subject-verb-object (SVO) languages, and the

major reordering challenge is the switching of adjectives and nouns: for instance, *maison bleue* becomes *blue house*. Such local reordering is handled well by phrase translation and the language model, which would prefer *a blue house* over *a house blue*.

For other language pairs, reordering is a big problem. On the one hand there are languages with different fixed sentence structures, for instance Arabic is VSO, Japanese is OSV. On the other hand there are languages with relatively free word order. In German, the verb has a fixed position, but subject and object may occur anywhere else in the sentence.

Clearly, syntax, the theory of sentence structure, should guide **restructuring** when translating between languages with different sentence structures. In this section, we discuss methods that make use of syntactic annotation to restructure sentences to better fit traditional phrase-based models.

restructuring

10.3.1 Reordering Based on Input-Language Syntax

An example of the reordering challenges when translating **German to English** is given in Figure 10.6. Here, we parse a German sentence (main clause and subclause) with a German parser, flatten the parse structure, so that all the clause-level constituents line up on the same level, and examine how these have to be reordered when translating the sentence to English.

German–English

Note for instance the verb movements. In the German main clause, the verb complex is broken up into the auxiliary *werde* (English *will*) at the second position and the main verb *aushändigen* (English *pass on*) at the final position of the clause. In English, both have to be combined and placed after the subject. In the German subclause, the verb complex *übernehmen können* (English *include can*) appears at the end; it needs to be moved forward and its two words have to be switched.

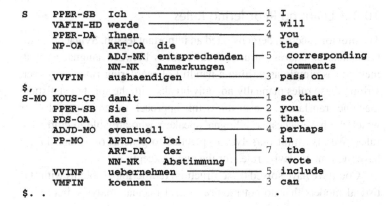

Figure 10.6 Reordering required for German–English: Clause structure for a German sentence annotated with English word translation and English order for the clause-level constituents.

English has a fairly fixed word order. Note the positions we assigned to each constituent in the example of Figure 10.6. For the word translations we have chosen, there are practically no other English target positions where they can be placed without distorting the sentence.

Therefore, the following should be a successful strategy to address reordering from German to English: First, we parse the German sentence to identify its clauses and its clause-level constituents. Then, we reorder the sentence following a set of rules into a German sentence in English sentence order. Finally, a phrase-based statistical machine translation system should be able to do a much better job at translating the sentence.

reordering rules   Collins *et al.* [2005] propose the following **reordering rules** for German–English:

1. In any verb phrase move the head verbs into the initial position.
2. In subordinate clauses, move the head (i.e., the main verb) directly after the complementizer.
3. In any clause, move the subject directly before the head.
4. Move particles in front of the verb (German typically places the particles at the end of the clause).
5. Move infinitives after the finite verbs.
6. Move clause-level negatives after the finite verb.

This approach rests on the assumption that we can reliable parse German and that we can find rules that reliably place constituents in the right order. In practice, we have only imperfect solutions to these two tasks. Parsing performance for German is below 90%, and rules may not apply if we have to deal with idiomatic expressions that do not follow the same syntactic patterns or other exceptions. Still, the gains from applying this approach outweigh the harm done by parsing errors or exceptions.

10.3.2 Learning Reordering Rules

The previous section demonstrated an important lesson. Syntactic annotation lets us address structural differences between languages, with methods as simple as writing a handful of reordering rules. However, writing these rules manually not only breaks with the spirit of statistical machine translation, it also limits this approach to language pairs for which we have access to bilingual speakers who are able to craft such rules. We also limit ourselves in practice to general rules and do not have the time to devise rules for the many exceptions.

Could we have solved these structural reordering problems with statistical models that do not require careful manual analysis, but rather

learning reordering

learn reordering automatically from parallel corpora? Intuitively, the syntactic annotation that we add is essential for detecting simple but powerful rules. The added annotation lets us formulate rules over categories such as *finite verbs*, instead of having to learn special rules for every single finite verb.

We can annotate parallel corpora with syntactic information using automatic tools (tools which in turn often employ statistical models trained on manually annotated data). Since we have evidence that this annotation is useful for addressing the reordering problem, let us discuss how we can exploit it in a statistical framework.

Given a sentence-aligned corpus, we obtain both word alignments and syntactic annotation with automatic methods. This allows us to spot syntactic patterns that help us to reorder each input sentence into the order of its output sentence. Typically, we will be able to learn a large array of rules of varying generality and reliability, so we need to establish preferences for some rules over others and eliminate rules that do more harm than good. Probabilistic scoring comes to mind.

The methods we discuss below, as well as the previous method of hand-crafted rules, assume that we build a reordering component to be used in a pre-processing step. This component reorders both training and testing data, so that less reordering is required by the main statistical machine translation engine.

10.3.3 Reordering Based on Part-of-Speech Tags

A basic form of syntactic annotation is the labeling of each word with its **part of speech**. This allows us not only to distinguish verbs from nouns, but also to make more fine-grained distinctions such as infinitive and participle verb forms. Some languages have more types than others, and some part-of-speech tag sets are richer than others, so expressiveness of part-of-speech information varies.

part-of-speech tags

Much of the reordering that has to occur when translating can be compactly captured with part-of-speech information. One typical example is the reordering of nouns and adjectives needed when translating from French to English. For German–English too, we can formulate reordering in terms of rules based on part-of-speech tags.

See Figure 10.7 for an illustration. In our example, the two words *übernehmen können* are reordered when translating into the English *can include*. Given the word alignment between the German and English sentence, as well as the additional annotation of the German words with part-of-speech tags, we are able to induce the rule VVINF VMFIN → VMFIN VVINF.

Figure 10.7 Induction of a reordering rule based on part-of-speech tags: According to the word alignment, the two words *übernehmen können* flipped during translation. Given the additional part-of-speech tag annotation, this example suggests a more general reordering rule for infinitives and modal verbs.

Figure 10.8 Induction of a rule with a gap: The main verb in German may be many words away from the auxiliary. Learning different rules for all possible intervening part-of-speech sequences is not practical, but a rule with a gap (expressed in the rule as a sequence of arbitrary part-of-speech tags *X**) captures all these cases.

In a parallel corpus of reasonable size, there are many occurrences of the German part-of-speech sequence VVINF VMFIN. In each example, the underlying words may either be reordered or not. If we collect statistics over these cases, we can estimate straightforwardly how reliable this reordering rule will be on new test data. We may collect only rules with sufficient, reliable evidence, or we may collect all rules along with their application probability.

Not all reordering takes place between neighboring words. The case of German–English especially provides many examples of **long-distance reordering**. For instance in verb constructions involving an auxiliary and a main verb, any number of words may intervene between the auxiliary and the main verb in German. In English, however, except for the occasional adverb (*will certainly confirm*), the auxiliary and main verb are next to each other.

See Figure 10.8 for an illustration taken from our example sentence. The German auxiliary *werde* and main verb *aushändigen* are separated by a number of words (four, to be precise). In English their translations occur next to each other: *will pass on*. Instead of learning different rules for all possible intervening part-of-speech sequences, a more compact solution is to learn a rule with a gap: in this case, VAFIN X* VVFIN → VAFIN VVFIN X*. The symbol X* in the rule indicates a sequence of any kind of part-of-speech tags.

While this seems at first like an elegant solution, we find on closer examination that allowing rules with gaps poses some challenges:

long-distance reordering

- There are many more potential rules with gaps than rules without. For a sentence of length n, there are $O(n^2)$ contiguous sequences, but $O(n^4)$ sequences with one gap and $O(2^n)$ sequences with an arbitrary number of gaps.

- In practice, we would like to be more specific about gaps, for instance restricting maximum size and disallowing certain part-of-speech tags in the sequence (for instance, no verbs). These restrictions, however, increase the number of potential rules even more.

- Once rules are established, we are confronted with the problem that many rules may apply to a test sentence. Even if we sort rules according to their reliability (or some other measure), the same rule may apply multiple times in same sentence (for instance, because the sentence contains multiple auxiliaries and main verbs). Deciding if and when rules apply is not straightforward.

Rules based on part-of-speech tags have been shown to be helpful in practice if properly restricted. The problem of the complexity of the space of possible rules (or the complexity of models) will continue to emerge throughout our search for more syntactically informed modes of translation.

10.3.4 Reordering Based on Syntactic Trees

An essential property of language is its **recursive structure**. All parts of a sentence can be extended. The extensions in turn can be extended further, and so on. The canonical basic sentence consists of a subject, verb, and maybe a few objects. Each subject and object can be extended to include relative clauses, which structurally resemble the basic sentence. Other qualifiers such as adverbs, adjectives, and prepositional phrases may be sprinkled throughout.

recursive structure

Linguistic theory addresses the structure of language with a formalism that represents sentences not as linear sequences of words but as hierarchical structures, so-called trees.

For our problem at hand, reordering during translation, **syntactic trees** provide a better basis for reordering rules than the part-of-speech tags discussed in the previous section. Recall that the rules of Collins *et al.* [2005] (Section 10.3.1) use not only part-of-speech concepts such as *infinitive verb*, but also the vocabulary of syntactic tree structures such as *verb phrase* and *head word*.

syntactic tree

To repeat an example from the previous section, limiting ourselves to part-of-speech tags leads us to create awkward rules such as

VAFIN X* VVFIN → VAFIN VVFIN X*

The wild card X* is introduced to account for the fact that any number of words may lie between the finite verb (in the second position of the clause) and the infinitive main verb (at the end of the clause) – a

Figure 10.9 Syntax tree representation of a German sentence: The clause-level constituents that need to be reordered when translating to English line up directly below the top node.

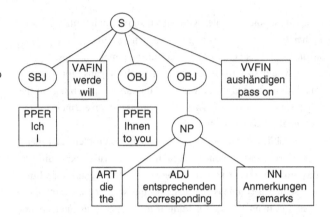

Figure 10.9 Syntax tree representation of a German sentence: The clause-level constituents that need to be reordered when translating to English line up directly below the top node.

direct consequence of the recursive structure of language, which allows the insertion of various arguments and adjuncts.

A tree structure files adjuncts away at lower levels, making the core clause structure more transparent. In Figure 10.9, immediately below the clause node (S), we find the clause-level constituents: subject (SBJ), auxiliary and main verb (VAFIN and VVFIN), and the two objects (OBJ). The two object noun phrases consist here of one and three words, but they may be of any complexity.

The reordering rule above may be rewritten using the annotation of the tree structure to give a rule that avoids wild cards and that is more precise:

SUBJ VAFIN OBJ* VVFIN → SUBJ VAFIN VVFIN OBJ*

Let us now take a closer look at the kinds of rules we may want to learn from syntactic tree structures. Theoretically, any number of elements in the input language sentence can be moved anywhere. Consequently, the number of possible rules easily becomes too large to handle. Therefore, in practice, we have to restrict the types of rules we want to learn.

child node reordering

A common restriction is to limit restructuring to **child node reordering**, meaning the reordering of nodes with the same parent, but no more extensive restructuring. This means, to continue with our example, that a single rule may move the German word *aushändigen* (English *pass on*) directly after the word *werde* (English *will*) but not directly after the word *entsprechenden* (English *corresponding*), which is nested in a subtree. The first movement affects the single parent node S, whereas the second movement involves multiple parent nodes. See Figure 10.10 for an illustration of this restriction.

Xia and McCord [2004] propose a method for learning syntactic reordering rules. They allow rules for any subset of nodes with the same parent. This restriction allows rules such as:

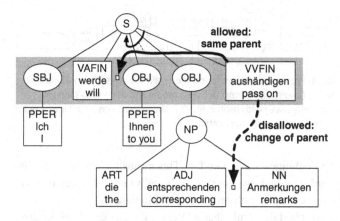

Figure 10.10 Typical restriction for syntactic restructuring rules: Only reordering of nodes with the same parent are allowed, not major restructuring across the tree.

- PPER VAFIN → VAFIN PPER
- VAFIN PPER NP VVFIN → VAFIN VVFIN PPER NP
- PPER NP VVFIN → VVFIN PPER NP
- VVINF VVFIN → VVFIN VVINF

We may want to include lexical information in these rules:

- PPER(*Ihnen*) NP VVFIN → VVFIN(*Ihnen*) PPER NP
- ADJD(*perhaps*) VVINF VVFIN(*can*) → VVFIN(*can*) ADJD(*perhaps*) VVINF

Note that with this framework for rules, which may apply to any subset of the children nodes of a parent, the number of possible rules is exponential with regard to the number of children for each parent. This is still substantially less than the number of unrestricted rules over subsets of words – which would be exponential in the sentence length, hence practically infeasible for all but the shortest sentences.

Given a parallel corpus, we collect many rules. For each rule, we can determine if it is generally reliable or not, say, by computing the likelihood of the right-hand side of the rule given the left-hand side. When applying rules to a test sentence, some rules may stand in conflict. We may prefer specific rules over more general ones, or we may choose which rule to apply according to the relative reliability of the rules.

10.3.5 Preserving Choices

There is a fundamental problem with separating the reordering task into a pre-processing component. Whatever mistake we make in these components will be passed along as a hard decision to the statistical machine translation system. However, some of the reordering performed on the input may be faulty – owing perhaps to unreliable rules, or to faulty syntactic annotation.

One principle behind statistical modelling is to avoid hard choices. In a probabilistic environment, early decisions can be reversed later

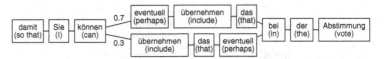

Figure 10.11 Preserving choices for nondeterministic rules: Given a rule that moves adverbs (*eventuell/perhaps*) between modal and main verb (*können übernehmen/can include*) with probability 0.7, the input is converted into a word lattice with and without rule application.

when all probabilities are factored in. This means for our current problem of reordering that, in some cases, (usually) reliable rules may not allow us to construct a high-probability translation.

For example, take a rule that addresses the movement of adverbs, which are often placed differently in German and English. In English, adverbs that qualify the main verb often (but not always) occur between the modal and main verbs (*can perhaps include*).

Consider what this means for our example in Figure 10.11. After applying all verb-related reordering, we face the choice of applying a rule that moves the adverb. If the rule is reliable with probability 0.7, we would want to apply it, since on average it improves matters.

But instead of simply making a hard decision, our experience with probabilistic models tells us that it is better to pass along both choices, weighted with their probabilities. One way to encode these choices is by passing along a **word lattice** instead of a word sequence. The preference for one choice over another is encoded as the path probability in the lattice. This means that we need to have a decoder that is able to translate word lattices. A fall-back solution would be to pass along n-best lists.

A final word about reordering in statistical machine translation systems. We may be inclined to disallow reordering in the main system (i.e., perform monotone translation) and to trust fully the reordering component. In other cases, we may simply restrict reordering to short movements, or not restrict reordering all. Experimentation helps us to make this determination.

10.4 Syntactic Features

Syntactic annotation may be exploited in a pre-processing stage, as discussed in the sections above. Conversely, we may use syntactic information in post-processing. In this scenario, the basic statistical machine translation model provides a number of possible candidate translations and a machine learning method using **syntactic features** may allow us to pick the best translation.

word lattice

syntactic feature

10.4.1 Methodology

The general outline of the approach is:

1. We use a baseline statistical machine translation model (for instance, a phrase-based model) to generate an n-best list of candidate translations.
2. We use automatic tools to add syntactic information, such as morphological analysis, part-of-speech tags, or syntactic trees.
3. We define a set of features and compute feature values for each candidate translation.
4. In a machine learning approach we acquire weights for each feature using a training set of input sentences, each paired with candidate translations and their feature representation.
5. Given a test sentence, we generate candidate translations and their feature representations. The feature weights allows us to pick the (hopefully) best translation.

Methods for generating candidate translations (Section 9.1) and re-ranking (Section 9.1.3) are discussed elsewhere in the book; here we want to focus on the type of syntactic features that may be useful.

10.4.2 Count Coherence

To illustrate what we mean by syntactic features, let us return to our example sentence. In Figure 10.12 the first clause of the sentence is translated by a baseline machine translation system into five choices.

This n-best list of candidate translations does contain a correct translation (number 5), but it is preceded by translations that are all faulty to some degree. The goal of re-ranking is to find features that distinguish the correct translation from the faulty ones, so that those may be discounted and the correct translation ranked first.

The first candidate translation (*I pass you the corresponding comment*) is a correct English sentence. However, it has the noun *comment* in singular form, while the corresponding German original *Anmerkungen* is in plural form.

Let us now define a feature that detects this problem. First, we need to annotate source and target with **count information**:

count

Ich werde Ihnen die entsprechenden Anmerkungen aushändigen.

1. *I pass you the corresponding comment.*
2. *I pass you this corresponding comments.*
3. *I passes you the corresponding comment.*
4. *I to you the corresponding comments.*
5. *I pass you the corresponding comments.*

Figure 10.12 Re-ranking with syntactic features: Given five candidate translations, how can we define syntactic features, so that the correct translation (currently ranked 5th) moves up as best translation.

F: *Ich*/SGL *werde Ihnen*/SGL-PL *die entsprechenden Anmerkungen*/PL
  aushändigen

E: *I*/SGL *pass you*/SGL-PL *the corresponding comment*/SGL.

We assume that the baseline system also gives us the word alignment between input and output sentence, so we know that the following three pronouns and nouns are aligned:

- Ich/SGL – I/SGL
- Ihnen/SGL-PL – you/SGL-PL
- Anmerkungen/PL – comment/SGL

The problem is the last noun, which is plural in the German input and singular in the English candidate translation. We want to detect these types of incoherences. To this end, we define a feature for each noun pair (e, f):

$$h_{\text{COUNT}}(e, f) = \begin{cases} 1 & \text{if count}(e) \neq \text{count}(f) \\ 0 & \text{if count}(e) = \text{count}(f) \end{cases} \qquad (10.5)$$

We ultimately want to have features for sentence pairs $(\mathbf{e}, \mathbf{f})$, so we sum the feature values for all nouns in a sentence:

$$h_{\text{COUNT}}(\mathbf{e}, \mathbf{f}) = \sum_{(e, f) \in (\mathbf{e}, \mathbf{f})} h_{\text{COUNT}}(e, f) \qquad (10.6)$$

The value of this feature for the first candidate translation in Figure 10.12 is 1, and it is 0 for the correct 5th candidate translation. We expect the machine learning method to learn a significantly large negative weight for this feature, so that the faulty translation is ranked lower, and the correct candidate translation can take over.

Note that agreement in count between input and output nouns is not a hard constraint. To give one example, in English the noun *police* is always plural, while its German equivalent *Polizei* is always singular. The argument for defining features with weights instead of hard constraints is the same as the argument for probabilistic modeling. There will always be exceptions, so we only want to introduce a general bias that will be beneficial in most cases, and to allow stronger contrary evidence to override it.

10.4.3 Agreement

Let us move on to slightly more complex features. The second candidate translation contains the phrase *this corresponding comments*. Even without looking at the input sentence, we know that this is faulty, since the noun phrase contains the singular determiner *this* and the plural determiner–noun agreement noun *comments*. In other words, we have an **agreement** violation within the noun phrase.

The agreement error is between multiple words, so simple word features such as part-of-speech tags do not give us enough information to detect it. We need to know that the determiner and the noun are part of the same basic noun phrase. The task of detecting such basic noun phrases is called chunking. A chunker will provide the following additional annotation to the English candidate translation:

[*I*/SGL] *pass* [*you*/SGL-PL] [*this*/SGL *corresponding comments*/PL] .

Given this additional annotation, we proceed to define a feature for each noun phrase and detect whether it contains an agreement violation or not. The sentence-level feature value is the count of all noun phrase agreement violations.

The third translation (*I passes you the corresponding comment.*) has an agreement violation of a different kind. The subject is first person singular, but the verb is third person singular. Again, we are talking about the syntactic relationships between words, but chunking does not provide sufficient information here to make the connection between the two words. What is required is some form of at least shallow syntactic parsing.

A dependency parser will provide the following additional annotation:

```
    subject   object     object
[ I/SGL ]   pass   [ you/SGL-PL]   [ this/SGL corresponding comments/PL]
```

With this type of annotation it is straightforward to define features for **subject–verb agreement** violations.   subject–verb agreement

10.4.4 Syntactic Parse Probability

In this discussion of syntactic features, we have slowly moved towards more and more sophisticated syntactic annotation. Linguistic theory typically represents the syntax of a sentence in a tree structure. Such tree structures may also be useful in determining the grammaticality of a candidate translation.

We presented some theories of grammar in Section 2.2.2, and the next chapter will provide a different approach to statistical machine translation using tree structures. In context-free grammars, a syntactic tree is represented by a set of rule applications, such as:

$$S \rightarrow \text{NP-SUBJECT V NP-OBJECT}$$

In a statistical model, we assign a probability to each rule application, representing the conditional probability of the right-hand side of the rule, given the left-hand side. The product of all rule application probabilities gives the likelihood of a specific English sentence and tree.

$$p(\text{TREE}) = \prod_i \text{RULE}_i \qquad (10.7)$$

What does that tree probability represent? It is similar to the n-gram language model; both measure how likely it is that this particular sentence (and its best tree) occurs. Hence, we could call it a **syntactic language model**. Note that syntactic language models share some of the problems of n-gram language models, such as their preference for short sentences with common words.

syntactic language model

Arguably, we may need to build syntactic language models differently from the common approach to statistical parsing, from which current statistical syntactic models originate. In statistical parsing, we optimize the model to reduce parsing errors; i.e., we would like to find the best tree given a sentence. In syntactic language modeling, we would like to assess the likelihood that a sentence and tree is good English, so we may want to optimize on perplexity, as in language modeling. Actually, what we really want is the probability that a given sentence is grammatical, i.e., how likely its best possible syntactic tree is to be well formed.

Recent research has shown at most moderate gains from the straightforward use of syntactic language models, and of syntactic features in general. One concern is that the tools that are used (for instance statistical syntactic parsers) are not built for the purpose of detecting grammaticality. These tools are built to work with correct English, and their application to machine translation output often leads to unexpected results. For instance, a part-of-speech tagger may assign unusual part-of-speech tags to a sequence of words, since it will try to assign a grammatical sequence of tags.

Another major concern with the re-ranking approach is the quality of the n-best list. Even 1,000 or 10,000 candidate translations may not be sufficient to contain the grammatically correct translation we are looking for, but may rather contain endless variations of lexical choices. This is to some degree a consequence of the exponential complexity of statistical machine translation, especially due to reordering. Given that reordering is the problem for which we expect major gains from syntactic models, applying syntactic information in a post-processing stage may be too late in the process.

10.5 Factored Translation Models

So far in this chapter we have discussed methods that utilize linguistic knowledge (in the form of special handling or additional annotation) during pre-processing and post-processing stages. From a search

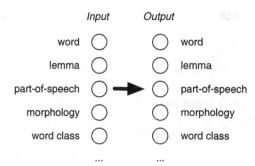

Input   Output

word   word
lemma   lemma
part-of-speech ➡ part-of-speech
morphology   morphology
word class   word class
...   ...

Figure 10.13 Factored translation models represent words as vectors of factors, allowing the integration of additional annotation.

perspective, however, it is desirable to integrate these stages into one model. Integrated search makes it easier to find the global optimal translation, which is less likely to be found when passing along one-best or n-best choices between the stages.

Factored translation models integrate additional linguistic markup at the word level. Each type of additional word-level information is called a **factor**. See Figure 10.13 for an illustration of the type of information that can be useful. The translation of lemma and morphological factors separately would help with sparse data problems in morphologically rich languages. Additional information such as part-of-speech may be helpful in making reordering or grammatical coherence decisions. The presence of morphological features on the target side allows for checking agreement within noun phrases or between subject and verb.

As we argue above, one example that illustrates the shortcomings of the traditional surface word approach in statistical machine translation is the poor handling of morphology. Each word form is treated as a token in itself. This means that the translation model treats, say, the word *house* completely independently of the word *houses*. Instances of *house* in the training data do not add any knowledge about the translation of *houses*.

In the extreme case, while the translation of *house* may be known to the model, the word *houses* may be unknown and the system will not be able to translate it. Although this problem does not show up as strongly in English – due to the very limited morphological inflection in English – it does constitute a significant problem for morphologically rich languages such as Arabic, German, Turkish, Czech, etc.

Thus, it may be preferable to model translation between morphologically rich languages on the level of lemmas, and thus pool the evidence for different word forms that derive from a common lemma. In such a model, we would want to translate lemma and morphological information separately, and to combine this information on the output side to ultimately generate the output surface words.

factored translation models

factor

Figure 10.14 Example factored model: Morphological analysis and generation is decomposed into three mapping steps (translation of lemmas, translation of part-of-speech and morphological information, generation of surface forms).

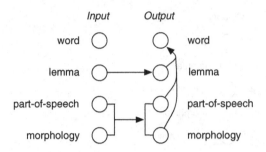

Such a model can be defined straightforwardly as a factored translation model. See Figure 10.14 for an illustration. Note that factored translation models may also integrate less obviously linguistic annotation such as statistically defined word classes, or any other annotation.

10.5.1 Decomposition of Factored Translation

The direct translation of complex factored representations of input words into factored representations of output words may introduce sparse data problems. Therefore, it may be preferable to break up the translation of word factors into a sequence of **mapping steps**. The steps either **translate** input factors into output factors, or **generate** additional output factors from existing output factors.

mapping steps

translate

generate

Given the example of a factored model motivated by morphological analysis and generation, the translation process is broken up into the following three mapping steps:

1. **Translate** input lemmas into output lemmas.
2. **Translate** morphological and part-of-speech factors.
3. **Generate** surface forms given the lemma and linguistic factors.

One way to implement factored translation models is to follow strictly the phrase-based approach, with the additional decomposition of phrase translation into a sequence of mapping steps. Translation steps map factors in input phrases to factors in output phrases. Generation steps map output factors within individual output words. All translation steps operate on the phrase level, while all generation steps operate on the word level. One simplification is to require that all mapping steps operate on the same phrase segmentation of the input and output sentences.

Factored translation models build on the phrase-based approach. This approach implicitly defines a segmentation of the input and output sentence into phrases. See the example in Figure 10.15.

Let us now look more closely at one example, the translation of the one-word phrase *häuser* into English. The representation of *häuser*

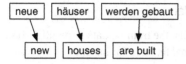

Figure 10.15 Example
sentence translation by a
standard phrase model:
Factored models extend this
approach.

in German is: surface-form *häuser* | lemma *haus* | part-of-speech *NN* |
morphology *plural*.

The three mapping steps in our morphological analysis and generation model may provide the following mappings:

1. **Translation:** Mapping lemmas
   - *haus → house, home, building, shell*
2. **Translation:** Mapping morphology
   - *NN\plural-nominative-neutral → NN\plural, NN\singular*
3. **Generation:** Generating surface forms
   - *house\NN\plural → houses*

   - *house\NN\singular → house*

   - *home\NN\plural → homes*

   - ...

We call the application of these mapping steps to an input phrase
expansion. Given the multiple choices for each step (reflecting the   expansion
ambiguity in translation), each input phrase can be expanded into a
list of translation options. The German *häuser\haus\NN\plural* may be
expanded as follows:

1. **Translation:** Mapping lemmas
   { *?\house\?\?,   ?\home\?\?,   ?\building\?\?,   ?\shell\?\?* }
2. **Translation:** Mapping morphology
   { *?\house\NN\plural,   ?\home\NN\plural,   ?\building\NN\plural,*
   ?\shell\NN\plural,   ?\house\NN\singular, ... }
3. **Generation:** Generating surface forms
   { *houses\house\NN\plural,   homes\home\NN\plural,*
   buildings\building\NN\plural,   shells\shell\NN\plural,
   house\house\NN\singular,   ... }

Although factored translation models follow closely the statistical
modeling approach of phrase-based models (in fact, phrase-based models are a special case of factored models), one main difference lies in
the preparation of the training data and the type of models learnt from
the data.

10.5.2 Training Factored Models

As for traditional phrase-based models, the training data (a parallel corpus) has to be annotated with additional factors. For instance, if we want to add part-of-speech information on the input and output sides, we need part-of-speech tagged training data. Typically this involves running automatic tools on the corpus, since manually annotated corpora are rare and expensive to produce. Next, we establish a word alignment for all the sentences in the parallel training corpus using standard methods.

Each mapping step forms a component of the overall model. From a training point of view this means that we need to learn translation and generation tables from the word-aligned parallel corpus and define scoring methods that help us to choose between ambiguous mappings.

Phrase-based translation models are acquired from a word-aligned parallel corpus by extracting all phrase pairs that are consistent with the word alignment. Given the set of extracted phrase pairs with *feature function* counts, various **feature functions** are estimated, such as conditional phrase translation probabilities based on relative frequency estimation or lexical translation probabilities based on the words in the phrases.

The models for the translation steps may be acquired in the same manner from a word-aligned parallel corpus. For the specified factors in the input and output, phrase mappings are extracted. The set of phrase mappings (now over factored representations) is scored based on relative counts and word-based translation probabilities. See Figure 10.16 for an illustration.

The generation models are probability distributions that are estimated on the output side only. In fact, additional monolingual data may be used. The generation model is learnt on a word-for-word basis. For instance, for a generation step that maps surface forms to part-of-speech, a table with entries such as *(fish,NN)* is constructed. As feature

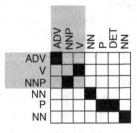

Figure 10.16 Training: Extraction of translation models for any factors follows the phrase extraction method for phrase-based models.

natürlich hat john – naturally john has   *ADV V NNP – ADV NNP V*

functions we may use the conditional probability distributions, e.g., $p(NN|fish)$, obtained by maximum likelihood estimation.

An important component of statistical machine translation is the language model, typically an n-gram model over surface forms of words. In the framework of factored translation models, such sequence models may be defined over any factor, or any set of factors. For factors such as part-of-speech tags, building and using higher order n-gram models (7-gram, 9-gram) is straightforward.

10.5.3 Combination of Components

Like phrase-based models, factored translation models are a combination of several components (language model, reordering model, translation steps, generation steps). Each component defines one or more feature functions that are combined in a log-linear model:

$$p(\mathbf{e}|\mathbf{f}) = \frac{1}{Z} \exp \sum_{i=1}^{n} \lambda_i h_i(\mathbf{e}, \mathbf{f}) \tag{10.8}$$

Z is a normalization constant that is ignored in practice. To compute the probability of a translation $\mathbf{e}$ given an input sentence $\mathbf{f}$, we have to evaluate each feature function h_i.

Let us now consider the feature functions introduced by the translation and generation steps. The translation of the input sentence $\mathbf{f}$ into the output sentence $\mathbf{e}$ breaks down into a set of phrase translations $\{(\bar{f}_j, \bar{e}_j)\}$.

For a translation step component, each feature function h_T is defined over the phrase pairs $(\bar{f}_j, \bar{e}_j)$ given a feature function τ:

$$h_T(\mathbf{e}, \mathbf{f}) = \sum_{j} \tau(\bar{f}_j, \bar{e}_j) \tag{10.9}$$

For a generation step component, each feature function h_G given a feature function γ is defined over the output words e_k only:

$$h_G(\mathbf{e}, \mathbf{f}) = \sum_{k} \gamma(e_k) \tag{10.10}$$

The feature functions follow from the feature functions (τ, γ) acquired during the training of translation and generation tables. For instance, recall our earlier example: a feature function for a generation model component that is a conditional probability distribution between input and output factors, e.g., $\gamma(fish,NN,singular) = p(NN|fish)$. The feature weights λ_i in the log-linear model are determined using a parameter tuning method.

10.5.4 Efficient Decoding

Compared to phrase-based models, the decomposition of phrase translation into several mapping steps creates additional computational complexity. Instead of a simple table lookup to obtain the possible translations for an input phrase, now multiple tables have to be consulted and their content combined.

translation option   In phrase-based models it is easy to identify the entries in the phrase table that may be used for a specific input sentence. These are called **translation options**. We usually limit ourselves to the top 20 translation options for each input phrase.

The beam search decoding algorithm starts with an empty hypothesis. Then new hypotheses are generated by using all applicable translation options. These hypotheses are used to generate further hypotheses in the same manner, and so on, until hypotheses are created that cover the full input sentence. The highest scoring complete hypothesis indicates the best translation according to the model.

expansion   How do we adapt this algorithm for factored translation models? Since all mapping steps operate on the same phrase segmentation, the **expansions** of these mapping steps can be efficiently pre-computed prior to the heuristic beam search, and stored as translation options. For a given input phrase, all possible translation options are thus computed before decoding (recall the example in Section 10.5.1, where we carried out the expansion for one input phrase). This means that the fundamental search algorithm does not change.

However, we need to be careful about combinatorial explosion of the number of translation options given a sequence of mapping steps. In other words, the expansion may create too many translation options to handle. If one or many mapping steps result in a vast increase of (intermediate) expansions, this may be become unmanageable.

One straightforward way to address this problem is by early pruning of expansions, and limiting the number of translation options per input phrase to a maximum number. This is, however, not a perfect solution. A more efficient search for the best translation options for an input phrase is desirable, for instance along the lines of cube pruning (see Section 11.3.7 on page 357).

10.6 Summary

10.6.1 Core Concepts

This chapter presented methods for dealing with a number of translation problems, where special treatment of language phenomena is required. We consider issues with letter translations (for numbers and names), word translation (caused by rich morphology and different definitions of words), and sentence structure (when languages differ significantly in word order).

The underlying assumption of methods presented previously is that sentences are sequences of tokens from a finite set. This is clearly not true for **numbers** and **names**. We propose special number and name translation components and their integration with **XML markup**. If languages differ in their writing systems, names may be **transliterated**. Transliteration may be implemented using **finite state transducers**. We distinguish between transliteration of foreign names and **back-transliteration**, i.e., the translation of English names spelled in a foreign writing system.

Rich **morphology** leads to large vocabulary sizes and a sparse data problem in translation. By splitting off or even removing **morphemes** in order to **simplify rich morphology** we reduce the problem when translating from a morphologically rich language into a poorer one. Otherwise, we may **translate morphology** by translating words and their morphological properties separately. Some languages (like German) allow the joining of separate words into one word, which may require us to employ **word splitting** when translating into English. Some languages do not separate words by spaces, so we need to use **word segmentation** methods.

If languages differ significantly in their word order, the reordering methods of phrase-based models may be insufficient. Instead, **reordering based on syntax** can be a more apt strategy. Using **reordering rules**, either hand-crafted or learnt from data, we can pre-process training and test data to better suit the capabilities of phrase-based models. Reordering rules can be learnt automatically based on syntax trees or part-of-speech tags. When dealing with the restructuring of syntax trees, the **child node reordering restriction** is often used to reduce complexity. When reordering test data before translation, we may want to preserve ambiguity by using **word lattices** as input.

Instead of dealing with syntactic problems in pre-processing, we can also use **re-ranking** methods to exploit **syntactic features** when picking the best translation out of a set of choices produced by a base model. This method allows us to check for **coherence** between input and output, for instance **count coherence**, to match singular and plural forms. We can also check grammatical **agreement** within noun phrases and between subject and verb. We can also use a full-fledged **syntactic language model**.

Factored translation models integrate additional annotation (linguistic or otherwise) as **factors** into an extension of phrase models. Phrase translations are broken up into **mapping steps**, which are either

generation steps or **translation steps**. These steps are modeled in the log-linear model as **feature functions**. We can require that all steps operate on the same phrase segmentation, so that translation options for all input phrases can be efficiently pre-computed in an **expansion** process.

10.6.2 Further Reading

Unknown words – Even with large training corpora, unknown words in the test data will appear. Habash [2008] points out that these come in different types, which require different solutions: unknown names need to be transliterated, unknown morphological variants need to be matched to known ones, and spelling errors need to be corrected. Another case are abbreviations, which may be expanded with a corpus-driven method [Karakos et al., 2008].

Transliteration with finite state machines – Early work in machine transliteration of names uses finite state machines. Our description follows the work by Knight and Graehl [1997b]. Such models can be extended by using a larger Markov window during mappings, i.e., using a larger context [Jung et al., 2000]. Schafer [2006] compares a number of different finite state transducer architectures. For closely related language pairs, such as Hindi–Urdu, deterministic finite state machines may suffice [Malik et al., 2008]. Transliteration can either use phonetic representation to match characters of different writing systems [Knight and Graehl, 1997a] or map characters directly [Zhang et al., 2004a]. Phoneme and grapheme information can be combined [Bilac and Tanaka, 2004]. Given small training corpora, using phonetic representations may be more robust [Yoon et al., 2007].

Transliteration with other methods – Improvements have been shown when including context information in a maximum entropy model [Goto et al., 2003, 2004]. Other machine learning methods such as discriminative training with the perceptron algorithm have been applied to transliteration [Zelenko and Aone, 2006]. Oh and Choi [2002] use a pipeline of different approaches for the various mapping stages. Lin and Chen [2002] present a gradient descent method to map phoneme sequences. Using phoneme and letter chunks can lead to better performance [Kang and Kim, 2000]. Li et al. [2004] propose a method similar to the joint model for phrase-based machine translation. Such a substring mapping model has also been explored by others [Ekbal et al., 2006], and can be implemented as bi-stream HMM [Zhao et al., 2007] or by adapting a monotone phrase-based translation model [Sherif and Kondrak, 2007b]. For different scripts for the same language, rule-based approaches typically suffice [Malik, 2006]. Ensemble learning, i.e., the combination of multiple transliteration engines, has been shown to be successful [Oh and Isahara, 2007].

Forward transliteration – The transliteration of Japanese names into English, or conversely the translation of English names into Japanese, is an ambiguous task; often no standard transliterations exist. Normalization of corpora can be useful [Ohtake *et al.*, 2004]. Another interesting problem, which has been studied for English–Chinese, is that the foreign name should not be rendered in a way that gives a negative impression by containing characters that have negative meaning [Xu *et al.*, 2006b]. Also, when transliterating names into Chinese, the original language of the name and its gender matters, which may be incorporated into a transliteration model [Li *et al.*, 2007b].

Training data for transliteration – Training data can be collected from parallel corpora [Lee and Chang, 2003; Lee *et al.*, 2004], or by mining comparable data such as news streams [Klementiev and Roth, 2006b,a]. Training data for transliteration can also be obtained from monolingual text where the spelling of a foreign name is followed by its native form in parenthesis [Lin *et al.*, 2004; Chen and Chen, 2006; Lin *et al.*, 2008], which is common for instance for unusual English names in Chinese text. Such acquisition can be improved by bootstrapping – iteratively extracting high-confidence pairs and improving the matching model [Sherif and Kondrak, 2007a]. Sproat *et al.* [2006] fish for name transliteration in comparable corpora, also using phonetic correspondences. Tao *et al.* [2006] additionally exploit temporal distributions of name mentions, and Yoon *et al.* [2007] use a Winnow algorithm and a classifier to bootstrap the acquisition process. Cao *et al.* [2007] use various features, including that a Chinese character is part of a transliteration a priori in a perceptron classifier. Large monolingual corpus resources such as the web are used for validation [Al-Onaizan and Knight, 2002a,b; Qu and Grefenstette, 2004; Kuo *et al.*, 2006; Yang *et al.*, 2008]. Of course, training data can also be created manually, possibly aided by an active learning component that suggests the most valuable new examples [Goldwasser and Roth, 2008].

Integrating transliteration with machine translation – Kashani *et al.* [2007] present methods to integrate transliteration into the main machine translation application. Hermjakob *et al.* [2008] give a detailed discussion about integration issues, including a tagger for when to transliterate and when to translate.

Morphology – Statistical models for morphology as part of a statistical machine translation system have been developed for inflected languages [Nießen and Ney, 2001, 2004]. Morphological features can be replaced by pseudo-words [Goldwater and McClosky, 2005]. Morphological annotation is especially useful for small training corpora

[Popović *et al.*, 2005]. For highly agglutinative languages such as Arabic, the main focus is on splitting off affixes with various schemes [Habash and Sadat, 2006], or by combination of such schemes [Sadat and Habash, 2006]. A straightforward application of the morpheme splitting idea may not always yield performance gains [Virpioja *et al.*, 2007]. Yang and Kirchhoff [2006] present a back-off method that resolves unknown words by increasingly aggressive morphological stemming and compound splitting. Denoual [2007] uses spelling similarity to find the translation of unknown words by analogy. Talbot and Osborne [2006] motivate similar work by reducing redundancy in the input language, again mostly by morphological stemming. Lemmatizing words may improve word alignment performance [Corston-Oliver and Gamon, 2004]. Using the frequency of stems in the corpus in a finite state approach may provide guidance on when to split [El Isbihani *et al.*, 2006], potentially guided by a small lexicon [Riesa and Yarowsky, 2006]. Splitting off affixes can also be a viable strategy when translating into morphologically rich languages [Durgar El-Kahlout and Oflazer, 2006]. Different morphological analyses can be encoded in a confusion network as input to the translation system to avoid hard choices [Dyer, 2007a,b]. This approach can be extended to lattice decoding and tree-based models [Dyer *et al.*, 2008b].

Generating rich morphology – Generating rich morphology poses different challenges. Often relevant information is distributed widely over the input sentence or missed altogether. Minkov *et al.* [2007] use a maximum entropy model to generate rich Russian morphology and show improved performance over the standard approach of relying on the language model. Such a model may be used for statistical machine translation by adjusting the inflections in a post-processing stage [Toutanova *et al.*, 2008]. Translation between related morphologically rich languages may model the lexical translation step as a morphological analysis, transfer and generation process using finite state tools [Tantuğ *et al.*, 2007a]. But splitting words into stem and morphemes is also a valid strategy for translating into a language with rich morphology as demonstrated for English–Turkish [Oflazer and Durgar El-Kahlout, 2007] and English–Arabic [Badr *et al.*, 2008], and for translating between two highly inflected languages as in the case of Turkman–Turkish language pairs [Tantuğ *et al.*, 2007b]. Translating unknown morphological variants may be learned by analogy to other morphological spelling variations [Langlais and Patry, 2007]. For very closely related languages such as Catalan and Spanish, translating not chunks of words but chunks of letters in a phrase-based approach achieves decent results, and addresses the problem of unknown words very well [Vilar *et al.*, 2007b].

Compounds – Languages such as German, where noun compounds are merged into single words, require compound splitting [Brown, 2002; Koehn and Knight, 2003a] for translating unknown compounds to improve machine translation performance [Holmqvist *et al.*, 2007]. When translating into these languages, compounds may be merged into single words [Stymne *et al.*, 2008].

Word segmentation – Segmenting words is a problem for languages where the writing system does not include spaces between words, as in many Asian languages. Zhang and Sumita [2008] and Zhang *et al.* [2008h] discuss different granularities for Chinese words and suggest a back-off approach. Bai *et al.* [2008] aim for Chinese word segmentation in the training data to match English words one-to-one, while Chang *et al.* [2008] adjust the average word length to optimize translation performance. Xu *et al.* [2008] also use correspondence to English words in their Bayesian approach.

Spelling correction – Accents in Spanish, umlauts in German, or diacritics in Arabic may not always be properly included in electronic texts. Machine translation performance can be improved when training and test data is consistently corrected for such deficiencies [Diab *et al.*, 2007].

Translating tense, case, and markers – Schiehlen [1998] analyses the translation of tense across languages and warns against a simplistic view of the problem. Murata *et al.* [2001] propose a machine learning method using support vector machines to predict target language tense. Ye *et al.* [2006] propose using additional features in a conditional random field classifier to determine verb tenses when translating from Chinese to English. Ueffing and Ney [2003] use a pre-processing method to transform the English verb complex to match its Spanish translation more closely. A similar problem is the prediction of case markers in Japanese [Suzuki and Toutanova, 2006], which may be done using a maximum entropy model as part of a treelet translation system [Toutanova and Suzuki, 2007], or the prediction of aspect markers in Chinese, which may be framed as a classification problem and modeled with conditional random fields [Ye *et al.*, 2007a]. Another example of syntactic markers that are more common in Asian than European languages are numeral classifiers (as in *three sheets of paper*). Paul *et al.* [2002] present a corpus-based method for generating them for Japanese and Zhang *et al.* [2008a] present a method for generating Chinese measure words. Dorr [1994] presents an overview of linguistic differences between languages, called divergences [Gupta and Chatterjee, 2003].

Translation of chunks and clauses – One approach to the translation of sentences is to break up the problem along syntactic lines, into clauses [Kashioka *et al.*, 2003] or syntactic chunks [Koehn and Knight, 2002a; Schafer and Yarowsky, 2003a,b]. This strategy also allows for special components for the translation of more basic syntactic elements such as noun phrases [Koehn and Knight, 2003b] or noun compounds [Tanaka and Baldwin, 2003]. Owczarzak *et al.* [2006b] and Mellebeek *et al.* [2006] break sentences into chunks, translate the chunks separately, and combine the translations into a transformed skeleton. Hewavitharana *et al.* [2007] augment a phrase-based model with translations for noun phrases that are translated separately.

Syntactic pre-reordering – Given the limitations of the dominant phrase-based statistical machine translation approach, especially with long-distance reordering for syntactic reasons, it may be better to treat reordering in pre-processing by a hand-crafted component; this has been explored for German–English [Collins *et al.*, 2005], Japanese–English [Komachi *et al.*, 2006], Chinese–English [Wang *et al.*, 2007a], and English–Hindi [Ramanathan *et al.*, 2008]. Zwarts and Dras [2007] point out that translation improvements are due to both a reduction of reordering needed during decoding and the increased learning of phrases of syntactic dependents. Nguyen and Shimazu [2006] also use manual rules for syntactic transformation in a pre-processing step. Such a reordering component may also be learned automatically from parsed training data, as shown for French–English [Xia and McCord, 2004], Arabic–English [Habash, 2007], and Chinese–English [Crego and Mariño, 2007] – the latter work encodes different orderings in an input lattice to the decoder. Li *et al.* [2007a] propose a maximum entropy pre-reordering model based on syntactic parse trees in the source language. It may be beneficial to train different pre-reordering models for different sentence types (questions, etc.)[Zhang *et al.*, 2008e]. Pre-processing the input to a machine translation system may also include splitting it into smaller sentences [Lee *et al.*, 2008].

POS and chunk-based pre-reordering – Reordering patterns can also be learned over part-of-speech tags, allowing the input to be converted into a reordering graph [Crego and Mariño, 2006] or enabling a rescoring approach with the patterns as features [Chen *et al.*, 2006b]. The reordering rules can also be integrated into an otherwise monotone decoder [Tillmann, 2008] or used in a separate reordering model. Such rules may be based on automatic word classes [Costa-jussà and Fonollosa, 2006; Crego *et al.*, 2006a], which was shown to outperform part-of-speech tags [Costa-jussà and Fonollosa, 2007], or they may be based on syntactic chunks [Zhang *et al.*, 2007c,d; Crego and Habash, 2008]. Scoring for rule applications may be encoded in the reordering graph, or done once the target word order is established which allows for rewarding reorderings that happened due to phrase-internal reordering [Elming, 2008a,b].

Syntactic re-ranking – Linguistic features may be added to an n-best list of candidate translations to be exploited by a re-ranking approach. This was explored by Och *et al.* [2004] and by Koehn and Knight [2003b] for noun phrases. Sequence models trained on part-of-speech tags [Bonneau Maynard *et al.*, 2007] or CCG supertags [Hassan *et al.*, 2007b] may also be used in re-ranking. To check whether the dependency structure is preserved during translation, the number of preserved dependency links or paths may be a useful feature [Nikoulina and Dymetman, 2008a].

Integrated syntactic features – If syntactic properties can be formulated as features that fit into the framework of the beam-search decoding algorithm, they may be integrated into a model. Gupta *et al.* [2007] propose reordering features for different part-of-speech types that flag different reordering behavior for nouns, verbs, and adjectives.

Factored translation – Factored translation models [Koehn and Hoang, 2007] allow the integration of syntactic features into the translation and reordering models. Earlier work already augmented phrase translation tables with part-of-speech information [Lioma and Ounis, 2005]. The approach has been shown to be successful for integrating part-of-speech tags, word class factors [Shen *et al.*, 2006b], CCG super-tags [Birch *et al.*, 2007], and morphological tags [Badr *et al.*, 2008] for language modeling. Complementing this, the source side may be enriched with additional markup, for instance to better predict the right inflections in a morphologically richer output language [Avramidis and Koehn, 2008]. More complex factored models for translating morphology have been explored for English–Czech translation [Bojar, 2007].

10.6.3 Exercises

1. (⋆) Given the word counts:

173	*age*	351	*package*	99	*website*
52	*home*	12	*site*	1012	*work*
199	*homework*	419	*web*	59	*workpackage*
17	*pack*	5	*webhome*	2	*worksite*

what are the possible splits for the words *homework, website, workpackage, worksite, webhome*. Based on the geometric average of word frequencies, what are the preferred splits?

2. (⋆) Given the corpus of German–English cognates:

Haus	house	Elektrizität	electricity	zirka	circa
Maus	mouse	Nationalität	nationality	Zirkel	circle
Hund	hound	Idealismus	idealism	Schule	school
Mund	mouth	Computer	computer	Schwein	swine

   (a) Draw a transliteration alignment by hand.
   (b) Determine the letter transition probabilities given the corpus as training data (ignore uppercase/lowercase distinction).
   (c) Find the best cognate transliterations for the words *Laus, Fund, Fakultät, Optimismus, Zirkus* according to your model.

3. (⋆) Given the factored mapping tables:

das Auto	the car
das Auto	the auto
das Auto	a car
das Auto	car
das Auto	auto

DET NN	DET NN
DET NN	DET NNS
DET NN	NN
DET NN	NNS

car/NN	car
car/NNS	cars
auto/NN	auto
auto/NNS	autos
a/DET	a
a/DET	an
the/DET	the

what are the possible translations for *das*/DET *Auto*/NN?

4. (⋆⋆) Using the cognate corpus from Question 2:
   (a) Implement a finite state transducer for mapping German cognates into English, using for instance the Carmel finite state toolkit.[2]
   (b) Improve your finite state transducer by combining it with a bigram letter model.

5. (⋆⋆) Instead of lemmatizing a morphologically rich language, we may simply stem the words by cutting off all but the first four letters. Check if this improves word alignment quality for statistical machine translation by building two machine translation systems: one baseline system and one system where words are stemmed during the word alignment stage. Use the Moses toolkit[3] and the Europarl corpus[4] for your experiment.

6. (⋆⋆) If English were written without spaces between words, we would need to employ a word segmentation step before we could use English text for statistical machine translation. Create an artificial corpus of such English by deleting all spaces. Implement a word segmentation method using

[2] Available at http://www.isi.edu/licensed-sw/carmel/
[3] Available at http://www.statmt.org/moses/
[4] Available at http://www.statmt.org/europarl/

(a) a lexicon of English words with counts;

(b) a lexicon of English words without counts;

(c) (★★★) no lexicon.

7. (★★★) Obtain a word-aligned parallel corpus and annotate one side with part-of-speech tags. Extract reordering patterns for part-of-speech sequences of length 2–4 words. For which patterns are words reliably reordered? You may use the Moses toolkit, the Europarl corpus (see Question 5) and the TreeTagger.[5]

---

[5] Available at http://www.ims.uni-stuttgart.de/projekte/corplex/ TreeTagger/

Chapter 11

Tree-Based Models

Linguistic theories of syntax build on a recursive representation of sentences, which are referred to as **syntactic trees**. However, the models for statistical machine translation that we presented in previous chapters operate on a flat sequence representation of sentences – the idea that a sentence is a string of words. Since syntactic trees equip us to exploit the syntactic relationships between words and phrases, it is an intriguing proposition to build models for machine translation based on tree structures.

syntactic tree

This line of research in statistical machine translation has been pursued for many years. Recently, some core methods have crystalized and translation systems employing tree-based models have been demonstrated to perform at the level of phrase-based models, in some cases even outperforming them.

In this chapter we will introduce core concepts of tree-based models. Bear in mind, however, that this is a fast-moving research frontier and new methods are constantly being proposed and tested. What we describe here are the underlying principles of the currently most successful models.

The structure of this chapter is as follows. We introduce the notion of synchronous grammars in Section 11.1, discuss how to learn these grammars in Section 11.2, and discuss decoding in Section 11.3.

11.1 Synchronous Grammars

Let us first lay the theoretical foundations for tree-based transfer models. A number of formalisms have been proposed to represent syntax grammar with tree structures. Such formalisms are called **grammars**, and in the case of formalisms that represent tree structures of a sentence pair in synchronous grammar two languages, they are called **synchronous grammars**.

11.1.1 Phrase Structure Grammars

Let us start with a quick review of phrase structure grammars, which we introduced along with the concept of context-free grammar rules in Section 2.2.2. See Figure 11.1 for an example sentence, annotated with its phrase structure tree, as produced by a syntactic parser.

phrase structure The name **phrase structure** derives from the fact that words are grouped in increasingly larger constituents in the tree, each labeled with noun phrase a phrase label such as **noun phrase** (NP), **prepositional phrase** (PP), prepositional phrase **verb phrase** (VP), or (on top) **sentence** (S). At the leaves of the tree, we verb phrase find the words, along with their part-of-speech tags. sentence

One formalism for defining the set of possible sentences and their context-free grammar syntactic trees in a language is a **context-free grammar**. A context- nonterminal symbol free grammar consists of **nonterminal symbols** (the phrase labels and terminal symbol part-of-speech tags), **terminal symbols** (the words), a start symbol (the sentence label S), and rules of the form NT → [NT,T]+, meaning mappings from one single nonterminal symbol to a sequence of terminal and nonterminal symbols.

One example of a context-free grammar rule is the rule NP → DET NN, which allows the creation of a noun phrase NP consisting of a determiner DET and a noun NN. In this case, all symbols are nonterminal. Note how the tree structure reflects the rule applications. Each nonleaf node in the tree is constructed by applying a grammar rule that maps it to its children nodes (hence, a top node in a rule application is called parent mode the **parent**).

The term context-free implies that each rule application depends only on a nonterminal, and not on any surrounding context. Taking context into account in grammar rules leads to a computationally more complex formalism, called context-sensitive grammars.

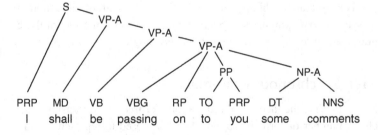

Figure 11.1 Phrase structure grammar tree for an English sentence (as produced by Michael Collins' parser, a popular and freely available tool).

11.1.2 Synchronous Phrase Structure Grammars

Synchronous grammars extend the idea of representing sentences with
trees to representing sentence pairs with **pairs of trees**. Let us start
with a simple example. A phrase structure grammar for English may
define noun phrases consisting of determiner, adjective, and noun with
the following rule:

pairs of trees

$$NP \rightarrow DET\ JJ\ NN$$

In French, adjectives may occur after the noun, so a French grammar
will contain this rule:

$$NP \rightarrow DET\ NN\ JJ$$

Suppose a sentence pair contains the French noun phrase *la maison
bleue*, which is translated as *the blue house*. We can capture this noun
phrase pair with a synchronous grammar rule:

$$NP \rightarrow DET_1\ NN_2\ JJ_3\ |\ DET_1\ JJ_3\ NN_2$$

This rule maps a nonterminal symbol (here a noun phrase NP) to a pair
of symbol sequences, the first for French and the second for English.
Each generated nonterminal symbol is indexed, so that we can identify which of the French nonterminals match which of the English
nonterminals (in a one-to-one mapping).

Rules that generate the leaves of the tree (the words) are defined in
the same way. We drop the indexes, since there is no further expansion:

$$N \rightarrow maison\ |\ house$$
$$NP \rightarrow la\ maison\ bleue\ |\ the\ blue\ house$$

Finally, nothing prevents us from mixing terminal and nonterminal
symbols on the right-hand side:

$$NP \rightarrow la\ maison\ JJ_1\ |\ the\ JJ_1\ house$$

A synchronous grammar for statistical machine translation is used similarly to a probabilistic context-free grammar in parsing. Each rule is
associated with a probabilistic score. There are many ways to estimate
probability distributions for rules, for instance the conditional probability of the right-hand side, given the left-hand side, or the conditional
probability of the English part of the right-hand side, given the French
part and the left-hand side. The overall score of a sentence pair (or
the English translation of a French sentence) is then computed as the
product of all rule scores:

$$SCORE(TREE, E, F) = \prod_i RULE_i \tag{11.1}$$

Typically, other scoring functions are also included in a statistical
machine translation model, most notably an n-gram language model.

We describe here synchronous grammars in a fairly general way. In the literature, such grammar formalisms for statistical machine translation have been proposed with restrictions to alleviate computational complexity, such as:

binary rule

- **Binary rules:** Only allow one or two symbols on the right-hand side. This restriction simplifies parsing complexity, a topic we will discuss in Section 11.3.
- **No mixing of terminals and nonterminals:** On the right-hand side, either only terminals or only nonterminals are allowed.
- **Set of nonterminals:** The set of nonterminals determines how sensitive the grammar is to syntactic distinctions between different types of phrases and part-of-speech tags. On one extreme, only a single nonterminal symbol x is allowed.

bracketing transduction grammar

A popular early version of synchronous grammars, the so-called **bracketing transduction grammar** (BTG), uses only binary rules, either resulting in at most two nonterminal or one terminal symbols (including the empty word), and a very restricted set of nonterminal symbols.

11.1.3 Synchronous Tree-Substitution Grammars

The synchronous phrase structure grammars described in the previous section have been successfully used in machine translation, especially if they are used as formal tree-based models without any actual syntactic annotation (phrase labels, etc.).

How suitable are they for a situation where we want to use real syntax trees for both input and output languages? Figure 11.2 displays

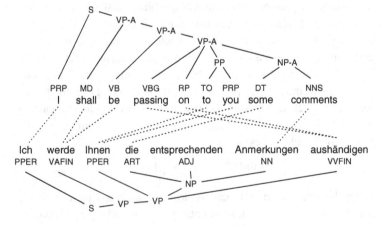

Figure 11.2 Two phrase structure grammar trees with word alignment for a German–English sentence pair.

the syntax trees for a German–English language pair. The sentences are fairly literal translations of each other, but the different placement of the main verb in German and English causes a certain degree of reordering.

First of all, let us look at how the translation of the verb *aushändigen* into the English *passing on* is nicely explained as reordering of the children of one VP node:

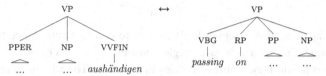

All the reordering in this sentence can be explained by a simple synchronous grammar rule:

$$\text{VP} \rightarrow \text{PPER}_1 \text{ NP}_2 \text{ } aush\ddot{a}ndigen \mid passing \text{ } on \text{ PP}_1 \text{ NP}_2$$

Note that this rule hides a problem we have with aligning the two VP subtrees. They do not have the same number of children nodes. The English translation of the German main verb consists of two words. If we want to describe the mapping of the VP subtrees with a purely non-terminal rule, we would have to map one German nonterminal to two English nonterminals. But this would violate our one-to-one mapping constraint for nonterminals on the right-hand side of the rule.

Let us look at a second example, the translation of the German pronoun *Ihnen* into the English prepositional phrase *to you*:

```
PPER       ↔        PP
  |                 /\
Ihnen            TO   PRP
                 |     |
                 to   you
```

Here, we use a trick to fit the rule into our synchronous phrase structure grammar formalism. By stripping out the internal structure of the English prepositional phrase, we arrive at the rule:

$$\text{PPER/PP} \rightarrow Ihnen \mid to \text{ } you$$

This rule simply ignores the part-of-speech tags on the English side; the prepositional phrase maps directly to the words. To preserve the internal structure, we need to include both the part-of-speech tags and the words on the English right-hand side. To put it another way, we want to use a rule like this:

```
PPER       ↔        PP
  |                 /\
Ihnen            TO   PRP
                 |     |
                 to   you
```

Let us look at another example. The mapping of the German *werde* to the English *shall be* implies the mapping of more complex subtrees. Here are the two tree fragments that contain these words:

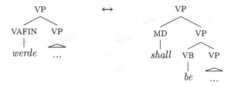

Capturing this mapping leads to a more complex rule. Since the left-hand side of a rule is a single constituent (here: VP), we need to incorporate these entire structures in the rules. The structures also include a VP as a leaf with additional material. For this, we use a non-terminal symbol on the right-hand side. This leads us to construct the following rule:

$$
\text{VP} \;\rightarrow\;
\left|
\begin{array}{cc}
& \text{VAFIN} \quad \text{VP}_1 \\
& | \\
& werde
\end{array}
\right|
\begin{array}{cc}
\text{MD} & \text{VP} \\
| & \\
shall & \text{VB} \quad \text{VP}_1 \\
& | \\
& be
\end{array}
$$

What are we doing here? We extend the synchronous phrase structure grammar formalism to include not only nonterminal and terminal symbols but also trees on the right-hand side of the rules. The trees have either nonterminal or terminal symbols at their leaves. All nonterminal symbols on the right-hand side are mapped one-to-one between the two languages.

synchronous tree substitution grammar

This formalism is called a **synchronous tree substitution grammar**, the synchronous version of the **tree substitution grammar** formalism for monolingual syntactic parsing.

Grammar rules in this formalism are applied in the same way as synchronous phrase structure grammar rules, except that additional structure is introduced. If we do not care about this additional structure, then each rule can be flattened into a synchronous phrase structure grammar rule. Applying the flattened rules instead would result in the same sentence pair, but with a simpler tree structure.

The reason why we should care about the tree structure expressed within synchronous tree substitution grammar rules is two-fold. In the input language tree structures act as constraints on when particular rules apply. In the output language they allow the construction of a syntax tree that corresponds to our common notion of grammatical representation, which enables us to assess the overall well-formedness of the sentence based on its syntactic structure.

Note that if we stay true to the given syntactic structure and only allow rules that have simple (nonterminal or terminal) symbols on the

right-hand side, then we effectively limit reordering within the model
to the swapping of children nodes directly under a parent. Such a
child node reordering restriction is common to many models that
have been proposed for translation, but it is generally assumed to be
too harsh. It requires that for all sentence pairs the input and output
syntactic trees are isomorphic in terms of child–parent relationships.
We can accommodate this with arbitrary tree structures, but not with
tree structures that follow linguistic principles in both input and output
languages.

child node reordering restriction

11.2 Learning Synchronous Grammars

In this section, we will describe in detail one method for **learning syn-chronous grammars** from parallel corpora. The method builds on word
alignments and resembles the way phrase-based statistical machine
translation models are acquired.

learning synchronous grammar

11.2.1 Learning Hierarchical Phrase Models

We present here how the learning of synchronous grammar rules
evolves from the method for phrase-based models that is described in
Section 5.2, starting on page 130. First, we want to build grammars that
have no underlying linguistic interpretation, but only use arbitrary non-terminals such as x. Our description is based mainly on work by Chiang
[2005].

See Figure 11.3a for an illustration of the method for traditional
phrase-based models. Given a word alignment matrix for a bilingual
sentence pair, we extract all phrase pairs that are consistent with the
word alignment. These phrase pairs are the translation rules in the
phrase-based models. There are various ways to estimate translation
probabilities for them – for instance, the conditional probability $\phi(\bar{e}|\bar{f})$
based on relative frequency of the phrase pair $(\bar{e},\bar{f})$ and the phrase $\bar{f}$ in
the corpus.

All the traditional phrase translation pairs form rules for a syn-chronous grammar. As already discussed, these are rules with only
terminal symbols (i.e., words) on the right-hand side:

$$\text{Y} \rightarrow \bar{f} \mid \bar{e}$$

We now want to build more complex translation rules that include both
terminal and nonterminal symbols on the right-hand side of the rule. We
learn these rules as generalizations of the traditional lexical rules.

See Figure 11.3b for an example. We want to learn a translation
rule for the German verb complex *werde aushändigen*. However, the

Figure 11.3 Extracting traditional and hierarchical phrase translation rules: We extend the method for phrase-based statistical methods described in Section 5.2. When extracting a larger phrase mapping using a block in the alignment matrix, subblocks may be replaced with the symbol x.

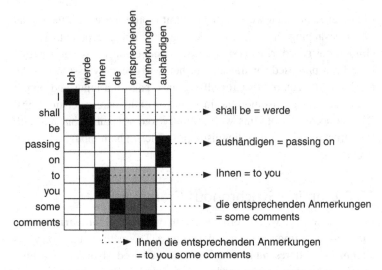

(a) Extracting traditional phrase translation rules

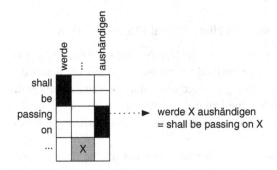

(b) Extracting hierarchical phrase translation rules

German words *werde* and *aushändigen* are not next to each other, but separated by intervening words. In traditional phrase models, we would not be able to learn a translation rule that contains only these two German words, since phrases in these models are contiguous sequences of words. A rule that contains *werde* and *aushändigen* also spans all intervening words:

Y → *werde Ihnen die entsprechenden Anmerkungen aushändigen*
| *shall be passing on to you some comments*

We now replace the intervening words with the nonterminal symbol X. Correspondingly, on the English side, we replace the string of English words that align to these intervening German words with the symbol X. We then proceed to extract the translation rule

Y → *werde* X *aushändigen* | *shall be passing on* X

This rule is a synchronous grammar with a mix of nonterminal symbols (here x) and terminal symbols (the words) on the right-hand side. It encapsulates nicely the type of reordering involved when translating German verb complexes into English.

Note that we have not yet introduced any syntactic constraints other than the principle that language is recursive, and this type of hierarchical translation rule reflects this property. We will add syntactic information in the next section, but let us first formally define the method of extracting hierarchical translation rules.

Recall from Section 5.2.2 on page 131 that given an input sentence $\mathbf{f} = (f_1, ..., f_{l_f})$ and output sentence $\mathbf{e} = (e_1, ..., e_{l_e})$, and a word alignment mapping A, we extract all phrase pairs $(\bar{e}, \bar{f})$ that are consistent with the word alignment:

$$(\bar{e}, \bar{f}) \text{ consistent with } A \Leftrightarrow$$
$$\forall e_i \in \bar{e} : (e_i, f_j) \in A \to f_j \in \bar{f}$$
$$\text{AND } \forall f_j \in \bar{f} : (e_i, f_j) \in A \to e_i \in \bar{e}$$
$$\text{AND } \exists e_i \in \bar{e}, f_j \in \bar{f} : (e_i, f_j) \in A \qquad (11.2)$$

Let P be the set of all extracted phrase pairs $(\bar{e}, \bar{f})$. We now construct hierarchical phrase pairs from existing phrase pairs. If an existing phrase pair $(\bar{e}, \bar{f}) \in P$ contains another smaller phrase pair $(\bar{e}_{SUB}, \bar{f}_{SUB}) \in P$, we replace the smaller phrase pair with a nonterminal symbol X, and add the more general phrase pair to the set P:

extend recursively:
$$\text{if } (\bar{e}, \bar{f}) \in P \text{ AND } (\bar{e}_{SUB}, \bar{f}_{SUB}) \in P$$
$$\text{AND } \bar{e} = \bar{e}_{PRE} + \bar{e}_{SUB} + \bar{e}_{POST}$$
$$\text{AND } \bar{f} = \bar{f}_{PRE} + \bar{f}_{SUB} + \bar{f}_{POST}$$
$$\text{AND } \bar{e} \neq \bar{e}_{SUB} \text{ AND } \bar{f} \neq \bar{f}_{SUB}$$
$$\text{add } (e_{PRE} + X + e_{POST}, f_{PRE} + X + f_{POST}) \text{ to } P \qquad (11.3)$$

The set of hierarchical phrase pairs is the closure under this extension mechanism. Note that multiple replacements of smaller phrases allow the creation of translation mappings with multiple nonterminal symbols. This allows us to build useful translation rules such as:

$$Y \to X_1 \ X_2 \ | \ X_2 \ of \ X_1$$

One note on the complexity of the hierarchical rules that are extracted from a sentence pair: since a rule may map any subset of input words (with nonterminal symbols filling in the gaps), an exponential number of rules are possible. To avoid rule sets of unmanageable size and to reduce decoding complexity, we typically want to set limits on possible rules. For instance, Chiang [2005] suggests the limits

- at most two nonterminal symbols;
- at least one but at most five words per language;
- span at most 15 words (counting gaps).

The limit on nonterminal symbols reduces the complexity of the size of the extracted rule set from exponential to polynomial. Typically, we also do not allow rules where nonterminal symbols are next to each other in both languages.

Models that use hierarchical rules, but no explicit syntax, have been shown to outperform traditional phrase-based models on some language pairs. They do seem to explain the reordering induced by certain words and phrases, especially in the case of discontinuous phrases (phrases with gaps).

11.2.2 Learning Syntactic Translation Rules

In the previous section we describe a method for learning synchronous grammar rules, but although these rules are formally forming a grammar, we did not use any of the syntactic annotation that we expect in a syntax-based translation model. Let us consider now how adding such annotation allows us to extract truly syntactic rules.

In addition to word alignments, we need to prepare the training data to include syntactic parse trees for each input and output sentence. Typically, we obtain these with automatic syntactic parsers, which are available for many languages. See Figure 11.4 for an illustration of our ongoing example sentence pair, annotated with word alignments and syntactic trees.

Covering phrases with a single node
Merging the notions of hierarchical phrase extraction with synchronous tree substitution grammars adds one constraint to the phrase extraction

Figure 11.4 Extracting syntactic translation rules: In addition to words, a rule also includes syntactic annotation. Since each half of the right-hand side of the rule has to be covered by a single constituent in the tree, the rule may also contain additional nonterminals.

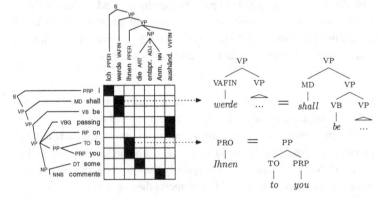

method. On the left-hand side of a grammar rule, we need one – and only one – nonterminal symbol. Since this nonterminal symbol expresses a node in both the input and the output syntax trees, it may consist of a pair of phrase labels (see an example of this in the next rule below). But we do need a unique phrase label for each language, which implies that, on the right-hand side, the rules generate complete subtrees governed by a single head node.

Let us take a closer look at how this plays out for a relatively simple rule. In the word alignment the German *Ihnen* is aligned to the English *to you*. Including the part-of-speech tags, we have the following mapping:

```
PRO    =    TO   PRP
 |           |    |
Ihnen       to   you
```

In the representation of the English phrase, we have two nodes. However, to be able to construct a grammar rule, we need a single node that includes the entire phrase. Fortunately, both nodes are children of the same prepositional phrase PP. So we are able to use this prepositional phrase node and have complete subtrees on both sides:

```
PRO    =        PP
 |            ⌒⌒⌒⌒
Ihnen       TO    PRP
             |     |
            to    you
```

The resulting rule is

```
                    | TO   PRP
PRO/PP  →  Ihnen    |  |    |
                    | to   you
```

Moving up the tree may result in additional nonterminals

Let us now consider a slightly more complicated example (also illustrated in Figure 11.4). In the word alignment, the German *werde* is aligned to the English *shall be*:

```
VAFIN   =   MD    VB
  |          |     |
werde      shall   be
```

Again, we need to cover the two English words under a single complete subtree. The smallest possible subtree is governed by a VP node, which includes the two words but also an additional VP:

We need to include this additional VP (the one in the bottom right-hand corner, on a level with VB) in the grammar rule that we are trying to construct. This VP node governs the words *passing on to you some comments*. These words align to the German words *Ihnen die entsprechenden Anmerkungen aushändigen*, which are also governed by a single VP in German.

Moving up the German tree by one level gives us the mapping

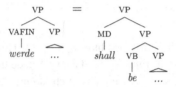

Since the two VP in the bottom right-hand corner of each language's syntax tree translate to each other, we end up with the rule

$$\text{VP} \;\rightarrow\; \begin{array}{c} \text{VAFIN} \;\; \text{VP}_1 \\ | \\ werde \end{array} \;\Bigg|\; \begin{array}{c} \text{MD} \qquad \text{VP} \\ | \qquad \land \\ shall \;\; \text{VB} \;\; \text{VP}_1 \\ | \\ be \end{array}$$

Rule generation from a phrase pair may fail

The method that we used to create a rule for a phrase pair may fail, even if the phrase pair is valid and consistent with the word alignment. One example is the mapping of the German *Ihnen die entsprechenden Anmerkungen aushändigen* to the English *to you some comments*. In both cases, we have to move up the tree to reach a parent node that includes all the words. We arrive at the mapping

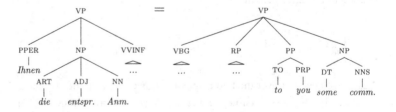

Here, the German VVINF is aligned to both the English VBG and RB. Since nonterminal symbols on the right-hand side must be mappings between unique nodes in the tree (and not 1–2 mappings, as in this case), we are not able to create a grammar rule.

Note that even if we are able to construct a rule for a given phrase pair, it may be overly complex. It may include so much additional structure and mapping of nonterminals that it will be rarely used in practice.

Formal definition

Above, we informally described a method for building grammar rules from a sentence pair that are consistent with the word alignment. This method is meant to convey an intuitive understanding of the resulting grammar rules, especially why these rules are sometimes overly complex or why we may not be able to construct rules for some aligned phrase pairs. We now conclude the topic of extracting syntactically annotated grammar rules with a formal definition of the set of syntax rules for a sentence pair.

Let us first define the **governing node** for a sequence of words. Given a sequence of words $w_1, ..., w_n$ and a syntax tree T, then a node $g \in T$ is a governing node for the words $w_1, ..., w_n$ if and only if the leaf nodes of the subtree under g are exactly the words $w_1, ..., w_n$.

governing node

Note that not every sequence of words will have a governing node. But it is also possible for a phrase to have multiple governing nodes in the case that one governing node has only one child, which is hence also a governing node.

We define the set of hierarchical phrase pairs in Equation (11.3) on page 339. For each hierarchical phrase pair $(\bar{e}, \bar{f})$ we are able to construct a synchronous grammar rule (a) if the phrases $\bar{e}, \bar{f}$ have governing nodes, and (b) if all phrases covered by nonterminals in the phrases $\bar{e}, \bar{f}$ have governing nodes.

On the left-hand side of the rule we use the node labels of the governing nodes of the full phrases $(\bar{e}, \bar{f})$ as nonterminal symbol. On the right-hand side we use the pair of sets of children subtrees under each governing node of the full phrases. We replace the nonterminals within the phrases with the node label of a governing node.

Note that this process of constructing synchronous tree-substitution grammar rules allows us also to construct rules that contain no terminal symbols (i.e., words).

Example: Given the synchronous phrase structure grammar rule

$$\text{Y} \rightarrow \text{X}_1 \text{ X}_2 \text{ } \textit{aushändigen} \mid \textit{passing on } \text{X}_1 \text{ X}_2$$

with the underlying tree structure

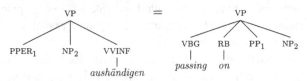

we construct the rule

$$VP \; \rightarrow \; \text{PPER}_1 \; \text{NP}_2 \; \underset{\textit{aushändigen}}{\text{VVINF}} \; \Big| \; \underset{\textit{passing}}{\text{VBG}} \; \underset{\textit{on}}{\text{RB}} \; \text{PP}_1 \; \text{NP}_2$$

Note that it is not possible to construct a rule for

$$\text{Y} \rightarrow \textit{aushändigen} \; | \; \textit{passing on}$$

11.2.3 Simpler Rules

In the previous two sections we described methods for building grammars for the cases where no syntactic annotation exists, and then extended this to the grammars where syntax trees are provided for both input and output languages. It is worth pointing out that there are different motivations for using syntax on either the input or the output side.

On the input side, syntax provides constraints on when certain rules apply. Before translation, we obtain the syntactic parse of the input sentence, and only rules that match this tree are available to the translation system. On the output side, syntax provides the means to build a tree structure for the output sentence. We would like to limit the output translation to grammatically correct English.

However, syntactic constraints can be too limiting. We may not be able to extract enough rules or the extracted rules may be too specific to be used during decoding. These constraints may limit our ability to exploit the training corpus effectively.

Hence, we may want to simplify syntactic rules in various ways.

semi-syntactic rule   **Semi-syntactic rules**: We may only want to syntactify either the input or the output language side of the rules. One practical reason for this may be the limited availability of reliable syntactic parsers. But for particular language pairs, either the input side or the output side may benefit more from syntactic annotation.

featurized rule   **Featurized rules**: Instead of using input-side syntax in the rules, we may want to integrate it as soft constraints in a featurized rule model, such as a maximum entropy model, as suggested for phrase-based models (see Section 5.3.6 on page 141).

Relabeling nonterminals: Nonterminal labels in syntactic grammars are typically motivated by the needs of syntactic parsing, where the words of a sentence are given and the syntactic structure has to be predicted. In machine translation, we are less concerned with the syntactic structure and more focused on predicting the right output sentence. Hence, we may want to use labels that are better at selecting the right output.

relabeling nonterminals

Binarization: Rules with many nonterminals on the right-hand side can be unduly specific. Think of adjective phrases with a specific number of adjectives or noun compounds with a fixed number of compounds. To learn more general rules, we may want to add internal nodes to the syntactic trees to have at most binary branching rules. Binarization would also help in decoding (see below in Section 11.3.8 on page 359).

binarization

Rules without internal structure: The rules we extract can have elaborate internal structure on the right-hand side since they are extracted from complex tree fragments. However, this structure does not matter, unless we care about the tree structure we generate in addition to the words we output. Hence, as already suggested above, we may want to flatten the rules, so that they are strings of terminal and nonterminal labels.

rules without internal structure

Back-off rules: In the worst case, the synchronous grammar we learn from a training corpus may fail to translate some input sentence. For more robust behavior of our model, we may want to introduce back-off rules, such as rules using the nonterminal X that matches anything. The grammar should discourage the use of the back-off rules, for instance by using a feature that flags their use.

back-off rule

11.2.4 Scoring Grammar Rules

For each sentence pair, we are able to extract a large number of grammar rules. As with phrase-based models, we now need to assign a score to each rule that indicates how reliable it is.

Given that a rule is in the format LHS $\rightarrow$ RHS$_f$ | RHS$_e$ the following probability distributions may be suitable as scoring functions for the grammar:

- Joint rule probability: $p(\text{LHS}, \text{RHS}_f, \text{RHS}_e)$;
- Rule application probability: $p(\text{RHS}_f, \text{RHS}_e | \text{LHS})$;
- Direct translation probability: $p(\text{RHS}_e | \text{RHS}_f, \text{LHS})$;
- Noisy-channel translation probability: $p(\text{RHS}_f | \text{RHS}_e, \text{LHS})$;
- Lexical translation probability: $\prod_{e_i \in \text{RHS}_e} p(e_i | \text{RHS}_f, a)$.

These conditional probability distributions can be estimated by maximum likelihood estimation using the rule counts. The lexical translation probability also requires that we remember the word alignment a to determine the alignment of each English word e_i.

A selection of these scoring functions can be included in a log-linear model that also includes the language model probability, and maybe a few other scoring functions. We then set the weight for each function with minimum error rate training.

11.3 Decoding by Parsing

In this section, we will describe a machine translation decoding algorithm for synchronous grammars. Just as we borrowed the formalism for tree transfer models from the statistical parsing world, we will adapt a popular algorithm for **syntactic parsing** to our decoding problem.

syntactic parsing

11.3.1 Chart Parsing

In tree transfer models, one fundamental element of the decoding process has changed compared to phrase-based models. In phrase-based models, we are able to build the translation from left to right. This is no longer possible given the synchronous grammar formalism we are using here. In particular, rules with gaps force us to produce English words at disconnected positions of the English output sentence.

However, one constraint we introduced for synchronous grammars allows us to use an efficient algorithm for decoding. We always have single constituents on the left-hand side of the grammar rules. Hence, when we build the tree from the bottom up, we are always able to create structures that are complete subtrees.

The constraint requiring single constituents on the left-hand side of rules also applies to the input language. Hence, we are always able to cover parts of the input sentence that are represented in the input syntax parse tree by complete subtrees. One important implication is that we are always able to cover contiguous spans of the input sentence.

chart parsing

The idea of **chart parsing** is to cover contiguous spans of the input sentence of increasing length. We record the translations of these spans in the **chart**. When creating **chart entries** for longer spans, we are able to build on the underlying smaller chart entries. This process terminates when we have covered the entire sentence. See Figure 11.5 for an illustration of the bottom-up chart decoding algorithm applied to a simple example. Given a set of six rules, we translate the German sentence *Sie will eine Tasse Kaffee trinken* into English.

We start by attempting to translate all single German words into English. For three of the words, we have synchronous grammar rules that match the German words and their part-of-speech tags. When translating these, we create chart entries that contain English words and

Grammar

PPER/PRO → *sie* | *she*   NP/NP →   ART   NN NN₁ | NP   PP

NN/NN → *Kaffee* | *coffee*   *eine* *Tasse* | DET   NN IN NN₁

VVINF/VB → *trinken* | *drink*   *a*   *cup* *of*

S/S → PPER VP | PRO VP

VP/VP → MD NP₁ VVINF₂ | VBZ   VP
              will   *wants*   TO   VB₂ NP₁
                                          to

Chart

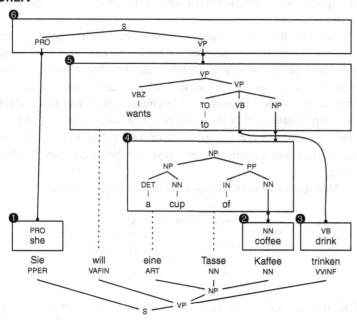

Figure 11.5 Translating with a synchronous tree substitution grammar by chart parsing: Chart entries are added bottom-up, first fully lexical rules (1–3), then partly lexical rules that build on top of them (4–5), and finally a nonlexical rule to build the sentence node (6).

their part-of-speech tags: By covering *Sie*/PPER we build the chart entry containing *she*/PRO, by covering *Kaffee*/NN we build the chart entry containing *coffee*/NN, and by covering *trinken*/VVINF we build the chart entry containing *drink*/VB.

Note that in a realistic synchronous grammar obtained from a parallel corpus, many more rules would apply and we would build many more chart entries. Let us ignore for now the issues of dealing efficiently with the complexity of the chart in a realistic case of competing rule applications.

Having applied all rules that match German spans of length one, we now move on to longer spans. There are no rules that apply to spans of length two, but one rule applies to the German three-word span *eine Tasse Kaffee*. Since we already translated *Kaffee*/NN into *coffee*/NN, we are able to apply the rule

$$\text{NP/NP} \rightarrow \left.\begin{array}{ccc} \text{ART} & \text{NN} & \text{NN}_1 \\ | & | & \\ \textit{eine} & \textit{Tasse} & \end{array}\right| \begin{array}{cc} \text{NP} & \text{PP} \\ \overset{\frown}{\text{DET} \quad \text{NN}} & \overset{\frown}{\text{IN} \quad \text{NN}_1} \\ | \quad\quad | & | \\ a \quad\quad cup & of \end{array}$$

The nonterminal NN$_1$ on the right-hand side of the rule matches the chart entry that we have already generated. We are able to check this by consulting the label of the chart entry (NN) and also the German parse tree that corresponds to the span covered by the chart entry. Since the rule applies, we are able to build a new chart entry that covers the entire German three-word span.

Consider the role a chart entry plays in the chart parsing process. From an algorithmic point of view, we care about the head node label of the subtree it contains and the span it covers. Internally the chart entry also contains the translation and pointers to other chart entries that were used to construct it. Recall that a chart entry represents not only the translation of a contiguous span of German words into a contiguous sequence of English words, but also the translation of a complete German subtree into a complete English subtree.

Moving on, the next rule application is more of the same:

$$\text{VP/VP} \rightarrow \left.\begin{array}{ccc} \text{MD} & \text{NP}_1 & \text{VVINF}_2 \\ | & & \\ \textit{will} & & \end{array}\right| \begin{array}{cc} \text{VBZ} & \text{VP} \\ | & \overset{\frown}{\text{TO} \quad \text{VB}_2 \quad \text{NP}_1} \\ \textit{wants} & | \\ & to \end{array}$$

The rule allows us to build a chart entry that covers a five-word German span. The rule contains two nonterminals NP$_1$ and VVINF/VB$_2$, which appear in a different order in the input and output languages. This causes the reordering of *a cup of coffee* and *drink*.

Finally, a nonlexical rule combines the pronoun *she* with the verb clause containing the rest of the sentence. This creates a chart entry that covers the entire input sentence with the sentence node label s, indicating a complete translation into a full English sentence.

11.3.2 Core Algorithm

chart decoding algorithm   The core **chart decoding algorithm** is sketched out in Figure 11.6. Chart entries are created for input spans of increasing length. For a given span in the chart, typically a large number of sequences of chart entries and input words are possible.

```
Input: Foreign sentence f = f₁,...f₁f, with syntax tree
Output: English translation e
 1: for span length l = 1 to lf do
 2:    for start=0 .. lf −1 do // beginning of span
 3:       end = start+l
 4:       for all sequences s of entries and words in span [start,end] do
 5:          for all rules r do
 6:             if rule r applies to chart sequence s then
 7:                create new chart entry c
 8:                add chart entry c to chart
 9:             end if
10:          end for
11:       end for
12:    end for
13: end for
14: return English translation e from best chart entry in span [0,lf]
```

Figure 11.6 Sketch of the core chart decoding algorithm.

For instance for the span 5–6 in our example from Figure 11.5, there are four **possible sequences**:

possible sequences

- word *Kaffee*, word *trinken*;
- word *Kaffee*, entry 3 (VB);
- entry 2 (NN), word *trinken*;
- entry 2 (NN), entry 3 (VB).

For each of the sequences, any number of rules may apply. Each applicable rule allows us to create a new chart entry. If our grammar contains unary nonlexical rules, we have to consider rule applications for the chart entries we just generated.

Note that in a realistic case, we would expect to have thousands of chart entries and millions of nodes, and hence many more possible sequences. In fact, an exhaustive listing of all sequences may be computationally too expensive. We explore efficient methods for chart decoding in the remainder of this chapter.

11.3.3 Chart Organization

The main data structure of the chart decoding algorithm is the chart. It consists of chart entries that may cover any of the $\frac{n(n+1)}{2}$ input spans (where n is the number of foreign input words). Given that a typical synchronous grammar provides many translations for each word or phrase, and many more rules for combining existing chart entries, it is easy to see that the number of chart entries grows explosively. We therefore have to **organize the chart** carefully and prune out bad entries early.

chart organization

Note that what we describe in this section has parallels to decoding for phrase-based models, which is covered in detail in Chapter 6. If you are unfamiliar with terms such as stack, recombination, pruning, or future cost estimation, please refer to the more extensive treatment in that chapter.

First of all, let us examine the properties of a chart entry. Each entry covers a span of input words. It contains the parse tree of the translation, which is a complete subtree. We typically store in the chart entry only the parts of the subtree that were added during the rule application that created the entry. Links to the underlying chart entries that were consumed during the rule application provide the remaining information.

When determining whether a chart entry can be used in a specific rule application, the only relevant information is its span and the constituent label of its English head node. We therefore organize the chart **stack** entries in **stacks** based on their coverage span. As with phrase-based decoding, you may want to organize stacks in other ways.

See Figure 11.7 for an illustration of the stack organization, which also shows how the core algorithm builds each new chart entry from chart entries below. The organization in stacks makes it easier to look up chart entries and also provides the basis for recombination and pruning.

11.3.4 Recombination

recombination Let us first consider the issue of **recombination**, i.e., the safe dropping of inferior chart entries that could not possibly be part of the best translation. Two chart entries are comparable for the purpose of recombination only if they cover the same span of input words and have the same head node label.

But the English words in the chart entries also matter. When applying a rule, we compute the values of various feature functions. One of them is the n-gram language model. When combining chart entries, the

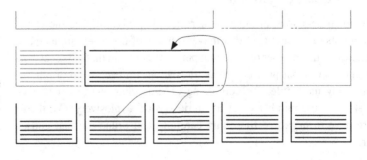

Figure 11.7 Organization of the chart in stacks: one stack per span (shown here), or one stack per span and head node label. New chart entries are generated from lower chart entries or words.

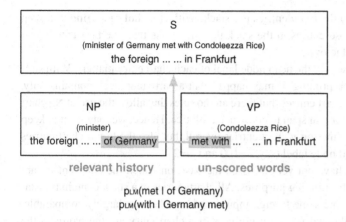

Figure 11.8 Language model computations when applying the grammar rule S → NP VP to build the new chart entry S. With a trigram language model, two words at the edge of a chart entry matter: the last two words of the left-hand entry are relevant history to score the first two words of the right-hand entry.

n–1 English words at the connecting edge of each chart entry have an effect on the language model probability.

See Figure 11.8 for an illustration of the language model computations when combining two chart entries (an NP and VP). The last two words of the left-hand chart entry are required as history to compute the language model probabilities of the not yet scored first two words of the right-hand chart entry.

Consequently, the following properties of chart entries have to match for recombination (where n is the order of the n-gram language model):

- span of input words covered;
- constituent label of English head node;
- first n–1 English words;
- last n–1 English words.

If two chart entries agree in all these properties, we may safely discard the weaker one. Recombination helps to reduce the search space, but by itself it does not reduce the complexity of the search when we have realistic grammar sizes sufficient to translate any but the shortest sentences.

11.3.5 Stack Pruning

The chart contains entries that cover any contiguous span of input words. We organize the chart entries in stacks corresponding to these spans, as illustrated in Figure 11.7. Due to the many possibilities in generating chart entries, the number of entries in each stack becomes unmanageable large.

We therefore have to discard chart entries that are likely to be too bad to be part of the best scoring translation. With **histogram pruning**,   histogram pruning threshold pruning   we keep the top *n* entries per stack. With **threshold pruning**, we keep only those entries in the stack that are worse than the best entry by at most a factor α.

However, the head node label of each chart entry matters. With simple stack pruning, it may happen that a particular stack contains only, say, NP chart entries, but there are no rules that allow the use of NP chart entries for that span to construct a full tree. Hence, we may want to keep not only the top *n* chart entries overall, but also the top *m* chart entries per head node label (say, $n=100$ and $m=2$).

We have not yet discussed the basis on which the chart entries are scored for pruning purposes. All chart entries in a stack contain translations of the same foreign input words, so they are largely comparable. One unknown for the usefulness of a chart entry are the words at the edges, which affect language model scores when the entry is used in a rule.

The initial words in a chart entry are a particular concern, because they lack the context to be adequately scored. For pruning purposes, cost estimate   however, we use a **cost estimate** that takes language model costs of unscored words into account. Since we have no context, we have to resort to lower order language models (unigram for first word, bigram for second word, etc.) for the estimation.

outside cost   We may also take **outside cost** into account. A stack may cover a span of foreign input words that are unlikely to be combined into an English output constituent. If we have some estimate of how likely chart entries with a given head node over a span are to be used in a good syntax tree, we can use smaller stacks for unlikely spans. Note the parallels with future cost estimation in phrase-based models. We will come back to outside cost estimation in Section 11.3.9.

11.3.6 Accessing Grammar Rules

The core chart decoding algorithm from Figure 11.6 contained the lines

4: **forall** sequences *s* of entries and words in span [start,end] **do**
5:     **forall** rules *r* **do**
6:         **if** rule *r* applies to chart sequence *s* **then**

Given the exponential number of sequences *s* and typically millions of grammar rules *r*, a straightforward implementation of these three lines would result in a very slow decoding process. We want to refine this part of the algorithm to have a more efficient solution.

Recall some sources of complexity:

- When combining a given set of stacks, many possible rules apply. Rules differ not only in the type of nonterminal head nodes of the chart entries that they combine, but also in the order and head label of the new chart entry, as well as potential additionally produced English output words. Applicable rules have to be accessed from a set that contains millions of rules. We discuss an efficient prefix data structure to represent a rule set immediately below.

- When applying a given rule to a given set of stacks, many different chart entries in the stacks may be used. We discuss the cube pruning method, which reduces this complexity by focusing on the most promising chart entries (Section 11.3.7 on page 357).
- To generate constituents over a given span, several combinations of underlying stacks are possible (recall Figure 11.15 on page 359 for an illustration). To address the problem that the number of combinations is exponential in the number of combined stacks, we discuss binarization of the grammar, or at least restricting the number of nonterminals (Section 11.3.8 on page 359).

Let us start with the first challenge, i.e., dealing with a very large rule set. Grammars extracted from modern training sets have somewhere between millions and billions of rules. We need to have an efficient algorithm to look up the rules that are applicable to a specific span in the chart.

The first step towards a solution to this problem is the use of a **prefix tree**, in which all the rules are stored. Figure 11.9 shows what such a data structure might look like. Each rule is broken up into its nonterminal mappings and input words that are consumed by the rule. For instance, stepping through the prefix tree starting with node NP, then

prefix tree

Prefix data structure

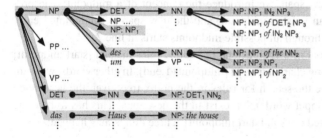

Rules

$$NP \rightarrow NP_1\ DET_2\ NN_3\ \mid\ NP_1\ IN_2\ NP_3$$
$$NP \rightarrow NP_1\ \mid\ NP1$$
$$NP \rightarrow NP_1\ des\ NN_2\ \mid\ NP_1\ of\ the\ NN_2$$
$$NP \rightarrow NP_1\ des\ NN_2\ \mid\ NP_2\ NP_1$$
$$NP \rightarrow DET_1\ NN_2\ \mid\ DET_1\ NN_2$$
$$NP \rightarrow das\ Haus\ \mid\ the\ house$$

Figure 11.9 Prefix tree for storing grammar rules: The six paths that are highlighted lead to the six rules displayed below the data structure.

nodes DET and NN, reaching the end point NP: NP_1 IN_2 NP_3, results in the lookup of the rule

$$NP \rightarrow NP_1 \ DET_2 \ NN_3 \ | \ NP_1 \ IN_2 \ NP_3$$

When looking up rules for a span, our path through the prefix tree is informed by the head node labels of the underlying chart entries and the input words. Note that when we are looking up rules for different spans that start at the same input word position, we follow the same path, and just stop at different points.

Earley parsing   This key insight forms the basis of the **Earley parsing** algorithm, which we adapt to the translation problem. The lookup of rules for spans at each step follows a principle derived from this insight: given any number of chart entries that we have already considered during the search for rules, the chart entries in the next span guide the path further along the prefix tree structure. For each span, we keep track of the locations in the prefix tree that match its underlying chart entries, which includes both complete rules and also intermediate points, which active rule   are called **active rules** or **dotted rules**, due to the notation used in the dotted rule   description of the algorithm.

See Figure 11.10 for the pseudo-code of the Earley parse-decoding algorithm. We build the chart from the bottom up, as discussed in previous sections of this chapter. This is done in the outer loops in lines 4–6, which iterate through spans [start,end] of increasing sizes. In this notation, the span [0,1] covers the first word of an input sentence.

As already indicated, we now want to combine search points in the rule prefix tree with new spans. To separate the already processed span and the new span, we introduce the concept of a midpoint: The processed span is [start,midpoint] and the new span is [midpoint+1,end]. The loop through all possible midpoints starts in line 7.

The goal now is to extend the dotted rules in span [start,midpoint] with existing chart entries in [midpoint+1,end]. In other words, we want to continue the search for rules in the prefix tree given the head node labels (or input words) that exist in the new span. This has to be done for all dotted rules in [start,midpoint]. Three things may happen:

1. None of the head node labels in the chart entries of span [midpoint+1,end] is found in the prefix tree. In this case, there is nothing to do.
2a. If we find a match in the prefix tree, we may reach complete rules. We apply the rule and add new chart entries to the span [start,end].
2b. If we find a match in the prefix tree, we may reach active (dotted) rules. We store these dotted rules (practically, pointers into the prefix tree) in the span [start,end].

```
Input: Foreign sentence f = f₁,...f₁f, with syntax tree
Output: English translation e
 1:  for i=0 .. length(f)-1 do // initialize chart
 2:    store pointer to initial node in prefix tree in span [i,i]
 3:  end for
 4:  for l=1..lf do // build chart from the bottom up
 5:   for start=0 .. lf − 1 do // beginning of span
 6:     end = start+l
 7:     for midpoint=start .. end-1 do
 8:       for all dotted rules d in span [start,midpoint] do
 9:         for all distinct head node nonterminals or input words h covering
                span [midpoint+1,end] do
10:           if extension d→ h exists in prefix tree then
11:             dnew = d→ h
12:             for all complete rules at dnew do
13:               apply rules
14:               store chart entries in span [start,end]
15:             end for
16:             if extension exist for dnew then
17:               store dnew in span [start,end] // new dotted rule
18:             end if
19:           end if
20:         end for
21:       end for
22:     end for
23:   end for
24:  end for
25:  return English translation e from best chart entry in span [0,lf]
```

Figure 11.10 Earley parsing algorithm adapted to decoding with synchronous grammars, which allows efficient lookup of all applicable rules.

To illustrate the Earley algorithm, let us take a look at the example in Figure 11.11, which shows some chart entries and dotted rules that are generated and stored during the execution of the algorithm when translating the input *das Haus des Architekten Frank Gehry*.

For one-word spans, such as the one spanning *Architekten*, we expect to find many translations, such as in this case *architect*. But for two-word phrases, such as *das Haus*, we also expect to find translations, here for instance *the house*. The seeding of the chart with phrase translations is akin to the workings of phrase-based models.

Searching the rule prefix tree for rules whose input part of the right-hand side starts with *das* or DET should also lead us down a promising path. Hence, we add the dotted rules *das•* and DET• to the span [0,1].

Notice what happens when we generate dotted rules for the span [0,2]. For instance, for the midpoint 1, we try to combine the dotted rule DET• from span [0,1] with the nonterminal head node NN of the chart entry *house* from span [1,2]. We expect many rules that start with a mapping of the input DET NN to outputs such as DET NN, so we will find a dotted rule DET NN•, which we add to the span.

Figure 11.11 Example of Earley parse-decoding: The top chart displays some of the dotted rules (shaded boxes) and chart entries (white boxes) generated during the translation process. The bottom chart shows the dotted rules (light shaded boxes), complete rules (dark shaded boxes) and chart entries (white boxes) generated for one translation of the input.

Some of the chart entries and dotted rules created

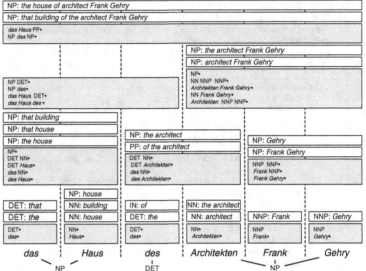

Rules and entries used for one derivation

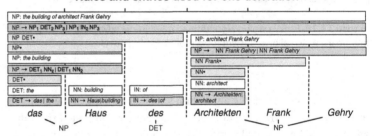

For the dotted rule DET NN•, there will likely be the complete rule NP → DET$_1$NN$_2$ | DET$_1$NN$_2$. Upon finding this rule, we can apply it to the chart entries DET:*the* and NN:*house*, resulting in the translation NP:*the house*. Refer to the figure for more examples.

A final note on the complexity of the algorithm: The loops of spans and midpoints are cubic with respect to the sentence length. The number of dotted rules is $O(C^R)$ where C is the number of nonterminals and R the rank of the grammar. Obviously a large rank R is a problem – more on that in the next section. The loop over the nonterminals of the chart entries in a span is linear with the total number of nonterminals and bounded by the maximum stack size.

11.3.7 Cube Pruning

Let us now continue our exploration of efficient methods for chart decoding by focusing our attention on applications of individual rules to create new chart entries from a sequence of stacks.

Note that in the following we use a simpler representation for synchronous grammar rules, which includes only the English output part of the right-hand side of the rules. The foreign input part may act as an additional constraint that would eliminate rules, but has no effect on the constructed English.

Check Figure 11.12 for an illustration of the application of binary rules, i.e., rules that combine two nonterminals. Fully nonterminal rules such as S → NP PP combine chart entries from two different stacks. If the first stack contains n NP chart entries and the second stack contains m VP chart entries, then $n \times m$ new chart entries can be generated.

The situation is similar if rules combine new words with chart entries. There may be many rules that translate a given foreign input sequence of words and combine it with a nonterminal, such as PP → *of* NP or PP → *by* NP. Again, if there are n such rules and m NP chart entries in the relevant stack, then $n \times m$ new chart entries can be generated.

If n and m are large, then we will generate many new chart entries, but we will discard most of them immediately. For instance, with a maximum stack size of 100, we may generate up to $100 \times 100 = 10,000$ new entries, but only store 100 after pruning.

So, perhaps we can do better by focusing on generating only the new chart entries that have a chance of ending up within the top 100. This is the idea behind **cube pruning**, which is illustrated in Figure 11.13.

cube pruning

Combining chart entries

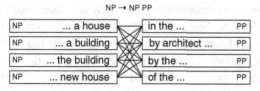

Combining chart entries with words from rules

Figure 11.12 Large numbers of possible chart entries: Each rule that combines chart entries leads to a quadratic number of new chart entries. The same situation arises if multiple rules combine words with chart entries.

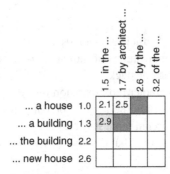

Figure 11.13 Cube pruning: Instead of exploring all possible combinations of chart entries, we start with the most likely (given actual costs and heuristics for remaining language model costs, here displayed using negative log), resulting in the cell in the top left-hand corner. Computing the costs for neighboring cells allows us to add the neighbor with best cost, and then move on to compute the costs for its neighbors (cells shaded in dark grey).

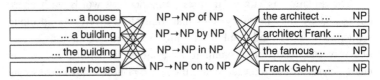

Figure 11.14 If a group of rules combines multiple nonterminals, here three, and differing output words, the resulting number of possible new chart entries becomes even larger, here $4 \times 4 \times 4 = 64$.

First, we sort the existing applicable chart entries in the stacks by their cost estimates (which include estimates of unscored language model costs). The most promising combination uses the top chart entries. The next most promising combinations use the next best entries. Since we may select second-best choices from any of the stacks, there are multiple next-best choices, so-called **neighbors**.

In cube pruning, we compute the costs of any neighbors, and then add the neighbor with the best cost. We then move on to compute the costs of that cell's neighbors, and iterate the process. We terminate after generating a fixed number of new chart entries (e.g., a fraction of the stack size), or if chart entries newly added to the stack are expected to be discarded due to stack pruning.

The term cube pruning derives from the three-dimensional case, illustrated in Figure 11.14 – the worst case if we group binary rules with the same nonterminals but differing output words. Cube pruning may be extended into even higher dimensions, allowing any number of nonterminals on the right-hand side of a synchronous grammar rule.

11.3.8 Binarizing the Grammar

The preceding section already touched on the issue of complexity of rules. Synchronous grammar rules, as we have defined them so far, can have several nonterminals on the right-hand side of the rule, mixed with word sequences. Consider, for instance, the following rule:

$$\text{NP} \rightarrow \textit{sowohl } \text{NP}_1 \textit{ als auch } \text{NP}_2 \mid \text{NP}_1 \textit{ as well as } \text{NP}_2$$

The decoding complexity of using such rules is related to the number of nonterminals on the right-hand side of the rule. The rule above has two nonterminals on the English output part. We refer to the number of elements in the output language part of a rule as the **rank** of the rule. The above rule, for instance, is a binary rule.

rank

Note that words on the right-hand side of the rule (either in the input or the output) do not have an effect on the rank of the rule, since they do not increase decoding complexity. However, if we group together rules whose nonterminals cover the same spans and whose nonterminals are the same, then we could say that the rank of this group of rules is one higher than the number of nonterminals on the right-hand side. While it plays out that way with respect to decoding as we discussed it above, it is not formally defined as such.

Problems with too large rules

Allowing any number of nonterminals on the right-hand side of synchronous grammar rules causes various computational complexity problems. It starts with the size of the grammar. Imposing no restrictions on rule extraction from a parallel corpus will result in many **large rules** that have no general applicability and are often just an artifact of erroneous alignment. Storing and accessing such large rule sets becomes a serious **resource burden**.

large rules

resource burden

Secondly, the number of possible new chart entries that can be generated with a rule grows exponentially in the number of elements (nonterminals or different word translations) in the rule, as Figure 11.14 illustrates. Cube pruning addresses this issue, but with increasingly large rules the risk of **pruning errors** grows.

pruning errors

Thirdly, with increasing rank of rules, the number of combinations of different stacks grows. See Figure 11.15 for an illustration of this. To

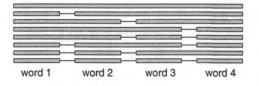

word 1   word 2   word 3   word 4

Figure 11.15 To create chart entries for longer spans, say, size 4, an exponential number of possible combinations of lower order stacks are possible. Here all $2^{4-1} = 8$ combinations are shown.

create new chart entries for a span that covers four words with a binary rule, three combinations of underlying stacks are possible: combining entries that cover the first word with entries that cover the next three words, entries from stacks 1–2 and 3–4, and entries from stacks 1–3 and 4.

Without any restrictions on the number of elements on the right-hand side of rules, there are 2^{n-1} **possible combinations** of lower order stacks possible. If we restrict ourselves to unary and binary rules, there are only n possible combinations.

possible combinations

Binarization of grammars

These considerations lead us to the conclusion that decoding would be much more manageable if we limit the grammar to unary and binary rules only. In fact, we do not lose any of the expressiveness of the grammar if we convert larger rules into binary rules, using a process called **binarization**.

binarization

Binarization of grammars is a well-known strategy in syntactic parsing. Take this example:

$$NP \rightarrow DET\ ADJ\ NN$$

This trinary rule may be binarized into two binary rules with the help of a new nonterminal, which we may want to call $\overline{NP}$.

$$NP \rightarrow DET\ \overline{NP}$$
$$\overline{NP} \rightarrow ADJ\ NN$$

Note that binarization does not change the expressiveness of the grammar. For each tree generated by the original grammar, there is a corresponding tree in the binarized grammar, and vice versa.

However, the introduction of a new nonterminal for every binarization may cause serious problems for efficient and accurate use of the grammar. So, instead, we may introduce the same new nonterminal $\overline{NP}$ for all NP rules. Keep in mind, however, that re-using nonterminals makes the grammar more expressive, i.e., it generates a larger set of trees.

We have only described the binarization of trinary rules. For larger rules, we apply this process recursively to eventually break them into binary rules.

Binarization of synchronous grammars

How does binarization work for synchronous grammar rules? Here is an example of a synchronous grammar rule:

$$NP \rightarrow DET_1\ NN_2\ ADJ_3\ \mid\ DET_1\ ADJ_3\ NN_2$$

As with monolingual binarization, we have to find a point at which to break the right-hand side into two sets:

$$NP \rightarrow DET_1 \star NN_2\ ADJ_3\ \mid\ DET_1 \star ADJ_3\ NN_2$$

which allows us to split the rule into two binary rules

$$NP \rightarrow DET_1\ \overline{NP}_2\ \mid\ DET_1\ \overline{NP}_2$$
$$\overline{NP} \rightarrow NN_1\ ADJ_2\ \mid\ ADJ_2\ NN_1$$

The binarization of rules with words is done the same way. Note again that we are concerned with the number of elements (nonterminals or word sequences) on the English output side only:

$$NP \rightarrow \textit{sowohl}\ NN_1\ \textit{als auch}\ NP_2\ \mid\ NN_1\ \textit{as well as}\ NP_2$$
$$\Downarrow$$
$$NP \rightarrow \textit{sowohl}\ NN_1\ \overline{NP}_2\ \mid\ NN_1\ \overline{NP}_2$$
$$\overline{NP} \rightarrow \textit{als auch}\ NP_2\ \mid\ \textit{as well as}\ NP_2$$

Not every synchronous grammar rule can be binarized. Take this example of a 4-ary rule:

$$X \rightarrow A_1\ B_2\ C_3\ D_4\ \mid\ B_2\ D_4\ A_1\ C_3$$

There is no way to split up the sequence of input nonterminals that allows a corresponding split of the sequence of output nonterminals. While it is possible to binarize any monolingual grammar, this is not the case for synchronous grammars. A 4-ary synchronous context grammar is more expressive than a 3-ary grammar. Each higher rank after that enables new rules that cannot be reduced to a lower-ranking grammar.

11.3.9 Outside Cost Estimation

Recall that in phrase-based model decoding we also consider a **future cost** estimate of how expensive it will be to translate the rest of the sentence. This is necessary because we store hypotheses that cover different parts of the sentence in the same stack, and we need to discount hypotheses that tackle the easy part of the sentence first.

future cost

In the chart-based decoding algorithm for tree-based models, all entries in a chart translate the same part of a sentence. However, the number of spans encountered when translating a sentence is quadratic in sentence length, and – since we need to distinguish chart entries with different head nodes – linear in the number of nonterminal symbols. To cut down the search space, we would like to reduce the number of spans we explore during the search. To do this, we need to

outside cost

consider the **outside cost**, an estimate of how expensive it will be to translate the rest of the sentence using translations for this particular span.

See Figure 11.16 for an illustration. For the given sentence, we may have translated *eine Tasse Kaffee* into an English noun phrase. Such a noun phrase will fit nicely into a full sentence translation, so the outside cost should be relatively small.

As with future cost estimation in phrase-based models, we are faced with having to compute the expected cost of translating the rest of the sentence without wanting to actually do the translation to get the estimate. Here, such estimation is even harder because there are important interactions between the nonterminal that heads the hypotheses for a span and the rest of the sentence.

multipass decoding

One approach is to perform **multipass decoding**. First, we decode with tight beams and a restricted grammar, say, a grammar with fewer nonterminals. In the subsequent passes we increasingly match the real grammar and increase beam sizes, but limit the use of badly scoring spans. In the final pass, we use the full grammar, but do not expand all spans, or at least focus the search on the most promising spans. In essence, the earlier passes give us outside cost estimates.

See Figure 11.17 of an example of the outside cost estimates we would expect for our example sentence. Chart entries over the span *will eine* will be less promising than the ones over the span *eine Tasse Kaffee*.

Figure 11.16 Outside cost estimation: Due to the large number of possible charts that need to be considered during the search, we may want to take into account the remaining cost to translate the whole sentence and prune charts accordingly.

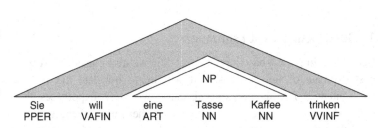

Figure 11.17 Outside cost estimates: More promising spans are displayed in darker colors.

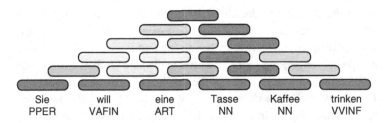

11.4 Summary

11.4.1 Core Concepts

This chapter presented tree-based models for statistical machine translation. The models are based on the notion of a formal grammar, which was already introduced in Chapter 2. Here, we extended the formalism of **phrase-structure grammars** into **synchronous grammars**, which create two trees at the same time – one of the input language and one of the output language of a machine translation application. We further extended the formalism to **synchronous tree-substitition grammars**, which allow the generation of non-isomorphic trees. This formalism overcomes the **child node reordering restriction** of flat context-free grammars.

We presented a method for **learning** synchronous grammar that builds on the method presented for phrase-based models. Starting with a word alignment and syntactic parse tree annotation for one or both of the languages, we extract grammar rules. In its simplest form, the **hierarchical phrase model**, the grammar does not build on any syntactic annotation. If syntactic annotation exists only for one of the languages, we call rules **semi-syntactic**. For given syntactic annotation, we need to find the **governing node** of each phrase to have a single nonterminal label on the left-hand side of rules. Rules are scored with methods similar to those used for phrase translations in a phrase model (i.e., conditional probability of the output side, given the input side).

Since we are building tree structures while translating with tree-based models, the translation process resembles syntactic parsing, and hence is often referred to as **parse-decoding**. In **chart parsing**, the organizing data structure is a **chart** with **chart entries** that cover continuous spans of the input sentence. If chart entries are equivalent from a search perspective, we can **recombine** them. In the **chart decoding algorithm**, we place the chart entries into stacks and apply **stack pruning**, either **histogram pruning** or **threshold pruning**.

To deal with the complexity of parse-decoding, we introduced several refinements. We store rules in a **prefix tree**, so we can efficiently look up all applicable rules given a set of input word spans (and corresponding stacks). In **cube pruning**, we do not exhaustively apply all rules to all matching chart entries, but focus on the most promising rules and entries. A grammar rule may contain a number of nonterminals on the right-hand side. This number is called the **rank**. Since rules with high rank cause computational complexity problems, we may resort to **binarization** of grammar rules.

11.4.2 Further Reading

Tree-based without syntax – Rooted in a finite state machine approach, head automata have been developed that allow for tree representation during the translation process [Alshawi, 1996; Alshawi et al., 1997, 1998, 2000]. Wang and Waibel [1998] also induce hierarchical structures in their statistical machine translation model. The use of synchronous grammars for statistical machine translation has been pioneered by Wu [1995, 1996, 1997] and Wu and Wong [1998] with their work on inversion transduction grammars (ITG) and stochastic bracketing transduction grammars (SBTG). A different formal model is multitext grammars [Melamed, 2003, 2004; Melamed et al., 2004] and range concatenation grammars [Søgaard, 2008]. Zhang and Gildea [2005] extend the ITG formalism by lexicalizing grammar rules and apply it to a small-scale word alignment task. Armed with an efficient A* algorithm for this formalism [Zhang and Gildea, 2006a], they extend the formalism with rules that are lexicalized in both input and output [Zhang and Gildea, 2006b]. Word alignments generated with ITG may also be used to extract phrases for phrase-based models [Sánchez and Benedí, 2006a,b]. Zhang et al. [2008d] present an efficient ITG phrase alignment algorithm that uses Bayesian learning with priors.

Generative models – Inspired by the IBM models, Yamada and Knight [2001] present a generative tree-based model that is trained using the EM algorithm, thus aligning the words in the parallel corpus while extracting syntactic transfer rules. Syntax trees are provided by automatically parsing the English side of the corpus in a pre-processing step. They also present a chart parsing algorithm for their model [Yamada and Knight, 2002]. This model allows the integration of a syntactic language model [Charniak et al., 2003]. Gildea [2003] introduces a clone operation to the model and extends it to dependency trees [Gildea, 2004].

Aligning subtrees – The use of syntactic structure in machine translation is rooted in earlier transfer and example-based approaches. There are many methods to extract subtrees from a parallel corpus, aided either by a word-aligned corpus or a bilingual lexicon and a heuristic to disambiguate alignment points. For instance, such efforts can be traced back to work on the alignment of dependency structures by Matsumoto et al. [1993]. Related to this are efforts to align syntactic phrases [Yamamoto and Matsumoto, 2000; Imamura, 2001; Imamura et al., 2003, 2004], hierarchical syntactic phrases [Watanabe and Sumita, 2002; Watanabe et al., 2002], and phrase structure tree fragments [Groves et al., 2004], as well as methods to extract transfer rules, as used in traditional rule-based machine translation systems [Lavoie et al., 2001]. The degree to which alignments are consistent with the syntactic structure may be measured by the distance in the dependency tree [Nakazawa *et al.*, 2007]. Tinsley *et al.* [2007] use a greedy algorithm that uses a probabilistic lexicon trained with the IBM models to align subtrees in a parallel corpus parsed on both sides. Zhechev and Way [2008] compare it against a similar algorithm. Lavie *et al.* [2008] use symmetrized IBM model alignments for the same purpose and discuss effects of alignment and parse quality.

Hierarchical phrase models – Chiang [2005, 2007] combines the ideas of phrase-based models and tree structure and proposes an efficient decoding method based on chart parsing. His hierarchical phrase-based model Hiero [Chiang *et al.*, 2005] makes no use of explicit annotation. Hierarchical rules may be extracted from sentence pairs in linear time [Zhang *et al.*, 2008c]. Some of the properties of such models and their relationship to phrase-based models are discussed by Zollmann *et al.* [2008]. Watanabe *et al.* [2006b] propose a model somewhat between traditional phrase models and hierarchical models, which allow for discontinuities in source phrases, but follow a traditional left-to-right search algorithm. They show performance competitive with phrase-based models [Watanabe *et al.*, 2006a,c]. Another adaptation of the hierarchical model approach allows only function words (or the most frequent words in the corpus) to occur in rules with nonterminals on the right-hand side, which allows a lexicalized but still compact grammar [Setiawan *et al.*, 2007]. As with phrase-based models, instead of setting the rule application probability by maximum likelihood estimation, we may train classifiers to include additional features [Subotin, 2008].

String to tree – Adding syntactic categories to target-side nonterminals in hierarchical phrase models leads to syntax-augmented models [Zollmann *et al.*, 2006]. Zollmann and Venugopal [2006] present a chart parse-decoding method for this approach. Galley *et al.* [2004] build translation rules that map input phrases to output tree fragments. Contextually richer rules and learning rule probabilities with the EM algorithm may lead to better performance [Galley *et al.*, 2006]. But adjusting the parse trees to be able to extract rules for all lexical matches may also be important – which requires the introduction of additional nonterminal symbols [Marcu *et al.*, 2006] or rules with multiple head nodes [Liu *et al.*, 2007]. Instead of using standard Penn tree bank labels for nonterminals, relabeling the constituents may lead to the acquisiton of better rules [Huang and Knight, 2006]. Since syntactic structure prohibits some phrase pairs that may be learned as syntactic translation rules, leading to less coverage, this may be alleviated by adjusting the rule extraction algorithm [DeNeefe *et al.*, 2007]. DeNeefe *et al.* [2005]

present an interactive tool for inspecting the workings of such syntactic translation models.

Tree to string – Tree-to-string models use a rich input language representation to translate into word sequences in the output language. As a soft constraint, similarity between the source syntax tree and the derivation tree during decoding may be used [Zhou *et al.*, 2008], or non-terminals in rule applications that match the source syntax tree could be flagged in a feature [Marton and Resnik, 2008]. Syntax-direction translation parses the input first and uses the parse structure to guide the output phrase generation [Huang *et al.*, 2006b,a]. Liu and Gildea [2008] extend this work by adding semantic role labels and changing parameter estimation. A simpler method follows the phrase-based approach but informs phrase selection with shallow source trees [Langlais and Gotti, 2006]. Given segmentation into phrases and a source syntax tree, both structural changes to the tree to fit the phrases and reordering of the restructured phrase tree may inform better translations [Nguyen *et al.*, 2008]. Building on the hierarchical phrase-based model, Zhang *et al.* [2007a] use syntactic annotation of the input to make a distinction between linguistic and non-linguistic phrases. Hopkins and Kuhn [2007] present a tree-to-string model with best-first search.

Tree to tree – As for the models mentioned above, rules for tree-to-tree models may be learned from word-aligned parallel corpora. To maximize the number of rules, alignment points from the intersection and union of GIZA++ alignments may be treated differently [Imamura *et al.*, 2005]. Probabilistic synchronous tree-insertion grammars (STIG) [Nesson *et al.*, 2006] may be automatically learned without any provided syntactic annotations. Synchronous tree substitution grammars (STSG) map tree fragments in the source to tree fragments in the target [Zhang *et al.*, 2007b]. Shieber [2007] argue for the use of synchronous tree adjoining grammars (S-TAG) as following the structure of printed bilingual dictionaries. This idea was already proposed by Shieber and Schabes [1990]. Relaxing the isomorphism between input and output trees leads to the idea of quasi-synchronous grammars (QGs) [Smith and Eisner, 2006b], which have been shown to produce better word alignment quality than IBM models, but not better than symmetrized IBM models. A similar relaxation is allowing multiple neighboring head nodes in the rules [Zhang *et al.*, 2008f,g]. Instead of using the 1-best or n-best syntactic parses of the source sentence, a forest of parse trees may be used during translation [Mi *et al.*, 2008].

Dependency structure – One example of statistical machine translation models based on dependency structures is the treelet approach [Menezes and Richardson, 2001; Menezes and Quirk, 2005a], and other researchers have found this a promising direction [Lin, 2004].

Tectogrammatical models are also based on dependency trees, but include morphological analysis and generation [Čmejrek *et al.*, 2003; Eisner, 2003]. By mapping arbitrary connected fragments of the dependency tree, the approach may be extended to apply the lessons from phrase-based models by mapping larger fragments [Bojar and Hajič, 2008]. This idea was pioneered in the dependency treelet model, which uses only source side dependency structures [Quirk *et al.*, 2005]. Such models have been shown to be competitive with phrase-based models [Menezes and Quirk, 2005b; Menezes *et al.*, 2006]. An extension of this model also allows fragments with gaps that are filled by variables, as in the hierarchical phrase-based model [Xiong *et al.*, 2007]. The dependency structure may also be used in a string-to-tree model: Shen *et al.* [2008] use rules that map into dependency tree fragments of neighboring words and additional restrictions, which allows the use of a dependency-based language model. Translating dependency tree fragments is also the idea behind synchronous dependency insertion grammars. Ding *et al.* [2003] and Ding and Palmer [2004] develop methods for aligning dependency trees, and then develop decoding algorithms [Ding and Palmer, 2005]. More recent work integrates the use of an n-gram language model during decoding [Ding and Palmer, 2006]. The generation of an output string from a dependency structure requires insertion of function words and defining an ordering. Hall and Němec [2007] present a generative model with a search algorithm that proceeds through stages. Chang and Toutanova [2007] apply a discriminatively trained model to the word ordering problem. Mapping into a dependency structure and its ordering gives better results than separating the two steps [Menezes and Quirk, 2007]. Bojar and Hajič [2008] present a dependency treelet approach trained with the aid of a parallel dependency tree bank.

Context features in rule selection – Chan *et al.* [2007] use a support vector machine to include context features for rules in a hierarchical translation model. Maximum entropy models may be used for the same purpose [Xiong *et al.*, 2008a; He *et al.*, 2008a]. Related work on featuring translation rules is cited in the further reading section of Chapter 5 on phrase-based models.

Binarizing synchronous grammars – Tree-based models that use syntactic annotation may benefit from binarization of the required rules. Binarization may be driven by the source side grammar [Zhang *et al.*, 2006a; Wang *et al.*, 2007b]. Instead of such synchronous binarization methods, binarization may also be driven by the target side [Huang, 2007]. A *k*-arization method with linear time complexity is proposed by Zhang and Gildea [2007]. Nesson *et al.* [2008] present a *k*-arization method for STAG grammars.

Decoding – The use of n-gram language models in tree-generating decoding increases computational complexity significantly. One solution is to do a first pass translation without the language model, and then score the pruned search hypergraph in a second pass with the language model [Venugopal *et al.*, 2007]. Our presentation of cube pruning follows the description of Huang and Chiang [2007]. Some more implementation details are presented by Li and Khudanpur [2008]. To enable more efficient pruning, outside cost estimates may be obtained by first decoding with a lower-order n-gram model [Zhang and Gildea, 2008]. Xiong *et al.* [2008c] introduce reordering constraints based on punctuation and maximum reordering distance for tree-based decoding.

Finite state implementations – Just as word-based and phrase-based models may be implemented with finite state toolkits, a general framework of tree transducers may subsume many of the proposed tree-based models [Graehl and Knight, 2004].

Complex models – Syntactical tree-based models may be viewed as a probabilistic build-up to more complex machine translation models that use richly annotated syntactic or dependency structures, or even some form of interlingua. These systems are usually built as a series of sequential steps [Zabokrtsky *et al.*, 2008]. Conversely, starting from such complex models, probabilistic components may be added. Using a traditional rule-based component for syntactic and semantic analysis of the input and a generation component for the output allows the training of translation models for mapping of f-structures [Riezler and Maxwell, 2006]. Cowan *et al.* [2006] propose a translation model that explicitly models clause structure as aligned extended projections and that is trained discriminatively.

Parallel tree banks – Cuřín *et al.* [2004] describe an effort to build manually a parallel corpus with syntactic annotation. The Prague Czech–English Dependency Treebank contains additional markup [Čmejrek *et al.*, 2005]. Similar projects to develop richly annotated parallel corpora are under way for Chinese–English [Palmer *et al.*, 2005] and Japanese–Chinese [Zhang *et al.*, 2005b].

Parse quality – Parse quality has obvious effects on the quality of syntax-based models. Quirk and Corston-Oliver [2006] show that relatively small tree banks of only 250 sentences give decent performance, and while there are gains with larger tree banks, they expect these gains to be diminishing with tree banks larger than the ones currently available, i.e., over 40,000 sentences.

Syntactic coherence between languages – Fox [2002] and Hwa *et al.* [2002] examine how well the underlying assumption of syntactic coherence between languages holds up in practice. In phrase-based systems, syntactic consitituents are not sufficient to map units between languages [Koehn *et al.*, 2003]. Also, for establishing mappings in tree-based transfer models, syntactic parsing of each side introduces constraints that may make it more difficult to match sentences [Zhang and Gildea, 2004]. When studying actual parallel sentences, the complexity of syntactic transfer rules to match them is often more complex than expected [Wellington *et al.*, 2006b]. Parallel tree banks are also a source of data for examining the parallelism between two languages, although the parallelism also depends on the annotation standards [Buch-Kromann, 2007]. Visualization and search of such tree banks may also provide important insights [Volk *et al.*, 2007].

11.4.3 Exercises

1. (⋆) Given the word-aligned sentence pair with syntactic annotation

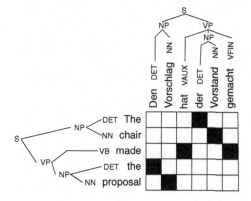

    (a) List all hierarchical phrase rules that can be extracted.
    (b) List all rules with target syntax that can be extracted.
    (c) List all rules with syntax on both sides that can be extracted.
2. (⋆) Given the following hierarchical phrase grammar rules

das	→	*that*	*das*	→	*the*
ist	→	*is*	*das ist*	→	*that 's*
Haus	→	*house*	*von*	→	*of*
Jane	→	*Jane*	X_1 *von* X_2	→	X_2 *'s* X_1
$X_1 X_2$	→	$X_1 X_2$			

   and the input sentence *das ist das Haus von Jane*, perform the chart decoding algorithm sketched in Figure 11.6 on page 349 by hand and draw all possible chart entries.
3. (⋆) Assuming only binary rules, what is the complexity of the chart decoding algorithm sketched in Figure 11.6 on page 349?
4. (⋆⋆) Implement an algorithm that extracts all syntactic rules from a word-aligned corpus that has been annotated with syntactic parse

trees either on the target or on both sides. Test this algorithm on a portion of the Europarl[1] corpus, after parsing its sentences, e.g., with the Berkeley parser.[2]

5. (★★) Implement a chart decoding algorithm for hierarchical phrase models. You may simplify this by ignoring hypothesis recombination and pruning when you test it on short sentences.

6. (★★★) A fully syntactified synchronous grammar may be more sparse and miss some essential rules. In this case, we may want to back off to hierarchical phrase rules that use only the nonterminal X. Given what you have learned about back-off in the context of language models in Chapter 7, how would you handle back-off in this case?

---

[1] Available at http://www.statmt.org/europarl/

[2] Available at http://nlp.cs.berkeley.edu/pages/Parsing.html

Bibliography

Abekawa, T. and Kageura, K. (2007). A translation aid system with a stratified lookup interface. In *Proceedings of the 45th Annual Meeting of the Association for Computational Linguistics Companion Volume Proceedings of the Demo and Poster Sessions*, pp. 5–8, Prague, Czech Republic. Association for Computational Linguistics.

Agarwal, A. and Lavie, A. (2008). Meteor, M-BLEU and M-TER: Evaluation metrics for high-correlation with human rankings of machine translation output. In *Proceedings of the Third Workshop on Statistical Machine Translation*, pp. 115–118, Columbus, Ohio. Association for Computational Linguistics.

Ahrenberg, L., Andersson, M., and Merkel, M. (1998). A simple hybrid aligner for generating lexical correspondences in parallel. In *Proceedings of the 36th Annual Meeting of the Association of Computational Linguistics (ACL)*.

Akiba, Y., Federico, M., Kando, N., Nakaiwa, H., Paul, M., and Tsujii, J. (2004a). Overview of the IWSLT04 evaluation campaign. In *Proceedings of the International Workshop on Spoken Language Translation*, pp. 1–12, Kyoto, Japan.

Akiba, Y., Sumita, E., Nakaiwa, H., Yamamoto, S., and Okuno, H. G. (2003). Experimental comparison of MT evaluation methods: RED vs. BLEU. In *Proceedings of the MT Summit IX*.

Akiba, Y., Sumita, E., Nakaiwa, H., Yamamoto, S., and Okuno, H. G. (2004b). Using a mixture of n-best lists from multiple MT systems in rank-sum-based confidence measure for MT outputs. In *Proceedings of COLING 2004*, pp. 322–328, Geneva, Switzerland. COLING.

Al-Onaizan, Y., Curín, J., Jahr, M., *et al.*, (1999). Statistical machine translation. Technical report, John Hopkins University Summer Workshop
http://www.clsp.jhu.edu/ws99/projects/mt/.

Al-Onaizan, Y. and Knight, K. (2002a). Machine transliteration of names in Arabic texts. In *Proceedings of the Workshop on Computational Approaches to Semitic Languages*, pp. 34–46, Philadelphia. Association for Computational Linguistics.

Al-Onaizan, Y. and Knight, K. (2002b). Translating named entities using monolingual and bilingual resources. In *Proceedings of the 40th Annual Meeting of the Association of Computational Linguistics (ACL)*.

Al-Onaizan, Y. and Papineni, K. (2006). Distortion models for statistical machine translation. In *Proceedings of the 21st International Conference on Computational Linguistics and 44th Annual Meeting of the Association for Computational Linguistics*, pp. 529–536, Sydney, Australia. Association for Computational Linguistics.

Alabau, V., Sanchis, A., and Casacuberta, F. (2007a). Improving speech-to-speech translation using word posterior probabilities. In *Proceedings of the MT Summit XI*.

Alabau, V., Sanchis, A., and Casacuberta, F. (2007b). Using word posterior probabilities in lattice translation. In *Proceedings of the International Workshop on Spoken Language Translation (IWSLT)*.

Albrecht, J. and Hwa, R. (2007a). A re-examination of machine learning approaches for sentence-level MT evaluation. In *Proceedings of the 45th Annual Meeting of the Association of Computational Linguistics*, pp. 880–887, Prague, Czech Republic. Association for Computational Linguistics.

Albrecht, J. and Hwa, R. (2007b). Regression for sentence-level MT evaluation with pseudo references. In *Proceedings of the 45th Annual Meeting of the Association of Computational Linguistics*, pp. 296–303, Prague, Czech Republic. Association for Computational Linguistics.

Albrecht, J. and Hwa, R. (2008). The role of pseudo references in MT evaluation. In *Proceedings of the Third Workshop on Statistical Machine Translation*, pp. 187–190, Columbus, Ohio. Association for Computational Linguistics.

Alshawi, H. (1996). Head automata and bilingual tiling: Translation with minimal representations (invited talk). In *Proceedings of the 34th Annual Meeting of the Association for Computational Linguistics (ACL)*.

Alshawi, H., Bangalore, S., and Douglas, S. (1998). Automatic acquisition of hierarchical transduction models for machine translation. In *Proceedings of the 36th Annual Meeting of the Association of Computational Linguistics (ACL)*.

Alshawi, H., Bangalore, S., and Douglas, S. (2000). Learning dependency translation models as collections of finite-state head transducers. *Computational Linguistics*, 26(1):45–60.

Alshawi, H., Buchsbaum, A. L., and Xia, F. (1997). A comparison of head transducers and transfer for a limited domain translation application. In *Proceedings of the 35th Annual Meeting of the Association for Computational Linguistics (ACL)*.

Amigó, E., Giménez, J., Gonzalo, J., and Màrquez, L. (2006). MT evaluation: Human-like vs. human acceptable. In *Proceedings of the COLING/ACL 2006 Main Conference Poster Sessions*, pp. 17–24, Sydney, Australia. Association for Computational Linguistics.

Arnold, D. J., Balkan, L., Meijer, S., Humphreys, R. L., and Sadler, L. (1994). *Machine Translation: An Introductory Guide*. Blackwells–NCC, London.

Arun, A. and Koehn, P. (2007). Online learning methods for discriminative training of phrase based statistical machine translation. In *Proceedings of the MT Summit XI*.

Aswani, N. and Gaizauskas, R. (2005). A hybrid approach to align sentences and words in English–Hindi parallel corpora. In *Proceedings of the ACL Workshop on Building and Using Parallel Texts*, pp. 57–64, Ann Arbor, Michigan. Association for Computational Linguistics.

Avramidis, E. and Koehn, P. (2008). Enriching morphologically poor languages for statistical machine translation. In *Proceedings of ACL-08: HLT*, pp. 763–770, Columbus, Ohio. Association for Computational Linguistics.

Axelrod, A., Yang, M., Duh, K., and Kirchhoff, K. (2008). The University of Washington machine translation system for ACL WMT 2008. In *Proceedings of the Third Workshop on Statistical Machine Translation*, pp. 123–126, Columbus, Ohio. Association for Computational Linguistics.

Ayan, N. F. and Dorr, B. J. (2006a). Going beyond AER: An extensive analysis of word alignments and their impact on MT. In *Proceedings of the 21st International Conference on Computational Linguistics and 44th Annual Meeting of the Association for Computational Linguistics*, pp. 9–16, Sydney, Australia. Association for Computational Linguistics.

Ayan, N. F. and Dorr, B. J. (2006b). A maximum entropy approach to combining word alignments. In *Proceedings of the Human Language Technology Conference of the NAACL, Main Conference*, pp. 96–103, New York City, USA. Association for Computational Linguistics.

Ayan, N. F., Dorr, B. J., and Habash, N. (2004). Multi-align: combining linguistic and statistical techniques to improve alignments for adaptable MT. In *Proceedings of the 6th Conference of the Association for Machine Translation in the Americas (AMTA 2004)*, pp. 17–26.

Ayan, N. F., Dorr, B. J., and Monz, C. (2005). NeurAlign: Combining word alignments using neural networks. In *Proceedings of Human Language Technology Conference and Conference on Empirical Methods in Natural Language Processing*, pp. 65–72, Vancouver, British Columbia, Canada. Association for Computational Linguistics.

Ayan, N. F., Zheng, J., and Wang, W. (2008). Improving alignments for better confusion networks for combining machine translation systems. In *Proceedings of the 22nd International Conference on Computational Linguistics (COLING 2008)*, pp. 33–40, Manchester, UK. COLING 2008 Organizing Committee.

Babych, B., Elliott, D., and Hartley, A. (2004). Extending MT evaluation tools with translation complexity metrics. In *Proceedings of COLING 2004*, pp. 106–112, Geneva, Switzerland. COLING.

Babych, B. and Hartley, A. (2004). Extending the BLEU MT evaluation method with frequency weightings. In *Proceedings of the 42nd Meeting of the Association for Computational Linguistics (ACL'04), Main Volume*, pp. 621–628, Barcelona, Spain.

Babych, B., Hartley, A., and Sharoff, S. (2007a). Translating from under-resourced languages: Comparing direct transfer against pivot translation. In *Proceedings of the MT Summit XI*.

Babych, B., Hartley, A., Sharoff, S., and Mudraya, O. (2007b). Assisting translators in indirect lexical transfer. In *Proceedings of the 45th Annual Meeting of the Association of Computational Linguistics*, pp. 136–143, Prague, Czech Republic. Association for Computational Linguistics.

Bach, N., Eck, M., Charoenpornsawat, P., *et al.*, (2007). The CMU TransTac 2007 eyes-free and hands-free two-way speech-to-speech translation system. In *Proceedings of the International Workshop on Spoken Language Translation (IWSLT)*.

Bach, N., Gao, Q., and Vogel, S. (2008). Improving word alignment with language model based confidence scores. In *Proceedings of the Third Workshop on Statistical Machine Translation*, pp. 151–154, Columbus, Ohio. Association for Computational Linguistics.

Badr, I., Zbib, R., and Glass, J. (2008). Segmentation for English-to-Arabic statistical machine translation. In *Proceedings of ACL-08: HLT, Short Papers*, pp. 153–156, Columbus, Ohio. Association for Computational Linguistics.

Bai, M.-H., Chen, K.-J., and Chang, J. S. (2008). Improving word alignment by adjusting Chinese word segmentation. In *Proceedings of the 3rd International Joint Conference on Natural Language Processing (IJCNLP)*.

Banerjee, S. and Lavie, A. (2005). METEOR: An automatic metric for MT evaluation with improved correlation with human judgments. In *Proceedings of the ACL Workshop on Intrinsic and Extrinsic Evaluation Measures for Machine Translation and/or Summarization*, pp. 65–72, Ann Arbor, Michigan. Association for Computational Linguistics.

Bangalore, S., Haffner, P., and Kanthak, S. (2007). Statistical machine translation through global lexical selection and sentence reconstruction. In *Proceedings of the 45th Annual Meeting of the Association of Computational Linguistics*, pp. 152–159, Prague, Czech Republic. Association for Computational Linguistics.

Bangalore, S., Kanthak, S., and Haffner, P. (2006). Finite-state transducer-based statistical machine translation using joint probabilities. In *Proceedings of the International Workshop on Spoken Language Translation*, Kyoto, Japan.

Bangalore, S., Murdock, V., and Riccardi, G. (2002). Bootstrapping bilingual data using consensus translation for a multilingual instant messaging system. In *Proceedings of the International Conference on Computational Linguistics (COLING)*.

Bangalore, S. and Riccardi, G. (2000). Stochastic finite-state models for spoken language machine translation. In *ANLP-NAACL 2000 Workshop: Embedded Machine Translation Systems*.

Bangalore, S. and Riccardi, G. (2001). A finite-state approach to machine translation. In *Proceedings of*

the Annual Meeting of the North American Chapter of the Association of Computational Linguistics (NAACL).

Bannard, C. and Callison-Burch, C. (2005). Paraphrasing with bilingual parallel corpora. In *43rd Annual Meeting of the Association of Computational Linguistics (ACL)*.

Baobao, C., Danielsson, P., and Teubert, W. (2002). Extraction of translation unit from Chinese–English parallel corpora. In *First SIGHAN Workshop on Chinese Language Processing*.

Bender, O., Hasan, S., Vilar, D., Zens, R., and Ney, H. (2005). Comparison of generation strategies for interactive machine translation. In *Proceedings of the 10th Conference of the European Association for Machine Translation (EAMT)*, Budapest.

Bender, O., Zens, R., Matusov, E., and Ney, H. (2004). Alignment templates: the RWTH SMT system. In *Proceedings of the International Workshop on Spoken Language Translation*, pp. 79–84, Kyoto, Japan.

Bertoldi, N., Cettolo, M., Cattoni, R., and Federico, M. (2007). FBK @ IWSLT 2007. In *Proceedings of the International Workshop on Spoken Language Translation (IWSLT)*.

Besacier, L., Mahdhaoui, A., and Le, V.-B. (2007). The LIG Arabic/English speech translation system at IWSLT 07. In *Proceedings of the International Workshop on Spoken Language Translation (IWSLT)*.

Bilac, S. and Tanaka, H. (2004). A hybrid back-transliteration system for Japanese. In *Proceedings of COLING 2004*, pp. 597–603, Geneva, Switzerland. COLING.

Birch, A., Callison-Burch, C., and Osborne, M. (2006a). Constraining the phrase-based, joint probability statistical translation model. In *5th Conference of the Association for Machine Translation in the Americas (AMTA)*, Boston, Massachusetts.

Birch, A., Callison-Burch, C., Osborne, M., and Koehn, P. (2006b). Constraining the phrase-based, joint probability statistical translation model. In *Proceedings of the Workshop on Statistical Machine Translation*, pp. 154–157, New York City. Association for Computational Linguistics.

Birch, A., Osborne, M., and Koehn, P. (2007). CCG supertags in factored statistical machine translation. In *Proceedings of the Second Workshop on Statistical Machine Translation*, pp. 9–16, Prague, Czech Republic. Association for Computational Linguistics.

Blackwood, G., de Gispert, A., Brunning, J., and Byrne, W. (2008a). European language translation with weighted finite state transducers: The CUED MT system for the 2008 ACL workshop on SMT. In *Proceedings of the*

Third Workshop on Statistical Machine Translation, pp. 131–134, Columbus, Ohio. Association for Computational Linguistics.

Blackwood, G., de Gispert, A., and Byrne, W. (2008b). Phrasal segmentation models for statistical machine translation. In *COLING 2008: Companion volume: Posters and Demonstrations*, pp. 17–20, Manchester, UK. COLING 2008 Organizing Committee.

Blatz, J., Fitzgerald, E., Foster, G., *et al.* (2004). Confidence estimation for machine translation. In *Proceedings of COLING 2004*, pp. 315–321, Geneva, Switzerland. COLING.

Blunsom, P. and Cohn, T. (2006). Discriminative word alignment with conditional random fields. In *Proceedings of the 21st International Conference on Computational Linguistics and 44th Annual Meeting of the Association for Computational Linguistics*, pp. 65–72, Sydney, Australia. Association for Computational Linguistics.

Blunsom, P., Cohn, T., and Osborne, M. (2008). A discriminative latent variable model for statistical machine translation. In *Proceedings of ACL-08: HLT*, pp. 200–208, Columbus, Ohio. Association for Computational Linguistics.

Bojar, O. (2007). English-to-Czech factored machine translation. In *Proceedings of the Second Workshop on Statistical Machine Translation*, pp. 232–239, Prague, Czech Republic. Association for Computational Linguistics.

Bojar, O. and Hajič, J. (2008). Phrase-based and deep syntactic English-to-Czech statistical machine translation. In *Proceedings of the Third Workshop on Statistical Machine Translation*, pp. 143–146, Columbus, Ohio. Association for Computational Linguistics.

Bonneau Maynard, H., Allauzen, A., Déchelotte, D., and Schwenk, H. (2007). Combining morphosyntactic enriched representation with n-best reranking in statistical translation. In *Proceedings of SSST, NAACL-HLT 2007/AMTA Workshop on Syntax and Structure in Statistical Translation*, pp. 65–71, Rochester, New York. Association for Computational Linguistics.

Brants, T., Popat, A. C., Xu, P., Och, F. J., and Dean, J. (2007). Large language models in machine translation. In *Proceedings of the 2007 Joint Conference on Empirical Methods in Natural Language Processing and Computational Natural Language Learning (EMNLP-CoNLL)*, pp. 858–867.

Brown, P. F., Cocke, J., Della-Pietra, S. A., *et al.* (1990). A statistical approach to machine translation. *Computational Linguistics*, **16**(2):76–85.

Brown, P. F., Cocke, J., Della-Pietra, S. A., *et al.* (1988). A statistical approach to language translation. In *Proceedings of the International Conference on Computational Linguistics (COLING)*.

Brown, P. F., Della-Pietra, S. A., Della-Pietra, V. J., and Mercer, R. L. (1991a). Word-sense disambiguation using statistical methods. In *Proceedings of the 29th Annual Meeting of the Association of Computational Linguistics (ACL)*.

Brown, P. F., Della-Pietra, S. A., Della-Pietra, V. J., and Mercer, R. L. (1993). The mathematics of statistical machine translation. *Computational Linguistics*, **19**(2):263–313.

Brown, P. F., Lai, J. C., and Mercer, R. L. (1991b). Aligning sentences in parallel corpora. In *Proceedings of the 29th Annual Meeting of the Association of Computational Linguistics (ACL)*.

Brown, R. D. (2002). Corpus-driven splitting of compound words. In *Proceedings of the Ninth International Conference on Theoretical and Methodological Issues in Machine Translation (TMI)*.

Buch-Kromann, M. (2007). Computing translation units and quantifying parallelism in parallel dependency treebanks. In *Proceedings of the Linguistic Annotation Workshop*, pp. 69–76, Prague, Czech Republic. Association for Computational Linguistics.

Callison-Burch, C., Bannard, C., and Schroeder, J. (2005a). A compact data structure for searchable translation memories. In *Proceedings of the 10th Conference of the European Association for Machine Translation (EAMT)*, Budapest.

Callison-Burch, C., Bannard, C., and Schroeder, J. (2005b). Scaling phrase-based statistical machine translation to larger corpora and longer phrases. In *Proceedings of the 43rd Annual Meeting of the Association for Computational Linguistics (ACL'05)*, pp. 255–262, Ann Arbor, Michigan. Association for Computational Linguistics.

Callison-Burch, C., Fordyce, C. S., Koehn, P., Monz, C., and Schroeder, J. (2007). (Meta-) evaluation of machine translation. In *Proceedings of the Second Workshop on Statistical Machine Translation*, pp. 136–158, Prague, Czech Republic. Association for Computational Linguistics.

Callison-Burch, C., Fordyce, C. S., Koehn, P., Monz, C., and Schroeder, J. (2008). Further meta-evaluation of machine translation. In *Proceedings of the Third*

Workshop on Statistical Machine Translation, pp. 70–106, Columbus, Ohio. Association for Computational Linguistics.

Callison-Burch, C., Koehn, P., and Osborne, M. (2006a). Improved statistical machine translation using paraphrases. In *Proceedings of the Human Language Technology Conference of the NAACL, Main Conference*, pp. 17–24, New York City, USA. Association for Computational Linguistics.

Callison-Burch, C. and Osborne, M. (2003). Bootstrapping parallel corpora. In Mihalcea, R. and Pedersen, T., editors, *HLT-NAACL 2003 Workshop: Building and Using Parallel Texts: Data Driven Machine Translation and Beyond*, Edmonton, Alberta, Canada. Association for Computational Linguistics.

Callison-Burch, C., Osborne, M., and Koehn, P. (2006b). Re-evaluating the role of BLEU in machine translation research. In *Proceedings of the 11th Conference of the European Chapter of the Association for Computational Linguistics*, Trento, Italy.

Callison-Burch, C., Talbot, D., and Osborne, M. (2004). Statistical machine translation with word- and sentence-aligned parallel corpora. In *Proceedings of the 42nd Meeting of the Association for Computational Linguistics (ACL'04), Main Volume*, pp. 175–182, Barcelona, Spain.

Cao, G., Gao, J., and Nie, J.-Y. (2007). A system to mine large-scale bilingual dictionaries from monolingual web pages In *Proceedings of the MT Summit XI*.

Cao, Y. and Li, H. (2002). Base noun phrase translation using web data and the EM algorithm. In *Proceedings of the International Conference on Computational Linguistics (COLING)*.

Carl, M. (2007). METIS-II: The German to English MT system. In *Proceedings of the MT Summit XI*.

Carl, M. and Fissaha, S. (2003). Phrase-based evaluation of word-to-word alignments. In Mihalcea, R. and Pedersen, T., editors, *HLT-NAACL 2003 Workshop: Building and Using Parallel Texts: Data Driven Machine Translation and Beyond*, Edmonton, Alberta, Canada. Association for Computational Linguistics.

Carpuat, M., Shen, Y., Yu, X., and Wu, D. (2006). Toward integrating word sense and entity disambiguation into statistical machine translation. In *Proceedings of the International Workshop on Spoken Language Translation*, Kyoto, Japan.

Carpuat, M. and Wu, D. (2005). Word sense disambiguation vs. statistical machine translation. In *Proceedings of the 43rd Annual Meeting of the Association for Computational Linguistics (ACL'05)*, pp. 387–394, Ann Arbor, Michigan. Association for Computational Linguistics.

Carpuat, M. and Wu, D. (2007a). Context-dependent phrasal translation lexicons for statistical machine translation. In *Proceedings of the MT Summit XI*.

Carpuat, M. and Wu, D. (2007b). Improving statistical machine translation using word sense disambiguation. In *Proceedings of the 2007 Joint Conference on Empirical Methods in Natural Language Processing and Computational Natural Language Learning (EMNLP-CoNLL)*, pp. 61–72.

Casacuberta, F. and Vidal, E. (2004). Machine translation with inferred stochastic finite-state transducers. *Computational Linguistics*, **30**(2):205–225.

Cattoni, R., Bertoldi, N., Cettolo, M., Chen, B., and Federico, M. (2006). A web-based demonstrator of a multi-lingual phrase-based translation system. In *Proceedings of the 11th Conference of the European Chapter of the Association for Computational Linguistics*, Trento, Italy.

Cer, D., Jurafsky, D., and Manning, C. D. (2008). Regularization and search for minimum error rate training. In *Proceedings of the Third Workshop on Statistical Machine Translation*, pp. 26–34, Columbus, Ohio. Association for Computational Linguistics.

Cettolo, M., Federico, M., Bertoldi, N., Cattoni, R., and Chen, B. (2005). A look inside the ITC-irst SMT system. In *Proceedings of the 10th Machine Translation Summit*, pp. 451–457.

Chai, C., Du, J., Wei, W., *et al.* (2006). NLPR translation system for IWSLT 2006 evaluation campaign. In *Proceedings of the International Workshop on Spoken Language Translation*, Kyoto, Japan.

Chan, Y. S. and Ng, H. T. (2008). MAXSIM: A maximum similarity metric for machine translation evaluation. In *Proceedings of ACL-08: HLT*, pp. 55–62, Columbus, Ohio. Association for Computational Linguistics.

Chan, Y. S., Ng, H. T., and Chiang, D. (2007). Word sense disambiguation improves statistical machine translation. In *Proceedings of the 45th Annual Meeting of the Association of Computational Linguistics*, pp. 33–40, Prague, Czech Republic. Association for Computational Linguistics.

Chang, J.-S. and Chen, H.-C. (1994). Using part-of-speech information in word alignment. In *Proceedings of the Conference of the Association for Machine Translation in the Americas*.

Chang, J. S. and Chen, M. H. (1997). An alignment method for noisy parallel corpora based on image processing techniques. In *Proceedings of the 35th Annual Meeting of the Association for Computational Linguistics (ACL)*.

Chang, P.-C., Galley, M., and Manning, C. D. (2008). Optimizing Chinese word segmentation for machine translation performance. In *Proceedings of the Third Workshop on Statistical Machine Translation*, pp. 224–232, Columbus, Ohio. Association for Computational Linguistics.

Chang, P.-C. and Toutanova, K. (2007). A discriminative syntactic word order model for machine translation. In *Proceedings of the 45th Annual Meeting of the Association of Computational Linguistics*, pp. 9–16, Prague, Czech Republic. Association for Computational Linguistics.

Chao, W.-H. and Li, Z.-J. (2007a). Incorporating constituent structure constraint into discriminative word alignment. In *Proceedings of the MT Summit XI*.

Chao, W.-H. and Li, Z.-J. (2007b). NUDT machine translation system for IWSLT2007. In *Proceedings of the International Workshop on Spoken Language Translation (IWSLT)*.

Charniak, E., Knight, K., and Yamada, K. (2003). Syntax-based language models for statistical machine translation. In *Proceedings of the MT Summit IX*.

Chatterjee, N. and Agrawal, S. (2006). Word alignment in English–Hindi parallel corpus using recency-vector approach: Some studies. In *Proceedings of the 21st International Conference on Computational Linguistics and 44th Annual Meeting of the Association for Computational Linguistics*, pp. 649–656, Sydney, Australia. Association for Computational Linguistics.

Chen, B., Cattoni, R., Bertoldi, N., Cettolo, M., and Federico, M. (2006a). The ITC-irst SMT system for IWSLT 2006. In *Proceedings of the International Workshop on Spoken Language Translation*, Kyoto, Japan.

Chen, B., Cettolo, M., and Federico, M. (2006b). Reordering rules for phrase-based statistical machine translation. In *Proceedings of the International Workshop on Spoken Language Translation*, Kyoto, Japan.

Chen, B., Federico, M., and Cettolo, M. (2007a). Better n-best translations through generative n-gram language models. In *Proceedings of the MT Summit XI*.

Chen, B., Sun, J., Jiang, H., Zhang, M., and Aw, A. (2007b). I^2R Chinese–English translation system for IWSLT 2007. In *Proceedings of the International Workshop on Spoken Language Translation (IWSLT)*.

Chen, B., Zhang, M., Aw, A., and Li, H. (2008a). Exploiting n-best hypotheses for SMT self-enhancement. In *Proceedings of ACL-08: HLT, Short Papers*, pp. 157–160, Columbus, Ohio. Association for Computational Linguistics.

Chen, B., Zhang, M., Aw, A., and Li, H. (2008b). Regenerating hypotheses for statistical machine translation. In *Proceedings of the 22nd International Conference on Computational Linguistics (COLING 2008)*, pp. 105–112, Manchester, UK. COLING 2008 Organizing Committee.

Chen, C. and Chen, H.-H. (2006). A high-accurate Chinese–English NE backward translation system combining both lexical information and web statistics. In *Proceedings of the COLING/ACL 2006 Main Conference Poster Sessions*, pp. 81–88, Sydney, Australia. Association for Computational Linguistics.

Chen, S. F. (1993). Aligning sentences in bilingual corpora using lexical information. In *Proceedings of the 31st Annual Meeting of the Association for Computational Linguistics (ACL)*.

Chen, S. F. and Goodman, J. (1998). An empirical study of smoothing techniques for language modeling. Technical Report TR-10-98, Computer Science Group, Harvard University.

Chen, Y., Eisele, A., Federmann, C., Hasler, E., Jellinghaus, M., and Theison, S. (2007c). Multi-engine machine translation with an open-source SMT decoder. In *Proceedings of the Second Workshop on Statistical Machine Translation*, pp. 193–196, Prague, Czech Republic. Association for Computational Linguistics.

Chen, Y., Shi, X., and Zhou, C. (2006c). The XMU phrase-based statistical machine translation system for IWSLT 2006. In *Proceedings of the International Workshop on Spoken Language Translation*, Kyoto, Japan.

Chen, Y., Shi, X., and Zhou, C. (2007d). The XMU SMT system for IWSLT 2007. In *Proceedings of the International Workshop on Spoken Language Translation (IWSLT)*.

Cheng, P.-J., Lu, W.-H., Teng, J.-W., and Chien, L.-F. (2004). Creating multilingual translation lexicons with regional variations using web corpora. In *Proceedings of the 42nd Meeting of the Association for Computational Linguistics (ACL'04), Main Volume*, pp. 534–541, Barcelona, Spain.

Cherry, C. (2008). Cohesive phrase-based decoding for statistical machine translation. In *Proceedings of ACL-08: HLT*, pp. 72–80, Columbus, Ohio. Association for Computational Linguistics.

Cherry, C. and Lin, D. (2003). A probability model to improve word alignment. In Hinrichs, E. and Roth, D., editors, *Proceedings of the 41st Annual Meeting of the Association for Computational Linguistics*, pp. 88–95.

Cherry, C. and Lin, D. (2006a). A comparison of syntactically motivated word alignment spaces. In *Proceedings of the 11th Conference of the European Chapter of the Association for Computational Linguistics*, Trento, Italy.

Cherry, C. and Lin, D. (2006b). Soft syntactic constraints for word alignment through discriminative training. In *Proceedings of the COLING/ACL 2006 Main Conference Poster Sessions*, pp. 105–112, Sydney, Australia. Association for Computational Linguistics.

Cherry, C. and Lin, D. (2007). Inversion transduction grammar for joint phrasal translation modeling. In *Proceedings of SSST, NAACL-HLT 2007 / AMTA Workshop on Syntax and Structure in Statistical Translation*, pp. 17–24, Rochester, New York. Association for Computational Linguistics.

Chiang, D. (2005). A hierarchical phrase-based model for statistical machine translation. In *Proceedings of the 43rd Annual Meeting of the Association for Computational Linguistics (ACL'05)*, pp. 263–270, Ann Arbor, Michigan. Association for Computational Linguistics.

Chiang, D. (2007). Hierarchical phrase-based translation. *Computational Linguistics*, 33(2).

Chiang, D., Lopez, A., Madnani, N., Monz, C., Resnik, P., and Subotin, M. (2005). The hiero machine translation system: Extensions, evaluation, and analysis. In *Proceedings of Human Language Technology Conference and Conference on Empirical Methods in Natural Language Processing*, pp. 779–786, Vancouver, British Columbia, Canada. Association for Computational Linguistics.

Chiao, Y.-C. and Zweigenbaum, P. (2002). Looking for candidate translational equivalents in specialized, comparable corpora. In *Proceedings of the International Conference on Computational Linguistics (COLING)*.

Chuang, T. C. and Chang, J. S. (2002). Adaptive sentence alignment based on length and lexical information. In *Proceedings of the ACL-02 Demonstration Session*.

Church, K. W. (1993). Char align: A program for aligning parallel texts at the character level. In *Proceedings of the 31st Annual Meeting of the Association for Computational Linguistics (ACL)*.

Civera, J., Cubel, E., Lagarda, A. L., *et al.* (2004). From machine translation to computer assisted translation using finite-state models. In Lin, D. and Wu, D., editors,

Proceedings of EMNLP 2004, pp. 349–356, Barcelona, Spain. Association for Computational Linguistics.

Civera, J. and Juan, A. (2006). Mixtures of IBM model 2. In *Proceedings of the 11th Conference of the European Association for Machine Translation (EAMT)*, Oslo, Norway.

Civera, J. and Juan, A. (2007). Domain adaptation in statistical machine translation with mixture modelling. In *Proceedings of the Second Workshop on Statistical Machine Translation*, pp. 177–180, Prague, Czech Republic. Association for Computational Linguistics.

Civera, J., Lagarda, A. L., Cubel, E., *et al.* (2006). A computer-assisted translation tool based on finite-state technology. In *Proceedings of the 11th Conference of the European Association for Machine Translation (EAMT)*, Oslo, Norway.

Cohn, T. and Lapata, M. (2007). Machine translation by triangulation: Making effective use of multi-parallel corpora. In *Proceedings of the 45th Annual Meeting of the Association of Computational Linguistics*, pp. 728–735, Prague, Czech Republic. Association for Computational Linguistics.

Collins, M. (2002). Discriminative training methods for hidden Markov models: Theory and experiments with perceptron algorithms. In *Proceedings of EMNLP*.

Collins, M., Koehn, P., and Kucerova, I. (2005). Clause restructuring for statistical machine translation. In *Proceedings of the 43rd Annual Meeting of the Association for Computational Linguistics (ACL'05)*, pp. 531–540, Ann Arbor, Michigan. Association for Computational Linguistics.

Corston-Oliver, S. and Gamon, M. (2004). Normalizing German and English inflectional morphology to improve statistical word alignment. In *Proceedings of the 6th Conference of the Association for Machine Translation in the Americas (AMTA 2004)*, pp. 48–57.

Costa-jussà, M. R., Crego, J. M., de Gispert, A., *et al.*, (2006a). TALP phrase-based system and TALP system combination for IWSLT 2006. In *Proceedings of the International Workshop on Spoken Language Translation*, Kyoto, Japan.

Costa-jussà, M. R., Crego, J. M., de Gispert, A., *et al.* (2006b). TALP phrase-based statistical translation system for European language pairs. In *Proceedings of the Workshop on Statistical Machine Translation*, pp. 142–145, New York City. Association for Computational Linguistics.

Costa-jussà, M. R., Crego, J. M., Vilar, D., Fonollosa, J. A. R., Mariño, J. B., and Ney, H. (2007). Analysis and system combination of phrase- and N-gram-based statistical machine translation systems. In *Human Language Technologies 2007: The Conference of the North American Chapter of the Association for Computational Linguistics; Companion Volume, Short Papers*, pp. 137–140, Rochester, New York. Association for Computational Linguistics.

Costa-jussà, M. R. and Fonollosa, J. A. R. (2006). Statistical machine reordering. In *Proceedings of the 2006 Conference on Empirical Methods in Natural Language Processing*, pp. 70–76, Sydney, Australia. Association for Computational Linguistics.

Costa-jussà, M. R. and Fonollosa, J. A. R. (2007). Analysis of statistical and morphological classes to generate weigted reordering hypotheses on a statistical machine translation system. In *Proceedings of the Second Workshop on Statistical Machine Translation*, pp. 171–176, Prague, Czech Republic. Association for Computational Linguistics.

Coughlin, D. (2003). Correlating automated and human assessments of machine translation quality. In *Proceedings of the MT Summit IX*.

Cover, T. M. and King, R. C. (1978). A convergent gambling estimate of the entropy of English. *IEEE Transactions on Information Theory*, 24(4):413–421.

Cover, T. M. and Thomas, J. A. (1991). *Elements of Information Theory*. Wiley Interscience, New York.

Cowan, B., Kučerová, I., and Collins, M. (2006). A discriminative model for tree-to-tree translation. In *Proceedings of the 2006 Conference on Empirical Methods in Natural Language Processing*, pp. 232–241, Sydney, Australia. Association for Computational Linguistics.

Crego, J. M., Costa-jussa, M. R., Mariño, J. B., and Fonollosa, J. A. R. (2005). N-gram-based versus phrase-based statistical machine translation. In *Proceedings of the International Workshop on Spoken Language Translation*.

Crego, J. M., de Gispert, A., Lambert, P., *et al.* (2006a). N-gram-based SMT system enhanced with reordering patterns. In *Proceedings of the Workshop on Statistical Machine Translation*, pp. 162–165, New York City. Association for Computational Linguistics.

Crego, J. M., de Gispert, A., Lambert, P., *et al.* (2006b). The TALP ngram-based SMT systems for IWSLT 2006. In *Proceedings of the International Workshop on Spoken Language Translation*, Kyoto, Japan.

Crego, J. M. and Habash, N. (2008). Using shallow syntax information to improve word alignment and reordering for SMT. In *Proceedings of the Third Workshop on Statistical Machine Translation*, pp. 53–61, Columbus, Ohio. Association for Computational Linguistics.

Crego, J. M. and Mariño, J. B. (2006). Integration of POS-tag-based source reordering into SMT decoding by an extended search graph. In *5th Conference of the Association for Machine Translation in the Americas (AMTA)*, Boston, Massachusetts.

Crego, J. M. and Mariño, J. B. (2007). Syntax-enhanced n-gram-based SMT. In *Proceedings of the MT Summit XI*.

Cromieres, F. (2006). Sub-sentential alignment using substring co-occurrence counts. In *Proceedings of the COLING/ACL 2006 Student Research Workshop*, pp. 13–18, Sydney, Australia. Association for Computational Linguistics.

Culy, C. and Riehemann, S. (2003). The limits of n-gram translation evaluation metrics. In *Proceedings of the MT Summit IX*.

Čuřín, J., Čmejrek, M., Havelka, J., and Kubon, V. (2004). Building a parallel bilingual syntactically annoted corpus. In *Proceedings of the International Joint Conference on Natural Language Processing (IJCNLP)*.

Dagan, I., Church, K. W., and Gale, W. A. (1993). Robust bilingual word alignment for machine aided translation. In *Proceedings of the Workshop on Very Large Corpora (VLC)*.

Daille, B. and Morin, E. (2008). An effective compositional model for lexical alignment. In *Proceedings of the 3rd International Joint Conference on Natural Language Processing (IJCNLP)*.

Daumé III, H., Langford, J., and Marcu, D. (2006). Search-based structured prediction. *Submitted to the Machine Learning Journal*.

Davis, M. W., Dunning, T. E., and Ogden, W. C. (1995). Text alignment in the real world: Improving alignments of noisy translations using common lexical features, string matching strategies and n-gram comparisons. In *Proceedings of Meeting of the European Chapter of the Association of Computational Linguistics (EACL)*.

Davis, P., Xie, Z., and Small, K. (2007). All links are not the same: Evaluating word alignments for statistical machine translation. In *Proceedings of the MT Summit XI*.

Déchelotte, D., Adda, G., Allauzen, A., *et al.* (2008). Limsi's statistical translation systems for WMT'08. In *Proceedings of the Third Workshop on Statistical*

Machine Translation, pp. 107–110, Columbus, Ohio. Association for Computational Linguistics.

Dejean, H., Gaussier, E., Goutte, C., and Yamada, K. (2003). Reducing parameter space for word alignment. In Mihalcea, R. and Pedersen, T., editors, *HLT-NAACL 2003 Workshop: Building and Using Parallel Texts: Data Driven Machine Translation and Beyond*, Edmonton, Alberta, Canada. Association for Computational Linguistics.

Delaney, B., Shen, W., and Anderson, T. (2006). An efficient graph search decoder for phrase-based statistical machine translation. In *Proceedings of the International Workshop on Spoken Language Translation*, Kyoto, Japan.

DeNeefe, S. and Knight, K. (2005). ISI's 2005 statistical machine translation entries. In *Proceedings of the International Workshop on Spoken Language Translation*.

DeNeefe, S., Knight, K., and Chan, H. H. (2005). Interactively exploring a machine translation model. In *Proceedings of the ACL Interactive Poster and Demonstration Sessions*, pp. 97–100, Ann Arbor, Michigan. Association for Computational Linguistics.

DeNeefe, S., Knight, K., Wang, W., and Marcu, D. (2007). What can syntax-based MT learn from phrase-based MT? In *Proceedings of the 2007 Joint Conference on Empirical Methods in Natural Language Processing and Computational Natural Language Learning (EMNLP-CoNLL)*, pp. 755–763.

DeNero, J., Gillick, D., Zhang, J., and Klein, D. (2006). Why generative phrase models underperform surface heuristics. In *Proceedings of the Workshop on Statistical Machine Translation*, pp. 31–38, New York City. Association for Computational Linguistics.

DeNero, J. and Klein, D. (2007). Tailoring word alignments to syntactic machine translation. In *Proceedings of the 45th Annual Meeting of the Association of Computational Linguistics*, pp. 17–24, Prague, Czech Republic. Association for Computational Linguistics.

DeNero, J. and Klein, D. (2008). The complexity of phrase alignment problems. In *Proceedings of ACL-08: HLT, Short Papers*, pp. 25–28, Columbus, Ohio. Association for Computational Linguistics.

Deng, Y. and Byrne, W. (2005). HMM word and phrase alignment for statistical machine translation. In *Proceedings of Human Language Technology Conference and Conference on Empirical Methods in Natural Language Processing*, pp. 169–176, Vancouver, British Columbia, Canada. Association for Computational Linguistics.

Deng, Y. and Byrne, W. (2006). MTTK: An alignment toolkit for statistical machine translation. In *Proceedings of the Human Language Technology Conference of the NAACL, Companion Volume: Demonstrations*, pp. 265–268, New York City, USA. Association for Computational Linguistics.

Deng, Y. and Gao, Y. (2007). Guiding statistical word alignment models with prior knowledge. In *Proceedings of the 45th Annual Meeting of the Association of Computational Linguistics*, pp. 1–8, Prague, Czech Republic. Association for Computational Linguistics.

Deng, Y., Xu, J., and Gao, Y. (2008). Phrase table training for precision and recall: What makes a good phrase and a good phrase pair? In *Proceedings of ACL-08: HLT*, pp. 81–88, Columbus, Ohio. Association for Computational Linguistics.

Denoual, E. (2007). Analogical translation of unknown words in a statistical machine translation framework. In *Proceedings of the MT Summit XI*.

Diab, M. and Finch, S. (2000). A statistical word-level translation model for comparable corpora. In *Proceedings of the Conference on Content-based Multimedia Information Access (RIAO)*.

Diab, M., Ghoneim, M., and Habash, N. (2007). Arabic diacritization in the context of statistical machine translation. In *Proceedings of the MT Summit XI*.

Ding, Y., Gildea, D., and Palmer, M. (2003). An algorithm for word-level alignment of parallel dependency trees. In *Proceedings of the MT Summit IX*.

Ding, Y. and Palmer, M. (2004). Automatic learning of parallel dependency treelet pairs. In *Proceedings of the International Joint Conference on Natural Language Processing (IJCNLP)*.

Ding, Y. and Palmer, M. (2005). Machine translation using probabilistic synchronous dependency insertion grammars. In *Proceedings of the 43rd Annual Meeting of the Association for Computational Linguistics (ACL'05)*, pp. 541–548, Ann Arbor, Michigan. Association for Computational Linguistics.

Ding, Y. and Palmer, M. (2006). Better learning and decoding for syntax based SMT using PSDIG. In *5th Conference of the Association for Machine Translation in the Americas (AMTA)*, Boston, Massachusetts.

Dorr, B. J. (1994). Machine translation divergences: A formal description and proposed solution. *Computational Linguistics*, **20**(4): 597–633.

Dorr, B. J., Pearl, L., Hwa, R., and Habash, N. (2002). DUSTer: A method for unraveling cross-language divergences for statistical word-level alignment. In Richardson, S. D., editor, *Machine Translation: From*

Research to Real Users, 5th Conference of the Association for Machine Translation in the Americas, AMTA 2002 Tiburon, CA, USA, October 6-12, 2002, Proceedings, volume 2499 of Lecture Notes in Computer Science. Springer.

Dreyer, M., Hall, K., and Khudanpur, S. (2007). Comparing reordering constraints for SMT using efficient BLEU oracle computation. In Proceedings of SSST, NAACL-HLT 2007/AMTA Workshop on Syntax and Structure in Statistical Translation, pp. 103–110, Rochester, New York. Association for Computational Linguistics.

Dugast, L., Senellart, J., and Koehn, P. (2007). Statistical post-editing on SYSTRAN's rule-based translation system. In Proceedings of the Second Workshop on Statistical Machine Translation, pp. 220–223, Prague, Czech Republic. Association for Computational Linguistics.

Dugast, L., Senellart, J., and Koehn, P. (2008). Can we relearn an RBMT system? In Proceedings of the Third Workshop on Statistical Machine Translation, pp. 175–178, Columbus, Ohio. Association for Computational Linguistics.

Duh, K. (2008). Ranking vs. regression in machine translation evaluation. In Proceedings of the Third Workshop on Statistical Machine Translation, pp. 191–194, Columbus, Ohio. Association for Computational Linguistics.

Duh, K. and Kirchhoff, K. (2008). Beyond log-linear models: Boosted minimum error rate training for n-best re-ranking. In Proceedings of ACL-08: HLT, Short Papers, pp. 37–40, Columbus, Ohio. Association for Computational Linguistics.

Durgar El-Kahlout, i. and Oflazer, K. (2006). Initial explorations in English to Turkish statistical machine translation. In Proceedings of the Workshop on Statistical Machine Translation, pp. 7–14, New York City. Association for Computational Linguistics.

Dyer, C. J. (2007a). The "noisier channel": Translation from morphologically complex languages. In Proceedings of the Second Workshop on Statistical Machine Translation, pp. 207–211, Prague, Czech Republic. Association for Computational Linguistics.

Dyer, C. J. (2007b). The University of Maryland translation system for IWSLT 2007. In Proceedings of the International Workshop on Spoken Language Translation (IWSLT).

Dyer, C. J., Cordova, A., Mont, A., and Lin, J. (2008a). Fast, easy, and cheap: Construction of statistical machine translation models with MapReduce. In Proceedings of

the Third Workshop on Statistical Machine Translation, pp. 199–207, Columbus, Ohio. Association for Computational Linguistics.

Dyer, C. J., Muresan, S., and Resnik, P. (2008b). Generalizing word lattice translation. In Proceedings of ACL-08: HLT, pp. 1012–1020, Columbus, Ohio. Association for Computational Linguistics.

Echizen-ya, H. and Araki, K. (2007). Automatic evaluation of machine translation based on recursive acquisition of an intuitive common parts continuum. In Proceedings of the MT Summit XI.

Echizen-ya, H., Araki, K., Momouchi, Y., and Tochinai, K. (2003). Effectiveness of automatic extraction of bilingual collocations using recursive chain-link-type learning. In Proceedings of the MT Summit IX.

Eck, M. and Hori, C. (2005). Overview of the IWSLT 2005 evaluation campaign. In Proceedings of the International Workshop on Spoken Language Translation.

Eck, M., Lane, I., Bach, N., et al. (2006a). The UKA/CMU statistical machine translation system for IWSLT 2006. In Proceedings of the International Workshop on Spoken Language Translation, Kyoto, Japan.

Eck, M., Vogel, S., and Waibel, A. (2006b). A flexible online server for machine translation evaluation. In Proceedings of the 11th Conference of the European Association for Machine Translation (EAMT), Oslo, Norway.

Eck, M., Vogel, S., and Waibel, A. (2007a). Estimating phrase pair relevance for translation model pruning. In Proceedings of the MT Summit XI.

Eck, M., Vogel, S., and Waibel, A. (2007b). Translation model pruning via usage statistics for statistical machine translation. In Human Language Technologies 2007: The Conference of the North American Chapter of the Association for Computational Linguistics; Companion Volume, Short Papers, pp. 21–24, Rochester, New York. Association for Computational Linguistics.

Efron, B. and Tibshirani, R. J. (1993). An Introduction to the Bootstrap. Chapman and Hall, Bora Raton.

Ehling, N., Zens, R., and Ney, H. (2007). Minimum Bayes risk decoding for BLEU. In Proceedings of the 45th Annual Meeting of the Association for Computational Linguistics Companion Volume Proceedings of the Demo and Poster Sessions, pp. 101–104, Prague, Czech Republic. Association for Computational Linguistics.

Eisele, A. (2005). First steps towards multi-engine machine translation. In Proceedings of the ACL Workshop on Building and Using Parallel Texts, pp. 155–158, Ann

Arbor, Michigan. Association for Computational Linguistics.

Eisele, A., Federmann, C., Saint-Amand, H., Jellinghaus, M., Herrmann, T., and Chen, Y. (2008). Using Moses to integrate multiple rule-based machine translation engines into a hybrid system. In *Proceedings of the Third Workshop on Statistical Machine Translation*, pp. 179–182, Columbus, Ohio. Association for Computational Linguistics.

Eisner, J. (2003). Learning non-isomorphic tree mappings for machine translation. In Matsumoto, Y., editor, *The Companion Volume to the Proceedings of 41st Annual Meeting of the Association for Computational Linguistics*, pp. 205–208.

Ekbal, A., Naskar, S. K., and Bandyopadhyay, S. (2006). A modified joint source-channel model for transliteration. In *Proceedings of the COLING/ACL 2006 Main Conference Poster Sessions*, pp. 191–198, Sydney, Australia. Association for Computational Linguistics.

El Isbihani, A., Khadivi, S., Bender, O., and Ney, H. (2006). Morpho-syntactic Arabic preprocessing for Arabic to English statistical machine translation. In *Proceedings on the Workshop on Statistical Machine Translation*, pp. 15–22, New York City. Association for Computational Linguistics.

Elming, J. (2008a). Syntactic reordering integrated with phrase-based SMT. In *Proceedings of the ACL-08: HLT Second Workshop on Syntax and Structure in Statistical Translation (SSST-2)*, pp. 46–54, Columbus, Ohio. Association for Computational Linguistics.

Elming, J. (2008b). Syntactic reordering integrated with phrase-based SMT. In *Proceedings of the 22nd International Conference on Computational Linguistics (COLING 2008)*, pp. 209–216, Manchester, UK. COLING 2008 Organizing Committee.

Elming, J. and Habash, N. (2007). Combination of statistical word alignments based on multiple preprocessing schemes. In *Human Language Technologies 2007: The Conference of the North American Chapter of the Association for Computational Linguistics; Companion Volume, Short Papers*, pp. 25–28, Rochester, New York. Association for Computational Linguistics.

Enright, J. and Kondrak, G. (2007). A fast method for parallel document identification. In *Human Language Technologies 2007: The Conference of the North American Chapter of the Association for Computational Linguistics; Companion Volume, Short Papers*, pp. 29–32, Rochester, New York. Association for Computational Linguistics.

Estrella, P., Hamon, O., and Popescu-Belis, A. (2007). How much data is needed for reliable MT evaluation? Using bootstrapping to study human and automatic metrics. In *Proceedings of the MT Summit XI*.

Federico, M. and Bertoldi, N. (2006). How many bits are needed to store probabilities for phrase-based translation? In *Proceedings on the Workshop on Statistical Machine Translation*, pp. 94–101, New York City. Association for Computational Linguistics.

Federico, M. and Cettolo, M. (2007). Efficient handling of n-gram language models for statistical machine translation. In *Proceedings of the Second Workshop on Statistical Machine Translation*, pp. 88–95, Prague, Czech Republic. Association for Computational Linguistics.

Filali, K. and Bilmes, J. (2007). Generalized graphical abstractions for statistical machine translation. In *Human Language Technologies 2007: The Conference of the North American Chapter of the Association for Computational Linguistics; Companion Volume, Short Papers*, pp. 33–36, Rochester, New York. Association for Computational Linguistics.

Finch, A., Akiba, Y., and Sumita, E. (2004). Using a paraphraser to improve machine translation evaluation. In *Proceedings of the International Joint Conference on Natural Language Processing (IJCNLP)*.

Finch, A., Denoual, E., Okuma, H., *et al.* (2007). The NICT/ATR speech translation system for IWSLT 2007. In *Proceedings of the International Workshop on Spoken Language Translation (IWSLT)*.

Finch, A. and Sumita, E. (2008). Dynamic model interpolation for statistical machine translation. In *Proceedings of the Third Workshop on Statistical Machine Translation*, pp. 208–215, Columbus, Ohio. Association for Computational Linguistics.

Fiscus, J. G. (1997). A post-processing system to yield reduced word error rates: Recognizer output voting error reduction (ROVER). In *Proceedings of the Conference on Automatic Speech Recognition and Understanding (ASRU)*, pp. 347–354.

Font Llitjós, A. and Vogel, S. (2007). A walk on the other side: Using SMT components in a transfer-based translation system. In *Proceedings of SSST, NAACL-HLT 2007/AMTA Workshop on Syntax and Structure in Statistical Translation*, pp. 72–79, Rochester, New York. Association for Computational Linguistics.

Fordyce, C. S. (2007). Overview of the IWSLT 2007 evaluation campaign. In *Proceedings of the*

International Workshop on Spoken Language Translation (IWSLT).

Fossum, V. L., Knight, K., and Abney, S. (2008). Using syntax to improve word alignment precision for syntax-based machine translation. In *Proceedings of the Third Workshop on Statistical Machine Translation*, pp. 44–52, Columbus, Ohio. Association for Computational Linguistics.

Foster, G. (2000a). Incorporating position information into a maximum entropy/minimum divergence translation model. In *Proceedings of the Fourth Conference on Computational Natural Language Learning and of the Second Learning Language in Logic Workshop*.

Foster, G. (2000b). A maximum entropy/minimum divergence translation model. In *Proceedings of the 38th Annual Meeting of the Association of Computational Linguistics (ACL)*.

Foster, G., Gandrabur, S., Langlais, P., Russell, G., Simard, M., and Plamondon, P. (2003). Statistical machine translation: Rapid development with limited resources. In *Proceedings of the MT Summit IX*.

Foster, G. and Kuhn, R. (2007). Mixture-model adaptation for SMT. In *Proceedings of the Second Workshop on Statistical Machine Translation*, pp. 128–135, Prague, Czech Republic. Association for Computational Linguistics.

Foster, G., Kuhn, R., and Johnson, H. (2006). Phrasetable smoothing for statistical machine translation. In *Proceedings of the 2006 Conference on Empirical Methods in Natural Language Processing*, pp. 53–61, Sydney, Australia. Association for Computational Linguistics.

Foster, G., Langlais, P., and Lapalme, G. (2002). User-friendly text prediction for translators. In *Proceedings of the Conference on Empirical Methods in Natural Language Processing (EMNLP)*, pp. 148–155, Philadelphia. Association for Computational Linguistics.

Fox, H. (2002). Phrasal cohesion and statistical machine translation. In *Proceedings of the Conference on Empirical Methods in Natural Language Processing (EMNLP)*, pp. 304–311, Philadelphia. Association for Computational Linguistics.

Fraser, A. and Marcu, D. (2005). ISI's participation in the Romanian–English alignment task. In *Proceedings of the ACL Workshop on Building and Using Parallel Texts*, pp. 91–94, Ann Arbor, Michigan. Association for Computational Linguistics.

Fraser, A. and Marcu, D. (2006). Semi-supervised training for statistical word alignment. In *Proceedings of the 21st International Conference on Computational Linguistics and 44th Annual Meeting of the Association for Computational Linguistics*, pp. 769–776, Sydney, Australia. Association for Computational Linguistics.

Fraser, A. and Marcu, D. (2007a). Getting the structure right for word alignment: LEAF. In *Proceedings of the 2007 Joint Conference on Empirical Methods in Natural Language Processing and Computational Natural Language Learning (EMNLP-CoNLL)*, pp. 51–60.

Fraser, A. and Marcu, D. (2007b). Measuring word alignment quality for statistical machine translation. *Computational Linguistics*, 33(3): 293–303.

Fukushima, K., Taura, K., and Chikayama, T. (2006). A fast and accurate method for detecting English–Japanese parallel texts. In *Proceedings of the Workshop on Multilingual Language Resources and Interoperability*, pp. 60–67, Sydney, Australia. Association for Computational Linguistics.

Fung, P. (1995a). Compiling bilingual lexicon entries from a non-parallel English–Chinese corpus. In *Proceedings of the Third Workshop on Very Large Corpora (VLC)*.

Fung, P. (1995b). A pattern matching method for finding noun and proper noun translations from noisy parallel corpora. In *Proceedings of the 33rd Annual Meeting of the Association for Computational Linguistics (ACL)*.

Fung, P. (1997). Finding terminology translations from non-parallel corpora. In *Proceedings of the Fifth Workshop on Very Large Corpora (VLC)*.

Fung, P. and Cheung, P. (2004a). Mining very-non-parallel corpora: Parallel sentence and lexicon extraction via bootstrapping and EM. In Lin, D. and Wu, D., editors, *Proceedings of EMNLP 2004*, pp. 57–63, Barcelona, Spain. Association for Computational Linguistics.

Fung, P. and Cheung, P. (2004b). Multi-level bootstrapping for extracting parallel sentences from a quasi-comparable corpus. In *Proceedings of COLING 2004*, pp. 1051–1057, Geneva, Switzerland. COLING.

Fung, P. and McKeown, K. R. (1994). Aligning noisy parallel corpora across language groups: Word pair feature matching by dynamic time warping. In *1st Conference of the Association for Machine Translation in the Americas (AMTA)*.

Fung, P. and Yee, L. Y. (1998). An IR approach for translating new words from nonparallel, comparable texts. In *Proceedings of the 36th Annual Meeting of the Association of Computational Linguistics (ACL)*.

Gale, W. A. and Church, K. W. (1991). A program for aligning sentences in bilingual corpora. In *Proceedings* of the 29th Annual Meeting of the Association of Computational Linguistics (ACL).

Gale, W. A. and Church, K. W. (1993). A program for aligning sentences in bilingual corpora. *Computational Linguistics*, **19**(1):75–102.

Gale, W. A. and Sampson, G. (1995). Good–Turing frequency estimation without tears. *Journal of Quantitative Linguistics*, **2**:217–237.

Galley, M., Graehl, J., Knight, K., Marcu, D., DeNeefe, S., Wang, W., and Thayer, I. (2006). Scalable inference and training of context-rich syntactic translation models. In *Proceedings of the 21st International Conference on Computational Linguistics and 44th Annual Meeting of the Association for Computational Linguistics*, pp. 961–968, Sydney, Australia. Association for Computational Linguistics.

Galley, M., Hopkins, M., Knight, K., and Marcu, D. (2004). What's in a translation rule? In *Proceedings of the Joint Conference on Human Language Technologies and the Annual Meeting of the North American Chapter of the Association of Computational Linguistics (HLT-NAACL)*.

Gamon, M., Aue, A., and Smets, M. (2005). Sentence-level MT evaluation without reference translations: beyond language modeling. In *Proceedings of the 10th Conference of the European Association for Machine Translation (EAMT)*, Budapest.

Ganchev, K., Graça, J. V., and Taskar, B. (2008). Better alignments = better translations? In *Proceedings of ACL-08: HLT*, pp. 986–993, Columbus, Ohio. Association for Computational Linguistics.

García-Varea, I., Och, F. J., and Casacuberta, F. (2001). Refined lexicon models for statistical machine translation using a maximum entropy approach. In *Proceedings of the 39th Annual Meeting of the Association of Computational Linguistics (ACL)*.

García-Varea, I., Och, F. J., Ney, H., and Casacuberta, F. (2002a). Efficient integration of maximum entropy models within a maximum likelihood training scheme of statistical machine translation. In Richardson, S. D., editor, *Machine Translation: From Research to Real Users, 5th Conference of the Association for Machine Translation in the Americas, AMTA 2002 Tiburon, CA, USA, October 6-12, 2002, Proceedings*, volume 2499 of *Lecture Notes in Computer Science*. Springer.

García-Varea, I., Och, F. J., Ney, H., and Casacuberta, F. (2002b). Improving alignment quality in statistical machine translation using context-dependent maximum entropy models. In *Proceedings of the International Conference on Computational Linguistics (COLING)*.

Gaspari, F. and Hutchins, W. J. (2007). Online and free! Ten years of online machine translation: Origins, developments, current use and future prospects. In *Proceedings of the MT Summit XI*.

Gaussier, E., Renders, J., Matveeva, I., Goutte, C., and Dejean, H. (2004). A geometric view on bilingual lexicon extraction from comparable corpora. In *Proceedings of the 42nd Meeting of the Association for Computational Linguistics (ACL'04), Main Volume*, pp. 526–533, Barcelona, Spain.

Ge, N., Ittycheriah, A., and Papineni, K. (2008). Multiple reorderings in phrase-based machine translation. In *Proceedings of the ACL-08: HLT Second Workshop on Syntax and Structure in Statistical Translation (SSST-2)*, pp. 61–68, Columbus, Ohio. Association for Computational Linguistics.

Germann, U. (2001). Building a statistical machine translation system from scratch: How much bang for the buck can we expect? In *Workshop on Data-Driven Machine Translation at 39th Annual Meeting of the Association of Computational Linguistics (ACL)*.

Germann, U. (2003). Greedy decoding for statistical machine translation in almost linear time. In *Proceedings of the Joint Conference on Human Language Technologies and the Annual Meeting of the North American Chapter of the Association of Computational Linguistics (HLT-NAACL)*.

Germann, U. (2007). Two tools for creating and visualizing sub-sentential alignments of parallel text. In *Proceedings of the Linguistic Annotation Workshop*, pp. 121–124, Prague, Czech Republic. Association for Computational Linguistics.

Germann, U. (2008). Yawat: Yet Another Word Alignment Tool. In *Proceedings of the ACL-08: HLT Demo Session*, pp. 20–23, Columbus, Ohio. Association for Computational Linguistics.

Germann, U., Jahr, M., Knight, K., Marcu, D., and Yamada, K. (2001). Fast decoding and optimal decoding for machine translation. In *Proceedings of the 39th Annual Meeting of the Association of Computational Linguistics (ACL)*.

Gildea, D. (2003). Loosely tree-based alignment for machine translation. In *Proceedings of the 41st Annual Meeting of the Association of Computational Linguistics (ACL)*.

Gildea, D. (2004). Dependencies vs. constituents for tree-based alignment. In Lin, D. and Wu, D., editors, *Proceedings of EMNLP 2004*, pp. 214–221, Barcelona, Spain. Association for Computational Linguistics.

Giménez, J. and Màrquez, L. (2006). The LDV-COMBO system for SMT. In *Proceedings of the Workshop on*

Statistical Machine Translation, pp. 166–169, New York City. Association for Computational Linguistics.

Giménez, J. and Màrquez, L. (2007a). Context-aware discriminative phrase selection for statistical machine translation. In *Proceedings of the Second Workshop on Statistical Machine Translation*, pp. 159–166, Prague, Czech Republic. Association for Computational Linguistics.

Giménez, J. and Màrquez, L. (2007b). Linguistic features for automatic evaluation of heterogenous MT systems. In *Proceedings of the Second Workshop on Statistical Machine Translation*, pp. 256–264, Prague, Czech Republic. Association for Computational Linguistics.

Giménez, J. and Màrquez, L. (2008a). Heterogeneous automatic MT evaluation through non-parametric metric combinations. In *Proceedings of the 3rd International Joint Conference on Natural Language Processing (IJCNLP)*.

Giménez, J. and Màrquez, L. (2008b). A smorgasbord of features for automatic MT evaluation. In *Proceedings of the Third Workshop on Statistical Machine Translation*, pp. 195–198, Columbus, Ohio. Association for Computational Linguistics.

Gimpel, K. and Smith, N. A. (2008). Rich source-side context for statistical machine translation. In *Proceedings of the Third Workshop on Statistical Machine Translation*, pp. 9–17, Columbus, Ohio. Association for Computational Linguistics.

Goldwasser, D. and Roth, D. (2008). Active sample selection for named entity transliteration. In *Proceedings of ACL-08: HLT, Short Papers*, pp. 53–56, Columbus, Ohio. Association for Computational Linguistics.

Goldwater, S. and McClosky, D. (2005). Improving statistical MT through morphological analysis. In *Proceedings of Human Language Technology Conference and Conference on Empirical Methods in Natural Language Processing*, pp. 676–683, Vancouver, British Columbia, Canada. Association for Computational Linguistics.

Good, I. J. (1953). The population frequency of species and the estimation of population parameters. *Biometrika*, **40**:237–264.

Goto, I., Kato, N., Ehara, T., and Tanaka, H. (2004). Back transliteration from Japanese to English using target English context. In *Proceedings of COLING 2004*, pp. 827–833, Geneva, Switzerland. COLING.

Goto, I., Kato, N., Uratani, N., and Ehara, T. (2003). Transliteration considering context information based on the maximum entropy method. In *Proceedings of the MT Summit IX*.

Goutte, C., Yamada, K., and Gaussier, E. (2004). Aligning words using matrix factorisation. In *Proceedings of the 42nd Meeting of the Association for Computational Linguistics (ACL'04), Main Volume*, pp. 502–509, Barcelona, Spain.

Graça, J. V., Caseiro, D., and Coheur, L. (2007). The INESC-ID IWSLT07 SMT system. In *Proceedings of the International Workshop on Spoken Language Translation (IWSLT)*.

Graehl, J. and Knight, K. (2004). Training tree transducers. In *Proceedings of the Joint Conference on Human Language Technologies and the Annual Meeting of the North American Chapter of the Association of Computational Linguistics (HLT-NAACL)*.

Groves, D., Hearne, M., and Way, A. (2004). Robust sub-sentential alignment of phrase-structure trees. In *Proceedings of COLING 2004*, pp. 1072–1078, Geneva, Switzerland. COLING.

Groves, D. and Way, A. (2005). Hybrid example-based SMT: the best of both worlds? In *Proceedings of the ACL Workshop on Building and Using Parallel Texts*, pp. 183–190, Ann Arbor, Michigan. Association for Computational Linguistics.

Groves, D. and Way, A. (2006). Hybridity in MT. Experiments on the Europarl corpus. In *Proceedings of the 11th Conference of the European Association for Machine Translation (EAMT)*, Oslo, Norway.

Gupta, D., Cettolo, M., and Federico, M. (2007). POS-based reordering models for statistical machine translation. In *Proceedings of the MT Summit XI*.

Gupta, D. and Chatterjee, N. (2003). Identification of divergence for English to Hindi EBMT. In *Proceedings of the MT Summit IX*.

Habash, N. (2007). Syntactic preprocessing for statistical machine translation. In *Proceedings of the MT Summit XI*.

Habash, N. (2008). Four techniques for online handling of out-of-vocabulary words in Arabic–English statistical machine translation. In *Proceedings of ACL-08: HLT, Short Papers*, pp. 57–60, Columbus, Ohio. Association for Computational Linguistics.

Habash, N. and Dorr, B. J. (2002). Handling translation divergences: Combining statistical and symbolic techniques in generation-heavy machine translation. In Richardson, S. D., editor, *Machine Translation: From Research to Real Users, 5th Conference of the Association for Machine Translation in the Americas, AMTA 2002 Tiburon, CA, USA, October 6-12, 2002, Proceedings*, volume 2499 of *Lecture Notes in Computer Science*. Springer.

Habash, N. and Sadat, F. (2006). Arabic preprocessing schemes for statistical machine translation. In *Proceedings of the Human Language Technology Conference of the NAACL, Companion Volume: Short Papers*, pp. 49–52, New York City, USA. Association for Computational Linguistics.

Haghighi, A., Liang, P., Berg-Kirkpatrick, T., and Klein, D. (2008). Learning bilingual lexicons from monolingual corpora. In *Proceedings of ACL-08: HLT*, pp. 771–779, Columbus, Ohio. Association for Computational Linguistics.

Hall, K. and Němec, P. (2007). Generation in machine translation from deep syntactic trees. In *Proceedings of SSST, NAACL-HLT 2007/AMTA Workshop on Syntax and Structure in Statistical Translation*, pp. 57–64, Rochester, New York. Association for Computational Linguistics.

Hamon, O., Hartley, A., Popescu-Belis, A., and Choukri, K. (2007a). Assessing human and automated quality judgments in the French MT evaluation campaign CESTA. In *Proceedings of the MT Summit XI*.

Hamon, O. and Mostefa, D. (2008). The impact of reference quality on automatic MT evaluation. In *COLING 2008: Companion Volume: Posters and Demonstrations*, pp. 37–40, Manchester, UK. COLING 2008 Organizing Committee.

Hamon, O., Mostefa, D., and Choukri, K. (2007b). End-to-end evaluation of a speech-to-speech translation system in TC-STAR. In *Proceedings of the MT Summit XI*.

Hanneman, G., Huber, E., Agarwal, A., *et al.* (2008). Statistical transfer systems for French–English and German–English machine translation. In *Proceedings of the Third Workshop on Statistical Machine Translation*, pp. 163–166, Columbus, Ohio. Association for Computational Linguistics.

HarperCollins (1998). *Harper Collins German Dictionary: German–English, English–German, Concise Edition*. HarperResource, Glasgow.

Haruno, M. and Yamazaki, T. (1996). High-performance bilingual text alignment using statistical and dictionary information. In *Proceedings of the 34th Annual Meeting of the Association for Computational Linguistics (ACL)*.

Hasan, S. and Ney, H. (2005). Clustered language models based on regular expressions for SMT. In *Proceedings of the 10th Conference of the European Association for Machine Translation (EAMT)*, Budapest.

Hasan, S., Zens, R., and Ney, H. (2007). Are very large n-best lists useful for SMT? In *Human Language Technologies 2007: The Conference of the North*

American Chapter of the Association for Computational Linguistics; Companion Volume, Short Papers, pp. 57–60, Rochester, New York. Association for Computational Linguistics.

Hassan, H., Ma, Y., and Way, A. (2007a). MaTrEx: the DCU machine translation system for IWSLT 2007. In *Proceedings of the International Workshop on Spoken Language Translation (IWSLT)*.

Hassan, H., Sima'an, K., and Way, A. (2007b). Supertagged phrase-based statistical machine translation. In *Proceedings of the 45th Annual Meeting of the Association of Computational Linguistics*, pp. 288–295, Prague, Czech Republic. Association for Computational Linguistics.

He, X. (2007). Using word-dependent transition models in HMM-based word alignment for statistical machine translation. In *Proceedings of the Second Workshop on Statistical Machine Translation*, pp. 80–87, Prague, Czech Republic. Association for Computational Linguistics.

He, Z., Liu, Q., and Lin, S. (2008a). Improving statistical machine translation using lexicalized rule selection. In *Proceedings of the 22nd International Conference on Computational Linguistics (COLING 2008)*, pp. 321–328, Manchester, UK. COLING 2008 Organizing Committee.

He, Z., Liu, Q., and Lin, S. (2008b). Partial matching strategy for phrase-based statistical machine translation. In *Proceedings of ACL-08: HLT, Short Papers*, pp. 161–164, Columbus, Ohio. Association for Computational Linguistics.

He, Z., Mi, H., Liu, Y., *et al.* (2007). The ICT statistical machine translation systems for IWSLT 2007. In *Proceedings of the International Workshop on Spoken Language Translation (IWSLT)*.

Hermjakob, U., Knight, K., and Daumé III, H. (2008). Name translation in statistical machine translation — learning when to transliterate. In *Proceedings of ACL-08: HLT*, pp. 389–397, Columbus, Ohio. Association for Computational Linguistics.

Hermjakob, U. and Mooney, R. J. (1997). Learning parse and translation decisions from examples with rich context. In *Proceedings of the 35th Annual Meeting of the Association for Computational Linguistics (ACL)*.

Hewavitharana, S., Lavie, A., and Vogel, S. (2007). Experiments with a noun-phrase driven statistical machine translation system. In *Proceedings of the MT Summit XI*.

Hewavitharana, S., Vogel, S., and Waibel, A. (2005). Augmenting a statistical translation system with a translation memory. In *Proceedings of the 10th Conference of the European Association for Machine Translation (EAMT)*, Budapest.

Hildebrand, A. S., Eck, M., Vogel, S., and Waibel, A. (2005). Adaptation of the translation model for statistical machine translation based on information retrieval. In *Proceedings of the 10th Conference of the European Association for Machine Translation (EAMT)*, Budapest.

Holmqvist, M., Stymne, S., and Ahrenberg, L. (2007). Getting to know Moses: Initial experiments on German–English factored translation. In *Proceedings of the Second Workshop on Statistical Machine Translation*, pp. 181–184, Prague, Czech Republic. Association for Computational Linguistics.

Hopkins, M. and Kuhn, J. (2007). Machine translation as tree labeling. In *Proceedings of SSST, NAACL-HLT 2007/AMTA Workshop on Syntax and Structure in Statistical Translation*, pp. 41–48, Rochester, New York. Association for Computational Linguistics.

Hu, X., Wang, H., and Wu, H. (2007). Using RBMT systems to produce bilingual corpus for SMT. In *Proceedings of the 2007 Joint Conference on Empirical Methods in Natural Language Processing and Computational Natural Language Learning (EMNLP-CoNLL)*, pp. 287–295.

Huang, B. and Knight, K. (2006). Relabeling syntax trees to improve syntax-based machine translation quality. In *Proceedings of the Human Language Technology Conference of the NAACL, Main Conference*, pp. 240–247, New York City, USA. Association for Computational Linguistics.

Huang, F. and Papineni, K. (2007). Hierarchical system combination for machine translation. In *Proceedings of the 2007 Joint Conference on Empirical Methods in Natural Language Processing and Computational Natural Language Learning (EMNLP-CoNLL)*, pp. 277–286.

Huang, F., Zhang, Y., and Vogel, S. (2005). Mining key phrase translations from web corpora. In *Proceedings of Human Language Technology Conference and Conference on Empirical Methods in Natural Language Processing*, pp. 483–490, Vancouver, British Columbia, Canada. Association for Computational Linguistics.

Huang, L. (2007). Binarization, synchronous binarization, and target-side binarization. In *Proceedings of SSST, NAACL-HLT 2007/AMTA Workshop on Syntax and Structure in Statistical Translation*, pp. 33–40, Rochester, New York. Association for Computational Linguistics.

Huang, L. and Chiang, D. (2007). Forest rescoring: Faster decoding with integrated language models. In *Proceedings of the 45th Annual Meeting of the Association of Computational Linguistics*, pp. 144–151, Prague, Czech Republic. Association for Computational Linguistics.

Huang, L., Knight, K., and Joshi, A. (2006a). Statistical syntax-directed translation with extended domain of locality. In *5th Conference of the Association for Machine Translation in the Americas (AMTA)*, Boston, Massachusetts.

Huang, L., Knight, K., and Joshi, A. (2006b). A syntax-directed translator with extended domain of locality. In *Proceedings of the Workshop on Computationally Hard Problems and Joint Inference in Speech and Language Processing*, pp. 1–8, New York City, New York. Association for Computational Linguistics.

Hutchins, W. J. (2007). Machine translation: a concise history. In *Computer Aided Translation: Theory and Practice*, C. S. Wai (ed.). Chinese University of Hong Kong.

Hutchins, W. J. and Somers, H. L. (1992). *An Introduction to Machine Translation*. Academic Press, London.

Hwa, R., Nichols, C., and Sima'an, K. (2006). Corpus variations for translation lexicon induction. In *5th Conference of the Association for Machine Translation in the Americas (AMTA)*, Boston, Massachusetts.

Hwa, R., Resnik, P., Weinberg, A., and Kolak, O. (2002). Evaluating translational correspondence using annotation projection. In *Proceedings of the 40th Annual Meeting of the Association of Computational Linguistics (ACL)*.

Hwang, Y.-S., Kim, Y.-K., and Park, S. (2008). Paraphrasing depending on bilingual context toward generalization of translation knowledge. In *Proceedings of the 3rd International Joint Conference on Natural Language Processing (IJCNLP)*.

Hwang, Y.-S. and Sasaki, Y. (2005). Context-dependent SMT model using bilingual verb-noun collocation. In *Proceedings of the 43rd Annual Meeting of the Association for Computational Linguistics (ACL'05)*, pp. 549–556, Ann Arbor, Michigan. Association for Computational Linguistics.

Imamura, K. (2001). Hierarchical phrase alignment harmonized with parsing. In *Proceedings of the 6th Natural Language Processing Pacific Rim Symbopium (NLPRS-2001)*, pp. 377–384.

Imamura, K., Okuma, H., and Sumita, E. (2005). Practical approach to syntax-based statistical machine translation. In *Proceedings of the Tenth Machine Translation Summit (MT Summit X)*, Phuket, Thailand.

Imamura, K., Okuma, H., Watanabe, T., and Sumita, E. (2004). Example-based machine translation based on syntactic transfer with statistical models. In *Proceedings of COLING 2004*, pp. 99–105, Geneva, Switzerland. COLING.

Imamura, K., Sumita, E., and Matsumoto, Y. (2003). Automatic construction of machine translation knowledge using translation literalness. In *Proceedings of Meeting of the European Chapter of the Association of Computational Linguistics (EACL)*.

Isabelle, P., Goutte, C., and Simard, M. (2007). Domain adaptation of MT systems through automatic post-editing. In *Proceedings of the MT Summit XI*.

Ittycheriah, A. and Roukos, S. (2005). A maximum entropy word aligner for Arabic-English machine translation. In *Proceedings of Human Language Technology Conference and Conference on Empirical Methods in Natural Language Processing*, pp. 89–96, Vancouver, British Columbia, Canada. Association for Computational Linguistics.

Ittycheriah, A. and Roukos, S. (2007). Direct translation model 2. In *Human Language Technologies 2007: The Conference of the North American Chapter of the Association for Computational Linguistics; Proceedings of the Main Conference*, pp. 57–64, Rochester, New York. Association for Computational Linguistics.

Jayaraman, S. and Lavie, A. (2005). Multi-engine machine translation guided by explicit word matching. In *Proceedings of the ACL Interactive Poster and Demonstration Sessions*, pp. 101–104, Ann Arbor, Michigan. Association for Computational Linguistics.

Jelinek, F. (1998). *Statistical Methods for Speech Recognition*. The MIT Press, Cambridge, MA.

Johnson, H., Martin, J., Foster, G., and Kuhn, R. (2007). Improving translation quality by discarding most of the phrasetable. In *Proceedings of the 2007 Joint Conference on Empirical Methods in Natural Language Processing and Computational Natural Language Learning (EMNLP-CoNLL)*, pp. 967–975.

Johnson, H., Sadat, F., Foster, G., *et al.* (2006). Portage: with smoothed phrase tables and segment choice models. In *Proceedings on the Workshop on Statistical Machine Translation*, pp. 134–137, New York City. Association for Computational Linguistics.

Jones, D. A., Anderson, T., Atwell, S., *et al.* (2006). Toward an interagency language roundtable based assessment of speech-to-speech translation capabilities. In *5th Conference of the Association for Machine Translation in the Americas (AMTA)*, Boston, Massachusetts.

Jones, D. A. and Rusk, G. M. (2000). Toward a scoring function for quality-driven machine translation. In *Proceedings of the International Conference on Computational Linguistics (COLING)*.

Jung, S. Y., Hong, S., and Paek, E. (2000). An English to Korean transliteration model of extended Markov window. In *Proceedings of the International Conference on Computational Linguistics (COLING)*.

Jurafsky, D. and Martin, J. H. (2008). *Speech and Language Processing (2nd edition)*. Prentice Hall.

Kaalep, H.-J. and Veskis, K. (2007). Comparing parallel corpora and evaluating their quality. In *Proceedings of the MT Summit XI*.

Kaji, H. (2004). Bilingual-dictionary adaptation to domains. In *Proceedings of COLING 2004*, pp. 729–735, Geneva, Switzerland. COLING.

Kaji, H. and Aizono, T. (1996). Extracting word correspondences from bilingual corpora based on word co-occurrence information. In *Proceedings of the 16th International Conference on Computational Linguistics (COLING)*.

Kang, I.-H. and Kim, G. C. (2000). English-to-Korean transliteration using multiple unbounded overlapping phoneme chunks. In *Proceedings of the International Conference on Computational Linguistics (COLING)*.

Kanthak, S., Vilar, D., Matusov, E., Zens, R., and Ney, H. (2005). Novel reordering approaches in phrase-based statistical machine translation. In *Proceedings of the ACL Workshop on Building and Using Parallel Texts*, pp. 167–174, Ann Arbor, Michigan. Association for Computational Linguistics.

Karakos, D., Eisner, J., Khudanpur, S., and Dreyer, M. (2008). Machine translation system combination using ITG-based alignments. In *Proceedings of ACL-08: HLT, Short Papers*, pp. 81–84, Columbus, Ohio. Association for Computational Linguistics.

Kashani, M. M., Joanis, E., Kuhn, R., Foster, G., and Popowich, F. (2007). Integration of an arabic transliteration module into a statistical machine translation system. In *Proceedings of the Second Workshop on Statistical Machine Translation*, pp. 17–24, Prague, Czech Republic. Association for Computational Linguistics.

Kashioka, H., Maruyama, T., and Tanaka, H. (2003). Building a parallel corpus for monologue with clause alignment. In *Proceedings of the MT Summit IX*.

Kauchak, D. and Barzilay, R. (2006). Paraphrasing for automatic evaluation. In *Proceedings of the Human*

Language Technology Conference of the NAACL, Main Conference, pp. 455–462, New York City, USA. Association for Computational Linguistics.

Kay, M. and Röscheisen, M. (1993). Text-translation alignment. *Computational Linguistics*, **19**(1):121–142.

Ker, S.-J. and Chang, J. J. S. (1996). Aligning more words with high precision for small bilingual corpora. In *Proceedings of the 16th International Conference on Computational Linguistics (COLING)*.

Khalilov, M., Hernández H., A., Costa-jussà, M. R., *et al.* (2008). The TALP-UPC N-gram-based statistical machine translation system for ACL-WMT 2008. In *Proceedings of the Third Workshop on Statistical Machine Translation*, pp. 127–130, Columbus, Ohio. Association for Computational Linguistics.

Kikui, G. (1998). Term-list translation using mono-lingual word co-occurrence vectors. In *Proceedings of the 36th Annual Meeting of the Association of Computational Linguistics (ACL)*.

Kikui, G. (1999). Resolving translation ambiguity using non-parallel bilingual corpora. In *Proceedings of the ACL Workshop on Unsupervised Learning in Natural Language Processing*.

Kim, J. D. and Vogel, S. (2007). Iterative refinement of lexicon and phrasal alignment. In *Proceedings of the MT Summit XI*.

Kim, S., Yoon, J., and Song, M. (2000). Structural feature selection for English–Korean statistical machine translation. In *Proceedings of the International Conference on Computational Linguistics (COLING)*.

Kim, Y.-S., Chang, J.-H., and Zhang, B.-T. (2002). A comparable evaluation of data-driven models in translation selection of machine translation. In *Proceedings of the International Conference on Computational Linguistics (COLING)*.

King, M., Popescu-Belis, A., and Hovy, E. (2003). FEMTI: Creating and using a framework for MT evaluation. In *Proceedings of the MT Summit IX*.

Kirchhoff, K., Duh, K., and Lim, C. (2006). The University of Washington machine translation system for IWSLT 2006. In *Proceedings of the International Workshop on Spoken Language Translation*, Kyoto, Japan.

Kirchhoff, K., Rambow, O., Habash, N., and Diab, M. (2007). Semi-automatic error analysis for large-scale statistical machine translation systems. In *Proceedings of the MT Summit XI*.

Kirchhoff, K. and Yang, M. (2005). Improved language modeling for statistical machine translation. In *Proceedings of the ACL Workshop on Building and Using Parallel Texts*, pp. 125–128, Ann Arbor, Michigan. Association for Computational Linguistics.

Kirchhoff, K. and Yang, M. (2007). The University of Washington machine translation system for the IWSLT 2007 competition. In *Proceedings of the International Workshop on Spoken Language Translation (IWSLT)*.

Kitamura, M. and Matsumoto, Y. (1996). Automatic extraction of word sequence correspondences in parallel corpora. In *Proceedings of the Fourth Workshop on Very Large Corpora (VLC)*.

Klementiev, A. and Roth, D. (2006a). Named entity transliteration and discovery from multilingual comparable corpora. In *Proceedings of the Human Language Technology Conference of the NAACL, Main Conference*, pp. 82–88, New York City, USA. Association for Computational Linguistics.

Klementiev, A. and Roth, D. (2006b). Weakly supervised named entity transliteration and discovery from multilingual comparable corpora. In *Proceedings of the 21st International Conference on Computational Linguistics and 44th Annual Meeting of the Association for Computational Linguistics*, pp. 817–824, Sydney, Australia. Association for Computational Linguistics.

Kneser, R. and Ney, H. (1995). Improved backing-off for m-gram language modeling. In *Proceedings of the IEEE International Conference on Acoustics, Speech and Signal Processing*, volume 1.

Knight, K. (1997). Automating knowledge acquisition for machine translation. *AI Magazine*, **18**(4):81–96.

Knight, K. (1999a). Decoding complexity in word-replacement translation models. *Computational Linguistics*, **25**(4):607–615.

Knight, K. (1999b). A statistical MT tutorial workbook. available at http://www.isi.edu/~knight/.

Knight, K., Chander, I., Haines, M., Hatzivassiloglou, V., Hovy, E., Iida, M., Luk, S. K., Okumura, A., Whitney, R., and Yamada, K. (1994). Integrating knowledge bases and statistics in MT. In *Proceedings of the Conference of the Association for Machine Translation in the Americas (AMTA 1994)*.

Knight, K. and Graehl, J. (1997a). Machine transliteration. *Computational Linguistics*, **24**(4):599–612.

Knight, K. and Graehl, J. (1997b). Machine transliteration. In *Proceedings of the 35th Annual Meeting of the Association for Computational Linguistics (ACL)*.

Koehn, P. (2004a). Pharaoh: a beam search decoder for phrase-based statistical machine translation models. In *Proceedings of the 6th Conference of the Association for Machine Translation in the Americas (AMTA 2004)*, pp. 115–124.

Koehn, P. (2004b). Statistical significance tests for machine translation evaluation. In Lin, D. and Wu, D., editors, *Proceedings of EMNLP 2004*, pp. 388–395, Barcelona, Spain. Association for Computational Linguistics.

Koehn, P. (2005). Europarl: A parallel corpus for statistical machine translation. In *Proceedings of the Tenth Machine Translation Summit (MT Summit X)*, Phuket, Thailand.

Koehn, P., Arun, A., and Hoang, H. (2008). Towards better machine translation quality for the German–English language pairs. In *Proceedings of the Third Workshop on Statistical Machine Translation*, pp. 139–142, Columbus, Ohio. Association for Computational Linguistics.

Koehn, P., Axelrod, A., Mayne, A. B., Callison-Burch, C., Osborne, M., and Talbot, D. (2005). Edinburgh system description for the 2005 IWSLT speech translation evaluation. In *Proceedings of the International Workshop on Spoken Language Translation*.

Koehn, P. and Hoang, H. (2007). Factored translation models. In *Proceedings of the 2007 Joint Conference on Empirical Methods in Natural Language Processing and Computational Natural Language Learning (EMNLP-CoNLL)*, pp. 868–876.

Koehn, P., Hoang, H., Birch, A., *et al.* (2007). Moses: Open source toolkit for statistical machine translation. In *Proceedings of the 45th Annual Meeting of the Association for Computational Linguistics Companion Volume Proceedings of the Demo and Poster Sessions*, pp. 177–180, Prague, Czech Republic. Association for Computational Linguistics.

Koehn, P. and Knight, K. (2000). Estimating word translation probabilities from unrelated monolingual corpora using the EM algorithm. In *Proceedings of Annual Meeting of the American Association of Artificial Intelligence (AAAI)*.

Koehn, P. and Knight, K. (2002a). ChunkMT: Machine translation with richer linguistic knowledge. Unpublished.

Koehn, P. and Knight, K. (2002b). Learning a translation lexicon from monolingual corpora. In *40th Annual Meeting of the Association of Computational Linguistics (ACL), Workshop of Unsupervised Lexicon Construction*.

Koehn, P. and Knight, K. (2003a). Empirical methods for compound splitting. In *Proceedings of the Meeting of the European Chapter of the Association of Computational Linguistics (EACL)*.

Koehn, P. and Knight, K. (2003b). Feature-rich statistical translation of noun phrases. In Hinrichs, E. and Roth, D., editors, *Proceedings of the 41st Annual Meeting of the Association for Computational Linguistics*, pp. 311–318.

Koehn, P. and Monz, C. (2005). Shared task: Statistical machine translation between European languages. In *Proceedings of the ACL Workshop on Building and Using Parallel Texts*, pp. 119–124, Ann Arbor, Michigan. Association for Computational Linguistics.

Koehn, P. and Monz, C. (2006). Manual and automatic evaluation of machine translation between European languages. In *Proceedings of the Workshop on Statistical Machine Translation*, pp. 102–121, New York City. Association for Computational Linguistics.

Koehn, P., Och, F. J., and Marcu, D. (2003). Statistical phrase based translation. In *Proceedings of the Joint Conference on Human Language Technologies and the Annual Meeting of the North American Chapter of the Association of Computational Linguistics (HLT-NAACL)*.

Koehn, P. and Schroeder, J. (2007). Experiments in domain adaptation for statistical machine translation. In *Proceedings of the Second Workshop on Statistical Machine Translation*, pp. 224–227, Prague, Czech Republic. Association for Computational Linguistics.

Komachi, M., Nagata, M., and Matsumoto, Y. (2006). Phrase reordering for statistical machine translation based on predicate-argument structure. In *Proceedings of the International Workshop on Spoken Language Translation*, Kyoto, Japan.

Kueng, T.-L. and Su, K.-Y. (2002). A robust cross-style bilingual sentence alignment model. In *Proceedings of the International Conference on Computational Linguistics (COLING)*.

Kumano, A. and Hirakawa, H. (1994). Building an MT dictionary from parallel texts based on linguistic and statistical information. In *Proceedings of the 15th International Conference on Computational Linguistics (COLING)*.

Kumar, S. and Byrne, W. (2002). Minimum Bayes-risk word alignments of bilingual texts. In *Proceedings of the Conference on Empirical Methods in Natural Language Processing (EMNLP)*, pp. 140–147, Philadelphia. Association for Computational Linguistics.

Kumar, S. and Byrne, W. (2003). A weighted finite state transducer implementation of the alignment template model for statistical machine translation. In Hearst, M. and Ostendorf, M., editors, *HLT-NAACL 2003: Main Proceedings*, pp. 142–149, Edmonton, Alberta, Canada. Association for Computational Linguistics.

Kumar, S. and Byrne, W. (2004). Minimum Bayes-risk decoding for statistical machine translation. In *Proceedings of the Joint Conference on Human Language Technologies and the Annual Meeting of the North American Chapter of the Association of Computational Linguistics (HLT-NAACL)*.

Kumar, S. and Byrne, W. (2005). Local phrase reordering models for statistical machine translation. In *Proceedings of Human Language Technology Conference and Conference on Empirical Methods in Natural Language Processing*, pp. 161–168, Vancouver, British Columbia, Canada. Association for Computational Linguistics.

Kumar, S., Deng, Y., Schafer, C., *et al.* (2004). The Johns Hopkins University 2004 Chinese–English and Arabic–English MT evaluation systems. In *DARPA/NIST Machine Translation Evaluation Workshop*.

Kumar, S., Och, F. J., and Macherey, W. (2007). Improving word alignment with bridge languages. In *Proceedings of the 2007 Joint Conference on Empirical Methods in Natural Language Processing and Computational Natural Language Learning (EMNLP-CoNLL)*, pp. 42–50.

Kuo, J.-S., Li, H., and Yang, Y.-K. (2006). Learning transliteration lexicons from the web. In *Proceedings of the 21st International Conference on Computational Linguistics and 44th Annual Meeting of the Association for Computational Linguistics*, pp. 1129–1136, Sydney, Australia. Association for Computational Linguistics.

Kupiec, J. (1993). An algorithm for finding noun phrase correspondences in bilingual corpora. In *Proceedings of the 31st Annual Meeting of the Association for Computational Linguistics (ACL)*.

Kutsumi, T., Yoshimi, T., Kotani, K., Sata, I., and Isahara, H. (2005). Selection of entries for a bilingual dictionary from aligned translation equivalents using support vector machines. In *Proceedings of the Tenth Machine Translation Summit (MT Summit X)*, Phuket, Thailand.

Labaka, G., Stroppa, N., Way, A., and Sarasola, K. (2007). Comparing rule-based and data-driven approaches to Spanish-to-Basque machine translation. In *Proceedings of the MT Summit XI*.

Lacoste-Julien, S., Taskar, B., Klein, D., and Jordan, M. I. (2006). Word alignment via quadratic assignment. In *Proceedings of the Human Language Technology Conference of the NAACL, Main Conference*, pp. 112–119, New York City, USA. Association for Computational Linguistics.

Lambert, P. and Banchs, R. E. (2005). Data inferred multi-word expressions for statistical machine translation. In *Proceedings of the Tenth Machine Translation Summit (MT Summit X)*, Phuket, Thailand.

Lambert, P. and Banchs, R. E. (2006). Tuning machine translation parameters with SPSA. In *Proceedings of the International Workshop on Spoken Language Translation*, Kyoto, Japan.

Lambert, P., Banchs, R. E., and Crego, J. M. (2007a). Discriminative alignment training without annotated data for machine translation. In *Human Language Technologies 2007: The Conference of the North American Chapter of the Association for Computational Linguistics; Companion Volume, Short Papers*, pp. 85–88, Rochester, New York. Association for Computational Linguistics.

Lambert, P., Costa-jussá, M. R., Crego, J. M., *et al.* (2007b). The TALP Ngram-based SMT system for IWSLT 2007. In *Proceedings of the International Workshop on Spoken Language Translation (IWSLT)*.

Lane, I., Zollmann, A., Nguyen, T. L., *et al.* (2007). The CMU-UKA statistical machine translation systems for IWSLT 2007. In *Proceedings of the International Workshop on Spoken Language Translation (IWSLT)*.

Langlais, P., Cao, G., and Gotti, F. (2005). RALI: SMT shared task system description. In *Proceedings of the ACL Workshop on Building and Using Parallel Texts*, pp. 137–140, Ann Arbor, Michigan. Association for Computational Linguistics.

Langlais, P., Foster, G., and Lapalme, G. (2000). Transtype: a computer-aided translation typing system. In *Proceedings of the ANLP-NAACL 2000 Workshop on Embedded Machine Translation Systems*.

Langlais, P. and Gotti, F. (2006). Phrase-based SMT with shallow tree-phrases. In *Proceedings of the Workshop on Statistical Machine Translation*, pp. 39–46, New York City. Association for Computational Linguistics.

Langlais, P. and Patry, A. (2007). Translating unknown words by analogical learning. In *Proceedings of the 2007 Joint Conference on Empirical Methods in Natural Language Processing and Computational Natural Language Learning (EMNLP-CoNLL)*, pp. 877–886.

Langlais, P. and Simard, M. (2002). Merging example-based and statistical machine translation: An experiment. In Richardson, S. D., editor, *Machine Translation: From Research to Real Users, 5th Conference of the Association for Machine Translation in the Americas, AMTA 2002 Tiburon, CA, USA, October 6-12, 2002, Proceedings*, volume 2499 of *Lecture Notes in Computer Science*. Springer.

Langlais, P., Simard, M., and Veronis, J. (1998). Methods and practical issues in evaluating alignment techniques. In *Proceedings of the 36th Annual Meeting of the Association of Computational Linguistics (ACL)*.

Lardilleux, A. and Lepage, Y. (2008). Multilingual alignments by monolingual string differences. In *COLING 2008: Companion volume: Posters and Demonstrations*, pp. 53–56, Manchester, UK. COLING 2008 Organizing Committee.

Lavie, A. and Agarwal, A. (2007). METEOR: An automatic metric for MT evaluation with high levels of correlation with human judgments. In *Proceedings of the Second Workshop on Statistical Machine Translation*, pp. 228–231, Prague, Czech Republic. Association for Computational Linguistics.

Lavie, A., Parlikar, A., and Ambati, V. (2008). Syntax-driven learning of sub-sentential translation equivalents and translation rules from parsed parallel corpora. In *Proceedings of the ACL-08: HLT Second Workshop on Syntax and Structure in Statistical Translation (SSST-2)*, pp. 87–95, Columbus, Ohio. Association for Computational Linguistics.

Lavie, A., Sagae, K., and Jayaraman, S. (2004). The significance of recall in automatic metrics for MT evaluation. In *Proceedings of the 6th Conference of the Association for Machine Translation in the Americas (AMTA 2004)*, pp. 134–143.

Lavoie, B., White, M., and Korelsky, T. (2001). Inducing lexico-structural transfer rules from parsed bi-texts. In *Workshop on Data-Driven Machine Translation at 39th Annual Meeting of the Association of Computational Linguistics (ACL)*.

Lee, C.-J. and Chang, J. S. (2003). Acquisition of English–Chinese transliterated word pairs from parallel-aligned texts using a statistical machine transliteration model. In Mihalcea, R. and Pedersen, T., editors, *HLT-NAACL 2003 Workshop: Building and Using Parallel Texts: Data Driven Machine Translation and Beyond*, Edmonton, Alberta, Canada. Association for Computational Linguistics.

Lee, C.-J., Chang, J. S., and Chuang, T. C. (2004). Alignment of bilingual named entities in parallel corpora using statistical models. In *Proceedings of the 6th Conference of the Association for Machine Translation in the Americas (AMTA 2004)*, pp. 144–153.

Lee, D., Lee, J., and Lee, G. G. (2007). POSSLT: A Korean to English spoken language translation system. In *Proceedings of Human Language Technologies: The Annual Conference of the North American Chapter of the Association for Computational Linguistics (NAACL-HLT)*, pp. 7–8, Rochester, New York, USA. Association for Computational Linguistics.

Lee, G. A. and Kim, G. C. (2002). Translation selection through source word sense disambiguation and target word selection. In *Proceedings of the International Conference on Computational Linguistics (COLING)*.

Lee, J., Lee, D., and Lee, G. G. (2008). Transformation-based sentence splitting method for statistical machine translation. In *Proceedings of the Workshop on Technologies and Corpora for Asia-Pacific Speech Translation (TCAST)*.

Lee, Y.-S. (2005). IBM statistical machine translation for spoken languages. In *Proceedings of the International Workshop on Spoken Language Translation*.

Lee, Y.-S. (2006). IBM Arabic-to-English translation for IWSLT 2006. In *Proceedings of the International Workshop on Spoken Language Translation*, Kyoto, Japan.

Lepage, Y. and Denoual, E. (2005). ALEPH: an EBMT system based on the preservation of proportional analogies between sentences across languages. In *Proceedings of the International Workshop on Spoken Language Translation*.

Lepage, Y. and Lardilleux, A. (2007). The GREYC machine translation system for the IWSLT 2007 evaluation campaign. In *Proceedings of the International Workshop on Spoken Language Translation (IWSLT)*.

Leusch, G., Ueffing, N., and Ney, H. (2003). A novel string-to-string distance measure with applications to machine translation evaluation. In *Proceedings of the MT Summit IX*.

Leusch, G., Ueffing, N., and Ney, H. (2006). CDER: Efficient MT evaluation using block movements. In *Proceedings of the 11th Conference of the European Chapter of the Association for Computational Linguistics*, Trento, Italy.

Leusch, G., Ueffing, N., Vilar, D., and Ney, H. (2005). Preprocessing and normalization for automatic evaluation of machine translation. In *Proceedings of the ACL Workshop on Intrinsic and Evaluation Measures for Machine Translation*, pp. 17–24, Ann Arbor, Michigan. Association for Computational Linguistics.

Li, B. and Liu, J. (2008). Mining Chinese–English parallel corpora from the web. In *Proceedings of the 3rd International Joint Conference on Natural Language Processing (IJCNLP)*.

Li, C.-H., Li, M., Zhang, D., Li, M., Zhou, M., and Guan, Y. (2007a). A probabilistic approach to syntax-based reordering for statistical machine translation. In *Proceedings of the 45th Annual Meeting of the*

Association of Computational Linguistics, pp. 720–727, Prague, Czech Republic. Association for Computational Linguistics.

Li, C.-H., Zhang, H., Zhang, D., Li, M., and Zhou, M. (2008). An empirical study in source word deletion for phrase-based statistical machine translation. In *Proceedings of the Third Workshop on Statistical Machine Translation*, pp. 1–8, Columbus, Ohio. Association for Computational Linguistics.

Li, H. and Li, C. (2004). Word translation disambiguation using bilingual bootstrapping. *Computational Linguistics*, **30**(1):1–22.

Li, H., Sim, K. C., Kuo, J.-S., and Dong, M. (2007b). Semantic transliteration of personal names. In *Proceedings of the 45th Annual Meeting of the Association of Computational Linguistics*, pp. 120–127, Prague, Czech Republic. Association for Computational Linguistics.

Li, H., Zhang, M., and Su, J. (2004). A joint source-channel model for machine transliteration. In *Proceedings of the 42nd Meeting of the Association for Computational Linguistics (ACL'04), Main Volume*, pp. 159–166, Barcelona, Spain.

Li, Z. and Khudanpur, S. (2008). A scalable decoder for parsing-based machine translation with equivalent language model state maintenance. In *Proceedings of the ACL-08: HLT Second Workshop on Syntax and Structure in Statistical Translation (SSST-2)*, pp. 10–18, Columbus, Ohio. Association for Computational Linguistics.

Liang, P., Bouchard-Côté, A., Klein, D., and Taskar, B. (2006a). An end-to-end discriminative approach to machine translation. In *Proceedings of the 21st International Conference on Computational Linguistics and 44th Annual Meeting of the Association for Computational Linguistics*, pp. 761–768, Sydney, Australia. Association for Computational Linguistics.

Liang, P., Taskar, B., and Klein, D. (2006b). Alignment by agreement. In *Proceedings of the Human Language Technology Conference of the NAACL, Main Conference*, pp. 104–111, New York City, USA. Association for Computational Linguistics.

Lin, C.-Y. and Och, F. J. (2004). ORANGE: a method for evaluating automatic evaluation metrics for machine translation. In *Proceedings of COLING 2004*, pp. 501–507, Geneva, Switzerland. COLING.

Lin, D. (2004). A path-based transfer model for machine translation. In *Proceedings of COLING 2004*, pp. 625–630, Geneva, Switzerland. COLING.

Lin, D. and Cherry, C. (2003). Proalign: Shared task system description. In Mihalcea, R. and Pedersen, T., editors, *HLT-NAACL 2003 Workshop: Building and Using Parallel Texts: Data Driven Machine Translation and Beyond*, Edmonton, Alberta, Canada. Association for Computational Linguistics.

Lin, D., Zhao, S., Van Durme, B., and Paşca, M. (2008). Mining parenthetical translations from the web by word alignment. In *Proceedings of ACL-08: HLT*, pp. 994–1002, Columbus, Ohio. Association for Computational Linguistics.

Lin, T., Wu, J.-C., and Chang, J. S. (2004). Extraction of name and transliteration in monolingual and parallel corpora. In *Proceedings of the 6th Conference of the Association for Machine Translation in the Americas (AMTA 2004)*, pp. 177–186.

Lin, W.-H. and Chen, H.-H. (2002). Backward machine transliteration by learning phonetic similarity. In *Proceedings of the Conference on Natural Language Learning (CoNLL)*.

Lioma, C. and Ounis, I. (2005). Deploying part-of-speech patterns to enhance statistical phrase-based machine translation resources. In *Proceedings of the ACL Workshop on Building and Using Parallel Texts*, pp. 163–166, Ann Arbor, Michigan. Association for Computational Linguistics.

Lita, L. V., Ittycheriah, A., Roukos, S., and Kambhatla, N. (2003). tRuEcasIng. In Hinrichs, E. and Roth, D., editors, *Proceedings of the 41st Annual Meeting of the Association for Computational Linguistics*, pp. 152–159.

Liu, D. and Gildea, D. (2005). Syntactic features for evaluation of machine translation. In *Proceedings of the ACL Workshop on Intrinsic and Extrinsic Evaluation Measures for Machine Translation and/or Summarization*, pp. 25–32, Ann Arbor, Michigan. Association for Computational Linguistics.

Liu, D. and Gildea, D. (2006). Stochastic iterative alignment for machine translation evaluation. In *Proceedings of the COLING/ACL 2006 Main Conference Poster Sessions*, pp. 539–546, Sydney, Australia. Association for Computational Linguistics.

Liu, D. and Gildea, D. (2007). Source-language features and maximum correlation training for machine translation evaluation. In *Human Language Technologies 2007: The Conference of the North American Chapter of the Association for Computational Linguistics; Proceedings of the Main Conference*, pp. 41–48, Rochester, New York. Association for Computational Linguistics.

Liu, D. and Gildea, D. (2008). Improved tree-to-string transducer for machine translation. In *Proceedings of the Third Workshop on Statistical Machine Translation*, pp. 62–69, Columbus, Ohio. Association for Computational Linguistics.

Liu, Y., Huang, Y., Liu, Q., and Lin, S. (2007). Forest-to-string statistical translation rules. In *Proceedings of the 45th Annual Meeting of the Association of Computational Linguistics*, pp. 704–711, Prague, Czech Republic. Association for Computational Linguistics.

Liu, Y., Liu, Q., and Lin, S. (2005). Log-linear models for word alignment. In *Proceedings of the 43rd Annual Meeting of the Association for Computational Linguistics (ACL'05)*, pp. 459–466, Ann Arbor, Michigan. Association for Computational Linguistics.

Llitjos, A. F., Carbonell, J., and Lavie, A. (2007). Improving transfer-based MT systems with automatic refinements. In *Proceedings of the MT Summit XI*.

Lopez, A. (2007). Hierarchical phrase-based translation with suffix arrays. In *Proceedings of the 2007 Joint Conference on Empirical Methods in Natural Language Processing and Computational Natural Language Learning (EMNLP-CoNLL)*, pp. 976–985.

Lopez, A. (2008a). Statistical machine translation. *ACM Computing Surveys*, **40**(3):1–49.

Lopez, A. (2008b). Tera-scale translation models via pattern matching. In *Proceedings of the 22nd International Conference on Computational Linguistics (COLING 2008)*, pp. 505–512, Manchester, UK. COLING 2008 Organizing Committee.

Lopez, A. and Resnik, P. (2006). Word-based alignment, phrase-based translation: What's the link? In *5th Conference of the Association for Machine Translation in the Americas (AMTA)*, Boston, Massachusetts.

Lü, Y., Huang, J., and Liu, Q. (2007). Improving statistical machine translation performance by training data selection and optimization. In *Proceedings of the 2007 Joint Conference on Empirical Methods in Natural Language Processing and Computational Natural Language Learning (EMNLP-CoNLL)*, pp. 343–350.

Lü, Y. and Zhou, M. (2004). Collocation translation acquisition using monolingual corpora. In *Proceedings of the 42nd Meeting of the Association for Computational Linguistics (ACL'04), Main Volume*, pp. 167–174, Barcelona, Spain.

Ma, Y., Ozdowska, S., Sun, Y., and Way, A. (2008). Improving word alignment using syntactic dependencies. In *Proceedings of the ACL-08: HLT Second Workshop on Syntax and Structure in Statistical Translation (SSST-2)*, pp. 69–77, Columbus, Ohio. Association for Computational Linguistics.

Ma, Y., Stroppa, N., and Way, A. (2007). Bootstrapping word alignment via word packing. In *Proceedings of the 45th Annual Meeting of the Association of Computational Linguistics*, pp. 304–311, Prague, Czech Republic. Association for Computational Linguistics.

Macherey, W. and Och, F. J. (2007). An empirical study on computing consensus translations from multiple machine translation systems. In *Proceedings of the 2007 Joint Conference on Empirical Methods in Natural Language Processing and Computational Natural Language Learning (EMNLP-CoNLL)*, pp. 986–995.

Macken, L., Lefever, E., and Hoste, V. (2008). Linguistically-based sub-sentential alignment for terminology extraction from a bilingual automotive corpus. In *Proceedings of the 22nd International Conference on Computational Linguistics (COLING 2008)*, pp. 529–536, Manchester, UK. COLING 2008 Organizing Committee.

Macken, L., Trushkina, J., and Rura, L. (2007). Dutch parallel corpus: MT corpus and translator's aid. In *Proceedings of the MT Summit XI*.

Macklovitch, E. (1994). Using bi-textual alignment for translation validation: the transcheck system. In *Proceedings of the Conference of the Association for Machine Translation in the Americas (AMTA 1994)*.

Macklovitch, E. (2004). The contribution of end-users to the transtype2 project. In *Proceedings of the 6th Conference of the Association for Machine Translation in the Americas (AMTA 2004)*, pp. 197–207.

Macklovitch, E., Nguyen, N. T., and Lapalme, G. (2005). Tracing translations in the making. In *Proceedings of the Tenth Machine Translation Summit (MT Summit X)*, Phuket, Thailand.

Madnani, N., Ayan, N. F., Resnik, P., and Dorr, B. J. (2007). Using paraphrases for parameter tuning in statistical machine translation. In *Proceedings of the Second Workshop on Statistical Machine Translation*, pp. 120–127, Prague, Czech Republic. Association for Computational Linguistics.

Majithia, H., Rennart, P., and Tzoukermann, E. (2005). Rapid ramp-up for statistical machine translation: Minimal training for maximal coverage. In *Proceedings of the Tenth Machine Translation Summit (MT Summit X)*, Phuket, Thailand.

Malik, M. G. A. (2006). Punjabi machine transliteration. In *Proceedings of the 21st International Conference on*

Computational Linguistics and 44th Annual Meeting of the Association for Computational Linguistics, pp. 1137–1144, Sydney, Australia. Association for Computational Linguistics.

Malik, M. G. A., Boitet, C., and Bhattacharyya, P. (2008). Hindi Urdu machine transliteration using finite-state transducers. In *Proceedings of the 22nd International Conference on Computational Linguistics (COLING 2008)*, pp. 537–544, Manchester, UK. COLING 2008 Organizing Committee.

Mann, G. S. and Yarowsky, D. (2001). Multipath translation lexicon induction via bridge languages. In *Proceedings of Annual Meeting of the North American Chapter of the Association of Computational Linguistics (NAACL)*.

Manning, C. D. and Schütze, H. (1999). *Foundations of Statistical Natural Language Processing*. The MIT Press, Cambridge, Massachusetts.

Marcu, D. (2001). Towards a unified approach to memory- and statistical-based machine translation. In *Proceedings of the 39th Annual Meeting of the Association of Computational Linguistics (ACL)*.

Marcu, D., Wang, W., Echihabi, A., and Knight, K. (2006). SPMT: Statistical machine translation with syntactified target language phrases. In *Proceedings of the 2006 Conference on Empirical Methods in Natural Language Processing*, pp. 44–52, Sydney, Australia. Association for Computational Linguistics.

Marcu, D. and Wong, D. (2002). A phrase-based, joint probability model for statistical machine translation. In *Proceedings of the Conference on Empirical Methods in Natural Language Processing (EMNLP)*, pp. 133–139, Philadelphia. Association for Computational Linguistics.

Mariño, J. B., Banchs, R. E., Crego, J. M., *et al.* (2005). Bilingual n-gram statistical machine translation. In *Proceedings of the Tenth Machine Translation Summit (MT Summit X)*, Phuket, Thailand.

Mariño, J. B., Banchs, R. E., Crego, J. M., *et al.* (2006). N-gram-based machine translation. *Computational Linguistics*, 32(4):527–549.

Martin, J., Johnson, H., Farley, B., and Maclachlan, A. (2003). Aligning and using an English–Inuktitut parallel corpus. In Mihalcea, R. and Pedersen, T., editors, *HLT-NAACL 2003 Workshop: Building and Using Parallel Texts: Data Driven Machine Translation and Beyond*, Edmonton, Alberta, Canada. Association for Computational Linguistics.

Martin, J., Mihalcea, R., and Pedersen, T. (2005). Word alignment for languages with scarce resources. In *Proceedings of the ACL Workshop on Building and Using Parallel Texts*, pp. 65–74, Ann Arbor, Michigan. Association for Computational Linguistics.

Martinez, R., Abaitua, J., and Casillas, A. (1999). Aligning tagged bitexts. In *Proceedings of the Sixth Workshop on Very Large Corpora (VLC)*.

Marton, Y. and Resnik, P. (2008). Soft syntactic constraints for hierarchical phrased-based translation. In *Proceedings of ACL-08: HLT*, pp. 1003–1011, Columbus, Ohio. Association for Computational Linguistics.

Matsumoto, Y., Utsuro, T., and Ishimoto, H. (1993). Structural matching of parallel texts. In *Proceedings of the 31st Annual Meeting of the Association for Computational Linguistics (ACL)*.

Matusov, E., Kanthak, S., and Ney, H. (2005). Efficient statistical machine translation with constrained reordering. In *Proceedings of the 10th Conference of the European Association for Machine Translation (EAMT)*, Budapest.

Matusov, E., Mauser, A., and Ney, H. (2006a). Automatic sentence segmentation and punctuation prediction for spoken language translation. In *Proceedings of the International Workshop on Spoken Language Translation*, Kyoto, Japan.

Matusov, E., Ueffing, N., and Ney, H. (2006b). Computing consensus translation for multiple machine translation systems using enhanced hypothesis alignment. In *Proceedings of the 11th Conference of the European Chapter of the Association for Computational Linguistics*, Trento, Italy.

Matusov, E., Zens, R., and Ney, H. (2004). Symmetric word alignments for statistical machine translation. In *Proceedings of COLING 2004*, pp. 219–225, Geneva, Switzerland. COLING.

Mauser, A., Vilar, D., Leusch, G., Zhang, Y., and Ney, H. (2007). The RWTH machine translation system for IWSLT 2007. In *Proceedings of the International Workshop on Spoken Language Translation (IWSLT)*.

Mauser, A., Zens, R., Matusov, E., Hasan, S., and Ney, H. (2006). The RWTH statistical machine translation system for the IWSLT 2006 evaluation. In *Proceedings of the International Workshop on Spoken Language Translation*, Kyoto, Japan.

May, J. and Knight, K. (2007). Syntactic re-alignment models for machine translation. In *Proceedings of the 2007 Joint Conference on Empirical Methods in Natural Language Processing and Computational Natural Language Learning (EMNLP-CoNLL)*, pp. 360–368.

McNamee, P. and Mayfield, J. (2006). Translation of multiword expressions using parallel suffix arrays. In

5th Conference of the Association for Machine Translation in the Americas (AMTA), Boston, Massachusetts.

Melamed, I. D. (1995). Automatic evaluation and uniform filter cascades for inducing n-best translation lexicons. In *Proceedings of the Third Workshop on Very Large Corpora (VLC)*.

Melamed, I. D. (1996a). Automatic construction of clean broad-coverage translation lexicons. In *Proceedings of the Conference of the Association for Machine Translation in the Americas*.

Melamed, I. D. (1996b). Automatic detection of omissions in translations. In *Proceedings of the 16th International Conference on Computational Linguistics (COLING)*.

Melamed, I. D. (1996c). A geometric approach to mapping bitext correspondence. In *Proceedings of the Conference on Empirical Methods in Natural Language Processing (EMNLP)*.

Melamed, I. D. (1997a). Automatic discovery of non-compositional compounds in parallel data. In *Proceedings of the Conference on Empirical Methods in Natural Language Processing (EMNLP)*.

Melamed, I. D. (1997b). A portable algorithm for mapping bitext correspondence. In *Proceedings of the 35th Annual Meeting of the Association for Computational Linguistics (ACL)*.

Melamed, I. D. (1997c). A word-to-word model of translational equivalence. In *Proceedings of the 35th Annual Meeting of the Association for Computational Linguistics (ACL)*.

Melamed, I. D. (1999). Bitext maps and alignment via pattern recognition. *Computational Linguistics*, 25(1):107–130.

Melamed, I. D. (2000). Models of translational equivalence among words. *Computational Linguistics*, 26(2):221–249.

Melamed, I. D. (2003). Multitext grammars and synchronous parsers. In *Proceedings of the Joint Conference on Human Language Technologies and the Annual Meeting of the North American Chapter of the Association of Computational Linguistics (HLT-NAACL)*.

Melamed, I. D. (2004). Statistical machine translation by parsing. In *Proceedings of the 42nd Meeting of the Association for Computational Linguistics (ACL'04), Main Volume*, pp. 653–660, Barcelona, Spain.

Melamed, I. D., Green, R., and Turian, J. P. (2003). Precision and recall in machine translation. In *Proceedings of the Joint Conference on Human Language Technologies and the Annual Meeting of the North American Chapter*

of the Association of Computational Linguistics (HLT-NAACL).

Melamed, I. D., Satta, G., and Wellington, B. (2004). Generalized multitext grammars. In *Proceedings of the 42nd Meeting of the Association for Computational Linguistics (ACL'04), Main Volume*, pp. 661–668, Barcelona, Spain.

Mellebeek, B., Owczarzak, K., Groves, D., van Genabith, J., and Way, A. (2006). A syntactic skeleton for statistical machine translation. In *Proceedings of the 11th Conference of the European Association for Machine Translation (EAMT)*, Oslo, Norway.

Menezes, A. and Quirk, C. (2005a). Dependency treelet translation: The convergence of statistical and example-based machine-translation? In *Proceedings of the Workshop on Example-based Machine Translation at MT Summit X*, Phuket, Thailand.

Menezes, A. and Quirk, C. (2005b). Microsoft research treelet translation system: IWSLT evaluation. In *Proceedings of the International Workshop on Spoken Language Translation*.

Menezes, A. and Quirk, C. (2007). Using dependency order templates to improve generality in translation. In *Proceedings of the Second Workshop on Statistical Machine Translation*, pp. 1–8, Prague, Czech Republic. Association for Computational Linguistics.

Menezes, A. and Richardson, S. D. (2001). A best-first alignment algorithm for automatic extraction of transfer mappings from bilingual corpora. In *Workshop on Data-Driven Machine Translation at 39th Annual Meeting of the Association of Computational Linguistics (ACL)*.

Menezes, A., Toutanova, K., and Quirk, C. (2006). Microsoft research treelet translation system: NAACL 2006 Europarl evaluation. In *Proceedings of the Workshop on Statistical Machine Translation*, pp. 158–161, New York City. Association for Computational Linguistics.

Mermer, C., Kaya, H., and Dogan, M. U. (2007). The TÜBITAK-UEKAE statistical machine translation system for IWSLT 2007. In *Proceedings of the International Workshop on Spoken Language Translation (IWSLT)*.

Mi, H., Huang, L., and Liu, Q. (2008). Forest-based translation. In *Proceedings of ACL-08: HLT*, pp. 192–199, Columbus, Ohio. Association for Computational Linguistics.

Mihalcea, R. and Pedersen, T. (2003). An evaluation exercise for word alignment. In *Proceedings of the HLT-NAACL 2003 Workshop on Building and Using Parallel Texts: Data Driven Machine Translation and Beyond*.

Miller, K. J. and Vanni, M. (2005). Inter-rater agreement measures, and the refinement of metrics in the PLATO MT evaluation paradigm. In *Proceedings of the Tenth Machine Translation Summit (MT Summit X)*, Phuket, Thailand.

Minkov, E., Toutanova, K., and Suzuki, H. (2007). Generating complex morphology for machine translation. In *Proceedings of the 45th Annual Meeting of the Association of Computational Linguistics*, pp. 128–135, Prague, Czech Republic. Association for Computational Linguistics.

Mohit, B. and Hwa, R. (2007). Localization of difficult-to-translate phrases. In *Proceedings of the Second Workshop on Statistical Machine Translation*, pp. 248–255, Prague, Czech Republic. Association for Computational Linguistics.

Moore, R. C. (2001). Towards a simple and accurate statistical approach to learning translation relationships among words. In *Workshop on Data-Driven Machine Translation at 39th Annual Meeting of the Association of Computational Linguistics (ACL)*.

Moore, R. C. (2002). Fast and accurate sentence alignment of bilingual corpora. In Richardson, S. D., editor, *Machine Translation: From Research to Real Users, 5th Conference of the Association for Machine Translation in the Americas, AMTA 2002 Tiburon, CA, USA, October 6-12, 2002, Proceedings*, volume 2499 of *Lecture Notes in Computer Science*. Springer.

Moore, R. C. (2003). Learning translations of named-entity phrases from parallel corpora. In *Proceedings of Meeting of the European Chapter of the Association of Computational Linguistics (EACL)*.

Moore, R. C. (2004). Improving IBM word alignment model 1. In *Proceedings of the 42nd Meeting of the Association for Computational Linguistics (ACL'04), Main Volume*, pp. 518–525, Barcelona, Spain.

Moore, R. C. (2005). A discriminative framework for bilingual word alignment. In *Proceedings of Human Language Technology Conference and Conference on Empirical Methods in Natural Language Processing*, pp. 81–88, Vancouver, British Columbia, Canada. Association for Computational Linguistics.

Moore, R. C. and Quirk, C. (2007a). Faster beam-search decoding for phrasal statistical machine translation. In *Proceedings of the MT Summit XI*.

Moore, R. C. and Quirk, C. (2007b). An iteratively-trained segmentation-free phrase translation model for statistical machine translation. In *Proceedings of the Second Workshop on Statistical Machine Translation*, pp. 112–119, Prague, Czech Republic. Association for Computational Linguistics.

Moore, R. C. and Quirk, C. (2008). Random restarts in minimum error rate training for statistical machine translation. In *Proceedings of the 22nd International Conference on Computational Linguistics (COLING 2008)*, pp. 585–592, Manchester, UK. COLING 2008 Organizing Committee.

Moore, R. C., Yih, W.-t., and Bode, A. (2006). Improved discriminative bilingual word alignment. In *Proceedings of the 21st International Conference on Computational Linguistics and 44th Annual Meeting of the Association for Computational Linguistics*, pp. 513–520, Sydney, Australia. Association for Computational Linguistics.

Munteanu, D. S., Fraser, A., and Marcu, D. (2004). Improved machine translation performance via parallel sentence extraction from comparable corpora. In *Proceedings of the Joint Conference on Human Language Technologies and the Annual Meeting of the North American Chapter of the Association of Computational Linguistics (HLT-NAACL)*.

Munteanu, D. S. and Marcu, D. (2002). Processing comparable corpora with bilingual suffix trees. In *Proceedings of the Conference on Empirical Methods in Natural Language Processing (EMNLP)*, pp. 289–295, Philadelphia. Association for Computational Linguistics.

Munteanu, D. S. and Marcu, D. (2005). Improving machine translation performance by exploiting non-parallel corpora. *Computational Linguistics*, 31(4):505–530.

Munteanu, D. S. and Marcu, D. (2006). Extracting parallel sub-sentential fragments from non-parallel corpora. In *Proceedings of the 21st International Conference on Computational Linguistics and 44th Annual Meeting of the Association for Computational Linguistics*, pp. 81–88, Sydney, Australia. Association for Computational Linguistics.

Murakami, J., Tokuhisa, M., and Ikehara, S. (2007). Statistical machine translation using large J/E parallel corpus and long phrase tables. In *Proceedings of the International Workshop on Spoken Language Translation (IWSLT)*.

Murata, M., Uchimoto, K., Ma, Q., and Isahara, H. (2001). Using a support-vector machine for Japanese-to-English translation of tense, aspect, and modality. In *Workshop on Data-Driven Machine Translation at 39th Annual Meeting of the Association of Computational Linguistics (ACL)*.

Nagata, M., Saito, K., Yamamoto, K., and Ohashi, K. (2006). A clustered global phrase reordering model for statistical machine translation. In *Proceedings of the 21st International Conference on Computational Linguistics and 44th Annual Meeting of the Association for Computational Linguistics*, pp. 713–720, Sydney, Australia. Association for Computational Linguistics.

Nagata, M., Saito, T., and Suzuki, K. (2001). Using the web as a bilingual dictionary. In *Workshop on Data-Driven Machine Translation at 39th Annual Meeting of the Association of Computational Linguistics (ACL)*.

Nakazawa, T., Kun, Y., and Kurohashi, S. (2007). Structural phrase alignment based on consistency criteria. In *Proceedings of the MT Summit XI*.

Nakov, P. (2008). Improving English–Spanish statistical machine translation: Experiments in domain adaptation, sentence paraphrasing, tokenization, and recasing. In *Proceedings of the Third Workshop on Statistical Machine Translation*, pp. 147–150, Columbus, Ohio. Association for Computational Linguistics.

Nakov, P. and Hearst, M. (2007). UCB system description for the WMT 2007 shared task. In *Proceedings of the Second Workshop on Statistical Machine Translation*, pp. 212–215, Prague, Czech Republic. Association for Computational Linguistics.

Nelder, J. A. and Mead, R. (1965). A simplex method for function minimization. *Computing Journal*, 7(4):308–313.

Nelken, R. and Shieber, S. M. (2006). Towards robust context-sensitive sentence alignment for monolingual corpora. In *Proceedings of the 11th Conference of the European Chapter of the Association for Computational Linguistics*, Trento, Italy.

Nesson, R., Satta, G., and Shieber, S. M. (2008). Optimal *k*-arization of synchronous tree-adjoining grammar. In *Proceedings of ACL-08: HLT*, pp. 604–612, Columbus, Ohio. Association for Computational Linguistics.

Nesson, R., Shieber, S. M., and Rush, A. (2006). Induction of probabilistic synchronous tree-insertion grammars for machine translation. In *5th Conference of the Association for Machine Translation in the Americas (AMTA)*, Boston, Massachusetts.

Ney, H. (2001). Stochastic modelling: From pattern classification to language translation. In *Workshop on Data-Driven Machine Translation at 39th Annual Meeting of the Association of Computational Linguistics (ACL)*.

Ney, H., Och, F. J., and Vogel, S. (2001). The RWTH system for statistical translation of spoken dialogues. In *Proceedings of the First International Conference on Human Language Technology Research*.

Nguyen, P., Mahajan, M., and He, X. (2007). Training non-parametric features for statistical machine translation. In *Proceedings of the Second Workshop on Statistical Machine Translation*, pp. 72–79, Prague, Czech Republic. Association for Computational Linguistics.

Nguyen, T. P. and Shimazu, A. (2006). Improving phrase-based statistical machine translation with morpho-syntactic analysis and transformation. In *5th Conference of the Association for Machine Translation in the Americas (AMTA)*, Boston, Massachusetts.

Nguyen, T. P., Shimazu, A., Ho, T. B., Nguyen, M. L., and Nguyen, V. V. (2008). A tree-to-string phrase-based model for statistical machine translation. In *CoNLL 2008: Proceedings of the Twelfth Conference on Computational Natural Language Learning*, pp. 143–150, Manchester, England. COLING 2008 Organizing Committee.

Niehues, J. and Vogel, S. (2008). Discriminative word alignment via alignment matrix modeling. In *Proceedings of the Third Workshop on Statistical Machine Translation*, pp. 18–25, Columbus, Ohio. Association for Computational Linguistics.

Nießen, S. and Ney, H. (2001). Toward hierarchical models for statistical machine translation of inflected languages. In *Workshop on Data-Driven Machine Translation at 39th Annual Meeting of the Association of Computational Linguistics (ACL)*, pp. 47–54.

Nießen, S. and Ney, H. (2004). Statistical machine translation with scarce resources using morpho-syntactic information. *Computational Linguistics*, 30(2):181–204.

Nießen, S., Vogel, S., Ney, H., and Tillmann, C. (1998). A DP based search algorithm for statistical machine translation. In *Proceedings of the 36th Annual Meeting of the Association of Computational Linguistics (ACL)*.

Nightingale, S. and Tanaka, H. (2003). Comparing the sentence alignment yield from two news corpora using a dictionary-based alignment system. In Mihalcea, R. and Pedersen, T., editors, *HLT-NAACL 2003 Workshop: Building and Using Parallel Texts: Data Driven Machine Translation and Beyond*, Edmonton, Alberta, Canada. Association for Computational Linguistics.

Nikoulina, V. and Dymetman, M. (2008a). Experiments in discriminating phrase-based translations on the basis of syntactic coupling features. In *Proceedings of the ACL-08: HLT Second Workshop on Syntax and Structure in Statistical Translation (SSST-2)*, pp. 55–60,

Columbus, Ohio. Association for Computational Linguistics.

Nikoulina, V. and Dymetman, M. (2008b). Using syntactic coupling features for discriminating phrase-based translations (WMT-08 shared translation task). In *Proceedings of the Third Workshop on Statistical Machine Translation*, pp. 159–162, Columbus, Ohio. Association for Computational Linguistics.

Nomoto, T. (2003). Predictive models of performance in multi-engine machine translation. In *Proceedings of the MT Summit IX*.

Oard, D. and Och, F. J. (2003). Rapid response machine translation for unexpected languages. In *Proceedings of the MT Summit IX*.

Och, F. J. (2002). *Statistical Machine Translation: From Single-Word Models to Alignment Templates*. PhD thesis, RWTH Aachen, Germany.

Och, F. J. (2003). Minimum error rate training in statistical machine translation. In Hinrichs, E. and Roth, D., editors, *Proceedings of the 41st Annual Meeting of the Association for Computational Linguistics*, pp. 160–167.

Och, F. J. (2005). The Google statistical machine translation system for the 2005 NIST MT evaluation. In *DARPA/NIST Machine Translation Evaluation Workshop*.

Och, F. J., Gildea, D., Khudanpur, S., *et al.* (2004). A smorgasbord of features for statistical machine translation. In *Proceedings of the Joint Conference on Human Language Technologies and the Annual Meeting of the North American Chapter of the Association of Computational Linguistics (HLT-NAACL)*.

Och, F. J. and Ney, H. (2000). Improved statistical alignment models. In *Proceedings of the 38th Annual Meeting of the Association of Computational Linguistics (ACL)*.

Och, F. J. and Ney, H. (2002). Discriminative training and maximum entropy models for statistical machine translation. In *Proceedings of the 40th Annual Meeting of the Association of Computational Linguistics (ACL)*.

Och, F. J. and Ney, H. (2003). A systematic comparison of various statistical alignment models. *Computational Linguistics*, 29(1):19–52.

Och, F. J. and Ney, H. (2004). The alignment template approach to statistical machine translation. *Computational Linguistics*, 30(4):417–449.

Och, F. J., Tillmann, C., and Ney, H. (1999). Improved alignment models for statistical machine translation. In *Proceedings of the Joint Conference of Empirical Methods in Natural Language Processing and Very Large Corpora (EMNLP-VLC)*, pp. 20–28.

Och, F. J., Ueffing, N., and Ney, H. (2001). An efficient A* search algorithm for statistical machine translation. In *Workshop on Data-Driven Machine Translation at 39th Annual Meeting of the Association of Computational Linguistics (ACL)*.

Och, F. J. and Weber, H. (1998). Improving statistical natural language translation with categories and rules. In *Proceedings of the 36th Annual Meeting of the Association of Computational Linguistics (ACL)*.

Och, F. J., Zens, R., and Ney, H. (2003). Efficient search for interactive statistical machine translation. In *Proceedings of Meeting of the European Chapter of the Association of Computational Linguistics (EACL)*.

Oflazer, K. and Durgar El-Kahlout, I. (2007). Exploring different representational units in English-to-Turkish statistical machine translation. In *Proceedings of the Second Workshop on Statistical Machine Translation*, pp. 25–32, Prague, Czech Republic. Association for Computational Linguistics.

Oh, J.-H. and Choi, K.-S. (2002). An English–Korean transliteration model using pronunciation and contextual rules. In *Proceedings of the International Conference on Computational Linguistics (COLING)*.

Oh, J.-H. and Isahara, H. (2007). Machine transliteration using multiple transliteration engines and hypothesis re-ranking. In *Proceedings of the MT Summit XI*.

Ohashi, K., Yamamoto, K., Saito, K., and Nagata, M. (2005). NUT-NTT statistical machine translation system for IWSLT 2005. In *Proceedings of the International Workshop on Spoken Language Translation*.

Ohtake, K., Sekiguchi, Y., and Yamamoto, K. (2004). Detecting transliterated orthographic variants via two similarity metrics. In *Proceedings of COLING 2004*, pp. 709–715, Geneva, Switzerland. COLING.

Okuma, H., Yamamoto, H., and Sumita, E. (2007). Introducing translation dictionary into phrase-based SMT. In *Proceedings of the MT Summit XI*.

Olteanu, M., Davis, C., Volosen, I., and Moldovan, D. (2006a). Phramer – an open source statistical phrase-based translator. In *Proceedings of the Workshop on Statistical Machine Translation*, pp. 146–149, New York City. Association for Computational Linguistics.

Olteanu, M., Suriyentrakorn, P., and Moldovan, D. (2006b). Language models and reranking for machine translation. In *Proceedings of the Workshop on Statistical Machine Translation*, pp. 150–153, New York City. Association for Computational Linguistics.

Orliac, B. and Dillinger, M. (2003). Collocation extraction for machine translation. In *Proceedings of the MT Summit IX*.

Ortiz-Martínez, D., García-Varea, I., and Casacuberta, F. (2005). Thot: a toolkit to train phrase-based statistical translation models. In *Proceedings of the Tenth Machine Translation Summit (MT Summit X)*, Phuket, Thailand.

Ortiz-Martínez, D., García-Varea, I., and Casacuberta, F. (2006). Generalized stack decoding algorithms for statistical machine translation. In *Proceedings on the Workshop on Statistical Machine Translation*, pp. 64–71, New York City. Association for Computational Linguistics.

Otero, P. G. (2005). Extraction of translation equivalents from parallel corpora using sense-sensitive contexts. In *Proceedings of the 10th Conference of the European Association for Machine Translation (EAMT)*, Budapest.

Otero, P. G. (2007). Learning bilingual lexicons from comparable English and Spanish corpora. In *Proceedings of the MT Summit XI*.

Owczarzak, K., Groves, D., van Genabith, J., and Way, A. (2006a). Contextual bitext-derived paraphrases in automatic MT evaluation. In *Proceedings of the Workshop on Statistical Machine Translation*, pp. 86–93, New York City. Association for Computational Linguistics.

Owczarzak, K., Mellebeek, B., Groves, D., van Genabith, J., and Way, A. (2006b). Wrapper syntax for example-based machine translation. In *5th Conference of the Association for Machine Translation in the Americas (AMTA)*, Boston, Massachusetts.

Owczarzak, K., van Genabith, J., and Way, A. (2007a). Dependency-based automatic evaluation for machine translation. In *Proceedings of SSST, NAACL-HLT 2007 / AMTA Workshop on Syntax and Structure in Statistical Translation*, pp. 80–87, Rochester, New York. Association for Computational Linguistics.

Owczarzak, K., van Genabith, J., and Way, A. (2007b). Labelled dependencies in machine translation evaluation. In *Proceedings of the Second Workshop on Statistical Machine Translation*, pp. 104–111, Prague, Czech Republic. Association for Computational Linguistics.

Palmer, M., Xue, N., Babko-Malaya, O., Chen, J., and Snyder, B. (2005). A parallel Proposition Bank II for Chinese and English. In *Proceedings of the Workshop on Frontiers in Corpus Annotations II: Pie in the Sky*, pp. 61–67, Ann Arbor, Michigan. Association for Computational Linguistics.

Pang, W., Yang, Z., Chen, Z., Wei, W., Xu, B., and Zong, C. (2005). The CASIA phrase-based machine translation system. In *Proceedings of the International Workshop on Spoken Language Translation*.

Papageorgiou, H., Cranias, L., and Piperidis, S. (1994). Automatic alignment in parallel corpora. In *Proceedings of the 32nd Annual Meeting of the Association for Computational Linguistics (ACL)*.

Papineni, K., Roukos, S., Ward, T., and Zhu, W.-J. (2001). BLEU: a method for automatic evaluation of machine translation. Technical Report RC22176(W0109-022), IBM Research Report.

Patry, A., Gotti, F., and Langlais, P. (2006). Mood at work: Ramses versus Pharaoh. In *Proceedings of the Workshop on Statistical Machine Translation*, pp. 126–129, New York City. Association for Computational Linguistics.

Patry, A., Langlais, P., and Béchet, F. (2007). MISTRAL: A lattice translation system for IWSLT 2007. In *Proceedings of the International Workshop on Spoken Language Translation (IWSLT)*.

Paul, M. (2006). Overview of the IWSLT06 evaluation campaign. In *Proceedings of the International Workshop on Spoken Language Translation*, Kyoto, Japan.

Paul, M., Doi, T., Hwang, Y.-S., Imamura, K., Okuma, H., and Sumita, E. (2005). Nobody is perfect: ATR's hybrid approach to spoken language translation. In *Proceedings of the International Workshop on Spoken Language Translation*.

Paul, M. and Sumita, E. (2006). Exploiting variant corpora for machine translation. In *Proceedings of the Human Language Technology Conference of the NAACL, Companion Volume: Short Papers*, pp. 113–116, New York City, USA. Association for Computational Linguistics.

Paul, M., Sumita, E., and Yamamoto, S. (2002). Corpus-based generation of numeral classifiers using phrase alignment. In *Proceedings of the International Conference on Computational Linguistics (COLING)*.

Paul, M., Sumita, E., and Yamamoto, S. (2004). Example-based rescoring of statistical machine translation output. In *Proceedings of the Joint Conference on Human Language Technologies and the Annual Meeting of the North American Chapter of the Association of Computational Linguistics (HLT-NAACL)*.

Paulik, M., Rottmann, K., Niehues, J., Hildebrand, A. S., and Vogel, S. (2007). The ISL phrase-based MT system for the 2007 ACL workshop on statistical machine translation. In *Proceedings of the Second Workshop on*

Statistical Machine Translation, pp. 197–202, Prague, Czech Republic. Association for Computational Linguistics.

Pérez, A., González, M. T., Torres, M. I., and Casacuberta, F. (2007a). An integrated architecture for speech-input multi-target machine translation. In *Human Language Technologies 2007: The Conference of the North American Chapter of the Association for Computational Linguistics; Companion Volume, Short Papers*, pp. 133–136, Rochester, New York. Association for Computational Linguistics.

Pérez, A., González, M. T., Torres, M. I., and Casacuberta, F. (2007b). Speech-input multi-target machine translation. In *Proceedings of the Second Workshop on Statistical Machine Translation*, pp. 56–63, Prague, Czech Republic. Association for Computational Linguistics.

Pérez, A., Guijarrubia, V., Justo, R., Torres, M. I., and Casacuberta, F. (2007). A comparison of linguistically and statistically enhanced models for speech-to-speech machine translation. In *Proceedings of the International Workshop on Spoken Language Translation (IWSLT)*.

Pianta, E. and Bentivogli, L. (2004). Knowledge intensive word alignment with KNOWA. In *Proceedings of COLING 2004*, pp. 1086–1092, Geneva, Switzerland. COLING.

Pierce, J. R. and Carroll, J. B. (1966). Languages and machines — computers in translation and linguistics. Technical report, Automatic Language Processing Advisory Committe (ALPAC), National Academy of Sciences.

Popescu-Belis, A. (2003). An experiment in comparative evaluation: humans vs. computers. In *Proceedings of the MT Summit IX*.

Popovic, M., de Gispert, A., Gupta, D., *et al.* (2006). Morpho-syntactic information for automatic error analysis of statistical machine translation output. In *Proceedings of the Workshop on Statistical Machine Translation*, pp. 1–6, New York City. Association for Computational Linguistics.

Popovic, M. and Ney, H. (2004). Improving word alignment quality using morpho-syntactic information. In *Proceedings of COLING 2004*, pp. 310–314, Geneva, Switzerland. COLING.

Popovic, M. and Ney, H. (2007). Word error rates: Decomposition over POS classes and applications for error analysis. In *Proceedings of the Second Workshop on Statistical Machine Translation*, pp. 48–55, Prague, Czech Republic. Association for Computational Linguistics.

Popović, M., Vilar, D., Ney, H., Jovičić, S., and Šarić, Z. (2005). Augmenting a small parallel text with morpho-syntactic language. In *Proceedings of the ACL Workshop on Building and Using Parallel Texts*, pp. 41–48, Ann Arbor, Michigan. Association for Computational Linguistics.

Press, W. H., Teukolsky, S. A., Vetterling, W. T., and Flannery, B. P. (1997). *Numerical Recipes: The Art of Scientific Computing*. Cambridge University Press, Cambridge.

Pytlik, B. and Yarowsky, D. (2006). Machine translation for languages lacking bitext via multilingual gloss transduction. In *5th Conference of the Association for Machine Translation in the Americas (AMTA)*, Boston, Massachusetts.

Qu, Y. and Grefenstette, G. (2004). Finding ideographic representations of Japanese names written in latin script via language identification and corpus validation. In *Proceedings of the 42nd Meeting of the Association for Computational Linguistics (ACL'04), Main Volume*, pp. 183–190, Barcelona, Spain.

Quirk, C. and Corston-Oliver, S. (2006). The impact of parse quality on syntactically-informed statistical machine translation. In *Proceedings of the 2006 Conference on Empirical Methods in Natural Language Processing*, pp. 62–69, Sydney, Australia. Association for Computational Linguistics.

Quirk, C. and Menezes, A. (2006). Do we need phrases? Challenging the conventional wisdom in statistical machine translation. In *Proceedings of the Human Language Technology Conference of the NAACL, Main Conference*, pp. 9–16, New York City, USA. Association for Computational Linguistics.

Quirk, C., Menezes, A., and Cherry, C. (2005). Dependency treelet translation: Syntactically informed phrasal SMT. In *Proceedings of the 43rd Annual Meeting of the Association for Computational Linguistics (ACL'05)*, pp. 271–279, Ann Arbor, Michigan. Association for Computational Linguistics.

Quirk, C., Udupa, R., and Menezes, A. (2007). Generative models of noisy translations with applications to parallel fragment extraction. In *Proceedings of the MT Summit XI*.

Ramanathan, A., Hegde, J., Shah, R. M., Bhattacharyya, P., and M, S. (2008). Simple syntactic and morphological processing can help English–Hindi statistical machine translation. In *Proceedings of the 3rd International Joint Conference on Natural Language Processing (IJCNLP)*.

Ramiírez, J., Asahara, M., and Matsumoto, Y. (2008). Japanese–Spanish thesaurus construction using English as a pivot. In *Proceedings of the 3rd International Joint Conference on Natural Language Processing (IJCNLP)*.

Rapp, R. (1995). Identifying word translations in non-parallel texts. In *Proceedings of the 33rd Annual Meeting of the Association for Computational Linguistics (ACL)*.

Rapp, R. (1999). Automatic identification of word translations from unrelated English and German corpora. In *Proceedings of the 37th Annual Meeting of the Association of Computational Linguistics (ACL)*, pp. 519–526.

Reeder, F. (2004). Investigation of intelligibility judgments. In *Proceedings of the 6th Conference of the Association for Machine Translation in the Americas (AMTA 2004)*, pp. 227–235.

Reeder, F. (2006a). Direct application of a language learner test to MT evaluation. In *5th Conference of the Association for Machine Translation in the Americas (AMTA)*, Boston, Massachusetts.

Reeder, F. (2006b). Measuring MT adequacy using latent semantic analysis. In *5th Conference of the Association for Machine Translation in the Americas (AMTA)*, Boston, Massachusetts.

Ren, D., Wu, H., and Wang, H. (2007). Improving statistical word alignment with various clues. In *Proceedings of the MT Summit XI*.

Resnik, P. (1999). Mining the web for bilingual text. In *Proceedings of the 37th Annual Meeting of the Association of Computational Linguistics (ACL)*.

Resnik, P. and Melamed, I. D. (1997). Semi-automatic acquisition of domain-specific translation lexicons. In *Fifth Conference on Applied Natural Language Processing (ANLP)*.

Riesa, J. and Yarowsky, D. (2006). Minimally supervised morphological segmentation with applications to machine translation. In *5th Conference of the Association for Machine Translation in the Americas (AMTA)*, Boston, Massachusetts.

Riezler, S. and Maxwell, J. T. (2005). On some pitfalls in automatic evaluation and significance testing for MT. In *Proceedings of the ACL Workshop on Intrinsic and Extrinsic Evaluation Measures for Machine Translation and/or Summarization*, pp. 57–64, Ann Arbor, Michigan. Association for Computational Linguistics.

Riezler, S. and Maxwell, J. T. (2006). Grammatical machine translation. In *Proceedings of the Human Language Technology Conference of the NAACL, Main Conference*, pp. 248–255, New York City, USA. Association for Computational Linguistics.

Robitaille, X., Sasaki, Y., Tonoike, M., Sato, S., and Utsuro, T. (2006). Compiling French-Japanese terminologies from the web. In *Proceedings of the 11th Conference of the European Chapter of the Association for Computational Linguistics*, Trento, Italy.

Rodríguez, L., García-Varea, I., and Gámez, J. A. (2006). Searching for alignments in SMT. A novel approach based on an estimation of distribution algorithm. In *Proceedings of the Workshop on Statistical Machine Translation*, pp. 47–54, New York City. Association for Computational Linguistics.

Rosti, A.-V. I., Matsoukas, S., and Schwartz, R. (2007a). Improved word-level system combination for machine translation. In *Proceedings of the 45th Annual Meeting of the Association of Computational Linguistics*, pp. 312–319, Prague, Czech Republic. Association for Computational Linguistics.

Rosti, A.-V. I., Xiang, B., Matsoukas, S., Schwartz, R., Ayan, N. F., and Dorr, B. J. (2007b). Combining output from multiple machine translation systems. In *Human Language Technologies 2007: The Conference of the North American Chapter of the Association for Computational Linguistics; Proceedings of the Main Conference*, pp. 228–235, Rochester, New York. Association for Computational Linguistics.

Rosti, A.-V. I., Zhang, B., Matsoukas, S., and Schwartz, R. (2008). Incremental hypothesis alignment for building confusion networks with application to machine translation system combination. In *Proceedings of the Third Workshop on Statistical Machine Translation*, pp. 183–186, Columbus, Ohio. Association for Computational Linguistics.

Sadat, F. and Habash, N. (2006). Combination of Arabic preprocessing schemes for statistical machine translation. In *Proceedings of the 21st International Conference on Computational Linguistics and 44th Annual Meeting of the Association for Computational Linguistics*, pp. 1–8, Sydney, Australia. Association for Computational Linguistics.

Sadat, F., Johnson, H., Agbago, A., et al. (2005). PORTAGE: A phrase-based machine translation system. In *Proceedings of the ACL Workshop on Building and Using Parallel Texts*, pp. 129–132, Ann Arbor, Michigan. Association for Computational Linguistics.

Sammer, M. and Soderland, S. (2007). Building a sense distinguished multilingual lexicon from monolingual corpora and bilingual lexicons. In *Proceedings of the MT Summit XI*.

Sánchez, J. A. and Benedí, J. M. (2006a). Obtaining word phrases with stochastic inversion translation grammars for phrase-based statistical machine translation. In *Proceedings of the 11th Conference of the European Association for Machine Translation (EAMT)*, Oslo, Norway.

Sánchez, J. A. and Benedí, J. M. (2006b). Stochastic inversion transduction grammars for obtaining word phrases for phrase-based statistical machine translation. In *Proceedings of the Workshop on Statistical Machine Translation*, pp. 130–133, New York City. Association for Computational Linguistics.

Sanchis, A., Juan, A., and Vidal, E. (2007). Estimation of confidence measures for machine translation. In *Proceedings of the MT Summit XI*.

Sarikaya, R. and Deng, Y. (2007). Joint morphological-lexical language modeling for machine translation. In *Human Language Technologies 2007: The Conference of the North American Chapter of the Association for Computational Linguistics; Companion Volume, Short Papers*, pp. 145–148, Rochester, New York. Association for Computational Linguistics.

Sato, K. and Nakanishi, M. (1998). Maximum entropy model learning of the translation rules. In *Proceedings of the 36th Annual Meeting of the Association of Computational Linguistics (ACL)*.

Schafer, C. (2006). Novel probabilistic finite-state transducers for cognate and transliteration modeling. In *5th Conference of the Association for Machine Translation in the Americas (AMTA)*, Boston, Massachusetts.

Schafer, C. and Yarowsky, D. (2002). Inducing translation lexicons via diverse similarity measures and bridge languages. In *Proceedings of the Conference on Natural Language Learning (CoNLL)*.

Schafer, C. and Yarowsky, D. (2003a). Statistical machine translation using coercive two-level syntactic transduction. In Collins, M. and Steedman, M., editors, *Proceedings of the 2003 Conference on Empirical Methods in Natural Language Processing*, pp. 9–16.

Schafer, C. and Yarowsky, D. (2003b). A two-level syntax-based approach to Arabic-English statistical machine translation. In *MT Summit IX Workshop on Machine Translation for Semitic Languages: Issues and Approaches*.

Schiehlen, M. (1998). Learning tense translation from bilingual corpora. In *Proceedings of the 36th Annual Meeting of the Association of Computational Linguistics (ACL)*.

Schrader, B. (2006). ATLAS – a new text alignment architecture. In *Proceedings of the COLING/ACL 2006 Main Conference Poster Sessions*, pp. 715–722, Sydney, Australia. Association for Computational Linguistics.

Schroeder, J. and Koehn, P. (2007). The University of Edinburgh system description for IWSLT 2007. In *Proceedings of the International Workshop on Spoken Language Translation (IWSLT)*.

Schulz, S., Marko, K., Sbrissia, E., Nohama, P., and Hahn, U. (2004). Cognate mapping – a heuristic strategy for the semi-supervised acquisition of a Spanish lexicon from a Portuguese seed lexicon. In *Proceedings of COLING 2004*, pp. 813–819, Geneva, Switzerland. COLING.

Schwenk, H. (2007). Building a statistical machine translation system for French using the Europarl corpus. In *Proceedings of the Second Workshop on Statistical Machine Translation*, pp. 189–192, Prague, Czech Republic. Association for Computational Linguistics.

Schwenk, H., Costa-jussà, M. R., and Fonollosa, J. A. R. (2006a). Continuous space language models for the IWSLT 2006 task. In *Proceedings of the International Workshop on Spoken Language Translation*, Kyoto, Japan.

Schwenk, H., Costa-jussa, M. R., and Fonollosa, J. A. R. (2007). Smooth bilingual *n*-gram translation. In *Proceedings of the 2007 Joint Conference on Empirical Methods in Natural Language Processing and Computational Natural Language Learning (EMNLP-CoNLL)*, pp. 430–438.

Schwenk, H., Dechelotte, D., and Gauvain, J.-L. (2006b). Continuous space language models for statistical machine translation. In *Proceedings of the COLING/ACL 2006 Main Conference Poster Sessions*, pp. 723–730, Sydney, Australia. Association for Computational Linguistics.

Schwenk, H., Fouet, J.-B., and Senellart, J. (2008). First steps towards a general purpose French/English statistical machine translation system. In *Proceedings of the Third Workshop on Statistical Machine Translation*, pp. 119–122, Columbus, Ohio. Association for Computational Linguistics.

Seneff, S., Wang, C., and Lee, J. (2006). Combining linguistic and statistical methods for bi-directional English Chinese translation in the flight domain. In *5th Conference of the Association for Machine Translation in the Americas (AMTA)*, Boston, Massachusetts.

Sethy, A., Georgiou, P., and Narayanan, S. (2006). Selecting relevant text subsets from web-data for building topic specific language models. In *Proceedings of the Human*

Language Technology Conference of the NAACL, Companion Volume: Short Papers, pp. 145–148, New York City, USA. Association for Computational Linguistics.

Setiawan, H., Kan, M.-Y., and Li, H. (2007). Ordering phrases with function words. In Proceedings of the 45th Annual Meeting of the Association of Computational Linguistics, pp. 712–719, Prague, Czech Republic. Association for Computational Linguistics.

Setiawan, H., Li, H., and Zhang, M. (2005). Learning phrase translation using level of detail approach. In Proceedings of the Tenth Machine Translation Summit (MT Summit X), Phuket, Thailand.

Shannon, C. E. (1948). A mathematical theory of communication. Bell System Technical Journal, 27(3):379–423.

Shannon, C. E. (1951). Prediction and entropy of printed English. Bell Systems Technical Journal, 30:50–64.

Shen, L., Sarkar, A., and Och, F. J. (2004). Discriminative reranking for machine translation. In Proceedings of the Joint Conference on Human Language Technologies and the Annual Meeting of the North American Chapter of the Association of Computational Linguistics (HLT-NAACL).

Shen, L., Xu, J., and Weischedel, R. (2008). A new string-to-dependency machine translation algorithm with a target dependency language model. In Proceedings of ACL-08: HLT, pp. 577–585, Columbus, Ohio. Association for Computational Linguistics.

Shen, W., Delaney, B., and Anderson, T. (2005). The MIT-LL/AFRL MT system. In Proceedings of the International Workshop on Spoken Language Translation.

Shen, W., Delaney, B., and Anderson, T. (2006a). The MIT-LL/AFRL IWSLT-2006 MT system. In Proceedings of the International Workshop on Spoken Language Translation, Kyoto, Japan.

Shen, W., Delaney, B., Anderson, T., and Slyh, R. (2007a). The MIT-LL/AFRL IWSLT-2007 MT system. In Proceedings of the International Workshop on Spoken Language Translation (IWSLT).

Shen, W., Zens, R., Bertoldi, N., and Federico, M. (2006b). The JHU workshop 2006 IWSLT system. In Proceedings of the International Workshop on Spoken Language Translation, Kyoto, Japan.

Shen, Y., Lo, C.-k., Carpuat, M., and Wu, D. (2007b). HKUST statistical machine translation experiments for IWSLT 2007. In Proceedings of the International Workshop on Spoken Language Translation (IWSLT).

Sherif, T. and Kondrak, G. (2007a). Bootstrapping a stochastic transducer for Arabic-English transliteration extraction. In Proceedings of the 45th Annual Meeting of the Association of Computational Linguistics, pp. 864–871, Prague, Czech Republic. Association for Computational Linguistics.

Sherif, T. and Kondrak, G. (2007b). Substring-based transliteration. In Proceedings of the 45th Annual Meeting of the Association of Computational Linguistics, pp. 944–951, Prague, Czech Republic. Association for Computational Linguistics.

Shieber, S. M. (2007). Probabilistic synchronous tree-adjoining grammars for machine translation: The argument from bilingual dictionaries. In Proceedings of SSST, NAACL-HLT 2007/AMTA Workshop on Syntax and Structure in Statistical Translation, pp. 88–95, Rochester, New York. Association for Computational Linguistics.

Shieber, S. M. and Schabes, Y. (1990). Synchronous tree-adjoining grammars. In 13th International Conference on Computational Linguistics, University of Helsinki, COLING, pp. 253–258.

Shin, J. H., Han, Y. S., and Choi, K.-S. (1996). Bilingual knowledge acquisition from Korean-English parallel corpus using alignment. In Proceedings of the 16th International Conference on Computational Linguistics (COLING).

Simard, M. (1999). Text-translation alignment: Three languages are better than two. In Proceedings of the Joint Conference of Empirical Methods in Natural Language Processing and Very Large Corpora (EMNLP-VLC).

Simard, M., Goutte, C., and Isabelle, P. (2007). Statistical phrase-based post-editing. In Human Language Technologies 2007: The Conference of the North American Chapter of the Association for Computational Linguistics; Proceedings of the Main Conference, pp. 508–515, Rochester, New York. Association for Computational Linguistics.

Simard, M. and Langlais, P. (2003). Statistical translation alignment with compositionality constraints. In Mihalcea, R. and Pedersen, T., editors, HLT-NAACL 2003 Workshop: Building and Using Parallel Texts: Data Driven Machine Translation and Beyond, Edmonton, Alberta, Canada. Association for Computational Linguistics.

Simard, M. and Plamondon, P. (1996). Bilingual sentence alignment: Balancing robustness and accuracy. In Proceedings of the Conference of the Association for Machine Translation in the Americas.

Singh, A. K. and Husain, S. (2005). Comparison, selection and use of sentence alignment algorithms for new language pairs. In *Proceedings of the ACL Workshop on Building and Using Parallel Texts*, pp. 99–106, Ann Arbor, Michigan. Association for Computational Linguistics.

Smadja, F., Hatzivassiloglou, V., and McKeown, K. R. (1996). Translating collocations for bilingual lexicons: A statistical approach. *Computational Linguistics*, **22**(1):1–38.

Smith, D. A. and Eisner, J. (2006a). Minimum risk annealing for training log-linear models. In *Proceedings of the COLING/ACL 2006 Main Conference Poster Sessions*, pp. 787–794, Sydney, Australia. Association for Computational Linguistics.

Smith, D. A. and Eisner, J. (2006b). Quasi-synchronous grammars: Alignment by soft projection of syntactic dependencies. In *Proceedings of the Workshop on Statistical Machine Translation*, pp. 23–30, New York City. Association for Computational Linguistics.

Smith, N. A. (2002). From words to corpora: Recognizing translation. In *Proceedings of the Conference on Empirical Methods in Natural Language Processing (EMNLP)*, pp. 95–102, Philadelphia. Association for Computational Linguistics.

Snover, M., Dorr, B. J., Schwartz, R., Micciulla, L., and Makhoul, J. (2006). A study of translation edit rate with targeted human annotation. In *5th Conference of the Association for Machine Translation in the Americas (AMTA)*, Boston, Massachusetts.

Søgaard, A. (2008). Range concatenation grammars for translation. In *COLING 2008: Companion volume: Posters and Demonstrations*, pp. 101–104, Manchester, UK. COLING 2008 Organizing Committee.

Somers, H. L. (1999). Review article: Example-based machine translation. *Machine Translation*, **14**:113–157.

Soricut, R., Knight, K., and Marcu, D. (2002). Using a large monolingual corpus to improve translation accuracy. In Richardson, S. D., editor, *Machine Translation: From Research to Real Users, 5th Conference of the Association for Machine Translation in the Americas, AMTA 2002 Tiburon, CA, USA, October 6-12, 2002, Proceedings*, volume 2499 of *Lecture Notes in Computer Science*. Springer.

Sproat, R., Tao, T., and Zhai, C. (2006). Named entity transliteration with comparable corpora. In *Proceedings of the 21st International Conference on Computational Linguistics and 44th Annual Meeting of the Association for Computational Linguistics*, pp. 73–80, Sydney, Australia. Association for Computational Linguistics.

Stroppa, N. and Way, A. (2006). MATREX: DCU machine translation system for IWSLT 2006. In *Proceedings of the International Workshop on Spoken Language Translation*, Kyoto, Japan.

Stymne, S., Holmqvist, M., and Ahrenberg, L. (2008). Effects of morphological analysis in translation between German and English. In *Proceedings of the Third Workshop on Statistical Machine Translation*, pp. 135–138, Columbus, Ohio. Association for Computational Linguistics.

Subotin, M. (2008). Generalizing local translation models. In *Proceedings of the ACL-08: HLT Second Workshop on Syntax and Structure in Statistical Translation (SSST-2)*, pp. 28–36, Columbus, Ohio. Association for Computational Linguistics.

Sumita, E., Shimizu, T., and Nakamura, S. (2007). NICT-ATR speech-to-speech translation system. In *Proceedings of the 45th Annual Meeting of the Association for Computational Linguistics Companion Volume Proceedings of the Demo and Poster Sessions*, pp. 25–28, Prague, Czech Republic. Association for Computational Linguistics.

Sun, J., Zhao, T., and Liang, H. (2007). Meta-structure transformation model for statistical machine translation. In *Proceedings of the Second Workshop on Statistical Machine Translation*, pp. 64–71, Prague, Czech Republic. Association for Computational Linguistics.

Sun, L., Jin, Y., Du, L., and Sun, Y. (2000). Word alignment of English–Chinese bilingual corpus based on chucks. In *Proceedings of the Conference on Empirical Methods in Natural Language Processing (EMNLP)*.

Sun, S., Chen, Y., and Li, J. (2008). A re-examination on features in regression based approach to automatic MT evaluation. In *Proceedings of the ACL-08: HLT Student Research Workshop*, pp. 25–30, Columbus, Ohio. Association for Computational Linguistics.

Surcin, S., Hamon, O., Hartley, A., *et al.* (2005). Evaluation of machine translation with predictive metrics beyond BLEU/NIST: CESTA evaluation campaign. In *Proceedings of the Tenth Machine Translation Summit (MT Summit X)*, Phuket, Thailand.

Suzuki, H. and Toutanova, K. (2006). Learning to predict case markers in Japanese. In *Proceedings of the 21st International Conference on Computational Linguistics and 44th Annual Meeting of the Association for Computational Linguistics*, Sydney, Australia. Association for Computational Linguistics.

Talbot, D. and Osborne, M. (2006). Modelling lexical redundancy for machine translation. In *Proceedings of the 21st International Conference on Computational*

Linguistics and 44th Annual Meeting of the Association for Computational Linguistics, pp. 969–976, Sydney, Australia. Association for Computational Linguistics.

Talbot, D. and Osborne, M. (2007a). Randomised language modelling for statistical machine translation. In *Proceedings of the 45th Annual Meeting of the Association of Computational Linguistics*, pp. 512–519, Prague, Czech Republic. Association for Computational Linguistics.

Talbot, D. and Osborne, M. (2007b). Smoothed Bloom filter language models: Tera-scale LMs on the cheap. In *Proceedings of the 2007 Joint Conference on Empirical Methods in Natural Language Processing and Computational Natural Language Learning (EMNLP-CoNLL)*, pp. 468–476.

Tanaka, K. and Iwasaki, H. (1996). Extraction of lexical translations from non-aligned corpora. In *Proceedings of the 16th International Conference on Computational Linguistics (COLING)*.

Tanaka, T. (2002). Measuring the similarity between compound nouns in different languages using non-parallel corpora. In *Proceedings of the International Conference on Computational Linguistics (COLING)*.

Tanaka, T. and Baldwin, T. (2003). Translation selection for Japanese–English noun–noun compounds. In *Proceedings of the MT Summit IX*.

Tantuğ, A. C., Adali, E., and Oflazer, K. (2007a). Machine translation between Turkic languages. In *Proceedings of the 45th Annual Meeting of the Association for Computational Linguistics Companion Volume Proceedings of the Demo and Poster Sessions*, pp. 189–192, Prague, Czech Republic. Association for Computational Linguistics.

Tantuğ, A. C., Adali, E., and Oflazer, K. (2007b). A MT system from Turkmen to Turkish employing finite state and statistical methods. In *Proceedings of the MT Summit XI*.

Tao, T., Yoon, S.-Y., Fister, A., Sproat, R., and Zhai, C. (2006). Unsupervised named entity transliteration using temporal and phonetic correlation. In *Proceedings of the 2006 Conference on Empirical Methods in Natural Language Processing*, pp. 250–257, Sydney, Australia. Association for Computational Linguistics.

Taskar, B., Simon, L.-J., and Klein, D. (2005). A discriminative matching approach to word alignment. In *Proceedings of Human Language Technology Conference and Conference on Empirical Methods in Natural Language Processing*, pp. 73–80, Vancouver,

British Columbia, Canada. Association for Computational Linguistics.

Tiedemann, J. (2003). Combining clues for word alignment. In *Proceedings of Meeting of the European Chapter of the Association of Computational Linguistics (EACL)*.

Tiedemann, J. (2004). Word to word alignment strategies. In *Proceedings of COLING 2004*, pp. 212–218, Geneva, Switzerland. COLING.

Tillmann, C. (2003). A projection extension algorithm for statistical machine translation. In Collins, M. and Steedman, M., editors, *Proceedings of the 2003 Conference on Empirical Methods in Natural Language Processing*, pp. 1–8.

Tillmann, C. (2004). A unigram orientation model for statistical machine translation. In *Proceedings of the Joint Conference on Human Language Technologies and the Annual Meeting of the North American Chapter of the Association of Computational Linguistics (HLT-NAACL)*.

Tillmann, C. (2008). A rule-driven dynamic programming decoder for statistical MT. In *Proceedings of the ACL-08: HLT Second Workshop on Syntax and Structure in Statistical Translation (SSST-2)*, pp. 37–45, Columbus, Ohio. Association for Computational Linguistics.

Tillmann, C. and Ney, H. (2000). Word re-ordering and DP-based search in statistical machine translation. In *Proceedings of the International Conference on Computational Linguistics (COLING)*.

Tillmann, C. and Ney, H. (2003). Word reordering and a dynamic programming beam search algorithm for statistical machine translation. *Computational Linguistics*, **29**(1):97–133.

Tillmann, C., Vogel, S., Ney, H., and Zubiaga, A. (1997). A DP-based search using monotone alignments in statistical translation. In *Proceedings of the 35th Annual Meeting of the Association for Computational Linguistics (ACL)*.

Tillmann, C. and Zhang, T. (2005). A localized prediction model for statistical machine translation. In *Proceedings of the 43rd Annual Meeting of the Association for Computational Linguistics (ACL'05)*, pp. 557–564, Ann Arbor, Michigan. Association for Computational Linguistics.

Tillmann, C. and Zhang, T. (2006). A discriminative global training algorithm for statistical MT. In *Proceedings of the 21st International Conference on Computational Linguistics and 44th Annual Meeting of the Association for Computational Linguistics*, pp. 721–728, Sydney, Australia. Association for Computational Linguistics.

Tinsley, J., Ma, Y., Ozdowska, S., and Way, A. (2008). MaTrEx: The DCU MT system for WMT 2008. In *Proceedings of the Third Workshop on Statistical Machine Translation*, pp. 171–174, Columbus, Ohio. Association for Computational Linguistics.

Tinsley, J., Zhechev, V., Hearne, M., and Way, A. (2007). Robust language pair-independent sub-tree alignment. In *Proceedings of the MT Summit XI*.

Tomás, J. and Casacuberta, F. (2006). Statistical phrase-based models for interactive computer-assisted translation. In *Proceedings of the COLING/ACL 2006 Main Conference Poster Sessions*, pp. 835–841, Sydney, Australia. Association for Computational Linguistics.

Tonoike, M., Kida, M., Takagi, T., Sasaki, Y., Utsuro, T., and Sato, S. (2006). A comparative study on compositional translation estimation using a domain/topic-specific corpus collected from the web. In *Proceedings of the 2nd International Workshop on Web as Corpus*, Sydney, Australia. Association for Computational Linguistics.

Toutanova, K., Ilhan, H. T., and Manning, C. D. (2002). Extensions to HMM-based statistical word alignment models. In *Proceedings of the Conference on Empirical Methods in Natural Language Processing (EMNLP)*, pp. 87–94, Philadelphia. Association for Computational Linguistics.

Toutanova, K. and Suzuki, H. (2007). Generating case markers in machine translation. In *Human Language Technologies 2007: The Conference of the North American Chapter of the Association for Computational Linguistics; Proceedings of the Main Conference*, pp. 49–56, Rochester, New York. Association for Computational Linguistics.

Toutanova, K., Suzuki, H., and Ruopp, A. (2008). Applying morphology generation models to machine translation. In *Proceedings of ACL-08: HLT*, pp. 514–522, Columbus, Ohio. Association for Computational Linguistics.

Tribble, A., Vogel, S., and Waibel, A. (2003). Overlapping phrase-level translation rules in an SMT engine. In *Proceedings of International Conference on Natural Language Processing and Knowledge Engineering (NLP-KE'03)*, Beijing, China.

Tsukada, H. and Nagata, M. (2004). Efficient decoding for statistical machine translation with a fully expanded WFST model. In Lin, D. and Wu, D., editors, *Proceedings of EMNLP 2004*, pp. 427–433, Barcelona, Spain. Association for Computational Linguistics.

Tsukada, H., Watanabe, T., Suzuki, J., Kazawa, H., and Isozaki, H. (2005). The NTT statistical machine translation system for IWSLT 2005. In *Proceedings of the International Workshop on Spoken Language Translation*.

Tsunakawa, T., Okazaki, N., and Tsujii, J. (2008). Building a bilingual lexicon using phrase-based statistical machine translation via a pivot language. In *COLING 2008: Companion volume: Posters and Demonstrations*, pp. 125–128, Manchester, UK. COLING 2008 Organizing Committee.

Tufis, D. (2002). A cheap and fast way to build useful translation lexicons. In *Proceedings of the International Conference on Computational Linguistics (COLING)*.

Tufis, D., Ion, R., Ceau su, A., and Stefanescu, D. (2006). Improved lexical alignment by combining multiple reified alignments. In *Proceedings of the 11th Conference of the European Chapter of the Association for Computational Linguistics*, Trento, Italy.

Turchi, M., De Bie, T., and Cristianini, N. (2008). Learning performance of a machine translation system: a statistical and computational analysis. In *Proceedings of the Third Workshop on Statistical Machine Translation*, pp. 35–43, Columbus, Ohio. Association for Computational Linguistics.

Turian, J. P., Melamed, I. D., and Shen, L. (2003). Evaluation of machine translation using maximum matching. In *Proceedings of the MT Summit IX*.

Uchimoto, K., Hayashida, N., Ishida, T., and Isahara, H. (2005). Automatic rating of machine translatability. In *Proceedings of the Tenth Machine Translation Summit (MT Summit X)*, Phuket, Thailand.

Uchimoto, K., Kotani, K., Zhang, Y., and Isahara, H. (2007). Automatic evaluation of machine translation based on rate of accomplishment of sub-goals. In *Human Language Technologies 2007: The Conference of the North American Chapter of the Association for Computational Linguistics; Proceedings of the Main Conference*, pp. 33–40, Rochester, New York. Association for Computational Linguistics.

Uchiyama, M. and Isahara, H. (2007). A Japanese–English patent parallel corpus. In *Proceedings of the MT Summit XI*.

Udupa, R., Faruquie, T. A., and Maji, H. K. (2004). An algorithmic framework for solving the decoding problem in statistical machine translation. In *Proceedings of COLING 2004*, pp. 631–637, Geneva, Switzerland. COLING.

Udupa, R. and Maji, H. K. (2006). Computational complexity of statistical machine translation. In

Proceedings of the 11th Conference of the European Chapter of the Association for Computational Linguistics, Trento, Italy.

Ueffing, N. (2006). Using monolingual source-language data to improve MT performance. In *Proceedings of the International Workshop on Spoken Language Translation*, Kyoto, Japan.

Ueffing, N., Haffari, G., and Sarkar, A. (2007a). Transductive learning for statistical machine translation. In *Proceedings of the 45th Annual Meeting of the Association of Computational Linguistics*, pp. 25–32, Prague, Czech Republic. Association for Computational Linguistics.

Ueffing, N., Macherey, K., and Ney, H. (2003). Confidence measures for statistical machine translation. In *Proceedings of the MT Summit IX*.

Ueffing, N. and Ney, H. (2003). Using POS information for SMT into morphologically rich languages. In *Proceedings of Meeting of the European Chapter of the Association of Computational Linguistics (EACL)*.

Ueffing, N. and Ney, H. (2005). Application of word-level confidence measures in interactive statistical machine translation. In *Proceedings of the 10th Conference of the European Association for Machine Translation (EAMT)*, Budapest.

Ueffing, N. and Ney, H. (2007). Word-level confidence estimation for machine translation. *Computational Linguistics*, 33(1):9–40.

Ueffing, N., Och, F. J., and Ney, H. (2002). Generation of word graphs in statistical machine translation. In *Proceedings of the Conference on Empirical Methods in Natural Language Processing (EMNLP)*, pp. 156–163, Philadelphia. Association for Computational Linguistics.

Ueffing, N., Simard, M., Larkin, S., and Johnson, H. (2007b). NRC's PORTAGE system for WMT 2007. In *Proceedings of the Second Workshop on Statistical Machine Translation*, pp. 185–188, Prague, Czech Republic. Association for Computational Linguistics.

Ueffing, N., Stephan, J., Matusov, E., *et al.* (2008). Tighter integration of rule-based and statistical MT in serial system combination. In *Proceedings of the 22nd International Conference on Computational Linguistics (COLING 2008)*, pp. 913–920, Manchester, UK. COLING 2008 Organizing Committee.

Utiyama, M. and Isahara, H. (2003). Reliable measures for aligning Japanese–English news articles and sentences. In Hinrichs, E. and Roth, D., editors, *Proceedings of the 41st Annual Meeting of the Association for Computational Linguistics*, pp. 72–79.

Utiyama, M. and Isahara, H. (2007). A comparison of pivot methods for phrase-based statistical machine translation. In *Human Language Technologies 2007: The Conference of the North American Chapter of the Association for Computational Linguistics; Proceedings of the Main Conference*, pp. 484–491, Rochester, New York. Association for Computational Linguistics.

Utsuro, T., Ikeda, H., Yamane, M., Matsumoto, Y., and Nagao, M. (1994). Bilingual text, matching using bilingual dictionary and statistics. In *Proceedings of the 15th International Conference on Computational Linguistics (COLING)*.

van der Eijk, W. (1993). Automating the acquisition of bilingual terminology. In *Proceedings of Meeting of the European Chapter of the Association of Computational Linguistics (EACL)*.

van Halteren, H. (2008). Source language markers in EUROPARL translations. In *Proceedings of the 22nd International Conference on Computational Linguistics (COLING 2008)*, pp. 937–944, Manchester, UK. COLING 2008 Organizing Committee.

van Zaanen, M. and Somers, H. L. (2005). DEMOCRAT: Deciding between multiple outputs created by automatic translation. In *Proceedings of the Tenth Machine Translation Summit (MT Summit X)*, Phuket, Thailand.

Varga, D., Halaácsy, P., Kornai, A., Nagy, V., Németh, L., and Trón, V. (2005). Parallel corpora for medium density languages. In *Proceedings of the RANLP 2005 Conference*, pp. 590–596.

Varga, I. and Yokoyama, S. (2007). Japanese–Hungarian dictionary generation using ontology resources. In *Proceedings of the MT Summit XI*.

Čmejrek, M., Cuřín, J., Hajič, J., and Havelka, J. (2005). Prague Czech–English dependency treebank: resource for structure-based MT. In *Proceedings of the 10th Conference of the European Association for Machine Translation (EAMT)*, Budapest.

Čmejrek, M., Cuřín, J., and Havelka, J. (2003). Czech–English dependency tree-based machine translation. In *Proceedings of Meeting of the European Chapter of the Association of Computational Linguistics (EACL)*.

Venkatapathy, S. and Bangalore, S. (2007). Three models for discriminative machine translation using global lexical selection and sentence reconstruction. In *Proceedings of SSST, NAACL-HLT 2007/AMTA Workshop on Syntax and Structure in Statistical Translation*, pp. 96–102, Rochester, New York. Association for Computational Linguistics.

Venkatapathy, S. and Joshi, A. (2007). Discriminative word alignment by learning the alignment structure and syntactic divergence between a language pair. In *Proceedings of SSST, NAACL-HLT 2007/AMTA Workshop on Syntax and Structure in Statistical Translation*, pp. 49–56, Rochester, New York. Association for Computational Linguistics.

Venugopal, A., Vogel, S., and Waibel, A. (2003). Effective phrase translation extraction from alignment models. In Hinrichs, E. and Roth, D., editors, *Proceedings of the 41st Annual Meeting of the Association for Computational Linguistics*, pp. 319–326.

Venugopal, A., Zollmann, A., and Stephan, V. (2007). An efficient two-pass approach to synchronous-CFG driven statistical MT. In *Human Language Technologies 2007: The Conference of the North American Chapter of the Association for Computational Linguistics; Proceedings of the Main Conference*, pp. 500–507, Rochester, New York. Association for Computational Linguistics.

Vickrey, D., Biewald, L., Teyssier, M., and Koller, D. (2005). Word-sense disambiguation for machine translation. In *Proceedings of Human Language Technology Conference and Conference on Empirical Methods in Natural Language Processing*, pp. 771–778, Vancouver, British Columbia, Canada. Association for Computational Linguistics.

Vilar, D., Leusch, G., Ney, H., and Banchs, R. E. (2007a). Human evaluation of machine translation through binary system comparisons. In *Proceedings of the Second Workshop on Statistical Machine Translation*, pp. 96–103, Prague, Czech Republic. Association for Computational Linguistics.

Vilar, D., Matusov, E., Hasan, S., Zens, R., and Ney, H. (2005). Statistical machine translation of European parliamentary speeches. In *Proceedings of the Tenth Machine Translation Summit (MT Summit X)*, Phuket, Thailand.

Vilar, D., Peter, J.-T., and Ney, H. (2007b). Can we translate letters? In *Proceedings of the Second Workshop on Statistical Machine Translation*, pp. 33–39, Prague, Czech Republic. Association for Computational Linguistics.

Vilar, D., Popovic, M., and Ney, H. (2006). AER: do we need to "improve" our alignments? In *Proceedings of the International Workshop on Spoken Language Translation*, Kyoto, Japan.

Virpioja, S., VÃd'yrynen, J. J., Creutz, M., and Sadeniemi, M. (2007). Morphology-aware statistical machine translation based on morphs induced in an unsupervised manner. In *Proceedings of the MT Summit XI*.

Vogel, S. (2003). Using noisy biligual data for statistical machine translation. In *Proceedings of Meeting of the European Chapter of the Association of Computational Linguistics (EACL)*.

Vogel, S. (2005). PESA: Phrase pair extraction as sentence splitting. In *Proceedings of the Tenth Machine Translation Summit (MT Summit X)*, Phuket, Thailand.

Vogel, S., Ney, H., and Tillmann, C. (1996). HMM-based word alignment in statistical translation. In *Proceedings of the 16th International Conference on Computational Linguistics (COLING)*.

Vogel, S., Zhang, Y., Huang, F., *et al.* (2003). The CMU statistical machine translation system. In *Proceedings of the Ninth Machine Translation Summit*.

Volk, M. and Harder, S. (2007). Evaluating MT with translations or translators. What is the difference? In *Proceedings of the MT Summit XI*.

Volk, M., Lundborg, J., and Mettler, M. (2007). A search tool for parallel treebanks. In *Proceedings of the Linguistic Annotation Workshop*, pp. 85–92, Prague, Czech Republic. Association for Computational Linguistics.

Voss, C. R. and Tate, C. R. (2006). Task-based evaluation of machine translation (MT) engines. Measuring how well people extract who, when, where-type ents in MT output. In *Proceedings of the 11th Conference of the European Association for Machine Translation (EAMT)*, Oslo, Norway.

Wang, C., Collins, M., and Koehn, P. (2007a). Chinese syntactic reordering for statistical machine translation. In *Proceedings of the 2007 Joint Conference on Empirical Methods in Natural Language Processing and Computational Natural Language Learning (EMNLP-CoNLL)*, pp. 737–745.

Wang, C. and Seneff, S. (2007). Automatic assessment of student translations for foreign language tutoring. In *Human Language Technologies 2007: The Conference of the North American Chapter of the Association for Computational Linguistics; Proceedings of the Main Conference*, pp. 468–475, Rochester, New York. Association for Computational Linguistics.

Wang, H., Wu, H., and Liu, Z. (2006a). Word alignment for languages with scarce resources using bilingual corpora of other language pairs. In *Proceedings of the COLING/ACL 2006 Main Conference Poster Sessions*, pp. 874–881, Sydney, Australia. Association for Computational Linguistics.

Wang, W., Knight, K., and Marcu, D. (2006b). Capitalizing machine translation. In *Proceedings of the Human*

Language Technology Conference of the NAACL, Main Conference, pp. 1–8, New York City, USA. Association for Computational Linguistics.

Wang, W., Knight, K., and Marcu, D. (2007b). Binarizing syntax trees to improve syntax-based machine translation accuracy. In *Proceedings of the 2007 Joint Conference on Empirical Methods in Natural Language Processing and Computational Natural Language Learning (EMNLP-CoNLL)*, pp. 746–754.

Wang, W. and Zhou, M. (2002). Structure alignment using bilingual chunking. In *Proceedings of the International Conference on Computational Linguistics (COLING)*.

Wang, W. and Zhou, M. (2004). Improving word alignment models using structured monolingual corpora. In Lin, D. and Wu, D., editors, *Proceedings of EMNLP 2004*, pp. 198–205, Barcelona, Spain. Association for Computational Linguistics.

Wang, Y.-Y. and Waibel, A. (1997). Decoding algorithm in statistical machine translation. In *Proceedings of the 35th Annual Meeting of the Association for Computational Linguistics (ACL)*.

Wang, Y.-Y. and Waibel, A. (1998). Modeling with structures in statistical machine translation. In *Proceedings of the 36th Annual Meeting of the Association of Computational Linguistics (ACL)*.

Wang, Z. and Shawe-Taylor, J. (2008). Kernel regression framework for machine translation: UCL system description for WMT 2008 shared translation task. In *Proceedings of the Third Workshop on Statistical Machine Translation*, pp. 155–158, Columbus, Ohio. Association for Computational Linguistics.

Wang, Z., Shawe-Taylor, J., and Szedmak, S. (2007c). Kernel regression based machine translation. In *Human Language Technologies 2007: The Conference of the North American Chapter of the Association for Computational Linguistics; Companion Volume, Short Papers*, pp. 185–188, Rochester, New York. Association for Computational Linguistics.

Watanabe, T., Imamura, K., and Sumita, E. (2002). Statistical machine translation based on hierarchical phrase alignment. In *Proceedings of the Ninth International Conference on Theoretical and Methodological Issues in Machine Translation (TMI)*.

Watanabe, T. and Sumita, E. (2002). Bidirectional decoding for statistical machine translation. In *Proceedings of the International Conference on Computational Linguistics (COLING)*.

Watanabe, T., Sumita, E., and Okuno, H. G. (2003). Chunk-based statistical translation. In Hinrichs, E. and Roth, D., editors, *Proceedings of the 41st Annual Meeting of the Association for Computational Linguistics*, pp. 303–310.

Watanabe, T., Suzuki, J., Sudoh, K., Tsukada, H., and Isozaki, H. (2007a). Larger feature set approach for machine translation in IWSLT 2007. In *Proceedings of the International Workshop on Spoken Language Translation (IWSLT)*.

Watanabe, T., Suzuki, J., Tsukada, H., and Isozaki, H. (2006a). NTT statistical machine translation for IWSLT 2006. In *Proceedings of the International Workshop on Spoken Language Translation*, Kyoto, Japan.

Watanabe, T., Suzuki, J., Tsukada, H., and Isozaki, H. (2007b). Online large-margin training for statistical machine translation. In *Proceedings of the 2007 Joint Conference on Empirical Methods in Natural Language Processing and Computational Natural Language Learning (EMNLP-CoNLL)*, pp. 764–773.

Watanabe, T., Tsukada, H., and Isozaki, H. (2006b). Left-to-right target generation for hierarchical phrase-based translation. In *Proceedings of the 21st International Conference on Computational Linguistics and 44th Annual Meeting of the Association for Computational Linguistics*, pp. 777–784, Sydney, Australia. Association for Computational Linguistics.

Watanabe, T., Tsukada, H., and Isozaki, H. (2006c). NTT system description for the WMT2006 shared task. In *Proceedings on the Workshop on Statistical Machine Translation*, pp. 122–125, New York City. Association for Computational Linguistics.

Weaver, W. (1947). Letter to Norbert Wiener.

Weaver, W. (1949). Translation. Reprinted in Locke and Booth (1955).

Wellington, B., Turian, J. P., Pike, C., and Melamed, I. D. (2006a). Scalable purely-discriminative training for word and tree transducers. In *5th Conference of the Association for Machine Translation in the Americas (AMTA)*, Boston, Massachusetts.

Wellington, B., Waxmonsky, S., and Melamed, I. D. (2006b). Empirical lower bounds on the complexity of translational equivalence. In *Proceedings of the 21st International Conference on Computational Linguistics and 44th Annual Meeting of the Association for Computational Linguistics*, pp. 977–984, Sydney, Australia. Association for Computational Linguistics.

White, J. S., O'Connell, T. A., and O'Mara, F. E. (1994). The ARPA MT evaluation methodologies: Evolution, lessons, and future approaches. In *Proceedings of the Conference of the Association for Machine Translation in the Americas (AMTA 1994)*.

Witten, I. H. and Bell, T. C. (1991). The zero-frequency problem: estimating the probabilities of novelevents in adaptive text compression. *IEEE Transactions on Information Theory*, **37**(4):1085–1094.

Wu, D. (1994). Aligning a parallel english-chinese corpus statistically with lexical criteria. In *Proceedings of the 32nd Annual Meeting of the Association for Computational Linguistics (ACL)*.

Wu, D. (1995). Trainable coarse bilingual grammars for parallel text bracketing. In *Proceedings of the Third Workshop on Very Large Corpora (VLC)*.

Wu, D. (1996). A polynomial-time algorithm for statistical machine translation. In *Proceedings of the 34th Annual Meeting of the Association for Computational Linguistics (ACL)*.

Wu, D. (1997). Stochastic inversion transduction grammars and bilingual parsing of parallel corpora. *Computational Linguistics*, **23**(3):337–404.

Wu, D. and Wong, H. (1998). Machine translation with a stochastic grammatical channel. In *Proceedings of the 36th Annual Meeting of the Association of Computational Linguistics (ACL)*.

Wu, D. and Xia, X. (1994). Learning an English–Chinese lexicon from a parallel corpus. In *Proceedings of the Conference of the Association for Machine Translation in the Americas*.

Wu, H. and Wang, H. (2004a). Improving domain-specific word alignment with a general bilingual corpus. In *Proceedings of the 6th Conference of the Association for Machine Translation in the Americas (AMTA 2004)*, pp. 262–271.

Wu, H. and Wang, H. (2004b). Improving statistical word alignment with a rule-based machine translation system. In *Proceedings of COLING 2004*, pp. 29–35, Geneva, Switzerland. COLING.

Wu, H. and Wang, H. (2005). Boosting statistical word alignment. In *Proceedings of the Tenth Machine Translation Summit (MT Summit X)*, Phuket, Thailand.

Wu, H. and Wang, H. (2007a). Comparative study of word alignment heuristics and phrase-based SMT. In *Proceedings of the MT Summit XI*.

Wu, H. and Wang, H. (2007b). Pivot language approach for phrase-based statistical machine translation. In *Proceedings of the 45th Annual Meeting of the Association of Computational Linguistics*, pp. 856–863, Prague, Czech Republic. Association for Computational Linguistics.

Wu, H., Wang, H., and Liu, Z. (2006). Boosting statistical word alignment using labeled and unlabeled data. In *Proceedings of the COLING/ACL 2006 Main Conference Poster Sessions*, pp. 913–920, Sydney, Australia. Association for Computational Linguistics.

Wu, H., Wang, H., and Zong, C. (2008). Domain adaptation for statistical machine translation with domain dictionary and monolingual corpora. In *Proceedings of the 22nd International Conference on Computational Linguistics (COLING 2008)*, pp. 993–1000, Manchester, UK. COLING 2008 Organizing Committee.

Xia, F. and McCord, M. (2004). Improving a statistical MT system with automatically learned rewrite patterns. In *Proceedings of COLING 2004*, pp. 508–514, Geneva, Switzerland. COLING.

Xiong, D., Liu, Q., and Lin, S. (2006). Maximum entropy based phrase reordering model for statistical machine translation. In *Proceedings of the 21st International Conference on Computational Linguistics and 44th Annual Meeting of the Association for Computational Linguistics*, pp. 521–528, Sydney, Australia. Association for Computational Linguistics.

Xiong, D., Liu, Q., and Lin, S. (2007). A dependency treelet string correspondence model for statistical machine translation. In *Proceedings of the Second Workshop on Statistical Machine Translation*, pp. 40–47, Prague, Czech Republic. Association for Computational Linguistics.

Xiong, D., Zhang, M., Aw, A., and Li, H. (2008a). Linguistically annotated BTG for statistical machine translation. In *Proceedings of the 22nd International Conference on Computational Linguistics (COLING 2008)*, pp. 1009–1016, Manchester, UK. COLING 2008 Organizing Committee.

Xiong, D., Zhang, M., Aw, A., and Li, H. (2008b). A linguistically annotated reordering model for BTG-based statistical machine translation. In *Proceedings of ACL-08: HLT, Short Papers*, pp. 149–152, Columbus, Ohio. Association for Computational Linguistics.

Xiong, D., Zhang, M., Aw, A., Mi, H., Liu, Q., and Lin, S. (2008c). Refinements in BTG-based statistical machine translation. In *Proceedings of the 3rd International Joint Conference on Natural Language Processing (IJCNLP)*.

Xu, B. (2005). Phrase-based statistical machine translation for MANOS system. In *Proceedings of the Tenth Machine Translation Summit (MT Summit X)*, Phuket, Thailand.

Xu, J., Deng, Y., Gao, Y., and Ney, H. (2007). Domain dependent statistical machine translation. In *Proceedings of the MT Summit XI*.

Xu, J., Gao, J., Toutanova, K., and Ney, H. (2008). Bayesian semi-supervised chinese word segmentation for statistical machine translation. In *Proceedings of the 22nd International Conference on Computational Linguistics (COLING 2008)*, pp. 1017–1024, Manchester, UK. COLING 2008 Organizing Committee.

Xu, J., Zens, R., and Ney, H. (2005). Sentence segmentation using ibm word alignment model 1. In *Proceedings of the 10th Conference of the European Association for Machine Translation (EAMT)*, Budapest.

Xu, J., Zens, R., and Ney, H. (2006a). Partitioning parallel documents using binary segmentation. In *Proceedings on the Workshop on Statistical Machine Translation*, pp. 78–85, New York City. Association for Computational Linguistics.

Xu, L., Fujii, A., and Ishikawa, T. (2006b). Modeling impression in probabilistic transliteration into Chinese. In *Proceedings of the 2006 Conference on Empirical Methods in Natural Language Processing*, pp. 242–249, Sydney, Australia. Association for Computational Linguistics.

Yamada, K. and Knight, K. (2001). A syntax-based statistical translation model. In *Proceedings of the 39th Annual Meeting of the Association of Computational Linguistics (ACL)*.

Yamada, K. and Knight, K. (2002). A decoder for syntax-based statistical MT. In *Proceedings of the 40th Annual Meeting of the Association of Computational Linguistics (ACL)*.

Yamamoto, H., Okuma, H., and Sumita, E. (2008). Imposing constraints from the source tree on ITG constraints for SMT. In *Proceedings of the ACL-08: HLT Second Workshop on Syntax and Structure in Statistical Translation (SSST-2)*, pp. 1–9, Columbus, Ohio. Association for Computational Linguistics.

Yamamoto, K., Kudo, T., Tsuboi, Y., and Matsumoto, Y. (2003). Learning sequence-to-sequence correspondences from parallel corpora via sequential pattern mining. In Mihalcea, R. and Pedersen, T., editors, *HLT-NAACL 2003 Workshop: Building and Using Parallel Texts: Data Driven Machine Translation and Beyond*, Edmonton, Alberta, Canada. Association for Computational Linguistics.

Yamamoto, K. and Matsumoto, Y. (2000). Acquisition of phrase-level bilingual correspondence using dependency structure. In *Proceedings of the International Conference on Computational Linguistics (COLING)*.

Yamamoto, K., Matsumoto, Y., and Kitamura, M. (2001). A comparative study on translation units for bilingual lexicon extraction. In *Workshop on Data-Driven Machine Translation at 39th Annual Meeting of the Association of Computational Linguistics (ACL)*.

Yang, F., Zhao, J., Zou, B., Liu, K., and Liu, F. (2008). Chinese–English backward transliteration assisted with mining monolingual web pages. In *Proceedings of ACL-08: HLT*, pp. 541–549, Columbus, Ohio. Association for Computational Linguistics.

Yang, M. and Kirchhoff, K. (2006). Phrase-based backoff models for machine translation of highly inflected languages. In *Proceedings of the 11th Conference of the European Chapter of the Association for Computational Linguistics*, Trento, Italy.

Yarowsky, D. (1994). Unsupervised word sense disambiguation rivaling supervised methods. In *Proceedings of the 32nd Annual Meeting of the Association of Computational Linguistics (ACL)*, pp. 189–196.

Yasuda, K., Sugaya, F., Takezawa, T., Yamamoto, S., and Yanagida, M. (2003). Automatic evaluation for a palpable measure of a speech translation system's capability. In *Proceedings of Meeting of the European Chapter of the Association of Computational Linguistics (EACL)*.

Yasuda, K., Zhang, R., Yamamoto, H., and Sumita, E. (2008). Method of selecting training data to build a compact and efficient translation model. In *Proceedings of the 3rd International Joint Conference on Natural Language Processing (IJCNLP)*.

Ye, Y., Fossum, V. L., and Abney, S. (2006). Latent features in automatic tense translation between Chinese and English. In *Proceedings of the Fifth SIGHAN Workshop on Chinese Language Processing*, pp. 48–55, Sydney, Australia. Association for Computational Linguistics.

Ye, Y., Schneider, K.-M., and Abney, S. (2007a). Aspect marker generation in English-to-Chinese machine translation. In *Proceedings of the MT Summit XI*.

Ye, Y., Zhou, M., and Lin, C.-Y. (2007b). Sentence level machine translation evaluation as a ranking. In *Proceedings of the Second Workshop on Statistical Machine Translation*, pp. 240–247, Prague, Czech Republic. Association for Computational Linguistics.

Yoon, S.-Y., Kim, K.-Y., and Sproat, R. (2007). Multilingual transliteration using feature based phonetic method. In *Proceedings of the 45th Annual Meeting of the Association of Computational Linguistics*, pp. 112–119,

Prague, Czech Republic. Association for Computational Linguistics.

Zabokrtsky, Z., Ptacek, J., and Pajas, P. (2008). TectoMT: Highly modular MT system with tectogrammatics used as transfer layer. In *Proceedings of the Third Workshop on Statistical Machine Translation*, pp. 167–170, Columbus, Ohio. Association for Computational Linguistics.

Zelenko, D. and Aone, C. (2006). Discriminative methods for transliteration. In *Proceedings of the 2006 Conference on Empirical Methods in Natural Language Processing*, pp. 612–617, Sydney, Australia. Association for Computational Linguistics.

Zens, R. and Ney, H. (2003). A comparative study on reordering constraints in statistical machine translation. In Hinrichs, E. and Roth, D., editors, *Proceedings of the 41st Annual Meeting of the Association for Computational Linguistics*, pp. 144–151.

Zens, R. and Ney, H. (2004). Improvements in phrase-based statistical machine translation. In *Proceedings of the Joint Conference on Human Language Technologies and the Annual Meeting of the North American Chapter of the Association of Computational Linguistics (HLT-NAACL)*.

Zens, R. and Ney, H. (2005). Word graphs for statistical machine translation. In *Proceedings of the ACL Workshop on Building and Using Parallel Texts*, pp. 191–198, Ann Arbor, Michigan. Association for Computational Linguistics.

Zens, R. and Ney, H. (2006a). Discriminative reordering models for statistical machine translation. In *Proceedings on the Workshop on Statistical Machine Translation*, pp. 55–63, New York City. Association for Computational Linguistics.

Zens, R. and Ney, H. (2006b). N-gram posterior probabilities for statistical machine translation. In *Proceedings on the Workshop on Statistical Machine Translation*, pp. 72–77, New York City. Association for Computational Linguistics.

Zens, R. and Ney, H. (2007). Efficient phrase-table representation for machine translation with applications to online MT and speech translation. In *Human Language Technologies 2007: The Conference of the North American Chapter of the Association for Computational Linguistics; Proceedings of the Main Conference*, pp. 492–499, Rochester, New York. Association for Computational Linguistics.

Zens, R., Ney, H., Watanabe, T., and Sumita, E. (2004). Reordering constraints for phrase-based statistical machine translation. In *Proceedings of COLING 2004*, pp. 205–211, Geneva, Switzerland. COLING.

Zens, R., Och, F. J., and Ney, H. (2002). Phrase-based statistical machine translation. In *Proceedings of the German Conference on Artificial Intelligence (KI 2002)*.

Zettlemoyer, L. and Moore, R. C. (2007). Selective phrase pair extraction for improved statistical machine translation. In *Human Language Technologies 2007: The Conference of the North American Chapter of the Association for Computational Linguistics; Companion Volume, Short Papers*, pp. 209–212, Rochester, New York. Association for Computational Linguistics.

Zhang, D., Li, M., Duan, N., Li, C.-H., and Zhou, M. (2008a). Measure word generation for English-Chinese SMT systems. In *Proceedings of ACL-08: HLT*, pp. 89–96, Columbus, Ohio. Association for Computational Linguistics.

Zhang, D., Li, M., Li, C.-H., and Zhou, M. (2007a). Phrase reordering model integrating syntactic knowledge for SMT. In *Proceedings of the 2007 Joint Conference on Empirical Methods in Natural Language Processing and Computational Natural Language Learning (EMNLP-CoNLL)*, pp. 533–540.

Zhang, D., Sun, L., and Li, W. (2008b). A structured prediction approach for statistical machine translation. In *Proceedings of the 3rd International Joint Conference on Natural Language Processing (IJCNLP)*.

Zhang, H. and Gildea, D. (2004). Syntax-based alignment: Supervised or unsupervised? In *Proceedings of COLING 2004*, pp. 418–424, Geneva, Switzerland. COLING.

Zhang, H. and Gildea, D. (2005). Stochastic lexicalized inversion transduction grammar for alignment. In *Proceedings of the 43rd Annual Meeting of the Association for Computational Linguistics (ACL'05)*, pp. 475–482, Ann Arbor, Michigan. Association for Computational Linguistics.

Zhang, H. and Gildea, D. (2006a). Efficient search for inversion transduction grammar. In *Proceedings of the 2006 Conference on Empirical Methods in Natural Language Processing*, pp. 224–231, Sydney, Australia. Association for Computational Linguistics.

Zhang, H. and Gildea, D. (2006b). Inducing word alignments with bilexical synchronous trees. In *Proceedings of the COLING/ACL 2006 Main Conference Poster Sessions*, pp. 953–960, Sydney, Australia. Association for Computational Linguistics.

Zhang, H. and Gildea, D. (2007). Factorization of synchronous context-free grammars in linear time. In *Proceedings of SSST, NAACL-HLT 2007 / AMTA*

Workshop on Syntax and Structure in Statistical Translation, pp. 25–32, Rochester, New York. Association for Computational Linguistics.

Zhang, H. and Gildea, D. (2008). Efficient multi-pass decoding for synchronous context free grammars. In *Proceedings of ACL-08: HLT*, pp. 209–217, Columbus, Ohio. Association for Computational Linguistics.

Zhang, H., Gildea, D., and Chiang, D. (2008c). Extracting synchronous grammar rules from word-level alignments in linear time. In *Proceedings of the 22nd International Conference on Computational Linguistics (COLING 2008)*, pp. 1081–1088, Manchester, UK. COLING 2008 Organizing Committee.

Zhang, H., Huang, L., Gildea, D., and Knight, K. (2006a). Synchronous binarization for machine translation. In *Proceedings of the Human Language Technology Conference of the NAACL, Main Conference*, pp. 256–263, New York City, USA. Association for Computational Linguistics.

Zhang, H., Quirk, C., Moore, R. C., and Gildea, D. (2008d). Bayesian learning of non-compositional phrases with synchronous parsing. In *Proceedings of ACL-08: HLT*, pp. 97–105, Columbus, Ohio. Association for Computational Linguistics.

Zhang, J., Zong, C., and Li, S. (2008e). Sentence type based reordering model for statistical machine translation. In *Proceedings of the 22nd International Conference on Computational Linguistics (COLING 2008)*, pp. 1089–1096, Manchester, UK. COLING 2008 Organizing Committee.

Zhang, M., Jiang, H., Aw, A., Li, H., Tan, C. L., and Li, S. (2008f). A tree sequence alignment-based tree-to-tree translation model. In *Proceedings of ACL-08: HLT*, pp. 559–567, Columbus, Ohio. Association for Computational Linguistics.

Zhang, M., Jiang, H., Aw, A., Sun, J., Li, S., and Tan, C. L. (2007b). A tree-to-tree alignment-based model for statistical machine translation. In *Proceedings of the MT Summit XI*.

Zhang, M., Jiang, H., Li, H., Aw, A., and Li, S. (2008g). Grammar comparison study for translational equivalence modeling and statistical machine translation. In *Proceedings of the 22nd International Conference on Computational Linguistics (COLING 2008)*, pp. 1097–1104, Manchester, UK. COLING 2008 Organizing Committee.

Zhang, M., Li, H., and Su, J. (2004a). Direct orthographical mapping for machine transliteration. In *Proceedings of COLING 2004*, pp. 716–722, Geneva, Switzerland. COLING.

Zhang, R., Kikui, G., Yamamoto, H., Soong, F., Watanabe, T., and Lo, W. K. (2004b). A unified approach in speech-to-speech translation: Integrating features of speech recognition and machine translation. In *Proceedings of COLING 2004*, pp. 1168–1174, Geneva, Switzerland. COLING.

Zhang, R. and Sumita, E. (2007). Boosting statistical machine translation by lemmatization and linear interpolation. In *Proceedings of the 45th Annual Meeting of the Association for Computational Linguistics Companion Volume Proceedings of the Demo and Poster Sessions*, pp. 181–184, Prague, Czech Republic. Association for Computational Linguistics.

Zhang, R. and Sumita, E. (2008). Chinese unknown word translation by subword re-segmentation. In *Proceedings of the 3rd International Joint Conference on Natural Language Processing (IJCNLP)*.

Zhang, R., Yamamoto, H., Paul, M., *et al.* (2006b). The NiCT-ATR statistical machine translation system for IWSLT 2006. In *Proceedings of the International Workshop on Spoken Language Translation*, Kyoto, Japan.

Zhang, R., Yasuda, K., and Sumita, E. (2008h). Improved statistical machine translation by multiple Chinese word segmentation. In *Proceedings of the Third Workshop on Statistical Machine Translation*, pp. 216–223, Columbus, Ohio. Association for Computational Linguistics.

Zhang, Y., Liu, Q., Ma, Q., and Isahara, H. (2005a). A multi-aligner for Japanese–Chinese parallel corpora. In *Proceedings of the Tenth Machine Translation Summit (MT Summit X)*, Phuket, Thailand.

Zhang, Y., Uchimoto, K., Ma, Q., and Isahara, H. (2005b). Building an annotated Japanese–Chinese parallel corpus a part of NICT multilingual corpora. In *Proceedings of the Tenth Machine Translation Summit (MT Summit X)*, Phuket, Thailand.

Zhang, Y. and Vogel, S. (2005a). Competitive grouping in integrated phrase segmentation and alignment model. In *Proceedings of the ACL Workshop on Building and Using Parallel Texts*, pp. 159–162, Ann Arbor, Michigan. Association for Computational Linguistics.

Zhang, Y. and Vogel, S. (2005b). An efficient phrase-to-phrase alignment model for arbitrarily long phrase and large corpora. In *Proceedings of the 10th Conference of the European Association for Machine Translation (EAMT)*, Budapest.

Zhang, Y. and Vogel, S. (2007). PanDoRA: A large-scale two-way statistical machine translation system for hand-held devices. In *Proceedings of the MT Summit XI*.

Zhang, Y., Vogel, S., and Waibel, A. (2003). Integrated phrase segmentation and alignment algorithm for statistical machine translation. In *Proceedings of International Conference on Natural Language Processing and Knowledge Engineering (NLP-KE'03)*, Beijing, China.

Zhang, Y., Zens, R., and Ney, H. (2007c). Chunk-level reordering of source language sentences with automatically learned rules for statistical machine translation. In *Proceedings of SSST, NAACL-HLT 2007/AMTA Workshop on Syntax and Structure in Statistical Translation*, pp. 1–8, Rochester, New York. Association for Computational Linguistics.

Zhang, Y., Zens, R., and Ney, H. (2007d). Improved chunk-level reordering for statistical machine translation. In *Proceedings of the International Workshop on Spoken Language Translation (IWSLT)*.

Zhao, B., Bach, N., Lane, I., and Vogel, S. (2007). A log-linear block transliteration model based on bi-stream HMMs. In *Human Language Technologies 2007: The Conference of the North American Chapter of the Association for Computational Linguistics; Proceedings of the Main Conference*, pp. 364–371, Rochester, New York. Association for Computational Linguistics.

Zhao, B., Eck, M., and Vogel, S. (2004a). Language model adaptation for statistical machine translation via structured query models. In *Proceedings of COLING 2004*, pp. 411–417, Geneva, Switzerland. COLING.

Zhao, B. and Vogel, S. (2003). Word alignment based on bilingual bracketing. In Mihalcea, R. and Pedersen, T., editors, *HLT-NAACL 2003 Workshop: Building and Using Parallel Texts: Data Driven Machine Translation and Beyond*, pp. 15–18, Edmonton, Alberta, Canada. Association for Computational Linguistics.

Zhao, B. and Vogel, S. (2005). A generalized alignment-free phrase extraction. In *Proceedings of the ACL Workshop on Building and Using Parallel Texts*, pp. 141–144, Ann Arbor, Michigan. Association for Computational Linguistics.

Zhao, B., Vogel, S., Eck, M., and Waibel, A. (2004b). Phrase pair rescoring with term weighting for statistical machine translation. In Lin, D. and Wu, D., editors, *Proceedings of EMNLP 2004*, pp. 206–213, Barcelona, Spain. Association for Computational Linguistics.

Zhao, B. and Xing, E. P. (2006). BiTAM: Bilingual topic AdMixture models for word alignment. In *Proceedings of the COLING/ACL 2006 Main Conference Poster Sessions*, pp. 969–976, Sydney, Australia. Association for Computational Linguistics.

Zhao, B., Zechner, K., Vogel, S., and Waibel, A. (2003). Efficient optimization for bilingual sentence alignment based on linear regression. In Mihalcea, R. and Pedersen, T., editors, *HLT-NAACL 2003 Workshop: Building and Using Parallel Texts: Data Driven Machine Translation and Beyond*, Edmonton, Alberta, Canada. Association for Computational Linguistics.

Zhechev, V. and Way, A. (2008). Automatic generation of parallel treebanks. In *Proceedings of the 22nd International Conference on Computational Linguistics (COLING 2008)*, pp. 1105–1112, Manchester, UK. COLING 2008 Organizing Committee.

Zhou, B., Xiang, B., Zhu, X., and Gao, Y. (2008). Prior derivation models for formally syntax-based translation using linguistically syntactic parsing and tree kernels. In *Proceedings of the ACL-08: HLT Second Workshop on Syntax and Structure in Statistical Translation (SSST-2)*, pp. 19–27, Columbus, Ohio. Association for Computational Linguistics.

Zhou, L., Lin, C.-Y., and Hovy, E. (2006). Re-evaluating machine translation results with paraphrase support. In *Proceedings of the 2006 Conference on Empirical Methods in Natural Language Processing*, pp. 77–84, Sydney, Australia. Association for Computational Linguistics.

Zhou, Y., He, Y., and Zong, C. (2007). The CASIA phrase-based statistical machine translation system for IWSLT 2007. In *Proceedings of the International Workshop on Spoken Language Translation (IWSLT)*.

Zollmann, A. and Venugopal, A. (2006). Syntax augmented machine translation via chart parsing. In *Proceedings on the Workshop on Statistical Machine Translation*, pp. 138–141, New York City. Association for Computational Linguistics.

Zollmann, A., Venugopal, A., Och, F. J., and Ponte, J. (2008). A systematic comparison of phrase-based, hierarchical and syntax-augmented statistical MT. In *Proceedings of the 22nd International Conference on Computational Linguistics (COLING 2008)*, pp. 1145–1152, Manchester, UK. COLING 2008 Organizing Committee.

Zollmann, A., Venugopal, A., Paulik, M., and Vogel, S. (2007). The syntax augmented MT (SAMT) system at the shared task for the 2007 ACL workshop on statistical machine translation. In *Proceedings of the Second Workshop on Statistical Machine Translation*, pp. 216–219, Prague, Czech Republic. Association for Computational Linguistics.

Zollmann, A., Venugopal, A., Vogel, S., and Waibel, A. (2006). The CMU-UKA syntax augmented machine translation system for the IWSLT-06. In *Proceedings of the International Workshop on Spoken Language Translation*, Kyoto, Japan.

Zwarts, S. and Dras, M. (2007). Syntax-based word reordering in phrase based statistical machine translation: Why does it work? In *Proceedings of the MT Summit XI*.

Zwarts, S. and Dras, M. (2008). Choosing the right translation: A syntactically informed classification approach. In *Proceedings of the 22nd International Conference on Computational Linguistics (COLING 2008)*, pp. 1153–1160, Manchester, UK. COLING 2008 Organizing Committee.

Author Index

Index

Printed in the United States
by Bookmasters

Printed in the United States
By Bookmasters